PSYCHOLINGUISTICS

SECOND EDITION

Jean Berko Gleason
Boston University

Nan Bernstein Ratner
University of Maryland

EDITORS

HARCOURT BRACE COLLEGE PUBLISHERS

Fort Worth   Philadelphia   San Diego   New York   Orlando   Austin   San Antonio

Toronto   Montreal   London   Sydney   Tokyo

Publisher	Earl McPeek
Associate Acquisitions Editor	Lisa Hensley
Product Manager	Don Grainger
Developmental Editor	Susan R. Petty
Project Editor	Elaine Richards
Art Director	Sue Hart
Production Manager	Andrea A. Johnson

Cover image: © Gary A. Bartholomew/Westlight

ISBN: 0-15-504106-1

Library of Congress Catalog Card Number: 97-73099

Address for orders:
Harcourt Brace College Publishers
6277 Sea Harbor Drive
Orlando, FL 32887-6777
1-800-782-4479

Address for editorial correspondence:
Harcourt Brace College Publishers
301 Commerce Street, Suite 3700
Fort Worth, TX 76102

Web site address:
http://www.hbcollege.com

Harcourt Brace & Company will provide complimentary supplements or supplement packages to those adopters qualified under our adoption policy. Please contact your sales representative to learn how you can qualify. If as an adopter or potential user you receive supplements you do not need, please return them to your sales representative or send them to: Attn: Returns Department, Troy Warehouse, 465 South Lincoln Drive, Troy, MO 63379.

Printed in the United States of America

7 8 9 0 1 2 3 4 5 6   039   9 8 7 6 5 4 3 2 1

PREFACE

The second edition of *Psycholinguistics* has been revised and updated to reflect the changing nature of the field as it is seen by the experts who have contributed chapters. It also has many new features that have been added in response to suggestions from our readers.

The introductory chapter contains expanded sections on linguistics and contemporary linguistic theory. We have included a completely new chapter on discourse processing (Chapter 6) that covers many kinds of connected language in addition to conversational discourse, including the latest work on narrative. Each chapter has new references to recent cutting-edge work in psycholinguistics, and there are many new charts, tables, and graphic presentations that help make difficult concepts clearer. We have also added a variety of features that make the book more user-friendly and helpful for instructors and students alike. These include interesting information set apart typographically in boxes within the body of the chapter, as well as key words, discussion questions, and suggested activities at the end of each chapter.

Psycholinguistics is the discipline that investigates and describes the psychological processes that make it possible for humans to master and use language. The revolution in cognitive science has led researchers from many different backgrounds to study language processing. In preparing the second edition of this book, our aim has been to create a current and introductory level text to acquaint readers with the core concepts and range of topics that constitute the discipline of psycholinguistics. Course work in the psychology of language historically has been an upper-level or graduate school undertaking, but now there is increasing enrollment by undergraduates interested in the cognitive sciences. This book was designed to be used in both undergraduate and graduate courses in psycholinguistics, as well as in more general courses in cognitive science, cognition, human communication, language and mind, speech perception and production, and similar topics.

Psycholinguistics is a young and rapidly growing field. There are now so many psycholinguistic subspecializations that it would be difficult for only one or two authors to cover the entire field in a timely and authoritative fashion, especially if we prefer authors to be active researchers in the areas they write about. We enlisted researchers with expertise in the topics chosen for inclusion in this text to write chapters in their own specialties. The authors have written contemporary chapters that will introduce students without prior background in linguistics or cognitive science to the basic issues of concern to psycholinguists. Each chapter provides a perspective on the major questions that confront researchers working in the area and carefully explains the research methods used to obtain answers to such questions. Each chapter also contains models that have been developed to explain major psycholinguistic functions and some hands-on exercises or demonstrations to help bring the topics alive. We have tried in all instances to provide a perspective on the field, rather than an indoctrination, and we have chosen co-authors who are not so wedded to their own theoretical positions that they cannot present the views of others.

The book is divided into ten chapters:

Chapter 1 Introduction to Psycholinguistics: What Do Language Users Know? In this chapter we present an overview of the field of psycholinguistics as well as a basic description of the components of language. Readers who have already had courses in linguistics will find familiar material here. To make the book accessible in an introductory context we have included contemporary linguistic concepts as well as a historical perspective on the changes that the field has undergone in the last few years.

Chapter 2 The Biological Bases of Human Communicative Behavior. Language is a social activity, but it also depends on our uniquely human brains. This chapter presents basic neurolinguistic information. The reader will become familiar with the neural structures that support language; with the methods that have been used to localize language function in the brain; and with the fascinating history, dating to antiquity, of observations about the relation between brain damage and aphasia, the loss of communicative abilities.

Chapter 3 Speech Perception. Language is hierarchically structured: comprehension relies upon multiple processes. At the top of the pyramid lie inference and context—we often know what a person is saying to us based purely on expectation. At the bottom of the hierarchy lie our most fundamental decoding skills—the ability to detect language, to segment the stream of speech, and to assign individual sounds we hear to the sounds and words of our language. Chapter 3 explores the basic processes involved in speech perception at this level. It also presents research on computer-generated speech, as well as several important models of speech perception.

Chapter 4 Words and Meaning: From Primitives to Complex Organization. This chapter is divided into two major sections. The first explores our mental dictionary, including descriptions of research that reveals how words are stored and accessed. The second half of the chapter deals with the fascinating topic of meaning. The authors present major theories of lexical access and some of the best known philosophical and scientific approaches to the study of meaning.

Chapter 5 Sentence Processing. Earlier chapters have described how we isolate and recognize individual speech sounds and how we combine them to produce or recognize the words of our language. Chapter 5 takes us through the next step: producing and recognizing connected speech, at the sentence level. Some of the interesting questions considered in this chapter include how we are able to produce coherent sentences so rapidly, typically at 100 words per minute, and how we are able to listen to such rapid speech and decode it.

Chapter 6 Sentences Combined: Text and Discourse. Once we have dealt with the topic of sentence processing, the next logical step in our description of language processing is to understand how we produce and comprehend connected speech beyond the sentence level. Chapter 6 discusses and describes our complex abilities at this high level of the language hierarchy. Among the topics included in this chapter are memory and context, ambiguity, metaphor, irony, and various discourse genres, such as narrative, humor, and explanations. No discussion of discourse would be complete without some mention of social class and gender differences, and they are examined here as well.

Chapter 7 Speech Production.   This chapter describes the processes involved in turning an idea into a spoken utterance. It discusses the stages of planning an utterance, the mental units involved, and such fascinating questions as how far in advance we choose our words when we begin speaking. Several important models of speech production are evaluated, and the authors provide insights into the kind of evidence researchers have used to develop their models, including information derived from experiments, from slips of the tongue, and from speakers' hesitations and disfluencies in speaking.

Chapter 8 Language Acquisition.   This chapter deals with one of the most basic psycholinguistic questions—how children, in the course of just a few years, are able to acquire complex language. The authors trace children's language development from their earliest attempts to communicate, even before they have real words, to their acquisition of complex propositional language. Theoretical positions vary widely in this field, and the range of language acquisition theories is sampled and described.

Chapter 9 A Psycholinguistic Account of Reading.   Perhaps no other invention has changed the course of history in the way that writing has. The topics of Chapter 9 are reading and writing. The authors discuss the history of writing systems, and they describe the discovery of the alphabetic principle: that one letter can stand for a single sound in the language. The major topic of the chapter is how readers process written language. A number of models of the development of the reading process in children also are presented here.

Chapter 10 Bilingualism and Second Language Acquisition.   A psycholinguistic discussion of language processing would not be complete without consideration of bilingualism and second language learning. As the author points out, monolingualism, so common and pervasive in the United States, is the exception around the world. Most of the people of the world are to some extent bilingual. In addition to discussing theories of bilingualism and second language learning, this chapter asks (and answers) a number of interesting questions: Is it possible to be perfectly bilingual, to have native–like proficiency in two languages? Is there an optimal age to learn a second language? What are the characteristics of very good second language learners? Is second language learning similar in psycholinguistic terms to first language learning?

These ten chapters were chosen to reflect the wide range of topics considered as domains within psycholinguistic inquiry, including some topics often given little or no coverage in introductory texts—neurolinguistics, speech perception, reading, and second language acquisition. Within these chapters, our intention was to develop an understanding of the major issues confronting researchers in the field, rather than an exhaustive summary of work to date. Thus, the text is introductory in intent and is meant to begin rather than end a student's study of the psychology of language.

The text is accompanied by a detailed and useful instructor's manual (including test questions of varying types) and a stimulus tape with examples of some of the phenomena and research paradigms discussed in the chapters.

In the course of editing this revision, we have become indebted to a large number of people. Our first thanks go to our distinguished colleagues who contributed chapters to this volume. We are also grateful to the editorial and marketing staff at Harcourt Brace, particularly to Lisa Hensley, Susan R. Petty, Elaine Richards, and Don Grainger. We thank also Mary Perry at Boston University and Mary Donaldson, Phyllis Bonelli, and Maria Dixon at the University of Maryland. And, of course, we thank our families.

For helpful comments and suggestions for improvement, we thank Catherine Doughty, Georgetown University; William Frawley, University of Delaware; Judith Goodman; University of Missouri—Columbia; Ken Kallio, State University of New York—Geneseo; Michael W. O'Boyle, Iowa State University; Neal Perlmutter, Northeastern University; Dan Swift, Vision Research Graphics; and Shari Speer, University of Kansas.

ABOUT THE AUTHORS

William Orr Dingwall received his PhD in linguistics from Georgetown University. He served as co-director of the linguistics program and later as associate professor of hearing and speech sciences at the University of Maryland, College Park. His areas of research and publication are brain and language and the evolution of language. He has also served as an editor for the journal *Brain and Language*.

Victoria Fromkin is a professor of linguistics at the University of California, Los Angeles, where she has served as department chair and vice chancellor for graduate programs. She is a past president of the Linguistic Society of America, a fellow of the American Academy of Sciences, the American Association for the Advancement of Science, the New York Academy of Science, the American Psychological Society and the Acoustical Society of America. She is the author (with Robert Rodman) of *An Introduction to Language* (5th Ed.) and has published over one hundred books, monographs and papers on topics in phonetics, phonology, speech errors, processing models, aphasia and the brain/mind/language interface.

Jean Berko Gleason is a professor of psychology and director of the graduate program in human development at Boston University, where she has also served as department chair. Her PhD is from Harvard/Radcliffe. A past president of the International Association for the Study of Child Language, she is currently president of the Gypsy Lore Society. She has conducted research and published widely in the fields of aphasia, language development in children, gender differences in parents' speech, and cross-cultural differences.

Roberta Michnick Golinkoff is H. Rodney Sharp Professor of Education, Psychology and Linguistics at the University of Delaware. After obtaining her PhD at Cornell University, she was a post-doctoral fellow at the Learning Research and Development Center at the University of Pittsburgh. With Dr. Kathy Hirsh-Pasek, she is the co-author of *The Origins of Grammar: Evidence from Early Language Comprehension*. Among her many publications are works on children's early comprehension strategies and on the development of the lexicon.

Kathy Hirsh-Pasek is a professor of developmental and cognitive psychology and director of the Infant Language and Perception Laboratories at Temple University. Since she received her PhD from the University of Pennsylvania, she has co-authored two books and has written dozens of articles in the area of early language development.

Allyssa McCabe is associate professor of psychology at the University of Massachusetts Lowell. She has also taught at Harvard University and at Tufts University. She received her PhD in psycholinguistics from the University of Virginia. She is co-editor of the journal *Narrative Inquiry* and the author of many books and articles. Her current research is on narrative and metaphor.

Bhuvana Narasimhan recently completed her doctoral dissertation in the Program in Applied Linguistics at Boston University. She has taught at several universities in Boston, and her research includes child language development and lexical semantics in cross-cultural perspective.

Nan Bernstein Ratner is associate professor and chair of hearing and speech sciences at the University of Maryland, College Park. She received her doctorate in applied psycholinguistics from Boston University. A fellow of the American Speech, Language and Hearing Association, she has focused her research and publications on speech and language production disorders, fluency, and language acquisition in children.

Lauretta M. Reeves is an associate professor in the Department of Psychology at Rowan University in Glassboro, New Jersey. Her research interests and publications are in reference and lexical acquisition, particularly in the area of semantic and syntactic factors that contribute to noun learning in infants.

Catherine Snow is the Henry Lee Shattuck Professor of Education at the Harvard Graduate School of Education. Her PhD is from McGill University. She has served on the National Academy of Sciences Committee to Establish a Research Agenda for Language Minority Children and chairs the Committee on the Prevention of Reading Difficulties in Children from Birth to Eight. She is director of a ten-year longitudinal study of literacy development in children from low-income families. She is editor of the journal *Applied Psycholinguistics* and is also past president of the International Association for the Study of Child Language. Her many books and papers are in the areas of bilingualism, language development, and literacy.

Debra Titone is a senior research associate at Brandeis University. Her PhD in experimental psychology is from the State University of New York at Binghamton. Dr. Titone has published articles on spoken word recognition, and how the brain supports higher-level language processes such as contextual sensitivity, nonliteral language, and discourse comprehension. She has taught at the State University of New York at Binghamton and the State University of New York, College at Oneonta.

Frank Vellutino is a professor of psychology and director of the Child Research and Study Center at the University of Albany, State University of New York. His research interests include memory and language processes, the causes and correlates of dyslexia, word identification, and the cognitive and linguistic foundations of reading ability. His recent publications include works on word identification and semantic and phonological coding in poor and normal readers.

Arthur Wingfield is a professor of psychology and a member of the teaching and research faculty of the Volen National Center for Complex Systems at Brandeis University. He holds a doctorate in philosophy from Oxford University in England. Dr. Wingfield's honors have included a MERIT Award from the National Institute on Aging and a research award from the American Speech, Language, and Hearing Association. He has authored or co-authored two books on memory and cognition as well as numerous journal articles on language processing and memory, with a special focus on speech processing in adult aging. He has most recently co-edited a volume on word-finding deficits in aphasia.

Maryanne Wolf is a professor in the Department of Child Study at Tufts University and director of the Center for Reading and Language Research there. She received her doctorate from the Harvard Graduate School of Education. The recipient of major teaching awards, she currently heads a large research project on curriculum development in reading disabilities intervention that will involve hundreds of children in Boston, Atlanta, and Toronto. Her research and publications are in the areas of developmental neurolinguistics, reading, and neuropsychology and cognition.

Grace Yeni-Komshian is professor of hearing and speech sciences at the University of Maryland, College Park. She received her PhD in psychology from McGill University. She has published widely in a number of areas of psycholinguistics, including speech perception and child phonology. Her current research focuses on bilingualism.

CONTENTS

Chapter 1

AN INTRODUCTION TO PSYCHOLINGUISTICS: WHAT DO LANGUAGE USERS KNOW?   1

Nan Bernstein Ratner   University of Maryland at College Park
Jean Berko Gleason   Boston University
Bhuvana Narasimhan   Boston University

Chapter 2

THE BIOLOGICAL BASES OF HUMAN COMMUNICATIVE BEHAVIOR 51

William Orr Dingwall *The University of Maryland at College Park*

Chapter 3

Chapter 4

WORDS AND MEANING: FROM PRIMITIVES TO COMPLEX ORGANIZATION   157

Lauretta M. Reeves   Rowan University
Kathy Hirsh-Pasek   Temple University
Roberta Golinkoff   University of Delaware

Chapter 5

SENTENCE PROCESSING   227

Arthur Wingfield & Debra Titone
Department of Psychology and Volen National Center for Complex Systems
Brandeis University

Chapter 6

Chapter 7

Chapter 8

Chapter 9

Chapter 10

Chapter 1

An Introduction to Psycholinguistics: What Do Language Users Know?

Nan Bernstein Ratner
University of Maryland at College Park

Jean Berko Gleason
Boston University

Bhuvana Narasimhan
Boston University

INTRODUCTION

Language is so basic to our existence that life without words is difficult to envision. Because speaking, listening, reading, and writing are such fundamental aspects of our daily lives, they seem to be ordinary skills. Executed easily and effortlessly, language use guides us through our day. It facilitates our relationships with others and helps us understand world events and the arts and sciences. However, as this book will demonstrate, even the simplest forms of language use are based on complicated processes; for instance, answering, "Tigers," in response to the toddler who points at some zoo animals and says, "What's that?" involves many mysteries: How did we come up with the word so quickly from among the many thousands of words in our vocabularies? Assuming that the word is stored somewhere in our brain, is it stored whole or in pieces? How do we know we have the right word when we have selected it? If we make a slip of the tongue or mistake in naming the tigers, why are we more likely to say, "Lions, oops, I mean tigers," than "chair," or, like the raven, "nevermore"? When we thank a colleague by saying, "I really appreciate your help on this project" (or, perhaps, "Thanks a bundle, buddy"), what processes underlie our choice of words and the way we combine them? How does our thought—in this case, a sense of gratitude—become encoded into a message? Similarly, when we hear the words, "That bench has just been painted," how do we determine what the message means and what it implies about the fact that we are, alas, sitting on the bench? Finally, why, on some occasions, will a speaker deliberately pick what would appear to be the wrong word for a situation, such as when a parent calls our tiger "a big kitty" when speaking to a young speaker of the language? From the speaker's thought to her message, from her words to her listener's understanding, the communicative function entails multiple stages of formulation, execution, and decoding. It is an easy and natural skill, but one that is difficult to explain fully or to describe.

In this chapter, we begin by outlining the domain of psycholinguistic inquiry. What is the discipline known as psycholinguistics? What do psycholinguists study? Our brief introductory descriptions will preview the more detailed coverage given to major issues in psycholinguistics found in Chapters 2 through 10.

We will next establish what we mean when we talk about language production, comprehension, and acquisition. What exactly is a language? All human languages share important formal properties: they are structured, symbolic systems. Further, every human language has conventions or rules that govern proper use of its subsystems. These subsystems include a sound system, or **phonology;** rules for word formation, or **morphology;** a vocabulary and meaning system, **lexicon** and **semantics;** rules for sentence formation, **syntax;** and rules for how to use language appropriately in social settings, **pragmatics.**

After drawing a sketch of the typical language user's knowledge, we will discuss why psycholinguists must often resort to complex experimental designs to understand how people process language. The experimental approach is necessary because our own **metalinguistic awareness** (or knowledge about language) is limited, and we typically are not conscious of the psychological processing that underlies language use. For instance, we cannot find out which additional words in our lexicon are also activated when we hear the word *cow* just by thinking about it, but we can devise an experiment that provides some answers to this and other questions about the organization of our internal dictionary.

Most of our discussions of language processing will use examples that illustrate how English is understood and produced. But clearly, English is just one of the world's languages, and many important variations among languages must be accommodated within general models of language processing. We will briefly address this issue and explore its ramifications both in this chapter and in later ones. The differences, for example, between oral and gestural (or signed) languages have extremely important implications for theories of language comprehension, production, and acquisition. In the same vein, differences between oral language processing and the acts of reading or writing must be accounted for in our models.

Finally, we will review the recent evolution of psycholinguistics as a discipline. Although many of the questions posed by psycholinguists have been considered by scientists and philosophers since ancient times, the field of inquiry that we call psycholinguistics is of recent origin. We will trace its roots in psychology and linguistics, as well as its early development.

WHAT IS PSYCHOLINGUISTICS?

The Domain of Psycholinguistic Inquiry

Linguistics is the discipline that describes the structure of language, including its grammar, sound system, and vocabulary. The field of **psycholinguistics,** or the psychology of language, is concerned with discovering the psychological processes by which humans acquire and use language. Conventionally, psycholinguistics addresses three major concerns (Clark & Clark, 1977; Tanenhaus, 1989):

1. *Comprehension: How people understand spoken and written language.* This is a broad area of investigation that involves scrutiny of the comprehension process at many levels, including investigation of how speech signals are interpreted by listeners (**speech perception,** discussed in Chapter 3), how the meanings of words are determined (**lexical access,** Chapter 4), how the grammatical structure of sentences is analyzed to obtain larger units of meaning (**sentence processing,** Chapter 5), and how longer conversations or texts are appropriately formulated and evaluated (**discourse,** Chapter 6). Concerns specifically relevant to how written language is processed are also part of this domain, and are discussed in Chapter 9.

2. *Speech production: How people produce language.* The chapters that follow suggest that it is somewhat easier to study comprehension than production; we can use controlled language stimuli and then analyze patterns of accuracy and error, response time, and other behaviors to arrive at an estimate of how listeners process language. However, it is more difficult to gain insight into how concepts are put into linguistic form; the process is largely hidden from observation, and speakers' verbal expressions, even in response to rather controlled eliciting stimuli, vary considerably. As Chapter 7 will indicate, we learn most about the probable nature of the speech production process from speakers' mistakes (**speech errors** or false starts) and from breaks in the ongoing rhythm of connected speech (**hesitation** and **pausal phenomena,** or **speech disfluencies**).

3. *Acquisition: How people learn language.* The major focus in this domain has been on how children acquire a first language (**developmental psycholinguistics**). First language acquisition is covered in Chapter 8 of this volume, and Chapter 10 surveys what we know about the process of acquiring subsequent languages (foreign language learning). Developmental psycholinguistics has become, by itself, a formidably large discipline with a wide array of journals, texts, and monographs specifically addressed to this issue.

In addition to these areas of inquiry, the search for the neurological bases of human language functioning continues. Where do language formulation and understanding reside in the brain? What anatomical structures underlie normal development and use of the full range of language skills? **Neurolinguistics** investigates the anatomical and physiological correlates of language behaviors. As Chapter 2 demonstrates, great strides have been made in identifying particular areas of the human brain associated with specific linguistic abilities.

The ultimate goal of psycholinguistic inquiry is, of course, to develop an integrated account of how competent language understanding and use occur and how young children acquire these abilities so rapidly. There are many reasons why understanding this process is a goal still to be met: Language is one of our most complex systems of behavior. Additionally, the research tools and techniques best used to study particular language skills do not lend themselves readily to the full array of skills found in communicative interactions. For example, methods that work well to investigate the comprehension of certain syntactic structures by mature adult listeners often don't work well or at all for the study of language understanding in young children or the process of speech production by either adults or children. The best models of human language capacity make use of converging evidence from adult comprehension and production and from child language acquisition.

LANGUAGE

What Is Language?

A baby cries because she is wet. A bee performs its "waggle dance" to inform others in the hive where nectar can be found. A cat scratches the door of the cupboard where the cat food is kept when she is hungry. A dog barks to be let out. A parakeet says, "Pretty bird!" as he views himself in the mirror. A child says, "I hate tofu, and I won't eat it."

Which of these represents the use of language? Certainly each example communicates a message to those who receive it. But most of us would agree that only the last example truly exemplifies the use of language. What most distinguishes human language from these other communicative acts?

Human language is characterized by its *hierarchical structure.* By this we mean that the message is divisible into smaller units of analysis. The child's utterance is a sentence that contains smaller discrete elements such as words and sounds, and these can be recombined to make other utterances (for example, "I won't eat tofu. I hate it."). All human languages are characterized by such structural properties. Conversely, it is difficult to analyze the "substructure" of infant or animal cries. Although some substructure may appear to exist in the bee's dance and the bird's replication of human speech, such messages lack the *infinite creativity* of human language. Competent language users are able to produce and understand a virtually unlimited number of well-formed sentences in their language.

And all human languages express the full range of speakers' experiences, even imaginary ones. Such is not the case (as far as we can tell) with animal languages. The parakeet is not free to discuss the weather with you, nor can he even paraphrase his message and say, "I'm a pretty bird," or "You're not a bird." Although the bee is adept at directing its fellow bees to nectar, it is incapable of warning them that an irate homeowner is coming after them with a can of insecticide. It may (or may not) possess such knowledge, but it lacks a sufficiently rich system of symbols and rules for their combination to allow transmission of a large variety of concepts.

The structural properties of any language include rules for using it properly; thus language is a *rule-governed* system of behavior. There is no right or wrong way to bark or cry (though some versions may be more annoying than others). Conversely, the rules of English specify that the child in our example may *not* say, "Tofu I like not, eat and it won't I." English, like other languages, has conventions for knowing what words must be included and for ordering those words in sentences. These rules are quite *arbitrary* in nature; no real reason exists why English should require the particular grammatical conventions it does. For example, English is considered to have a basic word order in which subjects precede verbs and objects follow verbs (what is typically called **S-V-O word order**), although not all English sentences conform to this ordering. However, the tendency to put subjects before verbs in English sentences is no more "logical" than an insistence that the verb should come first, followed by the subject, as happens to be the case in Arabic. Furthermore, the particular words used to describe entities, actions, and attributes in any language are also arbitrary. There is no good reason why a tree should be called *tree,* and of course in languages other than English, it is not. The words of a language are **symbols** that substitute one thing (in this case, the string of sounds in the word *tree*) for another (the concept of a tall plant with branches, bark, and leaves). Both the grammar and vocabulary of any language represent arbitrary conventions that the users of a language agree to abide by. Languages do not vary infinitely; there appear to be constraints on the nature of possible linguistic rules that reflect the nature of human cognition (Chomsky, 1981). Universal characteristics of human cognition and perception probably also underlie the presence in all languages of syntactic categories such as *noun* and *verb* (Greenberg, 1963). Properties shared by all languages are called linguistic **universals.**

These characteristics of language give it many other properties not shared by animal communication or infant cries. When both speaker and hearer (or writer and reader) share the same rule system, message transmission can be not only creative but usually unambiguous, its meaning clear. What the child is telling his parents about tofu is quite explicit; there is little doubt about his meaning. But a crying infant's parents will say, "I wonder what's wrong with the baby?" and try checking her diaper, burping her, or offering a bottle until they determine the meaning of her message, or at least until she stops crying. The same is true for the dog whose bark may not clearly inform its owner whether he needs to go out, needs more water, or sees a squirrel in the backyard. Language also allows us to talk about absent, or **displaced** concepts. We can converse about the upcoming election without having the candidates present; we can discuss purchasing a new sofa without physically looking at one. In this regard, human language is quite different from animal communication systems, whose communicative behaviors require elicitation by environmental stimuli.

Is Language Species-Specific?

Bertrand Russell once remarked, "No matter how eloquently a dog may bark, he cannot tell you that his parents were poor but honest." One of the properties attributed to language is that it is a uniquely human behavior. Virtually all human beings spontaneously acquire a language without overt instruction and relatively quickly during childhood, unless they possess handicapping conditions. Researchers have not yet isolated any natural form of animal communication that embodies all of the features of language we have discussed. They have probed the communicative systems of many animals, searching for the linguistic properties that define human language. Although bees, birds, whales, dolphins, and nonhuman primates are capable of fairly sophisticated message exchanges (Akmajian, Demers, Farmer, & Harnish, 1995; Demers, 1989), their capacities fall short of those of young children.

There have been attempts to teach human language to animals, particularly primates. It is true that some of the signing apes (Terrace, 1979; Rumbaugh, 1977) produce brief utterances that relate to their current intents (for example, "Tickle Nim"), but, as Demers (1989) notes, it is the unbounded productivity of new and varying messages so characteristic of human language activity that is largely missing from animal communication systems. Animal communication is typically context or stimulus dependent; vocalizations are likely to occur under narrowly specified conditions. We have much to learn from the study of animal languages and from attempts to teach human language to primates; currently, the most promising work is being conducted with bonobos, or pygmy chimpanzees, which display extraordinary communicative talents (Savage-Rumbaugh & Lewin, 1994). Most researchers agree that nonhuman primates can learn to use and comprehend vocabulary. However, it is a matter of spirited debate whether any nonhuman primate has learned to manipulate syntax as well as a typical two-year-old child (Akmajian, Demers, Farmer, & Harnish, 1995; Pinker, 1994).

Distinguishing Between Language and Speech

Although some authors say that language is sound (Dinneen, 1967) or that the medium of language is sound (Bolinger & Sears, 1981), this is not necessarily true. Most of the world's languages *are* spoken or oral, and for most individuals speaking precedes and is of greater importance than reading or writing. However, some human languages are *signed* or gestural. These languages, of which **American Sign Language (ASL)** is one example, have the same basic linguistic features found in oral human languages. Thus, like spoken languages, they are rule-governed, arbitrary systems of communication with hierarchical substructuring that are capable of infinite creativity and spontaneously acquired by infants exposed to them.

Many discussions in this book will require the extremely important distinction between *language* and *speech*. In some chapters we will specifically be concerned with how people decode the sounds of language; in others we will investigate how people respond to written language. In many cases, we will draw parallels between what we know about oral language comprehension and production and the processing of sign languages.

WHAT SPEAKERS AND LISTENERS KNOW: A BRIEF SURVEY OF LINGUISTICS

Linguistics is the study of language in its various aspects. As a science, its primary concern is the *structure* of a particular language or of languages in general. By structure we mean the rules for forming acceptable utterances of the language. Linguists take as their data what people say and what people find acceptable in language use. They work from actual language examples and individual intuitions about whether such examples are well formed to develop general accounts of the grammar of a language. In this sense, linguistics is *descriptive,* rather than *prescriptive*. That is, linguists attempt to account for what we actually say and what we find acceptable or poorly formed rather than to formulate language rules that we all must live by. By *acceptable* or *well formed* we mean that speakers agree that a particular utterance can indeed be said in a particular language, and we make no judgment about whether or not it *should* be said. Many of our experiences in English grammar classes were of the prescriptive sort, in which we were cautioned about dangling participles. The goal of linguistics is not to ensure that people follow a standard set of rules in speaking, but rather to develop parsimonious models to explain the language that people actually use and appreciate as well formed. In the next sections we will briefly survey the structural properties of human languages that must be accounted for in understanding how language is used and acquired. We will discuss the role of linguistic theories in psycholinguistic research in later sections of this chapter and text.

Levels of Language Analysis

A psycholinguist who wishes to understand how a sentence such as *How do people communicate with one another?* is processed must first acknowledge that understanding it depends on several smaller tasks:

- The *sounds* of the message must be isolated and recognized.
- The *words* must be identified and associated with their meanings.
- The *grammatical structure* of the message must be analyzed sufficiently to determine the roles played by each word.
- The resulting *interpretation* of the message must be evaluated in light of past experience and the current context.

Only then can the utterance be considered "understood."

Linguists, philosophers, and psychologists have long appreciated that language is a complex system that can be considered at multiple levels of analysis. Every human language may be analyzed in terms of its **phonology** (sound system), **morphology** (rules for word formation), **lexicon** (vocabulary), **syntax** (rules for combining words into grammatically acceptable sequences), **semantics** (conventions for deriving the meanings of words and sentences), and **pragmatics** (rules for appropriate social use and interpretation of language in context). Linguists strive to develop descriptions of a language that capture its characteristics at each of these levels. Psycholinguists, in turn, seek to determine whether these levels or units of analysis are represented in the actual process of producing or understanding various forms of language. Some call this endeavor the search for the *psychological reality* of linguistic descriptions.

We may more readily appreciate the complex interaction of these systems by considering efforts to get by in a language we do not know. Anyone who has attempted to function in a foreign culture using only an English–foreign language dictionary knows the frustrating limitations of a list of words and their meanings. Below we will examine some of the many specific abilities that underlie competent use of language. As we do, it may become evident that, although using and understanding language is a relatively quick and easy task for most of us, many aspects of our linguistic knowledge are subconscious in nature.

Phonology

The words of a language are divisible into sound sequences, and part of language knowledge is an understanding of the particular sounds used in a language, as well as the rules for their combination. The study of how the sounds of a language are physically enunciated is known as **articulatory phonetics** and will be explored in Chapter 3. A great number of speech sounds are available to the world's languages. Although substantial diversity exists among the world's languages—numbers of consonants in a given language range between 6 and 95 and numbers of vowels range between 3 and 46—any single language employs a sound subset of approximately 23 consonants and 9 vowels (Maddieson, 1984). The distinctive sounds used in a language are its **phonemes.** Phonemes are contrastive; changing from one to another within a word produces either a change in meaning or a nonword. For example, the /p/ in *pit* serves to contrast *pit* from other English words such as *bit, sit,* and *kit,* which are similar in all respects except that they begin with different English phonemes. Most of us are familiar with the experience of trying to learn a second language whose **phonemic inventory** (sounds used in the language) differs from our own. For example, pronunciation of the French word *rue* (street), or German name *Bach* confronts English speakers with the need to produce phonemes (the sounds of the French *r* and *u,* and the German *ch*) that do not exist in their language. Figure 1.1 shows the phonemic inventory of English; Figure 1.2 provides the inventories of Hindi and Hawaiian for your comparison. Although the charts contain symbols that may be unfamiliar to you, we include the charts to illustrate one simple concept: English uses more phonemic contrasts than Hawaiian, but fewer than Hindi. Languages vary in the size and shape of their phonemic inventories.[1]

Speakers of a language must be able to produce all the meaningful sound contrasts of that language. They must also learn which sound contrasts are not meaningful. For example, English contains the phonemes /p/ and /b/, which actually are similar sounds: They are both bilabial stops (made by blocking air behind the lips), one unvoiced and the other voiced. ("Voiced" means made using laryngeal activity. Try saying /p/ and /b/ to yourself to appreciate the difference between these sounds.) Because we can find **minimal pairs** such as *pit* and *bit,* which differ only in respect to /p/ and /b/ and have different meanings, we know that /p/ and /b/ are different phonemes. But consider the English words *pot* and *spot.* Although it is not obvious to English speakers, the /p/ in these two words is not the same sound. More force is used when we say *pot,* and the resulting puff of air is called **aspiration.** Linguists write the sound in this word as [pʰ]. The /p/ of *spot* is produced without aspiration—it is *unaspirated.* Yet this sound contrast cannot be used to mark a difference in meaning in English, where the two sounds are separate **allophones** (variants of the same phoneme) rather than separate phonemes. It is important to note that some languages create a phonemic contrast out of differences that in other languages are only allophonic. In Hindi, sounds similar to the [p] and [pʰ] sounds in *spot* and *pot* are two distinct phonemes, as in the Hindi words *pal,* "moment," and *pʰal,* "fruit." Most English speakers would find it difficult to hear (and perhaps produce) this distinction; their experience with English has taught them to ignore variations in production of /p/. In a similar way, a Chinese speaker learning English may have trouble with the English phonemes /r/ and /l/, which share many acoustic properties; Chinese has only /l/. The Chinese speaker may find it difficult both to distinguish and produce /r/ and may instead use the well-learned native /l/ for both sounds, saying "lake" for both *lake* and *rake.* The French, Spanish, or Italian speaker whose language contains /i/ as in *sheep,* but not /I/ as in *ship* may find production of these different words of English difficult, saying

---

[1] According to some authorities, there actually are more phonemes in Hawaiian than are shown here, including long variants of all five vowels as well as diphthongs (see Schutz, 1981).

FIGURE 1.1

The phonemic inventory of English.

English									
Consonants / **Place of articulation**	Bilabial	Labio-dental	Dental	Dental/alveolar	Alveolar	Palatal	Velar	Glottal	Labio-velar
Voiceless (vl) plosive	P			t			k		
Voiced (vd) plosive	b			d			g		
vl. sibilant affricate						tʃ			
vd. sibilant affricate						dȝ			
vl. nonsibilant fricative		f	θ					h	
vd. nonsibilant fricative		v	ð						
vl. sibilant fricative					s	ʃ			
vd. sibilant fricative					z	ȝ			
Voiced nasal	m			n			ŋ		
vd. lateral approximant				l,r					
vd. central approximant						j			w

Manner of articulation (row label for the consonant rows)

Vowels	Front	Back
high	i	u
	I	U
mid	e	ə o
	ε	ʌ ɔ
low	æ	a

/ʃip/ for both words, as in, "I took a *sheep* to the Bahamas," when referring to what she did on spring break.

As a final example, assume that we are trying to instruct a computer to recognize speech so that we might talk to it rather than type our communications. Consider the case of the common English phoneme /t/. What does it sound like? Most of us have a canonical or idealized notion of what /t/ sounds like. But consider the sentence *Tom Burton tried to steal a butter plate.* There are several /t/ variants in this phrase, and they are not at all produced in an identical fashion. The allophones of /t/ include the

FIGURE 1.2

Phonemic inventories of Hindi and Hawaiian.

Hawaiian Consonants

	Bilabial	Dental/alveolar	Velar	Glottal	Variable place	Labial-velar
Voiceless plosive	p		k	ʔ		
Vl. nonsibilant fric.					h	
Voiced nasal	m	"n"				
Vd. lateral approx.		"l"				
Vd. central approx.						w

Vowels

High	i	u
Higher mid	"o"	
Lower mid	ε	
Low	a	

Hindi-Urdu Consonants

	Bilabial	Labio-dental	Dental	Dental/alveolar	Palato-alveolar	Retroflex	Palatal	Velar	Uvular	Glottal	Variable place
Voiceless plosive	p		t̪			ʈ		k	q²	ʔ²	
Vl. aspirated plosive	pʰ		t̪ʰ			ʈʰ		kʰ			
Voiced plosive	b		d̪			ɖ		g			
Breathy vd. plosive	bː		d̪ː			ɖː		gː			
Vl. sibilant affricate					tʃ						
Vl. asp. sib. affricate					tʃʰ						
Vd. sibilant affricate					dʒ						
Breathy vd. sib. affricate					dʒ						
Vl. nonsib. fricative		f²							χ²		
Vd. nonsib. fricative									ʁ²	ɦ	
Vl. sibilant fricative				"s"	ʃ²						
Vd. sibilant fricative				"z"²	ʒ²						
Voiced nasal	m			"n"							
Breathy vd. nasal	mː			nː							
Voiced trill				"r"							
Voiced flap						ɽ²					
Vd. lateral approximant				"l"							
Breathy vd. lat. approximant				"l"ː							
Vd. central approximant	β						j				

Vowels

	Long oral	Short oral	Diphthongs
High	iː uː	ɪ ɨ̇ ʊ	əe
Higher mid	eː oː		oo
Lower mid		ə	ə̃ẽ
Low	aː	a	õo

	Long nasalized	Short nasalized	
High	ĩː ũː	ɪ̃ ʊ̃	
Higher mid	ẽː õː		
Lower mid		ə̃	
Low	ãː	ã	

aspirated initial /t/ of *Tom.* They also include the **glottalized stop** usually found when /t/ lies between /ər/ and syllabic /n/ as in *Burton,* and the **palatalized** /t/ that usually results when /t/ precedes /r/ (as in *tried*). The words *tried to* illustrate the elongated single phoneme that may occur when /t/ is next to another /t/ or to /d/. In *steal* we find the unaspirated /t/ that occurs when /t/ is preceded by other sounds rather than in initial position. The /t/ in *butter* is characterized by the quick "flapped" production that tends to occur when /t/ lies between a vowel and /ər/. Finally, as the last sound in *plate,* we come to the **unreleased,** or *checked,* version of /t/ that is typical when /t/ is the final sound in an utterance. Note how the sound seems to be only partially pronounced as the sentence ends. These numerous variants of /t/ cause the competent speaker or listener of English little trouble. However, the computer has every reason to assume that, because they differ acoustically, sometimes in fairly major ways, they represent seven distinct phonemes. The competent user of English has learned to collapse these distinctions into one phonemic class and does not randomly produce the allophones in inappropriate contexts (for instance, does not attempt *Tom* with a glottal stop, flap, or unaspirated /t/). A computer must be explicitly instructed in such details of phonological knowledge, not a trivial task, as Chapter 3 notes.

If we consider the phonemic profiles of the three languages in Figures 1.1 and 1.2, we see that a speaker of Hindi learning English must, among other things, learn to ignore certain phonemic contrasts found in Hindi but not English, such as the presence or absence of aspiration. The Hawaiian speaker learning English will have to learn to produce and distinguish phonemes not present in his native language. The processes of acquiring meaningful phonemic contrasts and learning to ignore nonmeaningful contrasts both are essential to the successful use of a language.

Sequences of Sounds: Phonotactics

Phonology is more than the repertoire of sounds in a language; it includes rules for their lawful combination into words. Consider the predicament of a contestant on the popular television show *Wheel of Fortune* who must guess a letter when the following sequence is revealed: _TR_N_.

Some guesses are more likely to be successful than others. Many readers will suggest an S for the first slot, unconsciously mindful that no other initial consonant would be permitted to precede T and R in English. The most common guesses for final position are G, K, and D and E (T is also possible but has already been "guessed"). A common strategy for the middle slot is to see what belongs in the initial and final position and to consider what vowels (note that a vowel is assumed in this case) would result in an English word. Thus, if S is correct in the first slot and G is the right answer for the last slot, then good guesses for the vowel are I, O, or U; A and E result in a permissible sequence of sounds in English, but not a lexically meaningful solution. Note that a guess of E for the last slot in our example leads to the same dilemma: the sequences *strane, strene, strine, strone,* and *strune* do not mean anything in everyday English, although the phonotactics of English do not prevent these sequences. The rules of English definitely prohibit K from both the initial and medial slots of our example.

The importance of knowing the rules for combining sounds in a language extends well beyond ensuring successful competition on game shows or accurate completion of crossword puzzles. As Chapter 3 demonstrates, in ordinary conversation the identity of individual speech sounds is often unclear. Experimental research indicates that listeners are often confronted with the auditory equivalent of our game-show example; they hear some of the sounds but not all and must "fill in the blanks." The usually effortless and accurate solution to such puzzles is mediated by the listener's knowledge of the phonemic inventory, phonotactic constraints, and lexicon (vocabulary) as well as the context. Chapter 3 explores the complex deployment of these systems in the process of speech perception.

The phonological system of a language also includes rules for the interpretation of **prosody,** or intonation and stress patterns. In English, prosodic cues can signal grammatical contrasts such as the difference between statements and questions (*You're going,* vs. *You're going?*). Prosody can also express emotional content and emphasize particular items in speech. The role of prosody in language comprehension is touched upon in Chapters 3 and 5.

The Lexicon and Semantics

When people contemplate communication in a foreign language, often they reach for a dictionary. Dictionaries provide meanings for the words of a given language and provide labels for concepts that speakers wish to discuss. A more technical term for a dictionary is a *lexicon.* A capable speaker-hearer of a language possesses a vast and complicated mental lexicon whose nature is of great interest to psycholinguists. Most adults know the meanings of tens of thousands of words in their native language and can readily comprehend or access them for communicative purposes. **Semantics** is the study of word meanings and the ways in which words are related to one another in our mental lexicon. It also includes the study of sentential meaning in contemporary linguistics.

What a word "means" is not simply explained. How is it that one identifies certain objects as chairs, no matter how they may vary in construction (Bernstein, 1983)? When does an object deserve the label *cup,* rather than *glass* (Labov, 1973)? The difficult problem of explaining how people readily label easily perceived, concrete concepts such as *dog* or *furniture* is addressed in Chapter 4. We can also contrast the knowledge of concrete words with *abstract* notions—*friendship* or *patriotism*—and *relational* words such as *good* or *short.*

Although it is difficult to account for the process of associating meaning with such words, we can define them, and dictionaries routinely do. For example, *frustrate* means, among other things, "to baffle." Some English words, however, do not easily lend themselves to definition: In the sentence *John is frustrated by calculus,* what does *by* mean? In *I really love to sleep late,* what does *to* mean? Somehow, the term "mean" seems inappropriate in these contexts. Most people believe that these words simply make the sentence grammatical, and they are right. Linguists categorize words such as *table, penguin,* and *ecstatic* differently from words such as *the, for,* and *is.* The first group of words are **content words** and the second group are **function words.**

Content words have external referential meaning in the usual sense; they identify and describe. Function words serve particular functions within the sentence by making the relations between the content words clearer. The distinction between content and function words is psychologically meaningful, as Chapters 2, 4, and 7 discuss. We can distinguish between the processes used to retrieve these two types of words in comprehension and production.

Some words also have more than one meaning. Consider this old joke: "Time flies. You can't—they go too fast!" (Of course, we don't ordinarily time flies because, after all, they *do* go too fast.) Multiple meanings make puns, riddles, and other types of humor work. But what happens to the language comprehension process when it encounters a word with multiple entries in the lexicon? Chapter 4 addresses the consequences of such ambiguity.

Other properties of words appear to be psychologically meaningful as well. For example, concrete nouns such as *car* and abstract nouns such as *altruism* seem to be learned and used differently and may be differentially affected in the language of language-impaired individuals. The frequency with which a word is usually encountered in the language also appears to be a nonlinguistic but psychologically meaningful factor. Terms such as *traveling* and *itinerant* are roughly synonymous, but the first is more commonly used in English than the second. Chapter 4 explores frequency effects on lexical processing.

Many other normal conversational phenomena provide insight into the possible nature of our mental dictionary. Why is it that we sometimes cannot recall a word but know what its beginning sound is? What would lead a person to say "slickery" when she means to say "slippery"? Such *performance errors* actually provide some evidence for possible models of the way we use our mental lexicon in constructing messages, as discussed in Chapter 7.

Morphology: The Study of Word Formation

In many languages we can readily identify meaningful units that appear to be separable parts of words. In English, for example, if one is asked to arbitrarily divide the word *cats* into two units, most people will peel off the final *-s*. We readily recognize that it signifies the notion of plurality and can be appended to many other words we wish to pluralize. We can even make a plural of a nonsense word, like *Wug* in Figure 1.3. Other similar word endings in English are *-ing* as in *jumping,* and *-ed* as in *dropped.* Such suffixes are *grammatical morphemes*. In linguistics, a **morpheme** is the smallest unit of a language that carries definable meaning or grammatical function.

Some morphemes are complete words. You cannot divide *table* into smaller units that make sense, nor can you chop up *the*. Examples such as *cats* are different. *Cats* is comprised of two separable notions and is *multimorphemic,* a word that contains more than a single morpheme. However, the parts of *cats* are in a sense unequal. *Cat* can stand by itself in a sentence; *-s* cannot. We recognize this difference by calling a morpheme that can stand by itself a **free morpheme** and one that cannot a **bound morpheme.** Bound morphemes serve two distinct functions. When we attach certain

FIGURE 1.3

Your knowledge of morphology enables you to complete these phrases.

This is a Wug.

Now there is another one.
There are two of them.
There are two _ _ _ _.

This is a man who knows how to Naz.
He is Nazzing. He does it every day.
Every day he _ _ _ _ _ _.

This is a man who knows how to Rick.
He is Ricking. He did the same thing
yesterday. What did he do yesterday?
Yesterday he _ _ _ _ _ _.

bound morphemes to words, we change the word meaning or part of speech. For instance, when the scarecrow in the *Wizard of Oz* was awarded a degree of *thinkology,* this new noun was created by adding the bound morpheme *-ology* (the study of) to the verb *think.* Such morphemes that create a new meaning or change the grammatical function of a word are called **derivational morphemes:** They can be used to derive a new word. Common derivational morphemes such as *un-* and *-ly,* for instance, can turn a *happy* day into an *unhappy* one and adjectives into adverbs (*happy>happily*).

A second type of bound morpheme provides additional information about a word or its grammatical function. These **inflectional morphemes** are used in English to indicate number in nouns (*cat* vs. *cats*), possession *(Harrison* vs. *Harrison's),* verb tense *(jog/jogging; study/studied),* and subject-verb agreement *(I/you/we/they understand vs. he/she/it understands).* Comparatives such as *smarter* and superlatives such as *smartest* are also created from the root form *smart* by the application of inflectional morphemes.

The distinctions between content and function words and between free and bound morphemes appear to be psychologically significant when you examine language understanding and production, as Chapters 2, 4, 5, and 7 illustrate. Describing the root and bound morphemes that combine to create a word such as *unwaveringly* might seem merely an academic exercise, but, as Chapter 4 shows, evidence exists that the language comprehension process must include such a level of analysis to permit successful understanding of the word. Chapter 2 discusses how brain damage can differentially affect ability to produce and understand these different classes of morphemes. Additionally, Chapter 7 includes "slips of the tongue," or speech errors, to demonstrate how we retrieve these different classes of morphemes at different stages of the sentence formulation process during speech.

Syntax: Combining Words to Form Sentences

Let us return to the example of a traveler who attempts to get by in an unknown language—Hungarian, for example—by using an English–Hungarian dictionary. Learning a new vocabulary and pronunciation is certainly a challenge, but our traveler would find that learning to place the new words within the framework of a new grammar is even more difficult. For example, if we are in Budapest and can understand only the word *kocsi* (car) in what a person is telling us, we won't know if they are trying to tell us that our vehicle is impressive, parked illegally, or rolling down the driveway unattended.

Thus, not only is it important to learn the words of an unfamiliar language, but it is also crucial that we know how to combine words into acceptable sequences to convey propositional meaning. Syntax is the study of how words can be put together to produce the well-formed sentences of a language. Consider a sentence such as *John loves Mary*. This sentence consists of a linear string of words—*John, loves,* and *Mary*. However, we cannot combine these words randomly in English without changing the meaning or reducing grammatical acceptability. Consider the following sentences:

   a. John loves Mary
   b. Mary loves John
   c. *Loves John Mary

Of these, the first and second sentences are well formed (or grammatical). The asterisk indicates—following a common convention in linguistics—that the third sentence is not permissible in modern English. Furthermore, *John loves Mary* and *Mary loves John* have different meanings. Thus, changing the word order can either change the meaning of the sentence as in (a) and (b), or it can result in ill-formed (or ungrammatical) sentences as in (c). English imposes fairly strict constraints on word order. Typically the subject is followed by a verb and then its object. For this reason, English is sometimes called an S-V-O (Subject-Verb-Object) language.

However, note that even in English, this word order is not entirely rigid. The sentence *Mary showed John the picture* has an indirect object (IO). *John* intervenes before the object to produce the order of S-V-IO-O. A sentence such as *The man who lives next to my sister collects antique cars* also disrupts the typical S-V-O order in English. It interposes the center-embedded relative clause *who lives next to my sister* between the subject and the verb and object, which produces discontinuity in the S-V-O pattern. Furthermore, sentences such as *John clumsily opened the can* and *John opened the can clumsily* can have a similar meaning even if their word orders differ from one another (Finnegan, 1994).

Crystal (1987) notes that 75% of the world's languages are predominantly S-V-O (French, English, and Hebrew) or S-O-V languages (Tibetan and Korean). Less common primary sentence ordering patterns are V-S-O (Arabic and Welsh) and V-O-S (Malagasy). Languages whose sentences tend to begin with objects (O-V-S languages) are quite rare (Crystal, 1987), but there are some. One is Hixkaryana, a language spoken by approximately 400 people in remote areas of Brazil.

Some languages of the world have fairly variable word order (for example, Walpiri in Australia, or Latin). They allow the equivalents of *John loves Mary, Loves John Mary,* and *Mary loves John,* all with the same meaning (although with some differences in emphasis). How then do these languages express the difference in meaning between *Mary loves John* and *John loves Mary*? Unlike English, which uses word order to mark grammatical relations such as subject and object, these languages use bound morphemes such as **affixes** to mark grammatical roles in the sentence. Thus in Latin, the affix *-am* indicates the direct object in the following sentences, all of which mean, with various emphases, *The charioteer lashes the mare*:

a. Aurīga equ*am* verberat
b. Equ*am* aurīga verberat
c. Verberat aurīga equ*am*

As we shall see in Chapter 5, the implicit expectation that words follow a conventional order in English aids a listener immensely in arriving at a rapid and accurate interpretation of many sentences. We use typical word order patterns as a comprehension strategy in English (Clark & Clark, 1977). But if word order deviates from the norm, problems in interpretation or differences in emphasis can arise. For example, the active sentence *The tornado transported Dorothy* has a focus different from its almost synonymous passive, *Dorothy was transported by the tornado*. In later chapters we survey some of these issues and how the listener most efficiently resolves them.

Are there any constraints on how words can be combined other than the linear order of the words? Consider the following sentences:

a. The famous athlete may endorse the new sneakers.
b. The new sneakers, the famous athlete may endorse.
c. *Sneakers, the famous athlete may endorse the new.
d. *New sneakers, the famous athlete may endorse the.

Sentence (b) differs from (a) in that it *preposes* a part of the sentence (*the new sneakers*) in order to give it more emphasis (perhaps in contrast to old sneakers). However, there are constraints on which of the words in a sentence can be preposed. Only when we prepose *the new sneakers* as a unit can we get a grammatical sentence.

When we try to prepose any other part alone as in (c) or (d), we get ungrammatical sentences.

Syntacticians suggest that *the new sneakers* functions as a unit in the sentence because the words can only be moved around together. Such units are called **constituents,** and operations such as preposing that rearrange the order of words are sensitive to the constituent structure of the sentence. Constituents are like building blocks that can be put together to build up a sentence. Different types of constituents include noun phrases (for example, *the famous athlete*), verb phrases (for example, *endorse the new sneakers*), and prepositional phrases (for example, *in the stadium*), among others. These constituents consist of smaller units or lexical categories, such as noun, verb, preposition, and such. Sentences thus have a hierarchical structure—constituents can be combined into larger and larger units. This can be represented with the **phrase-structure tree** that is presented in Figure 1.4.

The small triangles represent the noun phrase (NP) constituents—*the famous athlete* and *the new sneakers*—in the sentence. The bigger triangle—*endorse the new sneakers*—is formed when the noun phrase *the new sneakers* combines with the verb *endorse* to form a verb phrase (VP). The verb phrase in turn combines with the auxiliary (Aux) *may* and the noun phrase *the famous athlete* to form the full sentence (S). The phrase-structure tree thus represents both the linear order of words along the bottom of the phrase-structure tree and the hierarchical structure by the branching of the (upside down) tree.

In addition to operations such as preposing, the description of basic phenomena in (most) languages—such as question formation *(who may endorse the new sneakers?)*, passivisation *(the new sneakers may be endorsed by the athlete)*, or relative

FIGURE 1.4

A basic phrase-structure tree.

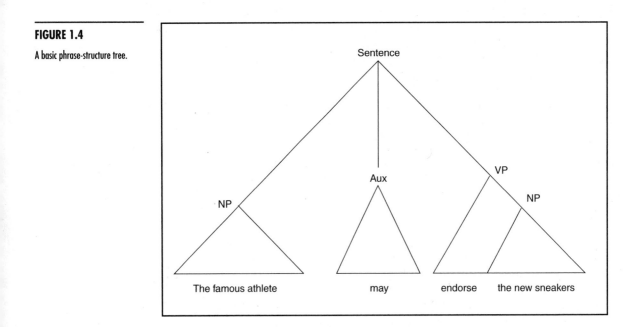

clause formation *(the new sneakers that the famous athlete may endorse)*—relies upon the hierarchical constituent structure of the sentence.

As we have noted, words form larger units called constituents that then combine to form a simple sentence (or a clause)—for example, *The professor was boring.* Entire clauses can also be embedded within one another to form **complex sentences** such as *The professor who taught the course was boring.* This sentence can be further elaborated to form *The professor who taught the course I took last semester was boring, The professor who taught the course on glottochronology I took last semester was boring,* and so on to infinity. Our language allows us to create sentences of infinite length constrained only by the limits of our energy or patience. Linguists describe the creativity of natural language in terms of a property called **recursion.** We are able to create completely new and possibly endless sentences by making use of a rule that recursively embeds one constituent, such as a clause, into another constituent of the same type. (That is, we can always go back to the sentence we have just created and add something new to it to produce longer and longer sentences.) Thus we could continue with the sentence by adding *Mildred thinks that* to form *Mildred thinks that the professor who taught the course on glottochronology I took last semester was boring.* We can also recursively embed constituents such as noun phrases and prepositional phrases into one another to produce a sentence such as *The student is working in the classroom across the hall from the office of the Dean.*

A related type of linguistic creativity is seen in **coordinate sentences,** in which we conjoin complete sentences rather than parts of sentences. For instance, a sentence such as *Jake swims* can be combined with the sentence *Sue sails* to create *Jake swims and Sue sails.* Or we can make even longer coordinate sentences such as *Jake swims and Sue sails and Bob canoes* or *Jake swims and Sue sails and Bob canoes, but Bill bikes,* and so on.

Why spend so much time discussing the ways in which sentences can be broken down into constituent structures? As the chapters that follow will show, such concepts appear to play a role in how sentences are actually understood and produced. Constituents are important building blocks in sentence comprehension and production processes.

Recombining constituents also allows us to creatively understand or produce completely novel utterances that we have never heard before. The sentence *The big aardvark stepped on my toe* is probably a sentence that you have never heard before. Hence you cannot have stored it in your memory. However, we are all able to understand such sentences and have little problem generating any number of utterly novel utterances. We know which orderings of constituents are permissible and which, like *aardvark my toe stepped on big the,* are not. How do we account for this ability? And how are a large number of possible orderings rapidly decoded?

One possible answer would be that we have implicit knowledge of certain *rules* that tell us how to combine a finite number of words into an infinite number of sentences. Over the years, linguists and psychologists have explored the possible rules that might explain the boundless creativity of human language by developing confined sets of rules, or grammars, that can convert a few basic linguistic forms into all the possible sentences a speaker-hearer might need to say or understand. Such rules must be **learnable**—that is, they must be formulated in a way that would account for how children are able to learn them in a short period of time with little explicit training. They must also fulfill the goal of **universality**—they must capture common features of the grammars of all languages.

SYNTACTIC THEORY IN THE 1960S: TRANSFORMATIONAL GRAMMARS. As Newmeyer (1986) notes, grammatical descriptions of languages prior to the 1960s showed little success in addressing the problem of explaining the infinite productivity of language or why some sentences that appear to mean similar things have different wording (that is, *John admires Fred; Fred is admired by John.*). One influential approach to a grammatical description of English was developed by the linguist Noam Chomsky (1957, 1965). Chomsky suggested that the knowledge of the grammar of one's language consists of an abstract system of rules and principles that is part of the speaker's grammatical **competence**. He distinguishes this type of knowledge from **performance,** which is related to "the actual use of language in concrete situations" (Chomsky 1965, p. 4). The kind of model that Chomsky proposed to describe this abstract mental competence was known as **Transformational Generative (TG) grammar,** or what has come to be known as Standard Theory (Chomsky, 1965).

The TG model posited that the grammar consists of two types of rules that allow us to *generate* various sentence types in a given language—*phrase-structure* rules and *transformational* rules. The phrase-structure rules are used to generate the most basic sentence types of English such as simple, active, affirmative declaratives. Phrase-structure rules specify the different kinds of constituents and categories and how they might combine to form a sentence. A (simplified) set of phrase-structure rules to generate the structure underlying a sentence such as *The famous athlete may endorse the new sneakers* is given below:

$$S \rightarrow NP\ Aux\ VP$$

$$NP \rightarrow (Art)\ (Adj)\ N$$

$$VP \rightarrow V\ (NP)$$

$$Aux \rightarrow Tense\ (Modal)$$

$$Tense \rightarrow \begin{cases} Past \\ Present \end{cases}$$

$$Art \rightarrow the$$

$$N \rightarrow athlete,\ sneakers$$

$$V \rightarrow endorse$$

$$Modal \rightarrow may$$

$$Adj \rightarrow new,\ famous$$

Based on Lester, 1971; Akmajian, Demers, Farmer, & Harnish, 1995.

These phrase-structure rules tell you that a sentence (S) consists of a noun phrase (NP), auxiliary (Aux), and a verb phrase (VP). The noun phrase consists of an optional article (Art) followed by an optional adjective (Adj) and a noun (N). The verb phrase consists of a verb followed optionally by a noun phrase. The auxiliary (Aux) consists of tense (either past or present tense), which may be followed by a modal verb. By substituting actual words for each of the category symbols, we construct the **deep structure** (underlying meaning) of the sentence: *The famous athlete + present tense + may + endorse + the new sneakers.* This can be represented, as in Figure 1.5, by a more elaborate version of the phrase-structure tree that we saw in Figure 1.4.

TG grammar also posited a second set of rules called transformational rules. Transformational rules were thought to apply to the underlying deep structure of the sentence in various ways to produce the **surface structure** (final spoken or written form) of the sentence. In order to **derive** the surface structure from the underlying structure *The famous athlete + present tense + may + endorse + the new sneakers,* TG suggested a transformational rule called the *affix-hopping rule* that attaches the *present tense* element to the modal element *may* to produce the surface structure of the sentence *The famous athlete may endorse the new sneakers.*

The two levels of representation in TG grammar—deep structure and surface structure—were used to capture the relationship between many sentence types in an economical way. The phrase-structure rules were used to generate simple, basic, declarative sentences. Sentence types related to these basic sentence types, such as questions, passives or relative clause constructions, were derived from these basic sentence types through various **transformations.**

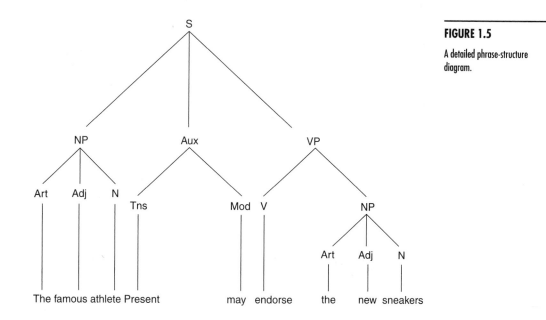

FIGURE 1.5

A detailed phrase-structure diagram.

For instance, an information question of the form *What may the famous athlete endorse?* would be derived by applying the *question* transformation that moved specified elements of the sentence at deep structure to other positions in the sentence at surface structure. This is shown below (based on Lester, 1971):

Phrase-structure rules

↓

Deep structure

The famous athlete may endorse SOMETHING

↓

Transformational rules

Replace SOMETHING with the wh-word WHAT

Move the modal auxiliary before the subject NP

Move the wh-word to the front of the clause

↓

Surface structure

What may the famous athlete endorse?

The concept of underlying representations such as deep structures was also useful in explaining the relationship between active–passive pairs such as *The famous athlete may endorse the new sneakers* and *The new sneakers may be endorsed by the famous athlete*. The active sentence type is generated at deep structure by the phrase-structure rules. The passive counterpart is derived from the underlying active sentence by a **passive transformation** that moves the object *the new sneakers* to the subject position, moves the subject *the famous athlete* into a *by-* phrase, changes the form of the verb to a past participle, and adds a form of the verb *be*. The similarity in meaning between the active and passive sentences arises because they both have the same deep structure, which is the level at which semantic interpretation occurs in the TG model.

Many other types of transformations were posited that added, deleted, or moved elements in the deep structure, some of which were optional and others of which were obligatory. Readable introductions to the principles of the Standard Theory of TG grammar can be found in Akmajian et al. (1995) and Baker (1995).

TG grammar offered interesting possibilities for the collaboration between linguists and psychologists. It made testable claims about whether certain sentences might be more difficult than others for speakers to produce or understand. It also made predictions about how children might move through stages in learning language, some of which were substantiated by studies of children's language development (Menyuk, 1968).

However, although TG grammar offered the exciting possibility of capturing our knowledge of language in a precise way that addressed the concepts of infinite creativity, learnability, and universality, it suffered from several problems (Webelhuth, 1995). For instance, it posited a large number of transformational rules, some with special conditions. Some transformations were quite complicated, and there were few constraints on how complex a transformational rule could be. Even a transformation as seemingly simple as the passive required four separate steps: insertion of an auxiliary, changing the form of the main verb, moving the object to subject position, and moving the subject to a prepositional phrase. When more than one transformational rule was applied to derive the surface structure of a sentence, the rules had to be ordered with respect to each other. For instance, the question *What may be endorsed by the famous athlete?* can be derived only if we apply the passive transformation *before* the question transformation. Furthermore, some transformations were obligatory (for example, the affix-hopping transformation), whereas others were optional (for example, the question and passive transformations). TG grammar was thus problematic from a learnability point of view because it posited so many different rules for a language learner to acquire in such a short time. It was not clear that all children are exposed to the kind of data needed to learn the precise form of these different rules or the conditions under which to apply them (Atkinson, 1992).

TG grammar also shed little light on theories of sentence processing (for a brief review, see Tanenhaus & Trueswell, 1995). The TG model was originally thought to provide the basis for a description of how speakers and listeners actually produce and understand sentences—it had potential psychological reality (Miller & Chomsky, 1963). For example, transformational grammarians hypothesized that passives and other constructions that required transformational derivations would take longer to process than simple, active sentences because listeners would have to "undo" the transformational derivations in order to understand them. That is, the perceptual complexity of the sentence would be related to the derivational complexity of the sentence (Miller, 1962). As we shall note later, many of the first modern psycholinguistic studies addressed this hypothesis, which was called the **Derivational Theory of Complexity** (DTC). The DTC proposed a direct relationship between the number of steps involved in the linguistic derivation of a surface structure and the time it would take to comprehend it.

Early experimental results were somewhat supportive of the Derivational Theory of Complexity (Miller & McKean, 1964; McMahon, 1963; Blumenthal, 1967; Wanner, 1974). However, subsequent tests of the predictions made by the Standard Theory suggested that the comprehension process did not necessarily reflect the proposed linguistic derivation of sentences (Slobin, 1966). Winograd (1972) suggested that although early transformational grammar was adequate in reflecting the logical structure of language, it implied the need for "astronomically large amounts of processing." The DTC assumed that structures that were more complex derivationally would take more time to process, a hypothesis that, as we have noted, was not clearly upheld. This may be because activities that are harder to do may not necessarily take longer to do. Berwick and Weinberg (1984) propose that more complex structures may simply tax the language-processing system more without taking longer to comprehend. Additionally, it may be possible to carry out multiple operations simultaneously by the language-processing system, a concept known as **parallel processing.** In the end, from the perspectives of both learnability theory and processing accounts, the original formulation of TG theory seemed unsatisfactory, although it dramatically changed the ways in which linguists attempted to describe syntactic knowledge.

SYNTACTIC THEORY IN THE 1970S AND 1980S.   It was also possible, of course, that the general premise of the DTC was sound but that the particular grammatical theory being used to describe utterances was not. TG theory underwent substantial modification during the 1970s and 1980s. Although many competing theories of syntax emerged (McCloskey, 1988), a major successor was Principles and Parameters Theory, also referred to as Government and Binding (GB) Theory, the earliest formulation of which appeared in *Lectures in Government and Binding* (Chomsky, 1981).

Although it retained many of the fundamental notions of "classical" transformational grammar, Principles and Parameters Theory (PPT) differed from earlier versions of the theory in several ways (Chomsky, 1981, 1986b; Haegeman, 1991; Napoli, 1993; Cook & Newson, 1996). Numerous differences exist between the Standard Theory and PPT, not all of which are relevant to the major issues discussed in the later chapters of this text. However, some major categories of changes do have important implications for current work in syntactic processing and the acquisition of language by children. In the following section we will discuss some specific aspects of PPT that bear on these topics.

First, the proliferation of phrase-structure rules and transformational rules that followed early TG proposals has been streamlined. Consider the numerous phrase-structure rules introduced on page 20. In particular, examine the rules for NP and VP:

$$NP \rightarrow (Art)\ (Adj)\ N$$

$$VP \rightarrow V\ (NP)$$

These rules express something we instinctively know, that a noun phrase must contain a noun, and a verb phrase must contain a verb, just as we know that prepositional phrases must contain prepositions, and so on. A simpler way of capturing this principle is to create phrase-structure rules of the following sort:

$$XP \rightarrow X\ \textit{Comp}$$

where *X* can be any of four major lexical categories (noun, verb, preposition, or adjective), *P* stands for *phrase,* and *Comp* represents *Complement* (a class of constituents that may be added to the phrase). If we do this, another regularity of English emerges. Verbs will always head (be to the leftmost position in) verb phrases, prepositions will always head prepositional phrases, and so on. Thus, we could say that English is a headfirst language, something it shares with many other languages of the world, but which crucially distinguishes it from other families of languages, such as Japanese, where the heads of phrases are always rightmost, or last (headlast). Discovering whether your language is headfirst or headlast can thus have important ramifications for the child's acquisition of syntax, as discussed in Chapter 8, because a simple rule predicts how all phrases of the language should be organized.

Second, the numerous transformational rules have been reduced to only one: *Move* α (alpha), which simply means "move something." Instead of many different rules, there are now limits on what can be moved (heads or phrases), and where they can "land" or be moved to. Additionally, movement of an element in the underlying structure of a sentence is hypothesized to leave a hole (empty category) where it once was, which linguists call a **trace.** For example, it seems clear that a sentence such as

What is John telling Mary?

conveys the meaning

John is telling Mary what?

Thus, a more accurate description of the sentence would be

$What_i$ is John telling Mary *Wh-trace$_i$*?

where the subscripts link (co-index) the item that has been moved and the trace left behind in its original position.

Some current psycholinguistic research has found evidence that readers seem to reactivate the trace in its original position when reading. How might they be shown to do this? Studies using two experimental techniques discussed later in this book—**event-related potentials** (ERPs), a measure of brain activity during sentence processing discussed in Chapter 2, and **priming** (discussed in Chapter 4)—suggest that readers seem to behave as though the moved element is recalled at the place that trace theory predicts to be its underlying representation (Fodor, 1995; Kluender & Kutas, 1993).

Principles and Parameters Theory also specifies that wh-words can only move to "landing sites" in the sentence that are "local"—that is, not too far from where they originated, where the notion "local" is defined in terms of a subtheory within PPT called Bounding Theory (for further details see Radford, 1988; Haegeman, 1991; Napoli, 1993; Cook & Newson, 1996). The notion of locality can be understood by comparing the following sentences:

a. $What_i$ may the famous athlete endorse e_i?
b. *$What_i$ does Mary hold the opinion that the famous athlete may endorse e_i?

For a question word such as *what* in (a), the only suitable landing site that is available is a node on the phrase-structure tree in the sentence initial position (the *e* represents the "trace" of the wh-word, and the subscript shows this relationship between the wh-word and the trace that it left behind when it moved). Contrast this with the relative ungrammaticality of (b). The wh-word has to move out of both an S *(the famous athlete may like what),* and an NP *(the opinion that the famous athlete may like what)* in order to get to its available landing site at sentence-initial position. Such "unbounded" movement is not allowed in English, and such constraints are stated by the principles of Bounding Theory, which places constraints on how far the wh-word can move (Atkinson, 1992). In this way, even though we allow free operation of Move-alpha, we restrict it by placing general constraints on its operation.

Another of the interesting developments in the theory is the increasingly important role accorded to the lexicon. The lexicon consists of words and fixed phrases in our language and a good deal of information about them. In Transformational grammar, as you will recall, deep structure was the output of the phrase-structure rules. In Principles and Parameters Theory, on the other hand, the form of d-structure is partially determined by the information in the lexical entries of words. That is, the information associated with individual words takes on the role that was previously played by phrase-structure rules, for instance, to specify the kinds and configurational position of constituents that may appear in a sentence. How does this work in PPT? Consider *The famous athlete may endorse the sneakers.* In PPT, the lexical entry for *endorse* specifies that *endorse* is a verb that expresses an action that involves someone doing the endorsing (the Agent), and the thing being endorsed (the Patient). (You can't just *endorse,* you have to endorse something.) Participants such as Agents and Patients are generally expressed as noun phrases (NP) in English (Grimshaw, 1981; Pesetsky, 1982; Chomsky, 1986b). Thus, the verb *endorse* has the following information associated with it:

Endorse: V;   Agent,   Patient

NP   NP

This information gets projected onto d-structure. That is, if we have a verb such as *endorse* in the sentence, we must also have an NP subject and an NP object in the sentence. We no longer need a separate phrase-structure rule to create a sentence outline at d-structure—we just need to look at the information associated with *endorse* in our mental lexicon.

Principles and Parameters Theory makes several fundamental assumptions with respect to learnability. Recall that one of the problems with Transformational Grammar was the vast array of language-particular and construction-specific rules that children had to acquire in a short time and with varying exposure to data. This made it hard to explain how language was acquired so rapidly with so little information available in the input about the correct formulation and application of these rules. PPT, in doing away with transformational rules, attempts to solve the problem by reducing the number of rules that the learner has to learn and replacing them with a few powerful and universal innate principles called **Universal Grammar,** or **UG.** UG radically limits the range of hypotheses that the language learner must choose among in order to construct a grammar of her language. In order to account for differences among languages, UG also includes **parameters,** each in the form of a grammatical yes–no choice, rather like switches, that learners must set in one way or the other to construct the grammar of their specific language. One possible parameter has already been discussed: whether languages organize their phrases with heads first, or heads last. Another such parameter is the Null Subject Parameter (Hyams, 1986). Some languages require that every sentence have an expressed subject, whereas other languages allow an inferred (or null) subject: For example, *It rains* in English is *Piove,* literally, "rains" in Italian. According to this theory, children "set" the null subject parameter for their own particular language on the basis of their early exposure to linguistic input.

Chomsky and, more recently, Crain (1991) argue strongly for the innateness of these principles and parameters. They suggest that the existence of universals in the world's languages and the early emergence of knowledge of syntactic structures in children in the absence of explicit instruction are evidence in favor of an innate UG. We will explore this issue more deeply in Chapter 8, "Language Acquisition."

Efforts to evaluate the psychological reality of PPT theory have been carried out mainly by linguists (see Berwick & Weinberg, 1984; Fodor, 1995; Frazier, 1988), who are often able to account for problematic results in older experimental studies that used TG grammar by referring to later versions of the theory. However, as Miller (1990) and Tanenhaus (1989) note, efforts by psychologists to use theories of grammar to study sentence comprehension in adults slowed somewhat as early versions of Transformational Grammar underwent dynamic reconfiguration during the mid-1970s and 1980s. More numerous efforts to evaluate claims made by current grammatical theory about the process of children's language acquisition will be discussed in greater detail in Chapter 8. Additionally, some attempts have been made to reconcile the performance patterns of adults whose language function has been impaired by brain damage (aphasics, Chapter 2), and children who are language-learning disabled, with the principles and predictions made by PPT grammar (Bates, Friederici, & Wulfeck, 1987; Leonard, Sabbadini, Volterra, & J. S. Leonard, 1988; Caplan & Hildebrandt, 1988; Grodzinsky, 1990). We will return to the role of grammatical theory in the history of psycholinguistic research in the final sections of this chapter.

Pragmatics and Discourse

We use language to inform, to promise, to request, to query; how language is used to accomplish various ends in the world is the domain of **pragmatics** (Austin, 1962). Pragmatics determines our choice of wording and our interpretation of language in different situations. Just as rules exist for creating grammatical sentences, linguistic conventions guide the appropriate use of language in various contexts. For instance, the politeness system in English is part of its pragmatics. A woman who says to her friend standing near the window, "It's hot in here," is probably asking her to open it. A parent who complains, "Your room is a total mess," usually intends the statement as an order to clean up the clutter. Indirect statements such as these contrast with the more direct, "Open the window," and "Clean up your room." Although it may appear to complicate conversation, we often consider it more polite in our system to use

SYNTACTIC THEORY IN THE 1990S

Syntactic theory in the 1990s has continued the trend started in the PPT model of the 1980s toward making simpler, more economical, and more powerful generalizations that lead to what has been termed the *Minimalist Program* (Marantz, 1995; Chomsky, 1995). A brief summary of the MP is provided here, although relatively little work in psycholinguistics has been carried out using this framework. Current formulations eliminate the levels of d-structure and s-structure and leave only Phonetic Form (PF) and Logical Form (LF) as "interface" levels of syntactic representation. Phonetic Form refers to the level of acoustic-articulatory representations, and Logical Form is the level at which semantic interpretation takes place. The derivation of a particular linguistic expression no longer involves several intermediate levels of representation. Rather, items from the lexicon enter into the computational system that then constructs the pair of interface representations, LF and PF (Chomsky, 1995). General principles based on notions such as simplicity and "economy" dictate which derivations are well formed and which ones will "crash." In essence, current syntactic theory formulates the minimal principles that generate well-formed pairings of sound and meaning in language.

In addition to developments within the transformational framework, current syntactic theory is also characterized by the growing importance of non-transformational theories such as Lexical-Functional Grammar (LFG), Head-driven Phrase Structure Grammar (HPSG), Construction Grammar, and Role and Reference Grammar (RRG), among others. Such theories, while differing among themselves in many respects, have in common a single level of syntactic representation, doing away with the transformational component entirely (so-called monostratal theories of syntax). These theories also differ from the transformational paradigm in the degree of importance they give to considerations such as processing or operations within the lexicon. Further details may be found in Horn (1983) for LFG, Pollard and Sag (1994) for HPSG, Goldberg (1995) for Construction Grammar, and Foley and Van Valin (1984) and Van Valin (1993) for RRG. Other grammatical theories that have had considerable influence on the field of syntax include Optimality Theory (Prince & Smolensky, 1993) and Relational Grammar (Perlmutter, 1983). Psychologists who conduct research on syntactic processing can choose among these grammatical models when designing their studies.

indirect phrasing to make requests of others. Such conversational modifications occasionally lead to communicative breakdowns in which the speaker's intent does not match the listener's interpretation (Tannen, 1990).

Knowledge of pragmatics also includes awareness of how we modify conversation when addressing different types of listeners. A greeting such as, "Hi, Sweetie, what's up?" is more likely to be uttered to your little sister than to the state trooper who has stopped you for speeding. Speech styles can vary with the context, the characteristics of the addressee, or the characteristics of the speaker, as well as with the medium of discourse (written or spoken, telephoned or face-to-face). These specially marked ways of speaking are called **registers.** Babytalk, foreigner talk, and the style used by some nurses talking to patients are but a few examples of different registers. Some registers typify casual interaction, whereas others are more appropriate to formal events. Conventions for language use with varying addressees include constraints on what is said and how it is phrased, as Chapter 6 demonstrates.

Much of our language use involves *discourse,* usually defined as verbal or written interactions longer than single utterances (see Chapter 6). Beyond the level of understanding single words or sentences, we more typically need to evaluate what we hear or read within a particular context and on the basis of our prior knowledge—we are thus able to make inferences. The situational setting or context of spoken messages is often crucial to their successful interpretation. "Success," in this sense, is taken as the hearer's full appreciation of the speaker's intent. The simple comment, "It's 8:15," assumes new dimensions if both speaker and hearer are sitting in traffic on the way to the airport to catch a plane scheduled to leave at 8:30.

The situational and world knowledge that conversational participants share determines the form and content of their utterances. When we refer to something, we usually must use a noun before we can meaningfully use a pronoun. The sentence, "Did you get it?" makes a poor opening gambit in conversation with a stranger on a bus, but it makes perfectly good sense when said to a child you just sent to the store to buy a loaf of bread. As a further example, pronouns commonly replace proper names in conversational interactions. The comment, "She's late again" is well formed and understood by students gazing at the empty podium where their instructor should be standing, but it is meaningless when the antecedent or reference for the pronoun cannot be determined.

Discourse conventions govern the way we understand and use connected language. The varieties of discourse, both written and spoken, are dealt with in Chapter 6.

Metalinguistic Capacity: The Ability to Analyze Our Own Language

Metalinguistic means, literally, "language about language." It is often difficult to explain our knowledge about language. Our talents for speaking well and understanding competently are aspects of our *linguistic* knowledge, whereas our ability to reflect upon our language—our understanding of how we do these things—represents an aspect of our *metalinguistic* knowledge. In this book we ask metalinguistic questions such as

"How do I understand the meaning of a word?"

"How do I find words when I want to talk about things?"

"Are some words easier or harder for people to understand?"

A linguistics text might simply note that English allows sentences such as *The guy who sits next to Susan is a geology major*, *I know a guy who is a geology major*, and *That John is a geology major surprises me*. This psycholinguistics text is more concerned with exploring what procedures a listener or reader might use in understanding what these sentences mean and independently generating comparable sentences and whether the sentences differ in their processing demands.

As you read this book, consider how effortlessly you understand the examples. Language use is a rapidly paced phenomenon. The task for the psycholinguist is to account for the discrepancy that often arises between the time required to produce or understand an utterance, and the time required to explain how this was accomplished! As an example of this, we can consider a simple sentence construction in English, the **tag question** (Akmajian & Heny, 1980). Tag questions have the following general form:

a. It's raining, *isn't it?*
b. He isn't going, *is he?*

If you are provided with additional starting points, you can easily provide the little "tags" that end them:

c. She doesn't like ice cream, _____?
d. They are expensive, _____?

But how do you know what to do? Try to form a rule that will generate the right answers to (c) and (d). Time yourself. Next consider whether or not your rule will "work" for the following:

e. Your little sister likes ice cream, _____?
f. The new people who moved in next door most certainly will want to be invited, _____?

If your first account was lacking in some way, estimate how much time it takes you to revise your rule to account for the right answers to (e) and (f). And if you find it difficult and time consuming, don't despair. It is difficult to develop succinct and accurate answers to such questions, even for linguists.[2] The major point we would like to make here is that saying and understanding such sentences is rather trivial; it is figuring

---

[2] The tag portion of the sentence reuses (or copies) parts of the original declarative. However, the subject noun of the original declarative is replaced by an appropriate corresponding pronoun. Note that the auxiliary (or helping verb) in (a) and (b) is the only part of the verb used; in (f), only the modal form *will* is used. In general, only the first part of the verb phrase is used to build the tag. Example (e) is problematic. In sentences where the verb is not the copula (verb *to be*) or has no auxiliary or modal elements, a helping verb (always derived from the verb *do*) must be "manufactured" to complete the tag; thus, we get *Your sister likes ice cream, doesn't she?* rather than **Your sister likes ice cream, likesn't she?* Note that in English the tag must be in the negative if the sentence is in the affirmative, and the tag must be affirmative if the sentence is in the negative!

out our subconscious strategies for doing such things that tantalizes the psycholinguist.

Linguistic exercises like the ones in this chapter demonstrate that much of our knowledge of the language is implicit and not easily available for self-examination. We can perform the task, but we cannot peer into the process and understand how it occurs. This distinction between linguistic and metalinguistic ability is both frustrating and fascinating to the psycholinguist and often requires us to develop special experimental techniques for indirectly measuring and describing the ways people generate and understand language.

Even when people think they know how they perform a linguistic task, they may not be correct. It is possible that you developed a rule for one of our examples that differed from our answer or was incomplete. Most people have no trouble producing all the phonemes of their language, but cannot produce a simple list of those phonemes. The process of "being metalinguistic" also seems more cumbersome than the process of speaking or listening. This dichotomy has its parallels in many other human endeavors. For example, one of us is a terrible tennis player. When an instructor finally despaired of improving our actual ability to play, she offered this advice: "Tell your opponent you really admire her serve. Then ask her whether she throws the ball up before or after she steps toward the line. Her serve won't be that great for the next few minutes while she thinks about it!"

LANGUAGE DIVERSITY
AND LANGUAGE UNIVERSALS

Because this book is written in English and because most of our readers will be most comfortable with English, we will concentrate heavily on research into the processes that underlie speaking and listening in English. However, in the broader perspective of human communicative behavior, this may provide an incomplete picture. As we noted earlier, languages differ markedly in their construction: Their sound systems may vary widely, their word formation rules and lexical inventories differ, and rules for ordering elements within sentences may differ from English. When possible we will attempt to note how the processing strategies used by speakers of different languages tell us more about either universal tendencies in linguistic processing or specific strategies that may be limited to a particular language. In general, more cross-linguistic research has been carried out in developmental psycholinguistics (cf. Slobin, 1985, 1992) than in the study of adult language comprehension and production, though effort is increasing in these areas (cf. MacWhinney & Bates, 1989).

The great variability found in human languages has prompted the search for linguistic universals or constant features that might characterize languages, their use, and their acquisition. As we noted in the section on linguistics, a *universal grammar* (UG) is "a system of principles, conditions, and rules that are elements or properties of all human languages . . . the essence of human language" (Chomsky, 1975, p. 29). UG is not merely a collection of absolute regularities across languages. It also specifies principles that may have differing realizations from language to language. A given language uses just one of the finite number of options (or parameters) specified by the principle.

Linguists continue to search for candidate rules for the universal grammar (Chomsky, 1986a). Recently, child language-acquisition research and second-language research have both become increasingly concerned with testing theories about the nature of the universal grammar (Hyams, 1986; Cook & Newson, 1996), thus attempting to link hypothetical linguistic universals with strategies seen in language learning.

Similar interest in what a psycholinguistic universal might look like has been pursued more intensely in the developmental domain than in study of adult language processing. A psycholinguistic universal might be based on cognitive and perceptual factors, as well as linguistic factors. Slobin (1973, 1985) proposed universal operating principles that govern the course of child language development. For example, he suggests that language learners pay *attention to the ends of words,* thus accounting for the usually early acquisition of inflectional morphemes in a wide variety of highly inflected languages. Another principle would lead children to *avoid discontinuous elements* in their speech such as embedded clauses (*The man who lives next to my sister is a doctor*) or discontinuous constructions such as the English present progressive (*Jimmy is going*) and the French (*Je ne suis pas*), where the *ne* and *pas* together signal negation. Thus, appropriate use of these forms would occur later in language development regardless of the language being learned.

Oral and Signed Language

One major way languages can differ is in whether they are spoken/heard (oral/aural) or encoded manually, as in sign language. Oral languages are more numerous, but the many signed languages in the world all differ crucially in their phonology (which in this case includes permissible handshapes, movement patterns, and placement of signs in space or in contact with the body), lexicon, and syntax (Bellugi & Klima, 1979; Wilbur, 1989). Of the signed languages, *American Sign Language* (ASL) has been studied the most extensively. As Figure 1.6 shows, in ASL the sign for *cat* is not at all like the Greek sign for *cat*. As some of the chapters to follow indicate, basic similarities exist in language processing, whether the language is signed or spoken. Brain damage often impairs spoken and signed communication in similar ways, suggesting a common neurological representation for the two types of language. "Slips of the tongue" and "slips of the hand" as well as verbal recall errors made by speakers and signers tend to be similar, thus bolstering our confidence in some accounts of language processing that were originally developed to account only for oral language. However, we can also ask whether the differing demands of gestural and oral language also require some different psycholinguistic strategies. Although this issue will be discussed only briefly, it is an area of great interest and importance in fully understanding the human capacity to learn, understand, and produce the full array of languages

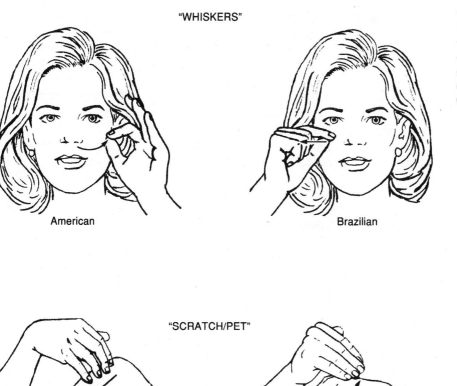

"WHISKERS"

American   Brazilian

"SCRATCH/PET"

Greek   Spanish

FIGURE 1.6

The sign for *cat* in four of the world's sign languages. The many sign languages of the world have differing phonologies, lexicons, and grammars.

used by diverse communities (Wilbur, 1989; Poizner, Klima, & Bellugi, 1987). Similarities between signed and spoken languages are an important area of inquiry for many psycholinguists.

Written Language

All human cultures possess either spoken or manual languages (or both). However, not all languages have an associated writing system, and it is evident that writing is a much more recent development in the history of humans than is speech. Written languages vary widely in their characteristics, but some broad categories of writing systems can be described (Crystal, 1987; Garman, 1990; Sampson, 1985).

The minimal unit, or building block, of any written system is the **grapheme.** Many writing systems reflect the phonological properties of the oral language they encode and are thus sound-based. A sound-based writing system that uses individual symbols, or letters, to represent the phonemes of a language is considered *alphabetic*. Written English is primarily an alphabetic system, although it is not completely regular in its representations. If it were, there would be no point in having spelling bees, because all words would be spelled just as they sound. An ideal alphabetic system would include a one-to-one correspondence between phonemes in the language and the symbols (or letters) used to represent them and enough different letters to represent all the phonemes. The English spelling system often has many different ways to spell one phoneme, and sometimes two different phonemes are represented by the same grapheme. For example, a sound such as /f/ may be written as *f, ph, gh,* or *ff*. The English phoneme /u/ is spelled many different ways in words such as *do, clue, blew, through, food,* and even *lieu*. On the other hand, the two different phonemes /θ/ and /ð/ are both spelled with a *th* in words such as *thigh* and *thy*. Figure 1.7 shows one child's efforts to conquer the English spelling system.

Many English spellings, though not completely alphabetic, provide information about the history and morphological connections of words. For instance, if the word *sign* were spelled "sayn," its relation to words such as *signal* and *signature* would be obscured. Other languages, such as Spanish and Hungarian, have more regular phoneme-grapheme correspondences.

The writing systems of some languages represent syllables rather than individual phonemes. Such systems (as seen in the Indian languages Kannada or Hindi) are called **syllabaries.** As Chapter 9 shows, there is evidence that readers of sound-based written material make grapheme-phoneme correspondences (associate graphemes or grapheme sequences with their appropriate pronunciation) during certain reading activities. Frequently encountered or irregularly spelled words may be processed differently.

Many of the world's languages possess writing systems that are not sound-based. Such systems link linguistic concepts (lexical and grammatical) with written symbols and are considered ideographic or logographic. Written Chinese is an example of such a system. Ideographic writing systems use **ideograms** to symbolize an idea or concept rather than a particular word, and logographic systems use **logograms** to represent whole words. We also use a few logograms in our writing system—for instance $ stands for *dollar*.

THE EVOLUTION OF PSYCHOLINGUISTIC INQUIRY

*W*hy study language? . . . Language is a mirror of the mind in a deep and significant sense. It is a product of human intelligence, created anew in each individual by operations that lie far beyond the reach of will or consciousness.

Chomsky, *Reflections on Language* (1975)

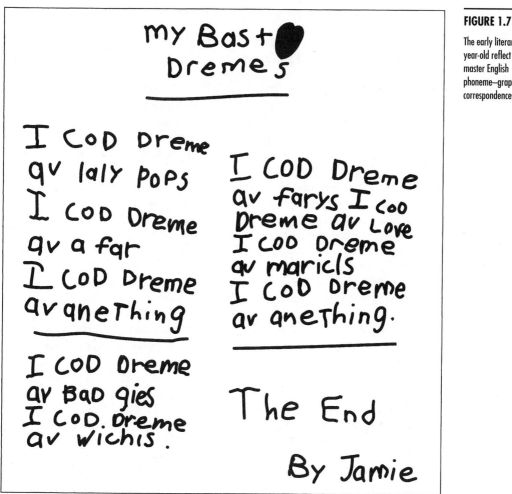

FIGURE 1.7

The early literary efforts of this 6-year-old reflect attempts to master English phoneme—grapheme correspondences.

Many of the questions that spur current psycholinguistic inquiry have been of enduring interest to philosophers, linguists, and scientists. The Greek philosopher Plato's *Cratylus* dialogue, written in the fourth century B.C., considers the relationships between names and the entities they represent. The participants in his dialogue disagree; one (an analogist) argues that the name of an object is part of its essential nature and not arbitrary. According to this view, careful etymology will reveal the reasons for names. Using English examples, we might show that a bedroom is so called because it is a room with a bed, and a blueberry is a berry that is blue. The analogists held that we could find the natural connections that underlie *mushroom* and *gooseberry* as well. The opposing "anomalists" in Plato's dialogue contended that names are linked to their referents merely through social convention, a view that was adopted by Aristotle.

The role of the brain in language functioning has been explored since the days of the Egyptian pharaohs, as Chapter 2 explains. The writings of Herodotus in the fifth century B.C. also suggest that at least one pharaoh, Psammetichus, was fascinated by the origins of human language. Chapter 8 recounts how he isolated two infants with a silent caretaker, hoping that left to their own devices the infants would produce their first words in the original language of humankind.

Some view psychologist Wilhelm Wundt (1832–1920) as the founder of modern psycholinguistics. Wundt developed the earliest theory of speech production and piloted the use of many experimental measures that are basic to psycholinguistic research, such as **reaction time (RT).** Reaction time studies will be covered in detail in later chapters. The premise that underlies the measurement of reaction time is that the time taken to process different experimental tasks reflects the degree of mental complexity involved in the task.

However deep its historical roots, however, the field of psycholinguistics is relatively young. Some researchers date its birth to the early 1950s (Brown, 1970; Tanenhaus, 1989; Miller, 1990), when psychologists and linguists met to discuss whether advances in experimental psychology could be applied to the study of language performance and comprehension. Psychology during the 1950s was strongly governed by behaviorist, or learning theory, principles that emphasized serial patterning in behavior. Though psychologists such as Hull, Watson, and Skinner differed in their specific accounts, all viewed learning as the outcome of successive stimulus-response-reinforcement chains. Behaviorist accounts of syntactic functioning based upon transitional probabilities (or the statistical likelihood that one word is likely to follow another) were advanced by Osgood (1963), Jenkins and Palermo (1964), and Staats (1971). Skinner (1957) formulated a behavioral model of language functioning that became particularly controversial. Its major focus was in predicting the conditions that elicit the use of a given word. As Fodor, Bever, and Garrett (1974) review in great detail, such theories faced many difficulties in explaining the complex nature of language production and understanding, as the following examples will show.

Learning theories were especially limited when attempting to account for the processing of phrases that contain discontinuous elements. For instance, an embedded relative clause interrupts the main clause in *The rider who fell off the horse broke a leg.* It is unclear in a sentence like this how *rider* can condition the word *broke,* which is five words away from it. Behavioral theories were also inadequate to account for elements that occur early in a phrase but are determined by later, nonadjacent elements. For example, it was difficult to account for the generation of questions such as "Are all the registered voters in this county Democrats?" in which the number agreement on the fronted auxiliary verb *are* clearly is determined by the speaker's use of a plural subject yet to come.

Finally, as Bever, Fodor, and Weksel (1965) noted, theories based on either association or on transitional probabilities do not predict the initial stages of language learning by children. For example, although *article + noun* sequences are extremely common in English, children's earliest utterances do not contain articles. More importantly, early child language often contains utterances that do not repeat anything the child has heard from adults. It is difficult to account for an utterance such as, "I do it Jamie self," by appealing to the learning of sequences of frequently associated items in the language. Nor is it readily apparent how children would achieve the ability to pluralize and otherwise inflect nonsense words such as *a wug/two wugs* (Berko, 1958) by mere regular observation of adult language patterns, although the learning principle of generalization has been invoked to do this.

Early behaviorally oriented psycholinguistic models were quickly challenged by rapid changes in linguistic theory. The emergence of the Transformational Generative grammatical framework (Chomsky, 1957; 1965) dramatically altered the study of language structure and its mental representation (Fodor, Bever, & Garrett, 1974; Newmeyer, 1986; Tanenhaus, 1989). Chomsky's (1957) *Syntactic Structures* and (1958) critique of Skinner's (1957) *Verbal Behavior* caused both linguists and psychologists to view language in new ways. Generative grammarians sought to include speakers' intuitions about grammatical and ungrammatical utterances, relationships that seem to exist between types of sentences in a language (such as between actives and their corresponding passives) and the problem of language acquisition by children.

The new transformational framework that guided much of linguistic theory for the next two decades was used by psychologists who attempted to determine whether the new approaches to describing the utterances of a language mirrored the mental operations required by speakers and hearers when they used the language. As mentioned earlier in our discussion of syntax, some initial findings suggested that listeners might mentally "undo" the grammatical transformations that linguists used to derive interrogative, passive, and negative sentences from simpler sentences (Miller & McKean, 1964; Clifton & Odom, 1966). Child language researchers such as Menyuk (1968) and Brown and Hanlon (1970) explored the possibility that language development was dependent upon the acquisition of transformations that operated on early acquired simple sentences to create more complex linguistic forms.

Research on transformations did not fully substantiate their mental representation, as we noted in our earlier discussion. That is, linguistic theory did not accurately predict subjects' responses in experiments or children's observed patterns of language development. Moreover, linguistic theory began to evolve and change extremely rapidly, making it difficult for psychologists to keep pace with new developments. As Miller (1990) and Tanenhaus (1989) note, the brief, close working relationship between linguistic theorists and psychologists began to erode by the early 1970s when their respective goals began to diverge markedly and their orientations toward human language became more distinct. Miller (1990, p. 321) simplifies what appear to be their current respective biases when he observes that, "Linguists and psychologists talk about different things. . . . Grammarians are more interested in what could be said than in what people actually say, which irritates psychologists, and psychologists insist on supplementing intuition with objective evidence, which irritates linguists."

During the 1970s, psychologists also discovered interactions among the various levels of linguistic analysis and the situational context in language processing, and they began to explore the nature of comprehension without reference to any particular theory of grammar. Work that examined the role of context in interpreting ambiguous speech signals (Games & Bond, 1976) and in making inferences—logical assumptions—from experimental sentences (Bransford, Barclay, & Franks, 1972) suggested that many kinds of information are used in the process of language understanding. Not all of these sources of information were adequately described by linguistic theory. Whereas the bulk of psycholinguistic work done in the 1960s had investigated syntactic processing, much of the work done in the 1970s concentrated on the mental organization of the lexicon and on the processing of text or discourse. Unlike syntax, these other areas of inquiry are less dependent upon the vagaries of current linguistic theory.

More recently, increasing attempts have been made to relate the principles of newer transformational grammars such as Government and Binding theory to adult sentence processing, child language acquisition, and language disorder. These attempts will be evaluated most extensively in the chapter that discusses child language acquisition (Chapter 8), where they have been most vigorously pursued.

THE ACQUISITION OF LANGUAGE BY CHILDREN

The rapidity with which children acquire language has fascinated scholars and parents for thousands of years. Although questions about the nature of child language learning and the methods of study used have varied, they embrace many recurring themes. As Chapter 8 notes, the nature–nurture controversy maintains a robust presence among child language researchers. Some (often called nativists) side with nature and maintain that language is basically innate, that children are born with a special, unique human talent that can extrapolate the grammar of a language without overt instruction or correction. Others stress the role of nurture and claim that adults teach language to children by using special kinds of simplified language with them and providing them with feedback when they have used the language well or poorly. An important component of Chomsky's early writings (1957, 1965) was its emphasis on the role of linguistic theory and the limits of behaviorist psychology in explaining the acquisition of language by children. He argued that Skinner's learning theory could not account for the rapid acquisition of an infinitely productive language faculty. A series of studies of children's language acquisition (Berko, 1958; Brown, 1965; Braine, 1965) did, in fact, show that children were developing grammatical systems that were quite orderly but different in the early stages from adult grammar, evidence often used to support Chomsky's views.

Chomsky also made two nativist claims that have spurred enduring controversy in the field of child language development. The first is what has become known as the *degeneracy problem* (Berwick & Weinberg, 1984). Simply put, Chomsky and others contended that children overhear language that is degenerate in that it contains many incomplete and ungrammatical sentences and that they have limited exposure to the full range of structures used by the language. Thus, language principles must be innate because the environment does not provide sufficient evidence for the child to permit competent language development. Further, a second problem was noted. The *negative evidence problem* argued that children do not receive overt instruction that some structures are not permissible in the language, either from parental correction of their errors (Brown & Hanlon, 1970) or from literal instruction (for example, "You can say X in English, but you can't say Y"). As Chapter 8 explores in great detail, both the validity and interpretation of such claims are a matter of spirited inquiry and debate within the field of child language acquisition.

SUMMARY

Language is an integral aspect of our human existence. Although the ability to formulate and understand language underlies almost every activity, the mental operations that enable language use are still poorly understood. Psycholinguistics explores the processes of language understanding, language production, and language acquisition.

In this chapter, we have briefly surveyed the broad domain of human language ability, which includes knowledge of the sound system of a language (its phonology), the vocabulary (its lexicon), rules for creating words (morphology), rules for including and sequencing words within sentences (syntax), and rules for using language appropriately within the social context (pragmatics).

The principles that govern appropriate use of each of these components of language are largely implicit, and most speaker-hearers have difficulty describing why they make certain judgments about good and poor examples of language use or how they generate or understand particular sentences. Our metalinguistic ability is usually quite poor, forcing psycholinguists to develop creative experimental strategies for better describing the mental operations that underlie language use. We will address these strategies, and what they reveal about how people use language, in the chapters that follow.

Relatively recent changes in linguistic theory in the late 1950s spurred the cross-disciplinary evolution of psycholinguistic inquiry. During the ensuing years, linguists and psychologists have attempted to apply developments in grammatical theory to models of language use and learning. Psychologists have additionally been concerned with issues in the use of language not generally addressed by linguistic theory, such as the role of context or experience in language processing.

The chapters that follow introduce the new student of psycholinguistics to the major questions that have been asked about how competent speaker-hearers of a language understand and produce sentences, the process of child language development, and the biological foundations that underlie language learning and use. We will additionally explore what is currently known about the processes of reading and second-language learning. These are important issues not just because it is interesting to understand how competent speakers and listeners use language, but because understanding human speech and language comprehension and use enables us to aid individuals whose communicative abilities are impaired and to develop computer programs that mimic the human mind's ability to understand spoken language. In this respect, the discipline of psycholinguistics faces an ever more interesting future.

KEY WORDS

Phonology
Morphology
Lexicon
Semantics
Syntax
Pragmatics
Metalinguistic awareness
Linguistics
Psycholinguistics
Speech perception
Lexical access
Sentence processing
Discourse
Hesitation
Pausal phenomena
Speech disfluencies
Developmental psycholinguistics
Neurolinguistics
S-V-O word order
Symbols
Universals
Displaced concepts
American Sign Language
Articulatory phonetics
Phonemes
Phonemic inventory
Minimal pairs
Aspiration

Allophones
Glottalized stop
Palatalized
Unreleased
Phonotactics
Prosody
Content words
Function words
Morpheme
Free morpheme
Bound morpheme
Derivational morpheme
Inflectional morpheme
Affix
Constituents
Phrase-structure tree
Complex sentence
Recursion
Coordinate sentence
Learnable
Universality
Competence
Performance
Transformational Generative grammar
Deep structure
Surface structure
Derive
Transformations

Passive transformation
Derivational Theory of Complexity
Parallel processing
Trace
Universal Grammar (UG)
Parameters
Registers

Metalinguistic
Tag question
Grapheme
Syllabaries
Ideograms
Logograms
Reaction time (RT)

SOMETHING TO THINK ABOUT

1. Why might a researcher want to try to teach a chimpanzee to use human language? How is human language different from animal communication systems? List and elaborate all the differences you can find.

2. Joe, age 8, says, "My favorite words are *pumpkin* and *pumpernickel!*" (Actually, he hates to eat the stuff.) Does he have metalinguistic awareness? Discuss some differences between linguistic and metalinguistic awareness and give examples of both.

3. Discuss the concept of *Universal Grammar*. What particular characteristics of human beings and their environment might contribute to the existence of Universal Grammar?

4. Some researchers have proposed that thought, or thinking, is accomplished using silent (subvocal) speech. Do you agree? Can you think without language? Give examples to illustrate your answer.

ACTIVITY 1

How do we form yes/no questions?
(Based on Radford, 1988)
Look at the following sentence pairs:

1a. John is at the concert.
1b. Is John at the concert?
2a. They are quite thirsty.
2b. Are they quite thirsty?

Based on these data, write a simple rule for making yes/no questions (questions that can be answered with a simple *yes* or *no*). Do this before reading further!

You probably wrote something like this:

Preliminary yes/no question rule:

Move the second element in the sentence to the sentence initial position.

Now let's look at more data:

3. The child is at the concert.
4. My little brothers are quite thirsty.
5. Many young people will go to the party.
6. The guests might want to go home.
7. The new employee didn't want to work.

What kind of yes/no questions can you form for these sentences? Does the above preliminary rule work for these sentences? No; it produces ill-formed questions such as *Child the is at the concert?*

How would you change the rule to form yes/no questions for sentences 3–7? What kind of constituents are phrases such as *the child* and *my little brothers* (verb phrase, noun phrase, prepositional phrase, and such)? Now, formulate a revised yes/no question rule based on the notion "constituent." Do this before reading on!

Revised yes/no question rule:

Move the element following the first noun phrase to sentence initial position.

Does this work for the sentences 3–7? It seems to.

Thus, the rule for yes/no question formation cannot be based only on the linear order of words but must also take into account the grouping of words in the sentence into cohesive units, or constituents of the sentence. The process of forming yes/no questions reveals the underlying organization of the sentence into such units.

Extra study topic: Look at the following sentences and evaluate whether or not your extended hypothesis works with them. How would you need to revise it? What new element would you need to introduce? Why? (For further details consult Akmajian, Demers, Farmer, & Harnish, 1995; Radford, 1988.)

1. She hopes to join the women's tennis team next year.
2. They walked home sadly.

ACTIVITY 2

Consider the following two examples. In English, we produce sentences such as (1) and (2) that appear well formed and synonymous:

1. Bill threw out the garbage.
2. Bill threw the garbage out.

Next, consider the following:

3. Bill looked out the window.
4. *Bill looked the window out.

Why is it that we can create a grammatical sentence such as (3) but not (4)? Most of us quickly judge (1), (2), and (3) as acceptable and (4) as ungrammatical. That seems to be the easy part of our language knowledge. It is explaining how and why we know that the first three sentences are well formed and the last is not that lies at the heart of much psycholinguistic research. *Answers:* The difference between the two sets of sentences lies in the two differing functions of the word *out.* In (1) and (2), *out* is not a preposition, as most readers assume. It is what is called a verb particle, a portion of a two-part verb. English has many two-part verbs, such as *throw out, call up, look up,* and *give back.* (Consider the difference in meaning between the sentences *He threw out the ball* and *He threw the ball.)* English permits the placement of verb particles, in most circumstances, either next to the verb, or after the object, as in (1) and (2). In (3), however, *out* functions as a preposition, which must always remain at the beginning of a prepositional phrase.

REFERENCES

Akmajian, A., Demers, R., Farmer, A., & Harnish, R. (1995). *Linguistics: An introduction to language and communication* (4th ed.). Cambridge, MA: MIT Press.

Akmajian, A., & Heny, F. (1980). *An introduction to the principles of transformational syntax.* Cambridge, MA: MIT Press.

Atkinson, Martin. (1992). *Children's syntax: An introduction to principles and parameters theory.* Oxford, UK; Cambridge, MA: Blackwell.

Austin, J. (1962). *How to do things with words.* Cambridge, MA: Harvard University Press.

Baker, C. L. (1995). *Introduction to generative-transformational syntax.* Englewood Cliffs, NJ: Prentice-Hall.

Bates, E., Friederici, A., & Wulfeck, B. (1987). Grammatical morphology in aphasia: Evidence from three languages. *Cortex, 23,* 545–574.

Bellugi, U., & Klima, E. (1979). *The signs of language.* Cambridge, MA: Harvard University Press.

Berko, J. (1958). The child's learning of English morphology. *Word, 14,* 150–177.

Bernstein, M. (1983). Formation of internal structure in a lexical category. *Journal of Child Language, 10* (2), 381–400.

Berwick, R., & Weinberg, A. (1984). *The grammatical basis of linguistic performance*. Cambridge, MA: MIT Press.

Bever, T., Fodor, J., & Weksel, W. (1965). Theoretical notes on the acquisition of syntax: A critique of "contextual generalization." *Psychological Review, 72,* 467–482.

Blumenthal, A. L. (1967). Prompted recall of sentences. *Journal of Verbal Learning and Verbal Behaviour, 6,* 203–206.

Bolinger, D. (1980). *Language: The loaded weapon*. London: Longman.

Bolinger, D., & Sears, D. (1981). *Aspects of language* (3rd ed.). New York: Harcourt Brace Jovanovich.

Braine, M. (1965). On the basis of phrase structure. *Psychological Review, 72* (6), 483–492.

Bransford, J., Barclay, J., & Franks, J. (1972). Sentence memory: A constructive vs. interpretive approach. *Cognitive Psychology, 3,* 193–209.

Brown, R. (1965). *Social Psychology*. New York: Free Press.

Brown, R. (1970). *Psycholinguistics*. New York: Free Press.

Brown, R., Cazden, C., & Bellugi, U. (1969). The child's grammar from I to III. In J. Hill (Ed.), *Minnesota Symposia on Child Psychology* (Vol. 2). Minneapolis: University of Minnesota Press.

Brown, R., & Hanlon, C. (1970). Derivational complexity and order of acquisition in child language. In J. Hayes (Ed.), *Cognition and the development of language*. New York: Wiley.

Caplan, D., & Hildebrandt, N. (1988). *Disorders of Syntactic Comprehension*. Cambridge, MA: MIT Press.

Chomsky, N. (1995). *The Minimalist Program*. Cambridge, MA: MIT Press.

Chomsky, N. (1988). *Language and problems of knowledge: The Managua lectures*. Cambridge, MA: MIT Press.

Chomsky, N. (1986a). *Knowledge of language: Its nature, origin and use.* New York: Praeger.

Chomsky, N. (1986b). *Barriers.* Cambridge, MA: MIT Press.

Chomsky, N. (1981). *Lectures on government and binding.* Dordrecht, Holland: D. Reidel Publishers.

Chomsky, N. (1975). *Reflections on language.* London: Temple-Smith.

Chomsky, N. (1965). *Aspects of the theory of syntax.* Cambridge, MA: MIT Press.

Chomsky, N. (1957). *Syntactic structures.* The Hague: Mouton.

Clancy, P. (1985). The acquisition of Japanese. In D. Slobin (Ed.), *The crosslinguistic study of language acquisition* (Vol. 1: *The data).* Hillsdale, NJ: Erlbaum.

Clark, H., & Clark, E. (1977). *Psychology and language: An introduction to psycholinguistics.* New York: Harcourt Brace Jovanovich.

Clifton, C., & Odom, P. (1966). Similarity relations among certain English sentence constructions. *Psychological Monographs, 80.*

Cook, V. J., & Newson, M. (1996). *Chomsky's universal grammar: An introduction.* Oxford, UK; Cambridge, MA: Basil Blackwell.

Crain, S. (1991). Language acquisition in the absence of experience. *Brain & Behavioral Sciences, 14,* 597–650.

Crystal, D. (1987). *The Cambridge encyclopedia of language.* Cambridge, MA: Cambridge University Press.

Demers, R. (1989). Linguistics and animal communication. In F. Newmeyer (Ed.), *Linguistics: The Cambridge survey. III. Language: Psychological and biological aspects.* Cambridge, MA: Cambridge University Press.

Dinneen, F. (1967). *An introduction to general linguistics* New York: Holt, Rinehart and Winston.

Finnegan, E. (1994). *Language: its structure, use and function* (2nd ed.). Fort Worth: Harcourt Brace College Publishers.

Fodor, J. (1995). Comprehending sentence structure. In L. Gleitman & M. Liberman (Eds.), *An invitation to cognitive science* (2nd ed.). *Language* (Vol. 1). Cambridge, MA: MIT Press.

Fodor, J., Bever, T., & Garrett, M. (1974). *The psychology of language: An introduction to psycholinguistics*. New York: McGraw-Hill.

Foley, W., & Van Valin, R. D. (1984). *Functional syntax and universal grammar*. Cambridge; New York: Cambridge University Press.

Frazier, L. (1988). Grammar and language processing. In F. Newmeyer (Ed.), *Linguistics: The Cambridge survey. II. Linguistic theory: Extensions and implications*. Cambridge: Cambridge University Press.

Garman, M. (1990). *Psycholinguistics*. Cambridge: Cambridge University Press.

Games, S., & Bond, Z. (1980). A slip of the ear: A snip of the ear? A slip of the year? In V. Fromkin (Ed.), *Errors in linguistic performance: Slips of the tongue, ear, pen and hand*. New York: Academic Press.

Goldberg, A. (1995). *Constructions: A construction grammar approach to argument structure*. Chicago: University of Illinois Press.

Greenberg, J. (Ed.). (1963). *Universals of language: Report of a conference held at Dobbs Ferry, NY, April 13–15, 1961*. Cambridge, MA: MIT Press.

Grimshaw, J. (1981). Form, function, and the language acquisition device. In C. L. Baker & J. J. McCarthy (Eds.), *The logical problem of language acquisition*. Cambridge, MA: MIT Press.

Greene, J. M. (1970). The semantic function of negatives and positives. *British Journal of Psychology, 61*, 17–22.

Grodzinsky, Y. (1990). *Theoretical perspectives on language disorders*. Cambridge, MA: MIT Press.

Haegeman, L. (1991). *Introduction to government and binding theory*. Oxford, UK; Cambridge, MA: Basil Blackwell.

Horn, G. M. (1983). *Lexical functional grammar*. Berlin, NY: Mouton.

Hyams, N. (1986). *Language acquisition and the theory of parameters*. Dordrecht, Holland: Reidel.

Jenkins, J., & Palermo, D. (1964). Mediation processes and the acquisition of linguistic structure. In U. Bellugi & R. Brown (Eds.), *The acquisition of language*. Chicago: University of Chicago Press.

Kluender, R., & Kutas, M. (1993). Subjacency as a processing phenomenon. *Language and Cognitive Processes, 8* (4), 573–640.

Labov, W. (1973). The boundaries of words and their meanings. In C. J. Bailey & R. Shuy (Eds.), *New ways of analyzing variation in English*. Washington, DC: Georgetown University Press, 340–373.

Leonard, L., & Loeb, D. F. (1988). Government-binding theory and some of its applications: A tutorial. *Journal of Speech and Hearing Research, 31* (4), 515–524.

Leonard, L. B., Sabbadini, L., Volterra, V., & Leonard, J. S. (1988). Some influences on the grammar of English- and Italian-speaking children with specific language impairment. *Applied Psycholinguistics, 9,* 39–57.

Lester, M. (1971). *Introductory transformational grammar of English*. New York: Holt, Rinehart and Winston.

MacWhinney, B., & Bates, E. (1989). *The cross-linguistic study of sentence processing.* Cambridge: Cambridge University Press.

Maddieson, I. (1984). *Patterns of sounds*. Cambridge: Cambridge University Press.

Marantz, A. (1995). The minimalist program. In G. Webelhuth (Ed.), *Government and binding theory and the minimalist program: Principles and parameters in syntactic theory.* Cambridge, MA: Blackwell.

McCloskey, J. (1988). Syntactic theory. In F. Newmeyer (Ed.), *Linguistics: The Cambridge survey. I. Linguistic theory foundations*. Cambridge: Cambridge University Press.

McMahon, L. (1963). *Grammatical analysis as part of understanding a sentence.* Harvard University doctoral dissertation.

Menyuk, P. (1968). *Sentences children use.* Cambridge, MA: MIT Press.

Miller, G. (1990). Linguists, psychologists, and the cognitive sciences. *Language, 66,* 317–322.

Miller, G. (1962). Some psychological studies of grammar. *American Psychologist, 17,* 748–762. Also in L. Jakobovits & M. Miron (Eds.), (1967), *Readings in the psychology of language*. Englewood Cliffs, NJ: Prentice-Hall.

Miller, G., & Chomsky, N. (1963). Finitary models of language users. In R. D. Luce, R. R. Bush, & E. Galanter (Eds.), *Handbook of mathematical psychology* (Vol. 2). New York: Wiley.

Miller, G., & McKean, K. (1964). A chronometric study of some relations between sentences. *Quarterly Journal of Experimental Psychology, 16,* 297–308.

Napoli, D. J. (1993). *Syntax: Theory and problems*. New York: Oxford University Press.

Newmeyer, F. (1986). *Linguistic theory in America* (2nd ed.). Orlando: Academic Press.

Osgood, C. (1963). On understanding and creating sentences. *American Psychologist, 18, 735–751.*

Perlmutter, D., (Ed.). (1983). *Studies in Relational Grammar* (Vol. 1). Chicago: University of Chicago Press.

Pesetsky, D. (1982). *Paths and categories.* MIT doctoral dissertation.

Pinker, S. (1994). *The language instinct: How the mind creates language*. New York: William Morrow.

Poizner, H., Klima, E., & Bellugi, U. (1987). *What the hands reveal about the brain*. Cambridge, MA: MIT Press.

Pollard, C., & Sag, I. (1994). *Head-driven phrase structure grammar.* Stanford: Center for the Study of Language and Information; Chicago: University of Chicago Press.

Premack, A. (1976). *Why chimps can read*. New York: Harper Colophon.

Prince, A., & Smolensky, P. (1993). *Optimality theory: Constraint interaction in generative grammar*. To appear, MIT Press. Technical Report-2, Rutgers University Cognitive Science Center.

Radford, A. (1988). *Transformational grammar: A first course.* Cambridge; New York: Cambridge University Press.

Rumbaugh, D. (Ed). (1977). *Language learning by a chimpanzee*. New York: Academic Press.

Sampson, G. (1985). *Writing systems*. London: Hutchinson Press.

Savage-Rumbaugh, S., & Lewin, R. (1994) *Kanzi, the ape at the brink of the human mind.* New York: Wiley.

Schutz, A. J. (1981). A reanalysis of the Hawaiian vowel system. *Oceanic Linguistics, 20,* 1–44.

Skinner, B. F. (1957). *Verbal behavior.* New York: Appleton-Century.

Slobin, D. I. (1966). Grammatical transformations and sentence comprehension in childhood and adulthood. *Journal of Verbal Learning and Verbal Behaviour, 5,* 219–227.

Slobin, D. I. (1973). Cognitive prerequisites for the development of grammar. In C. Ferguson & D. I. Slobin (Eds.), *Studies of child language development*. New York: Holt, Rinehart and Winston.

Slobin, D. I. (1985). *The crosslinguistic study of language acquisition* (Vol. 1: *The data;* Vol. 2: *Theoretical issues)*. Hillsdale, NJ: Erlbaum.

Slobin, D. (1992). *The crosslinguistic study of language acquisition* (Vol. 3). Hillsdale, NJ: Erlbaum.

Smith, N. (1989). *The twitter machine: Reflections on language*. Oxford: Basil Blackwell.

Staats, A. (1971). Linguistic-mentalistic theory vs. an explanatory S-R learning theory of language development. In D. Slobin (Ed.), *The ontogenesis of grammar*. New York: Academic Press.

Tannen. D. (1990). *But you just don't understand.* New York: Morrow.

Tanenhaus, M. (1989). Psycholinguistics: An overview. In F. Newmeyer (Ed.), *Linguistics: The Cambridge survey. III*. Cambridge: Cambridge University Press.

Tanenhaus, M., & Trueswell, J. C. (1995). Sentence comprehension. In J. L. Miller & P. D. Eimas (Eds.), *Speech, language, and communication.* San Diego: Academic Press.

Terrace, H. (1979). *Nim.* New York: Knopf.

Van Valin, R. (Ed.). (1993). *Advances in role and reference grammar.* Philadelphia: J. Benjamins.

Wanner, E. (1974). *On remembering, forgetting, and understanding sentences.* The Hague: Mouton.

Webelhuth, G. (1995). *Government and binding and the minimalist program: Principles and parameters in syntactic theory.* Cambridge, MA: Blackwell.

Wilbur, R. (1989). *American Sign Language: Linguistic and applied dimensions*. Boston: College-Hill Press.

Winograd, T. (1972). *Understanding natural language*. Edinburgh: Edinburgh University Press.

Chapter 2

THE BIOLOGICAL BASES OF HUMAN COMMUNICATIVE BEHAVIOR

William Orr Dingwall
The University of Maryland at College Park

INTRODUCTION

This chapter explores the anatomical and physiological bases of speech and language behavior. In other chapters, we are most concerned with asking *how* people understand spoken and written language, and how they produce it. Here we ask *where* such abilities lie within the brain. Can given communicative abilities be attributed to particular areas of the cerebral cortex? How does one determine where in the brain a particular function is encoded? Are particular speech and language abilities represented in a single discrete area, or multiple areas? What happens to communicative ability in the presence of brain damage? These and other questions will be addressed as we survey historical and current **neurolinguistic** (neurology of language) inquiry.

In the first section of this chapter, we note how early researchers first discovered and investigated the relation between brain and language. This section will also acquaint you with some of the basic "geography" of the human nervous system. Section two details the anatomy and physiology of the brain and describes some speech and language consequences of brain damage, which have the potential to allow us to see the roles that particular parts of the brain apparently play in language production and understanding. This section will also examine the question of whether we can assign the various components of language (articulation, naming, grammatical formulation, comprehension, and so on) to specific areas or interconnected combinations of areas within the human nervous system using the consequences of brain damage as a guide. Section three examines the relative contributions made by each of the two cerebral hemispheres to speech and language function, a concept termed **lateralization of function.** Section four explores recently developed experimental techniques that allow researchers to more precisely localize particular speech and language functions to specific areas within each hemisphere using subject responses during actual language tasks. Our final section explores the efforts of linguists, neurologists, and psychologists to integrate findings from both normal and language-impaired individuals to construct a rational model of the neurological bases of speech and language function.

LANGUAGE AND THE BRAIN: A HISTORICAL PERSPECTIVE

He is speechless, it means he is silent in sadness, without speaking.

(Case 22, the Edwin Smith Surgical Papyrus of 3000 B.C.)

The long history of the study of the relationship between language functioning and the brain (cf. Young, 1974; Clarke & O'Malley, 1968) is peopled with a cast of unforgettable characters of great intellectual insight. This section provides you with a brief overview of some of these individuals and their accomplishments.

Violence, unfortunately, provided us with our first insights into how the brain controls behavior. Starting with stones, and "progressing" to more advanced technology, humans have managed to inflict a wide variety of head injuries upon one another. From such injuries as well as the results of various diseases, observers noted, even in early times, particular patterns of behavior that followed brain damage.

Early Neurolinguistic Observations

Edwin Smith, an American, acquired in 1862 a papyrus scroll that many believe contains the first mention of the consequences of brain injury. Parts of this scroll have been dated to 3000 B.C. Forty-eight cases were discussed in this papyrus. Case 22 (quoted above) notes that the loss of speech skills was possible following head trauma. Many have regarded it as the first mention of **aphasia** (loss of language abilities due to brain damage). To this day, trauma (injury to the brain produced by external force) continues to provide us with insights into brain function.

The ancient Greeks offered little insight in their speculations about brain function, despite their contributions in many other areas of inquiry. For example, Aristotle (384–322 B.C.) claimed that the heart performed what we now know to be brain functions and that the brain was just a cooling system, a radiator. This theory led Shakespeare, centuries later, to query in the *Merchant of Venice:* "Tell me where is fancy bred, or in the heart or in the head?"

Hippocratic scholars (460–370 B.C.) correctly observed that brain injury often produced contralateral (opposite-sided) paresis (semiparalysis). They also noted that speech disturbances commonly accompanied left-side brain injury and right-side paresis. However, they never related these two crucial observations.

Herophilus and Galen, in the second century, developed the Ventricle or Cell Theory of brain function, which localized brain activity to its cavities, the ventricles, where cerebral spinal fluid (CSF) production takes place. It was Leonardo da Vinci (1452–1519) who disproved the Greek theory that the ventricles played a major role in brain functioning. Leonardo demonstrated this through animal dissections proving that the nerve tracts traveling from the retina of the eyes (the optic nerves) go nowhere near the ventricles.

By the eighteenth century almost all known language and speech disorders had already been described (Benton & Joynt, 1960). In the sixteenth century, a prominent medical scholar named Johann Schenk Von Grafenberg (1530–1598) was probably the first to point out that language disturbances due to brain damage (aphasia) were not due to paralysis of the tongue, thus distinguishing between aphasia and the neuromotor speech disorder we now call **dysarthria,** in which the ability to articulate speech sounds has been impaired.

At about the same time, G. Mercuriale (1588) first described what is now known as **pure alexia** or **alexia without agraphia.** He was astonished that his patient "... could write but could not read what he has written." In an age when scholars spoke Latin as well as their local language, the first cases of **bilingual aphasia** (aphasia affecting the use of two languages) were documented (Gesner, 1770; see Benton, 1981). This same scholar provided us with the first descriptions of **jargon aphasia** and **jargon**

agraphia, in which the affected patient's speech and writing contain seemingly meaningless nonsense words. The retained ability to recite overlearned materials such as prayers in the presence of severe aphasia was also noted by Peter Rommel in 1683. This retention of **automatic speech** has been documented countless times since then.

The view that language might be localized to a particular part of the brain, in particular the frontal lobes, was advanced in 1819 by Franz Josef Gall (1758–1828). This distinguished neuroanatomist, who was the first to point out the difference between white and gray matter in the brain, was also the founder of cranioscopy (better known today as phrenology). Gall believed that those particularly gifted in the memorization of verbal materials could be distinguished by prominent, even bulging eyes. His explanation for this "fact," years later, was hypertrophy (excessive growth) of the brain tissue in back of the eyes. Gall went on to postulate some 27 mental "organs" encompassing such traits as vanity, friendship, wisdom, and religion, which by hypertrophy or atrophy could affect the behavioral make-up of individuals.

As extraordinary as this view appears, it may well be correct in its basic outline. As Jerison (1977) has observed, the concept of localization of function in the brain still has validity. What is evidently incorrect is the type of mental faculties that Gall chose to localize. Language is undoubtedly localized in the brain in some complex manner but not, as we shall see, as a unitary phenomenon. However, Gall was able to document cases of trauma and stroke in the frontal cortex that resulted in loss of what he termed "verbal memory," thus providing much stronger evidence for the role of that portion of the brain in language functioning.

Localization of Function (Neurology in the Nineteenth and Twentieth Centuries)

During the nineteenth century researchers made the first concentrated attempts to understand how language was organized within the brain by studying aphasic patients. The first behavior of any type to be localized within the human brain was articulate (spoken) language (Young, 1974).

The French surgeon Pierre Paul Broca (1824–1880), who made this remarkable discovery, is portrayed in Figure 2.1 in a manner that undoubtedly would have pleased him. This statue, which unfortunately no longer exists, shows Broca measuring a human skull with a sliding caliper, one of the many instruments he invented for **craniometry** (measurement of skulls and brains).

As a founding father of what we now call physical anthropology, Broca was greatly intrigued with brain size and its relationship to age, sex, intelligence, race, and environment. This area of study is extremely controversial (see Hahn et al., 1979; Passingham, 1982, for recent overviews). Broca belonged to an anthropological society whose members examined human skulls and occasionally conducted research on the brains of deceased medical patients. Through such research they sought to attribute various behaviors either to the shape or size of the cranium or to sites of damage in the brain. It was during the meetings of this society in 1861 that another member, Dr. Ernest Aubertin, mentioned a patient of his who had a traumatic frontal cranial defect. When Aubertin applied light pressure to the frontal area while the patient was

speaking, he would stop in midword, only to begin speaking again once the compression ceased.

Shortly thereafter, Broca encountered a patient in Paris by the name of Leborgne. He had been a patient in a nursing home for some 21 years, and thus Broca was able to obtain an overview of the progression of his illness. The patient had been admitted at the age of 31 years because he had lost the ability to speak. He seemed to understand what was said to him but answered queries with the single syllable, "tan," accompanied by gestures. If sufficiently provoked, he was also capable of producing a few swear words.

Broca invited Dr. Aubertin to examine Leborgne in order to compare this patient's language deficit with the type that his fellow physician would expect to follow from a frontal lobe lesion. After his examination, Aubertin affirmed this diagnosis. When Leborgne died, Broca performed the autopsy and confirmed a striking frontal lobe lesion in the area of the third frontal convolution (gyrus) in the left hemisphere.

By 1863, Broca had studied 20 cases like that of Leborgne. In 19 of these, the lesion occupied the posterior part of the left third frontal convolution (Broca, 1863). A speech sample from what has come to be called a Broca's aphasic is provided in Table 2.1, together with other samples of disordered communication which we will discuss in the next section.

Note that the speech of the patient in Sample A appears halting, sparse, and devoid of recognizable sentence structure. This nonfluent, agrammatic type of output is

TABLE 2.1

Four Examples of
Communicative Disorders in
Speakers of English

A. **Broca's Aphasia.** Yes . . . ah . . . Monday . . . er . . . Dad and Peter H . . . (his own name), and Dad . . . er . . . hospital . . . and ah . . . Wednesday . . . Wednesday, nine o' clock. Ah doctors . . . two . . . an doctors . . . and er . . . teeth . . yah. (Patient's effort to explain that he came into the hospital for dental surgery.)

B. **Wernicke's Aphasia.** Well, this is . . . mother is away here working her work out here to get her better, but when she's looking, the two boys looking in the other part. One their small tile into her time here. She's working another time because she's getting, too . . . (Patient's description of a scene in which two children are stealing cookies while the mother's back is turned.)

C. **Jargon Aphasia.** All right. Azzuh bezzuh dee pasty hass rih tau dul too. Aulaz foley ass in duh porler dermass died duh paulmasty kide the, the, baidy pahsty bide uh . . . laidy faid uh . . . tiny bride. Uh . . . uh . . . orlihmin fee in a do . . . but uh, ordimis fihd and it was ahrdimidehsty by uhbuhtray dis (unintelligible) you do you know. (In answer to the question: What kind of work did you do?)

D. **Dementia.** Well, it's about half and half. It's a marble and it's half and half. Uhm, that uhm, I'm trying to think what the and ya know and I've been doing all this color work and uhm. I'm trying to think. There's a white and there's a black and there's a, uhm, uhm, I'm trying to think, uh, it, it's, like uhm, oh, what that called? Ym, more of a, oh damn, in the colors that I have in my book is uhm more vivid, and this is a little darker, and I'm trying to think, what's it called purple, more on the purple order this is (In answer to the question: Tell me about this marble.)

characteristic of Broca's aphasia. By 1885, Broca believed that he had amassed enough evidence to proclaim that for the vast majority of people *"nous parlons avec l'hemisphere gauche,"* ("We speak with the left hemisphere.") (Broca, 1885, p. 384).

Gall had not lateralized language to either frontal lobe. Broca made it clear that we are usually left-lateralized for articulate language (*la faculté du langage articule*), but not for the motor act of articulation, which he correctly stated depended to an equal degree on both hemispheres (Broca, 1885, p. 384).

Broca was also one of the first to relate lateralization of language to handedness. He did not do so in the simplistic manner of Dax (1836; see Benton, 1981), who said that language was always left-lateralized. Nor did he assume that right-handers are left-lateralized and left-handers are right-lateralized—a view that unfortunately has been repeatedly attributed to Broca as well. Rather, Broca related both handedness and lateralization of language to the precocious development of the left hemisphere. He also advanced the possibility of plasticity of brain function, stating:

> . . . a lesion of the left third frontal convolution, apt to produce lasting aphemia (Broca's term for aphasia) in an adult, will not prevent a small child from learning to talk. . . .
>
> (Broca, 1885, p. 392)

In the years since then, we have come to see additional examples of the flexibility of the young brain in responding to brain damage. Lenneberg (1967) went so far as to posit that there was a critical period for language acquisition, during which language learning occurred readily, and brain damage did not produce lasting communicative

A CRITICAL PERIOD FOR LANGUAGE DEVELOPMENT

Some support for the notion of a critical period beyond which language learning or recovery might be difficult was provided by the discovery, in 1970, of a young girl who had been brought up under conditions of extreme neglect and abuse. Between the ages of 2 and 13½, Genie was kept confined and was provided with little or no verbal interaction. Genie was unable to speak or understand language when removed from the home by social welfare workers. Although she was provided with intensive language stimulation and instruction following her rescue by authorities, she experienced great difficulty in learning expressive grammar, despite rather good progress in language comprehension and vocabulary development. A full discussion of this unfortunate but remarkable case is provided by Curtiss (1977) and Rymer (1992); Chapter 8 discusses Genie further.

disorder. As we shall see later in the chapter, children do appear to make remarkable recovery from brain injury, although subtle changes in linguistic ability may be detectable.

We have already said that even in ancient Greece, enough evidence existed to establish lateralization of function. Why was this association not made? Perhaps for the same reason that Broca's views were resisted when he announced them. For example, in discussing these views in 1865, Laborde (quoted in Berker et al., 1968) stated that he found it difficult to admit that "two parts of the same organ, whose situation, size, and detailed anatomical structures were absolutely identical and symmetrical, could have different functions."

The premise that the hemispheres are anatomically identical turns out to be false, and Broca himself first demonstrated that this was so. He completed analysis on thirty-seven brains and found that the mean weight of the right hemispheres was slightly greater than that of the left; however, the mean weight of the left frontal lobe was greater than the right (Broca, 1875). Both of these findings are supported by current research.

It is interesting to note that Leborgne's preserved brain was recently analyzed by a neuroimaging technique known as a CT scan or **computerized trans-axial tomography.** Figure 2.2 displays a horizontal section showing a massive lesion of the left frontal convolution (F3), which has come to be known as **Broca's area,** as well as the precentral gyrus and the insula (see Figure 2.10 for the precise location of Broca's area on the lateral surface of the cerebral cortex).

This modern CT scan analysis also shows another intact area of the brain implicated in language and speech processing by a neurologist contemporaneous with Broca. This area is now named after Carl Wernicke (1848–1904). Wernicke, a German, studied with Sigmund Freud (1856–1939) and Theodor Meynert (1833–1892), a neurologist who traced the auditory nerve—an elusive and most complex cranial nerve—which reaches from the ear to the cortex. The highest (most **rostral**) area of hearing

FIGURE 2.2

A horizontal section obtained via CT scan through the brain of Broca's patient, Leborgne, demonstrating involvement of the left third frontal convolution, precentral and postcentral gyri with sparing of Wernicke's area in the left first temporal gyrus (Signoret et al., 1984).

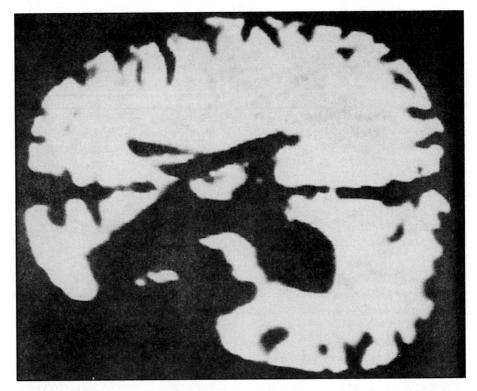

is known as **Heschl's gyrus** and is buried deep within the Sylvian fissure. The area of interest to Wernicke was contiguous with this cortical area for hearing. Damage to this area resulted in a complex of symptoms quite unlike those which Broca had observed.

A typical example of **Wernicke's aphasia** is illustrated in Sample B in Table 2.1. Unlike Broca's aphasics, these patients are fluent—so garrulous in fact that they have been termed **logorrheic.** For the most part, this patient's speech has discernible grammatical structure. However, it doesn't appear to make much sense; consider the somewhat random array of words in the phrase, "one their small tile into her time here." Whereas Broca's aphasics are acutely aware of their language problems, Wernicke's aphasics often are not and may even deny that they are ill (**anosognosia**). Both Broca's and Wernicke's aphasics have comprehension problems, but the problems are much more severe in Wernicke's aphasia. Many Wernicke's patients appear to understand at least some of what is addressed to them but wander further and further astray as they respond. Some patients produce jargon, as in Sample C, using "Jabberwocky" words that do not exist in English, such as *porler, demass,* and *ahrdimidehsty.* Even when such jargon is absent, their speech rapidly becomes meaningless and filled with inappropriate words.

As the speech samples and our discussions illustrate, Broca's and Wernicke's aphasia differ strikingly. The Broca's aphasic is nonfluent and uses language that seems sparse, labored, and agrammatic (missing important grammatical morphemes), although comprehension appears reasonable. The Wernicke's aphasic appears fluent and uses long complicated utterances that unfortunately make little sense. Their speech is apt to be full of **neologisms** (nonsense words). Finally, they appear quite disordered in their ability to understand both the speech of others and their own output.

Later, Wernicke, working with the neurologist Ludwig Lichtheim (1885), produced a classification of observed aphasias as well as those logically possible though not yet described (Wernicke, 1906). This classification is shown in Figure 2.3.

The Wernicke-Lichtheim model is based on neuroanatomical considerations and predicts the communicative consequences of injury to various parts of the brain. It has become the "classical model" of the aphasias within neurology and has been elaborated by the great American neurologist, Norman Geschwind (Geschwind, 1974). From its inception, the model had its detractors (Goldstein, 1948; Head, 1963; Cole & Cole, 1971) and, as you shall see, it is being attacked once again today. Although admittedly simplistic, the model has proved remarkably resilient (Goodglass, 1988). This may be because this model makes good neurological sense. It constitutes a first approximation to the final goal of localizing speech and language functions within the brain. The next section will survey the anatomical considerations that contribute to the development of such a model of the aphasias. In it, we will examine the anatomy of the brain and central nervous system and more closely analyze the behaviors that result from damage to various portions of this system.

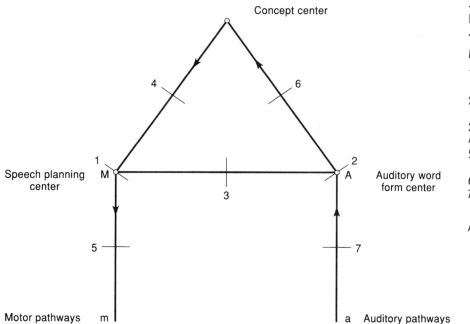

FIGURE 2.3

THE WERNICKE–LICHTHEIM MODEL OF THE APHASIAS

1. Cortical Motor Aphasia
   (= Broca's aphasia)
2. Cortical Sensory Aphasia
   (= Wernicke's aphasia)
3. Conduction Aphasia
4. Transcortical Motor Aphasia
5. Subcortical Motor Aphasia
   (= pure word mutism)
6. Transcortical Sensory Aphasia
7. Subcortical Sensory Aphasia
   (= pure word deafness)

Adapted from Lichtheim, 1885.

FUNCTIONAL NEUROANATOMY AND NEUROPATHOLOGY

. . . an enchanted loom where millions of flashing shuttles weave a dissolving pattern, always a meaningful pattern though never an abiding one; a shifting harmony of subpatterns.

(Herrington, Gifford Lectures, 1937–8)

The student who seeks to explore brain/behavior relationships should first understand the anatomy and physiology of the nervous system. Having gained a fairly detailed idea of how the human nervous system functions in the healthy individual, the next topic to approach is **neuropathology,** the study of what can go wrong with the system. From this study of such "experiments of nature" comes much of our knowledge of the human nervous system. Finally, an acquaintance with the available research techniques is useful. These range from detailed single-case studies through highly sophisticated neuropsychological experimentation to the use of advanced instrumentation employed in neurological diagnosis. A guide to the literature in these areas is provided in Dingwall (1981).

Neuroanatomical Structures Involved in Speech and Language

Figure 2.4 depicts the central nervous system (CNS)—that part of the nervous system housed within the bony structures of the skull **(cranium)** and vertebral column. Not only is it protected by these bony coverings, it is wrapped in three layers of membranes, the **meninges,** and floats in **cerebral spinal fluid (CSF)** produced in the four ventricles of the brain. Despite its minuscule weight, averaging about 3.5 pounds, the brain utilizes one-fifth of the body's blood supply.

The most rostral (from the Latin "toward the beak") structure, the cerebral cortex, is depicted at the very top of Figure 2.4. ("Cortex" is Latin for "bark," as in bark of a tree.) Its general appearance characterized by hills (gyri) and valleys (sulci or fissures) may have influenced its naming by medieval anatomists. (In fact, most of the basic structures of the central nervous system have names with down-to-earth meanings in Greek or Latin. Learning these meanings may help you remember the names.) Actually, the reason for the barklike appearance of the cortex, which is roughly 2.5 square feet in area, is dictated by folding a sheet of this size into the confines of the cranium.

The cortex, like almost every structure in the brain (and in the body), is paired—it has a left and right part. These two parts are the cerebral hemispheres, which are connected by fiber tracts (commissures), the most massive of which is known as the corpus callosum ("calloused body") shown in Figure 2.5.

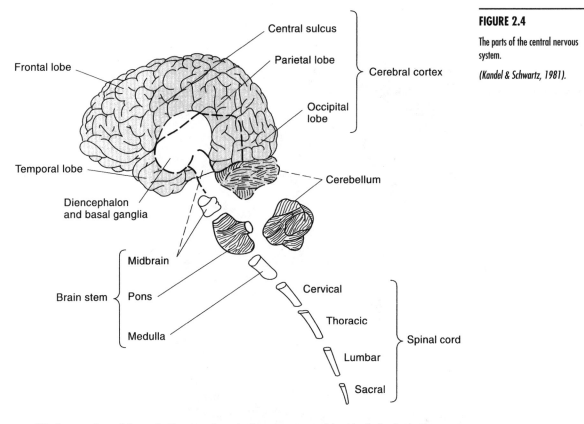

FIGURE 2.4

The parts of the central nervous system.

(Kandel & Schwartz, 1981).

We know that although the two hemispheres appear identical, in fact, they are not. The morphological (form) differences between them have now been extensively catalogued. Although language, in the vast majority of individuals, is lateralized to the left hemisphere, this is not true for articulation, which is subserved by both hemispheres. It is evident that handedness correlates in some manner with "brainedness." Language behavior is subserved by different cortical areas or loci located within different lobes of the cortex.

When Gall introduced the distinction between white and gray matter within the brain, he was referring to the nerve fibers and groups of nerve cells (neurons) respectively. Grossly, the brain resembles a layer cake with alternating layers of these two types of matter. As can be seen in Figure 2.4, and in more detail in Figure 2.6, at the very center of the brain is a mass of neurons, the **diencephalon** ("between brain"). This may be regarded as the first layer of gray matter. This paired structure is made up of a number of components which, among many other functions, serves as a way station for all incoming sensations—with the exception of smell (olfaction)—before they travel on to the cortex. It also plays a major role in providing motor feedback to the cortex. The **dorsal thalamus,** one of the components of the diencephalon, has been shown to be lateralized like the overlying cortex. Damage to the left side can produce

FIGURE 2.5

Is Your Left Hemisphere Different From Your Right?

Photo of human brain as seen from above, looking down on partially split corpus callosum.

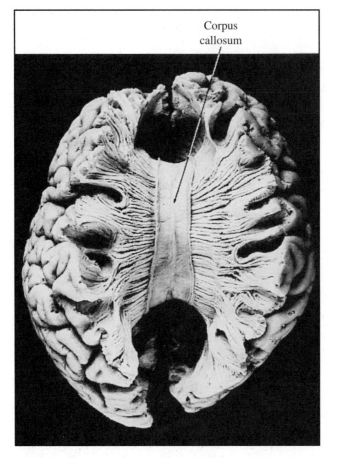

Corpus callosum

both aphasia and the articulation disorder dysarthria (Kennedy & Murdoch, 1989). The white matter layers of the brain are made up of ascending and descending fibers to and from the cortex. Those surrounding the diencephalon are known as the **internal capsule.**

The next layer of gray matter that we encounter is the **basal ganglia.** This complex structure not only plays a major role in the control of movement but also appears to be involved in cognitive functioning. Damage to the basal ganglia can result in poverty of movement **(hypokinesia),** as in Parkinson's disease, or too much movement **(hyperkinesia),** as in Huntington's chorea (dance), as well as tremor at rest. It is also known now that damage here can result in not only dysarthria but also aphasia.

Surrounding the basal ganglia is another white matter layer, the external capsule, beyond which lies the cortical mantle, the cerebral cortex. Below the cerebral hemispheres lies the cerebellum ("little brain"). (See Figures 2.4 and 2.7.) This structure is known to play a major role in motor control in conjunction with the basal ganglia, diencephalon, and the cortex itself. Damage to the cerebellum results in a

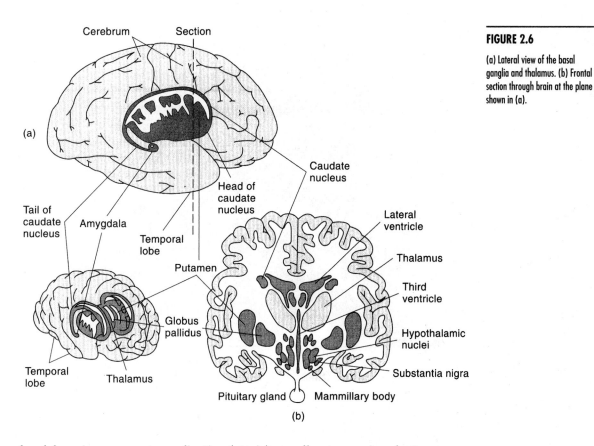

(a)

Cerebrum   Section

Tail of caudate nucleus

Amygdala

Temporal lobe

Putamen

Head of caudate nucleus

Caudate nucleus

Temporal lobe

Thalamus

Globus pallidus

Lateral ventricle

Thalamus

Third ventricle

Hypothalamic nuclei

Substantia nigra

Pituitary gland   Mammillary body

(b)

FIGURE 2.6

(a) Lateral view of the basal ganglia and thalamus. (b) Frontal section through brain at the plane shown in (a).

breakdown in movement coordination **(ataxia)** as well as tremor in voluntary movements. Dysarthria can result from damage to the cerebellum. Currently no language deficits have been reported from damage to this area.

At the very base of the brain is the **brain stem,** composed of the **midbrain, pons** ("bridge"), and **medulla** ("marrow"). This could be regarded as the most important part of the brain, as it controls the functioning of the heart and lungs.

The remainder of the central nervous system consists of the **spinal cord** housed within the vertebral column. It directly controls motor and sensory functions of the entire body with the exception of the face area. The human spinal cord is unfortunately **nonautonomous.** By this we mean that ultimately all functions of the body are controlled from the brain via the spinal cord. The spinal cord in humans cannot function independently of the brain. This is why a broken neck can lead to paralysis of the entire body below the neck.

The **peripheral nervous system (PNS)** encompasses those components of the nervous system that lie outside of the bony coverings of the central nervous system. This includes the **cranial nerves** that issue directly from the cranium and the **spinal nerves** that issue from the vertebral column. The cranial nerves are important in controlling such functions as vision, smell, hearing, and facial sensation. Specific cranial nerves

FIGURE 2.7

Sagittal section of the human brain showing the medial aspect of the left hemisphere.

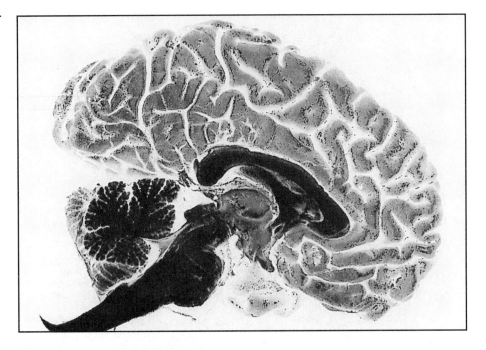

play crucial roles in **phonation** (laryngeal or voice activity) and tongue movement necessary for articulation.

How Speech Is Controlled by the Brain

Language is not the only species-specific aspect of human communicative behavior; speech is also specific to human behavior (Dingwall, 1975a). Darley et al. (1975b) have estimated that speech involves at least 100 muscles, each controlled by perhaps as many motoneurons. At a normal speech rate of about 14 sounds per second, this would mean that 140,000 neuromuscular events per second are required for speaking.

Research suggests (Kuypers, 1981) at least three distinct motor systems in all primates, including humans. One system controls individual movements of the fingers (digits); a second system controls independent movements of the hands and arms; and the third controls posture and bilateral trunk and limb movements.

A striking dissociation of these motor control systems is often seen in global aphasia, where a patient with little evidence of speech, language, or the ability to carry out individual limb movements to command (ideomotor praxis) can nevertheless respond to complex axial commands, such as stand up, turn around, go to the door, bow, and so on.

The best candidate for the motor control system of speech appears to be the first "finger" system. It is most highly developed in primates, particularly the chimpanzee and humans. It corresponds to the fibers of the pyramidal tract that cross over either in the brain stem or in the spinal cord in Figure 2.8. The fibers we are interested in are not only those that cross, but that also make direct contact on motoneurons either in the brain stem or spinal cord.

Let us examine this tract briefly. Note, first of all, the odd-looking creature perched at the top of the figure. This is the famous motor **homunculus** ("little man") schema of motor organization suggested by neurosurgeon Wilder Penfield (1891–1976), who mapped functional areas in the brain by electrically stimulating them. Because the brain itself is without pain receptors, such stimulation can be carried out on conscious patients under local anesthesia prior to medically necessary removal (ablation) of diseased neuronal tissue. Neurosurgeons must avoid damaging the speech and language areas of the cortex we have discussed, and one way to locate these areas is via **electrical stimulation of the brain (ESB).** Penfield was a pioneer in this area, and his book *Speech and Brain-Mechanisms,* which summarizes some of his findings, is well known (Penfield & Roberts, 1959). In it, the awkward little homunculus "lies across" areas of the cortex that appear to control the function of his various body parts. Note how large his head and tongue appear in relation to his trunk, for example; this is because proportionately more cortical area appears to be devoted to head and tongue functioning than to the torso. We may also note that although many areas adjacent to one another cortically subserve adjacent body parts (hip to knee to ankle to toes), the homunculus is not an exact photocopy of an actual person (consider the proximity of the neck and thumb to one another in their cortical representation, for example).

The aspect of the pyramidal tract that interests us in this discussion arises in part from the motor strip (Brodmann area 4) along which the homunculus lies, and in particular from that lower portion where the face and some of the speech organs are represented. Fibers from this area travel downward and cross at the level of the brain stem synapsing—making contact with—nerves (in this case, cranial nerves) that exit directly from the skull to control, among other things, the speech musculature. There are 12 pairs of cranial nerves in humans (other animals have more). Some are sensory; some, motor; some, both. In a tangential way, all could be said to be involved in some aspect of human communication. But we are only interested here in those involved in speech production. For example, the fifth cranial nerve (trigeminal) handles both motor function and sensation for portions of the jaw and face. The seventh (facial) nerve controls motor and sensory functioning of most of the facial musculature, enabling aspects of articulation and facial expression. The tenth (vagus) controls aspects of laryngeal function necessary for voicing, and the twelfth (hypoglossal) controls tongue movement necessary for articulation. The eighth cranial nerve is the auditory nerve, which has been discussed earlier. Still other cranial nerves are responsible for aspects of vision, eye movement, and olfaction (smell), which will not be described in detail.

Although some of the cranial nerves clearly must play some role in vocalization and articulation, they have not yet been studied in sufficient detail in humans or nonhuman primates to allow us to determine their precise role in speech production. The Czech physiologist J. Krmpotic (1959) noted that both the length of these nerves and

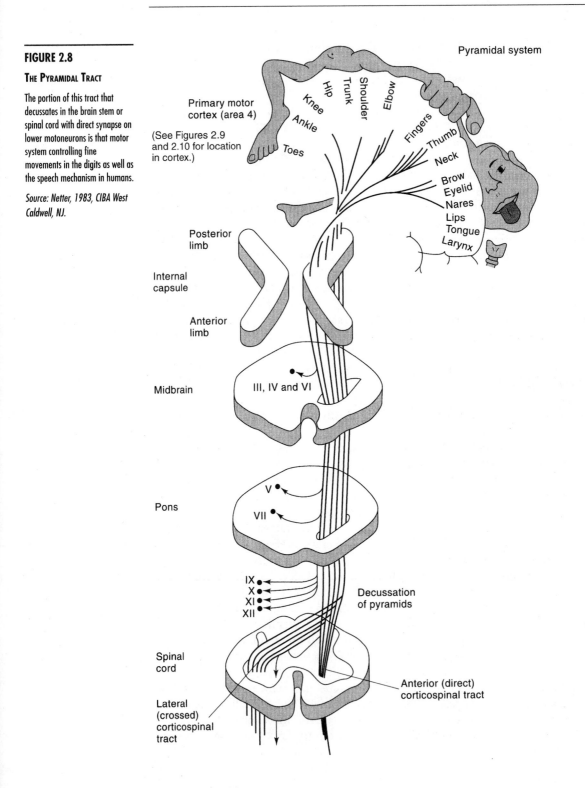

FIGURE 2.8

THE PYRAMIDAL TRACT

The portion of this tract that decussates in the brain stem or spinal cord with direct synapse on lower motoneurons is that motor system controlling fine movements in the digits as well as the speech mechanism in humans.

Source: Netter, 1983, CIBA West Caldwell, NJ.

Pyramidal system

Primary motor cortex (area 4)

(See Figures 2.9 and 2.10 for location in cortex.)

Hip · Knee · Ankle · Toes · Trunk · Shoulder · Elbow · Fingers · Thumb · Neck · Brow · Eyelid · Nares · Lips · Tongue · Larynx

Posterior limb

Internal capsule

Anterior limb

Midbrain — III, IV and VI

Pons — V, VII

IX, X, XI, XII

Decussation of pyramids

Spinal cord

Anterior (direct) corticospinal tract

Lateral (crossed) corticospinal tract

THE EVOLUTION OF HUMAN COMMUNICATIVE ABILITY

Another approach that may provide us with insight into how human communicative ability is mediated by the brain is to study communicative behavior in closely related species. It is unlikely that speech and language arose as a single genetic mutation; rather, it is much more likely that such a complex behavior developed gradually over time. Toulmin (1971) has offered the opinion that certain physiological behaviors once used for nonlinguistic purposes eventually became associated behaviorally with language functions.

Recent research using squirrel monkeys has identified areas that, when damaged, result in the disturbance or elimination of vocalization. Similar vocalization areas exist in man, and their damage results in similar consequences. The monkey's cingulate cortex and supplementary motor area (roughly equivalent to the human Brodmann area 6) appear to be necessary for the initiation of conditioned vocalization but not for the production of innate calls.

Control of nonhuman primate vocalization appears to terminate at subcortical levels, unlike human cortical representation of language abilities. Unilateral or bilateral destruction of areas of the monkey cortex comparable to the human language areas does not produce appreciable effects on their vocalizations (Steklis & Raleigh, 1979; Passingham, 1982; Dingwall, 1988).

---

their diameters vary greatly, two factors involved in speed of conduction of neural impulses. This raises the totally unresolved issue as to how the various aspects of the vocal tract are coordinated in the production of speech.

Neural Cells and Their Connections: The Ultimate Basis of All Behavior

The brain is composed of but two types of cells: nerve cells **(neurons)** and **glia** (glue cells). Humans do not win a prize for the largest number of these cells—other animals are larger than us in body size and brain weight. All these cells could be wired together, but they are not. Instead, a gap (the synapse) of minuscule proportion exists between one nerve cell and its processes (axons and dendrites) and the cells (often many) that are in contact with it. Across this gap, transmission occurs via chemical rather than electrophysiologic means. The chemical agents involved in this transmission are known as **neurotransmitters.** It is in this microscopic world of cells, their membranes and neurochemistry, that the true nature of our being may lie. Sherrington's comment at the beginning of this section mirrors the wonder he felt for the events transpiring in this realm.

One way of analyzing areas of the brain is in terms of **cytoarchitecture**—the organization of cells, their morphology and layering. One of the most often referenced "maps" of this type was produced by the German anatomist Korbinian Brodmann in 1909 (Figure 2.9). To this day, the numbers on this map (52 areas in all) are frequently used as reference points. The table accompanying this figure may aid you in gaining an initial understanding for the location and function of some of the areas Brodmann designated in the cerebral cortex.

What Can Go Wrong With the Brain: Neuropathology

Unfortunately, many things can go wrong with a system this complex. Table 2.2 lists some common types of neuropathology and the communication disorders with which they are associated.

Cerebrovascular diseases kill neurons by cutting off their blood supply, thus depriving them of glucose and oxygen. Other pathologies such as trauma, tumors, and hydrocephalus destroy neuronal tissue by producing within the cranium space-occupying masses that consist of blood, glial cells, or cerebrospinal fluid. Such masses can even result in herniation of neural tissue around the meninges or through the foramen magnum (the hole in the base of the skull through which the spinal cord connects with the brain stem). Some diseases, such as multiple sclerosis, affect conduction of nerve impulses by eating away at the myelin coverings of axons, composed of oligodendroglial cells in the CNS and Schwann cells in the PNS. Parkinsonism and Huntington's chorea result from neurotransmitter imbalances that affect the functions of the basal ganglia. Still other diseases such as myasthenia gravis come about from a decrease in neurotransmitter receptor sites on muscles. Thus, as you can see, if something can malfunction it will (see Gilroy & Holliday, 1982, for a concise and relatively comprehensive guide to neuropathology).

Examining the Consequences of Cortical Damage

We have already discussed Broca's aphasia (labeled *cortical motor aphasia* in Figure 2.3). Other common terms for this condition include expressive or nonfluent aphasia. Broca said that this condition resulted from a lesion of the third frontal convolution. This region lies directly in front of the face area of the motor strip, and is labeled *Broca's area* on Figure 2.10. A lesion to the motor strip itself can produce the neuromotor disorder of speech called dysarthria. Dysarthric patients have laborious and inaccurate articulation, though their ability to formulate language is intact.

The area that Wernicke said produced cortical sensory aphasia (synonyms: receptive or fluent aphasia), which we have discussed, is located in the posterior third of the first temporal gyrus. This area, which has been shown to extend into the deep valley called the Sylvian fissure, lies behind the cortical area for audition (Heschl's gyrus), and has become known as Wernicke's area in his honor. Slightly behind Wernicke's area lies the angular gyrus. The angular gyrus apparently plays a large role in the process of lexical access, or word retrieval, which is discussed in greater detail in Chapter 4. Damage to this area can produce a disorder known as anomia, in which the patient experiences difficulty in naming items, even though he can comprehend vocabulary reasonably well.

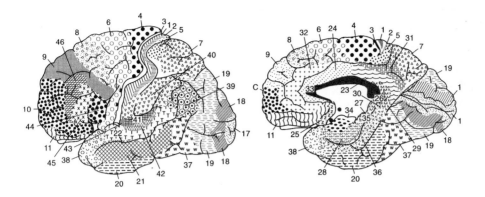

FIGURE 2.9

The cytoarchitectural maps of the lateral and medial surfaces of the human brain developed by Korbinian Brodmann (1909). The accompanying table provides information concerning the anatomical sites and functions of some of the 52 areas involved directly or indirectly with HCB.

BRODMANN AREA	ANATOMICAL LOCATION	FUNCTION
1, 2, 3	Postcentral gyrus	Primary sensori-motor area (Sm I)
4	Precentral gyrus	Primary motor-sensory area (Ms I)
6	Premotor cortex	Premotor area supplementary motor area (on medial surface) (Ms II)
8	Caudal part of middle frontal gyrus	Frontal eye field
9, 10, 11	Superior, middle, and inferior frontal gyri	Judgment, foresight, mood
17	Walls of calcarine sulcus	Primary visual area
18, 19	Occipital lobe	Visual association areas
39	Angular gyrus	Reading and writing (dominant hemisphere)
40	Supramarginal gyrus	Repetition (possibly due to disruption of arcuate fasciculus) (dominant hemisphere)
41	Heschl's gyrus	Primary auditory area
42	Belt of cortex surrounding Heschl's gyrus	Auditory association area
22	Superior temporal gyrus	Posterior third = Wernicke's area (dominant hemisphere)
44, 45	Third frontal gyrus (pars opercularis and triangularis)	Broca's area (dominant hemisphere)

TABLE 2.2

Types of Neuropathology and Their Associated Communicative Disorders

TYPES OF NEUROPATHOLOGY	TYPES OF COMMUNICATION DISORDERS
Cerebrovascular Disease (hemorrhage, aneurysm, atherosclerosis, arteriovenous malformation (AVM)	Aphasia, dysarthria, dementia[1]
Degenerative Disease (e.g., Alzheimer's, Pick's Disease)	Dementia
Trauma (penetrating and closed head injury [CHI])	Aphasia, dysarthria, language of confusion
Parkinsonism	Dementia and dysarthria
Multiple Sclerosis	Dysarthria
Hydrocephalus	Aphasia
Tumor (neoplasm) (benign or malignant)	Aphasia and/or dysarthria
Huntington's chorea	Dementia and dysarthria
Hereditary ataxias	Dysarthria
Amyotrophic lateral sclerosis (ALS)	Dysarthria
Myasthenia gravis	Dysarthria

[1]The communicative disorder associated with dementia is often referred to by the rather cumbersome term: *language of generalized intellectual impairment.*

Given these two different types of aphasias and the neuroanatomic sites associated with them, what other types of speech and language disorders might be possible?

Let us suppose that Wernicke's area and Heschl's gyrus are intact, but that the two are disconnected by some sort of lesion produced perhaps by a stroke or gunshot wound. Would the patient be able to hear? Yes. Heschl's gyrus is intact. Would she be able to understand what was said to her? No, because auditory signals are prevented from arriving at Wernicke's area by the lesion. This disorder is termed **subcortical sensory aphasia** in Figure 2.3 and is known as **pure word deafness** today. Patients with this disorder have been known to state: "I can hear what you say, but it just doesn't compute." Such patients can speak, write, and read normally. They may be able to distinguish nonspeech sounds but unable to interpret their own speech.

What might happen, on the motor (output) side, if Broca's area were disconnected from the face area of the motor strip or if the link between Wernicke's and Broca's areas were disrupted? In the first case, patients should have preserved comprehension of what is said to them, as Wernicke's area is intact; however, they should be incapable of volitional speech as well as repetition, because Broca's area can no longer control the motor output to the vocal tract. This is true because Broca's area is no longer connected with the motor strip. Lichtheim (1885, pp. 449–453) documents a number of such cases of subcortical motor aphasia.

In the second case, conduction aphasia, a quite different picture emerges. Because the speech production and auditory comprehension areas are intact, the output of such patients is reasonably well formed and they understand most of what they

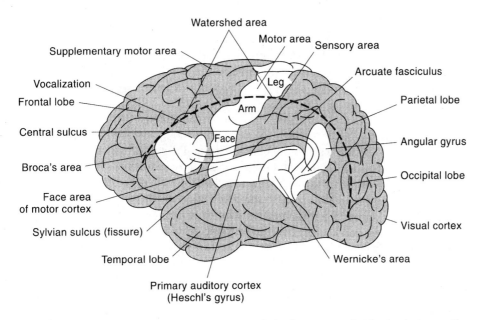

Watershed area
Motor area Sensory area
Supplementary motor area
Arcuate fasciculus
Leg
Vocalization
Frontal lobe
Arm
Parietal lobe
Central sulcus
Face
Angular gyrus
Broca's area
Occipital lobe
Face area
of motor cortex
Visual cortex
Sylvian sulcus (fissure)
Temporal lobe
Wernicke's area
Primary auditory cortex
(Heschl's gyrus)

FIGURE 2.10

Lateral view of the cerebral cortex of the left hemisphere showing the areas involved in language.

Adapted from Kandel and Schwartz, 1981.

hear. However, because messages cannot travel via the arcuate fasciculus between the auditory and speech production areas, they are basically unable to repeat what they hear, though they may understand the message.

Wernicke and Lichtheim also proposed a concept center that when damaged produces **dementia** or **agnosia.** A conversational sample from a patient with dementia is provided in Table 2.1, Sample D, along with our examples of aphasic output. Note that what appears lacking in this patient's language is conceptual, rather than linguistic. Thus, although the ability to produce language has been spared, the process of thought, or ideation, appears to have been disrupted.

We have already observed that brain damage can dissociate speech from language (dysarthria) and language from speech (jargon aphasia). Can you imagine speech and language without ideation or the converse? Such dissociations do occur.

Suppose an individual suffered damage to the vast majority of the region below the dashed line in Figure 2.10. This **perisylvian area** (the area surrounding the Sylvian fissure) contains most of the cortex exclusively devoted to language. Now also suppose that this damage is reversible. What might this disorder look like? Well, the patient has damage to Broca's area and Wernicke's area as well as everything in between. He should thus lose all speech and language abilities. This type of aphasia (which Wernicke did not postulate) occurs, and is known as **global aphasia.**

A patient with an unusual reversible aphasia of this type due to epilepsy, **paroxysmal aphasia,** has been documented by Lecours and Joanette (1980). Their case provides insight into not only the consequences of such an aphasia but also into the separability of thought and language processes. Brother John, a Catholic monk, periodically experiences "spells" that do not render him unconscious but rather globally aphasic. Lecours and Joanette describe one such spell during a train trip from Italy to

Switzerland. Despite the loss of speech production, comprehension, and reading ability, Brother John was able to get off the train at the appropriate stop, find his hotel, find yet another place to stay when informed by gestures that his hotel was full, and order supper in a restaurant by pointing to items on the menu and hoping to get something he would like! By the next morning, all of his language skills returned to normal.

This case offers striking support, as do other documented cases of global aphasia (cf. Gordon, 1990), for the retention of ideation or thought processes in the absence of language, and for the separability of linguistic and cognitive competence. Possible dissociations between cognitive and linguistic capacity are also discussed in Chapter 8, where we describe language acquisition in children.

The converse dissociation, retention of language abilities with little evidence of intact thought processes, has also been observed. The lesion in this case is above the dashed line in Figure 2.10 and has thus been termed isolation of the speech area or **mixed transcortical aphasia.** The most detailed description of such a case is found in Whitaker (1976). The patient, HCEM, who was found upon autopsy to have suffered from Pick's disease, was totally noncommunicative with no spontaneous speech and little evidence of language comprehension. She spent most of her days quietly watching television in the lounge of her nursing home.

One could demonstrate, however, that HCEM had not lost all aspects of communicative behavior. If one approached her and spoke to her directly, HCEM was **echolalic** (that is, she echoed or repeated what was said to her). The ability to repeat is the hallmark of all transcortical aphasias and was first suggested by Lichtheim (1885). Table 2.3 presents some of Dr. Whitaker's conversational exchanges with the patient.

In Sample A, you can see how adept HCEM is at repetition. In fact, she could even repeat foreign words but with an American accent! As Samples B and C demonstrate even more clearly, HCEM does not just echo. She repeats, applying the rules of her dialect of English. HCEM is not a parrot, but a human being who, although she has not lost the complex rule system of her native language, appears to be unable to use this linguistic "competence" to communicate.

HCEM's disorder, mixed transcortical aphasia, involves a combination of both transcortical motor aphasia and transcortical sensory aphasia. What distinguishes the

---

TABLE 2.3

EXAMPLES OF CONVERSATIONAL EXCHANGES WITH A PATIENT (HCEM) SUFFERING FROM MIXED TRANSCORTICAL APHASIA

A. HW: What's your name?
   HCEM: What's your name?
   HW: The car was bought by John.
   HCEM: The car was bought by John.

B. HW: *This is a yellow tencil.
   HCEM: yellow pencil
   HW: *That's a piece of dandy.
   HCEM: That's a piece of candy.

C. HW: *I talk to her yesterday.
   HCEM: I talked to her yesterday.
   HW: *She had four childs.
   HCEM: She had four children.

transcortical aphasias from other types of aphasia is the preservation of the ability to repeat. Thus, transcortical motor aphasia is like Broca's aphasia, and transcortical sensory aphasia is like Wernicke's aphasia in terms of the patients' communicative abilities, save for the transcortical patients' ability to repeat what is said to them. As the examples above show, HCEM can neither produce nor comprehend language; she is capable only of repetition.

LATERALIZATION OF FUNCTION

Nous parlons avec l'hémisphère gauche.

(Broca, 1865, p. 384)

As discussed earlier, Broca and Dax both introduced the idea that the two cerebral hemispheres, despite their apparent symmetry, might differ in function. In fact, Broca provided evidence for an anatomical asymmetry and furthermore noted the relationship between handedness and "brainedness."

Over the years, researchers have tried to relate brainedness not only to handedness and hand posture but also to age variances; gender, race (Tsunoda, 1985), and education differences (Bogen et al., 1972); human versus nonhuman; and so forth. Additionally, researchers have more closely examined the specific functions for which the two hemispheres appear to be specialized. Some communicative functions, as we shall see, do appear to reside in the nondominant (usually right) hemisphere.

Current evidence does suggest that the left and right hemispheres differ in some way in their function. This difference is clearly not dichotomous but ranges along a continuum. It does relate in some manner to some of the variables mentioned in the previous paragraph, but this correlation is far from completely clear.

It seems evident at this point that in the normal human brain both hemispheres are involved, perhaps to differing degrees, in language function. But it is also clear that such bihemispheric involvement may not be necessary for reasonably normal functioning. In the next section, we survey some of the experimental findings that lead to these conclusions.

Putting One Half of the Brain to Sleep: The Wada Test

Accurate knowledge of lateralization of language is crucial prior to surgery that may intrude upon the classical language areas. In 1949, Japanese neurosurgeon Juhn Wada developed a test for language dominance that involved injection of the drug sodium amytol (Wada, 1949). Originally, the injection was made in the **internal** or **common carotid arteries** in the neck. But now it is more common to inject the drug through a catheter threaded up into the internal carotid from a femoral artery in the thigh. The injection results in deactivation of the hemisphere ipsilateral (on the same side) to the side of injection.

The patient, who lies on the operating table with his legs drawn up, his forearms raised, and his fingers moving, is asked to count backwards. The injection generally produces immediate contralateral **hemiplegia** (paralysis of one side). The forearm and leg on the side opposite to the injection fall. In all instances counting is momentarily interrupted, but with nondominant deactivation, it resumes within 5 to 20 seconds. Yet if the dominant hemisphere is involved, dysphasic responses may persist for as long as 1–3 minutes. One common method of testing language functioning is by having the patient name objects projected on an overhead screen.

The results of such testing on two groups of patients studied by Rasmussen and Milner (1977) in Montreal are presented in Table 2.4 One group had no evidence of early left cerebral damage; the other did. The proportions of patients with left, right, and bilateral (both hemispheres) language representation are compared.

This table provides clear evidence of the relationship among three variables— handedness and age and language lateralization. On the basis of these results, it is clear that the vast majority of right-handed individuals display left lateralization for language. Although the majority of left-handed individuals and ambidextrous individuals without early brain damage are left-lateralized as well, a large proportion are right-lateralized or trilateral. A history of early left-hemisphere damage increases the possibility of bilateral or right hemispheric lateralization for language functions.

A recent study by Loring et al. (1990), using tasks that involve counting, comprehension, naming, and repetition, found that out of 103 patients, 79 had exclusive

TABLE 2.4

THE RESULTS OF SODIUM AMYTOL TESTING (THE WADA TEST) IN POPULATIONS DIFFERING IN HANDEDNESS AND EVIDENCE OF EARLY LEFT-HEMISPHERE DAMAGE

Source: Rasmussen and Milner, 1977.

Speech Lateralization as Related to Handedness in 262 Patients Without Clinical Evidence of Early Damage to the Left Cerebral Hemisphere				
		SPEECH REPRESENTATION		
Handedness	**No. of Cases**	**Left**	**Bilateral**	**Right**
Right	140	134 96%	0 0%	6 4%
Left or mixed	122	86 70%	18 15%	18 15%

Speech Lateralization as Related to Handedness in 134 Patients With Definite Clinical Evidence of an Early Left-Hemisphere Lesion				
		SPEECH REPRESENTATION		
Handedness	**No. of Cases**	**Left**	**Bilateral**	**Right**
Right	42	34 81%	3 7%	5 12%
Left or mixed	92	26 28%	17 19%	49 53%

left-hemisphere language representation, 2 had exclusive right-hemisphere language representation, and 22 had bilateral representation. Bilateral representation was much higher in left-handed individuals (nondextrals, 41.7%) than in right-handed individuals (dextrals, 18.7%).

The dramatic shift in dominance in nondextrals with early brain damage appears to support Broca's early view that the right hemisphere can assume many language functions if damage occurs early enough. How early is early enough? Rasmussen and Milner (1977) found that damage after five years of age rarely results in shift of laterality. Not only does age seem important; site of lesion also is important. According to their findings, only lesions within the perisylvian language and speech region result in shift of laterality. If damage to this region occurs before five years of age, the originally damaged perisylvian region may be surgically removed, if required, without producing aphasic disturbance.

Splitting Apart the Hemispheres: Commissurotomy

One neurosurgical procedure that has captured widespread public attention is known as **commissurotomy.** It was introduced in 1940 by the neurosurgeon Van Wagenen (1940) as a treatment to prevent the spread of electrical discharges associated with epilepsy from one hemisphere to another. By destroying the major commissures between the two hemispheres, including the corpus callosum, it was hoped that the spread of impulses, and thus the severity of the epileptic condition, could be contained.

The aim of this surgery was to disconnect the two cerebral hemispheres. Yet, after examining the first series of patients, Akelaitis, a psychologist, failed to find any major effects involving language (Akelaitis, 1964). At this point, some respected individuals in academe suggested that perhaps the only function the corpus callosum served was to hold the two hemispheres together!

It was actually Ronald Myers (1955) who first discovered that the estimated 200 million fibers of the corpus callosum don't just bind the hemispheres together. Take a look at Figure 2.11. Section the corpus callosum at the midline. Suppose you now present the subject with a picture of a common object as was done in the Wada Test. What do you think the subject will do? He should name it correctly, because, although the corpus callosum is sectioned, he can still scan the picture with his eyes. The optic tract decussates and thus the image of the picture goes to both hemispheres.

Myers sectioned both the corpus callosum and the optic chiasm in a group of laboratory animals. Let's assume we are doing the same and that we are operating on a monkey. Following the surgery, we cover one of the monkey's eyes and present it with a discrimination task: to distinguish between a triangle and a square. If he can do this, he will receive a reward—say, a candy. After many trials, he learns this task. Suppose we now cover the eye through which the monkey learned this discrimination and allow him to perform the task using the opposite, unpatched eye. What do you suppose will happen? With the other eye, the monkey now performs as if he had never been exposed to the task. Learning in one hemisphere totally fails to transfer to the other hemisphere.

Visual pathways are completely crossed so that when the eyes are fixated on a point, all of the field to the left of the fixation point excites the visual cortex in the right hemisphere and stimuli from the right visual field excite the left visual cortex. The visual cortexes can communicate via the corpus callosum, which connects the two hemispheres (Kimura, 1973).

Source: (a) "The Asymmetry of the Human Brain," by Doreen Kimura (91). Copyright 1973 Scientific American, Inc. All rights reserved.

(b) Graphic representation of (a).

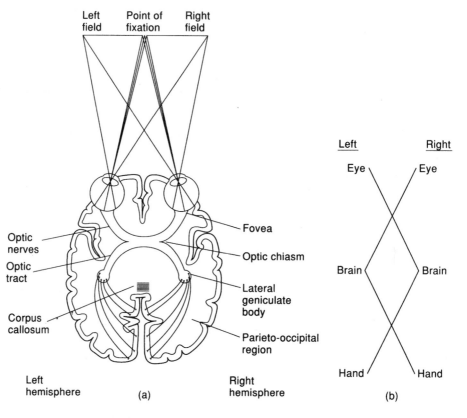

We cannot ethically transect the optic chiasm in a human being, but we can accomplish the same effect by having the subject fixate on a midpoint as shown in Figure 2.11. All information presented to the right visual field is then projected to the left (generally language-dominant) hemisphere and all information flashed in the left visual field is projected to the right (usually nondominant) hemisphere. Information must be presented at a rapid rate (approximately 50 milliseconds per stimulus) before the eyes have a chance to move from the fixation point. The device used to present stimuli in this manner is known as a **tachistoscope** or **T-scope.** The major paths of information flow under these conditions, from hand and eye to the brain, for example, are presented schematically in (b) of Figure 2.11. Much of the research on callosally sectioned (split-brained) patients has employed this type of task (cf. Springer & Deutsch, 1989).

A few examples may describe the general findings of such research. Suppose the word *heart* is flashed on the screen with a midpoint dividing the word: HE / ART. Can you already predict what the "split-brain" patients will say they have seen? Asked this question, they will *say,* "ART," and nothing more. Asked to point out with the *left* hand which word they have seen, subjects invariably point to HE rather than ART. Subjects cannot write words or the names of objects flashed to the nondominant hemisphere. However, the dominant hemisphere has no difficulty with these tasks.

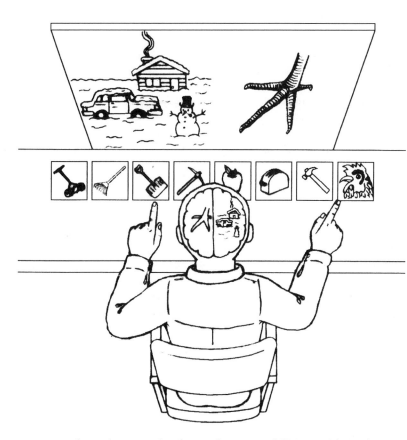

FIGURE 2.12

**HOW THE SPLIT BRAIN
INTEGRATES INPUT**

Information was presented simultaneously to the left and right visual fields of a split brain patient. When focusing on the dot in the midline, all information on the left goes to the right hemisphere and vice versa. The split brain subject is asked to point to the card that is most related to the picture. The left hand should point to what is being processed in the right hemisphere and vice versa because of contralateral control of motor function. All subjects did extremely well on such a task. What was of interest was how the subjects interpreted their choices. Asked why they picked a shovel and a chicken, the subjects answered, "You have to clean out the chicken shed with a shovel." What is going on here? What does this tell us about how the human brain operates?

Are we to assume from these results that no language abilities reside in the nondominant hemispheres of these patients? Not at all. Such patients can locate a requested object with the left hand when requested verbally even when the items are described in a circumlocutory manner (see Figure 2.12). Thus, when requested to find the thing that monkeys eat, subjects are able to locate a banana with the left hand behind a screen. Later, when the same piece of fruit is placed in this hand, it cannot be named. The nondominant hemisphere is capable of finding an item presented to it visually or tactually from among a list of words. This item cannot be named, however, until it is located on the list.

It thus appears that in the vast majority of these patients (there are exceptions) only the dominant hemisphere can produce verbal output, but the nondominant hemisphere is not without language abilities.

Taking Out Half the Brain: Hemispherectomy

It is difficult to imagine a more radical surgery on the brain than that of disconnecting the two cerebral hemispheres. But in 1927, Johns Hopkins neurosurgeon Walter Dandy introduced a procedure involving the total removal of an entire hemisphere

(hemispherectomy) for the treatment of intractable epilepsy, which appeared to originate from large areas of diseased tissue in one of the two hemispheres (Dandy, 1928). Upon hearing of this extraordinary operation, Dr. W. W. Keen, a fellow neurosurgeon, wrote him:

> March 21, 1928
> My dear Dandy:
> As I have told you before, you are rightly named. Here you are removing half of a fellow's brains and letting him go around just as usual. Whenever you get to the point when you can take out all the brains, I may consult you.
> Sincerely yours,
> W. W. Keen

(quoted in Fox, 1984)

Since that time, hundreds of such operations have been performed on children, as well as adults, for treatment of various neuropathologies.

In all cases of dominant hemispherectomy in adults, verbal output, while not totally obliterated, was severely affected. The same was true of writing. Comprehension appeared much less involved. However, gradual recovery of language abilities appeared almost complete if the surgery was performed early enough in the child's development, as was often the case (Smith, 1966). Such findings are consistent with the critical period hypothesis discussed earlier.

What is your reaction to such findings? Virtually half of the **telencephalon** (far brain) has been removed, but there are no lasting effects on speech and language, and it appears not to matter which hemisphere is removed as long as such surgery is performed early enough—before five years of age. I raise this question with you, because it seems reasonable that we have roughly the right amount of brain tissue to survive as a species, rather than twice as much as we need. Removing a massive amount of this tissue has got to affect a behavior as complex as communicative behavior—and, as is usually the case, with careful testing, it does. It is now evident that removal of the dominant hemisphere, no matter how early, does exact a toll.

Dennis and Whitaker (1976) studied language abilities in 3 children ages 9 and 10. They employed a wide variety of both standardized and specially developed tests of speech and language functioning. In one of these children, the right hemisphere had been removed; in the two others, the left hemisphere. In each case the operation had occurred before five months of age. It was found that all children did equally well on tasks involving phonological and semantic abilities. In the two patients whose left hemisphere had been removed, however, the right hemisphere did poorly on tasks involving any degree of syntactic complexity. One of the tasks involved detection of semantic and syntactic anomalies. All three subjects did well at correcting semantic anomalies such as *My favorite breakfast is radios with cream,* but only the left **hemidecorticates** demonstrated problems in detecting syntactic anomalies. Presented with the anomalous sentence *The best cars in Canada is a Ford and some Datsun,* one subject responded, "Wrong, it's a Mercury." These results seem to suggest that the right hemisphere is incapable of acquiring all aspects of language even when the left hemisphere is removed at an early age. However, as Broca postulated, the brain does demonstrate a great deal of plasticity in regard to language functions. The one exception appears to be syntax, that aspect of communicative behavior which many linguists regard as unique to our species.

All of the evidence we have presented so far relating to the organization of speech and language within the brain comes from individuals whose brains are damaged. In 1878, the British neurologist Hughling-Jackson issued a dictum that is probably the most frequently cited and frequently ignored in this field: "To locate the damage that destroys speech and to localize speech are two different things" (Hughling-Jackson, 1878). In fact we are now in a position to directly investigate Hughling-Jackson's caution through the use of neuroimaging techniques, which compare the effects of lesions in one part of the brain with metabolic activity at other loci. Preliminary findings do indicate metabolic abnormalities in presumably healthy tissue located at a distance from the lesion site **(diaschesis).** Thus, brain damage in one area may have consequences for brain functioning in another.

Listening With Both Ears: The Dichotic Listening Technique

Thus, what we need is evidence from normal individuals that will allow us to understand more fully what we see in cases of brain pathology. Luckily techniques exist that can provide us with such information.

One such technique is **dichotic listening.** The basic paradigm for this approach was created by the British psychologist Donald Broadbent (1954) in connection with his studies of attention. Broadbent presented subjects with a sequence of three digits to one ear, while simultaneously presenting another sequence to the opposite ear. Thus, one ear might be presented with a sequence such as 1–7-6 while the other ear received another sequence such as 8–5-2. Figure 2.13a shows a schematic diagram of this experimental procedure.

In administering this test to patients at the Montreal Neurological Institute, Kimura (1961) discovered that digits presented to the ear contralateral (opposite) to the dominant hemisphere were reported more accurately. This same effect was later observed in normal subjects.

Kimura attributed this effect to cerebral dominance, coupled with the greater strength of the contralateral pathways over the ipsilateral ones. When stimuli were presented monaurally, however, the right ear advantage was not observed. Kimura hypothesized that this occurred because the ipsilateral pathways are inhibited only under dichotic presentation. Strong support for this explanation is provided by studies of dichotic listening in commissurotomy (Sparks & Geschwind, 1968) and hemispherectomized patients (Curry, 1968). Such studies show a drastic decline in accuracy for the left ear. These results can only be attributed to inhibition at a peripheral level, as all other pathways from the ear ipsilateral to the dominant hemisphere do not exist in these patients (see Krashen, 1972, for a complete discussion of this topic). See Figure 2.13b.

FIGURE 2.13a

KIMURA'S MODEL OF DICHOTIC LISTENING IN NORMAL SUBJECTS

(a) Monaural presentation to the left ear is sent to the right hemisphere by way of contralateral pathways and to the left hemisphere by way of ipsilateral pathways. The subject reports the syllable "ba" accurately.

(b) Monaural presentation to the right ear is sent to the left hemisphere by way of contralateral pathways and to the right hemisphere by way of ipsilateral pathways. The subject reports the syllable "ga" accurately.

(c) In dichotic presentation, ipsilateral pathways are suppressed, so "ga" goes only to the left (speech) hemisphere and "ba" to the right hemisphere. The syllable "ba" is accessible to the left (speech) hemisphere only through the commissures. As a consequence, "ga" is usually reported more accurately than "ba" (a right-ear advantage).

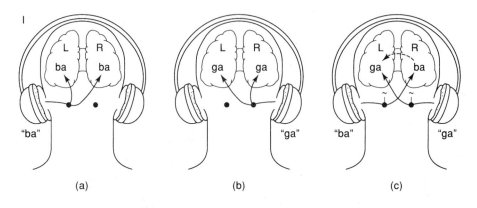

Combined results from the dichotic listening paradigm, tachistoscopic presentations, tests of observed hand movements, and tactile sensitivity of the two hands are presented in Table 2.5, which is adapted from Kimura (1973). The left hemisphere, as one might expect, more quickly and accurately processes words, whether presented aurally or in writing. It also does better at identifying letters. Perhaps surprisingly, the left hemisphere also seems to have an advantage when processing nonsense syllables and backward speech or when performing manual tasks while speaking. The right hemisphere appears to do better when asked to process musical stimuli, or human nonspeech stimuli (such as a cough). It also seems to show an advantage during visual-spatial processing tasks.

Some researchers have proposed a **functionalist hypothesis** to explain laterality. They suggest that the function served by a stimulus, rather than the physical characteristics of the stimulus, determines laterality of processing. This hypothesis suggests, for example, that only if tone is used to signal meaning differences in a language will it be lateralized to the dominant hemisphere. This is exactly what has been found in dichotic listening experiments comparing English and Thai speakers. Only in the Thai group was a right-ear advantage for tonal contrasts demonstrated (Van Lancker & Fromkin, 1978). However, Shipley-Brown et al. (1988) demonstrated a left-ear advantage not only for affective prosody (happy, angry, and sad readings of simple sentences such as: "The cat slept by the fire") but also for linguistic prosody (declarative, question, and continuation-type intonations of the same sentences).

What Functions Reside in the Nondominant Hemisphere?

As we have already seen in our study of commissurotomy and hemispherectomy patients, it is clear that linguistic processing is not entirely confined to the dominant hemisphere. Metabolic neuroimaging techniques, as we shall see, strongly support the view that both hemispheres are active during linguistic processing. Thus, laterality appears to be continuous rather than dichotomous.

Although aphasia is extremely rare from right-hemisphere lesions in right-handed individuals (approximately 4% of such individuals evince so-called crossed

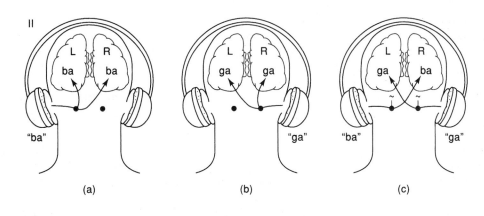

(a) (b) (c)

FIGURE 2.13b

DICHOTIC LISTENING IN SPLIT BRAIN SUBJECTS

(a) and (b) Monaural presentations operate as they do with normal subjects. Because both ipsilateral and contralateral pathways are unaffected by commissurotomy, the patient can accurately report a signal to either ear.
(c) In dichotic presentation, the ipsilateral pathways are suppressed (as in normal subjects), but "ba" is not accessible to the left (speech) hemisphere because the commissures are cut. Only "ga" is reported in complete right-ear advantage (Springer & Deutsch).

aphasia), such lesions do affect communication. Certain language functions are disturbed following damage to the right hemisphere. Many of these problems relate to less "structural" aspects of linguistic functioning. That is, patients with right hemisphere lesions do not appear to have problems with phonology, lexicon, or syntax but often seem to confuse the order of events in a story, are unable to formulate a moral for a story, and are impaired in their ability to draw inferences from a story. They also experience problems with ambiguous, metaphorical, and figurative terms, and tend to interpret them narrowly and literally. Thus, a "broken heart" may be understood as a cardiac condition! Finally, they experience difficulty in using and interpreting

MODALITY	LEFT/RIGHT HEMISPHERE TEST SCORE RATIO
Auditory	
words	1.88:1
nonsense syllables	1.73:1
backward speech	1.66:1
melodic pattern	1:1.19
human nonspeech sounds	1:1.08
Visual	
letters	1.23:1
words	1.47:1
two-dimensional point location	1:1.18
dot and form enumeration	1:1.20
matching of slanted lines	1:1.05
stereoscopic depth perception	1:1.28
Manual	
skilled movements	1.13:1
free movements during speech	3.10:1
tactile dot patterns (Braille)	Right advantage (initial findings)
nonvisual location	1:1.12

(from Kimura, 1973)

TABLE 2.5

SUMMARY OF LEFT/RIGHT HEMISPHERE TEST SCORES IN NORMAL, RIGHT-HANDED SUBJECTS IN THREE MODALITIES

prosodic cues in conversation. Intonation may be impaired, and use of stress and intonation to understand both the meaning and intent of utterances may be disordered. This may lead the patient with right-hemisphere damage to misinterpret sarcasm, for example. Problems with this paralinguistic domain of emotional expression may extend to difficulties in reading facial expression or gestural cues that accompany conversation (Code, 1987; Pimental & Kingsbury, 1989; Myers, 1986; Perecman, 1983).

The literature dealing with possible functions of the two hemispheres now is so vast that we can provide here only a few findings to initiate discussion. We have talked about some of the variables relating to laterality, such as handedness and age, but with great oversimplification. Broca's finding of morphological differences favoring the left hemisphere has been demonstrated for other language-related areas, in particular, the **planum temporale** which, buried in the Sylvian fissure, lies behind Heschl's gyrus (Geschwind & Levitsky, 1968). Strangely enough, if bigger means better, the right (nondominant) hemisphere wins! Broca, as usual, was correct in his observation that the right hemisphere is generally heavier. It also often has two Heschl's gyri, a larger superior temporal gyrus and parietal lobe as well as a greater volume of blood flow. It also matures earlier (Chi et al., 1977). However, none of these morphological differences has been directly related to function.

Many of the variables mentioned above, as well as others, may aid us in understanding "brainedness" in our species. One variable currently of some interest is gender. Do men and women differ in their lateralization patterns? There is evidence for hemispheric differences related to this variable in animals (Nottebohm & Arnold, 1976). Whether such differences exist in humans is, at present, unclear (Kolb & Whishaw, 1990). Possible differences are suggested by the following facts: Aphasia is more common after left-hemisphere damage in males than it is in females, suggesting that language functions may be more diffusely organized in women. The corpus callosum is also larger in females. In general, recovery from aphasia is better for women than for men. These and other observations about brain and language functioning in men and women continue to spur further research into gender differences (Kimura, 1992).

When Sign Language Users Become Aphasic

In all of our discussions, we have confined ourselves to the analysis of the consequences of brain damage on the production and comprehension of spoken language. What happens when a deaf sign-language user suffers damage to the areas of the brain normally associated with language processing in oral language users? Poizner, Klima, and Bellugi (1987) have investigated this question. The deaf signers they followed showed left-hemispheric specialization for language, just as right-handed oral-language users. Moreover, because many syntactic functions are coded using spatial cues in ASL, it might have been reasonable to suspect that they would be preserved if the right hemisphere, normally attributed with spatial processing, was spared. This, however, was not the case. Left-hemisphere damage had the potential to disrupt the use of space to convey syntactic information in deaf signers.

Intrahemispheric Localization of Function

. . . he (Gall) . . . developed a correct theoretical framework, which is his enduring contribution to the neurosciences: the concept of localized functional areas in the brain, including the cerebral cortex.

(Jerison, 1977)

To lateralize a function is to attribute it to a given hemisphere. To localize a function is to specify exactly where within the brain a function appears to reside. There is no doubt that many functions can be localized within the human brain and, for that matter, within all other vertebrate brains that have been studied.

However, even functions that seem relatively simple when compared to speech and language use have defied localization to one single area of the brain. Vision, for example, involves the entire occipital lobe, inferior portions of the temporal lobe, the frontal eye fields (Brodmann area 8), the cranial nerves for eye movement and other aspects of ocular motor function, the optic tectum, as well as parts of the parietal lobe and the lateral geniculate nucleus of the metathalamus. Vision is by no means a simple function, but compared to human communicative behavior, it seems simple indeed. Remember that vision constitutes but one of the input modalities involved in our complex form of communication. The specific localization of many speech and language functions has proven a formidable task.

Measuring Electrical Activity in the Brain

One longstanding method for examining brain activity during linguistic tasks has been the **electroencephalogram (EEG).** This method of monitoring electrical activity of the brain from electrodes placed on the scalp has been used to demonstrate differences between the hemispheres on language-related tasks (for example, Galin & Ornstein, 1972). More recently, researchers have turned their attention to monitoring electrical activity of the brain in specific, time-referenced response to a stimulus. **Event-related potentials (ERPs)** cast some light on the brain's behavior during language comprehension tasks (Garnsey, 1993; Kutas & van Petten, 1994). Using data on both the timing (latency) and strength (amplitude) of ERPs, researchers have found physical evidence that the brain responds differently to tasks involving syntactic and semantic processing. For example, ERPs differ when subjects are asked to read sentences that are syntactically or semantically ill-formed.

FIGURE 2.14

The following is a sample of Gail D.'s interchanges with the examiner, all in ASL. The examiner's probes are given in English translation; Gail D.'s signing is in English gloss for signs. The first drawing shows Gail D.'s awkward rendition and effortful articulation of the sign BROTHER, taken from her description of the picture.

EXAMINER:	What's that? [Pointing to the picture.]
GAIL D.:	THREE.
EXAMINER:	Who is that? [Pointing to the woman in the picture.]
GAIL D.:	MOTHER.
EXAMINER:	Who is that? [Pointing to the boy.]
GAIL D.:	BROTHER . . . BROTHER . . .

Correct form — Gail D.'s form

Brother — Brother

Effortful production typical of Gail D.'s signing.

Correct form — Gail D.'s form

Girl — Girl

Articulatory difficulty characteristic of Gail D.'s signing. In the example, Gail D. searches for the hand configuration and movement of the sign, although on occasion she produces the sign smoothly.

EXAMINER:	What else happened?
GAIL D.:	CAR . . . DRIVE . . . BROTHER . . . DRIVE . . . I . . . S-T-A-D. [Attempts to gesture "stand up."]
EXAMINER:	You stood up?
GAIL D.:	YES . . . I . . . DRIVE . . . [Attempts to gesture "wave goodbye."]
EXAMINER:	Wave goodbye?
GAIL D.:	YES . . . BROTHER . . . DRIVE . . . DUNNO . . . . [Attempts to gesture "wave goodbye."]
EXAMINER:	Your brother was driving?
GAIL D.:	YES. . . . BACK. . . . DRIVE . . . BROTHER . . . MAN . . . MAMA . . . STAY . . . BROTHER . . . DRIVE.
EXAMINER:	Were you in the car?
GAIL D.:	YES.
EXAMINER	Or outside?
GAIL D.:	NO.
EXAMINER:	In the car.
GAIL D.:	YES.
EXAMINER:	You were standing up with your mother?
GAIL D.:	NO . . . BROTHER . . . DRIVE . . . [Points in back.] . . . DEAF BROTHER . . . I . . .
EXAMINER:	Your brother didn't know you were in the car?
GAIL D.:	YES.
EXAMINER:	Your brother was driving and saw you in the back seat?
GAIL D.:	YES, YES. [Laughs.]
EXAMINER:	Oh, I see.

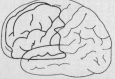

Gail D.

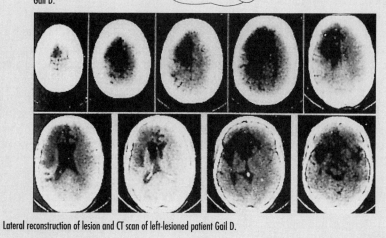

Lateral reconstruction of lesion and CT scan of left-lesioned patient Gail D.

Measuring Blood Flow in the Brain

We have utilized Broca's remarkably insightful nineteenth-century research as a kind of leitmotif in this chapter. In 1879, shortly before his death, he devised an instrument that he dubbed a **thermometric crown,** composed of six symmetrically arranged thermometers shielded with cotton, for precisely identifying functional as well as diseased areas of the brain. Broca proposed to measure increases or decreases in **regional cerebral blood flow (rCBF)** with this device; thus, we may regard his research as the first step in developing modern techniques for measuring this indicator of metabolic activity within the brain.

The blood flow of the brain is ultimately controlled by the metabolic activity of neuronal tissue. Several techniques are currently available for measuring regional cerebral blood flow to study functional changes within discrete areas of the brain during various behaviors. One method involves the injection of xenon 133, a radioactive isotope, dissolved in a saline solution, into the internal carotid artery. The Swedish group of Lassen, Ingvour, and Skinhj (1978) utilized an array of detectors to monitor gamma ray emission produced by the isotope. They worked under the assumption that the faster tissue clears (the steeper the decay curve), the faster the blood flow in a region.

How might we test the validity of such a procedure? We could first ask a subject to perform a relatively simple behavior, the localization of which within the cortex is presumed to be well established. Suppose we have him simply wiggle the fingers of his right hand. Where in the cortex would you expect an increase in blood flow? The increase should be in the hand area of the motor and perhaps sensory strip of the contralateral hemisphere. This is exactly what happens. The supplementary motor area also "lights up." In fact, this area appears to be involved bilaterally in all complex movements, whether of the foot, hand, mouth, or eyes (Orgogozo & Larsen, 1979). Lassen et al. (1978) postulate that this area may control the programming of complex movements, whereas the sensory cortex is the controller and the primary motor cortex is the executor of such movements.

These same investigators found that listening to simple words produces involvement of the auditory cortex in both hemispheres and speaking aloud adds three more areas: the face areas of the sensorimotor strips, the supplementary motor areas, and Broca's area in both hemispheres. Reading aloud adds the visual association cortex in the occipital lobes, as well as the frontal eye fields (Brodmann area 8) bilaterally.

This bilateral pattern of activation has also been demonstrated in a more recent study which, unlike the Lassen et al. study, examined rCBF in both hemispheres simultaneously during humming and automatic speech (repetition of the days of the week) (Ryding et al., 1987). Although both tasks activated the brain bilaterally, differences occurred in the regions of activation. An area that the investigators believed corresponded to Broca's area was activated in both tasks only on the left. In speech, the left hemisphere was most extensively activated in precentral (motor) regions, whereas the right hemisphere showed predominant activation of postcentral (sensory) regions.

Let us examine the results of two additional studies that employed an even more sophisticated method of monitoring cerebral blood flow. This method employs a scanning technique known as **positron emission tomography (PET),** which provides a three-dimensional representation of blood flow within the brain and allows monitoring of subcortical structures (Petersen, Fox, Posner, Mintun, & Raichle, 1989; Posner, Raichle, Petersen, Fox, & Mintun—reported in Posner & Raichle, 1994). Studies of the processing of single words presented aurally and visually were carried out in a hierarchical manner allowing for computer-assisted subtraction of what was hypothesized as simpler processing from more complex processing. In both sets of studies the researchers developed a set of experiments that were graduated in demand. In the first stage, subjects viewed a small fixation point on a television monitor while brain activity was measured using PET technology. In the second stage, the same subjects fixated on the point while common English nouns were displayed right below the fixation point, or were presented over headphones. In both conditions, the words were presented at the rate of 40 words per minute, and the subjects did not have to respond in any way; they were passive viewers and listeners. In the third stage, subjects were required to say words they heard or saw out loud. Finally, in the fourth stage, subjects were required to supply a verb that matched any nouns they heard or saw (for example, if the subjects saw cake, they might respond, "eat").

Visual images of brain activity were computed by subtracting the level of activity seen during the various tasks. Taking the level of activity at stage two from stage one allows display of the brain activity that accompanies the perception of spoken or written words. Subtracting the level of activity seen during task two from task three isolates the level of brain activity associated with speech production. Finally, subtracting the level of activity during the third task from the fourth task allows us to view the brain activity that accompanies lexical and grammatical selection (Posner & Raichle, 1994). Figure 2.15 shows the resulting pattern of brain activity.

As can be seen, perception of printed words largely activates a posterior portion of the brain associated with visual perception. Hearing words activated the temporal lobes bilaterally. The areas activated by visual and auditory presentation of words are quite discrete, but asking subjects to determine whether a visually presented set of stimuli rhyme (that is, *buy* and *sigh*) activates an area between the visual and auditory areas. Speaking "lights up" the motor areas of the brain, in particular, the primary motor cortex and the SMA. During the generation of verbs, large areas of the brain were activated including Broca's area, portions of the anterior cingulate, the posterior temporal lobes, and portions of the right cerebellum.

Figure 2.16 presents the lexical processing model that Petersen et al. propose to account for their findings. In it, different portions of the cortex are assumed to take primary responsibility for different speech and language tasks. If the task is to take auditory input and do something with it, such as tasks (b) through (d), then the primary auditory cortex first receives and processes the input, passing it next to the temporoparietal cortex, which analyzes its phonological structure. Its semantic interpretation is apparently derived in the anterior inferior left frontal cortex, while the

FIGURE 2.15

PET studies reveal brain activity associated with different language tasks (Posner & Raichle, 1994).

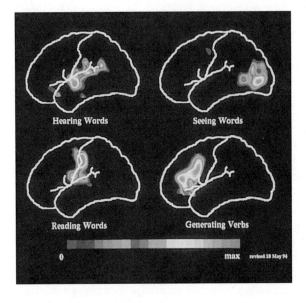

commands necessary to pronounce the word or its associate are generated first in the **supplementary motor area,** and next in the motor cortex. Visually presented input follows a somewhat different route. Early visual processing of the material is accomplished in the striate cortex, which sends its results to the **extrastriate cortex** for coding and further analysis by the semantic association areas mentioned earlier. We can also note from this model that information may flow in both directions from "level" to "level" of processing, allowing the system to check itself for possible analytical errors.

What do these results tell us about the role of the lateral surface of the cortex in speech and language functions? First it appears that both hemispheres are involved, though in differing degrees, in speech and language. We would expect this to be the case for early stages of auditory and visual processing as well as for motor (articulatory) output. We have also noted that the supplementary motor area (SMA) appears to be activated in a variety of complex motor tasks including speech. Previous rCBF studies had shown bilateral activation of the temporoparietal cortex (Wernicke's area) while listening to speech, as well as visual association areas (extrastriate cortex) while reading words. The earliest blood flow studies failed to detect metabolic changes in Broca's area; however, both the Ryding et al. and Petersen et al. studies note activation of this area in the left hemisphere. In addition, Petersen et al. observed left activation of the inferior prefrontal as well as anterior cingulate cortex during a task involving generating verbs compatible with nouns.

Researchers have also begun to use PET to investigate how various grammatical operations are carried out by the brain. Recently, PET scans were used to examine whether the formation of regular and irregular past tenses is handled in the same manner by the brain (Jaeger, Lockwood, Kemmerer, van Valin, Murphy, & Khalak, 1996). Results indicated that different portions of the brain were activated when trying to create past tenses for regular verbs, irregular verbs, and nonsense words. The authors noted that regular past tenses were formed relatively rapidly when compared with irregular forms, and hypothesized that, "Regular past forms . . . are computed on-line by a suffixation operation, whereas irregular past tense forms are computed some other way, most likely involving lexical access" (p. 477). In other words, the researchers found evidence that irregular past tenses may be stored as individual words. Chapter 4 discusses other experimental techniques for analyzing how morphological affixes are processed.

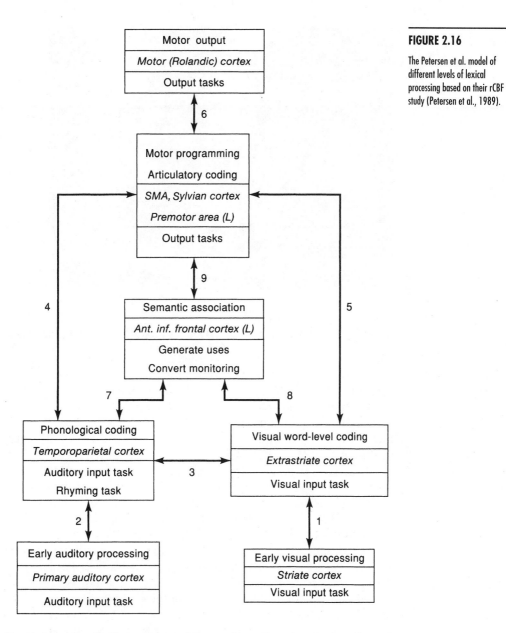

FIGURE 2.16

The Petersen et al. model of different levels of lexical processing based on their rCBF study (Petersen et al., 1989).

Some other interesting findings emerge from such studies. One is the effect of practice on brain activity. As Figure 2.17 shows, the rehearsal or practice of a linguistic task reduces brain activity while often increasing efficiency or accuracy of response. In some respects, this may be counter-intuitive. We tend to think of "brain power" when imagining a person who is quick or knowledgeable. In fact, increased efficiency corresponds with less brain activity, perhaps because the brain develops patterns or habits that allow more automatic performance. Chapter 4 explains how practice appears to affect the efficiency of lexical retrieval, in particular.

Practice diminishes the level of brain activity required to carry out a task (Posner & Raichle, 1994).

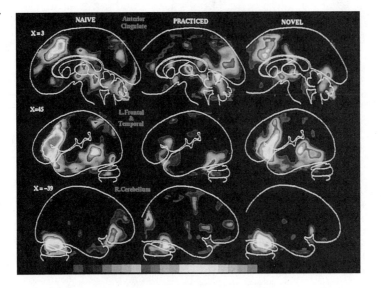

The Role of Subcortical Structures in Speech and Language

In addition to the areas on the lateral and medial surfaces of the cerebral hemispheres, it is now also evident that subcortical structures operate in some manner not only in speech but language functions as well. Dysarthrias resulting from damage to the basal ganglia (hypokinetic and hyperkinetic dysarthria) and the cerebellum (ataxic dysarthria) have long been documented (Darley et al., 1975a). It is now evident that dysarthria can also follow from thalamic hemorrhages and infarctions (Cappa & Vignolo, 1979). Articulation in such disorders may be slow, laborious, and inaccurate.

In addition to neuromotor speech disorders, it has recently been discovered that damage to the basal ganglia, thalamus, and surrounding white matter (internal capsule) may produce aphasic disturbances unlike those from purely cortical damage (Damasio et al., 1981; Naeser et al., 1982; Metter et al., 1983). Lesions of the thalamus result in preserved ability to repeat and relatively good auditory comprehension. However, spontaneous speech is of diminished quantity and characterized by word selection errors. Patients tend to avoid speaking unless it is absolutely necessary, and they produce semantic paraphasias, substituting inappropriate words for their intended targets when speaking. Lesions of the globus pallidus (part of the basal ganglia) also result in speech characterized by semantic paraphasias. Lesions involving other subcortical structures such as the internal capsule and caudate nucleus may result in dysarthria, which suggests that these structures may play some role in motor speech planning and execution. How these structures participate in language formulation is at present poorly understood. It is clear that both the basal ganglia and thalamus are lateralized in function. Whether their role in language functions is a distinct one or is involved with disruption of cortical functioning in general is not clear (Crossen, 1985; Murdoch, 1990).

Hellige (1993) notes that some types of cross-hemispheric communication can occur subcortically, below the level of the corpus callosum. He concludes that, "although

VIVE LA DIFFERENCE!

Men and women have been observed to perform differently on selected tasks. Doreen Kimura (1992) notes that women tend to score more highly than men on tasks related to language functions. Men appear to have a slight advantage on certain types of spatial tasks.

Aphasia occurs much more frequently in males after left-hemisphere damage than it does in females, and women tend to have a better prognosis for recovery from aphasia than do men, irrespective of which hemisphere has sustained the damage leading to the language impairment. This observation has led investigators to postulate that linguistic abilities are more bilaterally represented in women than in men (cf. Levy, 1972). This view has some anatomical support: women appear to possess larger interhemispheric connections via the corpus callosum than do men (cf. Allen, Richey, Chai, & Gorski, 1991).

Recent research that uses **functional magnetic resonance imaging (fMRI)** to measure cerebral blood flow more precisely than does PET (Shaywitz et al., 1995), further supports the notion that linguistic organization in male and female brains may differ somewhat. Blood-flow patterns were different when men and women completed a rhyme judgment task. Subjects were required to determine whether two nonsense word strings such as *lete* and *jete* rhymed. Researchers used a subtraction process similar to the one described in Posner et al. study and found that the inferior frontal gyrus (roughly equivalent to Brodmann areas 44 and 45) (cf. Figure 2.9) demonstrates activation lateralized to the left hemisphere in males but is bilaterally activated in the majority of the female subjects tested (see Figure 2.18). The Shaywitz et al. study is the first study to demonstrate consistent functional processing differences on a linguistic task by male and female subjects.

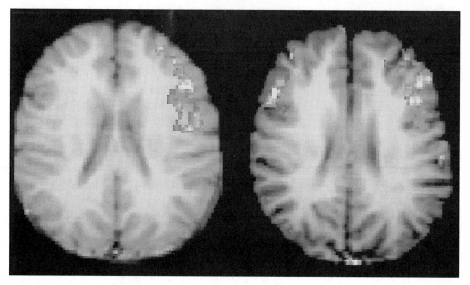

FIGURE 2.18

Brain activation patterns differ between men and women completing the same linguistic task.

information about the name . . . of a stimulus cannot be transferred from one hemisphere to the other subcortically, various other types of information can: for example, connotative and contextual information about an object, information about the category to which an object belongs, and information about the location of objects in space" (p. 204).

Ways of Viewing the Relationship Between Brain and Language

> . . . modern linguistic aphasiology has been developed by psychologists and linguists whose interests are in how language breaks down, and in what the pattern of breakdown reveals about normal language and its processing. Much work has gone on in this area without concern for the details of the correlation between symptoms and neural lesions.
>
> (Caplan, 1987, p. XI)

We approach the study of behavior in general and speech and language functioning in particular in various ways. Of the approaches that focus not only on external, observable behaviors but also allow for the investigation of the hidden, internal processes that produce such behaviors, we note a dichotomy, as old as time, between mind and brain. Disciplines such as psycholinguistics typically attempt to provide explanations of behaviors in terms of information-processing descriptions, whereas neurolinguistics seeks explanations for the same behaviors in terms of neurological processes. The approach exemplified in this chapter is most akin to neurolinguistics.

Linguistic Aphasiology

In the 1980s a quite different approach developed from a blending of **cognitive psychology** and **neuropsychology.** This new psychology subdiscipline, cognitive neuropsychology, has two basic aims: (1) to explain the patterns of impaired and intact cognitive performance seen in brain-injured patients in terms of damage to one or more of the components of a theory or model of normal cognitive functioning, and (2) to draw conclusions about normal, intact cognitive processes from the patterns of impaired and intact capabilities seen in brain-injured patients (Ellis & Young, 1988, p. 4). The study of language functions is but a part of this broader endeavor. The study of language within this approach has recently been termed linguistic aphasiology (Caplan, 1987).

Note while reading in later chapters that psycholinguists generally construct their models of language processing from the study of normal populations. Linguistic aphasiologists seek to accomplish the same end by studying brain-damaged populations. A basic tenet of their approach is that the mind is composed of a set of processing elements, modules, which are dissociable. This view, reminiscent of Franz Josef Gall's study of craniology discussed earlier in this chapter, has been revived in several versions by Chomsky (1980), Gardner (1983), and Fodor (1983).

These modules are held to be related to distinct areas of the brain. If we are to assume that brain damage can provide us with insight as to how complex cognitive processes such as language operate in normals, then as Caramazza (1984) makes clear, it must be that neural modules can be differentially damaged **(fractionation),** and that, given such damage, we can ascertain what specific linguistic ability has been lost **(transparency).** This is a tall order, and it is not at all certain that such an approach can accomplish its goals.

The models that result from this approach generally are unrelated to neurological structures, as was the case in the famous Wernicke-Lichtheim model. Researchers within this paradigm rightfully point out that these earlier diagram makers were overly simplistic in their analysis of language processes. Some say that what we need first is a better and more complete understanding of the processes involved in language production and comprehension (psycholinguistic findings) before they can be related successfully to neural structures (neurolinguistic findings). Research on both oral and sign language users, however, does suggest that differing aspects of language, such as lexical retrieval and grammatical encoding, can be dissociated and differentially impaired following brain damage.

Linguistic aphasiologists also critique the terminology of traditional aphasic syndromes on several grounds: (1) they are not specific enough in their analysis of the language dysfunctions under consideration, (2) many components of the syndrome need not be present for a patient to be placed within a category (e.g., agrammatism is not a necessary feature of Broca's aphasia), (3) many components are shared by different syndromes (e.g., anomia), and finally (4) many patients, perhaps given the inherent nature of diffuse brain damage itself, cannot neatly be classified under the criteria for any given syndrome. These critiques are well founded and have led many investigators to return to a detailed study of individual cases of brain damage, as opposed to group studies (Caramazza, 1984).

Consider the syndrome of Broca's aphasia. It often includes apraxia of speech, anarthria, dysarthria, and agrammatism, as well as disturbances of repetition, reading, and writing. Can such associated characteristics be decomposed in terms of differential lesion sites that make sense neurologically? The answer is yes in many instances. Thus, apraxia of speech appears to be associated with a lesion confined to Broca's area alone (for example, the left third frontal convolution). Although apraxia of speech usually co-occurs with aphasia, it can appear in isolation (Wertz et al., 1970). Broca's aphasics are often dysarthric but need not be. Finally, it is now clear that Broca's aphasia need not be characterized by agrammatism; in some cases, the speech errors of such patients involve major content items rather than grammatical elements. We thus need to investigate the lesion sites that result in this syndrome with and without agrammatism. Mohr (1976), in a review of autopsy records at the Massachusetts General Hospital, found that a lesion confined to Broca's area is insufficient to produce a persistent Broca's aphasia with all of the elements usually included in the syndrome. Rather, a much more widespread infarct is required encompassing, in addition to Broca's area, the insula and often the region underlying it, both pre- and post-central gyri as well as often anterior parietal cortex. (For an excellent introduction to cognitive neuropsychology including how this approach is applied to language, see Ellis & Young, 1988; for a more detailed discussion of this approach devoted solely to language, see Caplan, 1987; 1992. For examples of many of the techniques employed in the localization of functions mapped onto such models, see Kertesz, 1983.)

SUMMARY

What are we? What are we not? The dream of a shadow is man.

Pindaros

As noted at the beginning of this chapter, the brain may well be so complex as to defy its comprehension of itself. It is a complex physical structure composed of billions of cells, with a connectivity per cell that often exceeds many thousands of synapses complicated by differential chemical means of transmission. We must relate this structure to what is probably the most complex form of human behavior known—speech and language ability. Understanding this relationship in all its facets may well prove to be immensely difficult if not impossible—not only because of the awe-inspiring complexities involved, but also because the brain, like most natural phenomena, is characterized by a great deal of individual variation.

However, we do understand something about how speech and language ability is instantiated in our nervous system. We shall probably never understand this relationship totally, but we must try not only because it tells us something we want to know about ourselves, but also because what we learn may help to mend dysfunctions due to brain damage. What we have learned so far points to a complex and interconnected set of cortical and subcortical areas, each of which appears to subserve different aspects of the communicative process. Thus, discrete areas of the brain have been identified that play major roles in articulation, grammatical formulation, word finding, and speech comprehension. Additional areas may have special responsibility for tasks such as reading, writing, and the ability to repeat utterances.

The two sides of the brain, although comparable in size and form, appear to specialize in handling various language and nonlinguistic tasks. For most individuals, language appears to reside in the left hemisphere, although some linguistic skills, such as interpretation of discourse and figurative or humorous language, appear to be mediated by the right hemisphere. If the left hemisphere is damaged early enough in development, the right hemisphere is capable of assuming many, though not all, language functions that usually reside in the left side of the cortex.

Although the earliest evidence concerning lateralization and localization of language functions utilized analysis of brain damaged individuals, new procedures allow us to study cortical activity in normal subjects during specific linguistic and nonlinguistic tasks. From dichotic listening, tachistoscopic, and cerebral blood flow studies we obtain greater information about the neurological bases of normal language processing.

As linguistic theory continues to evolve, it will provide us with new theories to explore. New experimental techniques will undoubtedly be developed within psychology. Advances in statistical procedures will allow us to better interpret our data. Computer modeling of neural processes may provide us with new insights into how human beings accomplish similar tasks. One of the most exciting developments within neuroscience has been the proliferation of many new forms of neuroimaging. Just as we have become ever more adept at probing the universe around us, so we have advanced greatly in our investigation of the universe within us. Increased study of old and newly discovered disease processes that affect the brain will undoubtedly provide new perspectives on brain function. Interest is increasing in the study of those with exceptional language abilities and individuals with dissociated cognitive and linguistic abilities (Obler & Fein, 1988) as well as individuals who use a variety of different languages, including signed language (Poizner et al., 1987). The list of topics for study is constrained only by our own creativity. In regard to every aspect of brain and language function that is studied, it is important to utilize all available approaches—theoretical as well as experimental—whether from linguistics, psychology, or neuroscience.

The exploration of both the universe surrounding us and the one within us is active today as never before. In these new frontiers we may come closer than ever to interpreting "the dream of a shadow" that we are.

KEY WORDS

Neurolinguistic
Lateralization of function
Aphasia
Dysarthria
Pure alexia (alexia without
agraphia)
Bilingual aphasia
Jargon aphasia/agraphia
Automatic speech
Craniometry
Hypertrophy
Gyrus
Broca's aphasia
Plasticity of brain function

Computerized trans-axial tomography
(CT scan)
Broca's area
Rostral
Heschl's gyrus
Wernicke's aphasia
Logorrhea
Anosognosia
Neologism
Neuropathology
Cranium
Meninges
Cerebral spinal fluid (CSF)
Corpus callosum

Diencephalon
Dorsal thalamus
Internal capsule
Basal ganglia
Hypokinesia
Hyperkinesia
Ataxia
Brain stem
Midbrain
Pons
Medulla
Spinal cord
Nonautonomous
Peripheral nervous system (PNS)
Cranial nerves
Spinal nerves
Phonation
Homunculus
Electrical stimulation of the brain (ESB)
Neurons
Glia
Neurotransmitters
Cytoarchitecture
Cerebrovascular disease
Hydrocephalus
Foremen magnum
Multiple sclerosis
Myelin
Myasthenia gravis
Expressive (nonfluent) aphasia (see
    Broca's aphasia)
Dysarthria
Cortical sensory aphasia (see receptive,
    fluent, or Wernicke's aphasia)

Angular gyrus
Anomia
Subcortical sensory aphasia (pure word
    deafness)
Dementia
Agnosia
Perisylvian area
Global aphasia
Paroxysmal aphasia
Mixed transcortical aphasia
Echolalic
Internal (common) carotid arteries
Hemiplegia
Commissurotomy
Tachistoscope (T-scope)
Hemispherectomy
Telencephalon
Hemidecorticates
Diaschesis
Dichotic listening
Functionalist hypothesis
Planum temporale
Electroencephalogram (EEG)
Event-related potentials (ERPs)
Thermometric crown
Regional cerebral blood flow (rCBF)
Positron emission tomography (PET)
Supplementary motor area (SMA)
Extrastriate cortex
Cognitive psychology/neuropsychology
Fractionation
Transparency
Functional magnetic resonance
    imaging (fMRI)

SOMETHING TO THINK ABOUT

1. On the basis of what you have read, make a chart comparing the language abilities of individuals with Broca's and Wernicke's aphasia. Be sure to include examples of what their speech output might look like.

2. List the available techniques for determining where in the brain various aspects of language processing occur. For each, provide examples of the kind of information that can be gained.

3. Evaluate the claim for a critical period for language acquisition. What data support this claim? What are the possible implications of a critical period for language teaching and language rehabilitation?

ACTIVITIES

1. Marcel Kinsbourne, a neuropsychologist, has proposed a model of neural processing based on the concept of functional distance. This model would predict that verbal activities such as repeating sentences aloud should interfere with a task such as balancing a dowel rod on the index finger of the right hand (as opposed to the left hand) in right-handed subjects. From what you have learned so far, why should this be the case? This finding was supported by Kinsbourne and Cook (1971). Read this experiment and see if you can replicate its findings.

2. Kinsbourne's model also predicts that conjugate lateral eye movements would be differentially affected by verbal versus spatial tasks. In the task outlined in (1) above, verbal activity presumably would affect concurrent manual activity by activating the hand area of the motor strip. In the case of eye movement, verbal activity might affect eye movement due to activation of frontal eye fields. Indeed, Kinsbourne (1972) found this to be true. An opportunity to observe such eye movements might be found during television interviews. First of all, observe the lateral eye movements that occur in such individuals. See if they correlate in any way with the questions to which the individuals are responding or thinking about.

3. Surf the Web! As explained in greater detail in Chapter 8, "Language Acquisition," an open-access Internet archive of language data (CHILDES) and programs for their analysis (CLAN), was established in the late 1980s. Information on how to access the archive and use its programs can be found at http://childes.psy.cmu.edu/childes/. Additional information can be found in MacWhinney (1995), also referenced in Chapter 8. The CHILDES archive has many language samples from typically developing children learning their first language and an entire subdirectory of the database devoted to samples of language taken from individuals with language impairments. Examine data taken from aphasic patients in the Comparative Aphasia Project (CAP) or from the Holland corpus. Find examples of Wernicke's aphasia and Broca's aphasia performance. (The data sets also provide examples of anomic speech and language

samples taken from a wide variety of aphasic conditions.) To what extent do the patients in these databases confirm the profiles of impairment discussed in this chapter?

REFERENCES

Akelaitis, A. J. (1964). Study of gnosis, praxis, and language following section of corpus callosum and anterior commissure. *Journal of Neurosurgery, 1,* 94–102.

Allen, L., Richey, M., Chai, Y., & Gorski, R. (1991). Sex differences in the corpus callosum of the living human being. *Journal of Neuroscience, II,* 933–942

Bayles, K., & Kaszniak, A. (1987). *Communication and cognition in normal aging and dementia.* Boston: College-Hill.

Benton, A. (1981). Aphasia: Historical perspectives. In M. Sarno (Ed.), *Acquired aphasia.* New York: Academic Press.

Benton, A., & Joynt, R. (1960). Early descriptions of aphasia. *Archives of Neurology, 3,* 205–222.

Berker, E., Berker, A., & Smith, A. (1986). Translation of Broca's 1865 Report. Localization of speech in the third left frontal convolution. *Archives of Neurology, 43,* 1065–1072.

Bogen, J., Dezure, R., Tenhouten, W. D., & Marsh, J. (1972). The other side of the brain IV: The A/P ratio. *Bulletin of the Los Angeles Neurological Societies, 37,* 49–61.

Broadbent, D. (1954). The role of auditory localization in attention and memory span. *Journal of Experimental Psychology, 47,* 191–196.

Broca, P. (1863). Localisation des fonctions cérébrales: siège du langage articulé. *Bulletins de la Société d'Anthropologie de Paris, 4,* 200–203.

Broca, P. (1875). Sur le poids relatif des deux hémisphères cérébraux et leur lobes frontaux. *Bulletins de la Société d'Anthropologie de Paris, 10,* 534–536.

Broca, P. (1885). Du siège de la faculté du langage articulé dans l'hémisphère gauche du cerveau. *Bulletins de la Société d'Anthropologie de Paris, 6,* 377–393.

Brodmann, K. (1909). *Vergleichende Lokalisationslehre der Grosshirnrinde in ihren Prinzipien dargestellt auf des Zellenbaues.* Leipzig: J. A. Barth.

Caplan, D. (1987). *Neurolinguistics and linguistic aphasiology. An introduction.* New York: Cambridge University Press.

Caplan, D. (1992). *Language: Structure, processing and disorders.* Cambridge, MA: MIT Press.

Cappa, S., & Vignolo, L. (1979). Transcortical features of aphasia following left thalamic hemorrhage. *Cortex, 15,* 121–130.

Caramazza, A. (1984). The logic of neuropsychological research and the problem of patient classification in aphasia. *Brain and Language, 21,* 9–20.

Chi, J., Dooling, E., & Gilles, F. (1977). Gyral development of the human brain. *Annals of Neurology, 1,* 86–93.

Chomsky, N. (1980). Rules and representations. *The Behavioral and Brain Sciences, 3,* 1–61.

Clarke, E., & O'Malley, C. D. (Eds.). (1968). *The human brain and spinal cord: A historical study illustrated by writing from antiquity to the twentieth century.* Berkeley: University of California Press.

Code, C. (1987). *Language, aphasia, and the right hemisphere.* New York: Wiley.

Cole, M., & Cole, M. (Eds.). (1971). *Pierre Marie's papers on speech disorders.* New York: Hafner.

Crossen, B. (1985). Subcortical functions in language: A working model. *Brain and Language, 25,* 257–292.

Curry, F. (1968). A comparison of the performance of a right hemispherectomized subject and 25 normals on 4 dichotic listening tasks. *Cortex, 4,* 144–153.

Curtiss, S. (1977). *Genie. A psycholinguistic study of a modern-day "wild child."* New York: Academic Press.

Damasio, A., Damasio, H., Gush, F., Varney, N., & Rizzo, M. (1981). Atypical aphasia following lesions of the dominant striatum and internal capsule. *Neurology, 31,* 82.

Dandy, W. (1928). Removal of right cerebral hemisphere for certain tumors with hemiplegia: Preliminary report. *Journal of the American Medical Association, 90,* 823–825.

Darley, F., Aronson, A., & Brown, J. (1975a). *Audio seminars in speech pathology: Motor speech disorders.* Philadelphia: W. B. Saunders.

Darley, F., Aronson, A., & Brown, J. (1975b). *Motor speech disorders.* Philadelphia: W. B. Saunders.

Dennis, M., & Whitaker, H. (1976). Language acquisition following hemidecortication: Linguistic superiority of the left over the right hemisphere. *Brain and Language, 3,* 404–433.

Dingwall, W. (1975a). The species-specificity of speech. In D. Dato (Ed.), *Developmental psycholinguistics: Theory and applications* (pp. 17–62). Georgetown University Press.

Dingwall, W. (1975b). Broca's contributions to physical anthropology relating to the brain and its functions. *Working Papers in Biocommunication, 1,* 1–28.

Dingwall, W. (1981). *Language and the brain: A bibliography and guide.* New York: Garland.

Dingwall, W. (1988). The evolution of human communicative behavior. In F. Newmeyer (Ed.), *Linguistics: The Cambridge survey. III. Language: Psychosocial and biological aspects.* New York: Cambridge University Press.

Ellis, A., & Young, A. (1988). *Human cognitive neuropsychology.* Hillsdale, NJ: Erlbaum.

Fodor, J. (1983). *The modularity of mind.* Cambridge, MA: MIT Press.

Fox, W. (1984). *Dandy of Johns Hopkins.* Baltimore: Williams and Wilkins.

Galin, D., & Ornstein, R. (1972). Lateral specialization of cognitive mode. II. EEG frequency analysis. *Psychophysiology, 9,* 412–418.

Gardner, H. (1983). *Frames of mind: The theory of multiple intelligences.* New York: Basic Books.

Garnsey, S. (1993). Event related brain potentials in the study of language: An introduction. *Language and Cognitive Processes, 8* (4), 337–356.

Geschwind, N. (1974). *Selected papers on language and the brain.* Dordrecht, Holland: Reidel.

Geschwind, N., & Levitsky, W. (1969). Human brain: Left-right asymmetries in temporal speech area. *Science, 161,* 186–187.

Gilroy, J., & Holliday, P. (1982). *Basic neurology.* New York: Macmillan.

Goldstein, K. (1948). *Language and language disturbances.* New York: Grune and Stratton.

Goodglass, H. (1988). Historical perspectives on concepts of aphasia. In F. Boller & J. Grafman (Eds.), *Handbook of neuropsychology (Vol. 1)* (pp. 249–265). New York: Elsevier.

Gordon, B. (1990). Human language. In R. Kessner & D. Olton (Eds.), *Neurology of comparative cognition* (pp. 21–49). Hillsdale, NJ: Erlbaum.

Haggard, M. (1971). Encoding and the REA for speech signals. *Quarterly Journal of Experimental Psychology, 23,* 34–45.

Hahn, M., Jensen, C., & Budelk, B. (Eds.). (1979). *Development and evolution of brain size.* New York: Academic Press.

Head, H. (1963). *Aphasia and kindred disorders of speech.* New York: Hafner.

Hellige, J. (1993). *Hemispheric asymmetry: What's right and what's left.* Cambridge, MA: Harvard University Press.

Jackson, J. H. (1878). On affections of speech from disease of the brain. *Brain, 1,* 304–330.

Jaeger, J., Lockwood, A., Kemmerer, D., van Valin, R., Murphy, B., & Khalak, H. (1996). A positron emission tomography study of regular and irregular verb morphology in English. *Language, 72* (3), 451–497.

Jerison, H. (1977). Should phrenology be rediscovered? *Current Anthropology, 18,* 744–746.

Kennedy, M., & Murdoch, B. (1989). Speech and language disorders subsequent to subcortical vascular lesions. *Aphasiology, 3,* 221–247.

Kertesz, A. (Ed.). (1983). *Localization in neuropsychology.* New York: Academic Press.

Kimura, D. (1961). Cerebral dominance and the perception of verbal stimuli. *Canadian Journal of Psychology, 15,* 166–171.

Kimura, D. (1973). The asymmetry of the human brain. *Scientific American, 228,* 70–78.

Kimura, D. (1992). Sex differences in the brain. *Scientific American, 267,* 118–125.

Kinsbourne, M., & Cook, J. (1971). Generalized and lateralized effects of concurrent verbalization on a unimanual task. *Quarterly Journal of Experimental Psychology, 23,* 341–345.

Kinsbourne, M. (1972). Eye and head turning indicates cerebral lateralization. *Science, 176,* 539–541.

Kolb, B., & Whishaw, I. (1990). *Fundamentals of human neuropsychology.* New York: W. H. Freeman.

Krashen, S. (1972). *Language and the left hemisphere.* UCLA Work Pap. Phonetics, 24.

Krmpotic, J. (1959). Données anatomiques et histologiques relative aux effecteurs laryngopharyngo-buccaux. *Rev. Laryngol., 11,* 829–848.

Kutas, M., & van Petten, C. (1994). Psycholinguistics electrified: Event-related brain potential investigations. In M. A. Gernsbacher (Ed.), *Handbook of psycholinguistics.* New York: Academic Press.

Kuypers, H. (1981). Anatomy of the descending pathways. In V. Brooks (Ed.), *Handbook of physiology* (Vol. 11, Part 1) (pp. 597–666). Bethesda, MD: American Physiology Society.

Lassen, N., Ingvour, D., & Skinhj, E. (1978). Brain function and blood flows. *Scientific American, 239,* 62–72.

Lecours, A., & Joanette, Y. (1980). Linguistic and other psychological aspects of paroxysmal aphasia. *Brain and Language, 10,* 1–23.

Lenneberg, E. (1967). *Biological foundations of language.* New York: Wiley.

Levy, J. (1972). Lateral specialization of the human brain: Behavioral manifestations and possible evolutionary basis. In J. A. Kiger (Ed.), *The biology of behavior.* Corvallis: Oregon State University Press.

Lichtheim, L. (1885). On aphasia. *Brain, 7,* 433–484.

Loring, D. W., Meador, K., Lee, G., Murro, A., Smith, J., Flanigan, H., Gallagher, B., & King, D. (1990). Cerebral language lateralization: Evidence from intra-carotid amobarbital testing. *Neuropsychologia, 28,* 831–838.

Metter, E., Riege, W., Hanson, W., Kuhl, D., Phelps, M., Squire, L., Wasterlain, D., & Benson, D. (1983). Comparison of metabolic rates, language, and memory in sub-cortical aphasias. *Brain and Language, 19,* 33–47.

Mohr, J. (1976). Broca's area and Broca's aphasia. In H. Whitaker and H. A. Whitaker (Eds.), *Studies in neurolinguistics* (Vol. 1). New York: Academic Press.

Murdoch, B. E. (1990). *Acquired speech and language disorders.* New York: Chapman and Hall.

Myers, P. (1986). Right hemisphere communication impairment. In R. Chapey (Ed.), *Language intervention strategies in adult aphasia.* Baltimore: Williams and Wilkins.

Myers, R. (1955). Interocular transfer of pattern discrimination in cats following section of crossed optic fibers. *Journal of Comparative and Physiological Psychology, 48,* 470–473.

Naeser, M., Alexander, M., Helm-Estabrooks, N., Levine, H., Laughlin, S., & Geschwind, N. (1982). Aphasia with predominantly subcortical lesion sites. *Archives of Neurology, 39,* 2–14.

Nottebohm, F., & Arnold, A. (1976). Sexual dimorphism in vocal control areas of the songbird brain. *Science, 194,* 211–213.

Obler, L., & Fein, D. (1988). *The exceptional brain.* New York: The Guilford Press.

Orgogozo, J., & Larsen, B. (1979). Activation of the supplementary motor area during voluntary movements in man suggests it works as a supramotor area. *Science, 206,* 847–850.

Passingham, R. E. (1982). *The human primate.* San Francisco: W. H. Thomas.

Penfield, W., & Roberts, L. (1959). *Speech and brain-mechanisms.* Princeton, NJ: Princeton University Press.

Perecman, E. (Ed.). (1983). *Cognitive processing in the right hemisphere.* New York: Academic Press.

Petersen, S., Fox, P., Posner, M., Mintun, M., & Raichle, M. (1989). Positron emission tomographic studies of the processing of single words. *Journal of Cognitive Neuroscience, 1,* 153–170.

Pimental, P., & Kingsbury, N. (1989). *Neuropsychological aspects of right brain injury.* Austin, TX: Pro-Ed.

Pinel, J. (1990). *Biopsychology.* Boston: Allyn and Bacon.

Poizner, H., Klima, E., & Bellugi, U. (1987). *What the hands reveal about the brain.* Cambridge, MA: MIT Press.

Posner, M., & Raichle, M. (1994). Images of mind. New York: Scientific American Library, W. H. Freeman Company.

Rasmussen, T., & Milner, B. (1977). The role of early left-brain injury in determining lateralization of cerebral speech functions. *Annals of the New York Academy of Sciences, 299,* 355–369.

Ryding, E., Bradvik, B., & Ingvar, D. (1987). Changes of regional cerebral blood flow measured simultaneously in the right and left hemisphere during automatic speech and humming. *Brain, 110,* 1345–1358.

Rymer, R. (1992). A silent childhood-I. *The New Yorker,* April 13 (41–81); April 20 (43–77).

Shaywitz, B., Shaywitz, S., Pugh, K., Constable, R., Skudlarski, P., Fulbright, R., Bronen, R., Fletcher, J., Shankweiler, D., Katz, L., & Gore, J. (1995). Sex differences in the functional organization of the brain for language. *Nature, 373,* 607–609.

Sherrington, C. (1951). *Man on his nature.* Cambridge: Cambridge University Press.

Shipley-Brown, F., Dingwall, W., Berlin, C., Yeni-Komshian, G., & Gordon-Salant, S. (1988). Hemispheric processing of affective and linguistic intonation contours in normal subjects. *Brain and Language, 33,* 16–26.

Signoret, J. L., Castaigne, P., Lhermitte, F., Abelavet, R., & Lavorel P. (1984). Rediscovery of Leborgne's brain: Anatomical description with CT scan. *Brain and Language, 22,* 303–319.

Smith, A. (1966). Speech and other function after left (dominant) hemispherectomy. *Journal of Neurology, Neurosurgery and Psychiatry, 29,* 467–471.

Sparks, R., & Geschwind, N. (1968). Dichotic listening in man after section of neocortical commissures. *Cortex, 4,* 3–16.

Springer, S., & Deutsch, G. (1989). *Left brain, right brain.* New York: W. H. Freeman.

Steklis, H., & Raleigh, M. (Eds.). (1979). *Neurobiology of social communication in primates. An evolutionary perspective.* New York: Academic Press.

Toulmin, S. (1971). Brain and language: A commentary. *Synthese, 22,* 369–395.

Tsunoda, T. (1985). *The Japanese brain.* Tokyo: Taishukan Publishers.

Van Lancker, D., & Fromkin, V. (1978). Cerebral lateralization of pitch contrasts in tone language speakers and in musically trained and untrained English speakers. *Journal of Phonetics, 6,* 19–23.

Van Wagenen, W. P., & Herren, P. Y. (1940). Surgical division of commissural pathways in the corpus callosum: Relation to spread of epileptic attack. *AMA Archives of Neurology and Psychiatry, 44,* 740–775.

Wada, J. (1949). A new method for the determination of the side of cerebral speech dominance. *Igaka to Seibutsugaku, 24,* 221–222.

Wernicke, C. (1906). *Der aphasische Symptomenkomplex.* V. Leyden et al. (Eds.), 487–556. Berlin: Deutsche Klinik am Eingange des 20. Jahrhunderts, Bd. 6, Abt. 1

Wertz, R., Rosenbek, J., & Deal, J. (1970). *A review of 228 cases of apraxia of speech: Classification, etiology, and localization.* Presented at the American Speech and Hearing Association Convention, New York, NY.

Whitaker, H. (1976). A case of the isolation of the language function. In H. Whitaker & H. A. Whitaker (Eds.), *Studies in neurolinguistics* (Vol. 11). New York: Academic Press.

Young, R. (1974). *Mind, brain and adaptation in the 19th century.* Oxford: Clarendon Press.

Chapter **3**

SPEECH PERCEPTION

Grace H. Yeni-Komshian
The University of Maryland at College Park

INTRODUCTION

In this chapter, we explore the processes by which people decode spoken messages. When we listen to a lecture, view a movie, or participate in a conversation, we must attach meaning to the sounds we hear. In later chapters, we examine how the meanings of words are accessed and how the grammar of sentences is analyzed to understand the full sense of a message. But before these stages of language understanding can occur, we must first determine what sounds we have heard. Thus, in order to appreciate the advice, *"Don't slip on that banana peel!"* we need to realize that we have heard a sequence of speech sounds. Next, we may need to label these sounds as particular sounds of English. At some point, we must decide when a string of sounds has become a recognizable and meaningful word or sentence.

Although the process of decoding speech occurs rapidly, understanding how we accomplish the task is quite complex. In this chapter, we survey what is known about the process by which listeners assign identity to speech sounds. This basic stage in communication is complicated by the fact that the sounds of a language do not have constant, unvarying acoustic characteristics. A sound such as the English phoneme /t/ will sound different, for example, when spoken by different speakers and when it appears in different words. We examine this problem of variation within the speech signal, as well as other problems that make the understanding of speech by people or machines such a prodigious feat. Additionally, we discuss theories that have been developed to explain the process of speech perception in syllables and words and the potential contribution of these theories to the full task of understanding language.

THE HISTORICAL ROOTS
OF SPEECH PERCEPTION RESEARCH

Compared to many other areas of inquiry in psycholinguistics, speech perception research is extremely recent in origin. Willis (1829) and Helmholtz (1859) studied the physical properties of sound in the nineteenth century, but specific research into the way we perceive speech emerged just prior to and during the Second World War. Much of the pioneering work in speech perception depended on the development of equipment for speech analysis and **synthesis** (computer simulation of speech). The technology required to develop such devices was not available until the middle of the twentieth century, and the primary motivation for developing them was commercial. The first such machine was developed by Homer Dudley of Bell Telephone Laboratories, who called it a **vocoder,** a term derived from the words *voice* and *coder* (Dudley, 1936, 1939). Originally, the vocoder was designed to provide an efficient means of transmitting speech signals over long and expensive telephone circuits. It accomplished this task by analyzing and recoding the speech into a simpler signal that contained less information to be transmitted. Dudley and others quickly came to appreciate that natural speech contains **redundant** (multiply specified) information. This means that many factors may contribute to our recognition of a speech sound; only some of them need be present for speech to be interpreted, either in laboratory experiments or over the telephone. Dudley and his coworkers also discovered that they could use the vocoder to generate synthetic speech (Dudley, Reisz, & Watkins, 1939). This early attempt produced speech that had an unpleasant "electrical accent" and was difficult to understand (Schroeder, 1966).

The principles used to design the vocoder advanced the development of the **sound spectrograph.** This instrument analyzes audio signals according to the distribution of sound frequencies (spectrum) contained in the signal. In analyzing speech, the spectrograph displays *frequency* on the ordinate (y-axis), *time* on the abscissa (x-axis), and *amplitude* by the darkness of the markings. Speech analysis through the use of sound spectrography existed during the Second World War but was kept a military secret and became available to the public only after the war. An early model built at the Bell Telephone Laboratories could produce an instantaneous visible record of running speech. At that time the output was called *visible speech* (Potter, Kopp, & Green, 1947). It soon became clear that the moving visible pattern of speech sounds was impossible to "read," so the spectrograph was modified to produce a printout capable of displaying about two seconds of speech. The picture generated by a spectrograph is called a sound **spectrogram.** An example of a spectrographic display is provided in Figure 3.1. Spectrograms provide us with a stationary display of the speech signal that permits us to evaluate which aspects of the signal might be important for the perception of speech segments. At present, sound spectrography is most commonly carried out on desktop or laptop computers with one of several specialized software packages.

Thus, the roots of speech perception research lie in commercial and military interest in developing better communication systems. Through the years, as society has increased its use of audio equipment for work and leisure, machinery has been developed that can better analyze and recreate the speech signal. Much of this work is now done by the use of specialized computer programs. Commercial interest in speech perception continues because of the strong desire to develop computers that can understand speech and perhaps even identify speakers from their speech patterns. Current machine speech recognition capacity is limited either to restricted vocabularies produced by different speakers or to a broad vocabulary produced by speakers whose speech samples are initially stored in the computer.

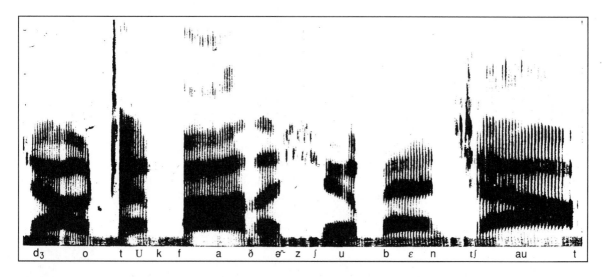

d₃   o   t   ʊ   k   f   a   ð   ɚ   z   ʃ   u   b   ɛ   n   tʃ   au   t

FIGURE 3.1

Spectrogram of the sentence, "Joe took father's shoe bench out." Note that the pauses (absences of energy) are not between words.

Source: V. C. Tartter (1986), Language Processes, NY: Holt, Rinehart and Winston, Figure 7.1, p. 210.

Major Questions in Speech Perception

How Do We Identify and Label Phonetic Segments?

In terms of its **acoustical** (sound) properties, human speech is a complex signal that contains many kinds of information at any single moment and varies continuously over time. Conversational speech in any language tends to be paced at 125–180 words per minute. At this rate of speech, we probably process approximately 25–30 phonetic segments per second (Liberman, 1970). To add to the problems inherent in decoding such a rapid and complex signal, conversational speech is a continuous signal. Let us return to Figure 3.1 for a moment. You will note that while there are numerous breaks in the visual pattern, individual sounds and words flow together in the spectrogram without easily identifiable boundary markers. The apparent gaps seen in Figure 3.1 are caused by specific articulatory movements associated with certain speech sounds and are not determined by the beginnings and ends of individual words. Articulatory movements for certain speech sounds (for example, oral stops and affricates) require periods of silence, and the visible breaks seen in Figure 3.1 are associated with these sounds.

Finding out how we manage to decode speech signals into phonetic units and derive meaningful words is a problem of great interest for speech perception research. Although the speech signal that reaches our ears varies more or less continuously over time, we perceive utterances as made up of discrete segments. We do not seem to have a major problem in segmenting speech into units of consonants and vowels, nor in identifying phonetic segments wherever they may appear in an utterance.

As a concrete example, let us consider the case of a student taking lecture notes. To do that, one needs to segment a continuous signal into the units that correspond to the English alphabet. The concern here is not how to spell the words, but how it is that one is able to hear a flowing, continuous signal and transform it into a *sequence of different speech segments.* Unlike print, speech does not contain cues for the beginning and end of words or of individual speech units, which we will call *phonetic segments.* When we speak, our articulatory gestures are smooth and continuous. If we were to write speech as it actually sounds, we might transcribe our lecture notes as follows: *Spokenwordsarenotseparatedbyspaceslikewordsareinprint.* Notice that it is difficult to read such a sentence because it is less obvious when words end and new words begin.

Even though it is relatively easy for us to segment speech, we should remember that phonetic segments are not like beads strung on a string, one segment after another. Rather, it is better to compare speech to a braid in which the properties that help us identify phonetic segments are tightly intertwined and overlap greatly. One of the greatest challenges for speech perception researchers is to determine how individual sounds are isolated (segmented) from the complex speech signal and how they are identified appropriately.

The "Lack of Invariance" Problem

It would be relatively easy to develop models of the speech perception process if each distinctive sound in a language was associated with a standard acoustic pattern. Unfortunately, neither speech nor its acoustic characteristics are that simple. Rather than displaying **invariant** (standard, unvarying) patterns, speech sounds vary considerably in their acoustic characteristics for several reasons. No simple one-to-one correspondence exists between the phonemes of a language and their acoustic realization. One important reason for this variation is that the production, and hence the acoustics, of the same phonetic segment varies depending on the context in which the segment is produced. That is, what we pronounce before and after a given segment affect the actual articulatory movements we make for the production of that segment. These context effects, which result in overlapping movements for speech, are called **coarticulation** effects. In Chapter 1 we explored the concept of **allophonic variation,** which is in part due to coarticulation effects. Allophonic variation occurs when speech sounds are embedded in certain contexts, such as initiating words, ending utterances, or when they are the neighbors of other specific sounds. The example given for this variability in phoneme realization was the sentence, "Tom Burton tried to steal a butter plate," with its many varieties of [t].

Next, the physical properties of speech sounds, especially vowels, vary according to whether they have been produced by men, women, or children, whose vocal tracts differ in size and configuration. It is thus somewhat surprising that we do not have problems in understanding speech produced by such diverse speakers, and speech perception researchers must account for our relative ease in processing these varying speech signals.

Another factor leading to variation in the acoustic properties of speech sounds is that we do not pronounce the same utterance in exactly the same way twice. This type of variation is characteristic of natural-sounding speech; removing these variations makes it sound artificial. In listening to others speak we appear to have no problem in dealing with this type of variation.

Yet another factor leading to variation in the speech signal stems from the properties of rapidly articulated conversational speech. There is a great difference between saying single words slowly and carefully and the way we actually pronounce words when we speak fluently. The acoustic characteristics of speech segments are reduced and much more variable in fluent speech than in careful enunciation of words. Speech perception research must explain how listeners process such "messy" samples of speech.

Solving the invariance problem can also lead to the development of machines that process spoken, rather than typed input. Consequently, solving the invariance problem is of great commercial interest. Attempts to get computers to recognize speech segments or words have not been tremendously successful because segments and words do not exist as stable acoustic patterns in fluent speech and cannot be easily recognized using pattern-matching techniques. Research has shown that segments that are clearly visible when words are spoken one at a time may be shortened, altered, deleted, or combined with other segments when the same words are produced in conversation (Klatt & Stevens, 1973; Reddy, 1976; Klatt, 1977). Thus, a machine cannot be programmed to search through a large but limited number of stored patterns and convert the patterns to phonetic segments and ultimately to words and sentences. The variations seen in conversational speech are so complex and diverse that at present no system available allows machines to recognize speech as you and I are able to do. Currently, such "intelligent" machines can only process a limited repertoire of words spoken one at a time using template-matching programs. A few systems can recognize a larger vocabulary, but they can process speech only from a single speaker who must first provide large samples of speech. Such **speaker-dependent** systems are seen in some newer "dictation programs" available for personal computers. A **speaker-independent** system can recognize more than a single speaker; at present these systems can process only a limited vocabulary, such as numbers. Some readers may have experienced telephone services that use a speaker-independent system; others may have explored newer programs for learning to pronounce foreign language vocabulary on home computers. (For a survey of research into this problem, see Schwab & Nusbaum, 1986; Zue, 1985, 1991.)

We should not end this section without pointing out that recent work appears to be pointing to invariant cues to identify stop consonants under specific conditions (Blumstein & Stevens, 1979, 1980; Stevens & Blumstein, 1981; Kewley-Port, 1982, 1983; Sussman, McCaffrey, & Matthews, 1991). Our ears may be using invariant cues for the identification of sounds, but perhaps new techniques are needed to isolate and describe them.

How Is Speech Perceived Under Less Than Ideal Conditions?

Conversational speech is quite variable in its acoustic characteristics. Sometimes speakers **underarticulate** (miss articulatory targets), so much so that the words lose much of their identifying information. Yet, listeners usually have little trouble understanding such speech samples. We will show how lexical, syntactic, and contextual information is used to interpret **ambiguous** (unclear speech) signals. Models of speech perception will need to explain how these other levels of processing contribute to the process of speech understanding.

In summary, the major research issues in speech perception research have to do with delineation of the mechanisms we use in segmenting and recognizing speech. These mechanisms are the basis for speech perception. Although the ultimate goal for some is to explain not only how we perceive but also how we understand spoken language signals, most of the available research has focused on investigating the perception of well defined samples of speech that are restricted as far as other aspects of language, such as meaning and syntax. Typically, studies have used syllables or single words as the experimental stimuli to be processed. The field has progressed enough to set the stage for a move toward using larger and meaningful units of speech in perceptual studies (Cole, 1980; Spoehr, 1981; Pisoni & Luce, 1987). Some of these studies will be discussed later on in the chapter. Before we can discuss the nature of speech perception, however, it is important to recognize how speech sounds are produced and how they are classified. We will also briefly explain the acoustical properties of the speech signal.

THE SPEECH SIGNAL

How Speech Is Produced

In this section, we briefly survey the process by which speech sounds are produced. How and where sounds are produced within our **vocal tracts** determines the acoustic properties of those sounds. Because of this, sometimes we can also work backwards and identify from its acoustic image on a spectrogram where and how a particular sound was articulated.

Let us first identify the body parts that are involved in speech production. Figure 3.2 is a diagram of most of the organs used in speech production that shows the places of articulation for English consonants. Starting at the bottom of Figure 3.2, you can see the **glottis,** which is part of the **larynx.** The larynx contains the **vocal folds,** and the glottis is the opening between the vocal folds where the folds meet when they vibrate to produce voice or **phonation.** You can also see the **pharynx,** the **nasal cavity,** and the various parts of the **oral cavity.** These include the **uvula,** the **velum** (or soft palate), the **hard palate,** the **alveolar ridge, tongue, teeth, and lips.** The area from the larynx to the lips is called the **vocal tract;** as can be seen in Figure 3.2, it is shaped like a bent tube.

There are three major systems for speech production: (1) the vocal tract, (2) the larynx, and (3) the **subglottal system,** which includes the lungs and associated muscles needed for inhalation and exhalation and the trachea or the windpipe. The subglottal system provides the air support for speech, which is produced on exhalation. Movements in these three systems are coordinated during the production of speech sounds.

FIGURE 3.2

A schematic drawing of the vocal tract. Places of articulation: 1, bilabial; 2, labiodental; 3, dental or interdental; 4, alveolar; 5, palatoalveolar; 6, palatal; 7, velar; 8, uvular; 9, glottal.

Source: An Introduction to Language *(4th ed.) (Figure 2.1, p. 36), V. Fromkin and R. Rodman, 1988, New York: Holt, Rinehart and Winston.*

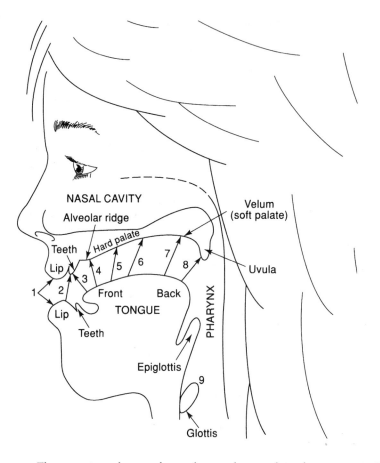

There are two classes of speech sounds: vowels and consonants. Vowels and consonants are produced differently. The major difference is that consonants are produced with more articulatory movement and more **constriction** (narrowing in a location in the vocal tract) than are vowels.

Linguists have further classified consonants and vowels according to various categories. One of the most common and basic systems is to classify sounds by where in the vocal tract they are made (**place of articulation**) and how they are made (**manner of production**). Table 3.1 lists most of the English consonants according to place of articulation and manner of production.

Place of Articulation

The numbers along the vocal tract in Figure 3.2 refer to the various places where constriction for different English consonants takes place. We call each of these locations *place of articulation*. Common places of articulation for English consonants are **bilabial** (closing the lips to create [p], [b], and [m]), **labiodental** (with the top teeth against

TABLE 3.1

ENGLISH CONSONANTS CLASSIFIED ACCORDING TO PLACE OF ARTICULATION AND MANNER OF PRODUCTION

		Place of articulation					
		Bilabial	**Labiodental**	**Interdental**	**Alveolar**	**Palatal**	**Velar**
Oral stop voiceless voiced		p (pin) b (bin)			t (tin) d (din)		k (kin) g (get)
Nasal stop voiced		m (map)			n (nap)		ŋ (sing)
Fricative voiceless voiced			f (fin) v (van)	θ (thin) ð (than)	s (sin) z (zone)	ʃ (shin) ʒ (leisure)	
Affricate voiceless voiced						tʃ (chin) dʒ (gin)	
Liquid voiced					l (law) r (raw)		
Glides voiced						j (yes)	w (we)

Manner of production (left vertical label)

the bottom lip, as in [f] and [v]), **interdental** (with the tongue protruding between the lips, in the production of [θ] and [ð], as in too*th* and *th*e), **alveolar** (with the tongue placed behind the upper teeth, as in [t], [d], [n], [s], [z], [l], and [r]), **palatal** (with the tongue against the palate, as in [ʃ] (hu*sh*), [ʒ] (lei*s*ure), [tʃ] (*ch*urch), [dʒ] (*j*ud*g*e), and [j] (*y*es), and **velar** (with the body of the tongue contacting the velum or soft palate, as in [k], [g], and [ŋ] as in si*ng*). The consonants listed in Table 3.1 are organized according to place of articulation.

Manner of Production

The source of acoustic energy for speech sound production comes from modulations in the air flowing from the lungs to the lips. The production of any sound involves the movement of air molecules. We breathe air into our lungs to serve as the power supply for the production of speech. The air flowing from the lungs to the lips is called the *air stream.* During regular quiet breathing, the vocal tract is open and the air flows out freely either through the nose or mouth. During speech production, however, some part (or parts) of the vocal tract constricts to a degree sufficient to impede the flow of air. The manner in which the constrictions are made in the vocal tract affects the air stream and results in different ways in which speech sounds can be produced. The consonants listed in Table 3.1 are also organized in terms of manner of production.

Some sounds are produced by modulating the air stream by the periodic opening and closing of the vocal folds at the glottis, also called glottal pulsing. As the vocal folds open and close, puffs of air are generated and flow through the oral cavity. These airflow pulses are **periodic** (occurring at regular intervals), rapid, and produce a sound that has a buzz-like quality. Sounds produced by the action of vocal-fold vibration are called **voiced** or phonated. In English, all vowel sounds and the consonants in Table 3.1 that are classified as voiced make use of the voiced sound source in their production. You can feel the vibration of your vocal folds by placing your fingers on your throat when you produce a sustained [z]. You can also feel the absence of vibration when you produce a sustained [s]. Try this procedure with the other pairs of voiced and **voiceless** fricatives and affricates; it is difficult to feel the difference between voiced and voiceless oral stops because they are short in duration. Also note that nasal stops, glides, and liquids are voiced; you can feel your vocal folds vibrate when you produce these consonants.

The rate at which glottal pulsing occurs during sound generation (phonation) is called the **fundamental frequency (FO).** Fundamental frequency is about 125 glottal pulses per second for adult males, about 200 pulses per second for adult females, and about 300 pulses per second for children. The perceived difference between the pitch of men, women, and children is based on the rate of glottal pulsing.

A second type of sound source is achieved when air is forced through a narrow constriction in the oral cavity. For example, in the production of [s], a narrow slit is formed between the tip of the tongue and the alveolar ridge. Air rushes through this slit. The flow of air creates a turbulent speech sound. The turbulence produces friction noise that has a hissing quality. The same thing happens if you blow air through a narrow constriction such as a slit through a grass blade or two sheets of paper. The turbulent airstream does not pulse periodically, but has random variations in airflow. This **aperiodic** (turbulent) sound source is the basis for the production of consonants called **fricatives** and **affricates.** Voicing and turbulence may be combined in the case of voiced fricatives and affricates, as Table 3.1 indicates.

In English, certain speech sounds are made by stopping the airflow completely for a short period of time and then abruptly releasing it. This third type of sound source, called a transient sound source, is used in the production of oral **stop consonants,** shown in Table 3.1. The production of these consonants requires a complete closure of the oral cavity, which in effect stops the airflow for a short period and increases air pressure. These movements are then followed by an abrupt release of the air stream, which creates the sound (burst). If we make similar articulatory movements as for oral stop consonants, but allow air to flow from the nasal cavity, we produce the nasal stops shown in Table 3.1.

Speech sounds that combine the gestures for stop consonants and fricatives are called affricates (in English [ʧ] as in *ch*in and [ʤ] as in *j*am). Speech sounds classified as **liquids** (*l*aw and *r*aw) have a voiced sound source and air flow that is minimally constricted. Sounds classified as **glides** (*y*es and *w*e) are the consonants closest to vowels because they allow the air to flow freely. However, the articulators move faster than for vowels. These consonants are listed in Table 3.1.

In contrast, airflow from the lungs is unobstructed when vowels are produced. Each vowel, however, is produced with a different configuration of tongue and lip movements. Vowels can also be classified in terms of articulatory movements. There are three distinguishing features in classifying vowels. The first is tongue height, which refers to whether the tongue is raised, as in [i] and [u], or lowered, as in [æ] and [a], during production. The second is tongue position, which refers to the part of the tongue that is most involved in producing the vowel; for example, the front part of the tongue is raised for [i], whereas the back of the tongue is raised for [u]. The third feature has to do with the position of the lips—whether they are pursed (rounded) or not rounded—for example, the lips are rounded for [u] and unrounded for [i]. Using this system, [i] is classified as high, front, and unrounded; [u] is classified as high, back, and rounded; [æ] as low, front, and unrounded; and [a] as low, back, and unrounded. The examples given above are for the four vowels ([i] as in *beet,* [u] as in *boot,* [æ] as in *bat,* and [a] as in *bah*) that best fit these descriptions. The remaining English vowels are also classified using this system.

Distinctive Features

Linguists have used concepts such as voicing or place of articulation to develop a system of **distinctive features** for describing speech sounds. For example, all sounds are characterized either by the feature +*voice* (voiced) or -*voice* (voiceless). Sounds are additionally described by other features such as whether the air stream exits the mouth or the nose. This produces the feature contrast +*oral/-oral.* Sounds classified as -*oral* would be the English nasal stops [m], [n], and [ŋ].

Sounds made with continuous airflow, such as vowels, fricatives, glides, and liquids, are noted by the feature +**continuant.** The stops, which require an abrupt stoppage of airflow in generating the transient sound source, receive the feature −**continuant.**

Place of articulation can also be captured by feature notation. Sounds made at the front of the mouth, such as [p], [b], and [m], are noted as +**anterior.** Sounds made by placing the tongue in contact with the palate ([t], [d], and [n]) are considered +**coronal.** By combining these features, we can arrive at a complete feature specification for a given English sound. For example, [b] could be described as:

$$
\begin{bmatrix}
+ \text{ oral} \\
- \text{ continuant} \\
+ \text{ voice} \\
+ \text{ anterior} \\
- \text{ coronal}
\end{bmatrix}
$$

We will not exhaustively survey the full range of distinctive features that have been developed to describe the sounds of English and other languages. However, it is interesting and important to note that common misperceptions of speech appear to reflect a change in the value of a single feature. That is, when we misperceive, we frequently are off by only one distinctive feature. The results of many experiments using single syllables as stimuli have demonstrated this phenomenon and have also delineated the order in which confusions between features are likely to occur (Miller & Nicely, 1955; Wang & Bilger, 1973). Later in the chapter we will see how misperceptions are perceived in fluent speech. Additionally, as Chapter 7 shows, some speech errors suggest that distinctive features may be real "building blocks" in the speech production process. It is possible to find examples of speech errors in which a given feature, such as voicing, is misplaced, which produces the unintended output, "Baul and Peth," for the intended sequence, "Paul and Beth."

Acoustic Properties of Speech Sounds

VOWELS: THE SIMPLEST CASE. The easiest way to demonstrate the acoustical properties of speech sounds is by describing single vowels. All speech sounds are composed of complex sound waves; that is, they contain many different frequencies simultaneously, like a musical chord that contains many notes. The vowels we hear are based on a modification of the sound source in a manner that is determined by the **resonant characteristics** of the oral cavity or vocal tract during the production of that sound.

What are resonant characteristics? We hear sound when air flows through any bounded area. The specific sound we hear is composed of the resonant frequencies associated with the size and shape of the space through which air is flowing. We have all heard the sounds made while filling a bottle with water. The change in sound while filling a bottle with water indicates to us that it is time to turn off the tap. That is, we have learned to assign meaning to these changes in sound. The sound changes are created by the change in the size and shape of the empty space in the bottle through which the air is flowing out. When the bottle is empty, the air in it is contained in a relatively large space. As you fill the bottle with water the air space gets smaller and the resonance characteristics change. The resonance of a relatively empty bottle is low pitched and the resonance of a bottle that is about to overflow is high pitched.

Let us now take the case of the voiced sound source, which is used in the production of all vowels. The frequency components, or **spectrum,** of this sound source at the glottis include the fundamental frequency (FO) and even multiples of the fundamental frequency. The multiples of the FO are called **harmonics.** Thus, if the FO is at 100Hz, the harmonics would be at 200Hz, 300Hz, 400Hz, 500Hz, and so on up to and beyond 8,000Hz. The unmodified spectrum at the sound source would have frequency components that are even multiples of 100Hz, though some of these frequencies would be of higher or lower **amplitude** (loudness). In the production of a vowel sound, for example [u] as in the vowel of the word *boot,* the shape of the vocal tract for producing [u] will determine the frequency components that will be prominent (resonate) when the airstream flows through that particular oral cavity and position of lips. The vocal tract shape for [u] (high, back, rounded) is such that bands of low frequency components will resonate. The bands of resonant frequencies for speech change in relation to the movement of our articulators while producing speech. These bands of resonant frequencies are called **formants.** The shape of the oral cavity is changed when we pronounce [i], [a], or any other speech sound. Figure 3.3 displays spectrograms of English vowels. Spectrograms display frequency on the vertical axis, time on the horizontal axis, and amplitude in the darkness of the markings. Formants (bands of resonant frequencies) are easily visible on the sound spectrograms: they are the horizontal dark bands.

The single vowels and diphthongs displayed in Figure 3.3 are organized according to their place of production. Figure 3.3A lists the front vowels. They range from high front to low front, ([i] as in *beet,* [e] as in *bait,* [I] as in *bit,* [ɛ] as in *bet,* [æ] as in *bat).* Similarly, in Figure 3.3B the back vowels are listed from high back to low back, ([u] as in *boot,* [o] as in *boat,* [U] as in *put,* [ɔ] as in *pour,* [ɑ] as in *bah).* Figure 3.3C shows the central vowels, ([ʌ] as in *putt,* [ə] as in *the,* [ɚ] as in *girl).* Finally, in Figure 3.3D the diphthongs are displayed ([iu] as in *view,* [ɔi] as in *boy,* [au] as in *cow,* [ai] as in *eye).* **Diphthongs** consist of two vowels articulated in smoothly changing sequence. As you examine the formants in Figure 3.3D, you can see that they are not flat, as in Figure 3.3A, B, and C; they curve upward or downward. The changes in formants of diphthongs reflect the changes in the resonance of the vocal tract as the speaker shifts from the first vowel to the second vowel. The vowels shown in Figure 3.3 were produced by a male who spoke in a deliberate and careful way. Even though these samples are not typical of conversational speech style, certain concepts are easier to illustrate using such simple examples. The most noticeable aspect of the individual patterns shown in Figure 3.3 is that each vowel appears to be characterized by at least three broad, dark, horizontal stripes. These stripes are the **vowel formants.** For each vowel, the first three formants are marked by small bars to help you locate them on the figure. Formants are numbered from low to high frequency such that the first formant (F1) is associated with the lowest frequency resonance band, the second formant (F2) with the next band of frequencies, and so on.

Vowels are differentiated by the relative position of the first two formants. Perceptually, the first two formants are sufficient for their identification. Thus, the combination of a low frequency F1 and a high frequency F2 is characteristic of [i], shown in Figure 3.3A. The pattern that identifies [u] consists of two low frequency formants, as in Figure 3.3B. Note that the frequency components of formants are affected by the size and shape of the vocal tract and to some degree by the fundamental frequency. Because of this, men, women, and children have different absolute values for the formants of given vowels. The fact that listeners can easily process vowels produced by men, women, and child speakers, whose vowels vary in absolute frequency,

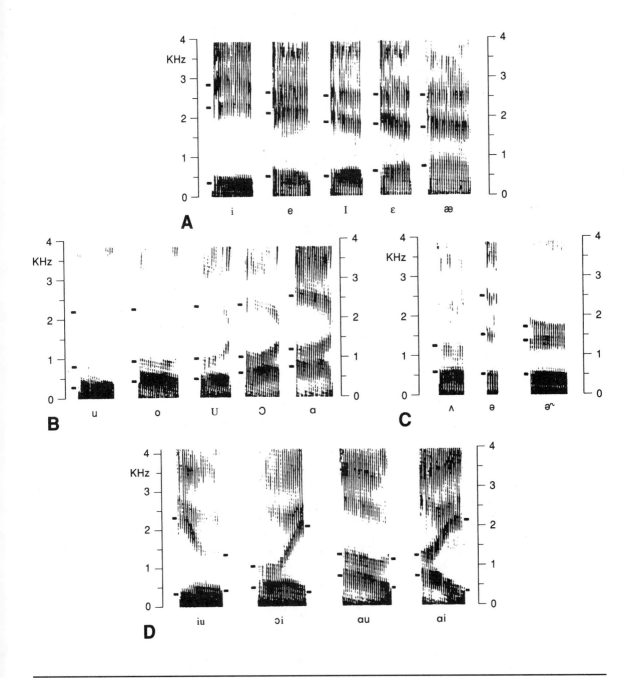

FIGURE 3.3

Spectrograms of examples of the vowels and diphthongs of American English. The approximate midvowel locations of the first three formants are indicated by the bars beside each spectrogram.

Source: Pickett, J. M. (1980). The Sounds of Speech Communication. *Baltimore: University Park Press, pp. 74–75.*

implies that a pattern-recognition system is in operation, rather than reference to absolute values. We call the ability of listeners to use pattern recognition to identify vowels spoken by different speakers **speaker normalization.**

Changes in the oral cavity for the production of different vowels in isolation are simple in comparison to the changes that take place in diphthongs, syllables, and conversational speech. Diphthongs, which are two vowels produced in a smooth glide, have formants moving from one vowel to another as described above and as shown in Figure 3.3D. These movements are called **formant transitions.** For example, for [iu], the formants begin in a pattern similar to that for [i] and move to end like the pattern for [u]. Formant transitions reflect the movements of the articulators and are faster and sharper in consonants than in vowels. In fact, single vowels produced in isolation, such as those in Figure 3.3A, B, and C, do not have formant transitions. These relatively flat formant patterns are called **steady states.** In fluent conversational speech, however, we hardly ever see vowels produced in steady state, and vowel formants have fairly sharp transitions going in and out of adjacent consonants. If you compare Figures 3.3 and 3.4, the differences in vowel formant patterns are evident.

Acoustic Characteristics of Consonants

Consonants are characterized by an array of different patterns on a sound spectrogram. Once more, we will start with more easily identifiable patterns, those associated with the fricatives [s] and [ʃ]. If you examine Figure 3.4, in which the speaker is saying, *"She sells sea shells,"* the turbulence associated with the fricatives [s] and [ʃ] is visible as dark, thick columns of aperiodic high frequency energy interspersed among the

FIGURE 3.4

Spectrogram of the phrase, "She sells sea shells."

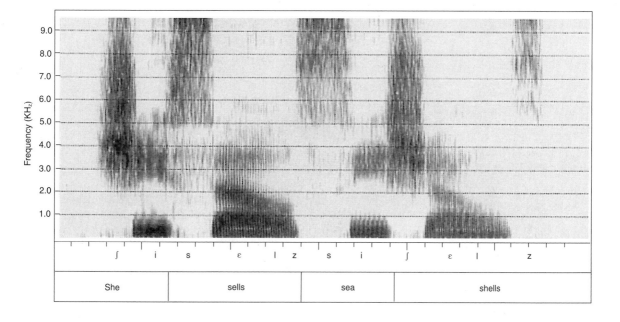

acoustic patterns associated with vowel formants. The difference between [s] and [ʃ] is signaled by the range of frequencies included in the columns. You will note that the range for [ʃ] dips lower in frequency than in [s]. As fricatives vary in their place of articulation, the range of frequencies seen in their spectrographic displays will also vary.

One visible feature of oral stop-consonant spectrographic displays is the thin vertical line associated with the sudden release of air pressure (the **burst**) just prior to the onset of the vowel. The burst is a rapid acoustic event and may not be visible because of low intensity. In Figure 3.5, the burst is not readily visible in *Bab*, clear in *gagged*, and fairly visible in *Dad*. For this reason, the stop consonants are sometimes more readily distinguished by the direction of second-formant transitions to their adjacent vowel sounds. In the sentence, "Bab gagged Dad," the second formants appear to rise upward from the release of the consonant to the vowel in *Bab*, they fall in *gagged*, and stay relatively level in *Dad*. It is these formant movements, or formant transitions, which appear to play a large role in deciding which stop consonant has been heard. The acoustic characteristics of the other consonants are not as easy to see as the examples given in Figures 3.4 and 3.5. For additional information on the acoustic characteristics of speech sounds see Pickett (1980), and Borden, Harris, and Raphael (1994).

Notice that in Figure 3.5, although the speaker said, "Bab gagged Dad," and listeners would agree that the intended message was heard, the acoustic display does not contain visible signs of the final consonants of the three words. This discrepancy is due to coarticulatory effects that take place in fluent speech. The speaker did not say each word one at a time, rather in the smooth flow of saying the phrase the speaker combined the articulatory gestures needed for the final [b] in *Bab* to the gestures needed for the initial [g] in *gagged*, and the same thing happened between the end of *gagged* and the beginning of *Dad*.

FIGURE 3.5

Spectrogram of the sentence, "Bab gagged Dad."

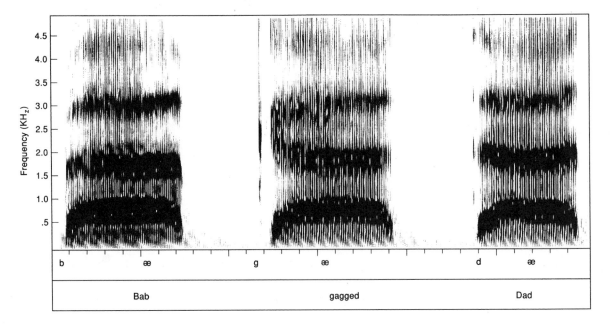

PERCEPTION OF PHONETIC SEGMENTS

In this section we address the perception of phonetic segments. As we have seen, the speech signal is complex and contains much information in the time, frequency, and amplitude domains. We have also seen that even though we can psychologically and linguistically identify segments or phonemes in fluent speech, the acoustic signal lacks visible markers that correspond to the segments. Furthermore, when we listen to someone, we not only hear the linguistic message but also the special characteristics of the speaker's voice and emotional state, although these are not necessary for determining the identity of the phonetic segments (phonemes) contained in the linguistic message.

One of the most important goals of research in this area has been to isolate specific aspects of the complex sound pattern necessary for the identity of a given phoneme. These critical parts of the complex sound pattern are called **acoustic cues.** Researchers required certain equipment before they could begin to work in this area. They needed speech analysis machines such as the sound spectrograph and also the capacity to synthesize speech according to precise specifications. The aim was to create speech stimuli that could be used to evaluate the perceptual relevance of acoustic cues.

The Role of Speech Synthesis in Perceptual Research

The collaboration of three pioneers in speech perception research at Haskins Laboratories signaled the start of research on the perceptual evaluation of acoustic cues. In the early 1950s, Franklin Cooper, an engineer, Alvin Liberman, a psychologist, and Pierre Delattre, a linguist, joined forces to study the perception of speech. It was true then and is true now that progress in speech perception relies on interdisciplinary cooperation.

They utilized the Pattern Playback Speech Synthesizer, constructed by Cooper and his colleagues (Cooper, Delattre, Liberman, Borst, & Gerstman, 1952). This machine synthesizes speech sounds by converting visual patterns to complex sound waves. The pattern playback device could synthesize speech from drawn formant patterns; it could also generate the sound associated with any pattern that one painted on its cellulose acetate belt. The researcher would paint a pattern on the belt, and the machine would play the pattern back. Figure 3.6 is a picture of the Pattern Playback Speech Synthesizer.

One of the first discoveries using this machine was that intelligible speech could be obtained from highly simplified spectrograms. For example, synthesis of the first and second vowel formants and appropriate formant transitions were enough to produce intelligible CV (consonant-vowel) syllables. This finding, like earlier observations about telephone transmission (Dudley, 1936, 1939) demonstrated that speech was highly redundant. Visual examples of two formant CV syllables, as drawn on the pattern playback, are illustrated in Figures 3.7 and 3.10. Needless to say, speech synthesis has progressed since development of the pattern playback synthesizer and now is done with computers.

FIGURE 3.6

F. S. Cooper painting a syllable on the Pattern Playback synthesizer. Speech was synthesized by converting patterns painted on acetate film loops into acoustic signals by a photoelectric system (Haskins Laboratories).

Source: Speech Science Primer (2nd ed.) (Figure 2.4, p. 21), G. J. Borden, K. S. Harris, and L. J. Raphael, 1994, Baltimore: Williams and Wilkins.

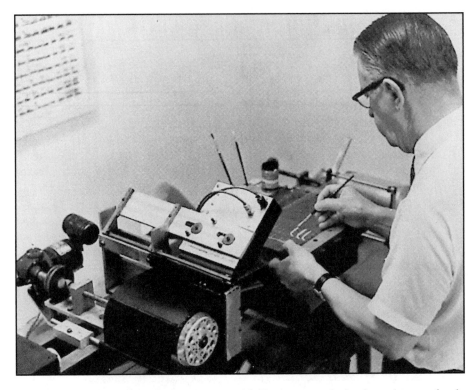

Early observations and experiments with the pattern playback made use of only two formant stimuli and were concerned with delineating the acoustic cues necessary to identify stop consonants synthesized with different vowels in the shape of CV syllables (Cooper et al., 1952; Liberman, Delattre, & Cooper, 1952). The researchers would paint a pattern and play it back to see if it produced the desired sound; if not, they would modify and replay the pattern until they got the desired sound. In this process they discovered the acoustic cues necessary to identify that particular speech sound. The resulting report by Liberman et al. (1952) anticipated and described many ideas that have become the foundation of research in speech perception. This initial work set the stage for charting the acoustic cues that perceptually differentiate one phoneme from another.

Ways in Which Speech Perception Is Tested

Many experiments in speech perception, including those that we will discuss in the following sections, have made use of two tasks: discrimination and identification. **Discrimination** tasks require the listener to indicate whether two stimuli are the same or different. The several methods for obtaining this type of information differ in the amount of memory required by the task. In discrimination, the listener can decide whether two stimuli are same or different without having to identify, label, or determine the meaning of the stimuli. **Identification** tasks require the listener to label or determine the identity of the stimulus. Thus, in identification the listener provides or selects a label and may use a lexicon for the decision. For example, listeners may be asked, "Write the word that you hear." In other situations they may receive a fixed number of alternatives and be asked to choose the alternative that best matches the label or identity of the stimulus, similar to a multiple-choice test question.

The speech perception studies we describe in detail in the following sections shed light on the complex procedures used in evaluating how listeners perceive speech. Like all studies covered in this chapter, these are based on adult speech perception.

Perception of Vowels

What is the most important part of the vowel signal in establishing its identity? The early studies made use of extended steady-state vowels as stimuli. One experiment made use of the pattern playback to synthesize the stimuli. The investigators wanted to find out how listeners respond to one- and two-formant steady-state stimuli (Delattre, Liberman, Cooper, & Gerstman, 1952). Listeners were able to perceive some vowels created with only a single formant. Low-frequency single formants were generally associated with back vowels, for example [u], [o], and higher-frequency single formants with front vowels, for example [i], [e]. This finding suggests that the frequency information contained in one formant is enough to provide the listener with the perception of a vowel, though not its exact identity. When stimuli that contained two formants were presented, however, agreement across listeners was high in identifying the stimuli as the particular vowel whose natural formant patterns had served as the model for the synthesis. This study and others that followed suggested that the steady-state portions of the first two formants of a vowel are the necessary and sufficient acoustic cues to determine its identity. As we shall see, this view was later modified as perception of more natural speech samples was investigated.

Steady States Versus Formant Transitions in Vowel Identification: An Illustrative Study

Recall that vowels contained in regular words are produced in the context of consonants. Acoustically this means that vowels are marked by formant transitions going in and out of the adjacent consonants and contain steady-state segments that are either short or not present at all. The next logical question, which was investigated about thirty years after the initial studies, was aimed at comparing the perceptual saliency of vowel steady states and formant transitions (Jenkins, Strange, & Edman, 1983). We will describe this study in some detail, not only because its findings are interesting, but also because it shows that controlled and precise stimuli can be created with real speech samples. In fact, at present both speech synthesis and computer control of real speech signals are common techniques for creating test stimuli for speech perception research.

As test stimuli, Jenkins et al. (1983) used CVC syllables that began and ended with [b] but contained nine different vowels (*beeb, bib, babe, bob,* and so on). A male speaker produced these nine syllables. With the use of a computer, the syllables were digitized and edited. Each syllable was then divided into three components: (a) the formant transitions from the initial consonant to the vowel, (b) the central vocalic (vowel) portion, and (c) the transition from the vowel to the final consonant. These three segments will be referred to as (a), (b), and (c). Listeners evaluated the following types of stimuli:

1. The unmodified original syllables, called *control syllables,* composed of segments (a) + (b) + (c);
2. *Silent-center syllables,* which consisted of segments (a) + silent gap + (c). The silent gap was as long as segment (b) for that syllable. This type of stimulus preserved the formant transitions and the actual duration of the vowel but did not contain the steady state information;
3. *Variable-center syllables,* which consisted of only the (b) portion of each syllable. These stimuli preserved the steady-state portion of the target vowel and its inherent duration;
4. *Fixed-center* stimuli were constructed by trimming segment (b) in each syllable to match the duration of the shortest target vowel. These stimuli preserved the steady-state portion of the vowels but did not contain durational information;
5. Finally, listeners evaluated *abutted syllables,* which were composed of segments (a) + (c). These stimuli did not contain any information concerning segment (b). That is, they did not contain a steady-state portion at all.

Groups of subjects were asked to identify the vowels in each type of test stimuli. The results showed that silent-center stimuli were identified as accurately as the original control syllables. Listeners made significantly more errors in identifying the variable-center (steady-state and temporal information) and abutted syllables than the original control syllables. The lowest accuracy level was for the fixed center (steady-state only) stimuli. The authors interpreted their results to indicate that formant transitions and vowel duration are more important cues to the identity of vowels than a fixed sample of the steady-state information. This finding has been replicated and extended in other studies. A more detailed account of more recent studies and a model of vowel perception can be found in Strange (1989a, 1989b).

This and other research on vowel perception suggest that perception of isolated sounds and continuous speech differ. What appeared to be an important acoustic cue for vowel identity (its steady state) in an isolated and extended segment of synthetic speech appears to be a less important acoustic cue in natural speech. Acoustic cues considered important when evaluating simplified speech (two formants only) may be less important when natural speech is considered (many formants). Thus, the history of research on vowel perception demonstrates that our understanding of how we process speech is bound to change as we improve and diversify our methods of investigation.

Current research approaches the characteristics of actual conversational speech sounds by using computer technology that edits natural speech to generate stimuli that are controlled and at the same time reflect the characteristics of normal conversation.

Perception of Consonants

In both conversational speech and laboratory studies, vowels are perceived more accurately than consonants. The intensity of the signal may play a role in the advantage seen in vowel identification. The acoustic energy associated with vowels is stronger by about six decibels (dB) than that with consonants. In addition, most consonants are shorter in duration than vowels. The short duration and lower amplitude of consonants make them harder to perceive than vowels.

Stop consonants have been studied extensively in speech perception research. We have already noted that in English the stops [b, d, g] are *+voice,* and [p, t, k] are *-voice.* All languages have oral stop consonants represented in their phonological system. Unlike other consonants, stops lose their identity when presented in isolation. For example, in a syllable such as [ba], it is impossible to separate the [b] portion from the [a] portion of the syllable. If one removes the entire vowel (transition plus steady state) from the syllable, the resultant segment sounds like a "chirp" rather than the phoneme [b]. Stop consonants in syllable initial position must contain a small piece of the transition segment in order to be perceived accurately. In other words, the acoustic signal from the articulation of the stop consonant *plus* the formant transitions into the adjacent vowel are necessary before we can hear the consonant. It is as if the consonant and the vowel information are merged together in the syllable, somewhat like the analogy of the braid mentioned earlier in this chapter. When the acoustic information of adjacent phonetic segments merges, the phonetic segment is described as being **encoded.** In our example, [b] would be considered encoded, because we can isolate no single acoustic segment that would sound like [b]. We can only extract the identity of [b] from the merged consonantal and vowel information. This means that the information about the consonant and the vowel is transmitted in parallel to the listener. This type of **parallel transmission** is most dramatically evident in highly encoded phonetic segments such as oral stop consonants. The formant transitions between the consonant and vowel appear to play a large role in deciding the identity of the stop consonant and the vowel.

Stop consonants are highly encoded; other consonants are encoded to a lesser degree. Even when isolated segments retain their phonetic identity, the acoustic signals of all consonants and vowels are affected by the characteristics of their adjacent phonemes. That is, all speech sounds change character to some degree as a function of the sounds with which they are produced, the phenomenon we have already called coarticulation.

Phoneme Identity Is Context Dependent

Since the late 1950s, a great deal of research has been devoted to other types of perceptual studies primarily concerned with determining the acoustic cues for all the

FIGURE 3.7

Two-formant syllables produced on the Pattern Playback synthesizer identified as [di] and [du]. Notice the difference in the beginning of the second formant of each syllable.

Source: Speech Science Primer (2nd ed.) (Figure 5.31, p. 213), G. J. Borden and K. S. Harris, 1984, Baltimore: Williams and Wilkins. Original figure from "The Grammars of Speech Language," by A. M. Liberman, 1970, Cognitive Psychology, 1, pp. 301–323.

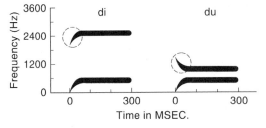

phonetic contrasts in English and other languages. Much empirical information has been accumulated on this subject matter. In this chapter we highlight two major general findings that have been repeatedly observed across different stimulus conditions and experimental techniques. The first finding is that acoustic cues are highly dependent on context effects. That is, not a single acoustic cue is present in all instances of a given phoneme. The acoustic cue for a phoneme changes as that phoneme is paired with other phonemes. In addition, research has shown that context-dependent variations are most pronounced in highly encoded speech sounds such as the stop consonants. For example, as illustrated in Figure 3.7, the acoustic patterns of the second formant transitions from the consonant into the vowel of [di] and [du] differ dramatically, yet listeners will agree that the consonant in these two syllables is the same [d]. This illustrates the effects of coarticulation and the "lack of invariance" problem described earlier in the chapter.

The second important general finding is that more than one acoustic cue exists for differentiating a phonetic contrast. This is true even when context effects are accounted for. As we shall see, **voice-onset-time (VOT)** is identified as the best single measure for signaling the difference between voiced and voiceless stop consonants in syllables such as [ba] versus [pa]. Additional cues, however, such as the amount of energy in the burst, onset frequency of the first formant, and rate of first formant transition, also contribute to the perception of voicing distinction in syllables (Lisker & Abramson, 1964; Summerfield & Haggard, 1974). This multiplicity of acoustic cues, which contributes to redundancy in the speech signal, is evident in many phonetic contrasts and appears to be the rule rather than the exception. Some theoretical accounts of speech perception have not as yet taken this empirical finding into consideration.

Voice-Onset-Time: An Important Acoustic Cue

Researchers have evaluated the perception of stop consonants extensively. One research aim was to determine the perceptual salience (importance) of specific acoustic cues used to distinguish among the various English stops. As we noted earlier, one way in which stops differ from one another is in whether they are voiced (*+voice,* accompanied by vocal-fold vibration) or voiceless (*−voice,* without vocal-fold vibration). In English, three pairs of stop consonants are identical except for the voicing feature. That is, [b] and [p], [d] and [t], and [k] and [g] are pairs of phonemes distinguished only by the feature *(voice)*. In each pair, the first sound is produced with accompanying vocal-fold vibration *(+voice)* and the second is not *(−voice)*.

Although it might appear that the presence or absence of voicing during stop production is a rather easy cue to the discrimination of sounds, describing listeners' actual discrimination between voiced/voiceless stop **cognates** (sounds that differ only in one feature, in this case the voicing feature) turns out to be more complex than anticipated. Researchers had already noted from spectrograms of speech samples that voicing distinctions were associated with different acoustic patterns depending on the phoneme and where in the word the contrast occurred. In the case of word initial contrasts, one parameter important for distinguishing between pairs such as [ba] and [pa], for instance, was **voice-onset-time (VOT).** In a stop-initial CV syllable, VOT represents the time between the release of air pressure (the burst) and the onset of vocal-fold vibration (voicing) for the adjacent vowel (Lisker & Abramson, 1964). On a spectrogram this is seen as the time between a sharp onset of broad-band energy (the burst) and the onset of the formant transition (onset of vocal-fold vibration). Figure 3.8 displays two spectrograms to illustrate this point. In both spectrograms, the initial consonant is an alveolar stop and the vowel is [i]. Which will be heard as [di] and which as [ti]? Figure 3.8A demonstrates a VOT of about 10 milliseconds—a 10 milliseconds gap between the stop burst and the onset of the following vowel's first formant. As we shall see, such a pattern is heard as [di]. Figure 3.8B shows a VOT of approximately 60 milliseconds, meaning that 60 milliseconds have elapsed between the stop burst and the onset of voicing for the following vowel; it is heard as [ti]. The horizontal bracket under each CV syllable marks the VOT region. VOT is demonstrably the best single acoustic cue that differentiates between syllable initial voiced and voiceless stop consonants not only in English but also for the stop consonants in other languages such as Dutch, Spanish, Hungarian, Tamil, Cantonese, Thai, and Eastern Armenian (Lisker & Abramson, 1964).

If all syllable-initial voiced stops had VOTs of zero, and all voiceless ones were characterized by VOTs of 60 milliseconds, explaining the discrimination of voicing would be relatively simple. However, the actual VOTs seen in stop production, even just for English, vary widely. Sometimes vocal-fold vibration (voicing) is initiated before the release of the burst in a voiced stop such as [d], and at other times voicing is initiated up to 30 milliseconds after the burst. On the other hand, voiceless stops such as [t] are characterized by VOTs that range between 40 and 100 milliseconds. Do listeners hear these sounds as different types of [d]s and [t]s? The answer turns out to be no. In order to explain how listeners evaluate the acoustic cue for voiced and voiceless initial stops, we shall discuss the findings of studies in which VOT values for stops in CV syllables were varied systematically such that the only difference among the stimuli was in VOT. The systematic variations in the VOT of each CV stimulus in the series form a continuum that is anchored by a voiced and a voiceless stop at either end of the series. Stimuli forming a continuum are synthesized and not based on natural speech, because we cannot control our articulators to produce the required systematic changes in VOT while keeping everything else in the syllable constant. The listeners

FIGURE 3.8

Spectrograms of the syllables [di] and [ti] to illustrate voice-onset-time (VOT). In each syllable the burst is seen as the dark vertical line to the left. The onset of voicing is indicated by the onset of the first formant (start of the segments that have regular striations). VOT is the distance between the burst and the onset of voicing (horizontal bracket starting at the burst of each syllable).

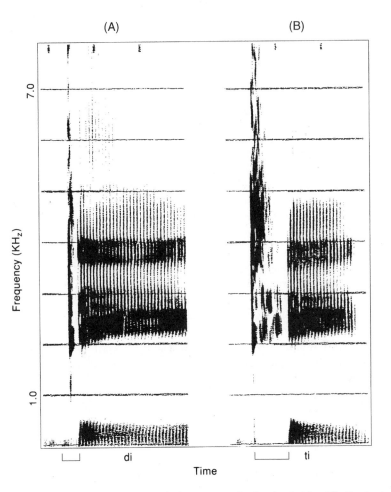

described in the experiments below were asked to both identify the test stimuli and to discriminate between pairs of stimuli.

Categorical Perception of Voicing Contrast

Many researchers have evaluated the perception of voicing in initial stop consonants (Liberman, Harris, Kinney, & Lane, 1961; Liberman, Harris, Eimas, Lisker, & Bastian, 1961; Liberman, Cooper, Shankweiler, & Studdert-Kennedy, 1967; Abramson & Lisker, 1970). In these studies, a synthesized continuum of 10 to 15 different VOT values was used as stimuli. For illustrative purposes, we will describe a simpler study based on the design of an experiment carried out by Yeni-Komshian and LaFontaine (1983), which used seven stimuli.

To establish the perceptual relevance of VOT as an important acoustic cue, seven stimuli along a continuum were constructed. In each case, the experimental syllable started with a burst and had three formant transitions leading into the vowel [i]; this would normally elicit the listener's perception of a CV syllable having an alveolar stop (either [d] or [t]). The first syllable was characterized by zero milliseconds VOT. That is, voicing for the following vowel was simultaneous with articulation of the stop consonant. The second through seventh stimuli were identical to the first stimulus, except that the VOT in each was 10 milliseconds longer for each subsequent stimulus. The result was a seven-stimuli continuum that varied only in VOT in 10 millisecond steps. These stimuli were then used to construct identification and discrimination tasks.

In a typical identification task involving a continuum such as this, the seven different stimuli in the continuum are presented in random order at least 10 times, creating an identification test that contains 70 trials. The subjects are usually given two alternatives, for example *di* or *ti,* to choose from and are asked to indicate which they have heard.

In the discrimination test, the subjects indicate whether a pair of stimuli are identical (same) or differ in any way (different). Some trials contain identical stimuli and others are composed of two different stimuli. The "different" trials may consist of pairs of stimuli varying by one step along the continuum (for example, stimuli 1 and 2) or two steps (for example, stimuli 1 and 3). The "different" and "same" trials would then be presented in random order at least 10 times. In this particular example we will count the two-step trials only. Even with this reduced number of pairings, the minimum number of trials would be 170, (100 "different" trials and 70 "same" trials). Thus, a discrimination test is much more time consuming to administer than an identification test.

The idealized results of such an experiment are shown in Figure 3.9. The identification scores (bars) are plotted in terms of percent [da] responses. We can see that stimuli 1, 2, and 3 were consistently identified as [da] and were never labeled as [ta]. On the other hand, stimuli 5, 6, and 7 were always labeled [ta] and never as [da]. In the case of stimulus 4, the results are mixed. In 50 percent of the trials it was heard [da], but the rest were heard as [ta]. In experiments such as this, it is not the case that the subject hears an in-between kind of speech sound. Rather, the perception of the stimulus is unstable; it is sometimes heard as [da] and at other times heard as [ta]. This perceptually unstable stimulus (stimulus 4 in our example) is called the **cross-over stimulus,** meaning it is the one that separates one phoneme category, [d], from the other phoneme category, [t]. Thus, these results indicate that the listeners classified stimuli 1, 2, and 3 in one phoneme category, [d]; and stimuli 5, 6, and 7 in a different phoneme category, [t]. The individual members within each phoneme category are physically different and each one is an allophone of that phoneme category. Thus, this type of an identification test would tell us the range and boundary of each phoneme category. The identification test also demonstrates that, for the listener, a group of physically different stimuli are consistently judged to be the same phoneme. Then, rather suddenly, the next stimulus in the continuum is perceived as a different phoneme. This sharp shift in perception is suggestive of a *perceptual discontinuity* across a continuously varying physical dimension. This pattern in response is characteristic of a perceptual phenomenon called **categorical perception.**

A reader might observe nothing special in the identification results. The listeners were given two options. They just divided the stimuli in the continuum into two piles

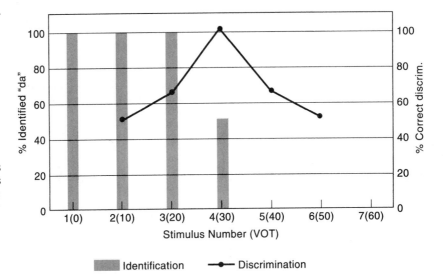

Idealized Results

in a manner that validates VOT as an acoustic cue for the voicing contrast in stops. One might suggest that, had the listeners been given the opportunity to describe the differences they heard among some of the stimuli, the results might have been different. Such comments are well taken as long as the results are limited to the identification test. To be able to establish whether stimuli in a continuum are perceived categorically, discrimination responses are necessary and these should fit a specific pattern. The results shown in Figure 3.9 (line graph) demonstrate the discrimination pattern typical of categorically perceived stimuli.

The line graph for the discrimination trials shown in Figure 3.9 is based on the results of the "different" trials. All subjects were highly accurate in indicating *same* when in fact the pair of stimuli were identical. This is what we would expect. All trials that contained physically different stimuli that on the identification task had been judged to fall within the same phoneme category (for example, the pairs of stimuli heard as [da] 1 and 3 and as [ta] 5 and 7) were discriminated at a chance level of accuracy. That is, about half the time they were judged to be the same and half the time as differing.

Trials that contained the crossover stimulus (for example, 2 and 4; 4 and 6) show better-than-chance accuracy (65 percent). The highest level of accuracy, called the **discrimination peak,** is for trials that contain a pair of stimuli from two different phoneme categories. In our example, it is the stimulus pair 3 and 5. The results for the discrimination trials demonstrate that the discrimination peak is situated at the boundary between the two phoneme categories.

Whereas the stimuli in pair 3 and 5 are discriminated highly accurately, it is somewhat surprising that a difference of the same magnitude (pairs 1 and 3 and 5 and 7) is not discriminated as accurately. In other words, perceptual discontinuity is demonstrated because a given amount of physical difference (in our example it is 20 milliseconds) does not have the same perceptual impact at all locations along the continuum. The listeners' ability to discriminate is not better than their ability to identify. What this means is that their discrimination of acoustic differences could be predicted from their performance on the identification test. A hallmark of categorical perception is that discrimination is not any better than identification.

In many perceptual domains, discrimination is better than identification. We can usually discriminate between two different stimuli much better than we can label or identify two different stimuli. Consider the following example from the visual domain: Let us imagine a series of photographs of two men who look somewhat alike. We could photograph each standing up with arms pressed against his sides. We could then take a second, third, and fourth photograph of each individual, asking each of them to raise his arms about 20 degrees for each photograph. The discrimination task would be to ask the viewer whether a pair of photographs were identical or not. The identification task would be to label the identity of the person in the picture. In this example you would not find it difficult to tell whether any two photographs of the *same* individual were identical or not (discrimination). In contrast, with speech stimuli such as [da] and [ta] your ability to tell whether two stimuli that you have already labeled [da] are the same or different is at chance level at best.

To summarize, the identification results establish the boundaries of the two phoneme categories ([d] and [t]) and confirm the validity of VOT as a relevant perceptual cue. The discrimination results, when viewed in relation to identification results, determine whether a phonetic contrast is perceived categorically.

Other Categorical Perception Studies

Through the years, many studies have used test procedures similar to those described above to examine the perception of other acoustic cues and to determine whether they are perceived categorically. The experiment that discovered categorical perception and inspired the numerous studies that followed was published by Liberman, Harris, Hoffman, and Griffith (1957). It investigated the perceptual consequences of second-formant transitions, rather than VOT. In the experiment, 14 two-formant CV syllables were synthesized on the Pattern Playback. These 14 stimuli differed only in the onset frequency and direction of the second-formant transitions. The vowel for all stimuli was [a]. A schematic representation of the continuum is shown in Figure 3.10. Note that the continuum spans three phoneme categories that differ in place of articulation. These stimuli were identified as [ba], [da], or [ga]. Figure 3.10 shows the range and boundary of each phoneme category (divisions are marked by arrows at the bottom of the figure). The results of the discrimination test showed two discrimination peaks that coincided with the two phoneme boundaries. The combined patterns of the identification and discrimination results indicated that speech sounds representing these three phoneme categories were perceived categorically.

The categorical perception studies that followed the original Liberman et al. (1957) study were limited only by the speech synthesis capabilities of the time. At one time the quality of synthesized stop consonants was much better than fricatives, liquids, and affricates. In time, just about all consonantal contrasts were investigated and found to be perceived categorically (for a detailed review, see Repp, 1984). With

FIGURE 3.10

Two formant syllables produced on the Pattern Playback synthesizer. The illustration is for a 14-step continuum. Each stimulus is numbered. The stimuli vary in the onset and direction of the second formant transition. This acoustic cue signals place of articulation for the stop consonants [ba], [da], and [ga]. The divisions marked by arrows at the bottom of the figure mark the phoneme boundaries.

Source: Listening, An Introduction to the Perception of Auditory Events *(Figure 9.3, p. 275),* S. Handel, 1989, Cambridge, MA: MIT Press.

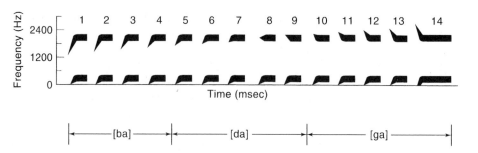

vowels, however, the results were complicated. In research using vowel stimuli, isolated and extended vowels were not perceived categorically (discrimination was better than identification). However, vowels of short duration (Pisoni, 1975) or in the context of consonants (Stevens & Ohman, 1969) were perceived categorically.

Table 3.2 lists the major acoustic cues for selected phonetic contrasts that have been studied and found to be perceived categorically. It is important to understand that these major acoustic cues are subject to context effects and other effects of coarticulation. The distinctions listed are based on pairs of single syllables that differ by one distinctive feature. Table 3.2 also demonstrates that the acoustic cues for voicing vary depending on the type of speech sounds (stops versus fricatives) and whether the contrast is word initial or word final.

Categorical Perception: Specific to Speech Sound Perception?

Researchers initially interpreted categorical perception as a phenomenon limited to the perception of speech sounds. According to this interpretation, speech is perceived in a special mode, the *speech mode,* in which we interpret the signal with reference to the motor movements involved in the production of that signal, and we automatically compute a phonetic label and discard the acoustic information. Thus, once physically different stimuli are given the same phonetic label, they are no longer distinguishable from each other. The motor theory of speech perception (Liberman, Cooper, Shankweiler, & Studdert-Kennedy, 1967), to be discussed later, relied heavily on this line of reasoning.

TABLE 3.2

MAJOR ACOUSTIC CUES FOR SELECTED VOICING AND PLACE CONTRASTS THAT ARE PERCEIVED CATEGORICALLY.

The syllables listed in the brackets are just one example for each of the contrasts.

CONTRAST	MAJOR ACOUSTIC CUE
Word initial voicing in oral stops [ba-pa]	Voice Onset Time
Word final voicing in oral stops [ab-ap]	Duration of preceding vowel
Place in oral stops [ba-da-ga]	Start and direction of the second formant
Place in nasal stops [ma-na]	Start and direction of the second formant
Voicing in final fricatives [as-az]	Duration of preceding vowel
Place in fricatives [sa-ʃa]	Frequency of the turbulent noise
Liquids [la-ra]	Frequency of the third formant

Other studies, however, have indicated that categorical perception is not a phenomenon demonstrated only with speech sounds produced by motor movements of our articulators. For example, categorical perception has been reported for complex nonspeech sounds (tones) that varied in sharpness of onset to make them sound as if they were plucked or bowed on a stringed instrument (Cutting & Rosner, 1974), for noise buzz sequences that vary on noise lead time (Miller, Weir, Pastore, Kelly, & Dooling, 1976), and for tones that vary on relative onset time (Pisoni, 1977). The general conclusion of these studies is that categorical perception is not limited to speech sounds. These and other studies that have addressed the question of whether categorical perception is special to speech and limited to humans (Kuhl & Miller, 1975) have emphasized the functioning of a general auditory component in speech perception (rather than the motor theory of speech perception). Handel (1989) provides an extensive evaluation of the available research on auditory perception of speech and nonspeech stimuli.

Other Applications of the Test Paradigms Used in Categorical Perception Studies

Other research questions have been investigated successfully using speech stimuli to form various continua in identification and discrimination tests. Investigations of phoneme boundaries for contrasts in languages other than English constitute one example. Abramson and Lisker (1970) compared perception by Thai and American English monolingual listeners of the same set of stimuli (a VOT continuum) that spanned a voicing contrast. The subjects were given the same identification and discrimination tasks. They found that Thai speakers identified and discriminated the test stimuli according to the phonology of the Thai language, which greatly differs from English. The phonetic boundaries for the Thai listeners differed from those of the English listeners. In other words, the speakers of these two languages perceived the same set of stimuli differently, and the differences were directly related to the phonological differences between the two languages. Other studies have been conducted to compare bilingual with monolingual listeners. These include an investigation of the perception of stop consonant voicing in Canadian French–English bilinguals (Caramazza, Yeni-Komshian, Zurif, & Carbone, 1973) and Spanish–English bilinguals (Williams, 1977, 1980). One question here is whether bilinguals identify stimuli differently according to their two languages. The studies with bilinguals generally show that they have a single perceptual system rather than two separate language-bound systems. The bilinguals' perceptual categories appear to be situated at a midpoint between the two categories set by the monolingual speakers of their two languages.

Other studies have considered the perception of [r] and [l] by Japanese–English bilinguals (Strange & Jenkins, 1978; MacKain, Best, & Strange, 1981; Strange & Dittman, 1984). In these studies, the test stimuli form a continuum spanning the [r] and [l] phonetic contrast. The results of these studies reveal the extent of the difficulties that Japanese listeners have in discriminating these speech sounds. The effect of special training on discrimination ability was also assessed by using the same research paradigms. These studies show fairly clearly the effects of linguistic experience on speech perception. They demonstrate that our perceptual capabilities relate directly to the phonology of the languages we speak. The language-specific honing of speech perception skills starts early in life, well before children say their first words, as Chapter 8 describes in greater detail. Speech perception research with native speakers of languages other than English or bilingual listeners whose second language is English is currently an active topic of investigation. Strange's recent (1995) book on speech perception and linguistic experience contains excellent chapters on this subject matter.

Another set of research issues that can be profitably investigated with the use of synthetic stimuli that span a continuum have to do with charting the extent of loss of normal speech perception by aphasics (Blumstein, Cooper, Zurif, & Caramazza, 1977; Yeni-Komshian & LaFontaine, 1983). Identification and discrimination test results demonstrate the degree to which phonetic boundaries are altered among aphasics. A typical result is that great individual differences exist among aphasics regarding their perceptual responses. Many aphasic listeners tend to have unstable responses for several stimuli in the phonetic boundary area. That is, their phonetic boundaries are not set as clearly as normal listeners'.

SPEECH PERCEPTION BEYOND A SINGLE SEGMENT

This section reviews the perception of speech signals longer than a single phoneme. We start with studies of the perception of two adjacent phonetic segments and conclude with studies of fluent speech. Almost all experiments reported in this section point to the role that our expectations play in speech perception. In our perception of normal conversational speech we weigh our knowledge of phonological sequences in English, the topic of conversation (semantic factors), and our expectations of appropriate syntactic structure to arrive at an image of what we have "heard."

The Perceptual Outcome of Coarticulation

As described earlier in this chapter, articulatory movements for different sounds within a word do not move in discrete series of separate gestures. Instead, there is temporal overlap of articulatory movements in producing a sequence of phonetic segments. This temporal overlap of articulatory movements results in coarticulation effects in which acoustic information of adjacent segments is transmitted in parallel to the listener. For a definition and detailed discussion of different types of coarticulation see Daniloff and Hammarberg (1973). The type of coarticulation discussed in this section is exemplified by the way we produce the [s] in words such as *see* and *Sue*. Try to say these two words in front of a mirror and pay attention to your lips while you produce the [s] portion of the syllable. You will see that your lips are in the position of a smile for the word *see* and puckered for the word *Sue*. These different articulatory gestures mean that the [s] in these two words is produced in two different ways. An experimental question is whether any information concerning the vowel in *Sue* is contained in the consonant that preceded it.

Several researchers have investigated issues related to the perception of coarticulated segments (Kuehn & Moll, 1972; LaRiviere, Winitz, & Herriman, 1975; Mann & Repp, 1980). The general technique for generating stimuli for such experiments is to start with samples of natural speech—for example the word *see* [si]—and to remove the vowel and leave the [s] segment as the stimulus. The listeners' task is to indicate whether they can hear the *excised* (removed) vowel from the consonant segment. Studies have demonstrated that listeners can identify the excised vowels in certain CV combinations, but not in others.

One investigation of this sort was carried out by Yeni-Komshian and Soli (1981). The stimuli were 12 CV syllables composed of four fricatives produced in three different vowel contexts (for example, [si, su, sa]). Computer editing procedures were used to generate the stimuli. All of the vowels were removed and 150-millisecond segments of just the fricative portions of the syllables were used as stimuli. One of the tasks in the experiment was to identify the excised vowel by listening to the fricative portion only. Results indicated that the vowels [i] and [u] were identified reliably in the fricative segments, but not the vowel [a]. This demonstrated that the fricative portion not only contained information about the consonant but also contained information about the identity of the following vowel. That is, information about the fricative and vowel is available simultaneously in the same acoustic segment. Here is another example of parallel transmission of information, a term used to describe the perceptual outcome of coarticulation.

Even though parallel transmission of information is common in speech, it appears that this additional source of perceptual information is available when articulatory compatibility exists between segments. When two adjacent segments can be produced with noncontradictory tongue movements, they are compatible. For example, the tongue is raised for both consonant and vowel in the production of [si] and [su]. However, when adjacent segments require contradictory tongue movements, they are incompatible and are not coarticulated. In our example, contradictory tongue movements are involved in the production of [sa], the tongue is raised for [s] and has to be lowered for [a]. This is the explanation given for why elements of [a] are not heard reliably in the excised [s] segment.

To summarize, coarticulatory effects do not exist uniformly across all adjacent segments and do not uniformly distribute perceptual information throughout the speech signal. Instead, when articulatory compatibility is possible, speakers naturally engage in coarticulation, and this may provide an additional source of perceptual information to the listener.

Perceptual Effects of Speaking Rate

The effects of speaking rate on segmental distinctions have been investigated and reviewed by Miller (1981). The acoustic characteristics of sounds alter as speaking rate increases. Changes from **citation form** (the way sounds are produced carefully in isolation) are more evident in vowels than in consonants. Nevertheless, all phonetic

SPEECH PERCEPTION IN LANGUAGE-LEARNING IMPAIRED (LLI) CHILDREN

As we will discuss in Chapter 8, the vast majority of children of normal hearing and intelligence achieve the milestones of first language learning with ease and no explicit instruction. About 3% to 6% of children, however, experience serious difficulties in various aspects of language function and fail to develop speech and language normally. These children are usually referred to as language-learning impaired (LLI) or specifically language impaired (SLI).

It is difficult to explain why LLI children have problems in speech and language; they score within normal limits on standardized tests for hearing and intelligence. The current general assumption is that their problem lies in subtle aspects of auditory-perceptual and cognitive-processing skills that are not tapped in standardized tests.

Paula Tallal and her colleagues (Merzenich, Jenkins, Johnston, Schreiner, Miller, & Tallal, 1996; Tallal & Piercy, 1973; Tallal, Stark, Kallman, & Mellits, 1980; Tallal, Miller, Bedi, Byma, Wang, Nagarajan, Schreiner, Jenkins, & Merzenich, 1996) suggest that LLI children, in comparison with normal developing children, have a deficit in processing rapidly changing or rapidly presented auditory or speech signals. For example, LLI children typically have difficulty in discriminating between speech signals such as [ba] and [da], whose identities are cued by rapid formant transitions that occur during the first 30 to 40 milliseconds of the syllable. When these same syllables are synthesized with the initial segments deliberately expanded to about 60 to 80 milliseconds, LLI children are reported to discriminate and identify these expanded syllables more accurately. The LLI children also benefit from a slower rate of input because they can discriminate and identify regular unexpanded syllables if they are provided with a longer interval between the syllables. The prediction made from these findings is that if LLI children were provided with adequate processing time (listen to expanded syllables and have longer intervals between stimulus events) they would not have difficulty in comprehending speech and language.

This prediction was recently tested by a group of researchers and clinicians who provided 5- to 10-year-old LLI children with concentrated and extended training. The training program made use of (a) speech stimuli synthetically modified to expand the duration of the transition portion and also to enhance the amplitude of the consonantal segments and (b) computer games designed to improve temporal processing abilities by training the children to process pairs of stimuli separated by increasingly shorter

(continued)

(continued from previous page)

intervals. At the end of a 4-week, 125-hour training period, 11 children in a training group demonstrated language score gains at a level not observed in 11 children assigned to play similar games that lacked the specially modified speech. The fact that the standardized test performance of most of the trained LLI children approached normal levels in a relatively short time led both Tallal et al. (1996) and Merzinich et al. (1996) to conclude that the apparent processing deficits of LLI children can be overcome by training.

The publication of these findings has created great excitement and controversy. On one hand, many parents of LLI children and clinicians working with LLI children are excited about the possibility of remediating the handicapping condition of impaired language understanding and production. On the other hand, the data are new and complex and can be interpreted in varying ways. Because the training program contained many different elements, it is unclear what aspect(s) of the program contributed to the improvement. Further, it is unclear how such a limited amount of training can so dramatically improve what children appear to know about language. Finally, it is unclear from the published data whether the children assigned to the control and training groups were equal regarding the nature of their deficits at the beginning of the program. These articles are listed below, as well as a critical review challenging Tallal's arguments regarding the underlying deficit in language learning and reading disabilities in children (Studdert-Kennedy & Mody, 1995).

Merzenich, M. M., Jenkins, W. M., Johnston, P., Schreiner, C., Miller, S. L., & Tallal, P. (1996). Temporal processing deficits of language-learning impaired children ameliorated by training, *Science, 271,* 77–80.

Studdert-Kennedy, M., & Mody, M. (1995). Auditory temporal perception deficits in the reading-impaired: A critical review of the evidence, *Psychonomic Bulletin & Review, 2,* 508–514.

Tallal, P., Miller, S. L., Bedi, G., Byma, G., Wang, X., Nagarajan, S. S., Schreiner, C., Jenkins, W. M., & Merzenich, M. M. (1996). Language comprehension in language-learning impaired children improved with acoustically modified speech, *Science, 271,* 81–84.

Tallal, P., & Piercy, M. (1973). Developmental aphasia: Rate of auditory processing and selective impairment of consonant perception, *Neuropsychologia, 11,* 389–398.

Tallal, P., Stark, R., Kallman, C., & Mellits, D. (1980). Perceptual constancy for phonemic categories: A developmental study with normal and language-impaired children, *Applied Psycholinguistics, 1,* 49–64.

segments undergo modification. What are these changes? All phonetic segments are shortened but even more so with vowels than consonants. Furthermore, shortening the inherent duration of vowels results in changes in the formant frequencies in the direction of the values for central vowels (see Figure 3.3C). The outcome for example is that the word *beat* may sound like *bit* when presented in isolation but like *beat* if it is presented as one of the words in a sentence that is spoken fast. This is because the listeners in this particular example (and in other perceptual studies of speaking rate) make perceptual adjustments for speeded speech. The typical research paradigm is to place a target stimulus (for example, a word) in a **carrier phrase** (standard, unvarying sentence) that is either fast or slow and instruct the listener to identify the target stimulus. Listeners apparently form certain expectations on the basis of the rate of the carrier phrase. Consequently, the same target stimulus may be identified as two different words or sound sequences depending on the rate of the carrier phrase. The shift in the perceptual response is directly related to the changes we make when we alter our rate of speaking.

Lexical and Syntactic Factors in Word Perception

Unlike perception of meaningless isolated phonetic segments, perception of meaningful words in connected fluent speech is influenced by higher-level knowledge of semantics and syntax. Early work in this area indicated that single words presented in noise are recognized more accurately in a sentence context than when spoken in isolation (Miller, Heise, & Lichten, 1951). In another study, words embedded in sentences were perceived more accurately than when the same words were excised from their sentences and presented in isolation (Pollack & Pickett, 1964). The researchers recorded conversations and excised individual words from the taped material. They then presented these isolated words to listeners for identification. Only about half of the excised words were recognized correctly. When the words were presented along with one or two neighboring words from the original conversational sentences, successful identification of the target words increased dramatically.

Words produced in conversational speech are less intelligible than isolated words because in fluent speech we pronounce words less precisely than in citation form. It is also clear from results such as these that in a sentence context, semantics and syntax help the listener decode individual words in fluent speech. What we call **top-down processing** (the use of semantic and syntactic information) as well as phonological **bottom-up processing** (using only acoustic information to decode the speech signal) operate jointly in everyday perception of conversation. Several models that attempt to account for the joint action of bottom-up and top-down processing of speech are discussed later in this chapter.

A classic demonstration of the effect of context on speech perception is a phenomenon called **phonemic restoration** (Warren, 1970). In this study, Warren replaced a phonetic segment (for example, the [s] in *legislature*) with a coughing sound of about the same intensity as the excised segment. The word was then presented in a sentence context and the subjects were asked to indicate where in the sentence the cough occurred. Surprisingly, subjects were not accurate in locating the cough. Their typical response was that they heard the full word *legislature;* the cough was heard as background noise. Thus, the subjects generated or *restored* a phoneme that was not part of the signal. The results were interpreted to suggest that when we listen to words, our expectations affect what we perceive. If we have most of the information necessary to specify a word, we mentally "smooth over" minor discrepancies in the speech signal.

The question is, then, under what circumstances do we detect irregularities or mispronunciations in words or sentences that we hear? Cole and his colleagues devised an ingenious method and carried out studies aimed at answering this question (Cole, 1973; Cole, Jakimik, & Cooper, 1978; Cole & Jakimik, 1980). The **listening for mispronunciation (LM)** detection task is an interesting way to examine the stimulus characteristics we pay attention to in recognizing words in the context of running speech. The subjects' main task is to listen for mispronunciations. This technique has been used to ask questions such as

> Which part of a word or a syllable do we pay attention to while listening to connected speech? (Answer: The initial part)
>
> Do we detect mispronunciations in predictable sequences better than in unpredictable sequences? (Answer: Yes)

Cole (1980) reports various examples of the uses of the LM procedure. We will concentrate on the one that has to do with inferring the relative perceptibility of different distinctive features in naturally produced fluent speech (Cole, Jakimik, & Cooper, 1978). This involved examining the results of different feature changes in target words in short stories. For example, to examine the perceptibility of the stop consonant voicing feature, the target word, *broom,* was systematically mispronounced. All mispronunciations resulted in phonologically permissible nonwords. That is, *b*room could be changed to *d*room, *t*room, or *f*room, but not to *s*room or *n*room, because *sr-* and *nr-* sequences are not acceptable in English. The mispronunciations were embedded in a 20-minute-long story. The subjects' task was to listen to the story and to push a button as soon as possible whenever they heard a mispronunciation.

The first experiment dealt with voicing in word-initial stops, fricatives, and affricates. Results suggested that voicing changes were detected most accurately for stops (*boot* to *poot*) (70%), followed by affricates (*chance* to *jance*) (64%), and least accurately for fricatives (*fin* to *vin*) (38%). The reduced ability to detect mispronunciations in fricatives may be due to their relatively weak acoustic signals. It is also true that few English words contrast minimally in the voicing characteristics of initial fricatives. Because this contrast is rare in the language, listeners may pay little attention to it.

Further experiments investigated place, voicing, and manner changes in initial consonants. In general, subjects were fairly accurate in detecting the mispronunciations based on place (80%–90%). Changes based on place differences (*take* to *pake*) were more perceptible than those based on voicing (*take* to *dake*). In addition, mispronunciations based on both place and voicing (*take* to *gake*) were detected no better than place changes alone. These findings elaborate and extend earlier research on perception of distinctive features (Miller & Nicely, 1955; Wang & Bilger, 1973) to the conversational speech level.

One other experiment compared the perception of mispronunciations in word-initial and word-final consonants. The changes involved place in nasals (*make* to *nake; drum* to *drun*) and voicing in stops (*dish* to *tish; split* to *splid*). The results indicated that for all comparisons, more than twice as many correct detections were made for word-initial (72%) mispronunciations than for word-final (33%). The poor detection of word-final consonant mispronunciation may be partially explained on acoustic grounds for oral stops but not for the nasal stops. These results appear to indicate that listeners pay more attention to beginnings of words rather than ends of words. It is suggested that the listener accesses a word candidate soon after hearing the beginning of the word and "fills in" for the end of the word. This particular finding was used by Marslen-Wilson (1987) in developing his Cohort Theory described later in the chapter.

Following a review of their research using the LM technique Cole and Jakimik (1980) conclude that words are recognized through the interaction of sound and knowledge. Sounds in the beginning of a word are used to access word candidates, sounds in a word are recognized sequentially, and once recognized, words provide semantic and syntactic constraints used to recognize the rest of the message (Cole & Jakimik, 1980, p. 161). These studies and others conducted by this team of researchers clearly demonstrate the joint influence of bottom-up and top-down processes operating when we listen to conversational speech.

We will end this section by describing an experiment to illustrate another interesting method for investigating the influences of bottom-up and top-down processing. This study was designed to examine the role of semantic influences in word identification. The test stimuli in Garnes and Bond (1976) were tokens in a 16-step continuum spanning the sequence *bait-date-gate*. The test stimuli were identical except for the starting frequency of the second formant, which was changed systematically in equal steps to signal place-of-articulation differences. These single-word stimuli were used in an identification test to define the boundaries for the three phoneme categories. These same 16 stimuli were also used as the last word in the following three carrier sentences:

1. Here's the fishing gear and the _____ .
2. Check the time and the _____ .
3. Paint the fence and the _____ .

Subjects were asked to indicate which of the three words they thought they heard at the end of each sentence. The results indicate that the unambiguous stimuli (those that were consistently identified as either *bait, date,* or *gate* when presented in isolation) were perceived accurately regardless of the carrier sentence. That is, subjects reported hearing semantically implausible sentences (for example, *"Paint the fence and bait."*) as long as the stimuli were unambiguous. Perception of the ambiguous stimuli (stimuli near the phoneme boundary or at the crossover), however, was influenced by the semantic message of the carrier sentence. Thus, for phonetically ambiguous stimuli, the semantic content of the carrier sentence affected the listener's perceptual judgment. This study shows that listeners use semantic information to aid in final decoding of the message. It also demonstrates the importance of semantic input in processing speech when the signal is not acoustically optimal, a condition that is common in regular conversational speech. Other studies on the role of the lexicon in speech perception are reviewed in Samuel (1986).

MODELS OF SPEECH PERCEPTION

In this section we describe several models that have been advanced to explain some of the mechanisms involved in speech perception. To date, none of the models is developed enough to explain the basic problems in speech perception or to account for the accumulated empirical information. First, we'll consider two early models that inspired and guided much of the research carried out up until the early 1980s. These are the *motor theory of speech perception* and *analysis-by-synthesis*. These two models and a more recent model called the *fuzzy logical model* view the process of perception rising through stages from the auditory input, to a phonological level, and up to word identification. This view is called bottom-up and does not incorporate the effects of lexical and other "higher-level" cognitive knowledge into the process of speech perception. A top-down view proposes that higher levels of knowledge play a significant role in speech perception. Models that incorporate the joint operation of multiple sources of information, including both bottom-up and top-down information, are called *interactive*. The main concern of interactive models is word recognition, whereas for bottom-up models, perception of phonetic segments is a major goal in itself. Most recent models incorporate an interactive approach. Two interactive models summarized briefly here are the *cohort model* and *TRACE model*. Other models in the literature and reviews of various speech perception models can be found in collections edited by Schwab and Nusbaum (1986) and Perkell and Klatt (1986). The brief review of models in this chapter relies primarily on Pisoni, 1978; Pisoni and Luce, 1986, 1987.

Motor Theory of Speech Perception

The main thesis of the motor theory is that, at some point in the speech perception process, speech signals are interpreted by reference to motor speech movements. This theory directly links the processes of speech production with speech perception by stating that we perceive speech in terms of how we produce speech sounds. This theory was advanced by Liberman and his colleagues at Haskins Laboratories (Liberman, Cooper, Shankweiler, & Studdert-Kennedy, 1967; Liberman, 1970). The theory was developed to deal with the absence of invariance between the acoustic signal and its phonemic representation, a problem we have already discussed. Liberman et al. (1967) emphasize differences in the acoustic signals of the same phoneme in various contexts. As discussed earlier, the acoustic patterns associated with [d] in the syllables [du] and [di] differ (see Figure 3.7), yet all listeners agree that the initial portion of the two syllables contains the same phoneme. If you pronounce these two syllables and pay attention to the movements of your tongue, you can feel a similarity in the motor movements of your tongue at the beginnings of the two syllables. This apparent similarity in motor gestures could then be used to counter the acoustic variance. Thus, the early form of the theory hypothesized invariance at the motor articulatory level of speech production. However, research in search of motor invariance did not produce the desired results. Later versions of the model hypothesized that the invariance most probably exists at an earlier neuromotor level, not at the actual stage of articulation, where motor commands to the articulators are made.

Another important assumption of the motor theory is that speech perception is phonetic and is different from auditory perception. According to the theory, speech is a special type of auditory stimulus for human beings; when we are exposed to it, we shift automatically to the *speech mode,* which uses different processes and criteria to evaluate speech, as opposed to music or other nonspeech sounds. Perceiving in the speech mode is innate and **species specific,** that is, it is a uniquely human property with which we are born. It enables us to link articulatory gestures involved in the production of a heard sound with the intended phonetic segment. The interpretation of categorical perception also relied on this special way human beings react to speech sounds. The motor theory motivated an extensive body of research on speech perception. The evidence accumulated from such research, however, has not provided strong support for the position that it is necessary to engage in some form of articulatory knowledge during perceptual processing of speech. Furthermore, arguments based on the special status of categorical perception, as discussed earlier, have not been upheld. More recent accounts of the motor theory that incorporate the idea of modularity are presented in Liberman and Mattingly (1985, 1989).

Analysis-by-Synthesis

The basic assumptions of the analysis-by-synthesis model proposed by Stevens (1960) and Stevens and Halle (1967) are similar to the motor theory in that speech perception and production are closely tied. This model assumes that we make use of an abstract distinctive features matrix in a system of matching that is crucial to the speech perception process. The major claim of the theory is that listeners perceive (analyze) speech by implicitly generating (synthesizing) speech from what they have heard and then compare the "synthesized" speech with the auditory stimulus. According to this model, the perceptual process begins with analysis of auditory features of the speech signal to yield a description in terms of auditory patterns. A hypothesis concerning the representation of the utterance in terms of distinctive features is constructed. In cases where phonetic features are not strongly influenced by context and thus contain an invariant attribute, the auditory patterns are tentatively decoded into phonemes. When no invariant attributes identify a phonetic feature, additional processing is required. A hypothesis concerning the distinctive feature representation of the utterance is formed. This message forms the input to a set of generative rules that synthesize candidate patterns, which are subsequently compared with the patterns of the original utterance at a neuroacoustical level rather than an articulatory level as in motor theory. The results of this match are sent to a control component that transfers the phonetic description to higher stages of linguistic analysis.

Analysis-by-synthesis is an abstract model of the speech perception process, and little direct empirical evidence has been found to support it. It is vague in its evaluation of speech perception as special and different from auditory perception. More recent versions of the theory hypothesize that the properties of speech can be uniquely and invariantly specified from the acoustic signal itself (Stevens & Blumstein, 1978; Blumstein & Stevens, 1979). Research continues into the problem of invariance, and several reports have shown evidence of invariance in stop-consonant characteristics (Blumstein & Stevens, 1979, 1980; Stevens and Blumstein, 1981; Kewley-Port, 1982; Sussman, McCaffrey, & Matthews, 1991). More work in this area will provide information regarding our ability to extract the identity of a given phonetic segment from apparently diverse acoustic signals related to that segment.

Fuzzy Logical Model

Speech perception, according to this model, is a prime example of pattern recognition (Massaro, 1987, 1989; Massaro & Oden, 1980). The model assumes three operations in speech perception: *feature evaluation, feature integration,* and *decision.* The model makes use of the idea of **prototypes,** which are summary descriptions of the perceptual units of language and contain a conjunction of various distinctive features. The features of the prototype correspond to the *ideal values* that a token should have if it is a member of that category. Continuously fed feature information is evaluated, integrated, and matched against prototype descriptions in memory, and an identification decision is made on the basis of the relative goodness of match of the stimulus information with the relevant prototype descriptions. The role of prototypes in determining the meanings of words is discussed in Chapter 4. According to this model, to recognize the syllable [ba], for example, the perceiver must be able to relate the information provided by the syllable itself to some memory of the category [ba], which is represented by a prototypical or idealized version of the syllable. *Feature evaluation* provides the degree to which each feature in the syllable matches the corresponding feature found in the prototype in memory. The outcome of *feature integration* consists of the degree to which each prototype matches the syllable. During *feature decision,* a relative "goodness of match" is made and the proportion of times the syllable is identified as an instance of the prototype is computed.

The model hypothesizes that multiple features corresponding to a given phonetic contrast are extracted independently from the wave form and then combined according to logical integration rules. These rules operate on *fuzzy truth values* so that information regarding a given feature may be represented in *degree of match,* rather than absolute identical *form.* This model stresses continuous rather than all-or-none information. Massaro's model thus attempts to account for the difficulties of mapping acoustic attributes onto higher-level representations by viewing phonetic perception as a probabilistic process of matching features to prototype representations in memory.

The three models just described are primarily concerned with perception of phonetic segments. Each model attempts to devise a means of correspondence between the acoustic speech signals and phonetic segments. In these models, the end results of phonetic segment identification are achieved without reference to meaning or syntax. The following two models are concerned with auditory word recognition. For these models the end result is a meaningful utterance rather than a meaningless syllable, for example. These models aim to describe the interaction between the processes of phoneme recognition and word recognition.

Cohort Model

This model of word recognition was developed by Marslen-Wilson and his colleagues (Marslen-Wilson & Welsh, 1978; Marslen-Wilson, 1987) and consists of two stages. In the first stage of word recognition, the acoustic-phonetic information at the beginning of a target word activates all words in memory that resemble it. For example, if the word is *drive*, then words beginning with [d] are activated (*dive, drink, date, dunk,* and so on). These activated words make up the "cohort." The activation of the cohort words is achieved on the basis of the acoustic information in the target word and is *not* influenced by other levels of analysis. The second stage of word recognition begins once a cohort structure is activated. In this second stage, all possible sources of information may influence the selection of the target word from the cohort. These interactive sources of information work toward *eliminating* words that don't resemble the target word. For example, further acoustic-phonetic information may eliminate some of the cohort words (*date* and *dunk*); and higher-level sources of information may appear and eliminate other members of the cohort that might not fit with the available semantic or syntactic information (*dive* and *drink*). Finally, word recognition is achieved when a single candidate remains in the cohort.

Marslen-Wilson has used his own and others' research on fluent speech perception, similar to the material presented earlier in this chapter (for example, Cole & Jakimik, 1980), in developing his theory. The theory has been revised and extended to take into account other sources of information, such as word frequency effects, which impinge on the word recognition process (Marslen-Wilson, 1987).

TRACE Model

This is a neural network model developed by Elman and McClelland (1984, 1986). It states that processing occurs through excitatory and inhibitory connections among numerous processing units called *nodes*. Phonetic or distinctive features, phonemes, and words constitute nodes that represent different levels of processing. Each node has a resting level, a threshold, and an activation level that signifies the degree to which the input is consistent with the unit that the node represents. In the presence of confirmatory evidence (input appropriate to the node), the activation level of a node rises toward its threshold; in the absence of such evidence, activation decays toward the resting level of the node.

Nodes within this system are highly interconnected, and when a given node reaches threshold, it may influence other nodes to which it is connected. Thus, a node that has reached threshold may raise the activation of some of the nodes to which it is connected, while lowering the activation of others. Connections between levels are excitatory and bidirectional. Thus, phoneme nodes may excite word nodes and word nodes may excite phoneme nodes. For example, excitation of nodes representing the phonemes [b] and [o] would conceivably lead to excitation of word nodes containing candidates whose first two sounds are [bo], such as *boat* and *bone*. Connections within levels, however, are inhibitory and bidirectional. Thus, the probability that a sound has been identified as a particular phoneme, such as [b], presumably lowers the activation levels of other nodes representing competing sounds such as [d] or [p]. This theory is still actively undergoing development, refinement, and evaluation (McClelland & Elman, 1986; Elman & Mc-Clelland, 1988; Massaro, 1989). (Note: Do not confuse the TRACE theory with the notion of traces in syntax (as described in Chapter 1), even though they are named similarly.)

SUMMARY

Human speech processing is a rapidly paced phenomenon that requires the listener to impose a phonemic identity on incoming sounds. As the sound sequences are identified, the listener can then decide which words are represented in the signal. This process is complicated because the speech typically shared between conversational participants is rapidly articulated, with great variation in the acoustic realization of phonemes.

Variation is induced by differences between speakers, by degree of care taken in articulation, and, most importantly, by the many changes in acoustic characteristics that occur when target sounds are coarticulated with other sounds in running speech. Models of speech perception must recognize and deal with the lack of invariance characteristic of spoken segments. Some have done this by suggesting that resemblance to a prototypical segment is sufficient for identification. Other researchers continue to search for invariant cues that may exist in the signal but have not yet been described.

Research also suggests lexical, syntactic, and contextual input to the speech perception process that operate in cases of unclear or unresolved acoustic information. Thus, what listeners expect to hear in a particular context is likely to affect what they think they actually heard. It is this flexible trading relationship among domains of linguistic knowledge that makes machine speech processing particularly formidable.

KEY WORDS

Synthesis

Vocoder

Redundant

Sound spectrograph

Spectrogram

Acoustics

Invariant

Coarticulation

Allophonic variation

Speaker dependent

Speaker independent

Underarticulate

Ambiguous

Vocal tract

Glottis

Larynx

Vocal folds

Phonation

Pharynx

Nasal cavity

Oral cavity

Uvula

Velum

Hard palate

Alveolar ridge

Subglottal system

Constriction

Place of articulation

Manner of production

Bilabial

Labiodental

Interdental

Alveolar

Palatal

Velar

Periodic

Voiced

Voiceless

Fundamental frequency (FO)

Aperiodic

Fricative

Affricate

Stop consonant (stop)

Liquid

Glide

Distinctive features

Continuant

Anterior

Coronal

Resonant characteristics

Spectrum

Harmonics

Amplitude

Formants

Diphthong

Vowel formants

Speaker normalization

Formant transitions

Steady state

Burst

Acoustic cues

Discrimination

Identification

Encoded

Parallel transmission

Voice-onset-time (VOT)

Cognates

Cross-over stimulus

Categorical perception

Discrimination peak

Citation form

Carrier phrase

Top-down processing

Bottom-up processing

Phonemic restoration

Listening for mispronunciation task (LM)

Motor theory of speech perception   *Prototype*
Analysis-by-synthesis   *Cohort model*
Species specific   *TRACE model*

SOMETHING TO THINK ABOUT

1. What is "the invariance problem" in speech perception? Describe the factors that contribute to the absence of invariance in the speech signal. What problems does this pose for developing computers that can understand speech?

2. Distinguish between top-down and bottom-up models of speech perception. What types of evidence suggest that speech is processed from the bottom up? What suggests that top-down processing may play a role?

3. Explain categorical perception of speech sounds. What aspects of speech are perceived categorically? What are the possible benefits to a processing system that demonstrates categorical perception?

ACTIVITIES

1. With a friend, try the following: First, each of you should make a list of random words and then a list of sentences. Stand at opposite corners of a rather large room with the lights off and play some background music to make listening more difficult. Take turns quietly reading the words and sentences to one another. Write down what you hear. Examine the accuracy of your responses. What kinds of mistakes did you make in hearing each other? How might they relate to the acoustical properties of speech sounds? Which was more accurate—hearing vowels or consonants, hearing words or sentences? Does performance improve if you turn the lights back on? Why do you think this happens?

2. Interact with a computer-assisted speech recognition system. Explain whether the system is speaker-dependent or speaker-independent. Evaluate the program's success in understanding speech. In what ways does the program mimic human speech perception abilities? In what ways does it differ from human speech perception?

REFERENCES

Abramson, A. S., & Lisker, L. (1970). Discriminability along the voicing continuum cross-language test. *Proceedings of the Sixth International Congress of Phonetic Science,* 569–573, Prague: Academia.

Blumstein, S., Cooper, W., Zurif, E., & Caramazza, A. (1977). The perception and production of voice onset time in aphasia. *Neuropsychologia, 15,* 371–383.

Blumstein, S. E., & Stevens, K. N. (1979). Acoustic invariance in speech production: Evidence from measurements of the spectral characteristics of stop consonants. *Journal of the Acoustical Society of America, 66,* 1001–1017.

Blumstein, S. E., & Stevens, K. N. (1980). Perceptual invariance and onset spectra for stop consonants in different vowel environments. *Journal of the Acoustical Society of America, 67,* 648–662.

Borden, G. J., Harris, K. S., & Raphael, L. J. (1994). *Speech science primer: physiology, acoustics, and perception of speech* (3rd ed.). Baltimore: Williams and Wilkins.

Caramazza, A., Yeni-Komshian, G. H., Zurif, E. B., & Carbone, E. (1973). The acquisition of a new phonological contrast: The case of stop consonants in French-English bilinguals. *Journal of the Acoustical Society of America, 54,* 421–428.

Cole, R. A. (1973). Listening for mispronunciations: A measure of what we hear during speech. *Perception and Psychophysics, 13,* 153–156.

Cole, R. A. (Ed.). (1980). *Perception and production of fluent speech.* Hillsdale, NJ: Erlbaum.

Cole, R. A., & Jakimik, J. (1980). A model of speech perception. In R. A. Cole (Ed.), *Perception and production of fluent speech* (pp. 133–163). Hillsdale, NJ: Erlbaum.

Cole, R. A., Jakimik, J., & Cooper, W. E. (1978). Perceptibility of phonetic features in fluent speech. *Journal of the Acoustical Society of America, 64,* 44–56.

Cooper, F. S., Delattre, P. C., Liberman, A. M., Borst, J. M., & Gerstman, L. J. (1952). Some experiments on the perception of synthetic speech sounds. *Journal of the Acoustical Society of America, 24* (6), 597–606.

Cutting, J. E., & Rosner, B. S. (1974). Categories and boundaries in speech and music. *Perception and Psychophysics, 16,* 564–570.

Daniloff, R., & Hammarberg, R. (1973). On defining coarticulation. *Journal of Phonetics, 1,* 185–194.

Delattre, P., Liberman, A. M., Cooper, F. S., & Gerstman, L. J. (1952). An experimental study of the acoustic determinants of vowel color; observations on one- and two-formant vowels synthesized from spectrographic patterns. *Word, 8,* 195–210.

Dudley, H. (1936). Synthesizing speech. *Bell Laboratories Record, 15,* 98–102.

Dudley, H. (1939). Remaking speech. *Journal of the Acoustical Society of America, 11,* 169–177.

Dudley, H., Reisz, R. R., & Watkins, S. S. A. (1939). A synthetic speaker. *Journal of the Franklin Institute, 227,* 739–764.

Eimas, P. D., & Miller, J. L. (Eds.). (1981). *Perspectives on the study of speech.* Hillsdale, NJ: Erlbaum.

Elman, J. L., & McClelland, J. L. (1984). The interactive activation model of speech perception. In N. Lass (Ed.), *Language and speech* (pp. 337–374). New York: Academic Press.

Elman, J. L., & McClelland, J. L. (1986). Exploiting lawful variability in the speech wave. In J. S. Perkell & D. H. Klatt (Eds.), *Invariance and variability in speech processes* (pp. 360–380). Hillsdale, NJ: Erlbaum.

Elman, J. L., & McClelland, J. L. (1988). Cognitive penetration of the mechanisms of perception: Compensation for coarticulation of lexically restored phonemes. *Journal of Memory & Language, 27,* 143–165.

Garnes, S., & Bond, Z. S. (1976). The relationship between semantic expectation and acoustic information. In W. Dressler & O. Pfeiffer (Eds.), *Proceedings of the Third International Phonology Meeting.* Innsbruck: Phonologische Tagung.

Handel, S. (1989). *Listening: An introduction to the perception of auditory events.* Cambridge, MA: MIT Press.

Helmholtz, H. (1859). Ueber die Klangfarbe der Vocale [On the quality of vowels]. *Ann. Phys. Chem., 108,* 280–290. See also Boring, E. G. (1942). *Sensation and perception in the history of experimental psychology.* New York: Appleton Century Crofts.

Jenkins, J. J., Strange, W., & Edman, T. R. (1983). Identification of vowels in "vowelless" syllables. *Perception and Psychophysics, 34* (5), 441–450.

Kewley-Port, D. (1982). Measurements of formant transitions in naturally produced stop consonant-vowel syllables. *Journal of the Acoustical Society of America, 72,* 379–389.

Kewley-Port, D. (1983). Time–varying features as correlates of place of articulation in stop consonants. *Journal of the Acoustical Society of America, 73,* 322–335.

Klatt, D. H. (1977). Review of the ARPA speech understanding project. *Journal of the Acoustical Society of America, 62,* 1343–1366.

Klatt, D. H., & Stevens, K. N. (1973). On the automatic recognition of continuous speech: Implications of a spectrogram-reading experiment. *IEEE Transactions. Audio Electroacoustics, AU-21,* 210–217.

Kuehn, D. P., & Moll, K. L. (1972). Perceptual effects of forward coarticulation. *Journal of Speech and Hearing Disorders, 15,* 654–664.

Kuhl, P. K., & Miller, J. D. (1975). Speech perception by the chinchilla: Voiced-voiceless distinction in alveolar plosive consonants. *Science, 190,* 69–72.

LaRiviere, C. J., Winitz, H., & Herriman, E. (1975). The distribution of perceptual cues in English prevocalic fricatives. *Journal of Speech and Hearing Disorders, 18,* 613–622.

Liberman, A. M. (1970). The grammars of speech and language. *Cognitive Psychology, 1,* 301–323.

Liberman, A. M., Delattre, P. C., & Cooper, F. S. (1952). The role of selected stimulus-variables in the perception of the unvoiced stop consonants. *American Journal of Psychology, 65,* 497–516.

Liberman, A. M., Harris, K. S., Hoffman, H. S., & Griffith, B. C. (1957). The discrimination of speech sounds within and across phoneme boundaries. *Journal of Experimental Psychology, 54,* 358–368.

Liberman, A. M., Harris, K. S., Eimas, P. D., Lisker, L., & Bastian, J. (1961). An effect of learning on speech perception: The discrimination of durations of silence with and without phonetic significance. *Language and Speech, 4,* 175–195.

Liberman, A. M., Hams, K. S., Kinney, J. A., & Lane, H. (1961). The discrimination of relative onset time of the components of certain speech and nonspeech patterns. *Journal of Experimental Psychology, 61,* 379–388.

Liberman, A. M., Cooper, F. S., Shankweiler, D. P., & Studdert-Kennedy, M. (1967). Perception of the speech code. *Psychological Review, 74,* 431–461.

Liberman, A. M., & Mattingly, I. G. (1985). The motor theory of speech perception revised. *Cognition, 21,* 1–36.

Liberman, A. M., & Mattingly, I. G. (1989). A specialization for speech perception. *Science, 243,* 489–494.

Lisker, L., & Abramson, A. S. (1964). A cross-language study of voicing in initial stops: Acoustical measurements. *Word, 20,* 384–422.

MacKain, K., Best, C., & Strange, W. (1981). Categorical perception of English /r/ and /l/ by Japanese bilinguals. *Applied Psycholinguistics, 2,* 369–390.

Mann, V. A., & Repp, B. H. (1980). Influence of vocalic context on perception of the [ʃ]–[s] distinction. *Perception and Psychophysics, 28,* 213–228.

Marslen-Wilson, W. D. (1987). Functional parallelism in spoken word recognition. *Cognition, 25,* 71–102.

Marslen-Wilson, W. D., & Welsh, A. (1978). Processing interactions and lexical access during word recognition in continuous speech. *Cognitive Psychology, 10,* 29–63.

Massaro, D. W. (1987). *Speech perception by ear and eye: A paradigm for psychological inquiry.* Hillsdale, NJ: Erlbaum.

Massaro, D. W. (1989). Testing between the TRACE model and the fuzzy logical model of speech perception. *Cognitive Psychology, 21,* 398–421.

Massaro, D. W., & Oden, G. C. (1980). Speech perception: A framework for research and theory. In N. J. Lass (Ed.), *Speech and language: Advances in basic research and practice* (Vol. 3) (pp. 129–165). New York: Academic Press.

McClelland, J. L., & Elman, J. L. (1986). The TRACE model of speech perception. *Cognitive Psychology, 18,* 1–86.

Miller, G. A., & Nicely, P. (1955). An analysis of perceptual confusions among some English consonants. *Journal of the Acoustical Society of America, 27,* 338–352.

Miller, J. L. (1981). Effects of speaking rate on segmental distinctions. In P. D. Eimas & J. L. Miller (Eds.), *Perspectives on the study of speech.* Hillsdale, NJ: Erlbaum.

Miller, G. A., Heise, G. A., & Lichten, W. (1951). The intelligibility of speech as a function of the context of the test materials. *Journal of Experimental Psychology, 41,* 329–335.

Miller, J. D., Weir, C. C., Pastore, R., Kelly, W. J., & Dooling, R. J. (1976). Discrimination and labeling of noise-buzz sequences with varying noise-lead times: An example of categorical perception. *Journal of the Acoustical Society of America, 60,* 410–417.

Perkell, J. S., & Klatt, D. H. (Eds.). (1986). *Invariance and variability in speech processes.* Hillsdale, NJ: Erlbaum.

Pickett, J. M. (1980). *The sounds of speech communication: A primer of acoustic phonetics and speech perception.* Baltimore: University Park Press.

Pisoni, D. B. (1975). Auditory short-term memory and vowel perception. *Memory and Cognition, 3,* 7–18.

Pisoni, D. B. (1977). Identification and discrimination of the relative onset time of two component tones: Implications for voicing perception in stops. *Journal of the Acoustical Society of America, 61,* 1352–1361.

Pisoni, D. B. (1978). Speech perception. In W. K. Estes (Ed.), *Handbook of learning and cognitive processes* (Vol. 6) (pp. 167–233). Hillsdale, NJ: Erlbaum.

Pisoni, D. B., & Luce, P. A. (1986). Speech perception: Research, theory, and the principal issues. In E. C. Schwab & H. C. Nusbaum (Eds.), *Pattern recognition by humans and machines: Vol. I* (pp. 1–50). Orlando: Academic Press.

Pisoni, D. B., & Luce, P. A. (1987). Acoustic-phonetic representations in word recognition. *Cognition, 25,* 21–52.

Pollack, I., & Pickett, J. M. (1964). The intelligibility of excerpts from conversation. *Language and Speech, 6,* 165–171.

Potter, R., Kopp, G., & Green, H. (1947). *Visible speech.* New York: Van Nostrand Reinhold (reprinted in 1966 by Dover Press).

Reddy, R. (1976). Speech recognition by machine: A review. *Proceedings of the IEEE, 64,* 501–531.

Repp, B. H. (1984). Categorical perception: Issues, methods, findings. In N. J. Lass (Ed.), *Speech and language: Advances in basic research and practice,* (Vol. 10), (pp. 243–335). New York: Academic Press.

Samuel, A. G. (1986). The role of the lexicon in speech perception. In E. C. Schwab & H. C. Nusbaum (Eds.), *Pattern recognition by humans and machines: Vol. 1.* (pp. 89–111). Orlando: Academic Press.

Schroeder, M. R. (1966). Vocoders: Analysis and synthesis of speech. *Proceedings of the IEEE, 54* (5), 720–734.

Schwab, E. C., & Nusbaum, H. C. (Eds.). (1986). *Pattern recognition by humans and machines: Vol. 1. Speech perception*, Series in Cognition and Perception. Orlando: Academic Press.

Spoehr, K. T. (1981). Word recognition in speech and reading: Toward a single theory of language processing. In P. D. Eimas & J. L. Miller (Eds.), *Perspectives on the study of speech* (pp. 239–282). Hillsdale, NJ: Erlbaum.

Stevens, K. N. (1960). Toward a model for speech recognition. *Journal of the Acoustical Society of America, 32,* 47–55.

Stevens, K. N., & Halle, M. (1967). Remarks on analysis by synthesis and distinctive features. In W. Wathen-Dunn (Ed.), *Models for the perception of speech and visual form* (pp. 88–102). Cambridge, MA: MIT Press.

Stevens, K. N., & Blumstein, S. E. (1978). Invariant cues for place of articulation in stop consonants. *Journal of the Acoustical Society of America, 64,* 1358–1368.

Stevens, K. N., & Blumstein, S. E. (1981). The search for invariant acoustic correlates of phonetic features. In P. D. Eimas & J. L. Miller (Eds.), *Perspectives on the study of speech* (pp. 1–38). Hillsdale, NJ: Erlbaum.

Stevens, K. N., & Ohman, S. E. G. (1969). Crosslanguage study of vowel perception. *Language and Speech, 12,* 1–23.

Strange, W. (1989a). Evolving theories of vowel perception. *Journal of the Acoustical Society of America, 85,* 2081–2087.

Strange, W. (1989b). Dynamic specification of coarticulated vowels spoken in sentence context. *Journal of the Acoustical Society of America, 85,* 2135–2153.

Strange, W. (Ed.). (1995). *Speech perception and linguistic experience: issues in cross-language research.* Baltimore: York Press.

Strange, W., & Jenkins, J. J. (1978). Role of linguistic experience in the perception of speech. In D. Walk & H. J. Pick, Jr. (Eds.), *Perception and experience* (pp. 125–169). New York: Plenum.

Strange, W., & Dittman, S. (1984). Effects of discrimination training on the perception of /r-l/ by Japanese adults learning English. *Perception and Psychophysics, 36,* 131–145.

Summerfield, Q., & Haggard, M. P. (1974). Perceptual processing of multiple cues and contexts: Effects of following vowel upon stop consonant voicing. *Journal of Phonetics, 2,* 279–295.

Sussman, H. M., McCaffrey, H. A., & Matthews, S. A. (1991). An investigation of locus equations as a source of relational invariance for stop place categorization. *Journal of the Acoustical Society of America, 90,* 1309–1325.

Wang, M. D., & Bilger, R. C. (1973). Consonant confusion in noise: A study of perceptual features. *Journal of the Acoustical Society of America, 54,* 1248–1266.

Warren, R. M. (1970). Perceptual restoration of missing speech sounds. *Science, 167,* 392–395.

Williams, L. (1977). The perception of stop consonant voicing by Spanish-English bilinguals. *Perception and Psychophysics, 21* (4), 289–297.

Williams, L. (1980). Phonetic variation as a function of second-language learning. In G. H. Yeni-Komshian, J. F. Kavanagh, & C. A. Ferguson (Eds.), *Child phonology, perception: Vol. 2* (pp. 185–215). New York: Academic Press.

Willis, R. (1829). On vowel sounds and on reed organ pipes. *Trans. Cambridge Philosoph. Soc., 3,* 231–268.

Yeni–Komshian, G. H., & LaFontaine, L. (1983). Discrimination and identification of voicing and place contrasts in aphasic patients. *Canadian Journal of Psychology, 37,* 107–131.

Yeni-Komshian, G. H., & Soli, S. D. (1981). Recognition of vowels from information in fricatives: Perceptual evidence of fricative-vowel coarticulation. *Journal of the Acoustical Society of America, 70,* 966–975.

Zue, V. W. (1985). The use of speech knowledge in automatic speech recognition. *Proceedings of the IEEE, 73,* 1602–1615.

Zue, V. W. (1991). From signals to symbols to meaning: On machine understanding of spoken language. *Proceedings of the 12th International Congress of Phonetic Sciences, 1,* 74–83.

Chapter 4

WORDS AND MEANING: FROM PRIMITIVES TO COMPLEX ORGANIZATION

Lauretta M. Reeves
Rowan University

Kathy Hirsh-Pasek
Temple University

Roberta Golinkoff
University of Delaware

> 'Twas brillig, and the slithy toves
> did gyre and gimble in the wabe,
> All mimsy were the borogroves,
> And the mome raths outgrabe.
> (Carroll, 1862, p.176)

INTRODUCTION

Most educated adults probably know between 75,000 (Oldfield, 1963) and 150,000 words (Seashore & Eckerson, 1940). These large vocabularies, however, do not contain *brillig* or *gimble*. Nevertheless, we know how to pronounce each of the nonsense words and sense whether each is functioning as a noun or verb or adjective. Do we, then, deduce meaning, however limited, from this passage from "Jabberwocky"? Further, if we can deduce information about fictional words, how much more can we know about real ones? In this chapter, we will address this question by discussing the organization and processing of words and of meanings.

Many people consider words as the building blocks of language; words and combinations of words allow us to symbolize objects and events in the world around us. The study of words and meaning (defined as **semantics** in Chapter 1) has a long and rich history dating back at least to the writings of Democritus *(On Words)* and Plato *(Cratylus)*.

One philosophical issue in the study of semantics is how words are bound to their meanings. For words such as *swish* the connection is obvious: the word sounds like the movement of water or draperies that it represents. Not all words have such an obvious connection to their meaning. A cat does not make sounds like [kæt] when it walks, purrs, or eats. Shakespeare remarked "that which we call a rose, By any other name would smell as sweet" (Shakespeare, 1975, p.1020). This famous quote hints at the arbitrary relationship between most words and the concepts to which they refer. Words typically lack the causal connection between sound and meaning that exists in onomatopoeia (for example, *kaboom*), although strong word-meaning links exist because of social convention. That is, we agree to call a humorous story with a punch line a "joke" so that we can communicate with other people who hold the same definition of *joke*. If someone offers to tell us a joke, we do not expect them to give a eulogy.

In this chapter, we use both psychological experiments and philosophical theorizing to obtain answers to questions such as: Where do we store words? How are they organized in our minds, and how do we recognize words that we see or hear? What is meaning? And how do words relate to meanings? The past two decades of research and writing on these topics have been particularly productive and have offered partial answers to these questions.

In the sections that follow we will pursue the difficult task of considering words and meaning separately (after all, we call things "words" because they convey a meaning). At the end of the chapter, we will link the two domains back together as we explore how listeners and readers process **lexical ambiguity**—words that have multiple meanings.

WORDS AND MEANINGS: SEPARATE BUT LINKED DOMAINS

Numerous findings, some anecdotal and some empirical, conclude that words and meanings are related but separate entities. Three lines of argument make this point. The first, the *translation* argument, suggests that any given language includes some words that do not depend on meaning for their existence and some meanings for which there are no single words. If meanings and words were tightly yoked all of the time, this could not be true. The second argument for a separation of words and meanings comes from the *imperfect mapping* illustration, which suggests that a given language can have many meanings for a specific word and many different words for a given meaning. Finally, the third argument for treating words and meanings as separate comes from the *elasticity* demonstration, which illustrates that a word meaning can change in different contexts. Let us briefly examine each of these arguments.

Most of us have experienced the *translation* argument. For example, the Yiddish word, *schlep,* requires a long-winded explanation in English "To move a heavy and usually bulky item from place to place." Those who have incorporated this Yiddish term into their vocabularies can talk about "schlepping" a load of books from class to class. Here we have a good *meaning* for which English possesses no single *word.* Similarly, we can create any number of words that have little meaning. In the poem cited above, *borogrove* offers one example. (*Borogrove* does have a meaning, according to Humpty Dumpty, but you'll have to wait until the end of the chapter to find out what it is.) We've all had the experience of recognizing a word as a word without knowing what it means. Thus, we can know words for which we have no meanings stored in our brain. For example, many people are uncertain of the meaning of *churlish* ("coarse, rude, and vulgar"). And many nonmusicians know that *adagio* is a word without knowing that it means "slowly."

Of the empirical demonstrations of the translation problem, two are particularly well known. The first comes from a study by Heider, now Rosch (1972), in which she investigated the language of the Dani, a modern-day Stone Age tribe who live in Indonesian New Guinea. Their language has only two color terms, *mola,* which designates bright, warm hues, and *mili,* which designates dark, cold hues. Does this limited color vocabulary imply that the Dani people perceive or recognize only two colors? No, it appears that the Dani can process more than just how dark or bright colors are.

In fact, Heider's (1972) research on the topic suggested that the Dani people see the color spectrum in exactly the same way that we do. A second celebrated example shows the impoverished English vocabulary for different kinds of snow. Whereas Eskimos have four different root words for snow, *aput* ("snow on the ground"), *quana* ("falling snow"), *pigsirpog* ("drifting snow"), and *qimuqsuq* ("a snow drift"), English speakers have only the lonely word *snow* (Boas, 1911; Pullum, 1990). In short then, the translation argument demonstrates the distinction between words and meanings because, although they are closely related, each can exist without the other.

The *imperfect mapping* illustration also refutes one-to-one mapping of words and meanings. Here we see many different meanings for a single word (ambiguity) and many words for a single meaning (synonymy). Thus, meaning can be marked in any number of different ways with language. One of the best illustrations of word ambiguity comes from the study of jokes and riddles. The success of some jokes hinges on setting up one meaning of a word when another is actually required (Fowles & Glanz, 1977; Hirsh-Pasek, Gleitman, & Gleitman, 1978; Shultz & Horibe, 1974). The following admittedly bad joke makes the point clear:

Doctor: Eyes checked?

Patient: No, they're blue.

The humor (such as it is) derives from the word *checked,* which has two meanings, one referring to the act of looking or examining and the other referring to a perceptual pattern. Experiments on word ambiguity demonstrate that people have multiple meanings available for words at any given time in processing. For example, Simpson (1981) found that in processing ambiguous sentences such as, "We had trouble keeping track of the *count,"* both meanings of the word—number of items and European nobleman—were called up from subjects' mental dictionary (although this need not be conscious and is demonstrable only through experimental techniques).

The other half of the imperfect-mapping illustration turns on the availability of two or more words for a single meaning, or synonymy. Although some argue against the existence of true synonyms (Clark, 1987), to many of us the words *sofa* and *couch* mean the same thing; so do the words *pail* and *bucket.*[1]

Finally, there is the *elasticity* argument, the demonstration that words can have varied meanings depending on the contexts in which they are found. Some clear examples are adjectives that modify different properties of words in different contexts. A "tall tale" is a story with exaggerated aspects to it, and the adjective *tall* clearly conveys something slightly different than when we describe a man as tall. Likewise, a "light" class load suggests that a student who is taking only a few classes has lots of free time, not that his or her schedule doesn't weigh much, as in a "light" child (see

---

[1] However, some words are more suited to certain contexts, and synonyms alter the meaning of the sentence itself (even if the words are identical in meaning). For example, "name" and "nomenclature" have identical meanings. However, Shakespeare's romantic quip, "A rose by any other name would smell as sweet," loses some of its poetic charge in, "A rose by any other nomenclature would smell as sweet." Again, the fact that meanings and words are not exclusively linked to one another leaves room for a separate examination of each domain.

Katz & Fodor, 1963). As these examples clearly show, word meanings sometimes hinge on the words that they appear with and are often context dependent. Thus, meanings and words are not unequivocally yoked.

Taken together, these three arguments suggest that words and their meanings, although closely related, are not identical. Having driven the wedge between these two types of psychological entities, it becomes possible to examine each domain separately. Indeed, within the field of psychology, these two topics have been differently treated. Research has typically studied how words are understood or recognized in speech or reading, whereas the study of meaning has concentrated on how these meanings are stored. In the discussion that follows, we look at the organization and processing of words in the mental *lexicon* (Greek for "dictionary"), and then ask about the representation of meaning within the mind. For notational clarity, whenever we refer to a specific word, we will italicize that word: *chicken.* Whenever we refer to the meaning of a particular word, we will enclose the meaning in quotation marks: "chicken." Thus, *chicken* refers to the name or word that we use. Presumably, if the English-speaking community decided en masse to change the name to *bukbuk,* no one would be deeply offended. However, changing the name would not change the meaning to which we are referring, it would still be a "chicken," defined as "a galvanatious bird," or offspring that has chickens as parents. No worldwide council could arbitrarily change these facts of definition, for once a chicken ceases to have parents who are chickens, its very essence is altered. Given that we can now talk separately about words and meanings, let's discuss what philosophers and psychologists say about words and their meanings.

THE STUDY OF WORDS

In this section on words, we explore (1) the form in which words are stored in our mental lexicon—for example, how complex words are constructed (in language production) or recognized (in language comprehension)—and (2) what factors contribute to the access or retrieval of words. Psychologists have used a variety of experimental techniques to study these issues. Let us first turn to a discussion of the theoretical issues that underlie this research.

Word Primitives

Let us begin by dissecting the sentence, *The impartial judge ruled the defendants guilty.* Is the action taking place now? Was more than one person convicted? Was the judge biased or not? Although the sentence is composed of only seven words, many of these words are complex and contain affixes that convey important information. For example, the suffixes *-ed* in *ruled,* and the *-s* on the end of *defendants* indicate that the judge's decision took place in the past and affected more than one guilty person. Furthermore, the prefix *im-* in *impartial* indicates that the judge was assumed to be making a fair and unbiased decision *(im- = not + partial)*. Accordingly, words such as *impartial, ruled,* and *defendants* are deemed multimorphemic words, where a **morpheme** is defined as the "smallest meaningful unit of language," a concept introduced in Chapter 1. Morphemes can be words in themselves (for example, *judge*) or simply appendages to words (for example, *-s* at the end of *judges or im-* at the beginning of *impartial*). Morphemes that can stand by themselves as words are called **free morphemes;** those that require attachment to other units are known as **bound morphemes.**

One hypothesis about **word primitives** (the smallest form in which a word is stored in the mental lexicon) argues that each word (even a multimorphemic word) is a separate entry (or **lexeme**) in our lexicons, and is thus its own primitive (Aitchison, 1987; Aronoff, 1976; Monsell, 1985; Sandra, 1990). This hypothesis states that each variant of a word (for example, *book, books, bookish, bookshelf,* and so on) has its own representation. When we produce multimorphemic words, such as *impartial* or *defendants,* we retrieve the plural form of the word directly. Likewise, according to this hypothesis, when we hear or read a word, we access its lexeme as a whole.

An alternative (and more widely held) hypothesis is that words are made up of constituent morphemes and that these morphemes serve as word primitives (MacKay, 1979; Murrell & Morton, 1974; Smith & Sterling, 1982; Taft, 1981; Taft & Forster, 1975, 1976). When we listen to someone speaking, we *decompose* words into morphemes in order to comprehend spoken language. This view of word primitives assumes that we "strip" a word of all affixes and then activate the root word *(rule)* plus the relevant bound morphemes *(-ed)*. Likewise, the decompositional view states that when we speak, we access individual morphemes and combine them to make up complex words.

The decompositional view of **morphemes as word primitives** has the advantage of **cognitive economy** (efficient use of cognitive resources), because not every variant of a word needs to be stored in the lexicon. Fewer lexical units are needed, because the bound morpheme *-s*, which indicates plural *defendants* in the sentence above, can also be combined with every other noun that can be pluralized. The word-as-word-primitive view would require at least *two* lexical entries for every noun—the root noun *and* its plural (for example, *table* and *tables; idea* and *ideas; forgery* and *forgeries*). This seems an illogical and unnecessary use of space. The alternative view argues that although storing multimorphemic words as separate entries may take up more memory space, it saves on processing time. That is, assembling *up-* and *grade* takes cognitive energy that can be saved if *upgrade* is stored as a single word.

EVIDENCE ABOUT WORD PRIMITIVES.   You now have two theories of what constitutes a word primitive: (1) Each word (even multimorphemic ones) has its own lexical entry, known as a lexeme; (2) constituent morphemes are individually stored in the lexicon so that words are decomposed (during comprehension) or composed (during production). The issue of whether whole words or individual morphemes function as word primitives may shed some light on the productivity exhibited by even the most novice users of language. Just as we are able to construct an infinite number of sentences because of our implicit knowledge of syntax, people are able to construct new words from their knowledge of morphology. If we asked you to change *snark* into a verb, you would have no trouble offering *snarking*. If the request was for an adjective, *snarkish* might come to mind; and for an adverb, *snarkfully* would fit. Knowledge of word primitives can also tell us where the cognitive system is devoting the most energy: With the lexeme view of words, much space would be devoted to maintaining multiple variations of words in the lexicon. The morpheme-as-primitive theory requires less storage space but greater capacity to perform the processes of constructing or decomposing words into their constituent morphemes.

What methods could be used to test whether people store whole words or morphemes in their lexicon? One technique is that of a **lexical decision task.** As you read the words below, tap with your right index finger to indicate Yes—the string of letters is a real word; tap with your left index finger to indicate No— the letter string is a nonsense word.

table

vanue

daughter

tasp

coref

hunter

You probably had no difficulty deciding Yes, No, Yes, No, No, Yes on the above entries. However, in a real lexical decision task, the letter strings would be presented on either a computer or **tachistoscope** (an apparatus that allows the experimenter to strictly control the duration of a stimulus), and your response would have been measured in milliseconds (one millisecond = one-thousandth of a second). The time it takes to respond Yes or No to each letter string is composed both of the time it takes to tap your respective index finger (or a computer key), time for **lexical access,** plus the decision time to tap with your left or right finger (to indicate Yes or No).

In the case of the real words—*table, daughter*—accessing your lexicon would have yielded recognition that these were indeed real words. Notice that although both *daughter,* and *hunter* have an *-er* ending, hunter is a multimorphemic word composed of *hunt* + *-er*, whereas *daughter* is only a single morpheme word that cannot be composed into *daught* + *-er*. It is therefore said to be a **pseudo-suffixed** word. Even more confusing might be *corner,* whose composition into *corn* (a legitimate word) plus *-er* would not yield the meaning of *corner* in the same way that *hunt* + *-er* divulges the meaning of *hunter.*

Many studies have found that it takes longer to process multimorphemic words than words composed of a single morpheme. In a speech production task, MacKay (1978) presented subjects with root morphemes (for example, *decide*) and asked them to respond with a variant of that word (for example, *decision*). The more morphologically complex the response, the longer the **reaction times.** For instance, *indecision,* which adds two bound morphemes to the root, would take longer to construct than *deciding,* which adds only one.

Which position one adopts, however—a decompositional view of morphology, or a whole-lexeme view—may depend on the kinds of morphemes being discussed. **Derivational morphemes** significantly alter the root morphemes to which they are added. For instance, the derivational prefix *dis-* changes *agree* and *interested* to their negatives *(disagree; disinterested)*. Many derivational morphemes also change the **grammatical class** of a word, as when the suffix *-er,* when added to *learn, hunt,* or *swim,* changes each verb into a noun. **Inflectional morphemes** (which all occur as suffixes in English) do not, however, significantly alter the root morphemes to which they are added. The *-s* or *-es* added onto words to indicate plurality is one such inflectional change. *Wish* and *wishes* are not completely different words, nor are *dolphin* and *dolphins.* Likewise, *-ed* or *-s* tacked onto the end of a verb merely changes its tense or person (for example, *jumped; swims*). Assessing whether people perform morpheme stripping (upon hearing and seeing a word) and morpheme assembly (when they produce speech) may depend on the kind of morpheme—derivational or inflectional—being discussed.

One experiment which supported a decompositional view of word storage found that words masquerading as multimorphemic items increase reaction times. Taft (1981) found that words such as *result* or *interest,* which appear to have prefixes (*re-* and *inter-,* respectively) took longer to respond to in a lexical decision task than either actual prefixed words (for example, *recall, interstate*) or unprefixed words (for example, *table, focus*). The search process for the pseudoprefixed words takes longer, argued Taft, because subjects strip away the *re-* or *inter-* and search for the root morphemes *sult* or *est,* which of course are not legitimate root morphemes.

Furthermore, when people make speech errors, morphemes often "float away" from each other. Substitutions of morphemes, such as *It waits to pay,* (for *It pays to wait.*) (Garrett, 1976, 1980), and perseverations of affixes, such as *ministers in the churches* (for *ministers in the church*) are quite common (Shattuck-Hufnagel, 1979). The migration of *-ed* in the example, *She wash upped the dishes,* (Aitchison, 1987) illustrates that many root and bound morphemes are independently retrieved and combined later in the speech production process. A decompositional view of the lexicon can also explain errors such as *The labrador bited the cat,* in which a person appears to be assembling morphemes based on a linguistic rule, rather than pulling *bited* out of the lexicon. Notice, however, that the errors cited above all involve inflectional suffixes (see Chapter 7 for more details of speech error data and analysis). Neuropsychological evidence of speech comprehension in Broca's aphasics also supports the concept that some root and bound morphemes are separately represented in the lexicon (Tyler, Behrens, Cobb, & Marslen-Wilson, 1990).

Thus some evidence indicates that people economically store morphologically complex words as individual morphemes, which are then combined (in speech production) or stripped (in comprehension). Might occasions arise, however, when it is beneficial to represent multimorphemic words as whole lexemes?

Frequently encountered affixes and compound words may indeed be stored whole as lexemes. In fact, to realize that many words (for example, *disguise; pardon*) were multimorphemic would require knowledge of Latin. For example, the common suffixed word *impossible* may be accessed as a single word, even though the less common *imperceptible* is processed through its separate morphemes (Carroll, 1986).

And what about **compound words,** such as *gingerbread,* which are clearly made up of two separate lexical entries? Sandra (1990), Monsell (1985), and Osgood and Hoosain (1974) found evidence that some compound words such as *butterfly* may have independent lexical entries in addition to entries for their morphemic constituents *(butter* and *fly).* Why? Because *butterfly* is **semantically opaque;** that is, its meaning is not simply a combination of the meanings of *butter* + *fly.* The words *buttonhole, teaspoon,* and *beanpole,* on the other hand, are **semantically transparent** complex words—their meanings are easily discernible from their constituent parts. A *buttonhole* is simply a hole for a button.

Semantic priming tasks have also been used to support a distinction in lexical storage and processing between semantically transparent and opaque terms. Semantic priming is analogous to hooking two cars together with battery cables: Some of the energy from the first car's battery gives an extra boost to the second car's start-up. Even if the second car would have started on its own, the energy traveling through the jumper cables makes it start up that much faster. Likewise, if we pair, or "hook up," two words related in meaning, recognition of one word will "jump start" recognition of associated words.

Semantic priming has been demonstrated through a variant on lexical decision tasks: Imagine that two people are participating in a lexical decision task. Each of them must make a decision about whether a pair of letter strings are both words or not. One subject receives the word *bread,* then *doctor;* the other receives *bread,* immediately followed by *butter.* Meyer and Schvaneveldt (1971) found faster response times to the second word when the first word was semantically related (for example, *bread–butter*) than when the two words were unrelated. The first word **primed** recognition of the second (semantically related) word. Semantic associates also have been found to prime semantically transparent compound words, but not semantically opaque compound words. For example, *pea* facilitated recognition of *beanpole,* but *bread* did not prime *butterfly* (Monsell, 1985; Osgood & Hoosain, 1974; Sandra, 1990). These findings support the idea that semantically transparent words such as *beanpole* are processed as two separate morphemes and semantically opaque terms are processed as a single morpheme.

Defense of a morpheme-stripping view may also have to hinge on the kinds of morphemes appended to root morphemes during lexical processing as opposed to those permanently appended and stored as independent lexical entries. For example, bound morphemes consist both of prefixes (the *un-* in *unhappy*) and suffixes (*-est* in *happiest*). Much evidence suggests that derivational endings (for example, *dis-, un-, -er, -ish*) are more firmly attached to root morphemes; inflectional morphemes are more likely to be added on as we speak. When people make word substitutions during speech errors, they tend to maintain the derivational suffixes of words, as in *provisional* for *provincial* (Aitchison & Straf, 1982). But, as noted earlier, inflectional suffixes float around during speech errors as if they were added on in the course of speech: "She wash upped the dishes" (Aitchison, 1987). In lexical decision tasks, it does not take any longer to recognize a derivationally suffixed word, such as *dust-y,* than a pseudosuffixed word, such as *fancy* (Manelis & Tharp, 1977). This is not to say that we can't have spare derivational morphemes separately stored in order to create new words as the need arises. For instance, *smiler* is not a common root + derivational morpheme combination, but we can both produce it and comprehend it with ease.

Furthermore, some of the differences between studies supporting a decompositional versus a lexeme view of the lexicon may depend upon task demands. Rubin, Becker, and Freeman (1979) found differences in lexical processing time between suffixed (for example, *sender*) and pseudosuffixed words (for example, *sister*) only when at least 50% of the experimental list was composed of suffixed words. This suggests that subjects may have resorted to the strategy of decomposing words into morphemes after noticing that many of the words in the list were multimorphemic.

SUMMARY.   It appears, then, that lexical processing tries to strike the best balance between cognitive economy in memory and economy in assembling and decomposing multimorphemic words. Inflectional suffixes such as *-ing* or *-s,* which do not significantly change the meaning or grammatical class of their root morphemes, are most likely to be appended (or stripped) during processing. Frequently occurring multimorphemic words *(disagree),* and those with derivational morphemes *(teacher),* however, often have separate lexical entries from their root morphemes. Compound words whose meaning cannot be discerned from the combination of the two constituents (called semantically opaque), such as *hippocampus,* may also have their own lexemes. Semantically transparent terms such as *firehouse* may be composed from their two independent morphemes. Furthermore, morpheme-stripping may be a strategy subjects adopt when they realize that many words in a list are morphologically complex. Task demands may thus alter normal lexical processing.

The cognitive system seems to strike a balance between saving mental "dictionary" space and saving processing energy. If commonly used multimorphemic words are stored as their own entries, this takes up more lexical space but saves combining morphemes every time we use (or hear or read) those words. On the other hand, storing every plural of every noun we know violates the concept of cognitive economy, and it may be simpler just to add the *-s* to nouns as we need it. Separate lexical storage of root and inflectional morphemes saves mental dictionary space but may not significantly tax the processing system during recombination (or decomposition) of those words. Why is this important? The ability to be creative with language and to create new words as needed dictates that we have a flexible system that can adopt different processing strategies as needed. The cognitive system thus balances between thrift in space and thrift in processing.

Factors Influencing Word Access and Organization

What if we were to ask you to create a computer model that mimicked the way in which your mental dictionary or lexicon was organized? Where would you begin? What principles might you use to sort those 150,000 words into separate files so that they could be retrieved when necessary? Would you first separate the words into files based on their initial **phoneme** or sound (for example, all the /s/ words would be stored together, or rhyming words like *name* and *same*)? Would you separate words into files according to semantic category (for example, fruits, animals), or semantic opposites (for example, salt–pepper)? Maybe you would attend to the frequency of words, so that the most commonly used words would be stored in their own file for easy access? What about dividing words into grammatical classes, so that *jump, tree,* and *sweet* would be in separate verb, noun, and adjective files, respectively, within the computer program? Or perhaps you would prefer a more flexible organization, so that word characteristics that influence retrieval would depend on your purposes at that time. That is, when you write poetry, you could access words by phonology or syllable or accent structure in order to construct rhymes and rhythms, but in delivering a speech, you could retrieve words based on the meaning you want to convey.

You may be thinking that you can sort words for retrieval in many different ways, and you are probably right. Models of lexical access need to account for this intuition and for various empirical findings that suggest that word recognition and retrieval are influenced by several key characteristics of words themselves. That is, factors such as the relative frequency of a lexical entry, its grammatical class, how it is pronounced, can all influence the speed and accuracy of access to that word. Some of these factors may influence lexical access directly; or they may influence the structure of the lexicon itself—how it is organized.

FREQUENCY.   Which word is more common: *predict* or *vilify? angry* or *puddle?* Multiple studies suggest that we tend to respond to high-frequency words more quickly than to low-frequency words in both lexical decision tasks (Rubenstein, Garfield, & Millikan, 1970) and naming tasks, where subjects are asked to read strings of letters aloud (Forster & Chambers, 1973). The effect of frequency on lexical processing is a robust experimental finding: While reading or listening to someone speak, subjects tend to recognize high-frequency words more quickly and easily than low-frequency words. Subjects with aphasia (discussed in Chapter 2) are typically more accurate at reading aloud high-frequency words than low-frequency words (for example, Ellis, Miller, & Sin, 1983).

Because of the consistency of these findings, frequency has played a major role in the development of models of lexical access. However, the presence of the **frequency effect** and the degree to which it affects lexical processing may depend on the type of task being studied. For example, Balota and Chumbley (1984) found large effects of frequency on lexical decision tasks, a moderate frequency effect in naming tasks, and only a small effect in category verification (where subjects respond True or False to statements such as, "A *canary* is a bird"). Because all three tasks involve lexical access, frequency should have affected all three to at least a moderate extent, argued Balota and Chumbley. They thus concluded processes that occur *after* lexical access, such as decision processes ("Is this a real word or isn't it?") or pronunciation, are responsible for frequency effects. The evidence taken as a whole suggests that frequency plays a role in lexical access, but the effects can be attenuated by subsequent lexical processing.

IMAGEABILITY AND CONCRETENESS AND ABSTRACTNESS.   As you read each of the following words, close your eyes and try to picture the object or idea portrayed by the words: *umbrella, lantern, freedom, apple, knowledge, evil.* Were *umbrella, lantern,* and *apple* easier to image? Did you have difficulty coming up with internal pictures for *freedom, knowledge,* and *evil?* If not, you probably imaged a symbol for the concept portrayed, such as the Liberty Bell for "freedom," rather than generate an image of the word meaning per se. This issue is sometimes divided into one of concreteness and abstractness; concrete words such as *apple* are more imageable, and abstract words such as *knowledge* are less easy to image. Paivio (1969) found that high-imagery words were more easily recalled in a memory test than low-imagery words. Bleasdale (1987) also found that, in a lexical decision task, words primed other words only when both words were of the same type, for example, concrete–concrete or abstract–abstract, but not concrete–abstract or vice versa. From this, he concluded that the lexicon is organized separately for concrete and abstract words.

The principle of imageability also interacts with the principle of frequency in word access; high-frequency high-imagery words (such as *student*) are best accessed and recalled; low-frequency low-imagery words (such as *excuse*) are least easily accessed. High-frequency low-imagery words (such as *justice*) and low-frequency high-imagery words (such as *elbow*) are somewhere in the middle (Paivio, 1969).

SEMANTICS.   As you read each of the following words, say aloud the first word that comes to mind:

   wet

   swift

   petal

   apple

   shoot

You may have said, "Dry, fast, flower, fruit, gun." If so, in each case you named a semantic associate (that is, a word related in meaning) of the initial words, even though *wet* and *dry* are related in a different way from *apple* and *fruit*. The first pair is based upon opposites in meaning; the second on category membership (see Miller, 1951, for a more detailed classification).

When adults (Jenkins, 1970) or children (Palermo, 1963) have been asked to engage in word association experiments, similar to the mini-experiment above, three major findings have occurred. First, subjects are most likely to respond with a semantically similar word (Ervin, 1957). This suggests a stronger connection among words based on meaning than on, say, perceptual similarity. When presented with *needle*, the likely candidates in a word association task are *thread, pin,* or *sew*, but not *nail* or *poker,* which resemble a needle. Second, subjects are most likely to free associate the completion of a pair: *salt* triggers *pepper,* and *king* triggers *queen.* Third, adults (but not necessarily children) are most likely to respond with a word of the same grammatical class as the target—noun with noun *(chair–table),* verb with verb *(run–jump),* and adjective with adjective *(dark–light).* There is no reason in principle why subjects in word association tasks would not choose similar sounding words (as in *wheedle* for *needle*), but they don't. These three findings reaffirm the notion that two main principles of word organization and access of lexical entries are *meaning* and *grammatical class.*

Freedman and Loftus (1971) found that subjects could name more (and more quickly) "Fruits beginning with P" than "P-words that are fruits." Listing the category word first better activated words beginning with a specific letter within that category. Hints about a word's semantic nature get us closer to the lexical entry for that word than do hints about its initial letter.

Further evidence for the role of semantics within lexical access and organization of the lexicon comes from brain-damaged patients. Marshall and Newcombe (1966) reported an aphasic patient who would often retrieve a semantic associate when reading. For example, he said, "sister," when trying to read *daughter;* "long," instead of *large,* and substituted "mauve" for *purple.* This is a common occurrence in many aphasics, and indicates a connection between words with related meanings within the lexicon.

Finally, recall the semantic priming effect, mentioned earlier. All of the available evidence suggests that word meaning and semantic connections among words in the lexicon greatly influence word access.

GRAMMATICAL CLASS.   Words also seem to be organized based on their grammatical class, such as whether they are nouns, verbs, or adjectives. Evidence for grammatical class as a lexical organizing principle comes from speech errors and tip-of-the-tongue states. Nouns tend to be substituted for nouns, as in, "She was my strongest *propeller* (proponent) during the campaign"; verbs for verbs, as in, "The nation's dictator has been *exposed* (deposed)"; and adjectives for adjectives, as in, "His mother is too *progressive* (possessive)." In word association tasks, adults most commonly respond to the stimulus word with a word of the same grammatical class (Ervin, 1957; Jenkins, 1970).

Related to the principle of grammatical class, words are sometimes divided into **open- and closed-class words,** a concept first explored in Chapter 1. **Open-class** words are the basic *content* words in the language expressed as nouns, verbs, adjectives, and adverbs. A language can contain an infinite number of these types of words, as new words get invented to explain new objects or **concepts** (for example, the words *computer* or *corporation* would have been of little use in Chaucer's day). As Aitchison (1987) analogizes, open-class words are the bricks of our sentences, closed-class words are the mortar. **Closed-class** words are *function* words that traditionally provide the architecture for our sentences but bear no content—words such as *the, and, from,* and so forth. They are so called because the set of words is "closed" in that it rarely admits new members. For example, when was the last time you learned a new preposition? Content words can be invented as the need arises. We had to invent the term *computer* to deal with modern technology, but the number of function words has changed little through time.

Bradley (1983) and colleagues (Bradley, Garrett, & Zurif, 1980) found no frequency effects for closed-class words in a lexical decision task, despite the fact that frequency effects for *open*-class words are a robust phenomenon (for example, Forster & Chambers, 1973). Further support for a lexicon organized according to closed- and open-class words comes from Broca's aphasics, who are selectively impaired predominantly in their production of closed-class words (see Chapter 2). For example, Gardner (1974) relates a speech sample from an aphasic patient trying to describe going home from the hospital on weekends:

"... Thursday, er, er, er, no, er, Friday ... Bar-ba-ra ... wife ... and, oh, car ... drive ... turnpike ... you know ... rest and ... tee-vee."

Notice that the sentence resembles a telegram in that it contains content words but little else.

In summary, the evidence from several experimental techniques converges to suggest that the grammatical category of a word may determine how it is stored and organized in relation to other words. And whether a word is open or closed class interacts with frequency to determine the likelihood of recognition or retrieval.

PHONOLOGY.   Although the emphasis thus far has been on frequency, meaning, and grammatical class as factors that influence lexical access, other means are available to us. Evidence indicates that words that sound alike, even though their first syllables are not identical, might also be connected or stored close together in the lexicon. One type of evidence for phonologically-based storage of lexical items comes from the so-called **"tip-of-the-tongue"** phenomenon (TOT). We have all experienced TOTs: we know what we want to say, but the word won't come. By inducing tip-of-the-tongue phenomena in the lab, Brown and McNeill (1966) found that subjects were more likely to approximate the target words with similar-sounding words than with similar-meaning words. For example, "sarong" would be more likely to be mentioned by subjects as a possible response for "sampan" than would "houseboat" or "junk," which have related meanings.

In speech errors, discussed in greater detail in Chapter 7, substitutions of similar-sounding words are quite common, as in *medication* for *meditation, cylinders* for *syllables, goof* for *golf, psychotic* for *psychological* (Tweney, Tkacz, & Zaruba, 1975). This is especially true when words have similar beginnings and endings, as though phonological cues are preserved as **access routes** within the lexicon. This is sometimes referred to as the "bathtub effect" (Aitchison, 1987), because the "head" and "foot" of the word are available, but the middle isn't, much like a person's body reclining in a bathtub. What may happen is that similar-sounding words are clustered together, and attempts to retrieve one may also activate its phonological neighbors. This follows not only for words that start with the same sound but also for words that sound alike but have different meanings (**homophones,** for example, *sale* and *sail*).

Access to the lexicon is flexible, and activation of lexical entries can occur using various criteria (although some principles of access may be more prevalent than others). Some principles, such as frequency and meaning, seem to permeate all other principles. In this respect they are more global aspects of the lexical system. We may use multiple principles of organization and access to accomplish all the jobs the lexicon is called on to perform. In modeling a computer simulation of a person's lexicon, one goal is for the program to provide information based on request. Words must be accessible through various means, depending on the task demands, and sometimes a request may require the use of several channels or principles at once. Next we'll examine the ways different theoretical models account for how all these principles operate within a single cognitive system. Let us now consider how the models of lexical access deal with the above findings.

Models of Lexical Access

When examined closely, how language users recognize a word's meaning—how it should be pronounced or written—is a much more impressive skill than we may initially have realized. Our lexicon must be an extremely organized place in order for speech (or comprehension) to occur as flawlessly as it normally does. The lexicon also serves multiple purposes: when reading it must yield information on word meaning based on the orthographic (that is, written) representation of a word; when listening to someone speak, we must recognize words from an auditory code. When we speak or write, words are activated based on the meaning we want to convey, and then translated into a phonological or orthographic code.

A viable model of lexical access must explain how the mind can act like a dictionary and a thesaurus, a poet's rhyming book, and a grammar book. Two major classes of models detail how words get accessed (or recognized) during reading or listening. Although they mostly emphasize how words are activated during language activities, these models also implicitly provide us with some hypotheses as to how the lexicon might be organized.

The first type of theory is typically referred to as a **serial search model.** It claims that when we encounter a word—while reading, for example—we look through a lexical list to determine whether the item is a word or not, and then retrieve the necessary information about the word (such as its meaning or grammatical class). Serial search means that the process takes place by scanning one lexical entry at a time, sequentially. The best known serial search model is **Forster's** (1976) **autonomous search model.**

The second type of model is known as a **parallel access (or direct access) model.** It proposes that perceptual input about a word can activate a lexical item directly, and that multiple lexical entries are activated in parallel. That is, a number of potential candidates are activated simultaneously, and the stored word that shares the most features with the perceived word wins. Most models then propose some kind of decision stage, during which the accessed word is checked against the input. Among the three major versions of direct-access models, the earliest version is John Morton's **logogen model.** Two other forms of direct-access model—connectionist models (for example, McClelland & Rumelhart, 1981) and cohort models (Marslen-Wilson, 1987)—are adaptations of the basic premises of the logogen theory.

Both types of models—serial search and parallel access—consider word recognition an automatic process, not subject to conscious examination. That is, we are not cognizant of "searching" through a lexical list or of "activating" numerous stored words during lexical access. At best, we are conscious only of the end result of these processes—when we realize that we "know" what the word is and what it means.

Let us examine those characteristics of words that influence their access and then discuss how the various models explain the empirical findings. We will compare the ways these two types of theories explain research findings about the factors involved in lexical access and how successful each is in accounting for the data.

Serial Search Models

Forster's (1976) autonomous search model of lexical access is best illustrated by comparing the lexicon to a library. A word, just like a book, can be in only one place in the lexicon/library, but its location can be determined from several catalog entries (for example, catalog entries for author, title, or subject matter). In the autonomous search model, these catalogs are known as "access files." Forster (1976) posited three major access files—*orthographic,* through which words are accessed by their visual features; *phonological,* through which words are accessed by how they sound; and *semantic/syntactic,* through which words can be retrieved according to their meaning and grammatical class. Given these three access files, lexical entries can be accessed during reading, listening, and speaking. These access routes can only be used one at a time (just as you can't look up books in more than one catalog at a time). That is, input from any modalities (visual or auditory) can only be used one at a time; it will not speed access time if you hear a word at the same time you read it. The orthographic and phonological access files mostly contain information about the beginning parts of words—the first few letters of their spelling (orthographic) or first few sounds with which they begin (phonological).

When a word is presented either visually or phonologically, a complete perceptual representation of the word is constructed and subsequently activated in the access file based on its initial letters or sounds. When you have derived the location of a word based on its access code (or its index in the library catalog, to carry out the library analogy), a search for the word entry in the master lexicon must still be conducted. Thus, Forster's model posits a two-stage process. Just as a person determines which section of the library a book is in, but still must search on the specific shelf, we find the general location of a lexical entry, but still must search for its unique location in the master lexicon. It is this entry (not the *partial* entry in the access files) which contains *all* linguistic information about the word (for example, its meaning, spelling, pronunciation, part of speech).

The master lexicon is assumed to be organized into "bins" or storage units, with the most frequent entries in that bin on the top. This is analogous to putting your books in stacks, with the most frequently used books on the top, and accounts for why high-frequency words are accessed more quickly than low-frequency words. When an access file directs the search to the appropriate lexical bin, entries are searched one by one until an exact match to the perceptual representation is found. Figure 4.1 depicts how this process takes place.

The process of lexical access proposed by sequential search models is thus more of a step-by-step process than that proposed by parallel search models.

When the relevant lexical entry in this serial model is retrieved, it is checked against the input (for example, the written word) in a **post-access check.** This process is analogous to an automatic spelling checker in a word-processing program. If correct, the search is discontinued. If incorrect, we have two response alternatives: Nonwords that in no way resemble legitimate words, such as *psbtu* can be confidently rejected. However, nonwords that resemble real words, as *coffey* resembles *coffee,* or *gallomp* resembles *gallop,* initiate a more exhaustive search. Experiments have shown that we require more time to reject these legal nonwords (sequences that could be words because they follow the phonotactics of English) than we do to accept legitimate words. According to the autonomous search model, the search for a word stops when its lexical entry is located. But in the case of legal nonwords, all possible lexical entries must be scanned before the letter string can be rejected, which delays response time.

Two other serial search models merit brief mentions: Becker's (1979) *verification model* is similar to Forster's, except that Becker tried to better account for priming effects by emphasizing that a semantically defined search can be conducted, aided by

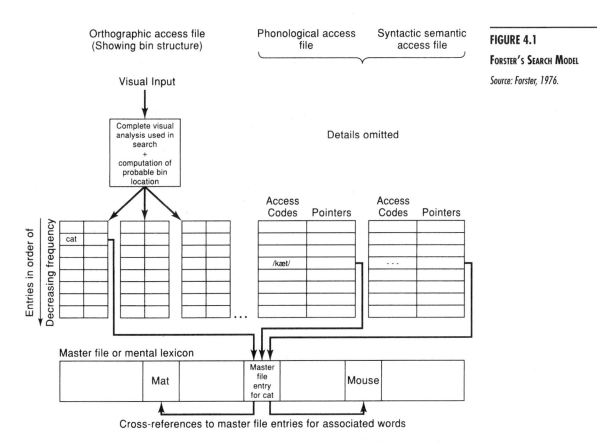

Orthographic access file
(Showing bin structure)

Phonological access
file

Syntactic semantic
access file

FIGURE 4.1

FORSTER'S SEARCH MODEL

Source: Forster, 1976.

Visual Input

Complete visual
analysis used in
search
+
computation of
probable bin
location

Details omitted

Access
Codes   Pointers

Access
Codes   Pointers

Entries in order of
Decreasing frequency

cat

/kæt/

- - -

Master file or mental lexicon

Mat

Master
file
entry
for cat

Mouse

Cross-references to master file entries for associated words

connections between associated words (for example, *doctor* and *nurse*) within the master lexicon. When one word is accessed, the system generates a list of potential words that *may* come next. This newly generated list is bound to be shorter than the list from a bin, thereby leading to quicker recognition of the second word in a priming pair *(doctor–nurse)* or to words suggested by the context of a sentence. Glanzer and Ehrenreich's (1979) model posits two dictionaries—a large, unabridged one composed of all words known to a person, and then a smaller pocket dictionary containing only high-frequency words. When confronted with a high-frequency word only the pocket dictionary need be used, which decreases search time.

Next we turn our attention to parallel access models. As we shall see, these models explain the various factors that influence lexical access in ways quite different from those proposed by serial search models.

Parallel Access Models

LOGOGEN MODEL.   Morton (1969, 1979) proposed that words are not accessed by determining their locations in the lexicon but by being activated to a certain **threshold.** Thus, a space analogy of lexical access such as we saw in Forster (1976) is replaced with a more electrical analogy—a word will "light up" when its activation is sufficient, in the same way that a lamp lights up when the electrical current is sufficiently strong. How does this activation occur, and what determines the threshold of a certain word?

Morton (1969) claimed that each word (or morpheme) has its own "logogen," which functions like a scoreboard, tabulating the number of features that a lexical entry shares with a perceptual stimulus. When a word is not being recognized, it is said to be in its resting level and has a zero feature count. Each logogen also has an individual threshold, which is the amount of "energy" that will be needed to access that lexical entry. As environmental input arrives when one is reading or listening to language, activation starts to accrue to each logogen based on the orthographic or phonological or semantic information being presented. All available information is accepted and summed *in parallel* as the various affected logogens race to the finish. Any logogen for which the total activation reaches a predesignated threshold, based on sufficient similarity to the stimulus word, is accessed. If several entries are activated to threshold, the one with the highest count wins and is "recognized." It then slowly returns to its resting level. The logogen model can thus account for semantic priming by allowing activation from one logogen to spread to related ones, and because it takes some time to return to a zero feature count, the primed target has a head start to recognition.

As depicted in Figure 4.2, Morton's logogen model provides no separate access routes by which to search a master list of lexical items.

FIGURE 4.2

THE LOGOGEN MODEL

The concept of direct access: The most well-known model of this class is John Morton's (1969, 1979) logogen model. It is called a direct-access model.

Source: Morton, 1970.

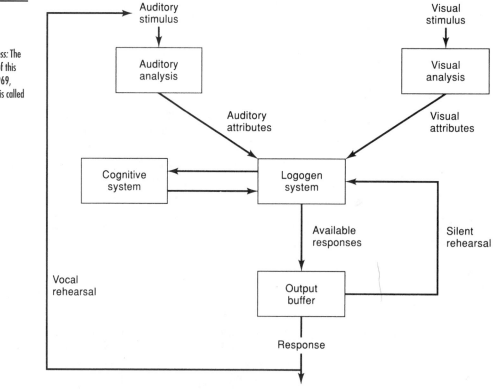

Rather, subjects make use of all available data—the context of a sentence suggests some meanings over others, the letters used in the orthographic representation of a word activate logogens with those same letter features. And all this information adds up to converge on (usually) a single candidate in the lexicon. Recall that in Forster's autonomous search theory (1976) access routes could be used only one at a time, whereas Morton's initial model permitted simultaneous summation of input from multiple modalities.

Why, then, are high-frequency words easier to access than low-frequency words? According to the logogen model, frequency effects are the result of the lowered threshold of the stored representation of a frequently used word. That is, it takes less activation to fire a high-frequency word than a low-frequency word. Such a lowering of the threshold takes place over a long period of time.

Priming, on the other hand, is accomplished by a quick and temporary lowering of the threshold of the logogens related to a prime. The logogen system itself does not contain semantic or associative data about words; rather, the cognitive system does (pictured as a separate "box" in Figure 4.2). However, when a word is accessed, the cognitive system receives this information and feeds information back to the linguistic system. Logogens that are related associatively or semantically to the prime receive increments to their logogens, and as a result require less perceptual input to achieve threshold. This results in quicker access times for primed words.

Morton's logogen model was the most influential of the parallel word access models and served as the basis for all of the parallel models that followed. As with any model, however, modifications were made to perfect the system. To show you how scientific progress forced changes in the model, consider the following example. The prediction of the original model that auditory presentation of a word would prime subsequent visual presentation of the same or related words turned out not to be the case, so the logogen model was revised in 1979 (Morton, 1979; Morton & Patterson, 1980) to constrain priming across modalities. Thus, although the model is good at explaining frequency and priming effects, its assumption that perceptual input is summed across modalities to achieve lexical access has been toned down, as suggested by new data. The newest version, depicted in Figure 4.3, posits separate input paths and logogens for words presented in visual channels versus auditory channels.

The initial logogen model also had difficulty accounting for how the linguistic system responds to nonwords. This required a further modification in the model. To ameliorate this problem, Coltheart, Davelaar, Jonasson, and Besner (1977) suggested a deadline within which words are recognized within the logogen system. If a stimulus word is not recognized within this deadline, it is rejected as a legal word. Nonword letter strings that most resemble words, such as *coffey,* cause more general activation in the logogen system. Such stimuli are rejected later and take even longer to reject than nonwords such as *hmrfi,* which do not resemble real words at all.

CONNECTIONIST MODELS.   A contemporary cousin of the logogen model comes from what is known as **connectionism.** Advocates of this approach in psychology, philosophy, computer science, and other fields, known as connectionists, use the analogy of the brain and neurons to develop models of cognition. Their computer models of cognitive processes (such as lexical access) are instituted in "neural nets" composed of **nodes** and connections between these nodes. Nodes are of three types: input nodes,

FIGURE 4.3

The later version of the logogen model. Nonlexical routes from input to response are not shown.

Based on Morton and Patterson, 1980.

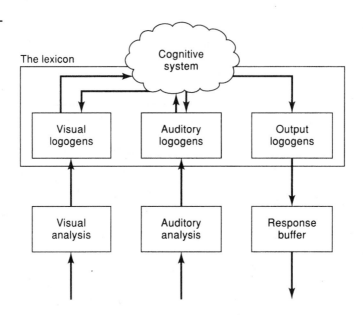

which process the auditory or visual stimuli; output nodes, which determine responses; and **hidden nodes,** which perform the internal processing between when we hear and see a word and when we respond to it. The hidden nodes do the lion's share of lexical processing as depicted (in simplified form) in Figure 4.4.

Connectionist models (for example, that of McClelland & Rumelhart, 1981) share many tenets of the logogen model, including direct access to lexical entries, simultaneous activation of multiple candidates, and the use of many types of information to access a target word. However, connectionists are more explicit in defining exactly the cognitive and linguistic architecture—that is, how words are represented. Each functional level of the hidden nodes represents different aspects of words—for example, their visual, orthographic, phonological, and semantic natures, and so forth. Processing proceeds from input to deciphering the raw perceptual input at a featural level (for example, does a written letter have a curved section?); nodes activated here then activate letter units that share those features (for example, *P, R, B, G,* and so forth), which in turn activate words which share those letters. Figure 4.5 shows how the word *time* might be recognized in a connectionist model.

Connections between layers, and between nodes in the same layer, can be either excitatory or inhibitory. Excitatory links are those that send activation onto other nodes attached to the original. For instance, if the feature "/" were activated, it would send energy onto all letter nodes that had this feature (for example, *A, M, W*). Inhibitory links, on the other hand, prevent further activation of the linked node. If one recognized the letter *A,* the letter node for *W* and *M* should be inhibited so that it does not compete with recognition of the *A.* The pattern of excitatory and inhibitory links allows lower units to feed into higher-level units (for example, letter features must be activated before word units can fire), but units within a layer compete with each other for activation during recognition of a given stimulus. When one representation

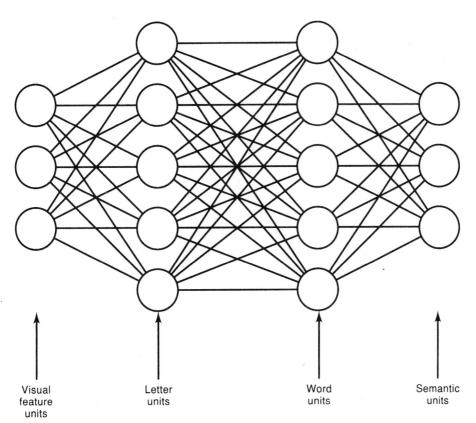

FIGURE 4.4

Connectionist network for word recognition depicting hidden nodes. Connections between nodes are strengthened or weakened as a function of experience.

Visual
feature
units

Letter
units

Word
units

Semantic
units

achieves threshold, it inhibits the firing of similar units with regard to a specific stimulus.

Connectionist models deal with frequency effects in a slightly different way than the logogen model—more frequently used word units have stronger connections to lower-level nodes, such as feature and letter nodes. High-frequency words thus receive more activation when those features and letters are activated. Priming and context effects are also explained the same way: When a node or connection is activated, a spread of activation occurs in all directions, incrementing representations that resemble the target visually, phonologically, semantically, and so forth. Connectionist models are also the only lexical access theory to, albeit implicitly, supply a theory of word organization: Organization is nothing more than the strength of connections between nodes (either word–word nodes, or word–feature nodes), based on past association.

COHORT MODEL.   The cohort model shares basic assumptions about lexical access with the logogen model but was designed to account only for *auditory* word recognition. Marslen-Wilson et al. (Marslen-Wilson, 1987; Marslen-Wilson & Welsh, 1978; Marslen-Wilson & Tyler, 1980, 1981) proposed that when we hear a word, all of its phonological neighbors get activated as well. Thus, upon hearing the sentence, "Paul got a job at the ca-. . . ," *candy, cash, candle, cashier, camp,* and many others would

FIGURE 4.5

A sketch of the interactive activation model of word perception. Units within the same rectangle stand for incompatible alternative hypotheses about an input pattern and are all mutually inhibitory. The bidirectional excitatory connections between levels are indicated for one word and its constituents.

Source: "Putting Knowledge in its Place: A Scheme for Programming Parallel Processing Structures on the Fly" by J. L. McClelland, 1985, Cognitive Science, 9, *p. 115. Copyright 1985 by Ablex Publishing. Reprinted by permission.*

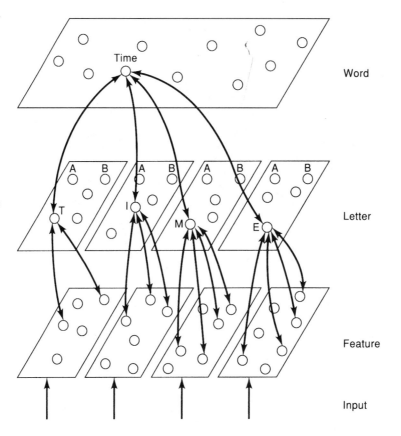

be available for selection. This set of words is known as the "word initial cohort" (though *cohort's* original meaning was a division of the Roman Army, here it refers to a "division" of words). Thus, as in the logogen model, multiple entries may be activated before the system settles on a final candidate. As with the other direct-access models, activation of a word is based on direct communication between the perceptual input and the lexical system.

One difference with the logogen model warrants discussion: Rather than the summing of partial inputs to logogens until adequate activation is achieved, all potential candidates for lexical access are activated by the perceptual input and then progressively eliminated. This elimination takes place in one of two ways—either the context of a spoken sentence narrows the initial cohort, or candidates are discarded as more phonological information comes in. In the latter case, as more of the spoken word is recognized, the cohort narrows. For example, if the phoneme /n/ was heard after the *ca-, candy* and *candle* (plus any other *can-* words) would be the only lexical items still possible from the initial cohort. The field of candidates continues to narrow as more stimulus information is received until only a single candidate remains. Figure 4.6 depicts the lexical elimination and access process for what might happen if one heard the sentence, "John was trying to get some bottles down

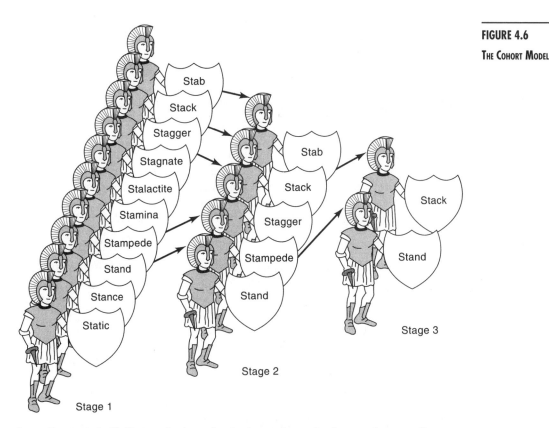

FIGURE 4.6

THE COHORT MODEL

Stab
Stack
Stagger
Stagnate
Stalactite
Stamina
Stampede
Stand
Stance
Static

Stage 1

Stab
Stack
Stagger
Stampede
Stand

Stage 2

Stack
Stand

Stage 3

from the top shelf. To reach them he had to *sta-...* "; the words preceding *sta-* would result in stage 3, where *stack* and *stand* are the only available remaining options.

Initially, the cohort model depended heavily on an exact match between a spoken word and its phonological representation in the lexicon. However, further study determined that people could recognize aurally presented words even if mispronounced, or if a sound (like a cough) blocked out part of the stimulus. The theory was subsequently revised (Marslen-Wilson, 1987) so that the system chooses the best match to fit an incoming word. This also makes the lexical access system less reliant on the word initial cohort. Under the original model, if a word did not make it into the first cohort, it had little chance of being chosen; now, as long as it shares enough features with the auditory stimulus, it can be selected for recognition.

Thus, like the logogen model and the connectionist model, the cohort model of lexical access posits that multiple candidates are activated in parallel. Unlike its cousins, the cohort model states that the list of word candidates is narrowed as the auditory input proceeds serially. It explains frequency and nonword effects in much the same way as the logogen theory. Context or priming is assumed to narrow the original set of candidates, and this shorter initial cohort leads to quicker recognition of a target word.

Having seen how the serial search and direct-access models deal with frequency, word class, phonology, and so forth, can we then determine which of the types of theories is best supported? It turns out that both types of models have something to recommend them. For example, one prediction of the serial search models is that only one access code can be used at a time. This means that hearing a word at the same time you are reading it will not facilitate reading recognition time. And research has indeed demonstrated a lack of priming between modalities (for example, Swinney, 1979).

Another test of the two kinds of models relates to the finding of **neighborhood effects.** Some words have many *neighbors* that are created by changing only a single letter of the target word. For instance, *mail* has many neighbors—*rail, bail, nail, fail, pail, hail, sail, tail, wail, mall, maid, maim,* and *main.* The word *film,* on the other hand, clearly lives in the country with few neighbors (only *firm* and *fill*). Serial search models would predict that large neighborhoods would increase access time because more entries would have to be perused before word recognition could take place. Parallel search models, however, would predict that spreading activation from numerous neighbors would facilitate eventual recognition of the target. Researchers (see review by Balota, 1994) consider faster recognition times for "city" words with many neighbors support for parallel search models.

Connectionist models, one form of the direct-access theories, provide the best explanation for semantic priming effects. The serial search model may prove too cumbersome for the efficiency with which lexical access is accomplished. However, some researchers argue that it may better account for some findings than direct-access models (see Forster, 1990, for a review). And neither serial nor parallel processing models are particularly adept at explaining the ability to pronounce nonwords, whose pronunciation cannot be in our dictionaries (see Henderson, 1982). As with word primitives, it could be that the task demands of an experiment greatly influence which predictions of serial versus parallel search models are supported. Both types of models provide numerous pathways to access words based on their frequency, grammatical class, phonology, and so on.

SUMMARY.   The factors that influence word access and lexical organization are addressed in both serial and parallel processing models. Both types of theories posit multiple access routes to lexical information—semantic, phonological, and so on—in order to account for the flexibility of the linguistic system. Although some aspects of the serial processing models (such as lack of intermodal priming) are supported, overall the trend is toward acceptance of parallel processing of information.

Separating Words and Meaning

Having discussed words, we now address meaning separately from the lexicon. You may envision this as a difficult task, because many meanings are best conveyed through language. However, let us reiterate that the two are not identical. Language may be heavily dependent on meaning (after all, words without meaning are called nonwords), but meaning is not as dependent on language. Let us draw a distinction between **signs** and **symbols:** Consider animal communication. A honeybee, through its dance, communicates the meaning that there is honey in a given direction and a certain distance from the hive. A deer running through the woods with his tail up represents the deer's belief that danger is nearby. Neither the honeybee nor the deer needs words to convey meaning. Likewise, nature provides its own instances of meaning without words. For example, bird tracks in the snow mean that birds have traveled that terrain; black clouds indicate that a storm is coming. These examples of meaning are often known as natural *signs*. Such signs have intrinsic meaning and can't help but convey the meanings that they do. Words, however, do not achieve their meaning naturally. Even though we may now agree on the association between a word and its meaning, assignment of words to world objects (or events) had an arbitrary beginning. That is, we know of no reason why the first person to apply the word *cat* to a furry creature with four legs that catches mice should not have originally called it a "table" or "snowflake." For this reason, words are known as *symbols* rather than signs.

Because of the separate but integral relations between words and meanings, the study of meaning is, in its own right, important to the study of words and language. We have already seen that much psychological evidence points to semantic meaning and semantic relatedness as major factors in word organization. Now we shall attempt to determine what features cause words, sentences, or larger linguistic units to *mean* what they do. Then we shall describe psychological theories of how meaning is stored in our minds.

MEANING

When we know the meaning of a word, what do we know? Take, for example, the term, *bachelor*. What does it mean to say, "Pierre is a bachelor"? We might easily respond that it means that Pierre is an unmarried male. Thus, "unmarried male" is the meaning of *bachelor*. But what about the Pope? Is he a bachelor, despite the fact that he has taken a vow never to get married? If we could modify our definition to include "eligible, unmarried male", then the Pope is not a bachelor. What about a divorced man? He is eligible *and* unmarried, but we typically don't think about people who have been married already (even though they no longer are) as bachelors. Social trends also complicate efforts to isolate the meaning of *bachelor*. Men and women may live together as partners without being married. Technically and legally, the men in these relationships are still eligible for marriage. But is it then accurate to portray them as *bachelors*? Isn't it misleading to state, "Despite having a lifelong relationship with Simone de Beauvoir, Jean-Paul Sartre died a bachelor"?[2]

You may begin to get a sense of how difficult it is to define even straightforward concepts such as *bachelor*. Every time we think we have the ultimate definition, we

---

[2] We are indebted to Robert Weisberg and Michael Tye for a discussion on defining features of *bachelor* that yielded many of our counterexamples.

can think of an example that the definition doesn't cover. Determining what constitutes meaning and formulating accurate definitions that cover *all* possible instances of a concept has been the difficult job of philosophers.

Before moving on to a philosophical and psychological analysis of meaning, an explanation may be useful about the association between words and concepts, and about the difference (and similarity) between concepts and categories. The meaning of a term is referred to as its **intension.** For example, there are two intensions of the concept *chair*—an object upon which we sit, and a person who heads a meeting or organization. The set of that to which a word applies is known as its **extension.** To continue our example, the extension of the first meaning of *chair* would be all the pieces of furniture you could point to and legitimately label "chair." This idea carries for the second meaning of *chair*—the extension of the term is all people who direct a meeting, organization, committee, or academic department.

One might think that the best route in establishing meaning is to start with the definition (or intension) of a concept and then pick out what in the world fits the definition. However, psychologists are interested in how people represent categories. And psychologists recognize that people may have categories that do not fit an exact definition. With this in mind, they often work backwards and gather information about how people extend terms in order to come up with a theory about the intension of concepts. Knowing how people apply concept words to objects can tell us about how they represent the meaning of concepts. For example, if it could be shown that people are quick to recognize apples, bananas, oranges, and pears as fruit, but not olives or cucumbers, we could look at what attributes that apples, bananas, oranges, and pears share that olives and cucumbers do not. This would yield a psychological theory of meaning (at least for the concept of fruit). Conversely, the theory could then be used to predict what other vegetative objects would be considered fruits by people. This is an illustration that one avenue to a theory of intension is to base it on research about extension.[3] For example, if removing the back from a chair causes it to be labeled a "stool," but sawing off one of its legs does not, then we can assume that the characteristic "having a back" is critical to people's concept of *chair,* but "having four legs" is not.

Using evidence from extension to infer the intension of a concept is easy for categories such as *kite:* What do all specific objects known as *kites* have in common? However, adjectival concepts such as *red* will be more problematic. *Red* defines a perceptual characteristic that can apply to apples, Valentine's Day cards, blood, velvet cloth, and so forth. However, these are *red objects* that yield examples of *red* but do not define it.

Because philosophers were the first to start thinking about theories of meaning, we will begin our discussion with a presentation of the major philosophical accounts of meaning.

Philosophical Theories of Meaning

REFERENCE THEORY.   If a friend asks you a question such as, "What is the meaning of the word *house?*" you might simply turn around and point to the nearest

---

[3] We do not want to argue that this is a viable way to develop a *philosophical* theory of meaning, however. It is only valid to ascertain people's *psychological* categories and criteria for those categories.

family-type dwelling. If so, you would be demonstrating a view that was prevalent in the early part of the century, known as the **reference theory of meaning.** This theory postulates that the meaning of a term is the object to which that term refers in the real world (that is, its **referent**). For example, *the Liberty Bell* and *Abraham Lincoln* point to or *denote* a specific object and person, respectively, whereas *geraniums* and *firefighters* point to or denote a class of things or people, respectively. Likewise, terms such as *red, round,* and *ripening* refer to actual properties of an object (or objects), such as a garden tomato. The theory thus draws a distinction between proper names that refer to a specific person or thing, category names that refer to a class of objects, and property names that refer to characteristics of objects or events.

If reference theory completely explained meaning, it would make the study of semantics rather concrete and easy: The meaning of a word is the object or property it denotes.

According to this view, terms that stand for the same object have the same meaning. Both the proper name *Mick Jagger* and the descriptions *lead singer of the Rolling Stones* and *husband of model Jerry Hall* point to or denote the same man. According to the reference view (as originally conceived), these two sets of words have identical meaning and we should be able to substitute one term for the other without changing the meaning of the sentence. Of course, the situation is not that easy. *Mick Jagger is the lead singer of the Rolling Stones* does not have the same meaning as *Mick Jagger is the husband of model Jerry Hall,* nor does it convey the same information as *Mick Jagger is Mick Jagger.* Thus, one problem with a strict reference view is that it does not explain how two terms can have the same referent (for example, the person Mick Jagger) and yet have different meanings (or "senses" in philosophical parlance).

Other problems arise with the reference view. For example, not all words *name* things—think of *and, not,* and *or.* Yet these words have meaning as used in ordinary speech: "Frank is going to the charity ball" means something different from "Frank is *not* going to the charity ball." "At the charity ball, Frank danced *on* a table," depicts an event other than "Frank danced *under* the table."

A second objection to this theory is that we can talk about things for which no real "objects" exist in the world, such as *freedom.* Although we can picture signs and symbols of freedom, such as the Liberty Bell or a raised flag, those images are not really the "thing" denoted by the word *freedom.* We also discuss objects that we infer to exist (such as quarks or black holes) but for which no real objects may exist per se. Thomas Hobbes, an early proponent of the referent theory, claimed that all terms that refer to nonreal objects (such as *angels*) are meaningless (Hobbes, 1651/1958). According to such a view, any discussions we might have about Hamlet, or unicorns, or Athena—the Greek goddess of wisdom and arts—would of necessity be meaningless. It's easy to agree with the King of Hearts in *Alice's Adventures in Wonderland,* who exclaimed, "If there's no meaning in it, . . . that saves a world of trouble, you know, as we needn't try to find any. And yet I don't know, . . . I seem to see some meaning in them after all" (Carroll, 1862/1990, p. 148). Clearly, we can discuss the fictional character of Hamlet (or unicorns or dragons) and communicate meaningfully with another person. And our conversational partner can comprehend our talk of "Hamlet," or "unicorns," even if these things don't exist. Such problems with the reference theory led philosophers to posit alternative views.

IDEATIONAL THEORY.   One remedy is to claim that what words actually denote are *ideas* rather than objects. According to the British philosopher John Locke (1690/1967, p. 225), "Words in their primary and immediate signification stand for nothing *but the ideas in the mind of him that uses them.*" Thus, the terms *Hamlet* and *unicorn* have meaning by virtue of our mental ideas about them, even if the objects themselves do not exist. This view is known as the **ideational theory of meaning.** Although it is a tempting alternative because it can take into account the imagined world, it is not itself without problems. If meaning is always in the head, how am I to know that we both mean the same thing when we use a hand gesture like waving or when we speak words or sentences? The ideational theory makes meaning—and the language used to convey meaning—private. Thus, we can never be entirely certain that other people correctly interpret our meanings, nor that we correctly interpret theirs. Language, after all, is often a public endeavor, and as in the examples of signs cited earlier in this chapter, some meanings are found in the real world, not just in one's head.

Alternative Theories: Meaning Is in the Public Domain

Both reference and ideational theories of meaning have been criticized for treating all meaningful terms and expressions as names. What of other words besides those that refer to properties or nouns, such as words that have meaning because of their role or function within language (for example, *not, the, a, and, because*)? Perhaps then, the meaning of names and properties derives from their participation in language as well. What gives words their meaning is often how they are used in conjunction with other words in the language.

This view is supported by philosophers such as Quine (1960), who postulated that the meaning of individual words can never be strictly derived. In his view, words, and even sentences, have no meaning independently, but are based on their connection to other words and sentences within the language. Another philosopher, Wittgenstein (1953), helped bridge philosophy and psychology in the study of semantics by claiming that meaning should be determined by how language terms are used by ordinary speakers. All competent speakers are assumed to use words in the same way. This concept is known as ***conventionality,*** the tendency for linguistic usage to be agreed upon by members of a community. Quine's and Wittgenstein's views have become influential in current psychological theorizing about semantics, as we shall see.

The reference and ideational theories have intrinsic appeal because we tend to think of the meaning of terms as objects or concepts we can point to or describe. Both, however, have their failings. Any philosophical theory of meaning must ultimately account for how word meanings are interconnected within a larger semantic and linguistic theory. For this reason, philosophers need psychologists, and vice versa, for adequate theorizing. Both armchair and empirical experiments are necessary.

As we did with words, let's now look at the building blocks (or primitives) of meaning, principles of meaning, and finally theoretical models that describe how concepts and meaning may be organized cognitively.

Conceptual Primitives

Three major issues address the study of meaning. The first is *what are the smallest units (or primitives) of meaning?* The study of the "building blocks" of concepts parallels exploration of the primitives of words. Recall that morphemes are considered the primitives of words, as complex words can be composed of several individual morphemes. The same is be true of concepts and **conceptual primitives,** referred to as **features.** Just as we know that *hopeful* is made up of the word parts, *hope + ful,* we realize that the concept *even number* has the featural definition of "divisible by 2."

The second issue is *whether concepts have clear boundaries or not,* so that, for example, it is evident what counts as a *cup* and what does not. This issue will be most important when comparing two main types of feature theories discussed later in this chapter—the classical view and the family resemblance view.

The third question asks *whether it is sufficient to represent a category as a list of features.* This issue has a parallel in the word primitives discussion: Just as we have knowledge of individual morphemes, we also have knowledge of which morphemes can be combined and which cannot. For instance, the morphemes *dis-* and *agree* can go together, but *un-* and *agree* cannot. Likewise, we can have knowledge of which features tend to co-occur within a concept. Most people realize that "has antennae" and "flies" are more likely to go together than are "has antennae" and "hibernates." Furthermore, people often have a greater ability to explain *why* conceptual features co-occur than why word primitives can co-occur (the exception would be scholars with a background in word etymology who know the Latin, Greek, and Germanic origins of contemporary words).

These issues, summarized in Table 4.1, will become clearer as we portray the differences between various feature theories. Let us first examine the feature theories and then discuss why meaning is represented in a more full-bodied way than feature theories claim.

Feature Theories

Feature theories hold that concepts can be defined by the prevalent attributes within a category. As in the morpheme-as-word-primitive view, most researchers believe in a **decompositional view of meaning** such that concepts are composed of bundles of smaller units called features. Thus, the meaning of *tree* is composed of attributes such as "having branches," "grew from tree seeds," "has leaves or needles," "has roots," and so on. Some characteristics that count as features can be designated as either *perceptual* (for example, "gray, large," like an elephant), *functional* ("used to

---

1. What are the smallest units of meaning?

2. Are concepts defined in a rule-like fashion, with clear conceptual boundaries?

3. Is it sufficient to represent a concept as a list of features?

TABLE 4.1

QUESTIONS ABOUT MEANING: CONCEPTUAL THEORIES

transport people," of vehicles), *microstructural* ("composed of hydrogen and oxygen molecules," of water) (Malt, 1990), or *societal/conventional* ("supreme ruler," of a king or queen). Features can also be considered meaningful units themselves (for example, "red" could be both a feature of blood and a concept itself), just as morphemes can be both meaningful units by themselves and the primitives of words. Several variations of these theories have developed (see below), but the emphasis on features has permeated most thinking on categories during the past 30 years.

Variations of Feature Theories

Although most philosophers and psychologists agree that concepts are themselves composites of features that serve to define each concept, there are disagreements about what features are necessary in defining each concept, and about the structure of meaning in the mind. Among the multiple theories of concepts and categorization (see Smith & Medin, 1981, for a thorough review), two main approaches are the **classical view** and Eleanor Rosch's **family resemblance theory.** In addition, because of perceived inadequacies of the classical and family resemblance views, there has developed a new class of theories that are less feature based and argue that we know more about concepts than what features are associated with them. According to this new breed of theory, we typically have additional higher-order information that causes us to weigh some features more than others, to know which features tend to co-occur (for example, laying eggs and having feathers). This new approach falls under knowledge-based theories of conceptual coherence.

Despite widespread agreement on a featural account of meaning, philosophers and psychologists diverge in their belief of what a theory of meaning must explain. Most philosophers are interested in determining what constitutes the *essence* of a concept. That is, what features distinguish one concept from another and what conditions must be met for an object to be considered an instance of that concept. Thus, any definition of a concept must be true in all possible circumstances and in all possible cases. Psychologists, on the other hand, are more interested in explaining how humans represent meaning in the mind and how they use and apply meaningful concepts. This has sometimes led to differences in the bases of philosophical and psychological theories of meaning, although philosophers and psychologists have begun to cooperate and to influence each other's views on meanings, as we shall see.

THE CLASSICAL VIEW.   Let us start with the following task: On a piece of paper, list all the attributes that a geometric figure must have to be considered a triangle.

Considering the features of a triangle is an excellent way to illustrate the classical view of categories. It states that any concept has necessary **and jointly sufficient features** that all instances of that concept share. All triangles, for example, (1) are closed figures, (2) have three sides, and (3) have angles that add up to 180 degrees. They *must* have these three features to be triangles (thus these features are singly *necessary* for something to be a triangle), and all objects that have all three features must be triangles (thus the three features listed above are jointly *sufficient* for considering something to be a triangle).

Beyond the existence of necessary features for each concept, the classical view makes some other strong claims. By way of example, all triangles are considered to be equally good triangles; no figure is considered to be a better instance of the concept *triangle* than any other. Thus, equilateral triangles are no better triangles than nonequilateral triangles because they all fulfill the necessary and sufficient conditions. Some figures, such as equilateral triangles, may be more common in a person's experience, and equal sides plus equal angles may be more *characteristic* of triangles, but this does not make them *better* triangles than others without these features. The distinction between necessary (or defining) and characteristic features is an important one, especially if we want to talk about how people process concepts.

Thus, proponents of the classical view consider features the smallest units of meaning. They also contend that concepts are defined in a rulelike fashion, with clear boundaries. The classical view states that concepts have definitely discrete boundaries; an item either has the necessary and sufficient features or it does not. If so, it is an instance of the concept; if not, it is not an instance of the concept. The classical view also postulates that a list of the necessary and jointly sufficient features adequately represents the meaning of a concept. This list can be used to determine category membership of new exemplars one encounters. Something is a triangle if it meets the criteria for being a triangle.

The classical view dates back at least to Aristotle, and is still the prevalent view held by many philosophers (see Katz & Fodor, 1963) and some psychologists (for example, Glass & Holyoak, 1975). It has, however, been challenged by Wittgenstein (1953) and his supporters, and by the empirical data that seem to suggest that people do not use necessary and sufficient features in categorization tasks (Rosch, 1975).[4]

THE FAMILY RESEMBLANCE VIEW.   Now try the following task: Take a minute to list (l) as many different birds as you can; and then (2) all characteristics or properties of the concept *bird* that come to mind.

Did bird names such as robins, sparrows, crows, bluejays pop into your head as you thought of all the members of the bird category? Do odd birds such as penguins, flamingos, and toucans appear toward the end of your list? If so, you are like most other people who participate in this task (Battig & Montague, 1969). Sometimes people even include bats, which are not birds at all but are birdlike in certain ways. Did your property list include features and attributes such as "can fly," "lays eggs," "has feathers," "builds nests," "is small," "has bones," "has skin," among others?

Now reexamine your list of bird features and check off the characteristics a bird *must* have in order to be considered a bird. Did you think it was necessary for birds to fly to fit the concept of *bird?* But ostriches and penguins don't fly. What about the feature of having feathers? Yet we refer to the Thanksgiving turkey on our table in November as a bird. Newly hatched chicks are also birds. You may have thought both

---

[4] One reason that philosophers have traditionally sided with the classical view and psychologists with the prototype view is a difference in academic missions. Philosophers are interested in the essence by which something gets its meaning, psychologists in how people use and store representations of meaning. Thus, both views may be correct—concepts may have necessary and sufficient conditions, but people may focus only on characteristic features.

flight and feathers were mandatory in order to be considered a bird. However, creatures that we definitely consider birds don't fit these conditions. Looking at your list of kinds of birds, it certainly appears *characteristic,* but not mandatory for birds to fly and lay eggs. Your lists of birds and bird attributes seem different from your list of criteria for what constitutes a triangle.

Many psychologists (for example, Lakoff, 1987; Rosch, 1973) consider the world, at least the world as represented in our minds, less clear-cut than the classical view of meaning would have us believe. If you listed all the features of all the birds on your list, there would be no, or few, features common to *all* instances of the concept *bird.* This, argues Rosch (1973, 1975; Rosch & Mervis, 1975), demonstrates the absence of necessary and sufficient conditions for *bird* and, indeed, for any natural concept. Instead, the emphasis is on **characteristic features**—attributes common to many exemplars of a category (as "having feathers" is true of *almost* all birds). Other features may be associated with a category (for example, "6-feet tall" with *bird* because ostriches have this attribute), even if they are not common. In Rosch's view, all attribute information would be stored within the meaning of a concept, but the features would be weighted according to their frequency within the category. The family resemblance view also emphasizes attributes easily accessible to people when they make category judgments. These most often are perceptual features (for example, "has feathers") and readily available facts (for example, "lays eggs").

Rosch's theory is based on the philosophical position of Wittgenstein (1953). Wittgenstein's most famous example of a concept with no defining or sufficient features is that of the concept *game.* The word *game* is applied to a variety of instances, from board games to soccer games to war games. Not every instance of a game shares a single feature or set of features. For example, you can think of counterexamples to every possible criterion of the concept *game.* Not all games are played on boards (for example, tennis), nor involve two or more people (for example, solitaire), nor are all games competitive (for example, ring-around-the-rosie). If you were to list all features of games, you could not find a set of necessary and sufficient features that defined all games but excluded all nongames.

This brings us to the second premise of the theory—from which the theory derives its name—that of *family resemblance* (Rosch, 1973, 1975; Rosch & Mervis, 1975). Rather than share a set of necessary and sufficient conditions, instances of a concept may overlap in some traits but not in others. A single term, such as *game,* refers to objects that resemble each other in the same way that members of a family resemble each other. You may have your mother's eyes, your father's mouth, and ears like your uncle and thus resemble each of them without them resembling each other. In Figure 4.7, you can see that the Smith brothers resemble each other even though no two brothers share a set of common features.

This claim was supported in an experiment by Rosch and Mervis (1975). They asked subjects to list all the attributes of twenty kinds of fruits and found no features common to all (as Wittgenstein would have predicted). For example, apples and oranges share a round shape, but bananas do not. Grapes and plums are both purple, but apples and watermelons are not. Cherries and grapes are the same size, which differs from the large size of a watermelon. You can see that the attributes of a single fruit

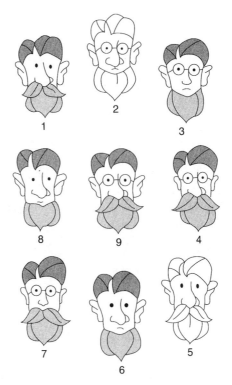

FIGURE 4.7

THE SMITH BROTHERS AND THEIR FAMILY RESEMBLANCE

The Smith brothers are related through family resemblance, though no two brothers share all features. The one who has the greatest number of the family attributes is the most prototypical. In the example, Brother 9 has all the family features: brown hair, large ears, large nose, mustache, and eyeglasses.

Source: Sharon Armstrong.

can overlap with those of many other fruits without sharing a single set of features with each and every fruit.

A third tenet of the family resemblance view is that some instances of a category or concept are more representative than others. Categories are said to have a ***graded structure***—some birds would appear on most everyone's lists (for example, robin, sparrow); others on few people's lists (for example, ibis), and some might be considered "intermediate" birds (for example, eagle, chicken, vulture). The *best* example of a concept or category is known as the **prototype.** Exemplars that have the most characteristic features for the category are also considered more prototypical. Rosch and Mervis (1975) found that the five most prototypical items of a category (for example, pants, shirt, dress, skirt, and jacket in the clothing category) had more features in common than did the five most peripheral members (hat, apron, purse, wristwatch, necklace). Furthermore, the most peripheral items of a category are apt to share features with other related categories. If we consider jewelry a close affiliate of the concept *clothing* we can see that two of the most peripheral members of *clothing*—wristwatch and necklace— can also be considered jewelry. This leads us to another tenet of the family resemblance theory—that of **fuzzy boundaries** (Lakoff, 1987). Some instances of one category can overlap significantly with other categories, in the way that tomatoes, cucumbers, and olives are all *fruit* concepts that seem to be equally well qualified for *vegetable* status.

An experiment by Armstrong, Gleitman, and Gleitman (Experiment 1, 1983) illustrates that many categories have a graded structure, where some exemplars are considered more typical of the category than others. And although we might expect a graded structure to be true of concepts such as *fruit* and *clothing,* we would not expect it of hard and fast categories that are better explained by the classical view. *Odd number* and *female,* for instance, are concepts that seem to have necessary and sufficient features by which they are defined.

Armstrong et al. asked people to rate category exemplars on a l (Best) to 7 (Worst) scale of how well each item represented the category. Not surprisingly, *apple* got a rating of l.3, whereas *olive* received a 6.5 rating. The surprise came in the ratings for exemplars of the well-defined categories: *13* was declared to be a better *odd number* than was *57!* And a *square* was rated more highly as a *plane geometry figure* than was an *ellipse.* The researchers thus found a graded structure to even well-defined categories (such as *odd number*) that do have necessary and sufficient features according to mathematicians. After all, any integer that, when divided by two, yields a remainder of one must be an odd number. To confirm the findings of the rating experiment, Armstrong, Gleitman, and Gleitman then asked subjects to engage in a **semantic verification task** in which participants read a statement about category membership and decide whether the statement is true or false. "A canary is a bird," is a true semantic verification statement; "A boot is a bird," is false. What is of interest is how quickly people respond to the true statements. Many studies have found, for example, that subjects are quicker to respond to prototypical items of a category (for example, "An apple is a fruit") than to peripheral items (for example, "A tomato is a fruit") (Rips, Shoben, & Smith, 1973). Again, even for well-defined categories, a graded structure was evident: "13 is an odd number" led to faster response times than "57 is an odd number"; and "A mother is a female," was verified more quickly than "A waitress is a female." Thus, people may represent even concepts with necessary and jointly sufficient features in a family resemblance way.

A further claim of this theory is that the prototype of a concept is used as a reference point to make category judgments (Rosch, 1975). If a new exemplar is similar enough to the prototype for that category, the new item will also be accepted. If you had never seen a flamingo before, you might still determine that it was a bird because it overlaps in a significant number of features with a robin (the prototype of the category *bird*).

We can now return to our three initial issues to discern how the prototype theory differs from the classical view. Both the classical and prototype views agree on the answer to the first question—that the primitive building blocks of concepts are features. However, the two disagree on the answer to the second question, about whether concepts are structured based on rules and whether conceptual boundaries are well defined. Whereas the classical view argues for strict boundaries and concepts defined by necessary and sufficient features, the prototype view states that emphasis on characteristic features makes concept boundaries fuzzy. Concepts are graded as to typicality within a category. On the third issue, the family resemblance view claims that a list of the most characteristic features of a category is sufficient to represent the meaning of the concept.

Thus far, then, we have discussed two theories of concept structure and category organization. Common to each of these approaches is the claim that features are central to the definition of concepts. To represent the units of meaning, we must first abstract the relevant bundles of features. Concepts are judged as similar to one another to the extent that they share the same features, and categories are formed from sets of similar concepts.

Knowledge-Based Approaches

The classical and family resemblance theories have provided impetus to research in concepts and categorization for the past 15 years. Recently, however, the very foundation of these views has been shaken by certain problems they cannot adequately address. Led largely by Medin and his colleagues (Murphy & Medin, 1985; Medin & Wattenmaker, 1987; Medin, 1989), a revolution is underway in our understanding of the nature of concepts. A knowledge-based approach emphasizes that categorization and knowledge of concepts is based on something deeper than perceptual features. It seeks to explain *how* and *why* individual items get grouped together under a category label. To gain some appreciation for this new movement in the field, it is important to first provide some criticism of the feature view and then to demonstrate how our inherent general knowledge about biology and our environment may supplement the feature approaches in explaining our conceptual judgments.

Several arguments make clear the problems with feature theories. The first, addressed by philosophers and psychologists alike, concerns the question, "What counts as a feature?" The most parsimonious explanation of concepts for the feature theorist would be that humans are equipped with a kind of finite alphabet of conceptual features that combine in any number of ways to yield all of the concepts that we could conceivably think about. Unfortunately, however, no such alphabet of meaning primitives has been discovered. Take the *bachelor* example as a case in point. Above it was suggested that *bachelor* can be decomposed into more primitive concepts *unmarried* and *man*. Is *unmarried* a primitive? Do we help the situation greatly by saying that *unmarried* can be decomposed into *not* and *married?* Where do we go from here? The problem of basic feature analysis becomes one of infinite regress.

A second problem that arises for the feature theorists is evident in the question, "Which of the available features should be chosen when representing a concept?" As with lexical access, conceptual judgments often depend on the *type of task* a subject participates in, and on the *context* in which an item is presented. For example, Barsalou (1982, 1987) argued that certain features and types of information about concepts may be differentially available depending upon the presentation context. We may not consider "floats" as a feature of the concept *basketball* unless we are told someone used a basketball as a life preserver. Likewise, subjects presented with the sentence, "The man lifted the heavy piano," were likely to respond more quickly "piano–heavy" in a lexical decision task than those presented with "The man tuned the piano" (Barclay, Bransford, Franks, McCarrell, & Nitsch, 1974). You can see some of the problems if you take just a moment to jot down all of the features that you can think of for the category *vegetable*. Were the characteristics "green, grows in my garden," and "put into salad" among your choices? These are excellent choices if your category of comparison is *furniture*. They are, however, less desirable choices if the comparison category is *fruit*, for apples can be green, and tomatoes can be put into salad, and cucumbers grow in your garden, and these are all fruits. The context of comparison in this task alters the features that we choose as representative of a particular concept.

The issues of task and context dependency also arise in a third example that damages the reputation of feature theories. In fact, you are already equipped with the relevant data. In the experiment mentioned earlier by Armstrong, Gleitman, and Gleitman (1983), subjects were willing to claim that 13 was a prototypical odd number and that mothers were "better" females than were comediennes. As Armstrong et al. (1983) pointed out, it may be necessary to make a distinction between their subjects' willingness to rate the characteristic quality of exemplars (like the numbers 13 or 57) and subjects' knowledge of a categorical description that defines a category. For example, mothers might be rated as more prototypical females, but if probed, almost all adult categorizers would claim that femaleness was based on specific genetic and anatomical features, not one's social role.

Finally, to borrow yet one more example, from Barsalou and Medin (1986), see if you can determine what features the following examples share: children, jewelry, portable television sets, photograph albums, manuscripts, and oil paintings. Did you say, "None"? They certainly don't share any obvious or perceptual features. And without sharing features, these concepts should not form a coherent category. Yet, when placed in the context, "things to take out of the home during a fire," they cohere quite naturally—with no featural similarities at all.

These examples point out the hazards of basing concept meaning upon feature lists, whether those feature lists contain necessary and sufficient attributes or merely characteristic features. First, features themselves are not well specified. Second, the choice and weighting of features is context- and task-dependent. And third (and perhaps most importantly), we know much more about the intension of a concept than a list of features suggests. We often know *why* a concept is associated with some features and not with others (for example, why birds have "wings," but not "wheels").

These concerns about features, and hence about feature theories, have led to the revolutionary idea that concepts must be represented and organized according to peoples' *theories about the world*. A theory is the underlying explanation for why bundles of features hang together, and allows us to make predictions about which features should co-occur and which should not. For instance, having gray hair may be characteristic of grandmothers without it being a defining feature. In order to be a grandmother, one must be the mother of a man or woman who has children of his or her own. Gray hair may be associated with grandmothers because as our children get old enough to reproduce, mothers age and as a result often develop gray hair. Features are merely the surface cues of more complex theoretical information about categories.

This shift in perspective, from feature theories to knowledge-based or theory-based theories, sets a new agenda for those studying conceptual coherence and category organization. What counts as a "theory" about a concept? How fully formed must our theories be before we can abstract the relevant features? Is there a time in development when we rely more crucially on the surface properties of objects only later to rely on the deeper theoretical relations behind these surface cues? While these questions are being hotly debated, two types of theories are being discussed in the literature: *psychological essentialism* and what we will call *psychological contextualism*. Let us briefly review each now.

PSYCHOLOGICAL ESSENTIALISM.   **Psychological essentialism** is the position advocated by Medin (Medin & Ortony, 1989; Murphy & Medin, 1985) that "people act as if things (for example, objects) have essences or underlying natures that make them the thing that they are" (Medin, 1989, p. 1476). It seems that people want to have a reason or an explanation for the ways they categorize the world. We want a reason why birds have wings, live in trees, and have beaks. For example, they are genetically endowed with a means for flying away from their predators. Indeed, even if people don't know the theory behind the features, they are committed to the notion that such a theory or essence exists and that it is discoverable (at least by scientists). Thus, people have a way of making sense out of the collection of features that they see and of using these features when they encounter them again as signposts for the theory.

To demonstrate the theory versus feature divide here, Medin and Shoben (1988) conducted an experiment in which they asked subjects to judge which terms were more similar: white hair and gray hair, or white clouds and gray clouds. The subjects claimed, despite the similarity in features across the two conditions, that white and gray hair were more similar—a finding that the authors interpret to be a consequence of a theory of aging. In short, then, overlapping characteristics are not as important as the underlying principles that *cause* those perceptual characteristics.

This position on psychological essentialism is actually derived from work by philosophers such as Quine (1977), Putnam (1973, 1975), and J. S. Mill (1843), who argue that extension labels are applied according to essential features, even if those features are not readily apparent. Someone may call a tomato a vegetable only until he is reminded that it is a fruit. To use one of Putnam's famous examples (Putnam, 1973, 1975), people may believe that gold has a particular microstructure by virtue of which it is gold. Any substance that is not known to have that structure (for example, brass) will not be called gold. It is not that people necessarily know what the microstructure of gold is; they rely on scientific experts to know that. It is enough to know that the microstructure *is* an essential feature. If the family resemblance view were entirely true, pirates who received 100 brass bars in exchange for a shipload of goods should have been just as happy as those who received 100 bars of gold—after all, they look the same! The belief in essential properties acts as a theory by which people label and categorize items, and these theories constrain and have causal links to more superficial or characteristic properties. That is, the characteristic yellow color of gold is dictated by its molecular structure. The molecular structure both defines the concept *gold, and* is the basis for the characteristic features associated with it (for example, its color, ability to be forged, and so on).

Much of the research on psychological essentialism comes from the developmental literature (Keil, 1989; Carey, 1985; Gelman & Markman, 1986, 1987; Murphy & Medin, 1985; Gelman & Coley, 1991). To illustrate the force of psychological essentialism, let's engage in another thought experiment paraphrased from work by Keil (1989). Think of all the features associated with *raccoon.* Now consider an actual raccoon; if I dye its fur so that it is black with a white stripe down its back, is it still a raccoon, or has it become a skunk? What if I sew a smelly sack inside it and teach it to spray the contents of the sack during times of danger? Has it remained a raccoon then? Now let's change our creature so that it no longer washes its food before it eats. At what point is the creature no longer a raccoon but something else, such as a skunk? You might argue that it is a raccoon until you change its DNA or the fact that it was born of raccoon parents. If so, you would be arguing in favor of essential features that occur in any instance of a concept that necessarily define that concept.

Keil (1987, 1989) actually posed the raccoon experiment to children. Although kindergartners (ages 5–6) were apt to rely on surface characteristics for making category assignments (as the family resemblance view predicts), by ages 8–10, children realized that essential biological features might determine skunkhood versus raccoonhood (as the psychological essentialist theory predicts). Keil argued that the results confirm evidence about conceptual development suggesting that from an early age children have theories. Very young children (kindergartners and younger) may know too little about DNA and genetic endowments, and are thus more likely to say that the deformed raccoon we discussed above was no longer a raccoon when all its characteristic features were changed (Keil, 1987, 1989). However, once this information is acquired, children develop a *theory* about a given domain (for example, animals). As a result, knowledge of the meaning of a concept shifts from knowing the most characteristic features of a category to having a general theory about why certain attributes occur. The theoretical reasons then predominate over features in making categorization judgments.

A belief in biological essence may prove to be a guiding factor in defining what Keil called **natural kind terms,** things found naturally in the world, like animals. In contrast, with **nominal terms** (also known as **artifacts**), which refer to objects invented by humans (for example, vehicles, furniture), a different picture emerges. Using a story analogous to the raccoon story, Keil tells children that a coffee pot is melted down and turned into a bird-feeder. In this example, the material of the two artifacts remains the same; what changes are both the shape and the function of the object. In this example, children of all ages (even as young as 5 years) were willing to accept that the coffee pot had now turned into a bird-feeder. Whereas the essence of biological categories will be genetic and anatomical; the essence of artifactual categories may be the function for which the object was designed—change the purpose or use, and you change the category.

In summary, then, psychological essentialism is the modern extension of feature theories. Features are embedded within richer mental constructs—theories—that organize meaning. Concepts are thus represented at many levels in the system, as correlated bundles of features *and* through an internal essence or theory of which these features are a part. Theories constrain the features; features do not construct the theories.

The work on psychological essentialism is largely being conducted with special attention to natural kind terms (Gelman & Coley, 1991), naive theories of biology, and naive theories of physics. One other class of theories is also gaining attention. These knowledge-based theories, what we have termed psychological contextualism, also go beyond individual feature analysis to ask how the context in which we find objects and events influences our meaning representations of those objects and events.

PSYCHOLOGICAL CONTEXTUALISM.   **Psychological contextualism** refers to the idea that certain contexts, either defined by goal or by culture, can provide the bond between features in a concept and concepts in a category. Several examples will illustrate this position. In the first, Labov (1973) presented subjects with pictures of cups (for example, teacups) and bowls, with some of the instances appearing to be part cup, part bowl—for example, wide like a bowl but with a handle. People categorized one of these hybrid objects as a cup if it was said to contain tea; a bowl if it was said to contain soup. Contextual knowledge influenced categorization. A second example is Barsalou's previously mentioned "things to take out of a burning house." Barsalou's point is that the objects in the collection—children, portable television sets, and jewelry—do not cohere into a group until some contextual goal links them. All concepts have both a set of context-independent features (for example, "bounces" and "round" for *basketball*) that are inextricably linked to the object, and a set of context-dependent features (for example "floats" for *basketball*) that can be called upon as needed. We rely on our knowledge of goals and past events to link these unusual features into a concept and the unusual set of concepts into a category. Hence, higher-order knowledge constrains the features that we choose and yokes them together with an underlying purpose (as in the burning-house example).

Just as contextual goals and memory serve as the knowledge base upon which conceptual relations are formed, so too can cultural goals. In a now classically cited example by Lakoff (1987), the Dyirbal language spoken in parts of Australia treats *women, fire,* and *dangerous things* as a coherent category, each preceded in the language by a unitary marker *balan.* The category appears to be based on elaborate associations among concepts, for example, birds also fit in the category *balan* because they are thought to be the spirits of dead human females. Although this categorization makes little sense to the Western mind, at least one writer, Dixon (1986) demonstrates that underlying this classification system there is a principled, though culturally constructed, way to classify things. (See Lakoff, 1987, pp. 92–102, for the anthropological hypotheses as to why these members are related.)[5]

These last three examples highlight the enormous flexibility and complexity inherent in the human conceptual system. They also demonstrate how our overall knowledge base interacts with conceptual features to create any number of viable categorization systems, from the biological to the sociological. To refer back to our initial questions in Table 4.1, the two knowledge-based theories claim that concepts have relevant features, but that these features do not define the category. As to question 2, Barsalou and Lakoff emphatically deny that concepts are defined in a rulelike way, with clear conceptual boundaries. Rather, concepts are constructed as needed for different contexts or goals (in Barsalou's theory), or on the basis of cultural criteria that may or may not be immediately evident (in Lakoff's theory). Both knowledge-based theories claim that a list of features is insufficient to represent an entire concept. Both psychological contextualism and psychological essentialism are committed to the view that deeper knowledge about conceptual coherence is necessary to make accurate and adult-level categorizations.

What we have seen in these newer versions of conceptual theory is a shift away from the more surface view that concepts are defined by independent bundles of features. In its place, the newer theories suggest that correlated sets of features that we observe in concepts are the product of our underlying knowledge and theories. By way

---

[5] Classifying the conceptual theories of Barsalou (1989) and Lakoff (1987) together under the heading of psychological contextualism blurs some essential distinctions between them. However, at the most general level, both of these theories demonstrate the ways in which contextual knowledge influences our construction of categories.

of example, psychological essentialism, particularly from the research on natural kind concepts, demonstrates how biological theories can form the basis for some of our conceptual knowledge. As Ghiselin (1969, p. 83) summarizes, "Instead of finding patterns in nature and deciding that because of their conspicuousness they seem important, we discover the underlying mechanisms that impose order on natural phenomena, . . . then derive the structure of our classification systems for this understanding" (in Gelman & Coley, 1991).

SUMMARY.   Summarizing the theories presented in this section, we find two broad classes of theories of conceptual structure. Some are feature-based approaches (for example, the classical view and family resemblance view) in which the features provide the basis of the theory of meaning. An alternate position is stated by theory- or knowledge-based approaches (psychological essentialism and psychological contextualism) in which features play a more ancillary role. In the former case, features are defining of the concept—a woman with gray hair, a twinkle in her eye, and pushing a baby stroller has a high probability of being a grandmother. In the knowledge-based approaches, perceptual or other salient features do not define concepts. A gray-haired woman pushing a stroller could only be a grandmother if she had given birth to a child who then grew to have a child.

As we noticed with the study of word primitives, concepts can sometimes be defined by feature primitives. However, this does not give a full picture of our mental representation of concepts. Just as the cognitive system dictates that some multimorphemic words are represented without a further breakdown, our knowledge of complex concepts will consist both of correlations of features, and the reasons for those correlations.

Whichever view we adopt, one point is clear from this discussion: If we are to understand conceptual structure, we must understand more than the concept alone. We must understand the relationship between concepts and how they are organized—into models (in the feature-based views) and into theories (in theory-based views). It is to the question of conceptual organization that we now turn.

Conceptual Organization

How are our concepts organized? Most of the models that we are about to look at use features as their building blocks, in part because they all preceded the more contemporary theory- and knowledge-based theories. Thus, we will only discuss the classical findings to give you the flavor of this literature. Chang (1986) provides a more thorough analysis of theories of semantic memory and their relative success in explaining the data. The most common methods of study have been semantic verification and semantic priming tasks. The models of **semantic organization** we will discuss are largely based on the findings of such experiments.

Models of Semantic Representation

HIERARCHICAL NETWORK MODEL.   The first cognitive model of semantic representation, by Collins and Quillian, appeared in 1969. An illustration of their approach to semantic representation appears in Figure 4.8. Individual concepts such as *animal* and *fish* are represented as "nodes," with the properties specific to each concept stored at the same level and connections between associated concepts. This **hierarchical network model** proposed that concepts are organized in our minds as "pyramids" of concepts, with broader, superordinate concepts (such as *animal*) at the top of the pyramid, and more specific, subordinate concepts (for example, *chihuahua*) at the bottom (Collins & Quillian, 1969, 1970, 1972). In the middle are basic level categories (such as *bird, dog, elephant,* and *fish*).

One important aspect of the model in Figure 4.8 is its emphasis on cognitive economy, a concept we have already introduced. Obviously, any member of a superordinate category such as *animal* will have all the features attributed to *animal,* plus its own features. However, in Collins and Quillian's semantic network, the features would only be stored at the higher-level concept in order to save space. For example, both birds and fish, by virtue of being animals, have all the features attributed to animals—having skin, being able to move, eat, and breathe. However, you do not see these features duplicated at the *birds* and *fish* nodes, because this would violate the concept of cognitive economy. In a now classic experiment, Collins and Quillian (1969) presented subjects with one of two types of semantic verification tasks. In the first, subjects were asked to judge category membership with statements such as, "A canary is a bird," or, "A canary is an animal." In the second, subjects were asked to

FIGURE 4.8

Example of a hierarchically organized memory structure.

Source: "Retrieval Time from Semantic Memory," by A. M. Collins and M. R. Quillian, 1969, Journal of Verbal Learning and Verbal Behavior, 8, pp. 240–248. Copyright 1969 by Academic Press. Reprinted by permission.

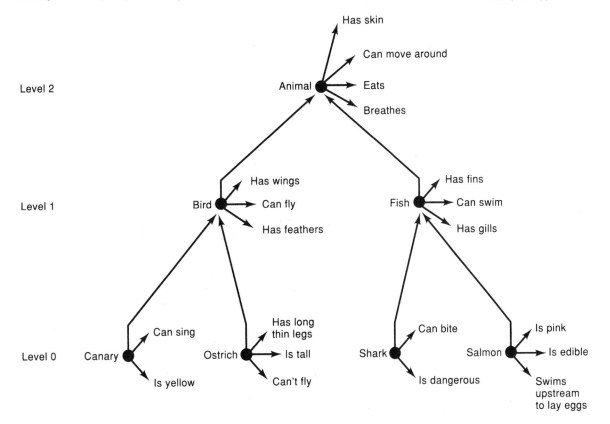

judge feature *attributes* of given concepts in property verification statements such as, "An ostrich has skin," or "An ostrich has feathers." To which of the two sentences in these experiments do you think subjects would respond more quickly (have a lower reaction time)? Why? What would the hierarchical network model predict?

Collins and Quillian were interested in judging "semantic distance effects." That is, looking at Figure 4.8 again, *canary* is further away from *animals* than it is from *birds.* Thus, according to the model, *A canary is an animal* should take longer to verify than *A canary is a bird* because in the former, two nodes must be traversed instead of just one. Property verification statements require us to go to the appropriate node before we can retrieve the features at that level. As with category statements, the number of nodes that must be traversed to determine feature attributes will determine reaction times. To verify *An ostrich has skin,* one must traverse two nodes up *(birds, animals),* and then note that *has skin* is an attribute of animals. To verify *An ostrich has feathers,* one only need go up one node to *birds* and note the features there. It should thus take longer to verify that an ostrich has skin than that it has feathers. It should also take longer to verify features than to verify category membership because not only must one move from node to node, but one must also retrieve features stored at that node. All these assumptions were found to be the case across numerous experiments (Collins & Quillian, 1969, 1970): The further the semantic distance between two concepts, the longer the reaction times in the semantic verification tasks. Additionally, property verification statements require longer time than category membership statements.

A second finding of interest in these experiments was the **category size effect.** That is, the larger the category, the longer time required for search. For example, because the concept *animal* embodies *all* instances of *birds,* as well as all instances of *fish, dogs, horses,* and so forth, it is of necessity a larger category than any of its member categories. Presumably, larger categories force us to muddle through more information before retrieving the relevant facts.

Several logical and empirical criticisms of the hierarchical network model of conceptual organization were responsible for modifying experimenters' views and for the creation of subsequent semantic network models that could better explain the data. One problem with the hierarchical network model is that it is too hierarchical and may only work for **taxonomic categories** such as *animals, dwellings, furniture,* and so forth, but not for more abstract concepts such as *virtue, good,* and *emotion.*

An important study by Conrad (1972) revealed other empirical and theoretical criticisms of the hierarchical network view. Conrad found that semantic distance effects were confounded by frequency effects of features. For example, subjects list the feature, "moves," as a feature of animals more frequently than "has ears," even though both are assumed to be stored at the *animals* node. Likewise, Conrad argued that the semantic distance effects found by Collins and Quillian (1969) need not be explained by semantic distance at all but by the strength of association between two concepts or between a concept and a feature. For example, "sings" may be verified as a property of *canary* more rapidly than "has skin" because singing is more frequently associated with *canary.*

Rips, Shoben, and Smith (1973; also Rosch, 1973) note that the hierarchical network model treats all members of a category as equal members of that category. Yet it seems clear that a German shepherd is a better instance of *dog* than is a chihuahua; a collie a more typical member than an afghan hound. Rips et al. (1973) argued that more typical members of a category should be verified more quickly than less typical members in semantic verification tasks. They did indeed find **typicality effects,** which were reflected in the reaction times of subjects who performed semantic verification tasks.

A third criticism of the hierarchical network theory is that it cannot account for *reverse* category size effects that turned up later (Smith, Shoben, & Rips, 1974). In some cases, subjects take longer to verify that an item is an instance of a superordinate category than it does to verify that it is an instance of a lower-level category. For example, subjects took less time to respond to, "A chimpanzee is a primate," than it did to, "A chimpanzee is an animal," even though *animal* would be stored at a higher category level than *primate* (Smith et al., 1974).

Problems with the hierarchical network model led some to postulate other models that had more explanatory power than a strict hierarchy could provide. The next major model to be developed was that of Smith, Shoben, and Rips (1974).

FEATURE COMPARISON MODEL.   Smith et al. (1974) also took a feature-oriented view of meaning. Instead of nodes, however, they postulated that concepts are represented as lists of features of two types, both (1) *defining* features, which are critical for inclusion in a category, and (2) *characteristic* features, which members of a category usually but do not necessarily have. For example, it is a defining feature of a professor to have an academic appointment, and characteristic but not necessary that the professor wear tweed. Likewise, it is necessary for birds to have skin and bones but not that they fly (think of chickens and penguins). In contrast to the hierarchical network theory, all features are assumed to be stored under all relevant concepts. Although this violates the assumption of cognitive economy, it renders the **feature comparison model** better able to account for some of the empirical findings.

According to Smith et al. (1974), semantic verification tasks are performed by comparing the number of overlapping features of two or more concepts. Feature comparison in semantic decision tasks is assumed to be a two-stage process. In the first stage, all the features—defining and characteristic—of two concepts are compared in a global comparison. A sufficient level of similarity produces a "yes" response. If the degree of similarity is too close to call, a second comparison step is instituted in which only the defining features of the two concepts are compared. Thus, this second stage would be slower and more evaluative than the first more global comparison. For example, refer to Figure 4.9 to see how a robin would be verified as a category member of *bird,* relative to how it would be verified in the hierarchical network model.

Because comparisons are based on similarity rather than category size, the feature comparison model can account for both category size effects and reverse category effects because its predictions are based on number of overlapping features between two concepts rather than distance. The model also predicts semantic distance effects; *collie* should be classified as a dog more quickly than an animal because more features overlap with the concept *dog.* The effects of typicality can also be explained; more typical members of a category would be verified more quickly because the number of overlapping features would be larger than for less typical members. For

FIGURE 4.9

Distinction between the feature comparison model and the hierarchical network model.

Source: "Theories of Semantic Memory," by E. E. Smith. In W. K. Estes (Ed.), Handbook of Learning and Cognitive Processes (Vol. 6). Copyright 1978 by Erlbaum. Reprinted by permission.

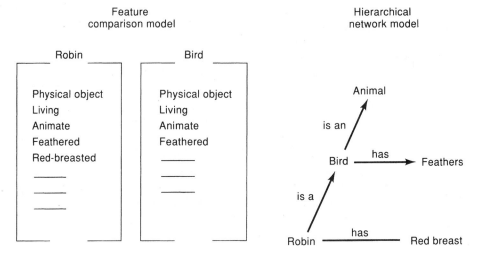

example, the concept of *robin* should share more features with *bird* than does *flamingo*.

Feature comparison theory is not without its share of problems. Most critical is an issue with which you are already familiar—whether or not there really are defining features of concepts. It is not always clear that humans rely on defining features (for example, "lays eggs" for *birds*) to make category judgments, and sometimes the distinction between defining and characteristic features is unclear.

Second, why couldn't we store category membership directly, as one of the features under a concept? That is, why couldn't we store "is a fish" as a feature under the concept *salmon?* That way, to decide that a salmon is a fish, we need only scan the list of *salmon* features rather than compare the feature lists from both concepts.

Another criticism of this model is that feature *lists* cannot account for all that people know about concepts; they also know that some features correlate more highly than others. Features are linked units, not independent units. For example, the features of "small" and "sings" are highly correlated for birds. Likewise, despite the fact that small spoons are considered more typical than large spoons, small *wooden* spoons are considered *less* typical than large wooden spoons (Rumelhart & Ortony, 1977). A theory such as the feature comparison view, which posits lists of independent features, cannot account for Rumelhart and Ortony's findings (Medin, 1989).

SPREADING ACTIVATION NETWORK MODEL.   In order to better account for the empirical findings that challenged his first semantic model, Collins, of Collins and Quillian (1969, 1970), developed a **spreading activation model** of semantic representation (Collins & Loftus, 1975). As in the earlier hierarchical network, concepts are represented as nodes and associated concepts are connected (see Figure 4.10). However, now properties such as *red, large,* or *transports people* are also nodes within this model, and in this way are treated as concepts in their own right. Relations between concepts (including concepts and feature concepts) are represented via connecting nodes, not the number of overlapping features as in the feature comparison view. The

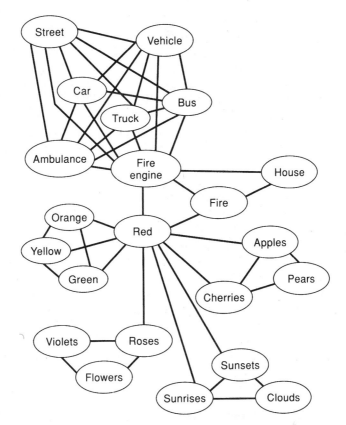

FIGURE 4.10

Example of a spreading activation model in which the length of each line (link) represents the degree of association between two concepts.

Source: "A Spreading Activation Theory of Semantic Processing," by A. M. Collins and E. F. Loftus, 1975, Psychological Review, 82, pp. 407–428. Copyright 1975 by the American Psychological Association. Reprinted by permission.

length of each line between nodes represents the degree of association between the two concepts—shorter lines mean stronger associations. Again, this distance is only metaphorical, and does not necessarily represent how far apart concepts are stored in the brain.

Like the hierarchical model, the spreading activation model is still an associated network. However, the structure is not that of a strict hierarchy, but a more complex web of concepts and relations between concepts. Note its resemblance to connectionist models of cognition such as the connectionist model of lexical access discussed earlier in the chapter. For example, the concept *flowers* is linked not only to *violets* and *roses,* but indirectly to *fire truck* via the *red* concept node. With regard to concepts, no distinction is made between defining and characteristic features; some connections simply appear stronger than others. The degree of association between nodes is represented by distance, with highly associated concepts, such as *canary* and *sings,* closer than more weakly associated concepts, such as *canary* and *skin.*

An important aspect of this model is the principle of spreading activation, from which it gets its name. Think of the model as a large electrical network. When a single concept is activated, the "electricity" spreads to connected concepts, decreasing in strength as it emanates outward. Assume that you are participating in a lexical access task. Through stimulus input the concept of *salmon* is activated.

Like the electricity in a circuit, all nodes connected to the concept *salmon,* such as *fish, animal, stream, pink, edible,* and *gills,* would be activated to a certain degree as well. Thus, the sentence, "A salmon has gills," should be quicker to verify than "A salmon has feathers." Why? Because once *salmon* is activated, *gills* will also receive some activation, whereas *feathers* will not. Likewise, "A salmon has gills," should be more quickly verified than "A salmon has skin," because *gills* are more highly associated with *salmon* and thus "closer" together in the network. Likewise, *cherry* would be confirmed more quickly than *fig* as *fruit* because *cherry* is closer to the subordinate category *(fruit),* because of its higher frequency and stronger association.

The strength of association between concepts (including property concepts), represented via degree of distance in the model, can explain category effects, reverse category effects, and typicality effects in categorization and semantic verification tasks. Notice that the spreading activation network can also be used to explain priming effects. In lexical decision tasks, it should take a shorter time period to recognize the word *nurse* if it follows the term *doctor,* than if it follows *bread,* because the concept node for *nurse* would have already been somewhat activated from *doctor.* Similar to the logogen and connectionist models of lexical access, semantic priming in the spreading activation model is accomplished by lowering thresholds.

You can see that a major advantage of such a model is its explanatory power in accounting for a wide variety of experimental findings. The spreading activation model is flexible enough to account for multiple access routes to concepts and their features and to explain many of the empirical findings related to lexical and conceptual research.

SUMMARY.   One gets a sense not only that meanings may be related through rigid taxonomic structures, but also that the best theories are ones flexible enough to account for all aspects of human performance. Many criteria can be imposed on the organization of concepts, in the same way that many criteria can be imposed on the organization of the lexicon. Task demands, contextual cues, and other factors can all influence what information is accessed and how. Theories that posit different points of access, association, and activation, as spreading activation models do, are bound to have more explanatory power than more rigidly designed models.

As you have seen, each problem space—language and meaning—raises a vast number of questions ripe for research effort. Having dissociated meaning and lexical symbols, let us discuss some final issues related to their reassociation.

A Special Problem for the Mental Lexicon: Lexical Ambiguity

There is no strict one-to-one mapping between words and meaning. Multiple words can supply the same meanings—*pseudonym, alias,* and *pen name* are equivalent in meaning. Likewise, a single word can have multiple meanings: *bank* can mean (l) a place to store money, (2) the side of a river, (3) what a race car driver does when he encounters a steep turn. Words such as *fox* (a mammal with reddish fur, or a clever and crafty person, or, in slang, a good-looking woman), *right* (correct or the opposite of left), and *drill* (a power tool, to use a tool to make a hole in wood, a practice exercise, or to engage in a practice exercise, as in the military) are said to be *lexically ambiguous* because each word in isolation does not indicate the intended meaning. One meaning of an ambiguous word can be more common than the others: *bank* is most frequently used to refer to a place where money is kept. In most cases, the multiple meanings of an ambiguous word share the same grammatical class. The meanings of *fox* listed above all are nouns. Other times, the different meanings of a word are from different grammatical classes: the noun *drill* refers to a power tool that makes holes, and the verb form describes what one does with that power tool. Many jokes (including the doctor joke about "Eyes checked?" at the beginning of this chapter) hinge on some words having two meanings. An obvious way in which the lexicon and meaning coalesce is in the study of how we process ambiguous words.

We use language to convey an intended meaning in the mind of the speaker or writer that can be accurately decoded by the listener or reader. Ambiguous words may foil comprehension because of their multiple meanings. However, we seldom encounter words in isolation; they tend to appear in sentences, and these sentences often provide a context for determining which of several meanings of a lexically ambiguous word is intended. For example, if I report, "The canoeist rowed up to the bank," it becomes evident from the mention of a canoeist and rowing which sense of *bank* is being used.

Much of the research into the processing of ambiguous words has used a **phoneme monitoring task,** in which subjects press a button every time they hear a particular phoneme, such as /b/. Foss (1969, 1970) placed some of the target phonemes after a word with multiple meanings, such as "The men started to *drill* before they were ordered to do so," and found that response times were longer than if the target phoneme appeared after a nonambiguous word. Although the sentence structure makes it clear that *drill* above is functioning as a verb, the sentence context does not specify which *interpretation* of the word is intended. It thus provides subjects with an "interpretive dilemma" (Simpson & Burgess, 1988) about whether *drill* refers to boring holes in wood, or to engaging in military exercises. We may not be conscious that two meanings of ambiguous words such as *drill* are being activated or "lit up" lexically, but the longer processing time in the phoneme monitoring task indicates that both meanings of ambiguous words are being activated, which then prevents subjects from responding as quickly to target phonemes. Foss's (1969, 1970) findings launched a mass of research on processing ambiguous words, in order to determine when and under what circumstances several meanings of a word are activated.

Sentence context usually constrains which interpretation an ambiguous word receives. For example, if Foss's sample sentence was modified to "The sergeant ordered the men to drill before they had recovered from morning exercises," it becomes evident that *drill* refers to military training and not to boring holes in wood. Would providing this contextual information have led to activation of only one meaning of *drill* and faster response times to the phoneme /b/ after it? The answer to this question is important to knowing what is happening during on-line processing of words and sentences. It is possible that subjects activate multiple meanings of a word even when the context makes it clear which meaning is intended.

There are two major theoretical camps about the role of context in influencing which of several meanings of lexically ambiguous words are activated. One camp (Glucksberg, Kreuz, & Rho, 1986; Schvaneveldt, Meyer, & Becker, 1976; Simpson, 1981), which we will call the **selective access view,** holds that context biases the interpretation of an ambiguous word, so that only the intended meaning is accessed. At a conscious level, we appear to consider only one interpretation of a word or sentence at a time. If Foss had used the sentence, "The carpenter ordered the men to drill before they were ready," most of us would report having generated an image of men with power tools piercing holes in boards. However, as you now know, much cognitive processing takes place beneath the level of consciousness.

The alternative view claims that even with context provided in a sentence or experimental task, multiple meanings of a lexically ambiguous term are activated (Onifer & Swinney, 1981; Seidenberg, Tanenhaus, Leiman, & Bienkowski, 1982; Swinney, 1979; Tanenhaus, Leiman, & Seidenberg, 1979). This second theory, the **exhaustive access view,** has more empirical support. Some of its advocates (for example, Simpson & Burgess, 1988) also claim meanings of an ambiguous word do not necessarily achieve activation threshold simultaneously; more frequently used meanings of the word, or those influenced by context, may achieve threshold *first,* although all meanings are activated in parallel. Context simply resolves the conflict between meanings in post-access processes.

CONTEXT.   The main empirical question, then, is whether the context surrounding an ambiguous word limits access to only the meaning intended by that context. Swinney (1979) asked subjects to participate in a **cross-modal priming study.** That is, they had to listen to sentences that contained ambiguous words and simultaneously participate in a visual lexical decision task. An example of stimuli is, "The man was surprised when he found several spiders, roaches, and other *bugs* in the corner of his room." Directly after the word *bugs* was heard, subjects saw either the word *ant,* or *spy,* or *sew* projected on the screen in front of them and had to perform a lexical decision task. Both *ant* and *spy* drew quicker responses than *sew,* even though only *ant* is the meaning consistent with the rest of the sentence. It appears multiple meanings of *bug* were activated, which then primed lexical recognition of words related to all interpretations of *bug.* Even though the insect-related interpretation of *bugs* is the dominant meaning, subjects unconsciously considered both interpretations.

Onifer and Swinney (1981) also noticed priming of both dominant and subordinate meanings of words, regardless of the context. For instance, lexical decision responses to both *round* and *noisy* were primed by either of the following sentences:

Dominant context: *The housewife's face literally lit up as a plumber extracted her lost wedding <u>ring</u> from the sink.*

Subordinate context: *The office walls were so thin that they could hear the <u>ring</u> of their neighbor's phone whenever a call came in.*

In this experiment, even associates of the less-frequently used meaning of ambiguous words were primed, regardless of whether the sentence context biased interpretation toward the dominant or subordinate meanings. Onifer and Sweeney (1981) concluded that meaning frequency has no effect on lexical interpretation until after both (or all) meanings of a word have been activated.

INTERACTION OF CONTEXT AND DOMINANT MEANING. Here is one humorous example of only the dominant (albeit erroneous) meaning of an ambiguous word being activated: While playing "Outburst," a game that requires contestants to yell out potential answers to a category, one of the authors of this book and her teammates received the category, "famous basketball centers." As the most frequent use of *center* refers to a place (as in convention center, Center for the Performing Arts), her team (to the great amusement of the opponents) began yelling out answers such as, "the Palestra in Philadelphia" as a renowned *place* where basketball was played. Of course, the intended meaning of the category clue was "famous people who have played the *position* of center in basketball," and the list included Kareem Abdul-Jabbar, Bill Walton, Wilt Chamberlain, and Shaquille O'Neal. Needless to say, no points were awarded to the author's team on that round. Even when context was clearly biased toward the subordinate meaning of *center* (though consistent with both meanings), the dominant interpretation of the ambiguous word won out. Of course, it is possible both meanings of *center* were activated, but only the one achieved threshold to become conscious.

The frequency of stored meanings of a word may interact with context to determine whether, and how quickly, multiple meanings are activated. In an eye-tracking task that measured the amount of time subjects spent fixated on a lexically ambiguous word, Duffy, Morris, and Rayner (1988) explored the difference between **balanced** and **polarized** homographs. Balanced ambiguous words are those whose several meanings are equally common (for example, *right* used to mean either correct or the opposite of left); polarized words are those for which one meaning predominates (for example, *yarn*—more commonly used to refer to a textile than to a folk tale). The ambiguous words were put into sentences either with or without a biasing context. A *before* biasing context would be, "The dragon was no longer in pain once the *scale* was removed," in which the beginning of the sentence leads to an interpretation of one meaning of the word. A nonbiasing context would provide no clues to the ambiguous word's interpretation until *after* the word appeared, as in the sentence, "Once the *scale* was removed, the dragon was no longer in pain." The context of the sentences was always tailored toward the subordinate meaning of a term (for example, a dragon's scale, rather than a scale for weighing).

In the *after* context condition, eye gaze was longer to the balanced ambiguous words than to control (that is, nonambiguous) words, which indicated that both interpretations were accessed in the absence of biasing context. Polarized words, however, did not receive additional looking times, presumably because the dominant meaning was adopted immediately. When context was available (in the *before* condition), eye gaze to the target word was longer only in the polarized condition. It appeared that even the dominant meaning of polarized words was accessed, despite the fact that the context in this condition was always tailored to the subordinate meaning (also see Dopkins, Morris, & Rayner, 1992; Miyake, Just, & Carpenter, 1994). The Duffy et al. (1988) experiment confirms that dominance is a major factor in early lexical access: Equally frequent meanings compete for interpretation when no context is available (in the balanced words, the *before* condition); and dominant meanings are immediately activated even when the context is biased against them (in the polarized words, the *after* condition, in which the context related to the subordinate meaning). Although this experiment suggests that sentence context can selectively access meaning of at least balanced ambiguous words, remember that eye gaze measures an early stage of lexical processing (which is important to the discussion below).

Like so many other studies, Tabossi, Colombo, and Job (1987) found that word associates of the dominant meaning were primed even when the context biased subjects to the subordinate meaning of the word. However, when the context was tailored to the dominant interpretation, they determined that only the dominant meaning was accessed, similar to the Duffy et al. findings.

The precedence of frequent meanings is a robust one: Simpson (1981) found that a strong biasing context was needed to overcome the dominance effect; the most frequent interpretations of a word are the first to be activated unless the context strongly steers subjects to the subordinate meaning. Because of its strength in lexical representation, the most frequent meaning of a word may always be accessed; less-frequent meanings may become active only in neutral or subordinate-biased contexts. This effect is akin to the importance of word frequency in lexical access models discussed in the earlier sections of this chapter (meaning dominance is really the same as "most frequently used interpretation").

OTHER FACTORS.   Whether the two interpretations of a lexically ambiguous item are from the same grammatical class or not also influences experimental findings. Seidenberg, Tanenhaus, Leiman, and Bienkowski (1982) determined that without a priming context, access was exhaustive. When a priming context was presented, both meanings of words with noun–verb interpretations (for example, *punch*) were activated, but only the contextually intended meaning of noun–noun meanings (for example, *spade*) was accessed. Seidenberg et al. claimed that the syntactic class of a word's meaning determines whether word access is exhaustive or selective, and not the context per se. Meanings of words with the same grammatical function (for example, noun–noun) compete for access in a way that word meanings from different grammatical classes (for example, noun–verb) do not.

TIME COURSE OF ACTIVATION.   A wealth of evidence indicates that processing of lexically ambiguous words leads to activation of multiple meanings (for example, Kinoshita, 1985; MacKay, 1966; Onifer & Swinney, 1981; Simpson & Burgess, 1985; Swinney, 1979), but also some evidence (for example, Duffy et al., 1988; Schvaneveldt, Meyer, & Becker, 1976; Tabossi et al., 1987) that context does constrain which word meanings are activated. Which is it, then? Does the research largely support exhaustive or selective access? Is there a way to explain all of the various findings?

Some of the discrepancies in experimental results may be resolved by looking at the time course of lexical access. *When* lexical access is tested can interact with (a) context, (b) the relative frequency of different interpretations of the word, and (c) whether the multiple definitions of a term are from the same grammatical class or not.

Simpson and Burgess (1985) attempted to test pure lexical access with a lexical decision task using prime-target pairs (for example, *bank–money,* or *bank–river*) without any sentence context. Which target was semantically primed depended on how soon after the lexically ambiguous prime it appeared. At 16 millisecond interstimulus interval (**ISI**)—that is, where the target appeared immediately after the prime went off—only dominant meanings were facilitated. In the example above, for instance, *money* would be recognized faster when it appeared after *bank* because *money* is related to the most common meaning of *bank*. However, with a 300 millisecond delay before the target appeared on the screen, both meanings were equally activated, and even the subordinate meaning *(river)* was primed. At longer ISIs, the dominant meaning appears to remain active while the less-frequent meaning subsides. Moreover, results showed an inhibition of meanings associated with the less-frequent meaning (Simpson & Burgess, 1988). That is, if *ball* appeared, and *dance* was not presented for 750 milliseconds, recognition of *dance* (related to the subordinate meaning of *ball*) was actually slower than if it had been preceded by an unrelated word (for example, *panel*).

It appears that multiple meanings of a word may be activated in parallel, with the dominant meaning "popping up" first. Evidence supports that this is an automatic process not influenced by subject intentions. Context sometimes may *speed* access to one of several meanings, but does not *restrict* access to all interpretations of an ambiguous word (Prather & Swinney, 1988). Such may have been the case in the Duffy et al. (1988) eye-gaze study in which the intended meaning of a balanced ambiguous word "beat out" the alternative (but equally frequent) interpretation. At longer delays, post-access processes, which may be under subject control, resolve ambiguities by concentrating on the intended meaning only. It is at this late stage that context may have the most influence (Simpson & Burgess, 1988). Several experiments that found a constraining effect of context on lexical access (for example, Schvaneveldt, Meyer, & Becker, 1976) may have been due to the length of time between primes and target words, which permitted contextually intended meanings to overcome unintended ones.

THE TIME COURSE OF SENTENCE CONTEXTS VERSUS WORD PAIRS.   Because of the biasing semantic influence sentences may exert prior even to presentation of a target ambiguous word, the time course of activation is slightly different in sentence studies. Recall that Simpson and Burgess (1985) found only the dominant meaning of an ambiguous word activated immediately after presentation, multiple meanings at 100–300 milliseconds, and only the meaning intended by the context (or prime) at 750 milliseconds. In contrast, Tanenhaus, Carlson, and Seidenberg (1984) and Swinney (1979) found immediate activation of multiple word meanings after reading a sentence; but only the contextually specified meaning of an ambiguous word remained by 200 milliseconds. Why the faster sequence of processing in the sentence conditions? Expectancy effects may begin activation of a word unit prior even to its interpretation, so that access to multiple meanings is available sooner than in word-pair studies.

SUMMARY.   Overall, the evidence suggests that activation of all meanings of ambiguous words takes place even in the face of biasing contexts. It thus appears that lexical ambiguity resolution is a dynamic process, with the various interpretations of a word racing against each other for access based on (1) frequency of meaning; and

(2) the degree to which context biases one interpretation over the other. Even though in most cases, we access multiple meanings of an ambiguous word, we do so at different rates. The evidence supports a model of exhaustive but brief access of all meanings of an ambiguous word. After the window of opportunity for multiple interpretations, context exerts its main influence on which of several meanings remains active. Two to three syllables after exposure to an ambiguous word (roughly 500–800 milliseconds), only a single meaning remains; the "unused" interpretation is not left hanging around indefinitely. Knowing the time course of lexical access within experiments may help resolve some of the discrepant findings.

Studies on lexical ambiguity are an effective way to determine the link between words (in their phonological or orthographic codes) and meanings. And the findings clearly have implications for models of lexical access discussed in the first half of the chapter (though an elaborated discussion is beyond our scope here). In lexical ambiguity, we again see the imperfect mapping between words and meanings, and also the ways in which the two domains interact. Thus lexical ambiguity provides a window into the complex processes that the human mind uses to navigate between our conceptual and linguistic systems. The study of lexical ambiguity also provides a vivid illustration of how language serves both communication and symbolic functions. To round off our discussion in this chapter, we now turn our attention to reestablishing the connection between words and meaning.

The Reciprocal and Influential Relationships of Words and Meaning

In the earlier sections of this chapter, we asked you to think separately about words and meaning, about language and the thoughts it represents. As you probably noticed, making a *complete* distinction between these two domains is almost impossible. Even our discussion of the lexicon suggested that word organization is permeated by discussions of meaning.

The relationship between words as communication symbols and conceptual meaning is a two-way street: Words influence the kind of meanings we can convey; and meanings dictate the development of words, which then spurs development of vocabulary as technology and civilization provide new objects and concepts.

The illustration that makes this point most clearly comes from an example with words offered by the philosopher Quine (1960) in his book *Word and Object.* To adapt his example for our purposes, imagine that you are a linguist in a foreign land, Kalaba, trying to decode a language about which you known nothing (Kalaban). Your job is a simple one (or so it seems). You need only link the sounds that you hear with the objects and events that you see. Suddenly, a rabbit hops by and the native speaker near you says, "Gavagai." "Aha," you think. "Perhaps 'gavagai' means rabbit." Shortly thereafter, another rabbit scurries by and again you hear, "Gavagai." Now you are certain and write the word in your vocabulary notebook.

Although you feel confident in your interpretation, Quine rightly casts doubt on your conclusion. The word *gavagai* could mean any number of things because label-to-word mapping is ambiguous. The term *gavagai* could be associated with any number of things or properties of the scene. For example, could it not refer to rabbit ears, or legs, or fur? Couldn't it also refer to the act of hopping that you saw both times? Even less likely, but possible, *gavagai* could refer to the movement of the rabbit relative to the background, or to the way the sun reflected off the rabbit fur in the two cases. These and many other referents could be valid meanings for the term *gavagai*. How, then, did you arrive so swiftly at a definite conclusion?

A recent body of work, mostly on the learning of object names, suggests that the very use of words and language constrains or limits the possibilities for **word–meaning mapping** (see Clark, 1983, 1987; Golinkoff, Mervis, & Hirsh-Pasek, 1994; Keil, 1989; Markman, 1989; and Merriman & Bowman, 1989, for reviews). The point of this research is that children come to favor certain meanings or mappings over others as they gain experience with language, a concept that we explore further in Chapter 8. Golinkoff et al. (1994) have postulated several key principles that word learners rely on in learning novel words: (1) the **reference principle** (a foundation of word learning) leads learners to assume that a word denotes or maps onto an object, event, or property. This is why you would assume that *gavagai* refers to something in the environment. (2) The **object scope principle** (or *whole object principle;* Markman & Wachtel, 1988) leads learners to look for a whole object rather than object parts as the referent. Thus you are more likely to see the rabbit as the referent in Quine's example above rather than the rabbit's ears, paws, or fur. (3) The **extendability principle** posits that children assume that a word refers not to a single object, action, or event, but to a *class* of objects, actions, and events. These classes can be defined in various ways, as **thematic associations** (for example, pen–paper) or taxonomically defined categories (for example, cow–sheep as animals). (4) The **categorical scope principle** leads learners to extend words to the same *kinds* of things (Markman & Hutchinson, 1984; Waxman & Gelman, 1986). For example, you would be most likely to assume your new word, *gavagai*, refers to all kinds of rabbits—brown ones, baby ones, floppy-eared ones—rather than to a thematic association (for example, rabbits and carrots). (5) The **novel name/nameless category principle** biases learners to assume that a novel word refers to an unnamed object in the environment rather than to an object that already has a name (Clark, 1987; Markman, 1989; Merriman & Bowman, 1989). Taken together, this body of research suggests that something about language directs attention to some meanings over others. Language itself alters the efficiency with which we organize concepts and contributes to greater depth of conceptual understanding.

Research on primates underscores this finding. Working with chimpanzees, Premack and Premack (1983) presented evidence that language-trained chimpanzees classify objects differently than do language-untrained chimps. Trained and untrained chimpanzees learned what is called a **match-to-sample** task, such as the one you see in Figure 4.11a. That is, when shown an apple as target, and then an apple and a banana as selections, the chimps were rewarded for choosing the apple because it matches the target apple. However, when shown a match-to-sample as in Figure 4.11b, where the match is to *half,* only the language-trained primate was able to group the half glass of water and the half apple together. Thus the mere presence of language seems to guide assumptions about meaning.

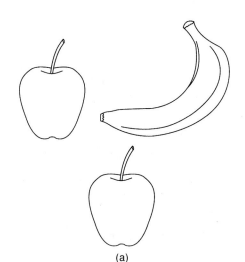

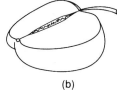

(a)

(b)

FIGURE 4.11

MATCH-TO-SAMPLE TASK

The studies presented above focus on ways in which word use and word knowledge might prime certain mappings between words and their meanings. Yet these findings can be viewed within an even larger arena of relations between language and thought. In one case, the use of language can change or determine how we think, as in the case of the Premacks' language-trained chimpanzees. Based on recent findings, Waxman and Gelman (1986) reported that the use of an adjective with a noun—even a novel adjective with a novel noun—leads children to look for subordinate classifications. The word *rose,* for example, refers to a taxonomic class that includes red roses, pink roses, and yellow roses, as well as climbing roses. Once an adjective is used, however, the field is narrowed to a particular type of rose as in the example of the climbing rose. Not only does the inclusion of adjectival markers therefore direct attention to certain meanings, but certain patterns of grammatical use lead to assumptions about meanings. Without knowing any of the words, to use a further example, you know that *X blixes Y* suggests some causal action with X as the actor and Y as the recipient of the action. Similarly, you know that *X and Y are blixing,* and that *X blixes with Y,* do not lead you to make causal assumptions. In fact, in the latter cases, you assume that X and Y are simply doing something together (*blixing*) (see Hirsh-Pasek & Golinkoff , 1996, for a more detailed discussion). The syntactic frames in which words are found reveal aspects of their meaning. According to Fischer, Gleitman, and Gleitman (1991; see also L. Gleitman, 1990), using these syntactic cues affords us high rate of accuracy in our attribution of meaning.

Conversely, the very makeup of our conceptual system works to influence the creation of words and language structures. Talmy (1975, 1985) noted that certain semantic properties are universally signaled by verbs. Verb systems of languages around the world specify *motion, manner, location,* and *cause* in various combinations. For example, some English verbs use a combination of motion and cause, as in the verbs, *blew, pulled,* or *kicked.* Others use motion and manner, or the way in which the motion occurs, as in *slid, swung,* and *swirled.* The conceptual structure embedded in the verb meaning serves to determine the prepositional structure.

This, in turn, determines the required syntax. By way of example, you can't think of *blowing* without thinking of an *agent* (for example, person or fan) who does the blowing and an *object* (for example, feather or dress) that is blown. Given this semantic base, any sentence or syntactic representation is bound to have a *subject noun* (the blower), a *verb* (the act of blowing), and a *direct object* (the thing being blown).

Psycholinguists are investigating these correlations between meaning and words and between meaning and syntax (Fischer, Gleitman, & Gleitman, 1991; Grimshaw, 1985; Pinker, 1989) in an effort to see how young learners might use their early knowledge of meaning and semantic structure to bootstrap their way into a knowledge of grammatical structure. The problem of understanding language acquisition is discussed in detail in Chapter 8. Again, the point is that just as language directs thought, properties of thought direct the composition of language.

SUMMARY

Language is like a cracked kettle upon which we beat out tunes for bears to dance to, while all the while we long to move the stars to pity.

Gustav Flaubert, *Madame Bovary*

As reflected by their joint coverage in this chapter, words and meaning are greatly intertwined within human communication. Flaubert may have been accurate in conveying our frustration in seeking and not always finding words (and combinations of words) that permit the intensity of poetic feeling we may have intended. Still, words remain our most effective and flexible way to communicate about events, thoughts, and emotions.

That is not to say that meaning cannot exist without language; a nine-month-old child can readily use pointing to communicate that she wants the toy perched on the table beyond her reach. And many a dog beats his owner to the door upon hearing the sound of a leash being rattled. However, individuals or species without language may be able to communicate only about a limited array of topics (Hauser, 1996). As discussed in the previous section, meanings confine words, and words influence the sophistication of our concepts.

One of the themes of this chapter has been that both words and concepts can be analyzed in terms of their primitives—morphemes in the case of words; features in the case of concepts. However, much evidence suggests that a purely decompositional view of these two domains cannot adequately cover the depth of either. The lexicon appears to contain both single- and multimorphemic entries for greater ease of word processing. Our conceptual system likewise stores information not only about the set of features characteristic of a given concept, but also about the ultimate causes for those features (for example, why a whale is a mammal and not a fish, even though it shares many features with fish). In this respect, knowledge-based theories supplement our surface understanding of the definitions of concepts.

We have, of course, much more to learn about the ways in which we represent words, about the nature of meanings, and about the connections between words, meaning, and language, and meaning and thought. Yet the past two decades of psycholinguistic research have taken us a long way toward formulating some tentative answers to the questions that philosophers posed long ago.

In closing, let us return to our opening example and reexamine whether this passage in "Jabberwocky" *really* has no meaning. You probably know what we are about to say: You know a great deal about the meanings of these sentences even before hearing our explanation (and Humpty Dumpty's):

> 'Twas brillig, and the slithy toves
> Did gyre and gimble in the wabe:
> All mimsy were the borogroves,
> And the mome raths outgrabe.

Just to get you started, you know that *gyre* and *gimble* are verbs and denote actions that must be able to be performed at the same time. You know this even before Humpty Dumpty informs Alice that they mean, "to go round and round like a gyroscope," and "to make holes like a gimlet," respectively. Furthermore, you know that *slithy* and *mimsy* are adjectives modifying the nouns *toves* and *borogroves*. How? Adjectives in English often take the morpheme *-y*, and the plural *-s* typically indicates the word is a noun. For further elucidation, *slithy* means both "lithe and slimy," *mimsy* is "flimsy and miserable." And according to Humpty Dumpty, a *borogrove* is a thin, shabby-looking bird with its feathers splaying out all over, while a *tove* is something like a badger, something like a lizard, and something like a corkscrew, that makes its nest under a sundial and lives on cheese. You get the picture. The rest of the interpretation we leave to your devices (or refer you to *Through the Looking Glass* for further exposition). Now, however, you see the words and not only have some idea about what they mean but how they are stored and accessed.

KEY WORDS

Semantics

Lexical ambiguity

Word primitives

Morpheme (free and bound)

Lexeme

Lexeme (as word primitive)

Morpheme (as word primitive)

Cognitive economy

Lexical decision task

Tachistoscope

Lexical access

Pseudo-suffixed

Reaction times

Derivational morphemes

Grammatical class

Inflectional morphemes

Compound words (semantically opaque and semantically transparent)

Semantic priming task
Primed
Phonemes
Frequency effect
Imageability effects
Open- and closed-class words
Tip-of-the-tongue (TOT)
Concepts
Access routes
Serial search model
Forster's autonomous search model
Parallel access (direct access) model
Logogen model
Post-access check
Threshold (for activation)
Connectionist models (connectionism)
Nodes
Hidden nodes
Cohort model
Neighborhood effects
Signs versus symbols
Intension
Extension
Reference theory of meaning
Referent
Ideational theory of meaning
Conventionality
Conceptual primitives
Features
Decompositional view of meaning
Classical view
Family resemblance theory

Necessary and jointly sufficient
    features
Characteristic features
Graded structure
Prototype
Fuzzy boundaries
Semantic verification task
Psychological essentialism
Psychological contextualism
Semantic organization
Hierarchical network model
Category size effect
Taxonomic categories
Typicality effects
Feature comparison model
Spreading activation model
Phoneme monitoring task
Selective access view
Exhaustive access view
Cross-modal priming study
Balanced and polarized (words)
Interstimulus interval (ISI)
Word-meaning mappings
Reference principle
Object scope principle
Extendability principle
Thematic associations
Categorical scope principle
Novel name/nameless category principle
Match-to-sample procedure
Conventionality principle
Ad hoc categories

SOMETHING TO THINK ABOUT

1. What is the relation between words and meanings? Is there an exact match between a word and a concept, or vice versa? Give examples and explanations.

2. Is it more likely that the word primitives stored in our lexicon are words (lexemes) or individual morphemes? Does the kind of word have any influence on which position you take? Explain.

3. What are the most important factors that influence lexical access? What experimental support is there for the primacy of these factors?

4. How do serial versus parallel search models of lexical access account for the main factors from the question above?

5. Contrast the classical and family resemblance theories of concepts with each other, and with the knowledge- (or theory-) based approaches.

6. Compare the models of semantic organization. Why is the spreading activation model considered the most flexible of the three?

7. How does the context of a sentence or word pair affect lexical access of ambiguous words? Which is better supported by the evidence: exhaustive or selective access of word meanings? Explain.

8. What appears to be the time course of lexical activation for words with multiple meanings?

ACTIVITIES

1. As this chapter and Chapter 1 demonstrate, speakers of a language have implicit understanding of how morphemes can be combined to create larger concepts. Consider the following words: *snark, blod, frep, plankle, lerb.*

   How would you adjust each of these words to fit into each of the following frames?
   1. Everyone agreed that she was the _____ woman on the volleyball team.
   2. At the conference, he delivered the opening speech _____.
   3. This wall is covered with _____. It is unbelievably _____. We need to _____ it.
   4. This person comes from (insert nonsense word). He is a _____.

   Construct more nonsense words and additional sentences into which they can be placed and modified as plurals, verb forms, modifiers, etc. Ask 10 adults and 10 children to complete the sentences. What, if any, are some common types of responses? Do responses at times differ from one person to the next? Why might this be?

2. Below are two lists of letter strings. Some are words, some are nonwords or arbitrary strings of letters. As you read each word to yourself, say aloud, "yes" if

the string is a word, "no" if the string is not a word of English. Using a stopwatch with a second hand, determine how long it took you to complete each list.

List 1: *gambasty, revery, voitle, chard, wefe, cratily, decoy, puldow, raflot, oriole, voluble, boovle, chalt, awry, signet, trave, crock, cryptic, ewe, himpola*

List 2: *mulvow, governor, bless, tuglety, gare, relief, ruftily, history, pindle, develop, gardot, norve, busy, effort, garvola, match, sard, pleasant, coin, maisle*

Consider your reaction times. Which list took longer to complete? Using information provided in this chapter, why do you think one list took longer than the other?

3. Perform a word association task. Ask 10 people to quickly provide 5 responses to the following words:

> wet
> swift
> petal
> apple
> shoot
> fire
> white

Examine their responses. In what way do such responses relate to models of lexical organization and retrieval discussed in this chapter?

4. Ask people to provide examples of the following concepts, as quickly as possible. See how many examples they can supply in 2 minutes. Do their responses shed light on notions such as prototypicality or defining features?

> fruit
> pets
> furniture
> mammals
> fish
> clothing

Ask children to do the same task. In what ways do their performances differ from adults'?

REFERENCES

Aitchison, J. (1984). The mental representation of prefixes. *Osmania Papers in Linguistics, 910* (*Nirmala* Memorial Volume), 61–72.

Aitchison, J. (1987). *Words in the mind: An introduction to the mental lexicon.* Oxford: Basil Blackwell.

Aitchison, J., & Straf, M. (1982). Lexical storage and retrieval: A developing skill. In A. Cutler (Ed.), *Slips of the tongue and language production.* Berlin: Mouton.

Armstrong, S., Gleitman, L., & Gleitman, H. (1983). What some concepts might not be. *Cognition, 13,* 263–274.

Aronoff, M. (1976). Word formation in generative grammar. *Linguistic Inquiry, Monograph 1.* Cambridge, MA: MIT Press.

Balota, D. (1994). Visual word recognition: The journey from features to meaning. In M. A. Gernsbacher (Ed.), *Handbook of psycholinguistics* (pp. 303–358). San Diego: Academic Press.

Balota, D. A., & Chumbley, J. I. (1984). Are lexical decisions a good measure of lexical access? The role of word frequency in the neglected decision stage. *Journal of Experimental Psychology, 10,* 340–357.

Barclay, J. R., Bransford, J. D., Franks, J. J., McCarrell, N. S., & Nitsch, K. (1974). Comprehension and semantic flexibility. *Journal of Verbal Learning and Verbal Behavior, 13,* 471–481.

Barsalou, L. W. (1982). Context-independent and context-dependent information in concepts. *Memory & Cognition, 10,* 82–93.

Barsalou, L. W. (1987). The instability of graded structure: Implications for the nature of concepts. In U. Neisser (Ed.), *Concepts and conceptual development: Ecological and intellectual factors in categorization.* New York: Cambridge University Press.

Barsalou, L., & Medin, D. (1986). Concepts: Fixed definitions or context-dependent representations? *Cahiers de Psychologie Cognitive, 6,* 187–202.

Battig, W. F., & Montague, W. E. (1969). Category norms for verbal items in 56 categories: A replication and extension of the Connecticut category norms. *Journal of Experimental Psychology Monograph, 80,* 1–46.

Becker, C. A. (1979). Semantic context and word frequency effects in visual word recognition. *Journal of Experimental Psychology: Human Perception and Performance, 10,* 340–357.

Bleasdale, F. A. (1987). Concreteness-dependent associative priming: Separate lexical organization for concrete and abstract words. *Journal of Experimental Psychology: Learning, Memory and Cognition, 13,* 582–594.

Boas, F. (1911). *The handbook of North American Indians.* (Smithsonian Institution, Bureau of American Ethnology, Bulletin 40). Washington, DC: U.S. Government Printing Office.

Bradley, D. C. (1983). *Computational distinctions of vocabulary type.* Bloomington, IN: Indiana University Linguistics Club.

Bradley, D. C., Garrett, M. F., & Zurif, E. B. (1980). Syntactic deficits in Broca's aphasia. In D. Caplan (Ed.), *Biological studies of mental processes.* Cambridge, MA: MIT Press.

Brown, R., & McNeill, D. (1966). The "tip of the tongue" phenomenon. *Journal of Verbal Learning and Verbal Behavior, 5,* 325–537.

Carey, S. (1985). *Conceptual change in childhood.* Cambridge, MA: MIT Press.

Carroll, D. W. (1986). *Psychology of language.* Monterey, CA: Brooks/Cole.

Carroll, L. (1862/1990). *Alice's adventures in Wonderland* and *Through the looking glass.* In M. Gardner (Ed.), *More annotated Alice.* New York: Random House.

Chang, T. M. (1986). Semantic memory: Facts and models. *Psychological Bulletin, 99,* 199–220.

Clark, E. (1983). Meanings and concepts. In J. H. Flavell & E. Markman (Eds.), *Handbook of child psychology, Vol. 3: Cognitive development* (pp. 787–840). New York: Wiley.

Clark, E. (1987). The principle of contrast: A constraint on language acquisition. In B. MacWhinney (Ed.), *Mechanisms of language acquisition.* Hillsdale, NJ: Erlbaum.

Collins, A. M., & Loftus, E. F. (1975). A spreading activation theory of semantic processing. *Psychological Review, 82,* 407–428.

Collins, A. M., & Quillian, M. R. (1969). Retrieval time from semantic memory. *Journal of Verbal Learning and Verbal Behavior, 8,* 240–248.

Collins, A. M., & Quillian, M. R. (1970). Facilitating retrieval from semantic memory: The effect of repeating part of an inference. *Acta Psychologia, 33,* 304–314.

Collins, A. M., & Quillian, M. R. (1972). Experiments on semantic memory and language comprehension. In L.W. Gregg (Ed.), *Cognition in learning and memory* (pp. 117–137). New York: Wiley.

Coltheart, M., Davelaar, E., Jonasson, J., & Besner, D. (1976). Access to the internal lexicon. In S. Dornic (Ed.), *Attention and performance, Vol. VI.* Hillsdale, NJ: Erlbaum.

Conrad, C. (1972). Cognitive economy in semantic memory. *Journal of Experimental Psychology, 92,* 149–154.

Dopkins, S., Morris, R. K., & Rayner, K. (1992). Lexical ambiguity and eye fixations in reading: A test of competing models of lexical ambiguity resolution. *Journal of Memory and Language, 31,* 461–476.

Duffy, S. A., Morris, R. K., & Rayner, K. (1988). Lexical ambiguity and fixation times in reading. *Journal of Memory and Language, 27,* 429–446.

Ellis, A. W., Miller, D., & Sin, G. (1983). Wernicke's aphasia and normal language processing: A case study in cognitive neuropsychology. *Cognition, 15,* 111–144.

Ervin, S. M. (1957). Grammar and classification. Paper presented at American Psychological Association annual meeting, New York, September.

Fischer, C., Gleitman, L., & Gleitman, H. (1991). On the semantic content of subcategorization frames. *Cognitive Psychology, 23,* 331–392.

Forster, K. I. (1976). Accessing the mental lexicon. In F. J. Wales & E. Walker (Eds.), *New approaches to language mechanisms* (pp. 257–287). Amsterdam: North-Holland.

Forster, K. I. (1990). Lexical processing. In D. Osherson & H. Lasnik (Eds.), *Language.* Cambridge, MA: MIT Press.

Forster, K. I., & Chambers, S. M. (1973). Lexical access and naming time. *Journal of Verbal Learning and Verbal Behavior, 12,* 627–635.

Foss, D. J. (1969). Decision processes during sentence comprehension: Effects of lexical item difficulty and position upon decision times. *Journal of Verbal Learning and Verbal Behavior, 8,* 457–462.

Foss, D. J. (1970). Some effects of ambiguity upon sentence comprehension. *Journal of Verbal Learning and Verbal Behavior, 9,* 699–706.

Foss, D. J., & Hakes, D. T. (1978). *Psycholinguistics: An introduction to the psychology of language.* Englewood Cliffs, NJ: Prentice-Hall.

Fowles, B., & Glanz, E. (1977). Competence and talent in verbal riddle comprehension. *Journal of Child Language, 4,* 433–452.

Freedman, J., & Loftus, E. (1971). Retrieval of words from long–term memory. *Journal of Verbal Learning and Verbal Behavior, 10,* 107–115.

Fromkin, V. (1973). *Speech errors as linguistic evidence.* The Hague: Mouton.

Gardner, H. (1974). *The shattered mind.* New York: Random House.

Garrett, M. F. (1976). Syntactic processes in sentence production. In R. J. Wales & E. Walker (Eds.), *New approaches to language mechanisms.* Amsterdam: North-Holland.

Garrett, M. F. (1980). Levels of processing in sentence production. In B. Butterworth (Ed.), *Speech production (Vol. 1).* New York: Academic Press.

Gelman, S. A., & Coley, J. D. (1991). Language and categorization: The acquisition of natural kind terms. In S. A. Gelman & J. P. Byrnes (Eds.), *Perspectives on language and thought: Interrelations in development* (pp. 146–196). Cambridge: Cambridge University Press.

Gelman, S. A., & Markman, E. M. (1986). Categories and induction in young children. *Cognition, 23,* 183–208.

Gelman, S. A., & Markman, E. M. (1987). Young children's inductions from natural kinds: The role of categories and appearances. *Child Development, 58,* 1532–1541.

Ghiselin, M. (1969). *The triumph of the Darwinian method.* Chicago: University of Chicago Press.

Glanzer, M., & Erhenreich, S. (1979). Structure and search of the internal lexicon. *Journal of Verbal Learning and Verbal Behavior, 18,* 381–398.

Glass, A. L., & Holyoak, K. J. (1975). Alternative conceptions of semantic memory. *Cognition, 3,* 313–333.

Gleitman, L. (1990). The structural sources of verb meanings. *Language Acquisition, 1,* 3–55.

Glucksberg, S., Kreuz, R., & Rho, S. (1986). Context can restrain lexical access: Implications for models of language comprehension. *Journal of Experimental Psychology: Learning, Memory and Cognition, 12,* 323–335.

Golinkoff, R., Mervis, C., & Hirsh-Pasek, K. (1994). Early object labels: The case for a developmental lexical principles framework. *Journal of Child Language, 21,* 125–155.

Grimshaw, J. (1985). Form, function and the language acquisition device. In C. L. Baker & J. McCarthy (Eds.), *The logical problem of language acquisition* (pp. 165–183). Cambridge, MA: MIT Press.

Hauser, M. (1996). *The evolution of communication.* Cambridge, MA: MIT Press.

Heider, E. R. (1972). Universals in color naming and memory. *Journal of Experimental Psychology, 93,* 10–20.

Henderson, L. (1982). *Orthography and word recognition in reading.* London: Academic Press.

Hirsh-Pasek, K., & Golinkoff, R. (1996). *The origins of grammar: Evidence from early language comprehension.* Cambridge, MA: Cambridge University Press.

Hirsh-Pasek, K., Gleitman, L., & Gleitman, H. (1978). What did the brain say to the mind? In A. Sinclair, R. J. Jarvella, & W. J. M. Levelt (Eds.), *The child's conception of language.* Berlin: Springer-Verlag.

Hobbes, T. (1651/1958). *Leviathan.* H. W. Schneider (Ed.). New York: Bobbs-Merrill.

Jenkins, J. J. (1970). The 1952 Minnesota word association norms. In L. Postman & G. Keppel (Eds.), *Norms of word association.* New York: Academic Press.

Katz, J., & Fodor, J. A. (1963). The structure of a semantic theory. *Language, 39,* 170–210.

Keil, F. C. (1987). Conceptual development and category structure. In U. Neisser (Ed.), *Concepts and conceptual development: Ecological and intellectual factors in categorization.* New York: Cambridge University Press.

Keil, F. C. (1989). *Concepts, kinds, and cognitive development.* Cambridge, MA: MIT Press.

Kinoshita, S. (1985). Sentence context effects on lexically ambiguous words: Evidence for a postaccess inhibition process. *Memory and Cognition, 13,* 579–595.

Labov, W. (1973). The boundaries of words and their meanings. In C. J. N. Bailey & R. W. Shuy (Eds.), *New ways of analyzing variations in English.* Washington, DC: Georgetown University Press.

Lakoff, G. (1987). *Women, fire and dangerous things: What categories reveal about the mind.* Chicago: University of Chicago Press.

Locke, J. (1690/1967). *An essay concerning human understanding.* A. S. Pringle-Pattison (Ed.). London: Oxford University Press.

MacKay, D. (1966). To end ambiguous sentences. *Perception and Psychophysics, 1,* 426–436.

MacKay, D. (1978). Derivational rules and the internal lexicon. *Journal of Verbal Learning and Verbal Behavior, 17,* 61–71.

MacKay, D. (1979). Lexical insertion, inflection, and derivation: Creative processes in word production. *Journal of Psycholinguistic Research, 8,* 477–498.

Malt, B. C. (1990). Features and beliefs in the mental representations of categories. *Journal of Memory and Language, 29,* 289–315.

Manelis, L., & Tharp, D. A. (1977). The processing of affixed words. *Memory and Cognition, 5,* 690–695.

Markman, E. (1989). *Categorization and naming in children.* Cambridge, MA: MIT Press.

Markman, E., & Hutchinson, J. E. (1984). Children's sensitivity to constraints on word meaning: Taxonomic vs. thematic relations. *Cognitive Psychology, 16,* 1–27.

Markman, E., & Wachtel, G. F. (1988). Children's use of mutual exclusivity to constrain the meanings of words. *Cognitive Psychology, 20,* 121–157.

Marshall, J. C., & Newcombe, F. (1966). Syntactic and semantic errors in paralexia. *Neuropsychologia, 4,* 169–176.

Marslen-Wilson, W. D. (1987). Functional parallelism in spoken word-recognition. *Cognition, 25,* 71–102.

Marslen-Wilson, W. D., & Tyler, L. K. (1980). The temporal structure of spoken language understanding. *Cognition, 8,* 1–71.

Marslen-Wilson, W. D., & Tyler, L. K. (1981). Central processes in speech understanding. *Philosophical Transactions of the Royal Society of London, B 295,* 317–332.

Marslen-Wilson, W. D., & Welsh, A. (1978). Processing interactions and lexical access during word recognition in continuous speech. *Cognitive Psychology, 10,* 29–63.

McClelland, J., & Rumelhart, D. (1981). An interactive activation model of context effects in letter perception. Part 1: An account of basic findings. *Psychological Review, 88,* 60–94.

Medin, D. L. (1989). Concepts and category structure. *American Psychologist, 44,* 1469–1481.

Medin, D. L., & Ortony, A. (1989). Psychological essentialism. In S. Vosniadou & A. Ortony (Eds.), *Similarity and analogical reasoning.* New York: Cambridge University Press.

Medin, D. L., & Schaffer, M. M. (1978). Context theory of classification learning. *Psychological Review, 85,* 207–238.

Medin, D., & Shoben, E. (1988). Context and structure in conceptual combination. *Cognitive Psychology, 20,* 158–190.

Medin, D. L., & Wattenmaker, W. D. (1987). Category cohesiveness, theories and cognitive archeology. In U. Neisser (Ed.), *Concepts and conceptual development.* Cambridge: Cambridge University Press.

Merriman, W. E., & Bowman, L. L. (1989). The mutual exclusivity bias in children's word learning. *Monographs of the Society for Research in Child Development, Serial No. 220, 54* (3–4), 1–123.

Meyer, D. E., & Schvaneveldt, R. W. (1971). Facilitation in recognizing pairs of words: Evidence of a dependence between retrieval operations. *Journal of Experimental Psychology, 90,* 227–234.

Mill, J. S. (1843). *A system of logic.* London: Longmans.

Miller, G. A. (1951). *Language and communication.* New York: McGraw-Hill.

Miyake, A., Just, M., & Carpenter, P. A. (1994). Working memory constraints on the resolution of lexical ambiguity: Maintaining multiple interpretations in neural contexts. *Journal of Memory & Language, 33* (2), 175–193.

Monsell, S. (1985). Repetition and the lexicon. In A. W. Ellis (Ed.), *Progress in the psychology of language (Vol. 1).* Hove and London: Erlbaum.

Morton, J. (1969). Interaction of information in word recognition. *Psychological Review, 76,* 165–178.

Morton, J. (1979). Facilitation in word recognition: Experiments causing change in the logogen model. In P. A. Kolers, M. E. Wrolstad, & H. Bouma (Eds.), *Processing of visual language.* New York: Plenum Press.

Morton, J., & Patterson, K. (1980). A new attempt at an interpretation, or, an attempt at a new interpretation. In M. K. Coltheart, K. Patterson, & J. C. Marshall (Eds.), *Deep dyslexia.* London: Routledge and Kegan Paul.

Murphy, G. L., & Medin, D. L. (1985). The role of theories in conceptual coherence. *Psychological Review, 92,* 289–316.

Murrell, G. A., & Morton, J. (1974). Word recognition and morphemic structure. *Journal of Experimental Psychology, 102,* 963–968.

Oldfield, C. R. (1963). Individual vocabulary and semantic currency. *British Journal of Social and Clinical Psychology, 2,* 122–130.

Onifer, W., & Swinney, D. (1981). Accessing lexical ambiguities during sentence comprehension: Effects of frequency of meaning and contextual bias. *Memory and Cognition, 9,* 225–236.

Osgood, C. E., & Hoosain, R. (1974). Salience of the word as a unit in the perception of language. *Perception and Psychophysics, 15,* 168–192.

Paivio, A. (1969). Mental imagery in associative learning and memory. *Psychological Review, 76,* 241–263.

Palermo, D. S. (1963). Word associations and children's verbal behavior. In L. P. Lipsitt & C. C. Spiker (Eds.), *Advances in child development and behavior (Vol. 1).* New York: Academic Press.

Pinker, S. (1989). *Learnability and cognition.* Cambridge, MA: MIT Press.

Prather, P. A., & Swinney, D. A. (1988). Lexical processing and ambiguity resolution: An autonomous process in an interactive box. In S. I. Small, G. W. Cottrell, & M. K. Tanenhaus (Eds.), *Lexical ambiguity resolution.* San Mateo, CA: Morgan Kaufman.

Premack, D., & Premack, A. J. (1983). *The mind of an ape.* New York: Norton.

Pullum, G. (1990, June). The great Eskimo vocabulary hoax. *Lingua Franca,* 28–29.

Putnam, H. (1973). Meaning and reference. *Journal of Philosophy, 70,* 699–711.

Putnam, H. (1975). The meaning of "meaning." In H. Putnam, *Mind, language, and reality: Philosophical papers (Vol. 2).* Cambridge, U.K.: Cambridge University Press.

Quine, W. V. O. (1960). *Word and object.* Cambridge, MA: MIT Press.

Quine, W. V. O. (1977). Natural kinds. In S. P. Schwartz (Ed.), *Naming, necessity, and natural kinds.* Ithaca, NY: Cornell University Press.

Rips, L. J., Shoben, E. J., & Smith, E. E. (1973). Semantic distance and the verification of semantic relationships. *Journal of Verbal Learning and Verbal Behavior, 12,* 1–20.

Rosch, E. H. (1973). On the internal structure of perceptual and semantic categories. In T. E. Moore (Ed.), *Cognitive development and the acquisition of language* (pp. 111–144). New York: Academic Press.

Rosch, E. H. (1975). Cognitive representations of semantic categories. *Journal of Experimental Psychology General, 104,* 192–233.

Rosch, E. H., & Mervis, C. B. (1975). Family resemblances: Studies in the internal structure of categories. *Cognitive Psychology, 7,* 573–605.

Rubenstein, H., Garfield, L., & Millikan, J. A. (1970). Homographic entries in the internal lexicon. *Journal of Verbal Learning and Verbal Behavior, 9,* 487–494.

Rubin, G. S., Becker, C. A., & Freeman, R. H. (1979). Morphological structure and its effect on visual word recognition. *Journal of Verbal Learning and Verbal Behavior, 18,* 757–767.

Rumelhart, D. E., & Ortony, A. (1977). The representation of knowledge in memory. In R. C. Anderson, R. J. Spiro, & W. E. Montague (Eds.), *Schooling and the acquisition of knowledge* (pp. 99–135). Hillsdale, NJ: Erlbaum.

Sandra, D. (1990). On the representation and processing of compound words: Automatic access to constituent morphemes does not occur. *The Quarterly Journal of Experimental Psychology, 42A,* 529–567.

Schvaneveldt, R., Meyer, D., & Becker, C. (1976). Lexical ambiguity, semantic context, and visual word recognition. *Journal of Experimental Psychology: Human Perception and Performance, 2,* 243–250.

Seashore, R. H., & Eckerson, L. D. (1940). The measurement of individual differences in general English vocabularies. *Journal of Educational Psychology, 31,* 14–33.

Seidenberg, M. S., Tanenhaus, M. K., Leiman, J. M., & Bienkowski, M. (1982). Automatic access of the meanings of ambiguous words in context: Some limitations of knowledge-based processing. *Cognitive Psychology, 14,* 489–537.

Shakespeare, W. (1975). Romeo and Juliet. In *The complete works of William Shakespeare.* Minneapolis: Amaranth Press.

Shattuck-Hufnagel, S. (1979). Speech errors as evidence for a serial-ordering mechanism in sentence production. In W. Cooper & E. C. T. Walker (Eds.), *Sentence processing.* Hillsdale, NJ: Erlbaum.

Shultz, T., & Horibe, F. (1974). Development of the appreciation of verbal jokes. *Developmental Psychology, 10,* 13–20.

Simpson, G. B. (1981). Meaning dominance and semantic context in the processing of lexical ambiguity. *Journal of Verbal Learning and Verbal Behavior, 20,* 120–136.

Simpson, G., & Burgess, C. (1985). Activation and selection processes in the recognition of ambiguous words. *Journal of Experimental Psychology: Human Perception and Performance, 11* (1), 28–39.

Simpson, G. B., & Burgess, C. (1988). Implications of lexical ambiguity resolution for word recognition and comprehension. In S. I. Small, G. W. Cottrell, & M. K. Tanenhaus (Eds.), *Lexical ambiguity resolution.* San Mateo, CA: Morgan Kaufman.

Smith, E. E., & Medin, D. L. (1981). *Categories and concepts.* Cambridge, MA: Harvard University Press.

Smith, E. E., Shoben, E. J., & Rips, L. J. (1974). Structure and process in semantic memory: A featural model for semantic decisions. *Psychological Review, 81,* 214–241.

Smith, P. T., & Sterling, C. M. (1982). Factors affecting the perceived morphemic structure of written words. *Journal of Verbal Learning and Verbal Behavior, 21,* 704–721.

Swinney, D. A. (1979). Lexical access during sentence comprehension: (Re)consideration of context effects. *Journal of Verbal Learning and Verbal Behavior, 18,* 645–659.

Tabossi, P., Columbo, L., & Job, R. (1987). Accessing lexical ambiguity: Effects of context and dominance. *Psychological Research, 49,* 161–167.

Taft, M. (1981). Prefix stripping revisited. *Journal of Verbal Learning and Verbal Behavior, 20,* 289–297.

Taft, M., & Forster, K. I. (1975). Lexical storage and retrieval of prefixed words. *Journal of Verbal Learning and Verbal Behavior, 14,* 638–647.

Taft, M., & Forster, K. I. (1976). Lexical storage and retrieval of polymorphemic and polysyllabic words. *Journal of Verbal Learning and Verbal Behavior, 15,* 607–620.

Talmy, L. (1975). Semantics and syntax of motion. In J. Kimball (Ed.), *Syntax and semantics (Vol. 4)* (pp. 181–238). New York: Academic Press.

Talmy, L. (1985). Lexicalization patterns: Semantic structure in lexical forms. In T. Shoben (Ed.), *Language typology and syntactic description (Vol. 3)* (pp. 57–149). Cambridge: Cambridge University Press.

Tanenhaus, M., Carlson, G., & Seidenberg, M. (1985). Do listeners compute linguistic representations? In D. R. Dawty, L. Karttunen, & A. M. Zwicky (Eds.), *Natural language parsing: Psychological, computational, and theoretical perspectives.* Cambridge, MA: Cambridge University Press.

Tanenhaus, M. K., Leiman, J. M., & Seidenberg, M. K. (1979). Evidence for multiple stages in the processing of ambiguous words in syntactic contexts. *Journal of Verbal Learning and Verbal Behavior, 18,* 427–440.

Tweney, R., Tkacz, S., & Zaruba, S. (1975). Slips of the tongue and lexical storage. *Language and Speech, 18,* 388–396.

Tyler, L. K., Behrens, S., Cobb, H., & Marslen-Wilson, W. (1990). Processing distinctions between stems and affixes: Evidence from a nonfluent aphasic patient. *Cognition, 36,* 129–153.

Waxman, S. R., & Gelman, R. (1986). Preschoolers' use of superordinate relations in classification. *Cognitive Development, 5,* 123–150.

Chapter **5**

SENTENCE PROCESSING

Arthur Wingfield & Debra Titone
*Department of Psychology and Volen National Center
for Complex Systems, Brandeis University*

INTRODUCTION

In Chapter 4 we saw how individual words may be correctly recognized and their meanings activated. The power of language as a tool for communication, however, comes when we combine these words into sentences and collections of sentences. Collections of sentences that tell a story or convey sequences of events are referred to as **discourse,** which is the topic of Chapter 6.

The scope of *this* chapter lies between these two levels of language analysis. In this chapter we look at how people understand speech at the sentence level. We call this **sentence processing:** the question of how listeners rapidly decipher the structure of sentences and gain access to the meaning of the sentence as a whole.

One of the most striking features of connected speech is the rapid rate at which it ordinarily arrives. Speech rates in everyday conversation typically average between 140 to 180 words per minute (wpm), and a television newsreader speaking from a prepared script can easily exceed 210 wpm. Even these rates pale beside the rapid-fire delivery of many commercials or the fast talking television weather persons with their charts and maps and little jokes. It is true that people generally find television weather reports a perceptual and conceptual blur. But this is due more to the sensory overload caused by the charts and maps and little jokes than it is to the high speech rates *per se* (Wagenaar, Varey, & Hudson, 1984).

The rapidity of natural speech input is not the only problem listeners must face. In fluent speech individual words run in together and often are not as clearly articulated as they might seem. When speech scientists analyze the speech waveforms of ordinary speech, the waveforms often lack regular breaks between the words, phrases, and other linguistic elements of spoken sentences. The perceptual isolation of individual words that we hear as we listen to connected speech must be imposed by the listener, often based on the meaning of the sentence as a whole. Chapter 3 discusses this problem in some detail.

To get a sense of this perceptual segmentation, try saying aloud the two sentences, "I *better* do my laundry," and "I *bet her* five dollars." If you say these sentences several times and listen to yourself carefully, you may hear that the italicized segments are pronounced identically. It is the sentence context in which the sounds are embedded that brings perceptual clarity to utterances such as these (Martin, 1990).

More than thirty years ago, Pollack and Pickett (1964) demonstrated the surprising lack of clarity in articulation of many words in connected speech. They made tape recordings of people's conversations, electronically spliced out single words, and presented each of the words in isolation to different people. They wanted to see how recognizable the words might be when heard without their surrounding linguistic context. The results were dramatic. In many cases the words not only were unrecognizable but barely sounded like words at all. When Pollack and Pickett played back the words again, but in their full sentence context, they sounded crystal clear. The acoustic information was the same. What differed was the availability of surrounding semantic and syntactic context that the listener could use as part of the perceptual process. As discussed in Chapter 3, the use of context to aid speech perception is sometimes called "top-down" processing (see also Chapter 9 for a description of top-down processing during reading). The other side of the coin is that speakers can adjust the clarity of their articulation depending on the predictability of the words in the sentence context (Lindblom, Brownlee, David, & Moon, 1992).

In laboratory experiments we can use a computer to artificially accelerate speech without disturbing its pitch. This technique reveals that, depending on the speech materials, people can successfully comprehend speech at even twice normal speaking rates (Chodorow, 1979; Wingfield, 1975). Maximum speech rates are limited more by the speaker's output capability than by the perceptual needs of the listener.

In spite of these demands, listeners can with apparent ease segment the speech stream to isolate the "words," decode the grammatical structure of the sentences, determine the semantic relations between the words, and perhaps resolve semantic ambiguities and draw logical inferences and implications that lie beyond the literal meanings of the sentences themselves—all at the rapid rate of normal speech.

Our goal in this chapter is to describe current theory and research on sentence processing and to explain how we can process sentences at such rapid rates.

STRUCTURAL PROPERTIES OF SENTENCES

One reason why we can process speech so rapidly is our ability to systematically make use of structure in natural language.

What do we mean by *structure* in language? We can define the structure of language in terms of sets of *rules* that tell us how words strung together can form a sentence and convey a meaning. When we speak of rules that give structure to language, we do not mean that a speaker consciously follows these rules when uttering a sentence. As Levelt (1989) has said, "A speaker doesn't have to ponder the issue of whether to make the recipient of *give* an indirect object (as in *John* gave *Mary the book*) or an oblique object (as in *John* gave *the book to Mary*)." Nor, Levelt goes on to suggest, does the retrieval of common words require much time or conscious effort (p. 22). These are "automatic" processes over which we exert little conscious control. Yet, for communication to occur, the speaker and the listener must share a common knowledge base, and each must have access to the same knowledge sets and rules.

Think for a moment of a simple "sentence" in the abstract, a sentence following the *noun-verb-noun* form. Think now of the same "sentence" but in the form of an action, *The first noun verbed the second noun*. Finally, let us instantiate this sentence with specific words:

The student read the book.

The teacher graded the test.

The teacher heard the student.

Although all three sentences take the form of *The noun verbed the noun,* the first two sentences are not reversible. That is, while you can say, "The student read the book," or "The teacher graded the test," you cannot say, "The book read the student," or "The test graded the teacher." Only the third sentence is reversible. You can just as easily say, "The student heard the teacher," as "The teacher heard the student." Some actions are possible, and some are not. Real-world knowledge can supply constraints that operate as part of the structure of our language.

These properties of language give rise to regularities in the language that make possible a degree of statistical prediction whenever we listen to natural speech. To illustrate, let us begin with the fact that the average college-educated adult may have a speaking vocabulary of 75,000 to 100,000 words (Oldfield, 1963). Suppose someone was about to say a word to you, and you had to guess what the word might be. If all words in the language were equally probable, the odds of it being any particular word would be between .00001 and .000013. Now, clearly, each word is not equally probable. Some words tend to be used much more frequently than others. In writing, the most frequently used word is *the,* and in spoken telephone conversations, it is *I.* In fact, the 50 most commonly used words in English make up about 60% of all the words we speak, and about 45% of those we write. We can put this another way: On average, we speak only about 10 to 15 words before we repeat a word (Miller, 1951).

Thus, some words are more predictable than others, even out of context. When words are heard within a context, the effect is even further increased. Imagine someone started to speak to you, but then stopped suddenly in midsentence. If you were asked at that point what you thought the next word might be, you might have a good idea. You could at least say what part of speech the next word might be, whether it would probably be a noun, a verb, an adjective, and so forth. Indeed, you would stand a good chance of correctly guessing the word itself. If someone said, "The train pulled into the . . . ," you might say "station," or you might say "tunnel." From your knowledge of language, you would, at the very least, have a high expectation for either a noun or an adjective.

Statistical Approximations to English

We can capture this predictive quality of natural language by giving people a few words of a sentence and asking them to guess what they think the next word might be. We then show this set of words to another person and ask him to guess the next word, and so on. In this way one can see what people's linguistic intuitions look like with varying amounts of preceding context.

For example, Moray and Taylor (1960) showed subjects the five words, "I have a few little," and asked the subjects to guess what they thought the next word of this sentence might be. One subject said, "facts." Moray and Taylor added the word *facts,* covered the first word, *I,* and showed ". . . have a few little facts _____" to another subject. This subject said, "here." A third subject saw the last set of five words: ". . . a few little facts here _____" and was asked to guess the sixth word. This process was continued until an entire 150-word passage was constructed. This example is called a *sixth-order approximation* to English, because each word was generated based on a context of five preceding words. Here is an extract from Moray and Taylor's sample. As you read it, it seems as if our artificial speaker is continually on the verge of saying something meaningful, but never quite does:

> I have a few little facts here to test lots of time for studying and praying for guidance in living according to common ideas as illustrated by the painting.

A second-order approximation, where subjects guess the most likely word of a sentence based on seeing only one word of context, would be somewhat less English-like:

> The camera shop and boyhood friend from fish and screamed loudly men only when seen again and then it was jumping in the tree.

You might ask what would happen if one created approximations to English after giving subjects a specific context, such as telling them that the words are from a political campaign speech, a romantic novel, or a legal document. The following is a fourth-order approximation to English (each word is based on three words of prior context only) when respondents were told the words were taken from a mystery novel:

> When I killed her I stabbed Paul between his powerful jaws clamped tightly together. Screaming loudly despite fatal consequences in the struggle for life began ebbing as he coughed hollowly spitting blood from his ears (Attneave, 1959, p. 19).

We have long known that increasing the likelihood of words by increasing contextual constraints, either with sentences or with statistical approximations to English, will make the words easier to remember (Miller & Selfridge, 1950), more audible under poor listening conditions (Rubenstein & Pollack, 1963), and more recognizable if they are presented visually for brief durations (Tulving & Gold, 1963; Morton, 1964).

Where Do People Pause When They Speak?

Clearly, listeners know a great deal about the structure of their native language. The speech we hear also has an intonation pattern and rhythm to it that can give the listener hints about what is about to be heard. One of these hints can come from the periodic appearance of pauses in spontaneous speech, whether they are "filled" with *uhms* and *ahs,* or by silence. They occur as the speaker thinks of what to say and how to phrase it.

Some estimates suggest that as much as 40 to 50 percent of speaking time is occupied by pauses that occur as we select the words we wish to utter. What happens to these natural pauses when we reduce the planning demands on the speaker? Reading aloud from a script does reduce the proportion of pausing, but it may be impossible for a speaker to speak sensibly without pausing at least 20% of the time (Butterworth, 1989, p. 128).

Systematic studies verify that the pauses in connected speech tend to occur just before words of low probability in the context, the "thoughtful" words that do not represent a run of association. They suggest that in fluent speech we do not pause to take a breath. Rather, we take the opportunity to breathe during natural pauses determined by the linguistic content of what we are saying (Goldman-Eisler, 1968). In short, although speech that departs from an expected pattern will be harder to predict, the nature of the speech act itself can signal the listener that such an event is upcoming. Chapter 7 will discuss these and other issues in greater detail.

The lesson to be drawn from this discussion is that sentence perception is a surprisingly active process, even though it is ordinarily accomplished rapidly and without conscious effort. Sentence processing represents a continual analysis of the incoming speech stream to detect the structure and meaning of speakers' utterances as they are being heard. In order to discover how sentence processing takes place, we must understand how the listener accomplishes syntactic and semantic processing. As we shall see, some theorists have claimed that we conduct syntactic structure and semantic analysis independently, and others have claimed that we ordinarily process them at the same time in an interactive fashion.

SYNTACTIC PROCESSING

Syntactic Resolution Is Necessary for Comprehension

Although the statistical properties of language say something about the consequences of the speaker's and listener's knowledge of language structure, they do not themselves explain this structure. During the 1960s some researchers attempted to use **transformational grammar** to fulfill this goal. These attempts made two important points relevant to our discussion: the difference between surface structure and deep structure, and the difference between competence and performance.

Surface Structure Versus Deep Structure

The first point was a distinction between the **surface structure** and the **deep structure** of a sentence. The surface structure of a sentence is represented by the words you actually hear spoken or read: the specific words we have chosen to convey the meaning of what it is we wish to say. The listener must "decode" this surface structure to discover the meaning that underlies the utterance—the "deep structure" of the sentence.

Some sets of sentences have different surface structures, but the same deep structure. An example would be the pair of sentences, *The boy threw the ball,* and *The ball was thrown by the boy.* The specific words used—the surface structures—are obviously different. The first sentence is a simple active declarative, and the second is a passive. In spite of this difference, both sentences focus on the fact that a boy threw a ball. The two sentences have different surface structures, but they convey the same meaning. They have the same deep structure.

By contrast, some sentences can have the same surface structure, but different deep structures. A well-known example is the sentence, *Flying planes can be dangerous.* This sentence could mean that it is dangerous to be a pilot, or it could mean that living near an airport can be dangerous.

The distinction between deep structure and surface structure makes an important point for our understanding of sentence processing. It tells us that sentence processing is conducted in two steps in which the listener analyzes the surface structure and uses this information to detect the deep structure. The latter step conveys the meaning of the sentence that is the primary goal of the communicator (Fodor, Bever, & Garrett, 1974).

Competence Versus Performance

The second point is that the way people produce language is not equivalent to their knowledge of language. Much of what we say consists of incomplete fragments that do not even approach a grammatical sentence (Goldman-Eisler, 1968). This does not mean that we lack the knowledge to produce a complete sentence, or that we do not know the difference between an ungrammatical fragment and a grammatical sentence. The specification of these rules is critical to an understanding of language **competence**—what the speaker knows about the structure of the language (Chomsky, 1957, 1965). A theory of **performance** requires an explanation of how we can understand speech, however incomplete and fragmentary it may be. A complete theory of sentence processing must thus take into account both competence and performance.

Syntactic Structure of Sentences

In order to understand a sentence, the listener or reader must determine its syntactic structure. The assignment of words in a sentence to their relevant linguistic categories is called **parsing** a sentence.

By way of example, take the simple declarative sentence, *The boy threw the ball.* Figure 5.1 shows a tree diagram for this sentence that indicates the form class (part of speech) of each word, how the words can be grouped into phrases, and finally, how the phrase relationships form the structure of the sentence. That is, it tells us that this particular sentence is composed of two major phrases. The first is the *noun phrase* (NP), consisting of the article, or determiner (Det), *The,* and the noun (N) *boy,* followed by a *verb phrase* (VP), which is composed of the verb (V) *threw* and the noun phrase, *the ball.*

This simple phrase-structure grammar shows that the noun phrase *(the boy)* and the verb phrase *(threw the ball)* form separate *units* of the sentence, in the sense that they derive from different higher-order nodes. The detection of such structures is an

FIGURE 5.1

A phrase-structure grammar for the sentence, *The boy threw the ball.*

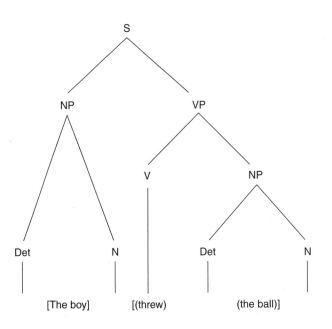

essential step for understanding the relationships between the objects and events within a sentence.

In many sentences, of course, recognition of the correct constituent boundaries is less clear than in this example. Some of these contain phrase-structure ambiguities, where different hypotheses about the intended structure of a sentence could give rise to different meanings. An example of this would be the sentence, *They are eating apples.* It is not immediately clear when you read this sentence if *eating* is part of the verb or if *eating* is an adjective that modifies the noun *apples,* as with apples that are all right to eat on their own *(eating apples)* versus apples that are good only as ingredients in cakes and pies *(cooking apples).* We can express this parsing distinction with the two phrase-structure diagrams for *They are eating apples* shown in Figure 5.2.

FIGURE 5.2

Two phrase-structure diagrams for the sentence, *They are eating apples.*

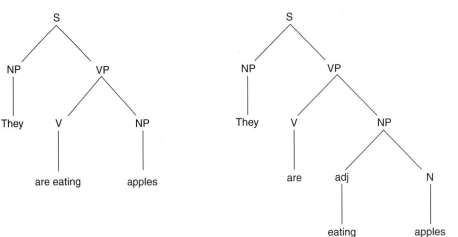

Most sentences are more complex than these simple examples. On the one hand, we might hear a sentence like that shown in Figure 5.2 transformed into a passive version, *(The ball was thrown by the boy)*, a passive negative version, *(The ball was not thrown by the boy)*, a negative question, *(Did the boy not throw the ball?)*, or a passive negative question, *(Was the ball not thrown by the boy?)*. All of these versions derive from the basic active declarative sentence, *The boy threw the ball*. A part of the sentence-processing task is to detect identities in underlying meanings of sentences in spite of differences in the surface structures represented by the different wordings of the sentences we might hear or read.

Complete understanding of a sentence must thus also take into account "trace" theory. (The trace theory referred to here is a syntactic theory first discussed in Chapter 1 and is quite different from the TRACE model of speech perception discussed in Chapter 3. See the glossary for definitions.)

Trace theory has three elements. The first is that linguistic constituents can move from one position to another as a speaker is organizing a sentence for production. The second is that this movement leaves a "trace" of the original constituent in the surface structure of the sentence. The third and final element is that detection of this trace by the listener is necessary for correct thematic role assignment. By this we mean that the sentence processor must reactivate the semantics of the correct lexical antecedent at the trace position (Chomsky, 1981; Nicol & Swinney, 1989). Consider, for example, the sentence, *The doctor treated the patient$_i$ from the new hospital who* (t_i) *had become suddenly ill.* The symbol t_i indicates that when you hear or read the word *who* you must link that word to the appropriate referent, in this case, *the patient*. Specifically, when you encounter *who* you must activate a "trace" (t_i) of the referent noun *patient*. Although making some inferences about missing or moved elements of a sentence may require conscious effort, simple inferences, such as correctly activating the meaning of a pronoun referent, typically occur rapidly and without awareness (Swinney & Osterhout, 1990).

An additional complicating factor is that many of the sentences with which we must deal have multiple clauses: *In order to achieve success, study and hard work are always necessary,* or, *The mechanic who knows how to fix the car that my friend bought last year left on vacation.* As we shall see, sentences such as these represent special processing problems.

Clausal Processing

One way the perceptual system can reduce the processing load is to break up incoming sentences into their constituent clauses. To get a sense of this, consider the sentence, *I was going to take a train to New York, but I decided it would be too heavy.* This old joke can still make people laugh because we process complex utterances in terms of smaller, more manageable units. It also demonstrates why comedians are referred to as having good "timing." This joke works best if the teller pauses for a few beats between delivering the first and the second clause.

Processing this sentence for meaning requires at least three operations. First, we take in and analyze the structure and meaning of the first clause, *I was going to take a train to New York,* and temporarily store the product of this analysis in memory.

Next, we analyze the second clause, *but I decided it would be too heavy,* and temporarily store the product of this analysis. (A combined temporary memory and mental work space is sometimes called "working memory.") Finally, we retrieve the stored representation of the first phrase and attempt to integrate it with the meaning of the second one. It is at this point that we begin to realize that it is funny. The delayed "double-take" people often exhibit after hearing this sort of joke—a look of confusion followed an instant later by amusement—is a measure of the time it takes for the incongruity to be appreciated.

This sense of processing speech by clauses is not just restricted to spoken language. When we look closely at people's reading strategies, we see that readers are also sensitive to boundaries between linguistic clauses. In a particularly interesting demonstration of this effect, Stine (1990) seated subjects in front of a computer that, when the space bar was pressed, would display on the screen the first word of a sentence the subject was told he or she would have to read, comprehend, and remember. With the next bar press, the first word of the sentence disappeared and the second word of the sentence appeared. This procedure continued, word by word, until the full sentence had been seen. Stine's interest was in the rate at which subjects felt ready for each subsequent word of the sentence. The computer automatically recorded subjects' word-by-word reading times as the time interval between successive bar presses for each word.

Figure 5.3 shows an example of these data for a group of university students reading the sentence, *The Chinese, who used to produce kites, used them in order to carry ropes across the rivers.* The jagged solid line running across the graph from left to right shows the average time (in milliseconds) that subjects dwelled on each word before pressing the bar for the next one. The dashed lines running above and below this average time show the range within which the majority of the reading times fell.

The pattern of word-by-word reading times across the sentence shows what we call a "scalloped" pattern: After reading the first NP (*The Chinese*), the subjects' time-per-

FIGURE 5.3

Average word-by-word reading times (RTs) for a sentence read by a sample of college-age readers. (The solid line indicates median reading time; dashed lines indicate 25th and 75th percentiles.)

Source: E. A. L. Stine, On-line processing of written text by younger and older adults. Psychology and Aging, 5, 1990: Fig. 1, pg. 73.

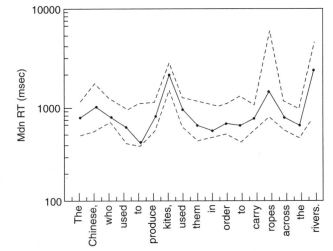

word reading rates increased until the completion of the first major clause boundary (ending with the word *kites*). At this point the reading rate slowed, presumably reflecting the readers' need for more time to process the clause content and to integrate this content with the preceding NP. Past this point, the subjects' reading rate again increased until the word *ropes* was reached. At this point subjects again dwelled on each word for a relatively long time, thus producing another scallop.

As Stine examined the patterns of reading times for many different sentences, she found an interesting generality. The more clauses (or chunks) a sentence contained, the higher was each successive peak, reflecting longer and longer processing times needed to integrate each new chunk into an increasingly rich coherence structure.

Although results such as these have been shown before (Aaronson & Scarborough, 1977; Haberlandt & Graesser, 1989), Stine's experiment was particularly interesting because it took as its starting point the fact that elderly adults often are less successful in remembering sentences than are young adults. For this reason, she also examined reading times for elderly adults matched with the young adults for years of education and general verbal ability. She found that subjects from both age groups were almost identical in the appearance of the scalloped pattern of their reading times: Both groups "chunked" the sentences into clauses in the same way. The difference was in the manner in which they allocated time at the peaks of the scallops as the number of chunks within the sentences increased. Whereas the young adults showed an essentially linear increase in the time spent at each successive peak, the older adults did not.

To Stine, this analysis suggested that although the older adults allocated time to organize information between peaks (for example, within clauses) just as the young did, they did not allocate time to integrate the information across chunks as effectively as did the young. The fact that the two groups differed in subsequent memory for the sentence content might thus be attributable to the way the sentences were organized as they were originally being read (Stine, 1990).

In speech, especially when the syntactic structure or the semantic content is complex, we can often wish that speakers would pause for us at major clause boundaries and give us time to digest what we have heard to that point. We can do this for ourselves by varying the dwell time on the words as we read a sentence—where we dwell, and for how long, depending on the structure of the sentence and the complexity of its content. We will return later to the topic of clausal processing of spoken sentences.

SENTENCE PARSING AND SYNTACTIC AMBIGUITY

In the previous section we saw how comprehenders extract syntactic structure from sentences in the form of clausal units. Comprehenders also extract syntactic structure while they are processing clauses word by word. Models of sentence parsing address how the syntactic functions of individual words determine the overall syntactic structure of clauses and sentences. Researchers have found that the way listeners and readers handle ambiguities can offer valuable insights into general processing principles in language comprehension.

Local Ambiguity Versus Standing Ambiguity

Syntactic ambiguity refers to cases where a clause or sentence may have more than one interpretation given the potential grammatical functions of the individual words. The occurrence of such ambiguities and the fact that language comprehension runs along smoothly in spite of these ambiguities have long been of interest in psycholinguistics. There are two types of syntactic ambiguity of interest. The first is referred to as **local ambiguity,** and the second is referred to as **standing ambiguity.**

Local ambiguity refers to cases where the syntactic function of a word, or how to parse a sentence, remains temporarily ambiguous until it is later clarified as we hear more of the sentence (Frazier & Rayner, 1989). For example, consider the sentence, *When Fred passes the ball, it always gets to its target.* This sentence is temporarily ambiguous when we hear the noun phrase, *the ball,* because it could be completed in two different ways, corresponding to two possible syntactic structures. For instance, another completion might be, *When Fred passes, the ball always gets to its target.* The ambiguity is referred to as local ambiguity because our uncertainty about the structure of the sentence is only temporary. When the reader or listener has encountered the phrase *it always gets* or *always gets* the ambiguity is resolved. If we are forced to remain uncertain for too long (if the disambiguating information doesn't arrive right away), we will find a sentence increasingly hard to understand. The sentence, *The rat the cat the dog chased bit ate the cheese,* is difficult because we must hold too many incomplete substructures before the sentence is finally complete and the full structure can be seen.

Abney and Johnson (1991) clearly summarize the complexities of memory requirements and parsing strategies in the resolution of local ambiguities. A parser could adopt a wait-and-see attitude, holding off making a decision until more information is available. This, however, would tax memory. On the other hand, a parsing strategy that keeps memory load to a minimum would increase the risk of making many preliminary parsing errors at points of local syntactic ambiguity. Some theorists, such as Frazier (1979), have emphasized the need to minimize memory requirements; others, such as Marcus (1980), have emphasized the need to avoid local ambiguities, hence putting a greater burden on memory.

Standing ambiguity refers to cases where sentences remain syntactically ambiguous even when all of the lexical information has been received. For example, the sentence, *The old books and magazines were on the bench,* remains ambiguous even when the sentence is finished. That is, it is not clear whether there should be a boundary after *books* (the books were old, but the magazines may not have been), or whether a boundary should follow *magazines* (making it clear that both the books and the magazines were old). Similarly, the sentence, *I saw the man with the binoculars,* does not make clear who has the binoculars. Sentences such as these can only be disambiguated by the broader context in which they are encountered.

MODELS OF SENTENCE PARSING

To understand how theorists have used ambiguous sentences to understand syntactic parsing, consider the sentence, *The old man the boats.* If you had trouble understanding this sentence, it is probably because you read *The old man* and assumed it was a noun phrase. When you reached the end of the sentence *(the boats)* and found no verb, you knew that either the sentence made no sense at all or your initial understanding of the sentence was wrong. If you went back and realized that *The old* is the noun phrase and *man* is the verb (meaning "to operate") the sentence made sense. Sentences that, like this one, are especially misleading when you first encounter them are called "garden path" sentences.

Let us think for a moment about how you might process a sentence such as *The old man the boats.* Most people's intuition is that we initially hear only one meaning of the sentence as we are listening to it. Because of this, when we reach the end of the sentence and discover we have done something wrong, we must go back and attempt to reparse the sentence in a different way. Alternatively, your intuition might tell you that as we listen to sentences that contain syntactic ambiguities we process *both* possible meanings, even though we are only consciously aware of one of them. In this case when we get to the end of the sentence and discover our interpretation was wrong, we could solve the problem by switching our attention to the alternative interpretation that has already been generated, albeit at the unconscious level.

Interestingly, versions of each of these two possibilities have been proposed in the psycholinguistics literature. A theory similar to the first possibility is sometimes referred to as the **garden path model** of sentence processing. A theory similar to the second possibility is sometimes referred to as the **constraint satisfaction model.**

Garden Path Model of Sentence Processing

According to the *garden path model* of sentence processing, the parser makes only one initial syntactic analysis of a word sequence. This initial parse is made on the basis of several rules and parsing principles. Two important principles in the garden path model are the **late closure principle** and the **minimal attachment principle.**

The *late closure principle* focuses on the way in which listeners (or readers) might determine when they have reached a major clause boundary. In doing this, one might attempt to "close" a clause boundary either at the earliest point possible or to hold off until the latest point possible. According to the late closure principle, listeners and readers tend to do the latter. When faced with a temporary sentence-beginning ambiguity such as *Because Jay always jogs a mile . . .* , we are more likely to assume that the clause boundary comes after *a mile,* as would be the case in the late closure sentence *Because Jay always jogs a mile, this seems like a short distance to him.* We are less likely to assume that the clause boundary comes after *jogs* as in the early closure sentence *Because Jay always jogs, a mile seems like a short distance to him.* For this reason, late closure sentences such as the first example will generally be easier to understand than early closure sentences such as the second example. Formally, the late closure principle states that one attempts to attach all incoming material to the phrase currently being processed (Frazier, 1987).

The late closure principle is actually a special case of a more general principle referred to as *minimal attachment*. This principle states that listeners or readers attempt to interpret sentences in terms of the simplest syntactic structure that is consistent with the input. This is done by using the fewest phrase-structure nodes possible. In the sentence, *Because Jay always jogs a mile, this seems like a short distance to him,* the noun phrase *a mile* attaches to the phrase already under construction *(Because Jay always jogs . . .).* This makes the sentence an easy one to understand. In contrast, the sentence *Because Jay always jogs, a mile seems like a short distance to him* is at odds with the minimal attachment principle. In this case, our understanding of the sentence requires that we establish an additional "node" that represents a whole new phrase in the sentence *(a mile seems like a short distance to him).* Readers will in general find this sentence harder to understand than the first one.

Constraint Satisfaction Model of Sentence Processing

In contrast to the garden path model of sentence parsing, the constraint satisfaction model says that more than one syntactic analysis of a word sequence may be generated during comprehension. Let us return to the sentence, *The old man the boats.* The constraint satisfaction model holds that, although we are only consciously aware of the noun phrase interpretation of *The old man,* the alternative interpretation of *old* as a noun and *man* as a verb has also been activated, but at a level below that of conscious awareness. According to the constraint satisfaction model, when we reach the end of the sentence and discover that we must have made a parsing error, we resolve the confusion by activating to a conscious level the alternative interpretation.

Note that the constraint satisfaction model does not suggest that readers or listeners automatically activate all possible parsing interpretations of a sentence. Rather, it is assumed that nonsyntactic information such as semantic context and expectancies influence the likelihood of alternative interpretations being generated (MacDonald, Pearlmutter, & Seidenberg, 1994; Trueswell & Tanenhaus, 1994).

We began this discussion by appealing to your intuition as to how one might deal with sentences containing syntactic ambiguities. Theorists have studied reading time for words in sentences to try to discover which of these theories more likely is correct. These studies seem to provide some support for both of the two models we have discussed.

READING TIME AS EXPERIMENTAL EVIDENCE.   Studies that measure eye movements during silent reading have provided support for the garden path model (Frazier & Rayner, 1982; Rayner, Carlson, & Frazier, 1983; Ferreira & Clifton, 1986; Rayner & Frazier, 1987). Consistent with the minimal attachment and late closure principles of the garden path model, for example, Frazier and Rayner (1982) have shown that reading times become significantly slower when the reader reaches an area of the sentence that is inconsistent with an attempt to use these two parsing principles. This is what we would expect to see if the readers had generated a single syntactic interpretation during their on-line comprehension of the sentence.

The garden path model holds that only one interpretation of a sentence will ordinarily be entertained, at least until such time as we discover that our original interpretation was incorrect (Ferreira & Clifton, 1986; Frazier & Clifton, 1996; Rayner, Garrod, & Perfetti, 1992). Some studies of reading times, however, suggest that, at least for some sentence types, readers construct multiple interpretations in ambiguous regions as they read the sentences. These studies also show that factors such as semantic context can override minimal attachment and late closure principles. Trueswell, Tanenhaus, and Garnsey (1994) have shown how semantic context can operate in interpreting the correct syntactic structure of a sentence. Good examples to illustrate this are sentences that contain what we call main verb/reduced relative ambiguities. In Trueswell et al.'s experiment, subjects read a sentence such as *The witness* examined *by the lawyer was useless* or *The evidence* examined *by the lawyer was useless*. According to the minimal attachment principle of the garden path model, readers process these two sentences no differently. This is so because the sentences have identical syntactic structures. In fact, they should both be difficult to process because neither is interpretable using the minimal attachment principle. However, Trueswell et al. (1994) found that reading times were faster for sentences of the second type than for sentences of the first type. This is so because the noun *evidence* constrains interpretation of the verb *examined*. This constraint is imposed by the semantic implausibility of an inanimate object performing an animate action. An animate object such as a *witness* can examine something, but an inanimate object such as *evidence* cannot.

Although spoken sentences can contain the same kind of syntactic ambiguities as written sentences, speakers can and usually do mark the intended boundary point by using such prosodic features as stress, intonation, and pauses. Beach (1991) illustrated this point by noting the way people spontaneously speak sentences that would certainly be syntactically ambiguous if you were reading them (Frazier & Rayner, 1982). The sentences, *The city council argued the mayor's position forcefully,* or *The city council argued the mayor's position was incorrect* are temporarily ambiguous because you do not know until after the word *position* whether or not a clause boundary should follow *argued*. When spoken aloud, however, natural stress can easily resolve such temporary ambiguity (Beach, 1991). Indeed, considerable evidence indicates that *prosodic* cues can operate effectively at the earliest stages of parsing and interpretation in sentence comprehension (Marslen-Wilson, Tyler, Warren, Grenier, & Lee, 1992).

MEANING: THE GOAL OF SENTENCE PROCESSING

The goal of sentence processing is to arrive at the meaning of the sentence. In formal terms, this means determining the semantic relationships between the rapidly arriving words. For this process to take place, the listener must analyze the acoustic information arriving at the ear in order to access the **lexicon,** the storehouse of our words and what we know about them, both at the semantic and syntactic levels. Our ultimate goal is to develop the **propositional representation** of the utterance—the relationship among the objects, actions, and events described by the sentence.

Studies of sentence processing suggest that under ordinary circumstances we strive to comprehend the meaning of a sentence as quickly as possible, and then we discard the surface structure to retain only the meaning. In one study, Sachs (1967) had subjects listen to paragraph-length stories that contained a critical test sentence. One story, for example, was about the invention of the telescope. It contained the target sentence, "He sent a letter about it to Galileo, the great Italian scientist."

As subjects listened to the passage, at a certain point a bell rang, and either the target sentence, or a sentence similar to it, was spoken. The subjects' task was to say whether or not they had heard this exact sentence in the passage. The recognition sentences bore four possible relationships to the target sentence: (a) the *identical sentence;* (b) *active/passive change,* in which the original sentence was changed from the active to passive form without changing the meaning (for example, "A letter about it was sent to Galileo, the great Italian scientist."); (c) *formal change,* in which the style of the wording was changed from the original sentence, but again without changing the meaning (for example, "He sent Galileo, the great Italian scientist, a letter about it."); or (d) *semantic change,* in which a sentence with similar wording to the original was presented, but with the meaning of the sentence changed (for example, "Galileo, the great Italian scientist, sent him a letter about it.").

Figure 5.4 shows the subjects' accuracy of detecting changes of each kind as a function of where in the original story the target sentence had occurred. When tested right after hearing the target sentence, the subject recognized any change from the original sentence. However, when the retention interval was increased and filled with greater amounts of interpolated material some changes were more difficult to detect than others. As time passed, subjects became less able to tell whether they were hearing the identical target sentence or a sentence in which the wording had been changed without changing the meaning (*active/passive* or *formal* changes). By contrast, any semantic change from the original was easily detected, even after relatively long intervals. The semantic relations derived from the sentences are important to people processing a sentence, and not the surface forms themselves. The former is durable in memory to a degree that the latter is not.

In some cases listeners do accurately remember the surface forms of sentences. Jokes and insults sometimes fall into this category as well as cases where the listener, for whatever reason, takes special care to focus on the surface features of an utterance (Murphy & Shapiro, 1994). In general, however, the importance of the meaning of a sentence over its surface form is easily demonstrated (Bransford & Franks, 1971; Bransford, Barclay, & Franks, 1972).

Numerous experiments have confirmed that immediate recall of sentences can be highly accurate, but that we can usually recover from long-term memory only the

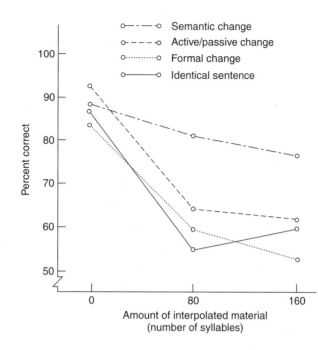

FIGURE 5.4

The ability to detect changes in a test sentence that involve either a change in wording *without* change in meaning (an active/passive or a formal change) or a change in wording *with* change in meaning (a semantic change). Accuracy is shown as a function of the amount of interpolated material received prior to testing.

Source: J. S. Sachs, Recognition memory for syntactic and semantic aspects of connected discourse. Perception and Psychophysics, 2, 1967: Fig. 2, pg. 441.

meaning, or "gist" of what we hear. Such experiments, however, do not necessarily mean that only the surface form of a sentence is initially stored in short-term memory. Indeed, Potter and Lombardi (1990) have argued that a conceptual representation of a sentence could be formed almost immediately and that reproduction of the surface form could be accomplished by *regenerating* the original words from this representation. That is, the immediate recall of a sentence may not be due to accessing a short-term verbatim representation that is simply "read off" word for word. It could be that short-term memory already holds a conceptual representation of the sentence and that apparent verbatim recall is the product of reconstructing the original sentence by piecing together in memory the sentence meaning and the fading traces of actual words and surface form.

If Potter and Lombardi are correct, this would imply that going back in memory to correct an initial parsing or interpretative error rests on our ability to correctly regenerate the original sentence, rather than simply reactivating a verbatim memory store. It is also possible that hearing a sentence is followed for a brief period by concurrent storage in memory of both semantic and surface representations, either of which can be tapped in a particular experiment (Potter, 1993; Wingfield, Tun, & Rosen, 1995).

Our point here is not that sentences may be represented conceptually in memory more quickly than some experiments might seem to imply. Our point is to reinforce the position that the goal of sentence processing is to extract meaning as quickly as possible, and that it is the conceptual representation of the utterance that is the primary focus of the memory system.

IS SYNTAX PROCESSED SEPARATELY FROM MEANING?

At the time when modern psycholinguistics was first developing, psychology as a whole was largely dominated by "serial" models of mental operations. The possibility of massively parallel computers and neural network modeling was still beyond the horizon. Most theories of the time dwelled on the idea of simpler, more easily visualized systems. In terms of language processing, it was common to see a four-stage model of sentence processing that followed the distinctions in general linguistics. These stages, which were assumed to operate in strict sequence, were processing at the level of phonology (the sound patterns of words), lexical processing (word identity or activation), syntactic processing (determination of grammatical structure), and semantic processing (processing the full utterance for meaning). Especially interesting was the proposal that syntactic processing must precede, and thus be conducted independently from, the semantic analysis of a sentence, where functional relationships are determined and meaning of the utterance becomes available. This was sometimes referred to as the principle of *syntactic autonomy* (Garrett, Bever, & Fodor, 1966).

In its earliest form, the idea of syntactic autonomy carried the implication that semantic analysis of a sentence could not begin until a major clause boundary or the end of the sentence had been reached (Fodor, Bever, & Garrett, 1974). This view led to attempts to demonstrate the importance of syntactic clauses at the earliest stages of sentence processing.

A favorite technique was to insert a click into a recorded sentence and then ask listeners to say at which point in the sentence they thought the click had occurred (Garrett, Bever, & Fodor, 1966). For example, a subject might hear the sentence given below, which consists of a dependent clause, "In order to catch his train," followed by an independent clause, "George drove furiously to the station." Subjects heard the sentence with a prerecorded click sound occurring either within the first clause (for example, position [1]), at the boundary between the two clauses (for example, position [2]), or somewhere in the second clause (for example, position [3]).

"In order to catch [1] his train, [2] George drove [3] furiously to the station."

Over the course of many such sentences, the study reliably demonstrated that subjects tended to be more accurate at saying where the click occurred when it had been presented between clauses than within a clause. Further, when subjects made a mistake in saying where a click had occurred, they tended to report the click as having occurred either at the boundary or closer to the boundary than it actually did. Why did the subjective impression of where the click occurred tend to "migrate" toward the major syntactic boundary of the sentence?

The so-called click studies were originally interpreted as demonstrating that major linguistic clauses represent the *perceptual units* of sentence processing. When steps were taken to eliminate the pauses and the changes in intonation pattern that usually accompany major clause boundaries, clicks located at clause boundaries were still more accurately localized than clicks presented within a clause (Garrett, Fodor, & Bever, 1966). Thus it was argued that the perceptual isolation of the linguistic clause was the first step in sentence processing, and formal syntactic structure alone was sufficient to tell the listener where the clause boundary had occurred.

Few paradigms in psycholinguistic research drew as much fire as did the early click studies. The questions were not based on whether or not clauses are important elements in sentence structure. They clearly are. The questions were, first, whether or not prosody is as unimportant to detecting syntactic boundaries of sentences as originally claimed, and second, whether these click effects reflected the way the sentences were actually perceived, or whether the click "migration" occurred in memory as the subject tried to recall where the click had occurred. For example, the migration effect is greatly reduced, although not completely eliminated, when subjects need not recall the entire sentence when saying where an extraneous sound had occurred, but instead may point at a script as they listen to the sentence. Prosody, as it turns out, also has a strong effect on the results (Wingfield & Klein, 1971).

THE ROLE OF PROSODY IN SENTENCE PROCESSING

Prosody is a general term for the variety of acoustic features—what we hear—that ordinarily accompany a spoken sentence. One prosodic feature is the *intonation pattern* of a sentence. *Intonation* refers to pitch changes over time, as when a speaker's voice rises in pitch at the end of a question or drops at the end of a sentence. A second prosodic feature is *word stress,* which is, in fact, a complex subjective variable based on loudness, pitch, and timing. Two final prosodic features are the pauses that sometimes occur at the ends of sentences or major clauses and the lengthening of final vowels in words immediately prior to a clause boundary (Cooper & Sorensen, 1981; Ferreira, 1993; Streeter, 1978).

Prosody plays numerous important roles in language processing. Prosody can indicate the mood of a speaker (happy, angry, sad, sarcastic), it can mark the semantic focus of a sentence (Jackendoff, 1972), and it can be used to disambiguate the meaning of an otherwise ambiguous sentence, such as *I saw a man in the park with a telescope* (Beach, 1991; Ferreira, Henderson, Anes, Weeks, & McFarlane, 1996; Wales & Toner, 1979).

A more subtle effect of prosody is the way it can be used to mark major clauses of a sentence. Consider the sentence, *In order to do well, he studied very hard.* If you say this sentence aloud, you will notice how clearly the clause boundary (indicated here by the comma) is marked by intonation, stress, and timing. Note especially how speakers automatically lengthen the final vowel in the word just prior to the clause boundary (in this case, the word *well*).

Although Garrett and his colleagues used an ingenious splicing technique to eliminate prosodic cues, this had the effect of underestimating their importance when such cues were present. When studies analogous to the click studies are conducted, but with the formal clause boundary and the prosodic marking for a clause boundary placed in direct conflict, clicks just as often migrate to the point marked by prosody as to the formal syntactic boundary (Wingfield & Klein, 1971).

Probably the experiment that cast the most dramatic doubt on whether or not the click studies were tapping on-line perceptual segmentation rather than reflecting a post-perceptual response bias was a study conducted by Reber and Anderson (1970). They found results parallel to the original click studies even when subjects were falsely told that the sentences they would hear contained "subliminal" clicks and asked to say where they thought these clicks had occurred. Although no clicks were actually presented, subjects more often reported having heard them at clause boundaries than within clauses.

It is certainly the case that clauses are important to the way people remember speech. In one series of experiments, subjects heard a tape-recorded passage that was stopped without warning at various spots in the passage. The moment the tape stopped, subjects were asked to recall as large a segment as possible of what had just been heard. Generally, subjects' recall was bounded by full clauses, just as one would expect if major linguistic clauses do have structural integrity (Jarvella, 1970, 1971). The importance of clause boundaries and other syntactic constituents can also be demonstrated by giving subjects tape-recorded passages and telling them to interrupt the tape whenever they want to immediately recall what they have just heard. In such cases, subjects reliably press the tape recorder pause button to give their recall at periodic intervals corresponding exactly with the ends of major clauses and other important syntactic boundaries (Wingfield & Butterworth, 1984).

We should not dismiss all elements of an autonomy principle out of hand. Indeed, we will later review evidence for some degree of autonomous processing in the form of activation of word meaning independent of the sentence context in which the word is embedded. Few writers today, however, espouse the early version of syntactic autonomy that implies that analysis at the semantic level must await completion of a full clause or sentence boundary in the speech stream.

We do not want to suggest that clauses are unimportant units in sentence processing. Rather, our question is whether both syntactic and semantic analyses occur together and continuously interact as we hear a sentence. Let us examine the principles of an interactive view of sentence processing before returning to the arguments for processing autonomy still current in the literature.

On-Line Interactive Models of Sentence Processing

We opened this chapter by stressing the speed with which spoken language must be comprehended when listening to everyday speech. In this regard we can see the attraction of an autonomy principle. "Autonomy" means *independence*. Would the fastest system be one in which an autonomous syntactic processor was allowed to run independently at its own rate? This might be the case if we imagined a rapid parser that would only slow down if it had to continually cross-check its operation against possible semantic interpretations derived from prior context. Or would sentence processing be faster if information from all levels of analysis could interact freely, with knowledge obtained at one level allowed to facilitate on-line processing at other levels? This latter idea is embodied in an **interactive model of language processing** (Tyler & Marslen-Wilson, 1977).

Both autonomous and interactive models would seem to have some virtue in a language-processing system that features speed, interpretive accuracy, and the least possible demands in terms of processing resources. As we indicated, we will review evidence that initial lexical activation, even in a sentence context, may represent an autonomous, automatic process that occurs free of interaction with other levels of sentence processing. On the other hand, equally persuasive evidence indicates that, at least at the level of conscious awareness, listeners make excellent use of prior context in their analysis of what is being heard.

An interactive view of sentence processing begins with **bottom-up processing,** as introduced in Chapter 3. This refers to the way in which the listener's sensory apparatus detects and analyzes the acoustic speech signal and processes it upward from the level of the acoustic waveform to the level of the recognition of phonemes, words, sentence structure, and finally, the recognition of semantic relations between the sentence elements that give rise to the sentence meaning. In our discussion of language structure, we also saw that listeners are quite adept at developing expectations of what they have yet to hear based on the structure and meaning of what they have already heard to that point. The term **top-down processing** refers to the potential use of such knowledge in order to speed, clarify, or otherwise facilitate the processing of emerging information from bottom-up sources.

Imagine you were trying to understand an indistinct voice over a noisy telephone line. You have impoverished bottom-up information. To the extent that you could utilize linguistic context to supplement this degraded information, we would refer to your success as being the product of an effective *top-down/bottom-up interaction.* Those who support an interactive model contend that knowledge-driven, top-down information and sensory-driven, bottom-up information interact continually, not only when the signal source is degraded. They also believe that all language processing is inherently interactive, even when the signal clarity is good. Such models are called *on-line interactive models* because they assume that semantic processing co-occurs with syntactic processing as the speech is being heard. *Off-line* processes also occur, but these refer to later interpretive, or retrospective operations that occur some time after the speech has been heard.

The comprehension system we are describing is one in which the listener carries out as much syntactic and semantic processing as possible as each word of the sentence is heard. As we activate the identity of each word, we determine its syntactic category and generate a hypothesis about the next syntactic element. Encountering the determiner, *the,* you have an expectation that a noun is upcoming, either as the next word or perhaps as the next word following an adjective modifying the upcoming noun. As each element arrives, you identify full noun phrases and verb phrases as soon as possible (Just & Carpenter, 1987; Thibadeau, Just, & Carpenter, 1982). An interactive model assumes not only that the meaning of the utterance is developed along with syntactic processing, but also that prior semantic operations facilitate subsequent parsing decisions.

Such a system would make use of all sources of information. One source might be the phonological information that affects word recognition, such as the acoustic coloring of sounds that results from their syllabic environment. Other sources of information include the syntactic frame that leads you to expect a word of a certain form class, as well as information based on the semantic constraints derived from the sentence meaning.

These interactions can account for the results of studies showing that prior context has a significant effect on the speed and ease with which a word seen or heard in a linguistic context can be recognized (Connine, Blasko, & Wang, 1994; Morton, 1969, 1970; Marslen-Wilson & Tyler, 1987).

In some interactive models, expectations generated by the linguistic and real-world context are thought to operate by influencing the recognizability of likely words even before any of their sensory information has been received (Morton, 1969; Becker, 1980). In other interactive models, context is assumed to operate only *after* the sensory information supplied by the first part of the word (the "bottom-up" portion of the mix) has activated a mental list of potential candidates. It is proposed that no matter how powerful a particular context might be, it will not influence the number of candidates initially activated on the basis of bottom-up information. Context can only operate by quickly eliminating initially activated possibilities that do not fit the ongoing context (Marslen-Wilson & Tyler, 1987).

Interactive models are thus a major alternative to the early clausal hypothesis that assumed that syntactic and semantic analyses are conducted independently and that analysis for meaning is not begun until a full sentence or clause boundary has been reached. In the interactive models, it is assumed that syntactic and semantic processing of sentences proceed together. The proponents of the interactive view believe that it is because we are able to mix the product of perceptual "bottom-up" analysis of the acoustic signal with "top-down" support from prior context that spoken sentences can be processed so rapidly.

Shadowing and Gating Studies

We can get a sense of top-down input whenever someone finishes a sentence for us. None of these interactive models, however, claim that this interactive process is conscious, or volitional, as it would be in this example. Rather, the interaction is assumed to be rapid and inaccessible to conscious awareness. How can we get a window on this on-line interactive processing so as to test the contention that prior context automatically places constraints on the perception of lower-level information?

One particularly ingenious study was conducted by Marslen-Wilson (1975), who had subjects listen to spoken passages and repeat what they were hearing as it was being heard. This is called **shadowing** (sometimes also called "echoing"). It may sound difficult, but it is in fact quite easy, and subjects rarely lag much behind the speech they are shadowing. Marslen-Wilson found that some subjects were "close" shadowers; they were able to speak almost simultaneously with what they were hearing. (We have known some children to do this to adult speech just to annoy the adults.)

Marslen-Wilson found that even his close-shadowing subjects would often spontaneously correct errors in pronunciation or grammar that had been intentionally placed into the recorded speech they were shadowing. To Marslen-Wilson, the important finding was that these unconscious corrections were made even before the incorrect word on the tape was fully completed. From the lags obtained, he estimated that recognition for words heard in context can occur within 200 milliseconds of their onset.

This time estimate was confirmed by Grosjean (1980) using a technique known as **gating.** Grosjean presented subjects with recorded sentences that included only the first 50 milliseconds of the last word in the sentence. The subject was asked to listen to the sentence and then to say what the last word of the sentence was. If the subject was unable to do this, the sentence was again presented, this time followed by the first 100 milliseconds of the last word, then the first 150 milliseconds, and so on, until the word could be correctly identified. This technique is called "gating" because in the early experiments an electronic "gate" was opened (and closed) to control the amount of the speech a subject would be allowed to hear.

Grosjean found that words in context could be recognized within 175 to 200 milliseconds of their onset, or when only half or less than half of their full acoustic signal had been heard. The average time for words out of context was 333 milliseconds. Although this may seem surprising, the fact is that only a limited number of words in the lexicon share the same initial sounds (the word-initial *cohort*). Further, this number decreases quite dramatically as more and more of a word onset is heard. For example, if you look in a standard dictionary and count the total number of different picturable nouns, you would find an average of 115 different nouns that share the same sounds in the first 50 milliseconds of the spoken word. After the first 100 milliseconds of the word onset has been heard the number drops to 43 words, then to 11 words after 200 milliseconds, and only 5 by 300 milliseconds (Wayland, Wingfield, & Goodglass, 1989). When we take into account the stress patterns of the words, the rate of reduction in word possibilities with increasing word-onset duration is even greater (Wingfield, Goodglass, & Lindfield, 1997). To put these figures in perspective, depending on speech rate, typical one-, two-, and three-syllable words may average between 550 to 830 milliseconds in full duration.

The effect of context would presumably be to reduce the initial cohort of possible words based on word-onset sounds, to those that could reasonably "fit" within the sentence frame heard (Tyler, 1984). Less clear is whether listeners reduce cohort size based on context alone, without phonological information (Morton, 1969); if context begins to take effect only after the beginning sounds have activated the full cohort (see Chapter 3 for description of "cohort" theory of spoken word recognition, Marslen-Wilson, 1987); or if context only operates after the word is fully specified and activated in the lexicon (Forster, 1979). The idea that context alone reduces cohort size is now thought unlikely. As Marslen-Wilson (1987) has suggested, real-world survival demands a bottom-up priority to some degree in the processing system. It is important that we are able to detect sounds that signal danger, no matter how unlikely they might be in a particular context.

How On-Line Is Gating?

The process we wish to understand, of course, is the real-time analysis of the speech input and the automated "core processes" involved in language understanding (Tyler & Wessels, 1985, p. 18). In gating, subjects typically have unlimited time to write down or to say aloud their answer after hearing a word-onset fragment. As we noted earlier, some theorists have argued that context functions only after the word has been accessed (Forster, 1979). If the subjects' responses in gating experiments are in fact produced only after a period of conscious (or unconscious) reflection, the effects of context seen in these studies could be occurring during a brief interval between the end of some automatic, context independent processes and the subjects' overt responses.

Gating has proven a useful technique in psycholinguistic research and a good review of this work can be found in Grosjean (in press). However, deciding whether gating taps on-line processes or later ones is not easy. Tyler and Wessels (1985) suggested that perhaps if subjects were forced to respond rapidly in a gating task, one might be on safer ground arguing that their responses did reflect the product of true on-line processing.

Their stimuli for this experiment consisted of gated words presented in the context of two prior sentences. The sentence pairs were selected such that one sentence of each pair would provide either a weak or a strong syntactic constraint and the other sentence of the pair would have wording that would make the target word either semantically anomalous or it would offer a minimal semantic context. (Because a strong semantic context can make any word-onset information redundant, they used only a weak semantic context for this experiment.)

The sentence pairing possibilities are listed here in decreasing order of their value in reducing the amount of word-onset information necessary for correct identification of a gated word (for example, *organize*). In the first type of sentence pairing, the gated word was not easily predictable from the semantic information in the first sentence, but its grammatical part of speech, or syntactic *form class,* was easily predictable from the syntactic information in the fragment of the second sentence (that is, minimal semantic constraint/strong syntactic constraint: *min sem/strong syn*). For example, the subject might hear, "The appointment with the dentist was canceled. John tried to . . ." followed by the target word *organize* presented in gated segments. Although *organize* is plausible from the semantic context of the first sentence, it is not highly predictable as *reschedule* might be. However, from the syntactic context of *John tried to . . .,* we would expect a verb because only a verb may grammatically follow *to.*

In the second type of sentence pairing, the gated word (for example, *organize*) was not easily predictable from the semantic information in the first sentence, nor was its part of speech totally predictable from the syntactic information in the fragment of the second sentence (minimal semantic constraint/weak syntactic constraint: *min sem/weak syn*). For example, the subject might again hear, "The appointment with the dentist was canceled," however, this time it would be followed by "John can . . . ." As we can see, the word *can* could be followed by a verb such as *organize*, or just as easily followed by an adverb such as *happily*.

In the third type of sentence pairing, the first sentence was semantically anomalous such that it had no constraining effect on the target word whatsoever (anomalous semantic information/strong syntactic constraint: *anom/strong syn*). However, the part of speech of the target word was easily predictable from the syntactic information in the beginning fragment of the second sentence. Here, the first sentence heard might be, "The breath with the lie shuffles only through," and the second sentence fragment, "The terrace tries to . . . ." We know that the target word is a verb, but beyond this we find no constraining information at the semantic level.

In the fourth type of sentence pairing, the first sentence is semantically anomalous and the part of speech is not heavily constrained by the syntactic information in the fragment of the second sentence (anomalous semantic information/weak syntactic constraint: *anom/weak syn*). An example sentence pairing of this type might be "The breath with the lie shuffles only through. The terrace can . . . ." In a final condition, gated words were presented with no linguistic context whatsoever *(no-context)*.

Here are the three steps Tyler and Wessels took to get fast responses and more immediate reactions within the gating paradigm. First, instead of repeatedly hearing the context sentences with increasingly larger word-onset fragments of the target word, each subject heard a given word fragment only once. The amount of word-onset information needed for identification in the various context conditions was determined by using large numbers of subjects, with different subjects receiving word-onset fragments of different sizes. Second, Tyler and Wessels used two measures of word identification. The first was the *isolation point,* which was defined as the smallest average gate size that allowed subjects to give the correct answer, regardless of how uncertain they might be of their answer. The second was the *recognition point.* This is a later point at which subjects not only gave the correct word but also rated their confidence in their judgment fairly highly. Finally, Tyler and Wessels contrasted *nontimed responses* (subjects were placed under no time pressure to give their responses) with *timed responses* (subjects were asked to respond as quickly as possible). Tyler and Wessels argued that timed responses at the isolation point might come closer to tapping on-line processing than the usual procedures of nontimed responses at the higher-confidence recognition point. Their results are shown in Figure 5.5.

When subjects give an overt response in an experiment, we can never be sure what sorts of processes may have preceded that response at a level inaccessible to conscious awareness. As we shall see in the next section, this is a problem that has plagued psycholinguistic investigators since the earliest days. Although Tyler and Wessels did observe the effects on gate sizes of timed versus nontimed responses and of using isolation versus recognition points, they were even more impressed with the

FIGURE 5.5

Mean isolation points and mean recognition points for gated words heard either with no context or with one of four combinations of types of linguistic context. Responses were either made at the subjects' own pace (nontimed) or when subjects were asked to respond as quickly as possible after hearing the target fragment (timed responses).

Source: L. K. Tyler and J. Wessels, Is gating an on-line task? Evidence from naming latency data. Perception and Psychophysics, 38, 1985: Fig. 1, pg. 220.

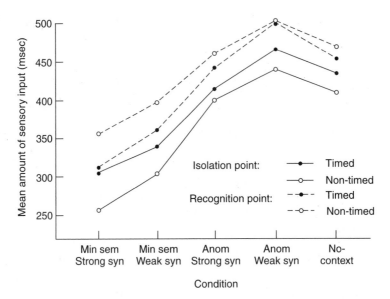

similarities in the gate sizes. Most important to them was that the pattern of the effects of linguistic context was the same, regardless of the length of the time lag before the response was given. On the basis of this reasoning, they concluded that the gating technique can be used to tap on-line processes.

Why did syntactic form-class constraints have such a small effect on word identification times? When Tyler and Wessels first found this effect in an earlier study (Tyler & Wessels, 1983), they interpreted the finding in terms of cohort theory. They accepted the likelihood that form-class constraints might be expected to reduce the initial cohort to just those words that belong to one, or a few possible syntactic categories. A syntactic constraint, however, would not ordinarily reduce the possible cohort size to the same degree as would a semantic constraint. To take a previous example, the semantic constraint offered by the sentence frame, *The train pulled into the . . .* , does more than constrain the next word to a noun, or to an adjective modifying a noun. It raises the likelihood of either one of two words occurring: *tunnel* or *station*.

In certain cases, syntactic information can specifically isolate the correct meaning of an ambiguous word, such as *watch*. This would be the case simply by knowing from the sentence structure whether the word is a noun or a verb. Even in such cases, however, Tyler and Wessels suggest that syntactic constraints do not seem to operate immediately. Indeed, they cite data from Seidenberg, Tanenhaus, Leiman, and Bienkowski (1982), who claim that effects of syntactic form-class disambiguation of this kind can be detected only some 200 milliseconds after a word has been identified (Tyler & Wessels, 1983, p. 418).

Because syntactic constraints had a relatively small effect in the Tyler and Wessels experiment, we should not forget the importance of syntax in ordinary language processing. As we have seen, syntactic information plays a key role in the listener's ability to develop the meaning of a sentence. As Tyler and Wessels cautioned when they obtained a similar finding in an earlier experiment, "Perhaps one moral of the present study is that an information source that is important in one aspect of the system does not need to be important in every aspect" (Tyler & Wessels, 1983, p. 418).

WHERE DOES CONTEXT OPERATE?

Modularity theorists are those who believe that input processes such as lexical activation are cognitively impenetrable. That is, these operations are performed rapidly, automatically, and uninfluenced by prior or collateral information. In cognitive theory, such modular processes are thus said to be "informationally encapsulated" (Fodor, 1983).

Although this level of cognitive theory is beyond the scope of this chapter, let us see how a modular process would operate in sentence processing. One version can be derived from an early proposal by Forster (1979), who defined what he believed to be three separate processing systems devoted to language processing. (The model had other elements that need not concern us here.)

The first system he called the *lexical processor*. It activates particular lexical (word) entries based on input from peripheral systems that deal with phonological input in speech (or orthographic input in writing). The output of the lexical processor is passed to the next level, a *syntactic processor*. This processor extracts information from the lexical output level in order to conduct a syntactic analysis of the sentence leading to a surface-structure representation. The final level of interest to us is that of a *message processor*. This was said to convert the linguistic representation into a conceptual, or meaning, structure that represents the semantic intention of the intended message.

In contrast with interactive models, in Forster's conceptualization no processor would have any information from operations conducted by any of the higher-level processors. In this scheme, for example, the lexical processor would work independently, or "autonomously" from both the syntactic and the message-level processors, and the syntactic processor would operate independently from the message processor. You can now see again the two contrasting views, both based on the speed of normal processing. The interactive model presumes that the only way people can handle speech so rapidly is because all levels of analysis are able to interact continuously with all other levels. The autonomous view suggests that lexical analysis is so rapid because it is not slowed by the need to integrate context as you process each word.

One way to view the autonomy question is to consider the possibility that while interactive processes might operate at a slower, conscious level of awareness of what we are hearing, the moment-to-moment analyses of the sentence's words are so fast and so automatic that the analysis at any one level is finished and its output delivered to the next higher level before any information from the higher levels could possibly be brought to bear on them. Both positions presume multiple levels of processing. One assumes that all of these levels are constantly interacting with each other (for example, that the lexical processor has at its disposal and can be influenced by semantic and message-level knowledge). The other position assumes that each processing level can be seen as an impenetrable, informationally encapsulated module, whose work is conducted autonomously from any other similarly modular process.

According to the autonomous theories, a clear limit exists on how contextual information could affect the bottom-up analysis at the word level. Specifically, linguistic or real-world context could contribute to the evaluation of the output of the lexical processor, but it would not influence the operations of the lexical processor that led to this output.

How could we peek into automatic unconscious processing activity to see whether or not semantic context is operating on a word the instant it is being heard rather than later? For example, would an ambiguous word heard in a sentence context have only its contextually constrained meaning activated (as would be predicted by an interactive model), or are even unlikely meanings of a word initially activated the instant the word is heard (as would be predicted by an autonomous model)?

An early experiment by Swinney (1979) illustrates one interesting approach to this question. In this study, Swinney attempted to show that at an immediate automatic level, semantic activation takes place independent of the context that precedes it. Swinney's experiment made use of the phenomenon of **priming,** the somewhat unmodular fact that the processing of a word will be facilitated by having just seen or heard another word that is semantically related to it (Meyer, Schvaneveldt, & Ruddy, 1975; Neely, 1977). One way to show this priming effect is to measure the speed of naming (that is, reading aloud) the second word. You will be faster reading aloud the word *nurse* flashed on a computer screen when it is preceded (either in writing or spoken through earphones) by the semantically related word *patient,* than if it is preceded by the unrelated word *saucer.* A second way to demonstrate semantic priming is to measure the speed with which you can decide whether or not a string of letters forms a real word. Using the above example, we could demonstrate the effect of semantic priming by showing that it takes you less time to decide that *nurse* is a real word (as opposed to the scrambled letters *surne*) if it is preceded by *patient* than if it is preceded by *saucer.* This word/nonword judgment is referred to as a **lexical decision task,** as introduced earlier in Chapter 4.

Swinney used a version of this task referred to as **cross-modal lexical priming.** His goal was to see whether a local linguistic context would constrain access to just the appropriate meaning of an ambiguous word as implied by the context, or whether other meanings of the ambiguous word would also automatically be activated. For example, many English words have homophones. (*Homophones* are pairs of words that have different meanings but that share the same sound.) At a conscious level, if you were hearing the word "bark" in the context of someone telling you about their new puppy, you would probably not be distracted by or even think of the fact that *bark* also has another meaning as the outer covering of a tree trunk. Could it be, however, that—even though it is inaccessible to conscious awareness—at the instant you heard the word "bark," *both* meanings of the word were momentarily activated?

Swinney first tape-recorded a person reading the following passage in a natural tone at a normal rate of speech:

Rumor had it that, for years, the government building had been plagued with problems. The man was not surprised when he found several spiders, roaches, and other bugs [1] in the [2] corner of the room.

The ambiguous word, of course, is the word *bugs,* which has at least two meanings known to most of us. One of these is the meaning of bugs in the sense of insects and the other is the term for a hidden microphone, a term introduced into the lexicon by numerous espionage stories and movies.

At the moment the word *bugs* was heard, Swinney flashed on a screen for a lexical decision, a word that was either related to the contextually appropriate meaning of *bugs* (for example, the word *ant*), a word related to the contextually inappropriate meaning (for example, *spy*), or a control word that was unrelated to either meaning (for example, *sew*). These visual probes were presented either immediately after the ambiguous word, at the position marked as [1], or at a point several syllables later [2].

Swinney found that for subjects who saw the probe words presented at position [1], the lexical decisions for both *ant* and for *spy* were significantly faster than for lexical decisions to a semantically unrelated control word such as *sew.* By the time several hundred milliseconds had passed (position [2]), however, only the word related to the contextually appropriate meaning of the word (for example, the word *ant*) was facilitated.

These results appear to support modularity at the lexical level. At the moment the spoken word was heard, there was a significant facilitation for lexical decisions to visually presented words that were related to both meanings of the ambiguous word even when the word had been preceded by what should have been a highly constraining lexical-semantic context. Some time after the word had been heard (position [2]), activation was present only for the contextually appropriate meaning of the word; the inappropriate meaning of the word had either rapidly decayed or rapidly been inhibited. Context did affect meaning, but only after a first stage of automatic "modular" activation.

In a series of follow-up experiments, Onifer and Swinney (1981) confirmed this earlier finding by including ambiguous words where one meaning is ordinarily more common than the other, presenting them also in strongly biasing contexts:

The postal clerk put the package on the scale [1] to see if [2] there was sufficient postage.

or

The dinner guests enjoyed the specially prepared river bass, although one guest did get a scale [1] caught in his [2] throat.

The results showed that even for subjects who heard the first sentence, where the sentence context implied the more frequent meaning of the word *scale,* both meanings of the word were activated at the instant in time indicated by position [1]. As before, for subjects who had the lexical decision tested at position [2], only the contextually appropriate meaning of the target word appeared to be activated.

To Swinney and colleagues, these data seemed to indicate a sentence-comprehension system composed of autonomous subsystems, called modules, that act automatically and are uninfluenced by higher-level processes. When an ambiguous word is heard, all of its meanings are activated. If a context is present, it operates only at a later point in time to select among possible meanings and to allow only the contextually appropriate one to come into conscious awareness. Although the technique of cross-modal lexical priming has received the most attention in the literature, a variety of experimental tasks have been used to support the general view that lexical access is automatic and uninfluenced, at least in its initial stages, by context. Simpson (1984) provides a good review of this early literature.

The cross-modal lexical priming technique has produced some interesting results and has made the important point that many operations may be going on at an unconscious automatic level, about which we have no conscious access. Why would all meanings of an ambiguous word be activated regardless of context? Recall that these ambiguous words were homophones: words such as *bug/bug* or *scale/scale* that are really two different words in the sense that they represent two different concepts, but that, when spoken, share the same sound pattern.

As we noted earlier, even if top-down information is important to language processing at one level, at another level our real-world survival would still demand a bottom-up priority in auditory processing. In times of danger we must be able to detect what is being heard rather than what is expected to be heard (Marslen-Wilson, 1987). You might not survive long if the unlikelihood of encountering a lion in your back yard would prevent you from correctly identifying its roar when you heard it.

Much can be said for a system that takes no chances, a system that activates every possible meaning of an acoustic input before using other information, such as context, to eliminate all but the appropriate interpretation. For nonhomophones that share only word onsets, the picture seems fairly simple. For example, hearing a word that begins with the sound *cap* may activate both *captain* and *capital* (and hence, in a priming study, prime both *salute* and *money*). However, by the time you have heard the full word, only one of these possibilities remains. This process has been studied using techniques that combine features of both gating and cross-modal lexical priming (Marslen-Wilson & Zwitserlood, 1989).

The results from cross-modal lexical priming do not negate the importance of prior context in sentence processing. What they do is to suggest the displacement of the effects in time. Context acted not to prevent automatic activation of both word meanings but to allow the listener to quickly select the correct one.

This view is an important one to modular theories of language processing, but the issue is not closed. Some researchers suggest that selective (pre)activation of the dominant meaning might occur if the context is sufficiently constraining (Simpson & Krueger, 1991; Tabossi & Zardon, 1993). Others argue a middle position: That sentence contexts do not preselect appropriate lexical entries, but that the process of eliminating the contextually inappropriate ones begins as the word is heard (Zwitserlood, 1989).

As we conclude this section, remember that both autonomous and interactive models have their adherents and that evidence supports both. At issue is not whether top-down support is available to immediate speech processing, nor whether some processes are automatic and autonomous. What is at issue is the exact microstructure of events in the first few hundred milliseconds of on-line operations. We can only report that the search is underway for the right microscope.

COMPREHENSION OF NONLITERAL MEANING

A distinction important to a discussion of sentence processing is the distinction between the **literal** meaning of an utterance and cases where sentences also have **nonliteral** meanings. One example of nonliteral meaning is sarcasm. We often hear people make statements such as, "It's a beautiful day today," when the weather is cold, windy, and damp. We intuitively know not to take the person's utterance at face value. We recognize from the context and the speaker's tone that the speaker is being sarcastic: We are expected to take the literal meaning and reverse it.

Idioms are another example of nonliteral meaning. Consider the sentence, *John kicked the bucket yesterday.* The literal meaning of the sentence is that a person, John, struck a pail with his foot. However, given that most speakers of English know that the phrase, *kick the bucket,* is an idiom, they would realize that this is a reference to someone having died.

Two other common types of nonliteral meaning are **metaphors** and **indirect requests.** *Metaphors* are formally defined as statements that are literally false but nevertheless convey a clearly understood meaning. We know what a person means by, "Billboards are warts on the landscape," even though we know that billboards are not really warts. Similarly, *indirect requests* are statements that literally ask one thing but figuratively ask another. If someone were to interrupt you right now and ask, "Do you know what time it is?" the appropriate answer is not to say "Yes." We recognize that the person is indirectly asking you to tell him what time it is.

In general, we have two accounts of how nonliteral meaning (or *figurative* language) is processed. One theory assumes a three-stage process. First, the individual determines the literal meaning of the sentence. Second, the individual determines whether the literal meaning seems appropriate to the context and circumstance surrounding the utterance. If this is not the case, a third stage is undertaken in which the individual rejects the literal truth value of the utterance and seeks a nonliteral interpretation (Searle, 1979). This kind of model implies that figurative language comprehension is secondary to, and qualitatively different from, literal language comprehension.

Although the three-stage model has some intuitive appeal, recent work with a variety of nonliteral forms such as idioms, metaphors, and indirect requests has cast doubt on the implications of this account. First, studies using cross-modal lexical priming have shown that figurative meanings of idioms often are available to listeners as rapidly as literal meanings (Cacciari & Tabossi, 1988; Titone & Connine, 1994a). These results clearly imply that listeners need not process the literal meaning of the phrase before understanding its figurative meaning. Second, the processes involved in understanding nonliteral language may be qualitatively no different from the processes involved in understanding literal language. Often the literal meaning helps us understand the figurative meaning, as it would for idioms such as *spill the beans,* in which the literal act of spilling beans is metaphorically related to the figurative act of revealing secrets (Blasko & Connine, 1993; Gibbs, Nayak, & Cutting, 1989; Glucksberg, 1995; Nunberg, Sag, & Wasow, 1994; Titone & Connine, 1994b; Titone & Connine, in press).

THE ROLE OF MEMORY IN LANGUAGE PROCESSING

Although most sentence processing is conducted rapidly as the speech is being heard, we have seen arguments for the necessity of a memory component in sentence processing to allow for necessary downstream operations. Martin (1990) has divided these needs into three categories.

Speech Perception and Lexical Identification

The first of these would be cases of ambiguous acoustic input in connected speech. We used one of Martin's examples earlier, the spoken sentence pair, "I *better* do my laundry," and "I *bet her* five dollars," in which the italicized segments are pronounced identically. Martin points out that often the linguistic context that follows the ambiguous region corrects the ambiguity. In a similar way, a poorly articulated word may not be recognized until more of the sentence following that word has been heard (Connine, Blasko, & Hall, 1991; Grosjean, 1985; Wingfield, Alexander, & Cavagelli, 1994). To make either form of recovery possible, the listener would have to retain the phonological information, albeit for a short period, until the clarifying information has been reached.

Syntactic Parsing and Retention of Phrases

In discussing the work of Sachs (1967) (Figure 5.4), we saw that memory for phonological and syntactic information fades at a much faster rate than does the representation of meaning. The more quickly a listener can develop the propositional representation of a sentence, the less dependent the listener will be on the rapidly fading trace of the surface features.

As we have seen, however, the drive to determine functional relations as quickly as possible runs the risk of premature closure on an incorrect meaning that will have to be corrected as more information is received. Earlier we gave examples of garden path sentences, sentences in which the wording (intentionally or not) invites people to take the wrong interpretive path at a point of local ambiguity. As we saw previously, such sentences are so hard to understand that people often are convinced that they are ungrammatical and meaningless.

Although a reader can reread a part of a sentence where a parsing confusion may arise, listeners do not have this luxury. Martin (1990) suggests that a brief memory representation for the surface form of the sentence would be necessary for any hope of repairing the initial parsing error.

Retention of Semantic Propositions

An erroneous initial parsing is not the only mistake an otherwise efficient sentence processor can make. No less costly to downstream comprehension can be an initial misinterpretation of a lexically ambiguous word, such as *case* being interpreted as *case* as in *suitcase,* versus *case* as in *legal case.* This error would lead to the wrong semantic proposition being formed, and the propositions derived from that misinterpretation would in turn have to be corrected after the error was discovered. In this case, a memory representation would allow the listener time to recover the original message for its reinterpretation at the propositional level. Sometimes propositions derived from a passage are difficult to remember, such as when semantic coherence among the content words is weak (Martin, 1990).

In addition to having the capability for correcting parsing errors, a transient memory representation allows integration of phrases and clauses to develop full utterance meaning (van Dijk & Kintsch, 1983). When the speech input is especially rapid or an unfamiliar word is encountered, words and phrases may continue to arrive even as we are still analyzing or attempting to integrate what we have already heard. Martin argues, quite reasonably, that some sort of memory buffer would be essential whenever on-line sentence processing lags behind the input.

How Specialized Is the Memory System Used for Sentence Processing?

The necessity of some sort of short-term or working memory for effective sentence processing seems persuasive (Just & Carpenter, 1992). How then can we account for reports of brain-damaged patients with severe short-term memory deficits who nevertheless show good ability for at least some aspects of sentence processing (Linebarger, Schwartz, & Saffran, 1983; Martin, 1987)?

Martin (1987) examined sentence comprehension for a group of brain-injured patients whose memory span for materials such as word lists had been tested and was known to be limited. The sentences she used varied in complexity from one-clause active sentences, *The boy pushed the girl,* to one-clause passive sentences, *The boy was pushed by the girl,* to sets of center-embedded relative clause constructions of the sort shown in Table 5.1.

Martin's task was to see whether a patient was able to assign a descriptive clause in a sentence to the correct person. For example, in sentence IV: Who had black hair, the man or the woman? As you can see, this task is not easy. The correct answer requires that we overlook the long intervening clause, *that was pushed by the man,*

SENTENCE TYPE	EXAMPLE OF SENTENCE USED
I.	The woman that had black hair pushed the man.
II.	The woman that pushed the man had black hair.
III.	The woman that had black hair was pushed by the man.
IV.	The woman that was pushed by the man had black hair.
V.	The woman that the man pushed had black hair.

while focusing on the long-distance dependency, *The woman . . . had black hair.* Note also that one's grasp of the sentence structure must be strong enough to overcome the potentially distracting association of the adjacent words, . . . *the man had black hair.* Role relations about the action verb were also tested: Did the man push the woman or did the woman push the man?

Relative-clause sentences should put greater demands on memory than the one-clause sentences. Not only are they longer, they are also center-embedded constructions, in which the embedded clause occurs between the main clause (head noun) and the verb. Information about the incomplete main clause must be retained in memory while the embedded clause is being processed.

Not all of Martin's subjects showed good comprehension, but short-term memory span was not the defining predictor of adequate comprehension and thematic role assignment. For example, two subjects had a memory span of only 2.2 items, versus the 7 or so items most adults can recall. One patient scored only 57% correct on a comprehension test of role relations in the simple active and passive sentences, and 54% correct on the relative-clause sentences. However, the other patient with exactly the same memory span scored 88% correct on the active and passive sentences and 93% correct on the relative-clause sentences.

Other reports have also appeared in the neuropsychological literature describing patients with limited short-term memories but with no apparent impairment in ordinary sentence comprehension (Butterworth, Campbell, & Howard, 1986). The same can be said for sentence processing and comprehension in normal aging where working memory capacity is often markedly limited (Stine & Wingfield, 1990).

It is thus clear that although some form of memory representation is required to effectively process language, it is likely that the nature of these representations must be quite complex. In particular, it would appear that the kind of memory representation required for language comprehension is not easily measured by our standard tests of ordinary memory capacity. A striking illustration of this point can be found in the results of an experiment by Waters and Caplan (1996).

The background for the Waters and Caplan experiment was based on the common presumption that sentences that require a "second-pass" analysis, such as the garden path sentences, might put especially heavy demands on working memory. Interestingly, Waters and Caplan (1996) probed this question, not with brain-damaged subjects, but with healthy young-adult college students who differed in their scores on a common test of working memory span (Daneman & Carpenter, 1980; Waters, Caplan, & Hildebrandt, 1987).

The subjects' task was to read a sentence that appeared printed on a computer screen and then to decide whether the sentence made sense or whether it was an anomalous sentence-like nonsensical sequence of words. The computer measured the time the subjects spent reading the sentences and the time it took them to press a "yes" or a "no" key depending on whether or not the sentence made sense.

Figure 5.6 shows the time it took subjects to read complex garden path sentences, and two types of control sentences that were not garden path sentences (Non–garden Path A and Non–garden Path B). These data are shown for three groups of subjects who differed in their measured spans of working memory.

We can see from Figure 5.6 that subjects took more time to read the garden path sentences than the non–garden path sentences. We can thus see that the reading time measure is sensitive to the greater comprehension difficulty imposed by garden path sentences. The major point, however, is that this measure of comprehension difficulty was not affected by whether the subjects tested as high, medium, or low in their working memory capacity. Waters and Caplan concluded that subjects' working memory capacity may relate to some verbally mediated tasks, but that this particular capacity does not influence the understanding of words, the resolution of syntactic structure, or the determination of meaning in even quite complex sentences.

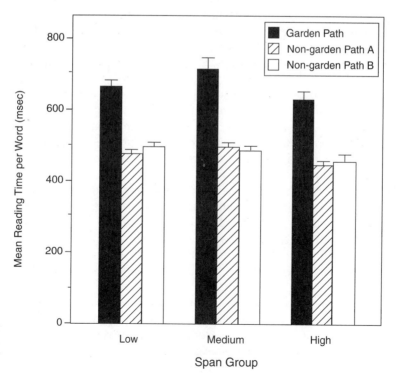

FIGURE 5.6

Mean reading time per word in milliseconds for garden path sentences and two types of non–garden path sentences (non–garden Path A and non–garden Path B). Subjects had either a low, medium, or high memory span.

Source: G. S. Waters and D. Caplan, Processing resource capacity and the comprehension of garden path sentences. Memory and Cognition, 24, 1996: Fig. 3, pg. 348.

Such results do not necessarily imply that memory is not important for sentence processing. What they do imply is that the memory structures used for temporary storage and recall of, for example, word lists, are not the same memory structures used to support on-line syntactic parsing and propositional analysis in natural language processing (Caplan & Waters, 1990; Martin, 1990; Waters & Caplan, 1996). You may recall Potter and Lombardi's (1990) point from earlier in the chapter that accurate short-term verbatim recall of a sentence does not mean that there is not yet a conceptual representation of the sentence in memory. At that time we raised the possibility that for a brief period there may exist concurrent storage of both semantic and surface representations of a sentence. It might thus be the case that one form of memory is damaged in the sorts of patients described by Martin and by Butterworth and his colleagues (a verbatim store that is measured by digit spans or word spans) and another form of memory (memory for semantic representations of sentences) is not.

A Processing Model
of Sentence Comprehension

Kintsch has offered the beginnings of a promising formulation of higher levels of analysis beyond syntax (Kintsch, 1988, 1994; van Dijk & Kintsch, 1983). This model proposes that in active speech perception (or in reading), linguistic input is processed in cycles on a segment-by-segment basis. As the phonological (or orthographic) stream arrives, it is rapidly recoded into propositions (or "idea units") consisting of a relational term (the *predicate*) plus a set of concepts to be related *(arguments)*. At the next stage, the connections among propositions are established and this relationship among the propositions is represented by a network referred to as a **coherence graph.** At this level, the propositions most important to the message structure are selected and other propositions connected to them are selected on the basis of shared arguments. Language is said to be coherent when its component propositions are rich in referential linkages.

Support for the belief that propositions serve as important units in sentence processing comes from the finding that the number of propositions contained in passages predicts the average reading time per word of written text (Kintsch & Keenan, 1973) and the speech rate at which rapidly spoken sentences can be understood and recalled (Stine, Wingfield, & Poon, 1986). It has also been shown that propositions at higher levels on a coherence graph are more likely to be recalled than propositions lower on the coherence graph. This would be a consequence of higher-level items receiving more processing cycles in working memory (Kintsch, 1994).

The importance of this model to our present discussion is the notion that in language processing, propositions are distributed across sentences, as well as within sentences. Language comprehension across sentences is referred to as discourse. It is to this topic that we will turn in Chapter 6.

SUMMARY

This chapter focused on sentence processing—the question of how listeners rapidly decipher the structure of sentences and gain access to their meaning. We saw that one striking feature of this process is the speed with which it is ordinarily conducted. Listeners have the ability to comprehend and integrate sentences and sentence elements as they are being heard, even though the sentences in ordinary conversation arrive at speech rates in excess of 100 words per minute.

Early studies of the statistical properties of language illustrated how we use knowledge of linguistic structure to develop expectations about the structure and meaning of what we hear. Such contextual constraints can facilitate rapid recognition of the speech input as well as serving to guide its later recall.

Determination of the syntactic structure of sentences is an essential step for understanding the meaning of a sentence. Experimental studies show that listeners ordinarily strive to determine the meaning of an utterance as quickly as possible and then to quickly discard its surface form from memory.

Many theorists believe that sentence comprehension is an active process in which the perceptual system continuously attempts to determine the structure and meaning of the sentence as it is being heard. Others argue that early levels of sentence processing, such as activation of word meaning, may be conducted independently of knowledge potentially available from prior linguistic context. These questions, as well as the role of memory processes in sentence comprehension, remain important questions for future research.

KEY WORDS

Discourse
Sentence processing
Transformational grammar
Surface structure
Deep structure
Competence
Performance
Parsing
Local ambiguity
Standing ambiguity
Garden path model
Constraint satisfaction model
Late closure principle

Minimal attachment principle
Lexicon
Propositional representation
Prosody
Interactive model of language
  processing
Bottom-up processing
Top-down processing
Shadowing
Gating
Priming
Lexical decision task
Cross-modal lexical priming

Literal meaning *Metaphors*
Nonliteral meaning *Indirect requests*
Idioms *Coherence graph*

SOMETHING TO THINK ABOUT

1. Create a set of second-, fourth-, and sixth-order statistical approximations to English. Make segments of different lengths, such as 10-, 12-, or 14-word "sentences." Now present these "sentences" to several friends (either spoken or in writing) and ask them to recall the "sentences" as accurately as possible. Are your subjects more accurate in recalling the higher-order approximations to English than the lower orders? Why do you think this is so? Sometimes subjects will "recall" a word that was not actually present in the stimulus. Does this give you a clue as to why higher-order approximations are recalled better than lower-order approximations?

2. One theory of sentence processing claims that when you hear a homophone (such as the word *bark*, which could refer to the bark of a dog or the bark of a tree) both meanings of the word are activated, even though the sentence context should clearly eliminate the wrong meaning. For example, the claim is that both meanings of the word *bark* will be activated regardless of whether the word is heard in the sentence, "The boy who climbed the tree bruised his knee on the sharp *bark*," or "The boy was frightened to go near the dog that had a loud *bark*." An assumption in this theory is that even though you may not consciously be aware of the inappropriate meaning of a word this does not mean that both meanings were not briefly activated the moment it was heard. Write an essay in which you evaluate this theory. Can you think of an experiment that could test this theory?

3. Listen carefully to the people around you during the day and keep a diary in which you list of all of the nonliteral statements you hear, such as metaphors and indirect requests (for example, "Do you have the time?" is actually a request to tell what time it is). How many examples have you come up with, and how many would you have been aware of if you had not been listening for them? How do you think we comprehend the nonliteral meanings of such utterances?

4. What role do you think prosody plays in everyday sentence comprehension? Give some examples of the use of prosody to mark a major syntactic boundary in a sentence and another example of the use of prosody to indicate the semantic focus of a sentence.

ACTIVITIES

1. An early technique researchers used to demonstrate the importance of syntactic clauses in sentence processing is to insert a click into a recorded sentence and ask listeners to say at which point in the sentence they thought the click had occurred (Garrett, Bever, & Fodor, 1966). Explore this syntactic phenomenon by conducting a "click" study of your own. First, create several sentences (containing independent and dependent clauses) of the following type: *In order to catch his train, George drove furiously to the station.* Next, create a written script of these sentences and record different versions using an ordinary tape recorder. Have a friend follow along with your prepared script and tap the microphone at various points in the sentence (thus creating a "click" to be detected in your experiment). Create different versions of each sentence by having your friend tap the microphone either within the first clause of the sentence, at the boundary between the two clauses, or somewhere in the second clause.

When you have finished preparing different versions of these sentences, play them back to several listeners and have them recall each sentence and report to you where the "click" was. How does accuracy of detecting the location of the click differ for different versions of your sentence? Does this pattern of accuracy change if subjects are given a script to follow along with while listening to these sentences? If so, based upon what you now know about syntactic processing, why?

2. Sachs (1967) showed that subjects' memory of the meanings of sentences is more durable than their memory of the surface forms of sentences, especially after the passage of time. However, Murphy and Shapiro (1994) found that under some circumstances listeners do focus on the surface forms of sentences (for example, jokes, insults). Use the following method to replicate the original Sachs (1967) experiment and test whether subjects are more likely to remember the surface forms of sentences when surface forms are likely to matter.

Create several stories that focus attention to the surface form of the last sentence of the passage (for example, stories that end with the punch line of a joke or an idiomatic expression), and several stories that do not focus attention to the surface form of the last word of the passage (for example, stories that end with factual statements such as "He sent a letter about it to Galileo, the great Italian scientist"). Similar to Sachs (1967), prepare test sentences for each of these stories that bear the following relationship to the passage-final sentences: (a) the *identical sentence,* (b) a *simple syntactic change* (for example, change an active sentence to a passive or vice versa— "A letter about it was sent to Galileo, the great Italian scientist"), (c) a *semantic meaning change* (for example, "Galileo, the great Italian scientist, sent him a letter about it").

Present a test sentence to subjects after they listen to each story, and ask them to decide whether the test sentence differs from what was presented in the original story. How does accuracy change for different kinds of test sentences and different kinds of stories? Based upon what you know of the original Sachs (1967) experiment, why would this be? Does the pattern of accuracy change for all target sentence and passage types if you present test sentences immediately following the passage or after a delay? Again, explain your findings.

REFERENCES

Aaronson, D., & Scarborough, H. S. (1977). Performance theories for sentence coding: Some quantitative models. *Journal of Verbal Learning and Verbal Behavior, 16,* 277–304.

Abney, S. P., & Johnson, M. (1991). Memory requirements and local ambiguities of parsing strategies. *Journal of Psycholinguistic Research, 20,* 233–250.

Attneave, F. (1959). *Applications of information theory to psychology.* New York: Holt, Rinehart and Winston.

Beach, C. M. (1991). The interpretation of prosodic patterns at points of syntactic structural ambiguity: Evidence for cue trading relations. *Journal of Memory and Language, 30,* 644–663.

Becker, C. A. (1980). Semantic context effects in visual word recognition: An analysis of semantic strategies. *Memory and Cognition, 8,* 493–512.

Blasko, D. G., & Connine, C. M. (1993). Effects of familiarity and aptness on the processing of metaphor. *Journal of Experimental Psychology: Learning, Memory, and Cognition, 19,* 295–308.

Bransford, J. D., & Franks, J. J. (1971). The abstraction of linguistic ideas. *Cognitive Psychology, 2,* 331–350.

Bransford, J. D., Barclay, J. R., & Franks, J. J. (1972). Sentence memory: A constructive versus interpretive approach. *Cognitive Psychology, 3,* 193–209.

Butterworth, B. (1989). Lexical access in speech production. In W. Marslen-Wilson (Ed.), *Lexical representation and process* (pp. 108–135). Cambridge, MA: MIT Press.

Butterworth, B., Campbell, R., & Howard, D. (1986). The uses of short-term memory: A case study. *Quarterly Journal of Experimental Psychology, 38A,* 705–737.

Cacciari, C., & Tabossi, P. (1988). The comprehension of idioms. *Journal of Memory and Language, 27,* 668–683.

Caplan, D., Vanier, M., & Baker, C. (1986). A case study of reproduction aphasia: II. Sentence comprehension. *Cognitive Neuropsychology, 3,* 129–146.

Caplan, D., & Waters, G. (1990). Short-term memory and language comprehension: A critical review of the neuropsychological literature. In G. Vallar & T. Shallice (Eds.), *Neuropsychological impairments of short-term memory,* (pp. 337–389). Cambridge: Cambridge University Press.

Chodorow, M. S. (1979). Time-compressed speech and the study of lexical and syntactic parsing. In W. E. Cooper & E. C. T. Walker (Eds.), *Sentence processing: Linguistic studies presented to Merrill Garrett* (pp. 87–111). Hillsdale, NJ: Erlbaum.

Chomsky, N. (1957). *Syntactic structures.* The Hague: Mouton.

Chomsky, N. (1965). *Aspects of a theory of syntax.* Cambridge, MA: MIT Press.

Chomsky, N. (1981). *Lectures on government and binding.* Dordrech, the Netherlands: Foris.

Connine, C. M., Blasko, D. G., & Hall, M. (1991). Effects of subsequent sentence context in auditory word recognition: Temporal and linguistic constraints. *Journal of Memory and Language, 30,* 234–250.

Connine, C., Blasko, D., & Wang, J. (1994). Vertical similarity and spoken word recognition: Multiple lexical activation, individual differences, and the role of sentence context. *Perception and Psychophysics, 56,* 624–636.

Cooper, W. E., & Sorensen, J. (1981). *Fundamental frequency in sentence production.* Berlin: Springer-Verlag.

Daneman, M., & Carpenter, P. A. (1980). Individual differences in working memory and reading. *Journal of Verbal Learning and Verbal Behavior, 23,* 569–578.

Ferreira, F. (1993). Creation of sentence prosody during sentence production. *Psychological Review, 10* (2), 233–254.

Ferreira, F., & Clifton C., Jr., (1986). The independence of syntactic processing. *Journal of Memory and Language, 25,* 348–368.

Ferreira, F., Henderson, J. M., Anes, M. D., Weeks, P. A., & McFarlane, D. K. (1996). Effects of lexical frequency and syntactic complexity in spoken-language comprehension: Evidence from the auditory moving-window technique. *Journal of Experimental Psychology: Learning, Memory and Cognition, 22,* 324–335.

Fodor, J. A. (1983). *Modularity of mind.* Cambridge, MA: MIT Press.

Fodor, J. A., Bever, T. G., & Garrett, M. F. (1974). *The psychology of language.* New York: McGraw-Hill.

Forster, K. I. (1979). Levels of processing and the structure of the language processor. In W. E. Cooper & E. C. T. Walker (Eds.), *Sentence processing: Psycholinguistic studies presented to Merrill Garrett* (pp. 27–85). Hillsdale, NJ: Erlbaum.

Frazier, L. (1979). *On comprehending sentences: Syntactic parsing strategies.* Bloomington: Indiana University Linguistics Club.

Frazier, L. (1987). Sentence processing: A tutorial review. In M. Coltheart (Ed.), *Attention and performance XII.* Hillsdale, NJ: Erlbaum.

Frazier, L., & Clifton, Jr., C. (1996). *Construal.* Cambridge, MA: MIT Press.

Frazier, L., & Rayner, K. (1982). Making and correcting errors during sentence comprehension: Eye movements in the analysis of structurally ambiguous sentences. *Cognitive Psychology, 14,* 178–210.

Frazier, L., & Rayner, K. (1989). Selection mechanisms in reading lexically ambiguous words. *Journal of Experimental Psychology: Learning, Memory and Cognition, 15,* 779–790.

Garrett, M. F., Bever, T. G., & Fodor, J. (1966). The active use of grammar in speech perception. *Perception and Psychophysics, 1,* 30–32.

Gibbs, R. W., Jr., Nayak, N., & Cutting, C. (1989). How to kick the bucket and not decompose: Analyzability and idiom processing. *Journal of Memory and Language, 28,* 576–593.

Glanzer, M., Fischer, B., & Dorfman, D. (1984). Short-term storage in reading. *Journal of Verbal Learning and Verbal Behavior, 23,* 467–486.

Glucksberg, S. (1995). Commentary on nonliteral language: Processing and use. *Metaphor and Symbolic Activity, 10,* 47–57.

Goldman-Eisler, F. (1968). *Psycholinguistics: Experiments in spontaneous speech.* New York: Academic Press.

Grosjean, F. (1980). Spoken word recognition processes and the gating paradigm. *Perception and Psychophysics, 28,* 267–283.

Grosjean, F. (1985). The recognition of words after their acoustic offset: Evidence and implications. *Perception and Psychophysics, 38,* 299–310.

Grosjean, F. (in press). Gating. *Language and Cognitive Processes.*

Haberlandt, K., & Graesser, A. C. (1989). Processing of new arguments at clause boundaries. *Memory and Cognition, 17,* 186–193.

Jackendoff, R. (1972). *Semantic interpretation in generative grammar.* Cambridge, MA: MIT Press.

Jarvella, R. J. (1970). Effects of syntax on running memory span for connected discourse. *Psychonomic Science, 19,* 235–236.

Jarvella, R. J. (1971). Syntactic processing of connected speech. *Journal of Verbal Learning and Verbal Behavior, 10,* 409–416.

Just, M. A., & Carpenter, P. A. (1987). *The psychology of reading and language comprehension.* Newton, MA: Allyn & Bacon.

Just, M. A., & Carpenter, P. A. (1992). A capacity theory of comprehension: Individual differences in working memory. *Psychological Review, 99,* 122–149.

Kintsch, W. (1988). The role of knowledge in discourse comprehension: A construction-integration model. *Psychological Review, 95,* 163–182.

Kintsch, W. (1994). The psychology of discourse processing. In M. A. Gernsbacher (Ed.), *Handbook of psycholinguistics.* San Diego: Academic Press.

Kintsch, W., & Keenan, J. (1973). Reading rate and retention as a function of the number of propositions in the base structure of sentences. *Cognitive Psychology, 5,* 257–274.

Levelt, W. J. M. (1989). *Speaking: From intention to articulation.* Cambridge, MA: MIT Press.

Lindblom, B., Brownlee, S., David, B., & Moon, S. J. (1992). Speech transforms. *Speech Communication, 11,* 357–368.

Linebarger, M., Schwartz, M., & Saffran, E. (1983). Sensitivity to grammatical structure in so-called agrammatic aphasics. *Cognition, 13,* 361–392.

MacDonald, M. C., Pearlmutter, N. J., & Seidenberg, M. S. (1994). The lexical nature of syntactic ambiguity resolution. *Psychological Review, 101,* 676–703.

Marcus, M. (1980). *A theory of syntactic recognition for natural language.* Cambridge, MA: MIT Press.

Marslen-Wilson, W. D. (1975). Sentence perception as an interactive parallel process. *Science, 189,* 226–228.

Marslen-Wilson, W. D. (1987). Parallel processing in spoken word recognition. *Cognition, 25,* 71–102.

Marslen-Wilson, W. D., & Tyler, L. K. (1987). Against modularity. In J. Garfield (Ed.), *Modularity in knowledge representation and natural language understanding.* Cambridge, MA: MIT Press.

Marslen-Wilson, W. D., Tyler, L. K., Warren, P., Grenier, P., & Lee, C. S. (1992). Prosodic effects in minimal attachment. *Quarterly Journal of Experimental Psychology, 45A,* 73–87.

Marslen-Wilson, W. D., & Zwitserlood, P. (1989). Accessing spoken words: The importance of word onsets. *Journal of Experimental Psychology: Human Perception and Performance, 15,* 576–585.

Martin, R. C. (1987). Articulatory and phonological deficits in short-term memory and their relation to syntactic processing. *Brain and Language, 32,* 159–192.

Martin, R. C. (1990). Neuropsychological evidence on the role of short-term memory in sentence processing. In G. Vallar & T. Shallice (Eds.), *Neuropsychological impairments of short-term memory* (pp. 390–427). Cambridge: Cambridge University Press.

Meyer, D. E., Shvaneveldt, R. W., & Ruddy, M. G. (1975). Loci of contextual effects on visual word recognition. In P. M. A. Rabbit & S. Dornic (Eds.), *Attention and performance V.* London: Academic Press.

Miller, G. A. (1951). *Language and communication.* New York: McGraw-Hill.

Miller, G. A., & Selfridge, J. A. (1950). Verbal context and the recall of meaningful material. *American Journal of Psychology, 63,* 176–185.

Moray, N., & Taylor, A. (1960). Statistical approximations to English. *Language and Speech, 3,* 7–10.

Morton, J. (1964). The effects of context on the visual duration threshold for words. *British Journal of Psychology, 55,* 165–180.

Morton, J. (1969). Interaction of information in word recognition. *Psychological Review, 76,* 165–178.

Morton, J. (1970). A functional model of human memory. In D. Norman (Ed.), *Models of human memory.* New York: Academic Press.

Murphy, G. L., & Shapiro, A. M. (1994). Forgetting of verbatim information in discourse. *Memory and Cognition, 22,* 85–94.

Neely, J. (1977). Semantic priming and retrieval from lexical memory: Evidence for facilitatory and inhibitory processes. *Memory and Cognition, 4,* 648–654.

Nicol, J., & Swinney, D. (1989). The role of structure in coreference assignment during sentence comprehension. *Journal of Psycholinguistic Research, 18,* 5–19.

Nunberg, G., Sag, I., & Wasow, T. (1994). Idioms. *Language, 70,* 491–534.

Oldfield, R. C. (1963). Individual vocabulary and semantic currency: A preliminary study. *British Journal of Social and Clinical Psychology, 2,* 122–130.

Onifer, W., & Swinney, D. (1981). Accessing lexical ambiguities during sentence comprehension: Effects of frequency-of-meaning and contextual bias. *Memory and Cognition, 9,* 225–236.

Pollack, I., & Pickett, J. M. (1964). Intelligibility of excerpts from fluent speech: Auditory versus structural context. *Journal of Verbal Learning and Verbal Behavior, 3,* 79–84.

Potter, M. C. (1993). Very short-term conceptual memory. *Memory and Cognition, 21,* 156–161.

Potter, M. C., & Lombardi, L. (1990). Regeneration in the short-term recall of sentences. *Journal of Memory and Language, 29,* 633–654.

Rayner, K., Carlson, M., & Frazier, L. (1983). The interaction of syntax and semantics during sentence processing: Eye movements in the analysis of semantically biased sentences. *Journal of Verbal Learning and Verbal Behavior, 22,* 358–374.

Rayner, K., & Frazier, L. (1987). Parsing temporarily ambiguous complements. *Quarterly Journal of Experimental Psychology, 39A,* 657–673.

Rayner, K., Garrod, S., & Perfetti, A. (1992). Discourse inferences during parsing are delayed. *Cognition, 45,* 109–139.

Reber, A. S., & Anderson, J. R. (1970). The perception of clicks in linguistic and nonlinguistic messages. *Perception and Psychophysics, 8,* 81–89.

Rubenstein, H., & Pollack, I. (1963). Word predictability and intelligibility. *Journal of Verbal Learning and Verbal Behavior, 2,* 147–158.

Sachs, J. S. (1967). Recognition memory for syntactic and semantic aspects of connected discourse. *Perception and Psychophysics, 2,* 437–442.

Searle, J. R. (1979). Metaphor. In A. Ortony (Ed.), *Metaphor and thought.* Cambridge: Cambridge University Press.

Seidenberg, M., Tanenhaus, M., Leiman, J., & Bienkowski, M. (1982). Automatic access to the meanings of ambiguous words in context: Some limitations of knowledge-based processing. *Cognitive Psychology, 14,* 489–537.

Simpson, G. B. (1984). Lexical ambiguity and its role in models of word recognition. *Psychological Bulletin, 96,* 316–340.

Simpson, G. B., & Krueger, M. A. (1991). Selective access of homograph meanings in sentence context. *Journal of Memory and Language, 30,* 627–643.

Stine, E. A. L. (1990). On-line processing of written text by younger and older adults. *Psychology and Aging, 5,* 68–78.

Stine, E. A. L., & Wingfield, A. (1990). How much do working memory deficits contribute to age differences in discourse memory? *European Journal of Cognitive Psychology, 2,* 289–304.

Stine, E. A. L., Wingfield, A., & Poon, L. W. (1986). How much and how fast: Rapid processing of spoken language by older adults. *Psychology and Aging, 86,* 303–311.

Streeter, L. A. (1978). Acoustic determinants of phrase boundary perception. *Journal of the Acoustical Society of America, 64,* 1582–1592.

Swinney, D. (1979). Lexical access during sentence comprehension: (Re)consideration of context effects. *Journal of Verbal Learning and Verbal Behavior, 18,* 645–659.

Swinney, D., & Osterhout, L. (1990). Inference generation during auditory language comprehension. In A. C. Graesser & G. H. Bower (Eds.), *Inference and text comprehension: The psychology of learning and motivation* (Vol. 25) (pp. 17–33). San Diego: Academic Press.

Tabossi, P., & Zardon, F. (1993). Processing ambiguous words in context. *Journal of Memory and Language, 32,* 359–372.

Thibadeau, R., Just, M. A., & Carpenter, P. A. (1982). A model of the time course and content of reading. *Cognitive Science, 6,* 157–203.

Titone, D. A., & Connine, C. M. (1994a). The comprehension of idiomatic expressions: Effects of predictability and literality. *Journal of Experimental Psychology: Learning, Memory, and Cognition, 20,* 1126–1138.

Titone, D. A., & Connine, C. M. (1994b). Descriptive norms for 171 idiomatic expressions: Familiarity, compositionality, predictability, and literality. *Metaphor and Symbolic Activity, 9,* 247–270.

Titone, D. A., & Connine, C. M. (in press). On the compositional and noncompositional nature of idiomatic expressions. *Journal of Pragmatics.*

Trueswell, J. C., & Tanenhaus, M. K. (1994). Toward a lexicalist framework of constraint-based syntactic ambiguity resolution. In C. Clifton, Jr., K. Rayner, & L. Frazier (Eds.), *Perspectives on sentence processing.* Hillsdale, NJ: Erlbaum.

Trueswell, J. C., Tanenhaus, M. K., & Garnsey, S. M. (1994). Semantic influences on parsing: Use of thematic role information in syntactic disambiguation. *Journal of Memory and Language, 33,* 285–318.

Tulving, E., & Gold, C. (1963). Stimulus information and contextual information as determinants of tachistoscopic recognition for words. *Journal of Experimental Psychology, 66,* 319–327.

Tyler, L. K. (1984). The structure of the initial cohort: Evidence from gating. *Perception and Psychophysics, 36,* 417–427.

Tyler, L. K., & Marslen-Wilson, W. D. (1977). The on-line effects of semantic context on syntactic processing. *Journal of Verbal Learning and Verbal Behavior, 16,* 683–692.

Tyler, L. K., & Wessels, J. (1983). Quantifying contextual contributions to word-recognition processes. *Perception and Psychophysics, 34,* 409–420.

Tyler, L. K., & Wessels, J. (1985). Is gating an on-line task? Evidence from naming latency data. *Perception and Psychophysics, 38,* 217–222.

van Dijk, T. A., & Kintsch, W. (1983). *Strategies of discourse comprehension.* New York: Academic Press.

Wagenaar, W. A., Varey, C. A., & Hudson, P. T. W. (1984). Do audiovisuals aid? A study of bisensory presentation on the recall of information. In H. Bouma & D. G.

Bouwhuis (Eds.), *Attention and performance X: Control of language processes.* Hillsdale, NJ: Erlbaum.

Wales, R., & Toner, H. (1979). Intonation and ambiguity. In W. E. Cooper & E. C. T. Walker (Eds.), *Sentence processing: Psycholinguistic studies presented to Merrill Garrett.* Hillsdale, NJ: Erlbaum.

Waters, G. S., & Caplan, D. (1996). Processing resource capacity and the comprehension of garden path sentences. *Memory and Cognition, 24,* 342–355.

Waters, G. S., Caplan, D., & Hildebrandt, N. (1987). Working memory and written sentence comprehension. In M. Coltheart (Ed.), *Attention and performance XII: The psychology of reading* (pp. 531–555). London: Erlbaum.

Wayland, S. C., Wingfield, A., & Goodglass, H. (1989). Recognition of isolated words: The dynamics of cohort reduction. *Applied Psycholinguistics, 10,* 475–487.

Wingfield, A. (1975). Acoustic redundancy and the perception of time-compressed speech. *Journal of Speech and Hearing Research, 18,* 139–147.

Wingfield, A., Alexander, A. H., & Cavagelli, S. (1994). Does memory constrain utilization of top-down information in spoken word recognition? Evidence from normal aging. *Language and Speech, 37,* 221–235.

Wingfield, A., & Butterworth, B. (1984). Running memory for sentences and parts of sentences: Syntactic parsing as a control function in working memory. In H. Bouma & D. G. Bouwhuis (Eds.), *Attention and performance X: Control of language processes.* Hillsdale, NJ: Erlbaum.

Wingfield, A., Goodglass, H., & Lindfield, K. C. (1997). Word recognition from acoustic onsets and acoustic offsets: Effects of cohort size and syllabic stress. *Applied Psycholinguistics, 18,* 85–100.

Wingfield, A., & Klein, J. F. (1971). Syntactic structure and acoustic pattern in speech perception. *Perception and Psychophysics, 9,* 23–25.

Wingfield, A., Tun, P. A., & Rosen, M. J. (1995). Age differences in veridical and reconstructive recall of syntactically and randomly segmented speech. *Journal of Gerontology: Psychological Sciences, 50B,* 257–266.

Zwitserlood, P. (1989). The focus of the effects of sentential-semantic context in spoken-word processing. *Cognition, 32,* 25–64.

Chapter **6**

SENTENCES COMBINED: TEXT AND DISCOURSE

Allyssa McCabe
University of Massachusetts, Lowell

INTRODUCTION

Consider the following examples of real discourse, one of which is readily comprehensible to interrogating lawyers, one of which is not. In both cases, however, you will understand that the groups of sentences are related to each other. This chapter will explain exactly how to understand that relationship.

1. In a courtroom, a member of a large-city police homicide squad testified as follows (from Barry, 1991):

Officer: I arrived there approximately—I believe it was 9:45 in the morning—
a.m. I was assigned by Sergeant E., who was the officer in charge, to
do the scene investigation. It was determined at that time that the
state police would be called, and I waited until about 12:40 . . . 12:10
when they arrived, and I assisted them in the scene investigation. My
partner did likewise.

Lawyer: Would you tell the jury what you observed about the scene?

Officer: The scene up in the area—it was in the northeast corner of a
fenced-in yard at [name of church] and in that area was found—
located two bodies located near the fence—the northern part of the
fence . . .”

2. In the same trial, another witness testified:

Lawyer: And what happened after he said that?

Witness: Well, just like I said, it still was—then that is when they put ’em on
the ground and stuff.

Lawyer: I am sorry?

Witness: That is when they put ’em on the floor.

Lawyer: Who put them on the floor?

Witness: Ordered them to get on the floor.

Lawyer: Yeah.

Witness: The victims.

. . .

Lawyer: Did it appear suspicious or strange to you that they would have this car?

Witness: Yeah, because he was drivin’ real fast like.

Lawyer: Who was driving fast?

DISCOURSE AND TEXT

Discourse refers to a "lengthy discussion of a subject, either written or spoken" (*American Heritage Dictionary,* p. 376), and **text** is defined as "any passage, spoken or written, of whatever length, that does form a unified whole" (Halliday & Hasan, 1976, p. 1). Thus, the two terms are synonymous. This chapter will address issues relevant to both oral and written texts or discourses; people respond to connected passages of discussion similarly regardless of whether such discussions are oral (typically called *discourse*) or written (more typically called *text*) (see Hidi & Hildyard, 1983).

Cohesion

Cohesion is defined as a semantic concept that "refers to relations of meaning that exist within the text and that define it as a text" (Halliday & Hasan, 1976, p. 4). Cohesive devices may refer either to upcoming text or, more commonly, back to prior text, which is known as **anaphora.** In the first excerpt, the officer uses "at that time" to refer back to "9:45 in the morning." In other words, cohesion consists of the various devices that glue a group of sentences together—the way that some words refer to other parts of the text *(reference),* the way that different words refer to the same thing *(substitution),* the gaps that speakers leave because they know their listeners can fill in those gaps *(ellipsis),* and the various connectives that link sentences together *(conjunctions).*

Halliday and Hasan delineated many types of cohesion. One of the most prominent types of cohesion is the use of various forms of *reference* (see Table 6.1). When a character or topic has been established, speakers or writers can use shorthand expressions as they continue to talk about it. One common way of accomplishing this is by using a pronoun to refer to a previously mentioned noun, a practice called **pronominal reference.** For example, the officer in the first excerpt refers once to the state police and then uses pronominal reference ("when *they* arrived"). In the second

TYPE	EXAMPLE
Reference	
Pronominal	Abby is a remarkable athlete. ***She*** swims, runs, and dances every day.
Demonstrative	***That*** was the best Spring Break ever.
Comparative	He's not ***as*** clever ***as I thought.***
Substitution	*He ordered her to stand up. She did* **so.**
Ellipsis	She has a beautiful voice. I don't [***have a beautiful voice***].
Conjunction	I thought I could ski well, ***but*** I couldn't.
Lexical	The child babbled in her crib. ***The little tyke*** made me laugh.

TABLE 6.1

TYPES OF COHESION

excerpt, the witness uses pronominal reference without first explicitly establishing referents for those pronouns, a practice common among working-class speakers who expect their listeners to collaborate in constructing a meaningful interchange by figuring out to whom such unspecified pronouns refer (Hemphill, 1989), but one that throughout the dialogue presents problems for the middle-class lawyer questioning him. Middle-class listeners expect speakers to be more explicit in their initial references.

Another form of cohesion is the use of *demonstratives,* meaning pronouns such as *this/these, that/those, here/there.* In the first excerpt, which follows a prolonged description of the murder scene, the officer uses a demonstrative to refer to the scene ("I arrived *there*"), as well as a *definite article* ("*the* scene investigation"). Elsewhere in the testimony, the officer uses a *comparative,* which refers to some contrast between present and previous objects ("[the grass was] twelve inches, *little higher.*").

Rather than continually repeating themselves, speakers often use a variety of expressions to refer to the same thing, which is called *substitution.* Substitution appears in the first excerpt when the officer uses "did likewise" to refer back to "assisted them in the scene investigation." Alternatively, speakers and writers often delete grammatical parts of sentences that would be unnecessarily repetitive, a type of cohesion known as *ellipsis.* The first excerpt is remarkable for the lack of this normal cohesive device; for example, it would have sounded more natural for the officer not to say "the scene investigation" twice). In the second excerpt, the witness uses (middle-class speakers might say misuses) ellipsis when he deletes the subject of a sentence ("Ordered them to get on the floor."). To create connections between sentences in a discourse, speakers also repeat the same words in different sentences (also called *reiteration*) or use clear synonyms; that is, they employ what Halliday and Hasan term *lexical cohesion* because it depends on the semantic relationships between certain words (for example, "I was assigned by *Sergeant* E., who was the *officer* in charge").

A particularly ubiquitous form of cohesion is the use of various conjunctions. Specifically, speakers use additive ("*and* in that area was found"), adversative ("He was dreading the square dance *but* he enjoyed it"), causal ("*because* he was drivin' real fast like."), and temporal ("*then* that is when they put 'em . . .") conjunctions to link sentences in discourse. Most of the time, these conjunctions denote some semantic connection between sentences. However, even young children put conjunctions to additional pragmatic use in discourse. For example, imagine you find yourself in a group of people who have been chatting easily. A discussion of politics ensues during which it is apparent that opinions diverge. The room falls silent. You decide to try to start the conversation up again with a new topic, "So," you say, "how about those Red Sox?" That *so* denoted no causal relationship; instead it was a way of signaling the opening of a new discourse. Young children (ages 4 through 9) use *so* about one third of the time for such pragmatic purposes as initiating or closing a topic of conversation, changing their focus, or letting speakers know that they are violating chronological recapitulation in narrative discourse (Peterson & McCabe, 1991), and they use other conjunctions to a lesser extent for similar purposes. In other words, units of discourse occur in the context of conversation, and from an early age speakers learn to tie such units (for example, narratives) together with cohesive devices just as they learn to tie sentences together within the discourses themselves.

Propositional Models of Text Processing

When people listen to or read a sentence, they remember its meaning, but typically they retain information about its grammatical form for only a brief time (Sachs, 1967) unless the syntactic form is itself meaningful (Slobin, 1968). For example, consider the following joke:

Why couldn't the mummy answer the telephone?
Because he was all tied up.

Note that the answer is a passive grammatical construction, which is typically altered in memory to become a simpler active form. However, in this case to change the form of the answer to an active one would be to ruin the joke. *Because his relatives tied him up after he died* just is not funny and, in fact, barely makes sense, and so prospective joke-tellers will remember the more difficult passive construction.

On the discourse level, a similar phenomenon occurs. That is, when people recall a text, they rarely recall it verbatim. Instead, they paraphrase and reduce it to a gist. Models have been developed to describe the way in which people process the texts they encounter (for example, Kintsch, 1974; Kintsch & van Dijk, 1978).

The basic unit for storing meaningful information in long-term memory is arguably the proposition, and the meaning of sentences and short paragraphs can be represented as a network of propositions (Kintsch, 1974). Although early accounts were somewhat ambiguous about what exactly a proposition was or where it came from, and although recent accounts would not exactly agree on the number of propositions to be found even in any one sentence, **propositions** are minimal units of information, in the form of relationships among concepts, that listeners derive from **parsing** sentences (Perfetti & Britt, 1995). Consider two ways of parsing a simple sentence into propositions (example taken from Perfetti & Britt, 1995):

Lyle pushed Paris out of his mind for three months.

Solution A:
1. PUSH (Lyle, Paris, out of his mind)
2. NUMBER OF (months, three)
3. EXTENT OF (1, 2)

Solution B:
1. PUSH (Lyle, Paris)
2. GOAL (1, out of mind)
3. NUMBER OF MONTHS (three)
4. EXTENT OF (2, 3)

Regardless of the exact manner in which individual subjects break sentences into their constituents—which then become propositions—propositions are formed by a combination of syntactic and semantic means.

Not all propositions in a discourse are equally important or likely to be recalled. In fact, ratings of the importance of a proposition correlate with the likelihood of their inclusion in the gists a subject recalls. Subjects usually (80% of the time) recall what they consider the most important propositions in a text. The more subordinate the position of a proposition in a text hierarchy, the less likely it is to be recalled (plummeting to 30%). Consider the following paragraph; try to extract the most important proposition in it as you read (from Estes, 1995, p. 41):

> Extra powerful shoulders that could give a decathloner an advantage in throwing the discus and shot can slow him in the sprints and hurdles. Thus, he must try to keep the tight, tapered calves of a sprinter even as he builds up strong hands for throwing the discus, shot, and javelin, and a barrel chest to pump air for endurance. A decathloner must develop a well-rounded athletic body that avoids overspecialization.

The most important proposition, a **macroproposition,** of this passage can be represented as the predicate *develop* and its arguments *decathloner* and *body.* This macroproposition has been found to be the best recognized proposition in the passage (Guindon & Kintsch, 1984). The passage includes many other **micropropositions** such as the following (note that the predicate is presented first, followed by its arguments):

1. give, advantage
2. build, hands
3. pump, air

Thus, we remember aspects of texts that we consider the most important better than we remember the details—an efficient approach considering how much information we must process.

Inferences

Not only do people regularly omit information they encounter, they elaborate upon it, drawing inferences about what was said or meant on the basis of their prior knowledge about the topic of discussion and rules of discourse. *Inferences* are deductions or guesses based on evidence in the text or derived from a person's preexisting knowledge. In the first dialogue at the outset of this chapter, we infer that the officer had a watch or saw a clock because he refers to the time events occurred. Can you infer anything else from the passage?

This tendency to draw inferences can cause discussions of an event after it happens to influence our memory. For example, Elizabeth Loftus and her colleagues (1980, p. 45) showed people films and later asked misleading questions about those films (for example, "How fast was the car going when it ran the stop sign?" or "How fast was the white sports car going when it passed the barn while traveling along the country road?"). People reported that they saw the stop sign or the barn even though the stop sign was really a yield sign and there was no barn at all. Loftus's use of the definite article *the* prompted people to infer that they had previously encountered a stop sign or barn. Similarly, asking subjects, "About how fast were the cars going when they smashed into each other?" biases subjects to report seeing fictitious broken glass, whereas substituting the verb *hit* does not.

Remembering

SCHEMATA.   In 1932, Bartlett published a book that eventually revolutionized the way psychologists thought about memory. Bartlett (1932, p. 44) argued that, "it is fitting to speak of every human cognitive reaction—perceiving, imaging, remembering, thinking and reasoning—as an *effort after meaning.*" He argued that memory is active, constructive, and schematically determined. Bartlett gave British people a North American Indian folk tale to recall repeatedly anywhere from 15 minutes to 10 years after they heard it. In their reproductions, subjects omitted much material, made many inferences, used more contemporary British phraseology than was in the original tale, and in these and other various ways made the tale more like a British story. Bartlett's findings have been supported and extended by more recent researchers. Adults better summarize and remember stories that come from their own culture than they do stories from other cultures when those other cultures have distinctly different expectations about storytelling forms. Such expectations are called **schemata** (Dube, 1978; Harris, Lee, Hensley, & Schoen, 1988; Kintsch & Greene, 1978). Schemata are, in other words, mental structures acquired through many experiences with an event or in routine social situations. Once acquired, schemata in turn guide people by setting up their expectations for what usually will happen and helping them interpret what does happen and remember what in fact did happen on particular occasions, both typical and unusual. Schemata are, in turn, continually modified by experiences.

Much evidence details the influence of culturally specific schemata on the interpretation and memory of stories. When preschool children of different ethnic backgrounds heard a story, for example, they retold it in distinctive ways (John & Berney, 1968). In a recent study (Invernizzi & Abouzeid, 1995), European North American children and Ponam children from Papua, New Guinea, read two European tales, which they retold in writing. As is typical of European North Americans in general, children from this culture gave the setting, precipitating events, attempts to reach a goal, the consequences, and the resolutions of the story. In contrast, Ponam children rationalized their recalls by giving extraordinary factual detail (five times as much as Americans) about settings, events, and outcomes, but, to a Westerner, appeared to miss the point, seldom repeating the consequence, resolution, or moral of the story because the latter is not something that is usually stated in their culture. Compare the following two retellings of "The Boy Who Cried Wolf" (from Invernizzi &

Abouzeid, 1995, p. 14). Note that the names of the boy and certain objects were changed to names more familiar to the Ponam children than to the American ones. Nonetheless, which do you think appears to "get the point of the story"?

Ponam:

> Once upon a time Kalai and his family they lived on an island. Kalai's mother always carried him everywhere. One day Kalai's mother and father went out fishing. Kalai's mother said, "Kalai, you are too small to go out fishing in the sea. You should stay home with your grandfather." Kalai was lonely on the beach. Kalai said, "How could I get my family home?" He sat down and decided to get his family home. He got his red laplap and ran down to the beach and waved his laplap to his family and said, "Fire, fire." His brother saw his laplap and went home. When they arrived they saw nothing.

American:

> Kalai was running up and down the beach yelling "Fire, fire." Everybody came home. The next day the same thing happened. They came home. The next day came, but the house caught on fire. He ran up and down the beach, but nobody came. Kalai kept waving the flag. Nobody came. Suddenly they saw the flames and the smoke and they came, but it was too late. Everything had burnt down to the ground, and his brother told him if he kept telling lies that nobody will come when you call for help.

CONTEXTS

Discourse as a Context

CONTEXT AND COMPREHENSION.

Remembering depends on understanding. That is, you cannot remember what you don't understand, a point students would be well-advised to take to heart before exams. Consider the following passage:

> With hocked gems financing him, our hero bravely defied all scornful laughter that tried to prevent his scheme. Your eyes deceive you, he had said, an egg, not a table correctly typifies this unexplored planet. Now three sturdy sisters sought proof, forging along sometimes through calm vastness, yet more often over turbulent peaks and valleys. Days became weeks as many doubters spread fearful rumors about the edge. At last, from nowhere, welcome winged creatures appeared, signifying momentous success (passage used by Dooling & Lachman, 1971).

Without any additional information, few individuals can comprehend this passage or remember much of it. However, individuals who are told in advance that the passage is about Christopher Columbus discovering America comprehend it readily and remember substantially more; in other words, their *schema* for early American history enables them to understand and therefore to remember the passage.

UNWRITTEN RULES OF DISCOURSE.   Paul Grice (1975) articulated four unwritten rules for efficient speech, otherwise known as **conversational maxims.** These maxims refer to concise directives on standards to be observed:

1. The Maxim of Quality: Speakers should tell the truth as they know it or acknowledge the uncertainty of what they are telling you.
2. The Maxim of Manner: Speakers should strive to be clear and unambiguous, not verbose and disorganized.
3. The Maxim of Quantity: Say all that is necessary or required but no more.
4. The Maxim of Relation: Speakers must confine themselves to what is relevant.

Although most of the time speakers and listeners, especially adults, seem tacitly, if unconsciously, to assume the applicability of these maxims, children can be quite blunt when they believe these maxims are violated. Preece (1992) documents numerous examples of children serving as critics of other children's narrations. Responding to a brother who claimed to have patted a bird, but who often departed from the truth in telling about his experiences, one child of about 7 years said, "He's doing the dream machine again—he's exaggerating too much!", which was her way of pointing out he had violated the maxim of quality in her view. Similarly, Preece (1992) notes that if the truth of an anecdote was in doubt, narrators could always expect pointed questions ("Is that true, what you just said?"), incredulity ("REALLY?"), playful charges of teasing ("You're teasing!"), and outright accusations of lying ("I bet, I bet! . . . Big fat lie!"). Preece (1992, p. 282) gives an example that can be construed to demonstrate one kindergartner's protest when the maxim of manner was violated by a playmate:

Kepman: Saint Nicholas was . . . was trying to pretend he was Saint Nicholas.

But then he went back to Saint Nicholas. I . . .

Bronwyn: Saint Nicholas went back to Saint Nicholas? He went back to

Saint—Saint Nicholas went back to his self? What's that mean?

That doesn't make sense.

Preece (1992) also gives an example of what might well be considered a kindergartner's protest of a violation of the maxim of quantity. Kepman announced that he would tell everyone the *Three Little Pigs* and began with a description of the pigs. Bronwyn at first listened happily but then protested, "You're forgetting the wolf. . . . You'll hafta start all over again."

Protests about violation of the maxim of relation (for example, "What's that [description of the vehicle a family took on vacation] got to do with where we went?") are also not uncommon in conversations at any age.

AMBIGUITY.   Discourse serves as a context, affecting sentence and word-level interpretation, tipping the interpretation of what would otherwise be ambiguous words or phrases in a certain direction. For example, some sentences can be interpreted *literally* (according to standard usage of the words) or *figuratively* (by deviating from what we understand to be the standard significance of the words for some special meaning or effect; following Abrams, 1971). Context can prompt readers to engage in one or the other (Keysar, 1994). For example, when you first read the Columbus passage above, you probably interpreted the phrase "three sturdy sisters" literally, imagining three hefty female siblings. Only after you read that the intended subject of the passage was the voyage of Columbus did you then interpret that same phrase metaphorically to refer to the three ships that composed Columbus's party.

METAPHORS.   **Metaphors** are an interesting form of discourse that has received attention in psychology for about 20 years, though most readers will have encountered discussion of them only in English classes. For example, in *The Scarlet Letter,* Nathaniel Hawthorne at one point compares Hester Prynne's beauty to a halo: "Those who had before known her, and had expected to behold her dimmed and obscured by a disastrous cloud, were astonished, and even startled to perceive how her beauty shone out, and made a halo of the misfortune and ignominy in which she was enveloped." Here *beauty* is the subject, or *tenor,* of the metaphor, and *halo,* the implicit comparison, is the *vehicle* of the metaphor. She really was beautiful, but she did not literally have a halo; rather, her beauty is compared to a halo. The *grounds* is the term used to describe the basis of the comparison (for example, that beauty stands aloft, as does a halo, and that both are angelic entities).

Of course, every student of English knows that such metaphors are common and important in literature. What makes metaphors of such keen psychological interest is that they also are common in discourse outside of literature. Metaphors are critical to science in many ways (see Hoffman, 1980, for a review). In such diverse contexts as psychotherapy interviews, political debates between presidential candidates, and the writings of children and adolescents, we find that every 100 words contains at least one novel metaphor (such as Hawthorne's) and several frozen metaphors (frozen in the sense that they are so commonplace that we do not typically notice that they are metaphoric, for example, the "mouth" of a river) (Pollio, Barlow, Fine, & Pollio, 1977).

The context in which a metaphor appears affects its interpretation and appreciation (McCabe, 1983, in press). Readers applaud Hawthorne's metaphor not only because of preexisting connections between tenor and vehicle concepts, but also because of its relationship to the whole passage (for example, that it conveyed the whole point of the passage, which was the surprising, ironically angelic appearance of the adulterous, ostracized Hester Prynne). The same principle applies outside of literary situations. Consider the following incident in which an otherwise apt metaphor backfired. A well-known nursery school hired a new director, who introduced some innovative educational practices. Many parents who had had children in the nursery school for some time became alarmed by what they saw as a departure from the educational values the school had held for years. The director held a meeting to discuss these parents' concerns, but during the meeting some outspoken parents became increasingly angry. To defuse that anger, a staff member offered a metaphor: "What we have here," he said, "is a clash between conservative and liberal educational values. There are those of you who are conservative, who do not wish to change this school in any way—" This man got no further. So-called conservative parents erupted, protesting that they had never voted Republican in their lives, that they had marched in numerous demonstrations, and so on. Unfortunately, the vehicle he chose—political approaches—so directly clashed with the real political approaches of this group that the tenor—educational practice at the nursery school—was for a time entirely forgotten. Discourse contexts heavily influence the meaning of terms, and effective communication must take such contextual factors into account.

IRONY.   **Irony** is another form of figurative language that illuminates the importance of context to meaning. Consider the case of a speaker who utters the ironic insult, "You're a fine friend," to someone who isn't. Dews and Winner (in press) account for all that happens in the process of interpreting this utterance to mean the opposite of what it literally says. They review many current theories that compare the comprehension of literal and nonliteral forms and argue in support of a multiple-meaning model of language processing. According to that model, both literal and nonliteral meanings are derived and must be processed, either simultaneously or in either order. Context, however, can affect the order of processing. Information such as knowledge of a particular ironic speaker's attitude toward a topic of remark may automatically trigger the intended critical evaluation before the speaker realizes that it conflicts with the positive literal meaning of the actual words.

SPEECH ACTS.   As Austin (1962) and Searle (1969) pointed out, speakers use language for many purposes—to inform, question, command, thank, apologize, congratulate, promise, offer, and marry people. When a preacher pronounces a couple husband and wife or a judge sentences a person to a term in prison, such speakers directly perform with those words an action that is quite dramatic. Most of the time, however, the actions performed by speech are much more subtle and far less immediate. If listeners do not appreciate the intended function of an utterance, speakers will consider them to have misunderstood the communication, even if they have recognized all the words uttered as well as their syntactic form. Direct **speech acts** are defined as those that use common syntactic forms to encode the common linguistic functions for which they are specifically designed. That is, speakers will often use declarative forms to inform listeners. For example, a witness might declare that, "The body was cold when I arrived." Typically, speakers use interrogative forms to request information. For example, the lawyer in the opening excerpt asks, "Who put them on the floor?" Imperative forms are the most direct way of commanding someone to do something such as, "Put your hand on the Bible and swear to tell the truth, the whole truth, and nothing but the truth."

Sometimes speakers choose not to use the syntactic form most closely matched to their intended purpose. A speech act in which the literal meaning of a sentence is not what speakers intend to communicate is called an *indirect speech act*. At one point during the testimony at the outset of this chapter, the lawyer says, "I am sorry?" not to genuinely apologize to the witness, but to command the witness to clarify his previous statement, which was not explicit enough for the lawyer to understand. Response to the literal meaning of such indirect speech acts often would be laughable. Consider how the jury would have responded had the witness said, "I accept your apology," instead of attempting to provide the additional information he thought the lawyer wanted.

Other common examples of indirect speech acts include the use of questions about a listener's ability or willingness to perform some action or statements about the circumstances that motivate a speaker's request in the first place. For example, a speaker might say, "Can you take out the garbage?" or, "Will you take out the garbage?" or even, "The garbage can is overflowing," instead of commanding someone to "Take out the garbage." Deborah Tannen (1990) reviewed studies that establish gender preferences regarding the desirability of using direct versus indirect speech acts to control someone else's actions. Specifically, boys and men tend to order each other around quite directly: "Get the stethoscope." In contrast, girls and women tend to prefer a less direct form: "Let's play doctor and use the stethoscope," or, "Let's take out the garbage." Tannen points out that women use such indirect forms to avoid confrontation with their listeners, but that this strategy often backfires when they use indirect forms with men. Men perceive that women are trying to get them to do something without coming right out and saying so, and often feel manipulated and threatened by what appears to them to be a devious strategy.

POLITENESS.   Brown and Levinson (1978) began a flurry of research with an article that claimed to provide a universal model of how speakers work to "save face" through various forms of politeness to listeners. "Face" is the image speakers want to present of themselves to others, a powerful emotional possession that can be lost, maintained, or enhanced in social interactions. **Politeness** means acting so as to take account of the feelings of others and includes both those actions concerned with *positive face* (the wish to be approved of) and *negative face* (the wish to be unimpeded, free from imposition, or left alone). Politeness is governed by power relations between individuals, the social distance between them, and the degree of imposition that might be involved. One negative politeness strategy is to minimize requests, using the indirect forms discussed in the previous section. Other forms are listed in Table 6.2.

As should be clear from the examples in Table 6.2, polite forms of address are sometimes wordy and take more time and effort than direct forms would. Thus, polite speech often violates the maxims laid out by Paul Grice (1975) for efficient speech, listed earlier. Deese (1984, p. 41) points out that in real public speech at city hall meetings or on radio talk shows, speakers often employ unnecessarily elaborate syntactic forms in the interests of politeness and face-saving (for example, "I feel that you believe that we understand your concerns."). Evidently many speakers believe that politeness and face-saving are worth considerable extra effort. Parents devote considerable effort to socializing their children in many politeness routines (for example, "What's the magic word?") from an early age (Gleason, Perlmann, & Greif, 1984).

Although politeness is arguably a universal concern, traditions differ distinctly from one culture to the next (Brown, 1987). Consider the case of a Chinese-American woman visiting China. She was shown around that country by a Chinese diplomat. At one point, they began crossing a busy street. All of a sudden, the woman noticed with horror a truck barreling down the street right at them. Imagine her further surprise

TABLE 6.2

TYPES OF POLITENESS

Source: Craig, Tracy, & Spisak, 1986.

POSITIVE POLITENESS

1. Notice or attend to Hearer: "You cut your hair."
2. Exaggerate interest, approval, or sympathy with Hearer: "How terrible that you missed your train."
3. Intensify interest to Hearer: Exaggerate facts, tell stories in present tense.
4. Use in-group identity markers: "Hey, dude, what's happening?"
5. Seek agreement: Select safe topics on which agreement is expected.
6. Avoid disagreement: "I'm not sure who I'm voting for."
7. Presuppose, raise, assert common ground: Gossip before getting down to business; presuppose shared knowledge, "The Sox were great."
8. Joke: Response to a long list of tasks to be performed: "So you're going to relax this weekend."
9. Assert or presuppose knowledge of and concern for Hearer's wants: "I know you'd want to help me out with this if you could, so that's why I'm here."
10. Offer, promise: "Look, I promise to come by and visit you when I get to Boston."
11. Be optimistic: "You'll stay with the baby, won't you?"
12. Include both Speaker and Hearer in the activity: "Let's take the garbage out."
13. Give or request reasons: "Why don't we go out for pizza?"
14. Assume or assert reciprocity: "You get coffee today. I did it yesterday."
15. Give gifts to Hearer: Sympathy, understanding, cooperation, goods.

NEGATIVE POLITENESS

1. Be conventionally indirect: "Would you please pass the salt?"
2. Question, hedge: "I wonder if you could help out?"
3. Be pessimistic: "I don't suppose you remember me taking your seminar five years ago."
4. Minimize the imposition: "Could I stay with you for just a little while?"
5. Give deference: "I must be stupid. Could you help me fix this?"
6. Apologize: "I'm sorry to ask you to move."
7. Impersonalize Speaker and Hearer: "Teachers have to grade students on the basis of the work they actually receive."
8. State the face-threatening act as a general rule: "There's no smoking in this section."
9. Nominalize: "Your poor performance on the exams" versus "You performed poorly."
10. Go on record as incurring a debt or as not indebting the Hearer: "I'd be eternally grateful if you would . . ."

at the diplomat's instructions: "Don't even look at him. Let him avoid us!" The Americanized woman found such life-threatening preoccupation with negative face-saving almost incomprehensible even though she recognized it as a typical Chinese concern. Mao (1994) argues that Chinese notions of face do not highlight the self as much as Brown and Levinson's definition of face suggests. Instead, Mao argues that Chinese face encodes a reputable image that individuals can claim for themselves as they interact with other members of their community. Furthermore, one part of Chinese notions of face—*mianzi*—cannot properly be understood in terms of negative face or claims to freedom of action so much as it must be understood as one's claim to the respect or prestige of the community. And although another aspect of Chinese notions of face—*lian*—bears a superficial resemblance to positive face, it is a much more serious concern; if one loses *lian,* one is most likely to suffer condemnation by the community because one's conduct will be considered extremely disagreeable or even immoral.

Individual Factors Affecting Discourse

CONVERSATIONAL STYLE.   Some people value the show of enthusiastic involvement in what speakers are saying. Such a preference involves the use of interruptions to show that a listener avidly follows what a speaker says, supports it, and is even able to extend it. Overlaps in such conversation are common and bother no one who shares this value. Such interruptions even facilitate the conversation between like-minded speakers. Tannen (1984) terms this a "high-involvement" style.

In contrast, other people value what Tannen (1984) terms a "high-considerateness" style of conversation, in which one and only one speaker talks at a time and interruptions are viewed as coercive attempts to take the conversational floor from a speaker. Priority is given to not imposing on other participants, instead of to showing enthusiastic involvement in what others are saying. As one might expect, clashes between speakers from these two different camps result in miscommunication on a routine basis.

GENDERLECT.   Robin Lakoff (1975) pointed out that women use more *tag questions* ("It is a nice day, *isn't it?*") than men, an observation that has received much—but not unmitigated—support. Women are also more polite because of socialization pressures not to "talk rough like a boy." Women tend to use more, and more varied, adjectives for color than men (for example, "That sofa is such a beautiful shade of salmon"), and to use more intensifiers (for example, "That was just a wretched experience"). Finally, Lakoff pointed out that the language people use to describe women differs from that used to describe men. For example, if someone says "The candidate fainted," we assume that the candidate is a woman because we also assume that men "pass out" rather than faint.

Tannen (1990) summarized research on the numerous ways in which men and women systematically miscommunicate, an effort that landed her book on the best-seller list for a long time. Although male and female speakers seem to share vocabularies, syntactic forms, and a general knowledge of the rules of discourse reviewed so far in this chapter, the success of Tannen's book is a good indication that the genders approach discourse with widely different expectations. For example, women often wish to engage in what Tannen calls "troubles talk," but men interpret their comments as a request for problem-solving suggestions. Tannen (1990, p. 49) tells the story of a woman who had a lump removed from her breast. After the operation, she told her sister that she found it upsetting to have been cut into and she was upset every time she looked at the stitches that had changed the contour of her breast. Her sister said, "I know. When I had my operation I felt the same way." The woman told her friend the same thing, and the friend replied, "I know. It's like your body has been violated." When the woman told her husband, however, he said, "You can have plastic surgery to cover up the scar and restore the shape of your breast," a comment that infuriated rather than comforted her, to her husband's complete puzzlement and distress. The two brought widely differing goals to the discourse event. Tannen also argues that women feel more need to talk in order to establish rapport (to connect, to negotiate relationships) with others, whereas men typically limit themselves to reporting what they find newsworthy. In general, women's greater talkativeness is a well-established gender difference (Hyde, 1988).

BILINGUAL ISSUES OF DISCOURSE.   When people are fluent in two or more languages, they often **code-switch,** which is to alternately speak one then another language. Speakers may switch languages for many reasons, including the topic of conversation and their audience. Ervin-Tripp (1968), for example, found that Japanese war brides living in the United States chose to speak Japanese when their listener was Japanese, especially when they wished to discuss Japanese topics such as Japanese festivals, cooking, and housekeeping; the Doll Festival; and street storytellers. However, if the topic was American housekeeping or cooking or shopping for food and clothing in the United States, these women tended to speak English, a tendency that was magnified if their audience was not Japanese. Sometimes politeness issues are at play and determine the choice of language. For example, Japanese students have commented that they switch into English if they feel obliged to refuse a request from their Japanese friends because such a refusal seems less rude than if it were made in Japanese.

Of course, sometimes choice of language spoken simply reflects the relative proficiency of bilingual speakers; people are likely to use a language they are proficient in speaking. In turn, proficiency in a language affects one's identification with other speakers of that language, and this identification affects such aspects of discourse as referential cohesion, mentioned at the outset of this chapter. For example, Imbens-Bailey (1995) found that to the extent that Armenian-American children and adolescents were proficient in Armenian, their parents' native language, they used *we* instead of *I* and *they* in narratives about Armenian cultural events. The following example from a 12-year-old girl who is not proficient in Armenian is typical:

"I remember crying that first day I was there [at Saturday School] . . . I think I was 8. I was old. I remember that. . . . They were just all talking in Armenian and I couldn't understand any of it" (Imbens-Bailey, 1995, p. 87).

In contrast, children who were proficient rarely used *I* in such narratives to refer to their own actions, preferring the *we* form, as in the following narrative by a 12-year-old boy:

> "There's like a couple of Armenian singers we go to. Famous Armenian singers that we go to them and concerts. . . . Recently, Baron Sarkis, because he has a band. We listen to them play. We went."

DIALECT.   **Dialect** is defined as a regional or socially conditioned variant of a language. Dialects may vary in their phonological, lexical, grammatical, and pragmatic conventions, but are generally mutually intelligible and often spoken by people who live in the same general geographical region. The difference between a dialect and a language is not clear, however. For example, Italian and Spanish are two different languages that are nonetheless mutually intelligible. Mandarin and Cantonese are not, although they are both considered dialects of Chinese. One whimsical linguist argued that a dialect becomes a language when its speakers get their own army (Foss & Hakes, 1978, p. 5).

From a linguistic point of view, every dialect—like every language—is a highly structured system, not an accumulation of errors caused by the failure of speakers to master the standard dialect. To prefer one dialect over another would be to display "dialectical chauvinism," just as to prefer your own native language to any other would be to display "linguistic chauvinism."

As linguists such as Labov (1972) point out, dialects such as African-American English vernacular have a logic and a set of rules every bit as complicated as that of Standard English. The differences between dialects have to do with how they negotiate the trade-off between work a speaker has to do (for example, mark plurality twice, once on the pronoun, once on the verb: *he comes* versus *they come*) and the work a listener has to do (listen carefully and catch each point in the conversation where information is not presented redundantly). African-American English vernacular has some redundancies that Standard English does not (for example, negatives must be marked at least twice, as in *I ain't never lost a fight*) and omits some redundancies required by Standard English (for example, omitted copulas, as in *Stan here right now*).

Many speakers of English learn to switch their dialects to suit the occasion, talking Standard English at school, for example, and their home dialect among friends and family. In fact, linguists may be the only people who perceive dialects to be equivalent. The 1997 controversy over the Oakland, California, school system's adoption of Ebonics (more technically known as African-American vernacular English, or AAVE) as a primary language has made this difference in the perceived prestige of dialects painfully clear. On a less-explosive level, George Bernard Shaw explored the difference in the prestige of dialects in his famous play, *Pygmalion,* and its musical version, *My Fair Lady.*

SOCIAL CLASS DIFFERENCES.   Bernstein (1974) argued that middle- and upper-class speakers use an **elaborated code** in discourse, which assumes little shared information on the part of speaker and listener and spells everything out in such detail that the discourse itself conveys necessary information. In contrast, Bernstein argued that lower-socioeconomic-class speakers employ what he termed a **restricted code.** In restricted code, speakers often do not specify the referents of pronouns before using them. As noted earlier, restricted-code speakers expect listeners to work at understanding what is said (Hemphill, 1989). For example, the witness in the second excerpt in the courtroom scene at the beginning of this chapter may have believed that the lawyers were not even trying to understand what he was telling them when he said ". . . that is when they put 'em on the floor."

ROLE.   Use of the restricted code may also have to do with the role assigned a person by a specific situation. For example, although the officer testifying in the opening excerpt clearly used an elaborated code, had he been a defendant instead of an expert witness, he might have testified using the restricted code so often characteristic of threatened, intimidated, relatively powerless individuals—particularly in situations in which they know that their own words might be used against them (Barry, 1991). That's what the following officer did in a hearing in which he was a defendant:

"It was my understanding that K. B. had told him where the gun was."

The judge requested clarification at several points ("Had told who where the gun was?") and finally instructed the trooper to use full names to keep the story straight.

GENRES

Discourse and text take many forms, and many ways exist to classify such forms. To refer to these forms of discourse, researchers have appropriated a term from literary criticism—**genre,** which means a "literary form" (Abrams, 1971).

Narrative

During the past 20 years, one genre—**narrative**—has received considerable attention. Narratives, as defined by McCabe (1991, pp. 1–2), usually concern real or pretend memories of something that happened, and therefore are often largely in the past tense. Some, however, are hypothetical, future-tense narratives and others are in the historical present. Narratives often contain a chronological sequence of events, but some narratives contain only a single event or skip around in time. Narrative is often a kind of language, although some narratives are musical, pictorial, or silently dramatic. Narratives contain descriptive, orientative information (for example, *This was about a year ago*) and evaluation (for example, *I was really scared*), as well as information about action sequences (for example, *He fell on the ice and slid all the way to the edge of the porch*).

Narratives serve many important functions (McCabe, 1996):

1. Narratives enable people to make sense of their experiences in ways that feel culturally satisfying. For example, if a woman has a car accident, chances are the first time she talks about it, she will be fairly incoherent. After talking about the experience with several supportive friends who ask questions and make some inferences about what must have happened, her account will become much more coherent, reflecting the fact that she has now made sense of the experience.
2. Narratives present the narrator in a particular light (for example, as hero or victim).
3. Narratives make past events present and abstract concepts vivid. Many journalists, historians, psychologists, and others have interviewed victims of the Holocaust in order to make that historical event present and vivid to younger individuals.
4. Narratives forge relationships. In fact, one index of your intimacy with another is the amount and kind of narratives you know about that person's life (McCabe, 1996).

The way people tell narratives depends on many factors, including their audience; the meaning of those narratives is jointly constructed between audience and narrator (Mishler, 1986).

Children begin to narrate memories at about 2 years of age (Nelson, 1989; Sachs, 1982), and they proceed to develop their narrative abilities over the next few years (Peterson & McCabe, 1983). At first narration tends to consist of reporting one event at a time. For example, a little 2-year-old girl told her mother, "I hied the big boy," informing her that she had just said hello to a waiter. By 31 months, children begin to chain two past events together. For example, a mother asked her 31-month-old son, "Did you like the puppy?" He said, "He taste my knee." She echoed this, "He tasted your knee?" Her son replied, "Yeth. An' puppy *chase* me."

At 3 and 4 years of age, children typically put together more than two events, but they often do so erratically by violating chronology, contradicting themselves, or leaving out important events. Consider the following narrative a little boy told to a friend of his parents when he was 3 years, 5 months old:

Friend: What did you do on your picnic?

Nicky: We just played hide and seek. We were just lost in the woods. We just found mushrooms. We wasn't lost anymore.

At 5 years, children almost always tell a well-ordered story, but they often end prematurely at the emotional climax of a narrative. The climax in the following two narratives involves getting a shot. Note that you feel dissatisfied at the end of Larry's story because you never find out how things turned out for the boy in the hospital:

Larry: And, um, and, uh, uh, you want to hear another one? I went to the hospital?

Interviewer: Sure.

Larry: Well, I don't like to go to the hospital, and, and I had to have a operation about *tonsils.* About my tonsils weren't getting very good. See, part of my food couldn't get down 'cause I had to take milk and this is—

Interviewer: The food couldn't get down?

Larry: Yeah, 'cause I had to take milk. Right here, two little bumps that were causing all the trouble. And I kept getting sore throats and colds so many *times,* and so we went and got those out. Man, we went *so early.* Nobody was up yet. Nobody, nobody was up 'cept us when we had the operation in the morning when nobody was up. 'Cept me and my dad and my grandma were up. Nobody, and my brother. Yeah, and, those were who were up, and nobody was else up 'cept the hospital was already up, yeah. I had to wait a few hours but, but while I was there they had brought stor—library stories along. And, and, then the doctor came in—one of the girl doctors—and gave me a shot like a mosquito bite. Anyway, you don't feel a mosquito bite, but she gave me one.

At 6 years of age, in European North American culture, children typically do go on to provide a resolution after the climax of a narrative, as in the following narrative (in which the climax is italicized). Note that the narrative is about one particular experience (one time the narrator went to the hospital), as is typical of European North American children:

Interviewer: Have you ever been in a hospital?

Donald: Uh-huh.

Interviewer: You have? Tell me about it.

Donald: When I got, when I drank glue. But, that's when I was about 1 or 2. Had to go to the hospital. They gave me some kind of pills to make me get all of it out. *Then I just went back home. They don't take too long. They just take about 1 minute. I, I, I, gue—, I*

guess it's, if the pills won't help you, gotta, gotta, they got to

operate on you. They didn't operate on me."

By 6 years, then, children tell a narrative that meets the basic requirements of canonical form in their culture (Berman, 1996; McCabe, 1996; Peterson & McCabe, 1983). However, narratives are complex constructions and cultures differ in the values they place on various aspects of narrative construction, notably preferred length, the number of experiences typically discussed in one narrative, and the relative emphasis placed on components of narration.

In Japan, for example, people prefer narratives that are not verbose and that concern several similar experiences (Minami & McCabe, 1991), as does the following one by an 8-year-old boy. The words in parentheses were pronouns and subjects omitted by the speaker, a practice known as ellipsis that is commonly practiced in Japan (Clancy, 1980). Japanese children are taught from an early age to rely on their listeners to empathize with them, so that not every detail of what they wish to communicate needs to be made explicit:

"As for the first (shot), you know, (I) got (it) at Ehime, you know. (It) hurt a lot. As for the second (shot), you know, (I) knew, you know, (it would) hurt, you know. Well, you know, (it) didn't hurt so much, you know. The next (one) didn't hurt so much, either. As for the last (one), you know, (it) didn't hurt at all."

In African-American communities, many speakers value performed narratives that also thematically link several similar experiences. In this cultural context, however, length is valued, as is clear in the following narrative by Vivian, a 9-year-old girl (Craddock-Willis & McCabe, 1996):

We went to the dentist before, and I was gettin' my tooth pulled, and the dentist said, "Oh, it's not gonna hurt." And he was lying to me. It hurt. It hurted so bad I coulda gone on screamin'. I don't know what it was like. I was like, "Oh, that hurt!" He said no, it wouldn't hurt. 'Cause last time I went to the doctor, I had got this spray. This doctor, he sprayed some spray in my mouth and my tooth appeared in his hand. He put me to sleep, and then I woke up. He used some pliers to take it out, and I didn't know. So I asked my sister how did the man take (it out)?

And so she said, "He used some pliers." I said, "Nah, he used that spray." She said, "Nope, he used that spray to put you to sleep, and he used the pliers to take it out." I was, like, "Huh, that's amazin'." I swear to God, I was so amazed. It was so amazing, right, that I had to look for myself. And then I asked him too. And he said, "Yes, I used some pliers to take out your tooth, and I put you to sleep so you wouldn't know. And that's how I did it." And I was like, "Ooouuu." And then I seen my sister get her tooth pulled. I was like, "Ooouuu" 'cause he had to put her to sleep to, hmm, to take out her tooth. It was the same day she got her tooth pulled, and I was scared. I was like, "EEE-hhhmmm." I had a whole bunch cotton in my mouth, chompin' on it 'cause I had to hold it to stop my bleeding. One day I was in school, I took out my own tooth. I put some hot water in it the night before I went to school. And I was taking a test. And then it came out right when I finished the test. And my teacher asked me, was it bleeding? I said, "No, it's not bleeding 'cause I put some hot water on it." And so my cousin, he wanted to take out his tooth, and he didn't know what to do, so I told him. "I'm a Pullin' Teeth Expert. Pull out your own tooth. But if you need somebody to do it, call me, and I'll be over."

Note that the length of her narrative and the number of dental experiences she discusses are both necessary to establish her main point; by the end, we agree heartily that she is in fact a "Pullin' Teeth Expert."

Although family members often appear in the narratives of children from all cultures, they play an especially prominent role in many narratives told by Spanish-speaking children (Silva & McCabe, 1996), as in the following excerpt from a 7-year-old El Salvadoran girl:

> "Well I (was) in the hospital, in the Mass. General Hospital—there where my Uncle Roberto works. That he has two children who are not twins, but who are only two children because first Robertico was born, who is named after his dad, and then Christopher was born. . . . But my Uncle Roberto have a dog who is one of those German ones, who is already two months old. And now, because the mom's name is Butterfly. She is with a man whose name is, who is my Uncle whose name is Juan. And by chance he gave him that dog. But look that dog, he bites Alex because he runs and bites much. *Here* he bit him, and he bites him even in the face and here in the arms."

When Spanish-speaking children and adults told a story prompted by a wordless picture book, they devoted a good deal of attention to scene-setting, that is, static descriptions of the locations of landmarks—more so than other cultures (Berman & Slobin, 1994). In other words, the focus on actions that was so prominent in the narratives of African-American and European North American children above is muted in some types of narratives told by Spanish-speaking children from various cultures in the United States.

Cultural differences pervade various kinds of storytelling in many other ways. For example, more so than in any other culture, Germans of all ages anchor narratives in the simple present tense (Bamberg, 1994). When composing a story prompted by a wordless picture book, the typical German practice is exemplified in the following excerpt produced by an adult (and translated into English preserving word order as much as possible):

> "When in the early morning then Hans and the dog wake up, they realize to their great fright, that Mrs. Frog through the opened window towards outside has run away."

In close scrutiny of the way children who speak different languages tell stories prompted by the same wordless picture book, you can see how children intensely, actively learn to put linguistic construction types to use for interpersonal, social purposes (Bamberg, in press).

By early elementary school, then, children tell stories that conform to particular cultural schemata for storytelling, schemata that in turn will determine how they hear and recall stories that they hear, as previously noted. Children essentially learn particular, culturally specific ways of "thinking for speaking" (Berman & Slobin, 1994).

Narrative development continues during adolescence, though much less is known about this time period. Adolescents will put narratives to such uses as gossip, where peers are evaluated behind their backs (Eder & Enke, 1991, pp. 499–500), as in the following exchange between two seventh-grade boys:

Barry: Yeah, Tommy Payson (the coach's son). He's a jerk.

Johnny: Who is he?

Barry: Tommy Payson, he was on my team. He's a jerk. I saw him at the movies with a girl. He was goin' (imitates boy with a goofy, jive walk), walkin' around. Oh, gosh.

(Everybody giggles.)

Johnny: What, well, isn't he any good?

Kevin: Not really.

Barry: No. He wears basketball shoes to baseball practice. It's pretty weird.

Kevin: Top Tens.

Barry: Yeah.

Kevin: Pretty weird.

Barry: Pretty weird.

Expository/Explanatory

Another important genre of thinking embodied in discourse is that which Bruner (1986) termed **paradigmatic.** Such thinking is logical, scientific, abstract, explanatory, or descriptive. The discourse that transmits such thinking is called argumentative or **expository discourse.** Beals and Snow (1994) investigated what they termed **explanatory talk** between parents and preschool-aged children during mealtime conversations, talk that included explanations of all of the following:

1. Intentions behind actions: "What's the spoon for? Sherbet?"
2. Requests or commands: "I said, stop the banging. That isn't to be played with. It's to eat with."

3. Questions or statements: "I told you you should have stuck with the leftovers. They're tastier today than they were yesterday, huh?"
4. Internal states: "[I'm not afraid to dunk] because I'm a big girl."

Explanatory talk also included

5. Causal explanations: "Sure have a big belly ache . . . I think I ate, had too much."
6. Definitions and descriptions: "[Your highness means] somebody who's really, really important—a queen and a princess, or something."
7. Evidential explanations: "Sally had gym today . . . (be)cause I saw her coming out of gym."
8. Procedural explanations: "You add a little water and you shake it up. That's how you get it to go when it's all stuck to the sides."
9. Explanations of the consequences of one's actions: "I said if you wanted to stay in the kitchen you had to remain quiet."

Although expository discourse or explanatory talk is conceptually distinct from narrative, in the real family conversations investigated the two genres were found to overlap to such an extent that the researchers argue that they draw on similar underlying skills. That is, almost all narrative utterances at dinner times were also considered explanatory, and 59% of explanatory utterances were found in narratives. The following excerpt demonstrates the overlap between explanation and narrative:

Grandma: And the thunder is when, uh, the angels are upstairs bowling. And that's one of them just got a spare.

Mother: Brad should get out his Berenstain Bear almanac and let Ma read it, and that'll tell her what thunder is, huh?

Grandma: Mmhm.

Mother: Tells all about thunder and . . .

Grandpa: That's the energy.

Grandma: Why should, why should he be brought up on a different story than you people were?

Brad: Because, that's because Mommy vacuuming it.

Grandpa: That's the energy, huh? Thunder is caused by energy in the clouds.

Brad: Yeah, yeah, but, but one day I was sleeping in my bed for, for a long, long time, and thunder and lightning came from outside, and I was trying to—(sneezes).

Mother: Oh, bless you.

Brad: . . . And I was trying to find something that was yellow outside in the dark all by itself. And it came out, and it was thunder and lightning, and I hided from it.

In this example the participants consider various possible explanations for thunder (angel myths, energy in the clouds). These explanations trigger a memory of a particular episode of lightning that Brad proceeds to narrate.

Humor

Humor or language play might well be considered a third genre. As with explanation and narrative, humor is conceptually distinct but in reality often overlaps with explanation and narrative. Even kindergarten children devote long stretches of talk to sound play, word play, role play, and verbal humor (Ely & McCabe, 1994). One little girl used repetitive word play playfully to provoke a laugh from her classmates: "Yuck, I hate bananas. They're icky, They're slimy. They're gooey." Other children tell traditional nursery rhymes or sing songs such as "Rain, Rain, Go Away," or "Clean Up." In role play, children adopt *registers,* which are variants of language typically used in certain social contexts or with particular kinds of listeners, such as the baby-talk register, the teacher register, or that of various animals. In their play, in other words, children demonstrate their burgeoning knowledge of the kinds of language associated with particular settings or social roles, both generalized (for example, generic "doctor talk") and particular (for example, talking like Kimberly, a Power Ranger). Finally, verbal humor includes traditional riddles, humorous repartee, and original comments such as, "What I like best about me is I lose teeth very fast." Of course, though the goal here is to make your audience laugh instead of to inform them (explanatory talk) or tell them a story, many jokes and riddles are explanations ("Why did the chicken cross the road?") or stories ("Did I ever tell you about the time? . . .").

CONCLUSION

Speakers must demonstrate to other speakers of their community not only that they know how to structure a sentence, but also that they know how to use language appropriate to a given situation—they know how and when to tell a story, how to take a turn in the conversation, to understand indirect and other nonliteral speech acts—in short to demonstrate competence negotiating all the aspects of discourse we have discussed in this chapter. To be accepted by their peers, people must demonstrate what has come to be called **communicative competence** (Hymes, 1972). Even children form impressions of personality characteristics on the basis of other children's discourse style (Hemphill & Siperstein, 1990).

SUMMARY

Discourse and text consist of sets of sentences about a single topic that are held together by diverse cohesive devices. When individuals hear or read discourse, they appraise the relative importance of various propositions, remembering the important ones, forgetting the less important. Not only do people omit information, they add inferences based on their knowledge of the world and of discourse rules. Memory for discourse is active, reconstructive, and dependent upon understanding. Individuals employ schemata drawn from their cultural experience to understand discourse. Discourse itself serves a context, influencing the interpretation of its constituents. Discourse also occurs in various contexts and is influenced by such variables of speakers and audience as bilingualism, gender, socioeconomic status, and role. Finally, the many genres of discourse serve a wide variety of important communicative functions.

KEY WORDS

Discourse
Text
Cohesion
Anaphora
Pronominal reference
Propositions
Parsing
Macroproposition
Microproposition
Schemata
Conversational maxims
Metaphor
Irony

Speech acts
Politeness
Code-switch
Dialect
Elaborated code
Restricted code
Genre
Narrative
Paradigmatic
Expository discourse
Explanatory talk
Communicative competence

SOMETHING TO THINK ABOUT

1. A naive view of language is that it is a system that consists of sounds combined into words that combine to form sentences that combine to form discourse. List all the ways that discourse affects how language sounds, the meanings of words, and the syntax of sentences.

2. How would you depict the relationships between discourse form, comprehension, and memory?

3. List all the ways mentioned in this chapter in which culture has been demonstrated to have a profound influence on discourse.

4. In *Pygmalion* (popularized as *My Fair Lady*), George Bernard Shaw transforms Liza Doolittle's way of speaking from that characteristic of the lower British classes to that characteristic of the higher ones. Was that transformation purely superficial or was Liza herself transformed in the process?

ACTIVITIES

Cohesion Markers

Find all markers of cohesion in the following personal narrative told by a 9-year-old European North American girl (taken from Peterson & McCabe, 1983):

Interviewer:	Did you ever get stung?
Didi:	Yeah, on my *very own birthday* I was *chased* by a yellow jacket. I didn't like it because it was on my *birthday* and everything, and I was getting chased all around. Mom kept *yelling* and *yelling* for me to come back. Because I was all the way out. I was about all the way down to my *friend*. And it started chasing me, going faster. I was in bare feet. I went chomping down the road and it, you know those kind, that rock with tar? And I was, I had I was kept about here because they started hurting, and so I finally got off the grass into the fence and I almost got *shocked* and it's *electric,* really *shocks* you. And I almost ran in it, about this close to it. Went back. Finally going to the house and I almost ran into my brother because he was a little bitty baby. Because he was blowing bubbles and he popped it. He was right there by the yellow jacket, and the yellow jacket came out and he was swatting

it, like, and he didn't know I was. I started running toward the door and he started *chasing* me!

Ghosts!

Read this North American Indian folk tale that Bartlett (1932, p. 65) presented to his subjects:

The War of the Ghosts

One night, two young men from Egulac went down to the river to hunt seals, and while they were there it became foggy and calm. Then they heard war-cries, and they thought: "Maybe this is a war-party." They escaped to the shore and hid behind a log. Now canoes came up, and they heard the noise of paddles, and saw one canoe coming up to them. There were five men in the canoe, and they said:

"What do you think? We wish to take you along. We are going up the river to make war on the people."

One of the young men said, "I have no arrows."

"Arrows are in the canoe," they said.

"I will not go along. I might be killed. My relatives do not know where I have gone. But you," he said, turning to the other, "may go with them."

So one of the young men went, but the other returned home.

And the warriors went on up the river to a town on the other side of Kalama. The people came down to the water, and they began to fight, and many were killed. But presently the young man heard one of the warriors say, "Quick, let us go home: that Indian has been hit." Now he thought, "Oh, they are ghosts." He did not feel sick, but they said he had been shot.

So the canoes went back to Egulac, and the young man went ashore to his house, and made a fire. And he told everybody and said, "Behold, I accompanied the ghosts, and we went to fight. Many of our fellows were killed, and many of those who attacked us were killed. They said I was hit, and I did not feel sick."

He told it all, and then he became quiet. When the sun rose he fell down. Something black came out of his mouth. His face became contorted. The people jumped up and cried.

He was dead.

Now, put away the story for a week. (Mark your calendar.) Without looking at it again, write out what you recall. Compare what you recalled with the original. Did you omit anything? If so, what? Did you insert any inferences or change words when you recalled the story? What sense did you make of it, especially the ending?

Metaphors

To give you a sense of how profoundly context can affect the meaning of terms, try the following exercise. Take an arbitrary group of nouns (from a dictionary, from one of those commercial magnetic poetry kits, etc.). Put them in a paper bag and randomly extract two at a time. Try to imagine a context in which one could serve as a metaphorical term for the other.

This exercise was the basis for an experiment (McCabe, 1977) which revealed that most college students could not only turn any two randomly paired concepts into metaphors, some students could turn even the most bizarre pairings into metaphors judged good by other students. Consider the following excerpt, in which embedding the metaphoric comparison of the highly dissimilar concepts *hydrant* and *elastic* works because of the way the writer embeds it in a slangy monologue:

> "Hey man it's hot out here today! You know, man, I am cookin', sizzlin' like a piece of bacon in a fryin' pan. This asphalt's so hot I got to get to that hydrant on 13th and Main or I'm gonna melt. You know I've seen six cars hit that hydrant and it ain't busted yet. Man, is it a sight to behold to see that thing bounce right back after it's been hit. That old *hydrant's* like the *elastic* in your underwear, man, bending and twisting but always bouncing back into position."

Or the way that another student imagined a character in whose experience the metaphoric comparison of the dissimilar concepts *ache* and *autograph* would seem natural:

> "My hometown doctor, Doc Wilson, was an old-fashioned country doctor. He knew all his patients carefully and individually. Each *ache* was as uniquely identified with a patient as was his or her *autograph*. Doc Wilson knew you inside and out."

Although numerous theories have been proposed that attempt to account for the appreciation of metaphor in terms of the similarity of the concepts it compares, this exercise demonstrates that it is the discourse context, not the preexisting similarity of words or the concepts they encode, that makes for a good metaphor (McCabe, 1983). When students read and interpret metaphors in the context of published works of fiction, they articulate many connections between the concepts that only emerge from the particular context in which they occur (Tourangeau & Rips, 1991), as well as many connections between the comparison and the extended context that led to their appreciation of that metaphor (McCabe, in press).

REFERENCES

Abrams, M. H. (1971). *A glossary of literary terms* (3rd ed.). New York: Holt, Rinehart and Winston.

American Heritage Dictionary of the English Language (New College Edition). (1978). Boston: Houghton Mifflin.

Austin, J. L. (1962). *How to do things with words.* New York: Oxford University Press.

Bamberg, M. (1994). Development of linguistic forms: German. In R. A. Berman & D. I. Slobin (Eds.), *Relating events in narrative: A crosslinguistic developmental study* (pp. 189–238). Hillsdale, NJ: Erlbaum.

Bamberg, M. (in press). *Narrative development: Six approaches.* Hillsdale, NJ: Erlbaum.

Barry, A. K. (1991). Narrative style and witness testimony. *Journal of Narrative and Life History, 1* (4), 281– 293.

Bartlett, F. C. (1932). *Remembering.* Cambridge, U.K.: Cambridge University Press.

Beals, D. E., & Snow, C. E. (1994). "Thunder is when the angels are upstairs bowling": Narratives and explanations at the dinner table. *Journal of Narrative and Life History, 4* (4), 331–352.

Berman, R. A. (1995). Narrative competence and storytelling performance: How children tell stories in different contexts. *Journal of Narrative and Life History, 5,* 285–314.

Berman, R. A., & Slobin, D. I. (1994). Becoming a native speaker. In R. A. Berman & D. I. Slobin (Eds.), *Relating events in narrative: A crosslinguistic developmental study* (pp. 611–643). Hillsdale, NJ: Erlbaum.

Bernstein, B. (1974). Class, codes, and control. *Theoretical studies towards a sociology of language* (2nd ed.). London: Routledge & Kegan Paul.

Blum-Kulka, S. (1982). Learning to say what you mean in a second language: A study of the speech act performance of learners of Hebrew as a second language. *Applied Linguistics, 3* (1), 29–59.

Bransford, J. D., & Johnson, M. K. (1972). Contextual prerequisites for understanding: Some investigations of comprehension and recall. *Journal of Verbal Learning and Verbal Behavior, 11,* 717–726.

Brown, P., & Levinson, S. (1978). Universals in language usage: Politeness phenomena. In E. N. Goody (Ed.), *Questions and politeness: Strategies in social interaction* (pp. 56–289). Cambridge, U.K.: Cambridge University Press.

Brown, R. (1987). Theory of politeness: An exemplary case. Invited address to Society of Experimental Social Psychologists. October.

Bruner, J. (1986). *Actual minds, possible worlds.* Cambridge, MA: Harvard University Press.

Clancy, P. M. (1980). Referential choice in English and Japanese narrative discourse. In W. L. Chafe (Ed.), *The pear stories: Cognitive, cultural, and linguistic aspects of narrative production* (pp. 127–202). Norwood, NJ: Ablex.

Craddock-Willis, K., & McCabe, A. (1996). Improvising on a theme: Some African-American traditions. In A. McCabe (Ed.), *Chameleon readers: Teaching children to appreciate all kinds of good stories* (pp. 98–115).

Craig, R. T., Tracy, K., & Spisak, F. (1986). The discourse of requests: Assessment of a politeness approach. *Human Communication Research, 12* (4), 437–468.

Deese, J. (1984). *Thought into speech: Psychology of a language.* Englewood Cliffs, NJ: Prentice-Hall.

Dews, S., & Winner, E. (in press). Attributing meaning to deliberately false utterances: The case of irony. In C. Mandell & A. McCabe (Eds.), *The problem of meaning: Cognitive and behavioral approaches.* Amsterdam: Elsevier.

Dooling, R. J., & Lachman, R. (1971). Effects of comprehension on retention of prose. *Journal of Experimental Psychology, 88,* 216–222.

Dube, E. F. (1982). Literacy, cultural familiarity, and "intelligence" as determinants of story recall. In U. Neisser (Ed.), *Memory observes.* San Francisco: Freeman.

Eder, D., & Enke, J. L. (1991). The structure of gossip: Opportunities and constraints on collective expression among adolescents. *American Sociological Review, 56,* 494–508.

Ely, R., & McCabe, A. (1994). The language play of kindergarten children. *First Language, 14,* 19–35.

Ervin-Tripp, S. M. (1968). An analysis of the interaction of language, topic, and listener. In J. A. Fishman (Ed.), *Readings in the sociology of language.* The Hague: Mouton.

Estes, W. K. (1995). A general model of classification and memory applied to discourse processing. In C. A. Weaver, S. Mannes, & C. R. Fletcher (Eds.), *Discourse comprehension: Essays in honor of Walter Kintsch* (pp. 35–48). Hillsdale, NJ: Erlbaum.

Foss, D. J., & Hakes, D. T. (1978). *Psycholinguistics: An introduction to the psychology of language.* Englewood Cliffs, NJ: Prentice-Hall.

Gee, J. P. (1991). A linguistic approach to narrative. *Journal of Narrative and Life History, 1* (1), 15–40.

Gleason, J. B., Perlmann, R. Y., & Greif, E. B. (1984). What's the magic word: Learning language through politeness routines. *Discourse Processes, 7,* 493–502.

Grice, H. P. (1975). Logic and conversation. In P. Cole & J. Morgan (Eds.), *Syntax and semantics: Speech acts* (Vol. 3) (pp. 41–58). New York: Academic Press.

Guindon, R., & Kintsch, W. (1984). Priming macropropositions: Evidence for the primacy of macropropositions in the memory for text. *Journal of Verbal Learning and Verbal Behavior, 23,* 508–518.

Halliday, M. A. K., & Hasan, R. (1976). *Cohesion in English.* London: Longman.

Harris, R. J., Lee, D. J., Hensley, D. L., & Schoen, L. M. (1988). The effect of cultural script knowledge on memory for stories over time. *Discourse Processes, 11,* 413–431.

Hawthorne, N. (1937). *The scarlet letter.* New York: Modern Library.

Hemphill, L. (1989). Topic development, syntax, and social class. *Discourse Processes, 12,* 267–286.

Hemphill, L., & Siperstein, G. (1990). Conversational competence and peer response to mildly retarded children. *Journal of Educational Psychology, 82,* 128–134.

Hidi, S. E., & Hildyard, A. (1983). The comparison of oral and written productions in two discourse types. *Discourse Processes, 1,* 97–117.

Hoffman, R. R. (1980). Metaphor in science. In R. P. Honeck & R. R. Hoffman (Eds.), *Cognition and figurative language.* Hillsdale, NJ: Erlbaum.

Hyde, J. (1988). Gender differences in verbal ability: A meta-analysis. *Psychological Bulletin, 104,* 53–69.

Hymes, D. (1972). Models of the interaction of language and social life. In J. J. Gumperz & D. Hymes (Eds.), *Directions in sociolinguistics.* New York: Holt, Rinehart and Winston.

Hymes, D. (1982). Narrative form as a "grammar" of experience: Native Americans and a glimpse of English. *Journal of Education, 2,* 121–142.

Imbens-Bailey, A. L. (1995). *Oral proficiency and literacy in an ancestral language: Implications for ethnic identity.* Unpublished doctoral dissertation, Harvard University, Cambridge, MA.

Invernizzi, M. A., & Abouzeid, M. P. (1995). One story map does not fit all: A cross-cultural analysis of children's written story retellings. *Journal of Narrative and Life History, 5* (1), 1–19.

John, V. P., & Berney, J. D. (1968). Analysis of story retelling as a measure of the effects of ethnic content in stories. In J. Helmuth (Ed.), *The disadvantaged child: Head Start and early intervention* (Vol. 2) (pp. 259–287). New York: Brunner/Mazel.

Keysar, B. (1994). Discourse context effects: Metaphorical and literal interpretations. *Discourse Processes, 18* (3), 247–269.

Kintsch, W. (1974). *The representation of meaning in memory.* Hillsdale, NJ: Erlbaum.

Kintsch, W., & Greene, E. (1978). The role of culture-specific schemata in the comprehension and recall of stories. *Discourse Processes, 1,* 1–13.

Kintsch, W., & van Dijk, T. A. (1978). Toward a model of discourse comprehension and production. *Psychological Review, 85,* 363–394.

Labov, W. (1972). *Language in the inner city.* Philadelphia: University of Pennsylvania Press.

Lakoff, R. (1975). *Language and women's place.* New York: Harper and Row.

Loftus, E. F. (1980). *Memory.* Reading, MA: Addison-Wesley.

Mao, L. R. (1994). Beyond politeness theory: "Face" revisited and renewed. *Journal of Pragmatics, 21,* 451–486.

McCabe, A. (1977). *Metaphor—Its goodness versus similarity and its relative nature.* Unpublished master's thesis, University of Virginia, Charlottesville.

McCabe, A. (1983). Conceptual similarity and the quality of metaphor in isolated sentences versus extended contexts. *Journal of Psycholinguistic Research, 12,* 41–68.

McCabe, A. (1991). Editorial. *Journal of Narrative and Life History, 1* (1), 1–2.

McCabe, A. (1996). *Chameleon readers: Teaching children to appreciate all kinds of good stories.* New York: McGraw-Hill.

McCabe, A. (in press). Narrative threads of metaphor. In C. Mandell & A. McCabe (Eds.), *The problem of meaning: Cognitive and behavioral approaches.* Amsterdam: Elsevier.

Minami, M., & McCabe, A. (1991). *Haiku* as a discourse regulation device: A stanza analysis of Japanese children's personal narratives. *Language in Society, 20,* 577–599.

Mishler, E. G. (1986). *Research interviewing: Context and narrative.* Cambridge, MA: Harvard University Press.

Nelson, K. (1989). Monologue as representation of real-life experience. In K. Nelson (Ed.), *Narratives from the crib* (pp. 27–72). Cambridge, MA: Harvard University Press.

Perfetti, C. A., & Britt, M. A. (1995). Where do propositions come from? In C. A. Weaver, S. Mannes, & C. R. Fletcher (Eds.), *Discourse comprehension: Essays in honor of Walter Kintsch* (pp. 35–48). Hillsdale, NJ: Erlbaum.

Peterson, C., & McCabe, A. (1983). *Developmental psycholinguistics: Three ways of looking at a child's narrative.* New York: Plenum.

Peterson, C., & McCabe, A. (1991). On the threshold of the storyrealm: Semantic versus pragmatic use of connectives in narratives. *Merrill-Palmer Quarterly, 37* (3), 445–464.

Pollio, H. R., Barlow, J. M., Fine, H. J., & Pollio, M. R. (1977). *Psychology and the poetics of growth: Figurative language in psychology, psychotherapy, and education.* Hillsdale, NJ: Erlbaum.

Preece, A. (1992). Collaborators and critics: The nature and effects of peer interaction on children's conversational narratives. *Journal of Narrative and Life History, 2* (3), 277–292.

Sachs, J. S. (1967). Recognition memory for syntactic and semantic aspects of connected discourse. *Perception and Psychophysics, 2,* 437–442.

Sachs, J. S. (1982). Talking about the there and then: The emergence of displaced reference in parent–child discourse. In K. E. Nelson (Ed.), *Children's language* (Vol. 3) (pp. 1–28). Hillsdale, NJ: Erlbaum.

Searle, J. R. (1969). *Speech acts: An essay in the philosophy of language.* New York: Cambridge University Press.

Shaw, G. B. (1913/1957). *Pygmalion.* Middlesex, UK: Penguin Books, Ltd.

Silva, M. J., & McCabe, A. (1996). Vignettes of the continuous and family ties: Some Latino American traditions. In A. McCabe (Ed.), *Chameleon readers: Teaching children to appreciate all kinds of good stories* (pp. 116–136). New York: McGraw-Hill.

Slobin, D. I. (1968). Recall of full and truncated passive sentences in connected discourse. *Journal of Verbal Learning and Verbal Behavior, 7,* 876–881.

Tannen, D. (1984). *Conversational style: Analyzing talk among friends.* Norwood, NJ: Ablex.

Tannen, D. (1990). *You just don't understand.* New York: Ballantine.

Tourangeau, R., & Rips, L. (1991). Interpreting and evaluating metaphors. *Journal of Memory and Language, 30,* 452–472.

Chapter 7

SPEECH PRODUCTION

Victoria A. Fromkin
University of California at Los Angeles

Nan Bernstein Ratner
University of Maryland at College Park

INTRODUCTION

In this chapter, we discuss the process by which a speaker turns a mental concept into a spoken utterance. It is more difficult to study speech production than to investigate speech perception or comprehension because of the difficulty in constructing experimental tasks that can reveal the complex steps in the process. Thus, psycholinguists interested in the speech production process must use less direct methods to gain insight into how this is accomplished. Researchers have historically relied on two kinds of data in the construction of speech production models—speech errors and speech disfluencies. These data have provided evidence for the units used in generating speech and for the stages that lie between the message the speaker wishes to convey and its spoken expression. This chapter discusses those data and their contribution to understanding production.

As Chapter 1 notes, knowing a language means knowing how to produce and comprehend an unlimited set of utterances. A competent speaker and listener does this effortlessly, without conscious knowledge of the complexities involved in the process. Further, as Chapter 4 notes, both the comprehension and production processes occur at extremely rapid rates: speech is typically generated at a rate of 150 words per minute (wpm) or greater (Maclay & Osgood, 1959). At such rapid rates, it's no surprise that occasional errors arise. When linguists refer to **mental grammar,** they refer to the internalized knowledge that permits us to simultaneously be both speaker and listener. Analysis of speech errors allows insight into the nature of this mental grammar.

From Concept to Expression

Speech[1] communication may be viewed as a "chain of events linking the speaker's brain with the listener's brain," as illustrated in Figure 7.1 (Denes & Pinson, 1963).

Figure 7.1 represents the nonlinguistic aspects of the speech chain, starting "in the speaker's brain [where] . . . appropriate instructions, in the form of impulses along the motor nerves are sent to the muscles of the vocal organs, the tongue, the lips and the vocal cords" (Denes & Pinson, 1963, p. 3), which in turn produce speech sound waves. In the case of signed communication, the neuromotor commands to the hands will produce signed gestures. We know a great deal about the physiological, articulatory, and acoustic aspects of these stages of speech production as a result of experimental phonetic research. But we are still far from understanding the processes by which speakers put the message they wish to convey into linguistic form or how their words and phrases are selected, constructed, and ordered. Nor do we fully understand what intermediate representations of the message look like at the different stages prior to neural excitation of the muscles.

---

[1] Linguistic communication may occur either via spoken or signed utterances. "Speech" or "speech production" as used here, therefore, refers to either the production of sounds or gestures, unless otherwise indicated.

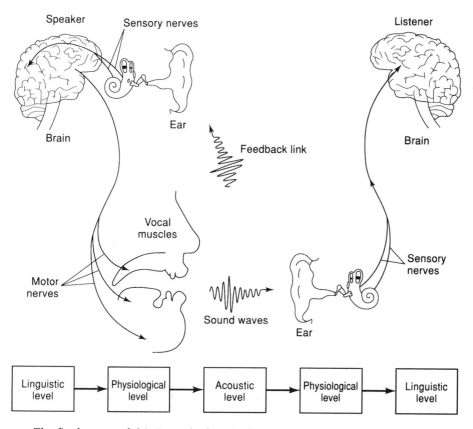

FIGURE 7.1

THE SPEECH CHAIN

The different forms in which a spoken message exists in its progress from the mind of the speaker to the mind of the listener.

The final stages of this "speech chain"—how the listener responds to the spoken message—were discussed in Chapters 3 through 5 on speech perception, lexical processing, and sentence processing, respectively. This chapter considers the process from the point of view of the speaker who "has to . . . arrange his [sic] thoughts, decide what he wants to say, and put what he wants to say into *linguistic form* . . . by selecting the right words and phrases to express its meaning, and by placing these words in the correct order required by the grammatical rules of the language . . ." (Denes & Pinson, 1963, p. 3).

The diagram of the speech chain in Figure 7.1 omits the initial and final stages of the process—the thoughts or nonlinguistic message that the speaker wishes to convey to the listener who, if all goes well, will receive that same message. As Pillsbury and Meader observed, " . . . man thinks first and then expresses his thought in words by some sort of translation. . . . Speech has its origin in the mind of the speaker . . . and the process . . . is completed only when the word uttered or spoken arouses an idea in the listener . . ." (1928, pp. 92–93). Although philosophers through the ages have speculated about the "language of thought" (Fodor, 1975), how concepts are represented in the mind remains a mystery. Numerous alternative views have been posited with little empirical evidence to support any one more than the rest. This chapter will therefore simply assume that speakers have some notion, concept, or message that they wish to convey but will not attempt to specify how it is represented before being encoded into linguistic form.

SOURCES OF DATA FOR MODELS OF SPEECH PRODUCTION

Speech Errors

It is of course no simple matter to try to understand any aspect of the mental processes involved in speaking. Lashley (1958) noted that "When we think in words, the thoughts come in grammatical form with subject, verb, object, and modifying clauses falling into place without our having the slightest perception of how the sentence structure is produced." Although Lashley was basically correct, it is not always the case that the thoughts come in correct grammatical form nor that we always select "the right words . . . to express (the) meaning" we wish to convey (Lashley, 1958). All of us have experienced, either as speakers or hearers, utterances that seem to have gotten mixed up on their way out. Consider the following examples in which we can compare what was actually said to what the speaker intended:

Intended utterance:	Actual utterance:
You have missed all my history lectures.	You have hissed all my mystery lectures.
Noble sons of toil	Noble tons of soil
You have wasted the whole term.	You have tasted the whole worm.
The dear old Queen	The queer old dean

Such errors in production, called **speech errors** or **slips of the tongue,** occur regularly in normal conversation. The above examples are all attributed to the Reverend William A. Spooner, the warden (head) of New College, Oxford University, England, from 1903 to 1924. Because he became "famous" for producing such errors, they are often called **spoonerisms.**

Although such errors may be funny (to the listener) or embarrassing or frustrating (to the speaker), they also provide indirect evidence for the units, stages, and cognitive computations involved in speech production. It is of interest to note that in a study of the speech produced in seminars, classes, business meetings, and similar contexts, in both planned talks and spontaneous conversation, Deese (1978, 1980) found that speakers used complete sentences, 98% of which were grammatically correct. Other researchers (for example, Garnham, Shillcock, Brown, Mill, & Cutler, 1981) find slips to be even less common than this. Yet an examination of the relatively small number of errors that people produce when speaking has led to greater insights

Rev. William Spooner was well known for his slips of the tongue.

into the production process than the study of error-free utterances. Various collections of errors are now used for analysis. Two of the largest collections are the UCLA corpus (Fromkin, 1988) and the MIT corpus (Garrett, 1988; Shattuck-Hufnagel, 1986).

Disfluencies

In addition to speech errors, many utterances are characterized by hesitations, repetitions, false starts, and "filler" words such as *um, well,* or *you know* (sometimes called **filled pauses**). Such disfluencies or nonfluencies are actually more common than we think—we tend not to notice them. Goldman-Eisler (1968) suggests that hesitations, sometimes called **unfilled pauses,** occur roughly every five words when people describe pictures. If speakers are conversing naturally, hesitations may appear every seven to eight words. However, their presence is rarely noted. As we shall see, such lapses in fluent speech production actually provide valuable insights into the units of speech production and permit us to evaluate how much of speech is mentally planned in advance of its production.

ISSUES IN SPEECH PRODUCTION

In trying to explicate what we know about the complex speech production process, questions arise: What are the basic elements, units, or hierarchy of units into which

humans translate the conceptual message? How are these units combined? What are the stages in real time by which we translate or encode a thought into an utterance? By what processes do we produce both well-formed and ill-formed structures (errors)? Do speech errors provide evidence to suggest that during speech production we use the units, components, and rules posited by linguistic theory as part of the mental grammar? These questions, which various models of speech production attempt to answer, are the focus of this chapter.

The Units of Speech Production

When we produce an utterance corresponding to some thought we wish to convey, we cannot go to a mental storage unit and pull out the appropriate stored message. The brain's finite storage capacity cannot warehouse an infinite set of utterances. Thus, we produce speech, most of which we have never said in just that way before, by stringing together, arranging, and rearranging a limited number of stored items. A major question in trying to understand the production process is to determine the size and nature of these units. Even a long memorized passage such as the Gettysburg Address or "Mary Had a Little Lamb" must be mentally represented by its constituent parts including sentences, clauses, phrases, words, morphemes, syllables, phonemes, and even phonological features, because, as we will see below, all of these units represent items that may be disordered or forgotten or remembered as fragments. As this chapter will explore, these units of language, which linguists use in describing the structure of language, are those discrete units out of which the semicontinuous physical speech signal is composed during the process of speech production.

The first known linguistic work to deal with speech errors was published in the 8th century by the Arab linguist Al-Ki-sa'i. More recently, speech errors have been analyzed by linguists and psycholinguists working under the assumption that these errors "... can give some clues to the particular mechanisms of language production, which in the abnormal case—in accordance with a general methodological principle—can lead to conclusions about the factors involved in normal functioning" (Bierwisch, 1982, p. 310).

Analysis of such errors shows, first of all, the discreteness of the units, which cannot normally be observed in error-free utterances. As Chapter 3 discussed, the speech signal is quite continuous, and locating the boundaries of any speech unit is difficult. However, when segments such as sounds or words are produced incorrectly or shift position within the utterance, they are more readily identifiable as separable units. Errors also reveal that utterances are composed of units of differing sizes and classes; segments of varying sizes appear to be vulnerable to slips of the tongue. Dell (1986) notes that, "slips of the tongue can be seen as products of the productivity of language. A slip is an unintended novelty. Word errors create syntactic novelties; morphemic errors create novel words; and sound errors create novel but phonologically legal combinations of sounds" (Dell, 1986, p. 286).

PHONEMIC SEGMENTS.   The literature on speech errors, going back to the first major collection of more than 8,000 German errors published by Meringer and Mayer (1895), provides countless examples of phonological errors in which single phonemic-sized segments are *anticipated* or *persevered.* In **anticipation errors,** sounds which will come later in the utterance inappropriately appear earlier than intended. In **perseveration errors,** a sound produced early in the utterance reappears in an incorrect location later in the utterance. Other error types include deleted or added phonemes or phoneme **exchange** (reverse) **errors,** as illustrated below: (Note: The intended utterance occurs to the left of the arrow; the actual utterance with the error appears on the right. C=consonant, and V=vowel in these examples.)

1. a reading list → a leading list (C anticipation)
2. a phonological rule → a phonological fool (C perseveration)
3. brake fluid → blake fruid (C cluster division and C exchange)
4. speech error → peach error (C deletion)
5. box of flowers → blocks of flowers (C anticipation and insertion; C cluster division)
6. fill the pool → fool the pill (vowel exchange)
7. Sue weeded the garden → sea weeded the garden (V anticipation)
8. annotated bibliography → annotated babliography (vowel perseveration)
9. drop a bomb → bop a dromb (consonant cluster—C exchange)
10. when you get old your spine shrinks → your shrine spinks (consonant cluster exchange)

It's impossible to account for such errors without positing that, for example, consonant clusters like the /br/ and /fl/ in example 3 are composed of individual segments that in the process of speaking are "split" and reversed. Note, however, that in examples 9 and 10, consonant clusters can also be disordered as a unit. The speech errors above illustrate an important point about the basic units of speech production: at some level, they correspond to our notions of phonetic segments, such as consonants, vowels, and consonant clusters (Stemberger & Treiman, 1986). We can divide the physical acoustic signal in the middle of a vowel, but such division does not occur when we speak, even when we catch ourselves in a false start or an error.

PHONETIC FEATURES.   The examples below illustrate that the *quark,* or most elementary unit of speech production, is even smaller than the segment, because **phonetic features** can independently be disordered. Phonetic features, sometimes called

distinctive features, are the attributes that combine to define the phonemes of a language. For example, /b/ in example 1 below can be described as having the features +consonantal, −continuant, +oral, +voice, and so forth. Taken together, these features define the segment /b/. Now consider the following speech errors:

1. big and fat → pig and vat (voicing reversal; +voicing → −voicing)
2. cedars of Lebanon → cedars of Lemadon (nasality reversal; −nasal → +nasal)
3. is Pat a girl → Is bat a curl (voicing reversal)
4. he's a vile person → he's a file person (voicelessness anticipation, +voice → −voice)

In example 1, the /b/ in the intended word *big* is a voiced bilabial stop and the /f/ in *fat* is a voiceless labiodental fricative. The /b/ and /f/ were not reversed; only the voicing feature was exchanged, which resulted in the production of the voiceless bilabial stop /p/ and the voiced labiodental fricative /v/. If we represent each feature as having a binary value, for example [+/−voicing], then in example 1 we see that the [+voicing] value of /b/ and the [−voicing] value of /f/ are reversed; all other feature values remain as the speaker intended. Thus, features must also be units in speech production.

One interesting finding about phonological feature errors is that features of consonants never exchange with or influence the features in vowels and vice versa. This fact supports the more recent views in phonological theory that suggest that segments have hierarchical structure, as opposed to earlier views that segments are bundles of unordered features (Clements, 1983; Archangeli, 1988; McCarthy, 1982).

Errors occurring in the production of American Sign Language (ASL) are similar to the kinds of errors discussed above. Thus, in Figure 7.2, the signer exchanged the hand configurations of two signs and kept other aspects of the sign as originally intended.

THE SYLLABLE.   It has been suggested that in addition to segments and features, syllables constitute "unit(s) in the phonemic programming system" (Nooteboom, 1969; MacKay, 1969; MacKay, 1970; Fromkin, 1968, 1971). Errors do occur in which syllables that have no morphemic status (have no meaning by themselves) are disordered:

1. unanimity of opinion → unamity of opinion (syllable deletion)
2. Morton and Broadbent point out → Morton and Broadpoint
3. Stockwell and Schacter → Schachwell and Stockter

Errors such as those above, in which nonmorphemic syllabic strings are disordered, are rare compared to other types of segmental errors. The major argument in support of the syllable as a processing unit is based on the fact that exchanged syllables seem to "obey a structural law with regard to syllable place"; that is, initial segments replace initial segments, and final syllables exchange with final syllables

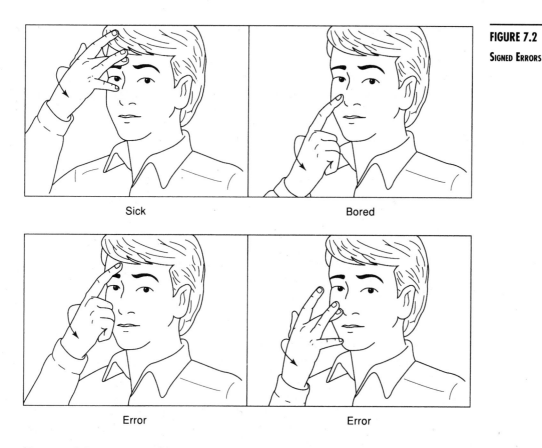

Sick

Bored

Error

Error

FIGURE 7.2

SIGNED ERRORS

(Boomer & Laver, 1968a, b). MacKay (1969) also found that the "syllabic position of reversed consonants was almost invariably identical."

The fact that in errors, syllable initial segments interact with initial segments, medial with medial, and final with final supports the "contemporary metrical theory (of phonology) in a straightforward way" (Garrett, 1988), further showing that linguistic theory and psycholinguistic processing interface in critical ways.

STRESS.   Controversy continues as to whether word and phrasal stress are manipulatable processing units. Fromkin (1977) argues—again from speech error data—that because stress can be disordered like other phonemic features, it should be viewed as an independent production unit. Such errors are exemplified below: (The stressed syllable is given in uppercase letters.)

1. apples of the Origin → apples of the oRIgin
2. moBILity → mobiLIty
3. eCONomists → ecoNOMists, I mean, eCONomists
4. phoNEtic → PHOnetic

Gandour (1977), in his study of speech errors in Thai, a tone language in which the pitch of a syllable may contrast meaning, shows that tone can also be disordered in slips of the tongue. Cutler (1980b), however, argues that what appears to be disordering of stress might really be a lexical error in which the wrong derived word is selected. For example, she would explain the stress error in example 3 as one in which the speaker incorrectly selected the word "ecoNOmics" instead of "eCONomists," and then corrected the selection error. However, one does find stress errors in which it is difficult to find related words with a different stress pattern.

Word, Morpheme, and Phrase Units in Speech Production.

Both speech error and disfluency patterns provide information about possible basic units used in generating sentences. We will review each of these types of data and explain how each contributes to an understanding of how a thought is eventually encoded into spoken utterances.

WORD SELECTION AND PLACEMENT ERRORS   No one would question that words are discrete units in the production process, even if errors such as those below were rare, which they are not.

1. tend to turn out → turn to tend out (word exchange)
2. I love to dance → I dance to love (exchange)
3. I really must go → I must really go (word movement)

In other kinds of speech errors, words are also misselected, which provides interesting evidence for the nature of lexical retrieval and the representation and organization of our mental dictionaries, issues which are discussed in Chapter 4.

LEXICAL SEARCH AND PAUSAL PHENOMENA   Lexical search, or the process by which the individual words are retrieved from the mental dictionary, is also reflected in patterns of speech disfluency. For example, hesitations (unfilled pauses) are more likely to occur before content words such as nouns, verbs, and modifiers, than before function words such as articles, helping verbs, and so forth (Maclay & Osgood, 1959). Pauses are also longer before content words than function words (Boomer, 1965). Such patterns suggest that the speaker does not yet have his lexical target available for the next stage in the production process. Further, hesitations are more likely to occur before less commonly used words in the language, suggesting a more difficult process of lexical access than for more frequently used words.

MORPHEMES AND SPEECH ERRORS   The basic unit of meaning in language is not the word but the morpheme; thus, all categories of morphological units serve as production building blocks. Stem morphemes, such as *easy* in the word *easily,* derivational morphemes such as the *-ly* in *easily* or *un-* in *unhappy,* and inflectional morphemes such as the plural endings in *ministers, churches,* or *priests* undergo rearrangement in different kinds of errors.

The separation of stem morphemes from affixes (inflectional or derivational prefixes or suffixes) shows that such affixes function as independent processing units, as the examples below reveal. Furthermore, the production of "possible" but nonoccurring derived forms shows that, at least in some cases, complex words may be formed during speech in addition to being selected from the mental dictionary.

Inflectional morpheme errors:

1. rules of word formation → words of rule formation
2. we have a lot of ministers in our church → we have a lot of churches in our minister
3. I'd forgotten about that → I'd forgot abouten that
4. cow tracks → track cows
5. it's not only us who have screws loose → . . . have screw looses

Derivational morpheme errors:

1. easily enough → easy enoughly
2. the introduction of the subject → the introducting of the subject
3. there's a good likelihood → there's a good likeliness
4. they can't quite make it → they can't quitely make it

GRAMMATICAL RULES   Rules of inflectional and derivational morphology *surface* in speech errors through production of nonoccurring, morphologically complex forms, and errors in morphological rule application (when a speaker fails to apply the rule when it fits or applies the rule when it does not fit). Here are some examples in which grammatical rules are misapplied:

1. the last I *knew* about it → . . . I *knowed* about it
2. I don't know that I'd *know* one if I *heard* it → . . . that I'd *hear* one if I *knew* it
3. bunnies [s=/z/] don't eat steak → steaks [s=/s/] don't eat bunny
4. an aunt's (/s/) money → a money's (/z/) aunt
5. he always keeps a pack → he always packs a keep
6. a watch*ed* (/t/) pot never boils → a pot*ted* (/əd/) watch never boils

In each of the above cases, although the speaker produces an error, the "slip" reveals knowledge of grammatical morphology, including how grammatical morphemes are to be pronounced when they are affixed to differing stems. Note that in example 3, while the plural is pronounced /z/ when the stem is *bunny,* it is pronounced /s/ when it "slips" to *steak.* Such an error additionally reveals something about the *stages* involved in speech production, an issue to which we will return later in this chapter.

The Phrase as a Planning Unit

THE PHRASE AS A UNIT IN SLIPS OF THE TONGUE. Various evidence supports the view that even larger linguistic structures function as units in the speech production process. We discuss below how these units are formed and the role they play in what has been called the planning aspects of speech; here we simply wish to point out that sentence constituents such as noun phrases, verb phrases, and prepositional phrases are in some way *marked off* as units when we speak. Consider, for example, the following speech errors, in which more than one word is involved.

1. A hummingbird was attracted by *the red color* of the feeder → *the red color* was attracted by *a hummingbird* of the feeder.
2. *My sister* went to *the Grand Canyon* → *the Grand Canyon* went to *my sister.*

Both examples show the exchange or reversal of two noun phrases. Interestingly, the noun phrases retain their internal organization, and two identical types of grammatical constituents are exchanged. One form of error that is theoretically possible, but never seen is that in which the final word of one constituent phrase and the first word of a following phrase are disordered, as in the following:

My sister went to *the Grand Canyon* → My *canyon* to the grand *sister went.*

The absence of such speech errors suggests that notions such as noun phrase, verb phrase, prepositional phrase, and so forth, represent types of units that play some role in the speech production process and that may be inadvertently exchanged.

SELF-CORRECTIONS AND RETRACINGS. It has also been observed that when a speaker notices an error and proceeds to correct it **(self-correction,** also called **retracing),** the correction is more apt to occur at the beginning of the syntactic constituent in which it occurs than at the actual error site. The speaker backtracks to the beginning of the constituent containing the speech error. Clark and Clark (1977) suggest that a speaker will self-correct by saying, "The doctor looked up Joe's nose—that is, up Joe's left nostril," rather than saying, "The doctor looked up Joe's nose, that is, left nostril." Although this is not always the case, the fact that most corrections do take place at the beginnings of syntactic phrases supports such units as one type of building block in the speech production process.

Similar findings were obtained in an earlier study conducted by Maclay and Osgood (1959) of repetitions in the recorded speech of speakers at a conference. They also found that when a speaker repeats himself, he most often goes back to a constituent break to begin the repetition. Thus, if a speaker intends to say, "Speech errors provide evidence for constituent boundaries" and stops after *evidence,* he will then say, "Speech errors provide evidence—(pause) provide evidence for, . . ." rather than, "Speech errors provide evidence (pause) evidence for . . ."

PAUSAL PHENOMENA. Pauses serve many functions in connected discourse. Speakers need to breathe every so often between utterances, and this is reflected in pause time. However, pausing is also a reflection of the language encoding process. Pauses are likely to occur at clause boundaries or other major structural breaks, as well as before certain lexical decision points, as discussed above (Goldman-Eisler, 1968; Boomer, 1965). This distribution is evident even when speakers are asked not to breathe during the production of short messages, thus removing the need to breathe as a factor in pausal phenomena (Grosjean, Grosjean, & Lane, 1979). Such positioning implies that speakers may be using the pause time to encode the following clause. Research by Lindsley (1975) suggests that speakers attempt to preplan their utterances before uttering them, and that such a strategy may demand lead time. Specifically, subjects in Lindsley's experiments took longer to initiate subject-verb captions for pictures than to initiate simpler subject captions. Such latency behaviors presumably reflect speakers' tendencies to pre-encode the verb that follows before producing sentential subjects.

Syntactically more complex speech tends to include more hesitations (unfilled pauses) and filled pauses (Rochester & Gill, 1973; Cook, Smith, & Lalljee, 1974), suggesting that more difficult constructions require more planning time for their execution. Indeed, experimental evidence suggests that some degree of pausing is *necessary* for successful speech production. Beattie and Bradbury (1979) designed an experiment in which speakers received feedback (in the form of a light) whenever they produced a pause of more than 600 milliseconds duration while narrating stories. The speakers, however, were not aware that this was the basis for the feedback; rather, they were told that the appearance of the light indicated poor storytelling. Even though speakers were instructed to view the light as indicative of storytelling ability, long pauses decreased by approximately 35% during the course of the experiment. However, the accuracy and quality of the speakers' output diminished in other respects, showing increased repetition and backtracking. By encouraging the speakers to avoid pauses, the experiment led to more production errors. Such a finding strongly suggests that pauses reflect active sentence planning effort on the part of speakers.

How Far Ahead Do We Plan?

Syntactic phrases have hierarchical structure—larger phrases include smaller phrases. A sentence or clause may be composed of constituent clauses, which in turn are composed of various syntactic phrases. An examination of speech errors in which words are exchanged, such as those in the section on word selection and placement errors on page 318, reveals that the largest percentage of such errors involves words in the same clause. Garrett (1975, 1976) found that 85% of word-exchange errors involved elements within a single clause; in Fromkin's corpus, 79% of such errors involved words in the same clause. This implies that speech is planned in clausal units. It must be noted, however, that 15% of the word-exchange errors in Garrett's corpus and 21% of those in the Fromkin corpus involved elements from more than one clause, which shows that before producing speech, the speaker plans quite far ahead and builds syntactic structures in advance.

Evidence from another source indicates that speech is planned in clausal units. In conversational speech, certain sequences of sounds often undergo rule-governed changes. For example, in English, a /d/ or a /t/ followed by a /y/ is often pronounced as /ʤ/ or /ʧ/ (did you → didzyu). However, such phonological processes apply less often across clause boundaries, indicating that the rules operate primarily within clausal units (contrast *The chef fixed the soup and then MADE YOUR sandwich* and *The chef fixed the soup and the MAID YOUR sandwich*) (Cooper & Paccia-Cooper, 1980).

Thus, both by observing spontaneous speech and through controlled experiments, the units involved in speech production are revealed: phonological segments and features, morphemes and words, and syntactic phrases and clauses.

WHAT SPEECH ERROR DATA SUGGEST ABOUT THE PROCESS OF SPEECH PRODUCTION

Even in attempting to determine the units used in production, we see that speech production is highly complex. The complexity is increased by how these units are accessed, selected, manipulated, and organized into hierarchical structures. We do not simply string them together, and even the errors we produce have constraints on what can occur. The question that any theory or model of speech production must address is how a speaker constructs an intended message out of these units. What are the stages of this process?

In trying to answer these questions, linguists and psycholinguists have constructed speech production models. A scientific model works only to the extent that it can account for the observable phenomena of interest and can predict further phenomena. Models can be simply descriptive or theoretical; the long-range goal in any empirical science is the construction of theoretical, explanatory models.

Speech Is Planned in Advance

Before examining some of the speech production models that have been developed, it may be helpful to summarize the data that such models must account for. First, anticipation and exchange errors (whether phonological, lexical, or syntactic) show that speech is not produced one unit at a time. As Lashley (1951) pointed out, prior to articulation the speaker must have access to a representation that includes more than one word, and in fact may include more than one clause. Furthermore, Lashley echoed Fournié's (1887) view of "speech (as) the only window through which the physiologist can view the cerebral life," and used the complex nature of language production to argue that an associative stimulus–response chain theory cannot account for the "multiplicity of integrative processes" underlying speech production. Lashley proposed "a series of hierarchies of organization: the order of vocal movements in pronouncing the word, the order of words in the sentence, the order of sentences in the paragraph" (Fournié, 1887, quoted by Lashley). The levels in this hierarchy can be viewed as stages in the production process, with the possibility of disordering occurring at any stage. A viable model of production must, therefore, posit all and only the necessary stages, showing which errors (and other disfluencies) could occur at which level or stage, and predict the form of the utterance representation at that level.

The Lexicon Is Organized Both Semantically and Phonologically

Second, in word substitution errors and word blends, words involved are semantically or phonologically similar or both. Fay and Cutler (1977), Cutler and Fay (1982), and Hurford (1981) show that in such speech errors the target word and substituted word share significantly similar initial segments, stress placement, morphological structure, and phonological form. Other studies (Fromkin, 1973, 1988; Garrett, 1988) also note the semantic similarities of affected words in slips of the tongue:

1. That's a horse of another color → . . . a horse of another race (semantic substitution)
2. Too many irons in the fire → too many irons in the smoke (semantic substitution)
3. White Anglo-Saxon Protestant → . . . prostitute (phonological substitution)
4. Grab/reach → greech (semantic blend)
5. Gin and tonic → gin and topic (phonological)
6. Arrested and prosecuted → arrested and persecuted (phonological/semantic)
7. At 4:30 we're adjourning the meeting → we're adjoining the meeting (phonological)
8. Stiffer/tougher → stougher or stuffer (semantic/phonological blend)
9. Edited/annotated → editated (semantic blend)

Chapter 4 discusses the representation and organization of morphemes and words in the mental lexicon and how these are accessed and retrieved during speech production and comprehension. The models of speech production discussed here assume that errors in lexical selection (retrieving the wrong word for a concept) are accounted for by the nature of lexical organization. That is, the choice of inappropriate lexical items may occur because synonyms, antonyms, and similar sounding words are stored in close proximity to a given target word, and thus may be retrieved in error. Such erroneous selection, however, must occur at a stage after the syntactic form class of the target words has been determined, because word substitutions and blends do not create ungrammatical strings, as the previous examples reveal. These examples illustrate that nouns substitute for nouns, verbs for verbs, and so forth. Such behavior indicates that the speaker has already determined the grammatical form class of a target word.

Some lexical selection errors seem to fall into the category of "Freudian slips," the result of unconscious "competing plans" (Baars, 1980), or nonlinguistic interference, either internally or externally induced. Such external influences may combine with linguistic factors, which could help to trigger their occurrence. A speaker's comment, "He made hairlines," produced in place of the intended, "He made headlines," when referring to a barber may be such an error. We know little about the ways in which linguistic and nonlinguistic factors intersect during speech and will thus leave this interesting issue until further research provides some answers.

Morphologically Complex Words Are Assembled

Other errors in which possible but nonoccurring morphologically complex words are produced also occur:

1. A New Yorker → a New Yorkan (cf. America/American)
2. The derivation of the surface form → the derival of the surface form (cf. recital or quittal)

As in the case of word-substitution errors, one can assume that these derivational errors occur in the lexicon prior to *lexical insertion* (the stage at which words are placed into the intended utterance). What they show is that the morphological rules for word formation posited by linguists are actively engaged during speech production, and that morphologically complex items are compiled, even if they are stored as wholes (with morphological boundaries included).

Some word substitutions occur that appear to be influenced by previous words in the string—they appear to be horizontally or *syntagmatically* conditioned:

1. It spread like wildfire → it spread like wildflower
2. Sesame-seed crackers → sesame street crackers
3. Chamber music → chamber maid
4. Gave birth at midnight → gave birth at midwife

Examples 1, 2, and 3 appear to be lexical selection errors similar to those in the previous example, if one assumes that *wildflower, sesame street,* and *chamber maid* are listed as noun compounds in the mental dictionary. One may then posit that the speaker selected a lexical entry that was listed in close proximity to the intended item. In example 4, however, the semantic relatedness between *birth* and *midwife* suggests that after *birth* was selected, as well as the intended *midnight, midwife* was incorrectly selected because of its phonological similarity and its active priming.

Errors involving word stem and affix morphemes were discussed in an earlier section. In particular, speech errors involving affix placement suggest that inflectional and derivational morphemes are stored and processed differently from words and word stems in the speech production process.

Although words and stems are often involved in exchanges or reversals, neither inflectional (for example, past tense, plural) nor derivational (for example, the *-er* of *singer)* morphemes are. For example, a past-tense marker does not appear to exchange position with a comparative form.

In the following examples of such exchanges, note that prepositions sometimes are exchanged, and pronouns, although they primarily exchange with pronouns, also may exchange with nouns or noun phrases.

1. Rules of word formation → words of rule formation
2. I left the cigar in my briefcase → I left the briefcase in my cigar
3. I don't know that I'd know one if I heard it → I don't know that I'd hear one if I knew it
4. Rubber hose and lead pipe → rubber pipe and lead hose
5. When the story hits the paper → when the paper hits the story

but **not:**

6. a big bird in the alder tree → the big bird in an alder tree

Note that in example 3 the verbs *know* and *hear* are shifted, but not in their inflected form; *heard* becomes *hear* and *know* becomes *knew*. That is, the verbs were exchanged (but the past-tense marker meant to be applied to *hear* remained behind) before the past-tense marker was applied to yield the final appropriate form of the new word, *knew*. Sentence 3 could only result from a discrete stage at which affixes are combined with their roots. This will be discussed again below.

In examples 1 and 3 above, and in those below, we see that inflectional morphemes may be "stranded" (left behind) in exchange errors; they are, however, seldom involved in exchanges.

1. Cow track<u>S</u> → track cow<u>S</u>
2. Minister<u>S</u> in our church → church <u>ES</u> in our minister
3. I hope<u>D</u> he would like Chris → I like<u>D</u> he would hope Chris

but **not:**

4. The boy<u>S</u> are go<u>ING</u> → the boy<u>ING</u> are goe<u>S</u>

Stranding errors reveal another phenomenon that must be accounted for in a viable production model. When grammatical morphemes are stranded, they are "fixed up" according to the phonological and morphological rules of the language (Fromkin, 1971; Bierwisch, 1982). Such "accommodations" also occur with some grammatical morpheme substitutions, anticipations, or perseverations:

An eating marathon → A meeting arathon

Note that when the initial segment of *marathon* is anticipated and inserted at the beginning of *eating,* the indefinite article does not surface as *a* (as it would have in the intended utterance) but as *an,* in keeping with the morphological rules of English. Similarly, when the stems in *cow track̲S̲* → track cow̲S̲ are exchanged, the stranded plural morpheme attached to *cow* is phonetically /z/, although had the exchange not occurred, the plural suffix for *track* would have been /s/. Thus, at the stage where the accommodation process occurs, these units must be marked as grammatical morphemes or the rule for appropriate phonological realization would not apply.

Affixes and Functors Behave Differently From Content Words in Slips of the Tongue

Garrett (1976, 1984, 1988) points out that affix morphemes and minor sentence elements (adverbs, intensifiers, determiners) may be "moved" or "shifted," whereas the major category stems and words (nouns, verbs, and adjectives) tend to be involved in exchange errors but seldom participate in shift errors. The following examples illustrate this tendency. Another difference between the two types of speech errors is pointed out by Cutler (1980), who notes that, whereas "exchanges preserve (phrasal) stress, shifts often distort it."

1. I frankly admit to being subjective → I admit to frankly being subjective
2. Did you stay up very late last night? → did you stay up late very last night?
3. I'd forgotten about that → I'd forgot abouten that
4. That would be the same as adding ten → as add tenning
5. if she wantS (-/s/) to come here → if she want to comeS (/-z/) here
6. Jerry'S (/-z/) Pancake House → Jerry Pancake'S (/-s/) House

Speech Errors Reflect Rule Knowledge

The remaining phenomena to be accounted for in a viable production model concern different categories of grammatical rules. It has already been shown that rules of inflectional and derivational morphology "surface" in speech errors through accommodation mechanisms and the creation of nonlexicalized, morphologically complex words. The productive use of such rules (or constraints on proper formation) is also shown in utterances where a regular rule has applied to an irregular or exceptional form, when a rule that should apply does not, or when a rule is mistakenly applied:

1. The last I KNEW about it → . . . I KNOWED about it
2. He SWAM in the pool → he SWIMMED in the pool
3. The CHILDREN are in the park → the CHILDS are—I mean the children are in the park
4. She was so DRANK when she called him
5. I don't know whether anyone has SAW the review

6. It took you longer to read it than it took me to WROTE it

7. How angry he is → how angry he AM

Such phonological specification of inflectional morphemes must occur at the same level as that at which the accommodation of stranded morphemes occurs—at the stage of representation before the **phonemicization** of these morphemes, the point at which the phonological composition of the target morphemes is specified.

The mental grammar accessed during production also includes syntactic rules and constraints that determine which sentences in a language are well formed or grammatical and which are not. These include movement rules, subcategorization constraints (for example, that a transitive verb must be followed by a noun-phrase object), selectional restrictions (for example, that some verbs, such as *love* or *cry,* must co-occur with an animate subject), among others. When speakers who "know better" violate these constraints, they produce ungrammatical sentences or syntactic speech errors:

1. Does it sound different → does it hear different

2. She swore me to secrecy → she promised me to secrecy

3. They seem to know where the problem is → they seem they know . . .

4. Turkish and German don't have the third dimension, so does Swedish.

5. It would be of interesting to see.

6. She made him to do the assignment over.

7. John is going, isn't it?

8. This is something that we should discuss about.

9. He not seem happy now.

10. It's almost all finished → it's all almost finished

11. She was waiting her husband for.

12. But when you will leave?

Some of these syntactically deviant sentences may arise from sentence blends, a combination of two sentence options into one. Example 3 may be a blend of *they seem to know/they know,* and 5 might be a blend of *it would be interesting/it would be of interest.* Such ill-formed syntax must arise at the level or stage in speech production when the syntactic structure of the utterance is being planned and constructed.

SPEECH PRODUCTION PROCESSING MODELS

Until investigators began to seriously examine speech error and other disfluency data, psycholinguistic processing was, for the most part, limited to the comprehension side of the speech chain. In 1976, MacNeilage and Ladefoged noted that, "Very little is known about the production of language" as opposed to the production of speech sounds. Only two pages in a basic introductory textbook on psycholinguistics by

Glucksberg and Danks (1975) were devoted to production. The first speculative model that attempted to specify stages and representations in production (Fromkin, 1968) was limited to the mapping of phonemic representations onto motor commands to the muscles.

In 1971, the first model that attempted to account for the major stages and levels of representation was published (Fromkin 1971, 1973), followed by a similar and more detailed model by Garrett (1976). Both were heavily based on speech error data and take a linguistic perspective, as opposed to a psychological one, on the process of speech production (Garrett, 1982; Garman, 1990). Other models more narrowly concerned with subsections or subprocessors of the overall model have been proposed. Shattuck-Hufnagel (1986) was concerned with accounting for phonological-segmental errors; Fay and Cutler (1977) provide a detailed account of word-substitution errors. In the next sections, we will review four alternative accounts of the speech production process.

The Utterance Generator Model of Speech Production

The *Utterance Generator model* proposed by Fromkin (1971) is presented in Figure 7.3. It attempted to account for most of the speech error patterns we have previously discussed (Fromkin, 1971). The Fromkin model distinguishes six stages at which different representations of the utterance occur. The rectangular boxes in the diagram stand for the representations at each level; the diamonds symbolize the processes that translate each level of representation into the one below. It is a top-down generator without any feedback loops. The large rectangular box labeled "Lexicon" will become better specified through aphasia research, further analysis of speech errors, and psycholinguistic experiments. As Chapter 4 and this chapter demonstrate, speech errors give us a much better idea about the organization and representation of lexical items (Fromkin, 1986, 1987, 1990; Emmorey & Fromkin, 1988). The stages, representations, and processes specified in the 1971 model are summarized below.

STAGE I. A MEANING TO BE CONVEYED IS GENERATED.   As mentioned earlier, we know little about the form of the conceptual message, and we therefore cannot specify what it looks like or how it is compiled. Butterworth (1980) believes that an adequate model of speech production should account for "competing plans" at the conceptual level or at other levels, the kinds of competing plans that might produce Freudian slips. The model could also allow the generation of more than one message at Stage I that could be mapped onto one or more syntactic structures at Stage II. This could lead to speech errors such as syntactic blending—*How long does that has to— have to simmer?*—or allow multirepresentations at any of the other levels.

STAGE II. THE MESSAGE IS MAPPED ONTO A SYNTACTIC STRUCTURE.   A syntactic outline of the message is created. Semantic features or constellations of such features will later be mapped onto these structures. One reason for generating the syntax before selecting words or stems from the lexicon is that the syntactic structure determines the form and grammatical category of the words that may be chosen. The

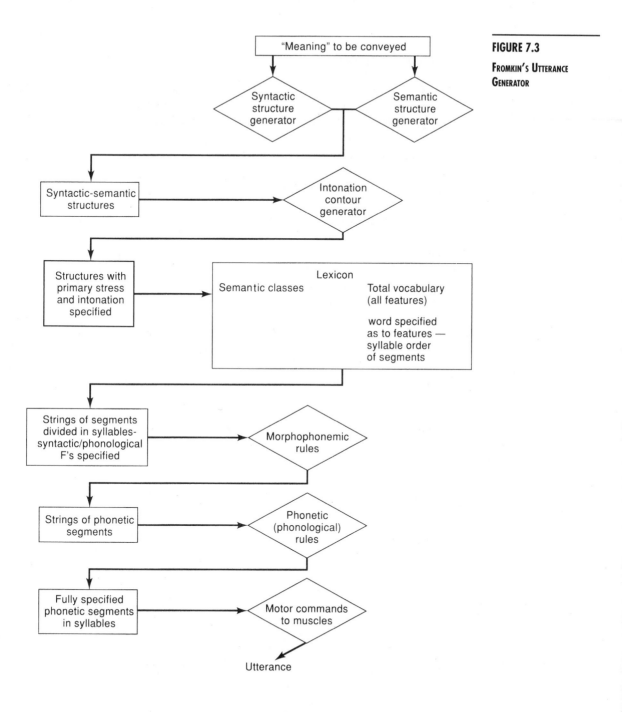

FIGURE 7.3

FROMKIN'S UTTERANCE GENERATOR

representation of the utterance at this level is thus a semantic–syntactic structure, with semantic and syntactic features marked at lexical nodes in the phrase marker.

STAGE III. INTONATION CONTOURS (SENTENCE AND PHRASAL STRESS) ARE GENERATED ON THE BASIS OF THE SYNTACTIC REPRESENTATIONS.

Intonation must be assigned before lexical selection occurs because the syntactically determined primary stress and intonation contours and lexical stress are independent of one another and exist on different prosodic tiers.

STAGE IV. WORDS ARE SELECTED FROM THE LEXICON.

The message is now represented as a syntactic structure, with semantic and syntactic features specified, and sentence and phrasal stress marked. Lexical items are now chosen on the basis of these semantic features and syntactic categories. The lexical items entered into this representation of the utterance are not fully specified, in the sense that their morphological affixes are not "spelled out" phonologically. The stems, however, are represented by phonemic segments with features specified and syllable positions serially ordered. Speech-error data discussed earlier show that the eventual phonological forms of the grammatical morphemes are not yet determined; in slips of the tongue, accommodations match morphological affixes to their stems using morphophonemic rules. Thus, the model proposes that grammatical morphemes are entered in their phonological shape at a later stage.

At this stage, errors may occur in which semantically or phonologically similar words may be selected instead of the intended words. It is also possible that in mapping these words onto the syntactic structures, phonological segments or features may be dislodged out of their specified sequential place.

STAGE V. PHONOLOGICAL SPECIFICATION.

At this level of representation, phonological pronunciation rules apply and produce fully specified phonetic segments in syllables as the output.

STAGE VI. GENERATION OF THE MOTOR COMMANDS FOR SPEECH.

The phonetic feature bundles (of segments or full syllables) are mapped onto motor commands to the muscles of the vocal tract to produce the intended (or deviant) utterance.

Such a model accounts for a large part of the data shown above as critical for a viable speech-production model. It specifies discrete planning units and explains why word substitutions tend to share phonological or semantic similarity. It accounts for the fact that phrasal stress is not disrupted when words shift or exchange position. The model predicts that grammatical morphemes could be stranded, as well as the phonological accommodation that occurs when this happens. It implicitly predicts the inclusion of words and stems and the exclusion of inflectional affixes in exchange errors by positing that at the stage where words and stems exchange, the grammatical morphemes are not yet phonologized. However, the model above does not account for the fact that major categories (nouns, verbs, adjectives) are not moved or shifted, whereas minor categories and inflectional morphemes are.

Sentences that result from possible sentence blends, such as *Where is the Grand Ball Room by any chance?*—a possible blend of *Where is the Grand Ball Room?* and *Do you know where the Grand Ball Room is by any chance?*— can be accommodated within the model by assuming the early attempt to generate multiple sentences, which become blended at a later stage. But as Butterworth (1982) points out, if the model allows initial generation of more than one sentence, we assume an "enormous proliferation of representations at lower levels, which requires the postulation of new mechanisms to sort them out in an appropriate way." Thus, the model still requires correction and enhancement.

The Garrett Model

In 1975, Garrett proposed a speech production model, also based on speech error data, that made explicit some of the implicit aspects of the Fromkin model and filled in some gaps in the model. Although it too requires refinement, this model has provided a major framework for further research in the field. Figure 7.4 presents the first version of the Garrett model, and Figure 7.5 the latest construction of the model (1984). The earlier model is presented because it includes statements of what the levels attempt to account for (Garrett, 1975, 1984).

Much overlap exists between the Fromkin and Garrett models. Both distinguish among three levels—a conceptual level, a language-specific sentence level, and a motor level of articulatory control (Garrett, 1980). At the conceptual level, Garrett's message source (Figure 7.4) and inferential processes and messages (Figure 7.5) correspond to Fromkin's *"meaning" to be conveyed.* At the sentence level, Garrett (1984) distinguishes between a *functional level*—"a multiphrasal level of planning in which the assignment of major lexical-class items to phrasal roles is accomplished." It is at this level that word exchanges involving words that have the same grammatical role occur.

A pronunciation-oriented representation occurs at the *positional level,* whereas in the Fromkin model, lexical items are retrieved with phonological form specified. In this model, it is at this level that sounds in words and sentence elements are assigned locations in the eventual surface sequence (Garrett, 1984, p. 177). At this level, form-based word substitutions (which are similar in form but not meaning) occur, as well as sound exchanges, stranding exchanges, and word and morpheme shifts.

In the Garrett model, the phonologization of grammatical morphemes takes place at the level of phonetic representation; this level is required to account for errors which show apparent alteration so that the eventual output conforms to the regular phonological constraints of the language.

Garrett's articulatory level corresponds to Fromkin's Stage VI, in which the motor commands to vocal tract produce the acoustic representation of the message.

Levelt's Model

In Levelt's (1989) model, message generation is initiated by the conceptualization of the utterance. During this early phase, an intention is conceived. The output of this

FIGURE 7.4

GARRETT'S 1975 MODEL

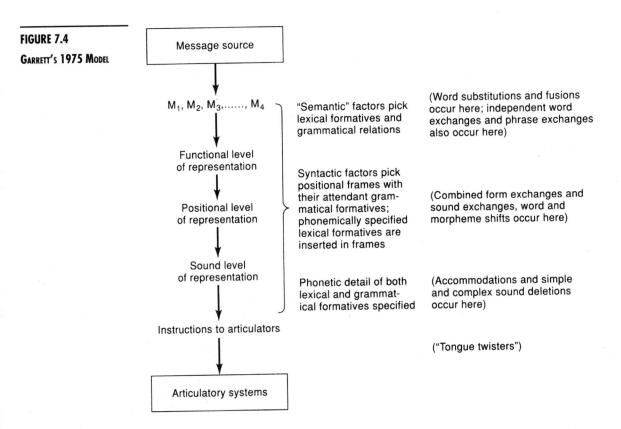

Utterance of a sentence

stage is called the *preverbal message,* which is fed to the *formulator.* The formulator is divided into two sub-components. The first is a grammatical encoder, which retrieves lexical items. Levelt distinguishes between the semantic and syntactic properties of items in the lexicon, bundled together to form **lemmas,** and the phonological information about the lemmas, which he believes are stored and accessed separately (called **lexemes**). Thus, a lemma contains an item's meaning as well as its syntactic properties, which are used to generate appropriate phrase structures. If a noun is selected, the outline of an appropriate noun phrase is generated from this selection; if a verb is selected, this drives the construction of an appropriate verb phrase. The grammatical encoder produces an appropriately ordered string of lemmas. This process is illustrated in Figure 7.6, which shows how the utterance, "She was handing him some broccoli," is assembled (from Bock & Levelt, 1994).

   The phonological encoder then takes the syntactic outline and generates a phonological plan for the utterance, which includes its eventual intonation and stress patterns. The *articulator* then executes the phonetic plan by conveying instructions to the neuromuscular system.

   Lemma information (semantic/grammatical characteristics) is retrieved before lexemic information (phonological properties of the word to be uttered). This can be

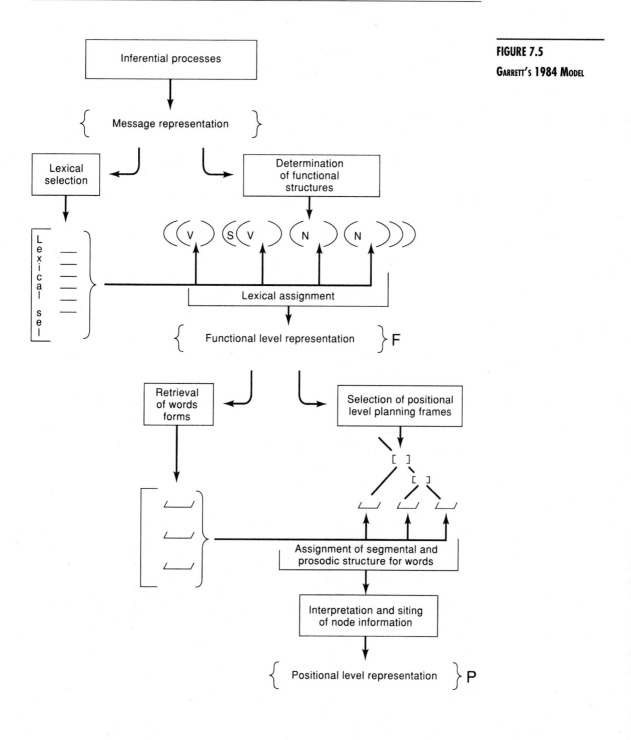

FIGURE 7.5
GARRETT'S 1984 MODEL

FIGURE 7.6

THE PRODUCTS OF FUNCTIONAL PROCESSING

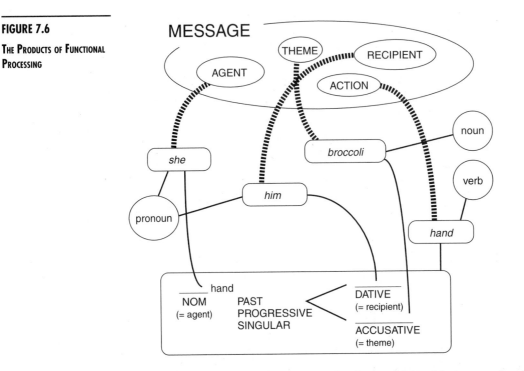

FIGURE 7.6

THE PRODUCTS OF FUNCTIONAL PROCESSING

supported by the results of experimental tasks in which subjects are primed at various points in word-naming tasks. Let us suppose that we want the subject to say the word *goat*. We can attempt to prime or facilitate this process by presenting the subject with semantically similar words, thus quickening the subject's response. In the typical case, priming with a semantically similar word, such as *sheep*, is successful only if the prime is shown before the target picture is presented. No priming results are seen if the picture has already been presented, indicating that the subject retrieves the lemma information rapidly. A schematic of Levelt's proposal for retrieving word names is shown in Figure 7.7.

Levelt further distinguishes a *speech-comprehension system* within his model of speech production. Its primary role is to monitor the output for errors. Levelt (1983, 1989) notes that attempts at self-correction while speaking suggest that speakers actively attend to **(self-monitor)** both intermediate forms of their intended utterances during processing, as well as their output. Nooteboom (1980) estimated that speakers detect up to about 75% of their phonological errors, but only about half of their lexical errors. Levelt offers the following utterances for example:

1. To the left side of the purple disk is a v—, a horizontal line.
2. How long does that has to—have to simmer?

The first suggests an error discovered before full articulatory realization, and the second demonstrates recovery from an error in a fully realized utterance.

Evidence for a monitoring function of speech comes from many sources. One type of evidence arises from experimental attempts to induce speakers to make speech

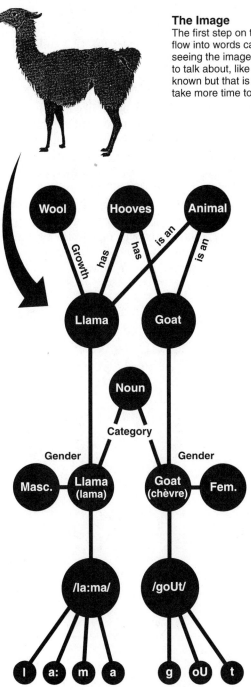

The Image
The first step on the path where thoughts flow into words can be thinking about or seeing the image of the thing you want to talk about, like a llama. A word that is known but that is not frequently used will take more time to recall.

FIGURE 7.7

Processes involved in word naming.

Adapted from Levelt's model of speech production.

Source: Dr. Willem Levelt/Max Planck Institute for Psycholinguistics

The Lexical Level, or Concept
The image activates the lexical module, or node, for llama, carrying all the information the brain has stored about llamas: an animal with hooves, wool, etc. Each node is believed to be a widely distributed network of connected neurons in the brain. Adjacent lexical nodes for related words, like sheep, goat, animal, etc., are also activated; the information is passed on to the next module for processing.

The Lemma Level
All the activated concepts are passed on to this level, where proper syntax is assigned to each one. These rules of language include word order, gender if appropriate, case markings, and other grammatical features. Meanwhile, the various activated concepts compete; usually the most highly activated wins, but the more competing concepts interfere, the longer it takes to generate the desired word.

The Lexeme Level
Turning the desired concept into a spoken word requires matching the syntactical elements from the lemma level to the sounds that make up a language, not just syllables but stresses, rhythms, and intonation. This is where the tip-of-the-tongue phenomenon occurs, perhaps because a given lexical node was not sufficiently activated to make it to the lexeme level.

errors. Baars, Motley, and MacKay (1975) used a **phonetic bias** technique. They asked readers to silently read lists of predictably-ordered, two-word strings such as *ball-dome, bath-dog,* and so forth. When subjects read aloud pairs that followed an inverted pattern, such as *darn-bore,* they occasionally responded, "barn-door." However, it is much less likely that a string such as *dart-board* will come out as *bart-doard,* presumably because the self-monitoring function checks to see if the output is lexically permissible. The editing function appears to work much like a spell-checker in a word-processing program. Its major concern is that the output contain legitimate words; it will allow through real words, even when they are not the correct selection for the phrase (just as word-processing programs will reject *the two boks* but allow *the too books* to pass freely through to print). However, if the experiment stimuli consist of nonsense words such as *bick-rint,* an error resulting in *rick-bint* (also nonsense forms) is as likely to occur as actual words produced, showing that the monitor "recognizes" that nonoccurring words are acceptable under these conditions.

Dell (1986) and others note that when speech is produced rapidly, the system has less time to spell-check its work. Thus, when speakers talk quickly, their speech errors tend to create more nonwords than if they are speaking more slowly.

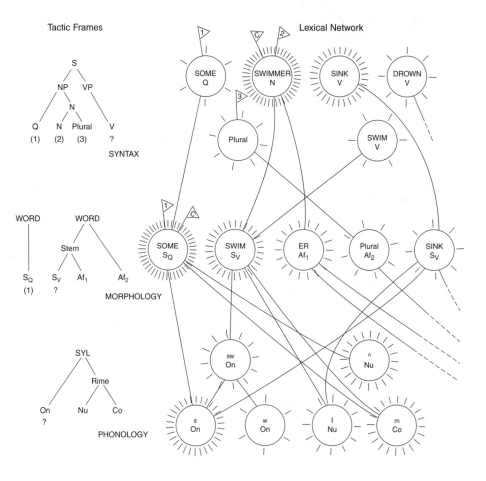

FIGURE 7.8

A moment in the production of the sentence, "Some swimmers sink." Tactic frames (left) specify an ordered set of categorically labeled slots. The numbered slots have already been filled in; a numbered flag (an order tag) has been placed on each node in the lexical network that stands for an item filling a slot. The question mark indicates the slot in each frame that is presently being filled. The highlighting surrounding the nodes reflects activation level, and the flag with a C on it marks the current node of each level. Each node is labeled for membership in some category: Syntactic categories for words are (Q)uantifier, (N)oun, (V)erb, and plural marker; morphological categories for morphemes are (S)tem and (Af)fix; and phonological categories for sounds are (On)set, (Nu)cleus, and (Co)da. Many nodes have been left out to simplify the network, including nodes for syllables, syllabic constituents, and features.

Dell's Model

The concept of spreading activation was discussed in Chapter 4 as a possible model of lexical organization and retrieval. Dell's spreading activation model of speech production (Dell, 1986) is such a connectionist model. In this model, words (and possibly rules) are organized into networks, with connections between units based on semantic and phonological relatedness. Figure 7.8 shows a hypothetical network representation for the utterance, "Some swimmers sink." The activation of a concept spreads activation to those lexical items sharing semantic features with the thought to be conveyed. For example, the speaker's thought, "swimmer," activates, among other things, a class of nouns, a class of nominal affixes such as the plural, and a class of verbs. Because of spreading activation among all nodes in the network, selection of *swimmer* also to some extent activates *drown* and *swim,* in addition to *sink*. Activation of *swimmer* and *sink* also activates aspects of their grammatical usage, as well as their phonological forms.

Because activation is presumed to be bidirectional, it is theoretically possible to have interactions between semantic and phonological representations, leading to slips that share both phonological and semantic properties with the intended output. Some examples of this have been given earlier in the chapter. Researchers have long recognized that many slips are ambiguous in this way. In an unintentionally humorous slip, one of our colleagues told us that a hotel had posted the availability of "attractive roommates (roomrates) at only $90 per night." Is this error based on phonological or semantic similarity, or both? Dell (1995) shows how a lexical network could slip from the intended output *present* to the unintended production of *prevent* (Figure 7.9).

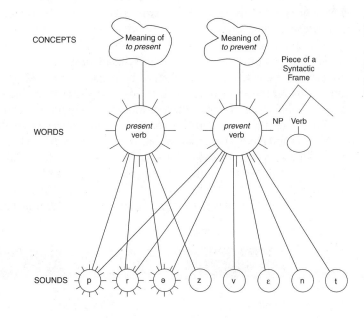

LEXICAL NETWORK

FIGURE 7.9

A piece of the lexical network shows how *present* might slip to *prevent* from the spreading of activation.

Some evidence indicates that recently retrieved lexical items can prime the speaker to make a slip. Motley and Baars (1976), using their **phonetic bias paradigm,** found that speakers were likely to create slips with semantic associations to items presented earlier. For example, the pair *get one* , in a list of *g–w* word pairs, was more likely to be "slipped" to *wet gun* if the semantically similar phrase *damp rifle* had occurred just prior to the target phrase. As Bohannon and Bonvillian (1997) note, you can easily demonstrate this tendency for "double priming" by testing a friend. Have the person say, "silk," out loud five times and then quickly force an answer to the question, "What do cows drink?" The answer is quite likely to be, "milk," which has been both phonologically and semantically primed (silk + cow), even though it is quite obviously wrong.

SUMMARY

This chapter has discussed the planning units and stages that form the bridge between a concept and its grammatical expression. The processes involved on the speaker's end of the speech chain elude easy description and explanation. One cannot go into speakers' brains and examine the mental processes and computations that are taking place when they are producing an utterance. Even the latest advances in CAT and PET scans, blood-flow analysis, and magnetic resonant imaging, all of which provide some idea of the neural activity in the brain when we are thinking, speaking, or listening, cannot tell us whether the speaker is constructing a noun phrase or a verb phrase, at what moment phrase construction occurs, or how it is accomplished.

In the attempt to understand this process, more and more linguists and psycholinguists have turned to speech error and other speech disfluency data. Deviant utterances serve as windows into the mind, showing that the semicontinuous speech signal is composed of discrete units of different sizes and kinds, that speech is not produced simply by uttering one sound, or syllable, or word at a time. Rather, these serially ordered elements are put together by means of fixed stages. By examining the constraints on the kinds of errors that occur, we have been able to construct models and posit what levels of representation and what computations can occur at each stage.

The models presented in this chapter still do not reveal all the complexities and constraints and kinds of representations that are computed in the course of producing even a single short utterance. However, by attempting to explain not only errorless production, but also those utterances that contain slips of the tongue or fluency failures, they point to the questions about the speech production process that are still unanswered, which is always the first step in the quest for understanding.

KEY WORDS

Mental grammar   *Slip of the tongue*
Speech error   *Spoonerisms*

Filled pauses
Unfilled pauses
Anticipation errors
Perseveration error
Exchange errors
Phonetic (distinctive) features
Self-correction

Retracing
Phonemicization
Lemmas
Lexemes
Self-monitor
Phonetic bias
Phonetic bias paradigm

SOMETHING TO THINK ABOUT

1. Discuss the suggestion that disfluencies are necessary for successful speech production.

2. How far in advance is speech planned? Evaluate the evidence that suggests that speech is preplanned before production.

3. Contrast the models of production advanced by Fromkin, Garrett, Levelt, and Dell. In what ways are they similar? In what ways do they differ? Which one most appeals to you, and why?

ACTIVITIES

1. Consider the kinds of speech errors discussed in this chapter. What kind of evidence do they provide for how words are represented in the mental lexicon, including such concepts as the discreteness of phonological features and segments, morphemes, words, and phrases? How do they support hypotheses that words are classified into syntactic classes (for example, noun, verb, adjective, determiner, and so forth) and semantic classes?

2. Have speakers attempt to read the following "twisters" three times rapidly and then repeat three times from memory (from Shattuck-Hufnagel, 1991). What kinds of errors were made? To what extent did the errors substantiate claims about the nature of speech errors that we have made in this chapter?
   1. How polite is the fame of the fib to police.
   2. Your lapel has the fame and the fib of Lapointe.
   3. This locale has a yen for a yacht by LaCoste.
   4. You collect if you yawn, but not yet, said Colleen.
   5. The rebuff was too wan since it's wet to rebuild.
   6. If the ribbon is wan it's too wet for a rebate.
   7. The balloon had no gun and could get the ballet.

8. From the belly a gun will not get me a ballot.
9. When the lubber is gone we can get him a lapel.
10. You defy me the tin and I talk to defend.

3. Consider the following tasks. In task 1, the subject is shown a list of color words and asked to read them. In task 2, the subject is shown circles of various colors and asked to name the colors. In task 3, the subject is shown color words, but each word is printed in a color other than that of the written word (that is, *red* is printed in green ink). The subject is asked to identify the *colors* of the stimulus items. In task 4, the subject is asked to view the same stimuli as in task 3 but to read the words. Predict which of these tasks will take longer. Explain your reasoning

 The difficulty most people experience with task 3 is known as the Stroop effect. It is consistent with the usual finding that reading words can be done more quickly than producing a word from a pictured stimulus. Reading the word in task 3 seems to inhibit easy retrieval of the ink color as requested. Develop an explanation of how this might happen.

4. It has been claimed that the two major classes of disfluencies, filled and unfilled pauses, tend to distribute differently in conversational speech. Tape record a speech sample from a friend or classmate. Examine where these two classes of disfluencies typically occur. Are there tendencies for various types of disfluencies to occur before certain types of words or at particular places in spoken sentences? What might this tell us about the role of such disfluencies in the process of speech production?

REFERENCES

Archangeli, D. (1988). Aspects of underspecification theory. *Phonology, 5,* 183–207.

Baars, B. J. (1980). The competing plans hypothesis: An heuristic viewpoint on the causes of errors in speech. In H. W. Dechert & M. Raupach (Eds.), *Temporal variables in speech.* The Hague: Mouton.

Baars, B., Motley, M., & MacKay, D. (1975). Output editing for lexical status from artificially elicited slips of the tongue. *Journal of Verbal Learning and Verbal Behavior, 14,* 382–391.

Beattie, G., & Bradbury, R. (1979). An experimental investigation of the modifiability of the temporal structure of spontaneous speech. *Journal of Psycholinguistic Research, 8,* 225–248.

Bierwisch, M. (1982). Linguistics and language error. In A. Cutler (Ed.), *Slips of the tongue and language production* (pp. 29–72). Amsterdam: Mouton.

Bock, K., & Levelt, W. (1994). Language production: Grammatical encoding. In M. A. Gernsbacher (Ed.), *Handbook of psycholinguistics* (pp. 945–984). San Diego: Academic Press.

Bohannon, J. N., & Bonvillian, J. D. (1997). Theoretical approaches to language acquisition. In J. B. Gleason (Ed.), *The development of language* (4th ed., pp. 259–316). Boston: Allyn & Bacon.

Bond, Z. S. (1969). Constraints on production errors. *Proceedings of the Chicago Linguistics Society, 5,* 302–305.

Boomer, D. (1965). Hesitation and grammatical encoding. *Language and Speech, 8,* 148–158.

Boomer, D. S., & Laver, J. D. M. (1968). Slips of the tongue. *British Journal of Disorders of Communication, 3,* 1–12.

Boomer, D. & Laver, J. (1968). Slips of the tongue. In V. Fromkin (Ed.), *Speech errors as linguistic evidence* (pp. 120–131). The Hague: Mouton.

Butterworth, B. (1980). Some constraints on models of language production. In B. Butterworth (Ed.), *Language production (Vol. 12): Speech and talk* (pp. 423–459). London: Academic Press.

Butterworth, B. (1981). Speech errors: Old data in search of new theories. *Linguistics, 19,* 627–662.

Butterworth, B. (1982). Old data in new theories. In A. Cutler (Ed.), *Slips of the tongue and language production* (pp. 73–108). Amsterdam: Mouton.

Clark, H. H., & Clark, E. V. (1977). *Psychology and language.* New York: Harcourt Brace Jovanovich.

Clements, G. N. (1988). Toward a substantive theory of features specification. In *Proceedings of the 18th Annual Meeting of the North East Linguistics Society.* Amherst, MA.

Clements, G. N., & Keyser, S. J. (1983). *CV phonology: A generative theory of the syllable.* Cambridge, MA: MIT Press.

Cook, M., Smith, J., & Lalljee, M. (1974). Filled pauses and syntactic complexity. *Language and Speech, 17,* 11–16.

Cooper, W. E., & Paccia-Cooper, J. (1980). *Syntax and speech.* Cambridge, MA: Harvard University Press.

Cooper, W. E., Paccia, J. M., & Lapointe, S. G. (1978). Hierarchical coding in speech timing. *Cognitive Psychology, 10,* 154–177.

Cowan, N., Braime, J. D. S., & Levitt, I. (1985). The phonological and metaphonological representation of speech: Evidence from fluent backward talkers. *Journal of Memory and Language, 24,* 689–698.

Cutler, A. (1979). The psychological reality of word formation and lexical stress rules. *Proceedings of the Ninth International Congress of Phonetic Sciences* (Vol. 2, pp. 79–85). Copenhagen: Institute of Phonetics.

Cutler, A. (1980a). Syllable omission errors and isochrony. In H. W. Dechert & M. Raupach (Eds.), *Temporal variables in speech* (pp. 183–290). The Hague: Mouton.

Cutler, A. (1980b). Errors of stress and intonation. In V. A. Fromkin (Ed.), *Errors in linguistic performance: Slips of the tongue, ear, pen, and hand* (pp. 67–80). New York: Academic Press.

Cutler, A. (Ed.). (1982). *Slips of the tongue and language production.* Amsterdam: Mouton.

Cutler, A., & Fay, D. (1982). One mental lexicon, phonologically arranged: Comments on Hurford's comments. *Linguistic Inquiry, 13,* 107–113.

Deese, J. (1978). Thought into speech. *American Scientist, 66,* 314–321.

Deese, J. (1980). Pauses, prosody and the demands of production in language. In H. W. Dechert & M. Raupach (Eds.), *Temporal variables in speech.* The Hague: Mouton.

Dell, G. S. (1986). A spreading activation theory of retrieval in sentence production. *Psychological Review, 93,* 283, 321.

Dell. G. S. (1995). Speaking and misspeaking. In L. Gleitman & M. Liberman (Eds.), *An invitation to cognitive science. Vol. 1: Language* (2nd ed., pp. 183–208). Cambridge, MA: MIT Press.

Denes, P. B., & Pinson, E. N. (1963). *The speech chain.* Baltimore: Waverly Press.

Emmorey, K., & Fromkin, V. A. (1988). The mental lexicon. In F. Newmeyer (Ed.), *Linguistics: The Cambridge survey III* (pp. 124–149). Cambridge: Cambridge University Press.

Fay, D., & Cutler, A. (1977). Malapropisms and the structure of the mental lexicon. *Linguistic Inquiry, 8,* 505–520.

Fodor, J. (1975). *The language of thought.* New York: Thomas Crowell.

Fodor, J., Bever, T., & Garrett, M. G. (1974). *The psychology of language: An introduction to psycholinguistics and generative grammar.* New York: McGraw-Hill.

Fournié, M. (1887). *Essai de psychologie.* Paris.

Fromkin, V. A. (1968). Speculations on performance models. *Journal of Linguistics, 4,* 47–68.

Fromkin, V. (1971). The nonanomalous nature of anomalous utterances. *Language, 47,* 27–52.

Fromkin, V. (Ed.). (1973). *Speech errors as linguistic evidence.* The Hague: Mouton.

Fromkin, V. A. (1977). Putting the emPHAsis on the wrong sylLAble. In L. M. Hyman (Ed.), *Studies in stress and accent* (pp. 15–26). Southern California Occasional Papers in Linguistics #4.

Fromkin, V. A. (Ed.). (1980). *Errors in linguistic performance: Slips of the tongue, ear, pen, and hand.* New York: Academic Press.

Fromkin, V. A. (1985). Evidence in linguistics. In R. H. Robins & V. A. Fromkin (Eds.), *Linguistics and linguistic evidence* (pp. 18–38). Newcastle upon Tyne: Grevatt & Grevatt.

Fromkin, V. A. (1987). The lexicon: Evidence from acquired dyslexia. *Language, 63,* 1–22.

Fromkin, V. A. (1988). The grammatical aspects of speech errors. In F. J. Newmeyer (Ed.), *Linguistics: The Cambridge survey* (Vol. II, pp. 117–138). Cambridge: Cambridge University Press.

Gandour, J. (1977). Counterfeit tones in the speech of Southern Thai bidialectals. *Lingua, 41,* 125–143.

Garman, M. (1990). *Psycholinguistics.* Cambridge: Cambridge University Press.

Garnham, A., Shillcock, R., Brown, G., Mill, A., & Cutler, A. (1982). Slips of the tongue in the London-Lund corpus of spontaneous conversation. In A. Cutler (Ed.), *Slips of the tongue and language production* (pp. 251–263). Berlin: Mouton.

Garrett, M. (1975). The analysis of sentence production. In G. Bower (Ed.), *Psychology of learning and motivation: Vol. 9.* New York: Academic Press.

Garrett, M. (1976). Syntactic processes in sentence production. In R. Wales & E. Walker (Eds.), *New approaches to language mechanisms* (pp. 231–256). Amsterdam: North Holland.

Garrett, M. (1980a). The limits of accommodation. In V. Fromkin (Ed.), *Errors in linguistic performance: Slips of the tongue, ear, pen, and hand* (pp. 263–271). New York: Academic Press.

Garrett, M. (1980b). Levels of processing in sentence production. In B. Butterworth (Ed.), *Language production I* (pp. 177–220). London: Academic Press.

Garrett, M. (1982). Production of speech: Observations from normal and pathological language use. In A. Ellis (Ed.), *Normality and pathology in cognitive functions.* London: Academic Press.

Garrett, M. F. (1984). The organization of processing structure for language production. In D. Caplan, A. R. Lecours & A. Smith (Eds.), *Biological perspectives on language* (pp. 172–193). Cambridge: MIT Press.

Garrett, M. F. (1988). Processes in language production. In F. J. Newmeyer (Ed.), *Linguistics: The Cambridge survey III. Language: Psychological and biological aspects* (pp. 69–96). Cambridge: Cambridge University Press.

Glucksberg, S., & Danks, J. (1975). *Experimental psycholinguistics.* Hillsdale, NJ: Erlbaum.

Goldman-Eisler, F. (1968). *Psycholinguistics: Experiments in spontaneous speech.* New York: Academic Press.

Grosjean, F., Grosjean, L., & Lane, H. (1979). The patterns of silence: Performance structures in sentence production. *Cognitive Psychology, 11,* 58–81.

Hurford, J. R. (1981). Malapropisms, left-to-right listing, and lexicalism. *Linguistic Inquiry, 12,* 419–423.

Lapointe, S. G., & Dell, G. S. (1989). A synthesis of some recent work in sentence production. In G. N. Carlson & M. K. Tanenhaus (Eds.), *Linguistic structure in language processing* (pp. 107–156). Dordrecht, Boston, London: Klower.

Lashley, K. S. (1951). The problem of serial order in behaviour. In L. A. Jeffress (Ed.), *Cerebral mechanisms in behaviour* (pp. 112–136). New York: Wiley.

Lashley, K. S. (1958). Cerebral organization and behaviour in the brain and human behaviour. *Proceedings of the Association for Research in Nervous and Mental Diseases, 36,* 1–18.

Levelt, W. (1983). Monitoring and self-repair in speech. *Cognition, 14,* 41–104.

Levelt, W. (1989). *Speaking: From intention to articulation.* Cambridge, MA: MIT Press.

Lindsley, J. (1975). Producing simple utterances: How far ahead do we plan? *Cognitive Psychology, 7,* 1–19.

MacKay, D. (1969). Effects of ambiguity on stuttering: Toward a model of speech production at the semantic level. *Kybernetick, 5,* 195–208.

MacKay, D. (1970). Spoonerisms: The structure of errors in the serial order of speech. *Neuropsychologia, 8,* 323–350. Reprinted in V. Fromkin (Ed.), *Speech errors as linguistic evidence.* The Hague: Mouton.

MacKay, D. (1972). Lexical insertion, inflection, and derivation: Creative processes in word production. *Journal of Psycholinguistic Research, 8,* 477–498.

Maclay, H., & Osgood, C. E. (1959). Hesitation phenomena in spontaneous English speech. *Word, 15,* 19–44.

MacNeilage, P., & Ladefoged, P. (1976). The production of speech and language. In E. C. Carterette & M. P. Friedman (Eds.), *Handbook of perception, 7,* 75–120. New York: Academic Press.

McCarthy, J. (1982). Prosodic templates, morphemic templates, and morphemic tiers. Part I. H. van der Hulst & N. Smith (Eds.), *The structure of phonological representations, I and II.* Dordrecht: Foris.

Meringer, R. (1908). *Aus dem Leben der Sprache.* Berlin: Behrs Verlag.

Meringer, R., & Mayer, K. (1895). *Versprechen und Verlesen: eine psychologisch-linguistische Studie.* Stuttgart: Göschense Verlagsbuchhandlung. [New edition 1978, A. Cutler & D. Fay. (Eds.). Amsterdam: Benjamins.]

Motley, M., & Baars, B. (1976). Semantic bias effects on the outcomes of verbal slips. *Cognition, 4,* 177–187.

Nooteboom, S. G. (1969). The tongue slips into patterns. In A. G. Sciarone, A. J. van Essen, & A. A. van Raad (Eds.), Nomen Society, *Leyden studies in linguistics and phonetics* (pp. 114–132). The Hague: Mouton.

Nooteboom, S. (1980). Speaking and unspeaking: Detection and correction of phonological and lexical errors in spontaneous speech. In V. Fromkin (Ed.), *Errors in linguistic performance.* New York: Academic Press.

Pillsbury, W. B., & Meader, C. L. (1928). *The psychology of language.* New York: Appleton.

Rochester, S., & Gill, J. (1973). Production of complex sentences in monologues and dialogues. *Journal of Verbal Learning and Verbal Behavior, 12,* 203–210.

Shattuck-Hufnagel, S. (1986). The role of word-onset consonants: Speech production priming. In E. Keller & M. Moprik (Eds.), *Motorsensory processes.* Hillsdale, NJ: Erlbaum.

Shattuck-Hufnagel, S. (1991). The role of word structure in segmental serial ordering. In W. Levelt (Ed.), *Lexical access in speech production* (pp. 213–260). Cambridge, MA: Blackwell.

Stemberger, J. P. (1982). The nature of segments in the lexicon: Evidence from speech errors. *Lingua, 56,* 235–259.

Stemberger, J. P., & Treiman, R. (1986). The internal structure of word-initial consonant clusters. *Journal of Memory and Language, 25,* 163–180.

Chapter 8

LANGUAGE ACQUISITION

Jean Berko Gleason
Boston University

Nan Bernstein Ratner
University of Maryland

INTRODUCTION

Adults have always been fascinated by the almost miraculous unfolding of language in children. Although born completely without language, by the time they are 3 or 4 years old, children typically have acquired thousands of vocabulary words, complex grammatical and phonological systems, and equally complex rules for how to use their language appropriately in many social settings. These accomplishments occur in every known society, whether literate or not, in every language from Afghan to Zulu, and in almost all children, regardless of the way in which they are reared. The tools of modern linguistics and psychology have enabled us to say a good deal about *what* children learn, and the stages they may go through on the way to adult communicative competence. But we still have many unanswered questions about *how* children actually acquire language. How do they determine what words mean, or how to produce grammatical utterances that they have never heard or produced before? Researchers have been unable to agree as to *why* children learn language: Do children learn language because adults teach it to them? Or because they are genetically programmed to acquire language? Do they learn complex grammar simply because it is there, or do they learn in the service of some need to communicate with others? **Developmental psycholinguistics** is the discipline devoted to the study of language acquisition by children, and it is the topic of this chapter. Developmental psycholinguists have described the way in which children acquire language, which is in fact a quite orderly process, and they have attempted to discover the biological and social processes that make language development possible, or, perhaps, inevitable.

RESEARCH METHODS IN THE STUDY OF LANGUAGE DEVELOPMENT

Diaries and Parental Reports

The first studies—some as early as the 18th century—were almost invariably based on observations of the author's own children and were kept in the form of diaries. During the 19th century and the first half of the 20th century, many psychologists kept diary records of their children (see Bar-Adon & Leopold, 1971, for summaries of fascinating early studies such as Charles Darwin's careful notes on his son's language development). Diaries remain a valuable way to trace the development of language in individual children. One of the most famous diary studies was conducted by Werner Leopold (1948), whose work traced his daughter Hildegarde's acquisition of both English and German.

Diaries can be a valuable adjunct to other research on children's language. By themselves, diaries can be misleading; the temptation to write what is unusual or interesting, rather than what is daily and ordinary, is hard to resist. More recently, researchers have augmented and improved diary studies by giving parents who participate in language studies checklists of the words that their children are likely to acquire during their first years (Bates, Dale, & Thal, 1995; Dale, 1991; Rescorla, 1989). The checklists help parents organize their observations and remind them of the more ordinary but important things their children say that they might otherwise overlook.

Observational Data

Spurred by the dramatic changes in linguistic theory during the early 1960s discussed in Chapter 1, developmental psycholinguists began to collect tape-recorded observational data on children's language and to conduct experimental research based on children's abilities to produce and comprehend specific structures of English. The goal of much of this research was to reconcile the findings of such observational and experimental research with the predictions made by the new transformational grammars.

Some of the landmark work in developmental psycholinguistics is based on small numbers of children who were intensively observed over a number of months or years. In the 1960s at Harvard University, Roger Brown headed a project that studied the language of three children who were called Adam, Eve, and Sarah (Brown, 1973). Researchers recorded the children monthly in their homes and brought the tape recordings back to the laboratory to be transcribed. The transcriptions were studied in a weekly seminar that led to many early studies of children's developing grammatical systems. Adam, Eve, and Sarah's earliest attempts at language fostered our earliest understanding of how children acquire basic sentence structures in English, such as questions and negatives, how they acquire the grammatical morphology of English, and the possible role of adult models and feedback in the process of language development (for a complete account, see Brown, 1973; Kessel, 1988).

FIGURE 8.1

Adam, Eve, and Sarah; Brown's study children.

Eve

Adam

Sarah

Similar intensive observational studies of small numbers of English-speaking children constituted the bulk of much child language acquisition research during the 1960s (Braine, 1963; Bloom, 1970; Miller & Ervin, 1964). Although other research methods using larger numbers of subjects have characterized the study of child language both during and since that time, intensive scrutiny of small numbers of children has continued to be a major research paradigm in the field for several reasons. First, it is often necessary to study a child's linguistic attempts intensively over time to obtain a representative sample of abilities. We cannot ask children to produce their current version of an imperative or question by simply saying, "Ask me a question," for example! This makes it difficult to construct a study that will examine the typical question asked by 2-year-old children. Second, because children's earliest attempts at language are unlike adult language in both structure and pronunciation, great care must be taken to annotate in a transcript what the researcher believes the child *meant to say,* as well as how he said it. The current context, previous context, responses of adults in the environment, and factors such as pronunciation and gestural support may all be extremely relevant to understanding the child's behavior. Such a broad array of concerns is not easily coded when large numbers of children are being observed. Thus, the study of child language development can be seen as relatively detail-intensive, which has led many researchers to confine their observations to small numbers of children. Thankfully, the results of such "small n" studies are not usually in great disagreement. We will note here, and discuss in further detail later in the chapter, the rather remarkable finding that many of the behaviors observed in Adam, Eve, and Sarah's speech were in fact consistent with the results of studies of many other children observed in later years.

By the mid-1980s, many finely detailed transcripts of early child language attempts had been compiled, some of which proved useful in investigating questions the original researcher had not necessarily envisioned. The Child Language Data Exchange System (CHILDES) was developed to enable child language researchers to examine and pool language transcripts already in existence (MacWhinney & Snow,

1985). Thus, Brown's transcripts are now available to the entire child language research community, and continue to provide data for current research questions (Pinker, 1991). CHILDES collects data in many languages and on normally and atypically developing children. The computerized databank enables researchers to test their hypotheses on many subjects and provides increased precision, standardization, and automation of the many data analyses concurrently developed to describe the samples. A more detailed guide to the CHILDES database and the computer programs designed to analyze the computerized transcripts can be found in MacWhinney (1995). Figure 8.2 shows a sample transcript and the home page of the CHILDES website.

Interviews

In general, we explore children's language systems indirectly, at least in part because their metalinguistic capacities are limited; it would be difficult to ask them what their rules are or what they find acceptable. A classic example is provided by a researcher's query of Adam (Brown & Bellugi, 1964):

Interviewer: Now Adam, listen to what I say. Tell me which is better . . .

    some water or a water.

Adam: Pop go weasel.

However, when we want to study children's **metalinguistic** development, it is appropriate to ask direct questions—the nature of the child's response enables us to ascertain the stage of metalinguistic development. In one famous metalinguistic study, Papandropoulou and Sinclair (1974) asked children metalinguistic questions (questions about language) such as, "What is a word?" "What is a long word?" and, "What is a short word?" They found that young children gave responses such as *river* for the long word, and only later came to recognize a difference between the word and its referent. If you ask a 3-year-old, "What is your favorite word?" she is liable to say, "Candy." A child of 6 or 7 is more likely to produce a word whose phonetic form appeals to her, even if its referent does not. One of our favorite words (not things) is *pumpernickel.* Our least favorite, most unappetizing word is *luscious.*

Experimental Techniques

Various experimental techniques assess infant and child language knowledge. These techniques differ widely, from observation of the child's physiological response to stimuli (that is, looking or, heart-rate changes) to procedures that ask the child to supply words for pictures or activities or to point to pictures that match an auditory stimulus. Because experimental techniques are so numerous and reflect the particular aspect of language the experimenter wishes to assess, we will cover them in greater detail in the sections that follow.

FIGURE 8.2A

A sample CHILDES transcript.

@Begin
@Participants: CHI Adami Child, MOT Nan Mother, SIS Jamie Sister, FAT Bob Father
@Age of child: 4;3.
@Date: 10-APR-1991
@Coder: Rachel Brown
@Coding: CHAT 1.0
*CHI: toy-s.
%pho: toiz.
%mod: toiz.
*CHI: after [*] my book.
%pho: afU mai bUk.
%mod: &ft3 mai bUk.
%gls: we will play after my book.
*CHI: this [*] is not [*] my book.
%pho: dIs Iz nad mai bUk.
%mod: DIs Iz nat mai bUk.
%gls: this is not my book.
*MOT: this is not your book?
*CHI: you-'re [*] just say-ing it.
%pho: n3r dZAS SejIN It.
%mod: j3r dZAs sejIN It.
%gls: you're just saying it.
*MOT: Well these are the pictures of our trip to Disney World.
*CHI: i want [*] two april-s in my xxx.
%pho: ai wAnt tu eprOlz In mai xxx.
%mod: ai want tu eprAlz In mai xxx.
%gls: i want two aprils xxx.
*CHI: xxx.
%pho: In dIs bO.
%mod: xxx.
%gls: xxx.
*MOT: you want two aprils?
*MOT: maybe we can give Jamie a different april.
*MOT: i might have a different april.
*MOT: what did you say about april?
*MOT: what's funny about april's name?
*CHI: me tell april.
%pho: ni [*] ter [*] eprO [*].
%mod: ai tEl eprAl.
%gls: I tell april.
*MOT: you did what April?
*CHI: me [*] tell [*] april [*] ‹is› [/] is on a calendar [*] day.
%pho: ni ter eprO iz iz an e kaundO de.
%mod: mi tel eprAl iz iz an e k&lInd3 de.
%gls: i tell april she is a calendar day.
*MOT: you're going to tell april that her name is on a calendar?
*CHI: yes.
%pho: jEs.
%mod: jEs.
%gls: yes.
%com: mother laughs.

Child Language Data Exchange System (CHILDES)

This is the home page for the Child Language Data Exchange System (CHILDES). From here you can access:

- the CHILDES database. Here you will find an enormous amount of child language transcript data from scores of projects in dozens of languages. Everything is in a consistent format called "CHAT" that facilitates the running of the "CLAN" programs.
- data files in the database are combined and compressed into .zip files. If you are lucky, your web browser already knows how to transfer and unpack .zip files. If not, you may need to learn how to set it up to "pass off" these files to a helper application like WinZip or StuffIt. If you are using a Macintosh, you may need a freeware copy of StuffIt Expander which you can get from here. If you are using MS-DOS, you can get a copy of pklte112.exe from here. If you are using Windows, you may need a copy of WinZip, which you can get from their site.
- the CLAN programs for analysis of the files in the CHILDES database. These files are in a self-extracting zip file for MS-DOS and .sea format for Macintosh.
- "The CHILDES Project: Tools for Analyzing Talk" by Brian MacWhinney, published by Lawrence Erlbaum Associates in 1995 and continuously updated for distribution over the net. The manual is in .pdf format and to read it you need to have a copy of Adobe Acrobat Reader 3.0 or higher installed. You can download a copy of Acrobat from Adobe's Web Site at www.adobe.com where you select the free software button. The full manual is just over 1 MB in size, so please be patient while it transfers over the net. You can transfer it to your machine by holding down the option key on the Macintosh or the shift key on Windows.
- Related resources on the study of Child Language Development as well as email addresses for child language researchers

The CHILDES system has developed a variety of computational tools that facilitate the sharing of transcript data, increase the reliability of transcriptions, and automate the process of data analysis. These new computational tools have brought about significant changes in the way that research is conducted in the child language field. Moreover, these tools have equally revolutionary potential for the areas of second language learning, adult conversational interactions, sociological content analyses, and language recovery in aphasia.

If you are accessing the InterNet from Europe, you may find it faster and more reliable to access CHILDES at one of the mirroring sites organized by Steven Gillis in Antwerp in Belgium, by Hidetosi Sirai in Chukyo in Japan, or by Colette Noyau at the Paris X server in France with a partial FTP mirror. People who use these data are asked to abide by these rules.

1. You must become a member of the CHILDES system by contacting Brian MacWhinney at macw@cmu.edu and giving your address, email address, phone number, and some information about the use you are making of the data.
2. You should acquire a copy of the second edition of the CHILDES manual that was published by Lawrence Erlbaum in March 1995. The cost is $35.00 and you can order by phoning 800 926-6579. You can also order the CHILDES CD-ROM from Erlbaum for $39.95.
3. Cite the manual in articles based on the use of the database. Also cite particular articles designated for particular corpora.
4. Assist in the growth of the database by contributing new corpora and urging your colleagues to contribute new corpora.

Please send questions and comments about CHILDES to Brian MacWhinney at macw@cmu.edu.

FIGURE 8.2B

The home page of the CHILDES website. The URL is http://poppy.psy.cmu.edu/childes/index.html.

Research Design

The design of studies can be either cross-sectional or longitudinal. **Longitudinal studies**—such as Brown's study of Adam, Eve, and Sarah—track development in the *same* subjects as they grow older. Longitudinal designs are necessary to answer certain kinds of questions, such as those that deal with the effects of children's early linguistic environment on their later acquisition of language. For instance, a longitudinal design was used to show that infants whose mothers spoke to them frequently and in short sentences at 9 months (time 1) performed better on tests of language comprehension at 18 months (time 2) than did infants of less talkative mothers (Murray, Johnson, & Peters, 1990). Longitudinal studies are usually limited in the number of individuals they can study.

Cross-sectional studies ask questions such as "How do 2-, 3-, and 4-year-old children interpret passive sentences?" They do not follow an individual 2-year-old over time to determine the answer, but instead gather groups of 2-, 3-, and 4-year-old children and assess their abilities on the task in question. They obtain a great deal of data in a short time, rather than over months or years. Studying many subjects also makes it more likely that study results can be generalized—rather than perhaps particularized to a small group of children. Cross-sectional studies include at least two groups of subjects: in order to study the development of tag questions cross-sectionally, for instance, the speech of a group of 3-year-olds and a group of 4-year-olds could be compared for their use of the tags.

Cross-sectional and longitudinal studies can be either observational or experimental. In **observational studies,** the researcher tries not to interfere with a child's natural use of language. **Naturalistic** observational studies focus on real-life situations. One example is the use of routines such as "What's the magic word?" in the speech of 24 families at home having dinner (Berko Gleason, Perlmann, & Greif, 1984). Such studies provide insight into the experiences that shape the child's linguistic socialization.

Controlled observational studies are often administered in a laboratory playroom where the setting and props are the same for all subjects. In an illustrative study, differences were observed between fathers' and mothers' speech to young language-learning children. Men and women were asked to play with their children in a laboratory playroom using particular toys provided by the research project (Bernstein Ratner, 1988). Fathers used less common vocabulary than did mothers, and repeated the names of items less often. The impact of parental input style on children's language development continues to be of great interest to many researchers, as we will discuss later in the chapter. A different type of controlled observational study might ask children to repeat adult sentences to see how well they can approximate the model (for example, Slobin & Welsh, 1971; Tager-Flusberg & Calkins, 1990). Research of this type tends to suggest that children's imitations reflect the grammatical tendencies of their spontaneously generated speech.

Experimental studies, by contrast, involve interference on the part of the researcher to discover if a particular condition does cause a predicted outcome. The **experimental group** of subjects receives a treatment chosen by the experimenter, and, for comparison purposes, a **control group** of subjects receives no special treatment. A researcher who wanted to know if training can make a difference in children's acquisition of tag questions, for instance, could split a group of 3-year-olds into a control group and an experimental group. The experimental group would receive some sort of training: They might be read stories in which many kinds of tag questions are modeled. The control group would get no special treatment. Finally, both groups could be engaged in puppet play in which the child is asked to add the tag questions to statements made by the examiner: "John can ride a bike, *can't he?*" "The dog isn't very big, *is it?*" and so forth (see Dennis, Sugar, & Whitaker, 1982, for an actual study of tag question acquisition). If the trained group performs significantly better than the control group the evidence would support the suggestion that training can cause earlier development of tag questions. Many such positive studies would have implications for theories that claim that grammatical development is innately determined and unaffected by environmental factors. In the example provided in the section above, we would have to overtly train parents to use different kinds of vocabulary with children and compare the children's pre- and postexperimental vocabulary patterns to ascertain what effect different naming strategies have on language development.

THE DEVELOPMENT OF SPEECH PERCEPTION

Methods for Studying Speech Perception in Infants

As discussed in Chapter 3, adult responses to speech stimuli can tell us much about the process of speech perception. Adults label sounds ("That's a [*b*]") or judge sounds to be the same or different. Infants cannot perform such tasks. How do we determine how infants process speech?

Infants demonstrate certain behaviors when a sound is novel or new to them. One is a higher rate of pacifier-sucking. Using this fact, researchers can perform **categorical perception** experiments on young infants (you may wish to review this concept, first discussed in Chapter 3). They will equip a pacifier with a device that measures the rate and strength of the sucking response. Next, they will play a speech sound (for example, *"ba"*) for the infant to hear. When the infant first hears this novel sound, she usually sucks vigorously. As the sound is repeated over and over, the infant's interest in it satiates and the sucking rate declines, a phase known as **habituation.** Once the sucking rate has declined, a new stimulus is played (for example, *"pa"*). If the infant's rate of sucking on the pacifier continues to decline, researchers assume that the infant does not discriminate this sound from the original sound. Conversely, if the infant's sucking rate increases, we assume that the infant considers this sound new and novel; that is, we presume the infant has discriminated between the two stimuli. Using this research design, called the **high-amplitude sucking paradigm (HASP)** (Eimas, Siqueland, Jusczyk, & Vigorito, 1971), researchers have been able to demonstrate that human infants are able to discriminate **voice-onset-time (VOT)** (Eimas et al., 1971) and place of articulation (Eimas, 1974) in an adult-like fashion at an early age (under 3 months). Another method, **cardiac deceleration,** is used in much the same way. Infants' heart rates slow and then accelerate when they are presented with novel stimuli, and researchers can record heart-rate responses to sounds much as they do in HASP experiments.

Slightly older infants are now usually tested using the **conditioned head-turn procedure** (see Polka, Jusczyk, & Rvachew, 1995, for an in-depth discussion of this technique), which can be employed with infants 6–18 months of age. In this procedure, a stimulus sound is presented repeatedly to the child. When a sound contrast is introduced, it is accompanied by the activation of an animated visual distractor located to the side of the child's line of vision. Eventually, the child learns to anticipate that sound changes provoke the interesting visual display, and the child will turn her head to look for it when she hears a sound change. Figure 8.3 demonstrates this technique.

How Speech Perception Develops

PRENATAL AUDITORY EXPOSURE AND LEARNING.   Infants can actually hear before they are born, and can demonstrate a preference for their own mothers' voices shortly after birth (Lecanuet & Granier-Deferre, 1993). They can also discriminate between utterances spoken in the mother's native language as opposed to a foreign language (Mehler et al., 1988) by about 4 days of age, which implies a certain amount of *in utero* learning. As we will note in a later section of this chapter, if some aspects of language learning occur in the womb, it becomes difficult to evaluate what aspects of language ability are an inherent part of human knowledge and what aspects are learned through exposure to the environment (Locke, 1993).

EARLY SPEECH PERCEPTION.   Chapter 3 discusses the complexities of categorical perception of speech sounds. Within a short period of time after birth, infants can demonstrate, through HASP experiments, that they perceive voice-onset-time (VOT) much as adults do, as well as utilize formant transition cues to discriminate sounds made in differing places of articulation. Similarly, they discriminate between male and female voices and between stimuli that differ in intonation contour (Kuhl, 1980). Infants also show an early preference for language that is broken into clausal chunks, rather than segmented randomly (Hirsh-Pasek et al., 1987). Such an ability is an example of a possible **bootstrapping strategy,** in which a child uses one ability (discovering clause boundaries) to make further advances in language analysis (beginning to analyze the internal structure of clauses). Finally, infants appear to understand the phonotactic regularities of their language (which sounds can appear next to other ones) by about 9 months of age, before the production of first words (Jusczyk, Luce, & Charles-Luce, 1996).

LINGUISTIC SPECIALIZATION.   As early as the first weeks of life, infants are able to make fine distinctions among speech sounds, to distinguish, for example, between voiced and unvoiced phonemes such as /p/ and /b/ in English. In fact, infants are able to make distinctions that adults cannot. Janet Werker (1984) and her colleagues have shown that Canadian babies can distinguish Czech [/ř/] from [/ʒ/], even though Canadian adults cannot hear the difference between these sounds (the first is a combination of [r] and [ʒ], as in the composer Dvořak's name, and the second is the sound [ʒ], as in the word *azure*). Thus, Werker and her colleagues have shown that infants 8 to

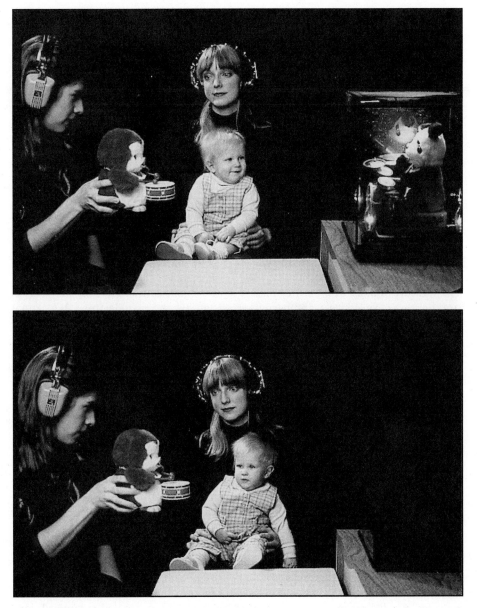

FIGURE 8.3

Changes in infant eye gaze can signal discrimination of sound differences.

10 months of age have the ability to discriminate phonemes that are not in the local language, whereas the adults in the community cannot. This ability begins to disappear by the end of the first year, when the infant has begun to learn the sounds of the language around her. Thus, **perceptual loss** is a consequence of the infant's continued interaction with her native language.

Apparently infants come prepared to hear all possible distinctions; they cannot know what language community they will be born into. When they learn their native language this special phonetic sensitivity vanishes. Work recently completed by Kuhl, Williams, Lacerda, Stevens, and Lindblom (1992) suggests that infants are beginning to narrow their perception of sounds to those in their target native language before they even begin talking, much earlier than had been previously presumed.

THE CHILD'S LEXICON

Before First Words

Parents in our society tend to anticipate their children's competencies. Not only do they assume that burps are conversational turns, they also impute intentions to their children well before the intentions are actually there. For example, they may say of a howling 2-month-old, "She wants her daddy." Late in the first year infants begin to demonstrate true intentions and to express them in a variety of prelinguistic ways. They gesture or point at what they want, they may make consistent word-like sounds, use their eyes expressively, and become persistent when misunderstood. We cannot always tell what an infant may be trying to express, but researchers believe that these early attempts at communication include both **protodeclaratives** (language about something) and **protoimperatives** (requests that something be done for or given to the infant) (Bates, 1979).

First Words

Children begin to produce recognizable words of their language at about 1 year of age (see Figure 8.4). By 18 to 20 months, they typically have acquired approximately 50 words, and by age 2, an average child knows 200–300 words (Barrett, 1995), a steep rise in the rate of lexical growth. The dramatic increase in children's lexicons that typically follows the acquisition of the first 50 words is sometimes called the vocabulary "spurt" (Dromi, 1987).

Despite the diversity of communities in the world, the first words spoken by children are similar both in their phonetic form and in the kinds of meanings that underlie them. First words, for instance, rarely contain consonant clusters and are more likely to consist of **open syllables** (a consonant followed by a vowel) rather than closed syllables, or syllables ending in consonants. Nelson (1973) noted that early words tend to refer to objects within the child's environment that the child can actively interact with. Early words serve important *functions* for the child. Thus, for both phonological and semantic reasons, a word such as *carpet* is an unlikely candidate for first word. A single word, such as, "More?" may be produced with an adult-like questioning intonation contour and function as a reduced version of the adult request, "May I have more please?" The one-word stage of language development is sometimes called the **holophrastic** stage to describe this use of single-word "sentences."

FIGURE 8.4

Between her first and sixth birthdays, this child will master a large proportion of her adult language capacity.

Children who are learning a sign language as their first language may begin to use words slightly earlier than children learning oral languages (Bonvillian, Orlansky, & Novack, 1983). This suggests that the ability to produce the first words may depend, to some extent, on the development of oral motor coordination, which is somewhat slower than manual coordination.

Once language development is under way, researchers have noted regular patterns in the ways young children progress toward full adult competence. The work of Brown and his colleagues has revealed the similarity of children's early utterances in a great variety of languages around the world (Brown, 1973; DeVilliers & DeVilliers, 1973; Slobin, 1985, 1992). At the earliest stage, children produce one meaningful word at a time, and that word is inevitably a concrete **content word** (such as *kitty* or *mommy*), but certainly not a **function word** such as *of* or *the,* or an abstract word such as *truth*. Early words are embedded in the child's environment or the "here and now."

Even at the single-word stage, children appear to be using their language to signal a variety of intentions, such as **negation, recurrence, nonexistence,** and **notice.** In other words, they can refuse something *("No!"),* ask for more of something *("More!"),* comment on the disappearance of something *("Gone!"),* or call attention to something or someone *("Hi!").*

Some researchers have suggested a qualitative difference between the meanings of the first few words a child learns and those that come somewhat later (that is, during the vocabulary spurt). They propose, using data from diary studies, that the earliest words are mostly restricted to discussion of ongoing context or words that engage the child in social interaction with the parent, such as *peek-a-boo* or *please*. Many children appear not to make **referential use of language** until after they have learned their earliest words. That is, in their earliest word productions, they do not use language to refer to absent objects or enlarge the meanings of words beyond their original context (Kamhi, 1986).

COMPREHENSION LEADS PRODUCTION.   We can seriously underestimate the lexical knowledge of a toddler if we estimate vocabulary size from spoken language only. Studies that compare parental report of children's word comprehension with their production suggest that children understand more than five times as many words as they actually produce (Benedict, 1979; Bates, Dale, & Thal, 1995). This trend will be true of children's acquisition of syntactic concepts as well.

CHARACTERISTICS OF EARLY VOCABULARY AND THEIR DETERMINANTS.   The early lexicon tends to look quite "nouny" for many children learning English (Nelson, 1973). This was long thought to reflect the inherent conceptual and linguistic complexity of verbs when compared to nouns (Gentner, 1982), but may also reflect the tendency for English-speaking parents to emphasize nouns when speaking to young children and to place them at the ends of utterances, where they carry more salience. Children who learn languages in which verbs occur more frequently and in sentence final position appear to have more verbs in their early lexicons (Snow, 1995).

Early nouns also tend to be exemplars of what have been called **basic level categories** (Mervis, 1983). That is, children first learn words such as *dog* and *car;* only later do they learn subordinate members of these categories such as *poodle* and *convertible* and superordinate terms such as *animal* and *vehicle.*

Finally, children do show individual variation in the types of words that comprise their earliest lexicons. Some children acquire relatively more social terms, such as *hi, bye-bye,* and *peek-a-bo*o, and others acquire relatively more nouns. Some children do not experience a dramatic vocabulary spurt, but acquire words in a more linear and continuous fashion. Although we can see general patterns in lexical acquisition, individual children may show preferences for learning and using their own distinct set of words.

HOW DO CHILDREN DETERMINE WHAT WORDS MEAN?   It doesn't take long for a child to assign *some* form of meaning to a new word. In some studies, children have shown that they understand some portion of a word's adult meaning after only one presentation. This rapidity of learning is sometimes called "rapid mapping," "zap mapping," or "quick incidental learning" (QUIL) (Carey & Bartlett, 1978; Rice, 1987). Children's early use of words allows us to evaluate whether children assign adult-like meanings to words. Often, they do not.

Overextension refers to the child's use of a word to refer to an overly large class of items or concepts. For example, a child might call all four-legged, hairy animals *doggies,* or all men *daddies.* Overextension is quite common in children's productions. Some researchers propose that up to one third of children's early words have overly general meanings (Anglin, 1977; Rescorla, 1980). Overextensions allow researchers to hypothesize what a child believes a particular word means. If a child calls horses, cows, wolves, and lions *doggies* but does not call pigs or elephants *doggies,* it is possible to speculate that the feature of obvious furriness is an inherent part of the child's semantic representation for *doggie.* Less common, but still frequently observed, is **underextension.** This is when a word is used to refer to fewer items or concepts than appropriate. A child may use *duck* to refer to his stuffed duck but not a picture of a duck, or *bottle* to refer only to baby bottles made of plastic (Anglin, 1983). Sometimes children mistakenly map an overheard word to a completely wrong meaning in the adult language **(mismatch).** For example, one child saw his first bicycle at a party for a child named Mikey. For a time afterward he called all tricycles and bicycles *Mikeys.* Although it has been argued that overextension appears only in children's expressive language, some experimental evidence suggests that children's understanding of words may also be overly broad (Fremgen & Fay, 1980). M. Bernstein (1983) showed that some young children were apt to label any items that could be sat on (such as sofas, benches, and swings) as "chairs."

HOW TO LEARN WHAT WORDS MEAN: SOME POSSIBLE STRATEGIES.   What strategies do children use to determine what words mean and how they should be used? Some hypothetical principles of early lexical learning include the following (Golinkoff, Mervis, & Hirsh-Pasek, 1994):

Reference: Assume that words map to (refer to) objects, actions and attributes.

Extendibility: Assume that words label more than just the original referent; assume that they label a class of objects or concepts.

Object scope: Assume that words that appear to map to objects map to whole objects, not just portions of the object.

Categorical scope: Assume that words can be extended to objects in the same basic level category as the original referent.

Novel name—nameless category: Assume that novel words map to concepts for which you do not yet have a name.

Conventionality: Assume that speakers prefer specific rather than general terms.

Because we believe that children do not suddenly switch from one type of lexical representation to another as they grow, children's early words enter into the debate about how words are represented in adults' minds, an issue discussed in Chapter 4. An original proposition was that children acquired **semantic features** for words (Clark, 1973). Early on, children have few features for many words; this predicts that they will overextend many words. In the case of *doggie,* when size and typical domestic context are added to the child's features for the word, horses, lions, and wolves will no longer be labeled inappropriately. In the case of the underextended *bottle,* removal of the features +plastic, +baby's will bring the meaning of the word into conformity with adult usage. However, semantic feature theory, as seen in Chapter 4, is difficult to apply to many words of the language. Further, some children's overextensions do easily relate to missing features. **Prototype** theory was also discussed in Chapter 4 and has also been proposed as an organizing principle for children's lexical learning. However, it is most successful at predicting why children learn and sometimes overextend referential words and less successful at explaining how children learn other classes of words.

How Do Children Determine the Part of Speech of a Novel Word?

The contexts in which children encounter new nouns are relatively favorable for making linkages between objects and names. Adults look at, point to, and interact with items that they name for children. In an experiment by Gillette and Gleitman (reported by Gleitman & Gillette, 1995), adult subjects viewed a videotape interaction between a mother and a young child without hearing the soundtrack. They were able to reliably determine when the mother was uttering particular nouns. However, learning the meanings of verbs can be more difficult, particularly verbs that encode hidden states such as *think, see, feel,* or *want.* Many researchers now believe that some aspects of verb learning, such as whether a verb is transitive or intransitive, rely on analysis of syntax of its surrounding sentence as much as the context in which it has been heard (Gleitman & Gillette, 1995). Children can use morphological inflections to predict whether words are nouns or verbs by age 2 1/2 (Golinkoff, Diznoff, Yasik, & Hirsh-Pasek, 1992). Children also can exploit knowledge of their grammar and lexical formation to coin new words (see Table 8.1). For example, they may turn a noun into a verb (as in "brooming the floor"). They can use their growing stock of morphological inflections to create modifiers, some of which exist in the language, others that don't but could (Clark, 1995, Tables 14.5, 14.6).

Some Words Are More Difficult to Learn Than Others

Not all words are equally easy for children to learn. Using both evidence from children's spontaneous speech and comprehension tasks, we know that children show a preference for using and understanding **concrete vocabulary** terms (that is, words that refer to what can be seen, touched, or acted upon, such as *floor, dirty,* and *run*) before terms for abstract concepts (that is, *honesty* and *think*). Until they are somewhat older, children are also likely to have trouble with **relative concepts.** A relative term is one that changes meaning depending upon context. For example, an object cannot be inherently *big.* An elephant is big when compared to a mouse but is small when measured against the Washington Monument. Children tend to give **absolute meaning** to such words for the first few years (Carey, 1982). In other words, if they are shown an elephant standing next to the Washington Monument and asked if the elephant is big or little, they will choose big. A similar pattern exists in children's learning of kinship terms, which are inherently relational (no pun intended!). Haviland and Clark (1974) noted that it took children until age 7 or older to fully understand the meanings of kinship terms such as *niece* and *uncle,* which require the child to adopt a flexible perspective on meaning. Children often are 8 to 10 years old before they appreciate that the language includes **ambiguous words.** When they understand this fully, they often develop great interest in jokes and puns. Until this point, they may laugh if you tell them a joke (for example, "How do you turn a pumpkin into an-

(1) SC (2;4, as his mother prepared to brush his hair): *Don't hair me.*

(2) JA (2;6, seated in a rocking chair): *Rocker me, mommy.*

(3) SC (2;7, hitting baby sister with toy-broom): *I broomed her.*

(4) SC (2;9, playing with a toy lawnmower): *I'm lawning.*

(5) RG (3;0, of a bell): *Make it bell.*

(6) DM (3;0, pretending to be Superman): *I'm supermanning.*

(7) SC (3;1, watching a cement truck revolving, not pouring): *That truck is cementing.*

(8) SC (3;2, putting on his cowboy hat with a string-and-bead fastening): *String me up, mommy.*

(9) JM (3;2, realizing his father was teasing): *Daddy, you joked me.*

(10) FR (3;3, of a doll that disappeared): *I guess she magicked.*

(11) AG (3;7, of food on his plate): *I'm gonna fork this.*

(12) KA (4;0, pretending to be a doctor fixing a broken arm): *We're gonna cast that.*

(13) BS (4;0): *Maybe it rained or it fogged yesterday.*

(14) RT (4;0): *Is Anna going to babysitter me?*

(15) CE (4;11): *We already decorationed our tree.*

(16) KA (5;0): *Will you chocolate my milk?*

TABLE 8.1

Some Novel Verbs Coined by 2- to 5-Year-Olds.

Source: Clark (1995), collection of spontaneous child coinages.

other vegetable?—Throw it up in the air, and it comes down squash."), but they cannot explain why the joke is funny. They understand jokes as a social interaction, but do not yet have the linguistic sophistication to appreciate why jokes are humorous.

SPEED OF RETRIEVAL. Children have much smaller lexicons than adults, yet they appear to take a longer time to recognize and retrieve words in experimental tasks (Wiegel-Crump & Dennis, 1986). This may seem somewhat counterintuitive: it should be easier to look up words in a smaller dictionary than in a huge unabridged dictionary. However, as Chapter 4 notes, efficiency of retrieval probably depends upon efficient storage and access strategies, which undoubtedly improve with practice and age in much the same way that we discover more efficient routes to places we visit frequently.

Lexical Organization and Word Association

By the time children enter kindergarten, they know an estimated 14,000 words and will acquire 300 or so new words each year until they leave school (Clark, 1995). How do children organize this large and ever-growing lexicon?

Chapter 4 introduced the notion of semantic networks. Some evidence indicates that children begin organizing the lexicon into such networks. Clark (1993) observed that children sometimes add many new words to a single semantic domain within a relatively short time, such as multiple words for insects or aquatic creatures. One additional clue that children undergo some form of lexical reorganization during childhood is in their responses to word association tasks. Chapter 4 notes the common responses that adults make to stimulus words. They usually include providing antonyms, synonyms, and other members of the stimulus's lexical category. Such responses, in which subjects respond to nouns with other nouns, verbs with verbs, and so on, suggest that words with similar and contrasting meanings are stored "near one another" in the mental lexicon. We call such responses **paradigmatic** responses. Children tend to respond somewhat differently. If given a noun such as *dog,* children under age 5 are more likely to provide a word that follows it in sentences, such as *barks,* than to provide another noun that either specifies a type of dog, such as *collie,* or a common noun association, such as *cat* (Brown & Berko, 1960). We call this second type of response **syntagmatic.**

LEARNING TO MAKE AND UNDERSTAND SENTENCES

Assessing Syntactic Knowledge

We have already discussed methods that researchers use to analyze children's language development. Researchers can learn quite a lot from careful observation of what children say in naturalistic settings. Procedures exist to quantify the developmental complexity of a child's speech sample (Lee, 1974; Scarborough, 1989). However, if a child's speech lacks certain types of sentences or some grammatical inflections, it may be difficult to determine whether the child does not know these forms, or simply did not use them in that particular recording session. For this reason, other methods are often used to augment analysis of spontaneous language samples. For instance, a researcher might ask a child to complete a word or phrase to see if the child understands certain grammatical concepts. The Wug study (Berko, 1958), discussed in Chapter 1, did just that. It showed children a novel word such as *gutch,* and asked the child to complete the phrase, "Here is a *gutch.* Now I have another. I have two _____." Such a procedure is useful in determining whether or not a child understands how to create plurals, past tenses, or to derive parts of speech ("This *gutch* has a lot of *lerbs* on it. It is very _____.").

In other cases, researchers may ask children to imitate adult sentences. Past work by researchers such as Slobin and Welsh (1971) and Tager-Flusberg and Calkins (1990) has shown that children usually are unable to imitate a sentence that is above their level of syntactic development. Thus, a child who has not yet learned to invert subjects and auxiliary verbs to make grammatical English questions is likely to repeat, "Is the boy running down the street?" as, "The boy is running down the street?" A child who does not yet understand or use the passive form is likely to repeat, "The boy is pushed by the girl," as "The boy pushed the girl."

Methods for Assessing Syntactic Understanding

Historically, researchers have tested children's understanding of sentences by asking them to act sentences out using objects ("Show me *the car bumps the train*"), or to point to pictures (for example, the child might be asked to pick *the car bumps the train* from an array that also shows a train bumping a car, two cars bumping, and so on). However, children must be a certain age to reliably complete such tasks. Moreover, it is often difficult to portray verb concepts in picture-pointing tasks. More recently, researchers have tested young children's understanding of grammatical concepts through the **preferential looking paradigm** (Golinkoff, Hirsh-Pasek, Cavley, & Gordon, 1987, 1996). In this design, shown in Figure 8.5, a child sits on her parent's lap and faces two video monitors. A centrally mounted speaker provides a short linguistic stimulus that matches only one of the video clips. Research has shown that the infant will reliably focus on the video monitor that matches the auditory stimulus. Using such a design, Hirsh-Pasek and Golinkoff were able to demonstrate that infants who were at the one-word stage of expressive language development could comprehend word order relationships in S-V-O constructions. That is, they could correctly focus on the video that showed Big Bird pushing Cookie Monster (as opposed to the contrast video clip that showed Cookie Monster pushing Big Bird).

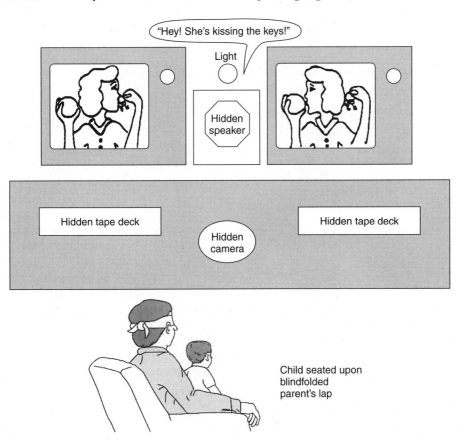

FIGURE 8.5

Even before they can construct sentences, infants recognize S-V-O construction in English by gazing at the televised image, which matches an audio message.

Moving From Words to Sentences

EARLY SENTENCES. Some time during their second year, after children have about 50 of these early words in their vocabularies, they begin to put them together into rudimentary two-word sentences (Brown, 1973). Words that they said in the one-word stage are now combined into short utterances. In English such utterances lack articles, prepositions, inflections, or any of the other grammatical modifications that well-formed adult language requires.

An examination of children's two-word utterances in many different language communities has suggested that everywhere in the world children at this age are expressing the same kinds of thoughts and intentions in the same kinds of utterances (Brown, 1973). The first two-word utterances tend to have the same kinds of meanings that the child expressed in the one-word stage:

> **Negation:** They say "no" to something: "No bed."
>
> **Recurrence:** They ask for more of something: "More milk."
>
> **Nonexistence:** They notice that something has disappeared: "All gone cookie."
>
> **Notice:** They call attention to something: "Hi, Daddy."

A little later in the two-word stage, another dozen or so kinds of meanings appear:

> They name an **actor and an action:** "Daddy eat."
>
> They **modify a noun:** "Bad doggie."
>
> They indicate **possession:** "David shoe."
>
> They specify a **location:** "Kitty table."
>
> They describe an **action and a location:** "Go store."
>
> They name an **action and an object,** leaving out the subject: "Eat lunch."
>
> They produce sentences consisting of an **actor and object,** leaving out the verb or action: "Mommy . . . lunch" (meaning Mommy is eating lunch).

At this stage, children acquiring English express these basic meanings, but they lack the grammatical forms of the language that indicate number, gender, and tense. Words that were previously uttered singly are produced in **telegraphic speech** combinations such as "Nice kitty" and "More cookie" (they sound like a telegram: *Send money car broke*). The sentences are limited in meaning (for example, they are not generally about events in the past or future) and are produced without function words or inflections.

As we discuss regular patterns of development here and elsewhere within this chapter, it is important to note that language acquisition is marked by individual variation as well as generalized developmental trends. Thus, some children seem to appreciate the "gestalt" of adult language patterns before being able to reproduce aspects of the grammar; such children may use adult-like prosody and "dummy sylla-bles" to fill in between those vocabulary items they are capable of producing, saying, [wan a kʊki] for "I want the cookie." Children with a more analytic style appear com-fortable producing "Want cookie," until they can incorporate the additional gram-matical elements into their output. Similarly, even when children use only single words to communicate, stylistic variation in the kinds of words most frequently used by children can be seen. Some children appear to build their initial lexicons by incor-porating many names for objects; other children may include proportionately more verbs or "social" items such as *hi, bye, please,* and so forth (Bates, Dale, & Thal, 1995; Nelson, 1973).

EARLY GRAMMAR.   English-speaking children's early utterances are markedly de-void of grammatical inflections, whereas children learning certain other kinds of lan-guages use such inflections earlier in the course of their language development. In languages with a much richer system of bound morphology, such as Turkish (Aksu-Koc & Slobin, 1985), Hungarian (MacWhinney, 1978), or Spanish (Johnson, 1991), much of the morphological system is used relatively error-free by age 2. Why should this be? Let us consider the case of English verbs. We (and the child) can say *talk* (which we will call the *bare-stem* version of the verb), as well as *talked, talking, talks,* and so forth. Additionally, the word *talks,* as in *She talks,* represents a deviation from our otherwise regular pattern that permits the bare-stem form of the verb in the pres-ent tense (for example, *I talk, you talk, we talk,* and so forth). In a language such as Spanish, bare stems are not permissible. That is, one must say *hablo,* habl**as,** *hablamos,* habl**a,** and so forth, when using the verb in any tense—present, past, or fu-ture. The underlying root, *habl-,* cannot exist in its uninflected form. Thus, children learning English and Spanish receive different cues regarding the importance of grammatical suffixes. A child learning Spanish quickly comes to appreciate the need for them because they are so pervasive; a child learning English, because she hears both inflected and uninflected forms of the root, may take longer to learn when they are necessary and when they are not.

Slobin (1985) proposes as one of his *operating principles* that govern child lan-guage acquisition that, "the more pervasive a morphological category is in a lan-guage, the more readily it will be learned" (p. 1194). He cites the example of Hebrew, in which gender must be marked in every utterance, and which affects proper forma-tion of subjects, verbs, modifiers, and plurals (Berman, 1985). In a language such as French, where gender is less obviously marked and multiple forms share the same pronunciation, children acquire gender marking later than those learning Hebrew (Clark, 1985).

In general, research such as that compiled by Slobin (1985, 1988) suggests that the emergence of grammar will be determined by numerous factors, including the *perva-siveness* and *regularity* of a language's grammatical constructions, the degree to which they "make semantic sense" (Slobin, 1973), and the relative *salience* of the grammati-cal concept. Those grammatical forms that are stressed are almost universally acquired before those that are not. Below, we will explore how such proposals accommodate general patterns of grammatical development in English and other languages.

Though the two-word stage has some universal semantic characteristics across all languages, what children acquire when they begin to acquire inflections and function words depends on the features of the language they are learning. English-speaking children learn the articles *a* and *the*. But a language such as Russian contains no articles. Russian grammar, conversely, has features that English lacks, such as different past-tense endings depending on whether the verb's subject is male or a female.

Some theorists (Hyams, 1986) believe not only that universal grammar (introduced in Chapter 1) specifies **parameters** or switches for some variable features of language, but that the parameters also have *default settings*. For instance, languages vary in respect to whether they require that the subject be expressed in any given declarative sentence. All English sentences require a subject, even when the subject lacks a real referent (such as the *it* in *It is raining*). Spanish, by contrast, is a *null subject* (so-called *pro-drop*) language and does not require a subject: Spanish speakers may and usually do structure statements such as, "Esta lloviendo" (literally "Is raining"). Hyams (1986), after surveying the early, often subjectless utterances of English-speaking children, hypothesizes that all children initially assume that their language is a pro-drop language; later evidence will cause English-language learners to reset their parameter to accommodate the mandatory expression of subjects in English declaratives.

When children learning a particular language begin to acquire grammatical markers, most of them do so in basically the same order within that language. In English, for instance, children tend to learn *in* and *on* before other prepositions such as *under,* and they learn the progressive tense *(-ing)* before other verb endings such as the past-tense marker *(-ed)*. Brown (1973), using data from Adam, Eve, and Sarah, proposed a uniform sequence of development in which phonologically regular and semantically simple concepts such as the present progressive *(-ing)* emerge before the past tense (which has multiple phonological representations—*walked -ed=/t/; played -ed=/d/;* and *patted -ed=/əd/*). In turn, the past will be acquired before the rather arbitrary *third person singular* marker (for example, *John walks*), which has both regular and irregular realizations (for example, *do/does*). The plural, which is conceptually simple, emerges before the possessive, which is somewhat more abstract. Rather arbitrary, unstressed, and semantically empty elements such as auxiliary verbs *(He is walking)* are relatively late acquisitions.

Because English contains relatively few grammatical morphemes, but uses them in the vast majority of well-formed sentences, Brown and other researchers have found it useful to track language development by reference to a measure known as **mean length of utterance (MLU).** This measure calculates the average length of a child's utterance in *morphemes,* rather than words, and tends to define stages of early language development.

After children begin to learn the regular plurals and pasts such as *horses* and *skated,* they create some regularized forms of their own, such as *mouses* and *eated*. This is generally referred to as **overregularization,** and it is excellent evidence that children are learning the *systems* of their language: They are producing words according to the basic *rules* of the language, rather than by simple imitation of the language they hear. Contributors to Slobin's (1985, 1988) volumes that survey language development cross-linguistically find overregularization of grammatical rules in all of the languages studied, including Hebrew, German, French, Hungarian, Japanese, Samoan, Polish, Turkish, Kaluli, and American Sign Language.

Learning to Make Sentences in English

Certainly, acquisition of morphological markers such as verbal inflections, articles, plurals, and so forth is necessary for the creation of well-formed sentences in English (and other languages). However, as Chapter 1 noted, English contains many types of sentences: those that negate, question, or take the form of the imperative. Additional major simple sentence types are **passives** *(The baby was frightened by the loud noise),* in which subject and object are inverted, or **datives** *(The man showed the student the room),* in which direct and indirect objects are inverted. Finally, English is characterized by varieties of **compound sentences,** in which conjunctions link multiple phrases *(John and Sue hike; Mary saw Tom and Joe; I will be late* because *I overslept.),* and by **complex sentences,** in which clauses are embedded within phrases *(The man* who lives down the street *is a doctor; I know the woman* whom you saw; That John passed any courses *surprised me).* In the next few sections we will briefly review acquisition of these many constructions. Research regarding the stages leading to mastery in the production and comprehension of these structures often suggests complex interactions between the syntactic and semantic complexity of such structures, their relative frequency (or lack of frequency) in conversational English, and children's use of nonlinguistic strategies in interpreting difficult constructions. More extensive reviews are provided by Tager-Flusberg (1996) and DeVilliers and DeVilliers (1985).

LEARNING TO SAY NO.   The development of negative sentence forms in English was originally traced by Bellugi (1967), using data from Adam, Eve, and Sarah. Most subsequent studies have generally agreed with her findings, which suggested three major stages in negative formation. These stages are not discrete and discontinuous, and children do not suddenly catapult from one to the next but rather make steady progress characterized by frequent use of a particular strategy as the child attempts to master the eventual adult form. In the first stage of negative formation, negative markers such as *no* and *not* simply precede the utterance, as in, "No cars there" and, "Not Fraser read it." In the next stage, as MLU approaches 3.0 words, negatives follow the main verb, and *can't* and *don't* appear within sentences, although apparently as unanalyzed elements (because *can* and *do* are not present in any utterances). Thus, the child may produce, "That not mine," "I no eat it," "I can't see." As children enter later stages of language development (roughly MLU 3.5–4.0 and beyond), they acquire the ability to place negative markers on the verbal auxiliary, creating forms such as *isn't.*

LEARNING TO ASK QUESTIONS.   Although it is possible to simply use a declarative sentence and modify its intonational structure when asking a question (for example, "He's coming?"), the usual question formation in English requires reordering of the subject and auxiliary of the corresponding declarative form. In general, well-formed *Yes/No questions* (for example, "Is Daddy going?") precede *Wh- questions*

Rules for Calculating Mean Length of Utterance. (From *A First Language* [p. 54] by R. Brown: 1973. Cambridge, MA: Harvard University Press. Reprinted by permission.)

1. Start with the second page of the transcription unless that page involves a recitation of some kind. In this latter case start with the first recitation-free stretch. Count the first 100 utterances satisfying the following rules.

2. Only fully transcribed utterances are used; none with blanks. Portions of utterances, entered in parentheses to indicate doubtful transcription, are used.

3. Include all exact utterance repetitions (marked with a plus sign in records). Stuttering is marked as repeated efforts at a single word; count the word once in the most complete form produced. In the few cases where a word is produced for emphasis or the like (*no, no no*) count each occurrence.

4. Do not count such fillers as *mm* or *oh*, but do count *no, yeah,* and *hi*.

5. All compound words (two or more free morphemes), proper names, and ritualized reduplications count as single words. Examples: *birthday, rackety-boom, choo-choo, quack-quack, night-night, pocketbook, see saw*. Justification is that there is no evidence that the constituent morphemes function as such for these children.

6. Count as one morpheme all irregular pasts of the verb (*got, did, went, saw*). Justification is that there is no evidence that the child relates these to present forms.

7. Count as one morpheme all diminutives (*doggie, mommie*) because these children at least do not seem to use the suffix productively. Diminutives are the standard forms used by the child.

8. Count as separate morphemes all auxiliaries (*is, have, will, can, must, would*). Also all catenatives: *gonna, wanna, hafta*. These latter count as single morphemes rather than as *going to* or *want to* because evidence is that they function so for the children. Count as separate morphemes all inflections, for example, possessive [s], plural [s], third person singular [s], regular past [d], progressive [Iŋ].

9. The range count follows the above rules but is always calculated for the total transcription rather than for 100 utterances.

(such as "Where is Daddy going?"), which require knowledge of the relevant *wh-* word as well as inversion of the subject and auxiliary. Some studies suggest that the relative semantic difficulty of words such as *why, how,* and *when*, which require understanding of causal and temporal concepts, causes them to emerge at a later stage in both production and appropriate comprehension than words such as *what, where,* and *who* (see DeVilliers & DeVilliers, 1985, for summary discussion).

The Role of Word Order Strategies in Sentence Formation and Comprehension

We have said that English primarily utilizes subject-verb-object word order in its sentences. Children exposed to English quickly appreciate this pattern, as Golinkoff et al.'s (1987) study of infants dramatically illustrates. The assumption that well-formed sentences will use S-V-O ordering has consequences for the acquisition of some sen-

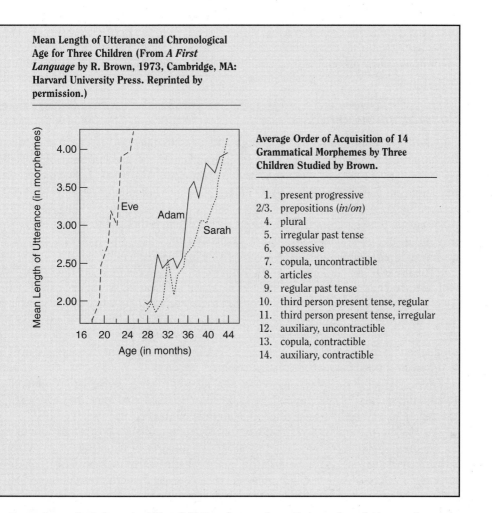

Mean Length of Utterance and Chronological Age for Three Children (From *A First Language* by R. Brown, 1973, Cambridge, MA: Harvard University Press. Reprinted by permission.)

Average Order of Acquisition of 14 Grammatical Morphemes by Three Children Studied by Brown.

1. present progressive
2/3. prepositions (*in/on*)
4. plural
5. irregular past tense
6. possessive
7. copula, uncontractible
8. articles
9. regular past tense
10. third person present tense, regular
11. third person present tense, irregular
12. auxiliary, uncontractible
13. copula, contractible
14. auxiliary, contractible

tence types that do not utilize S-V-O order, such as the passive, dative, and certain types of complex sentences.

Many studies suggest that children younger than age 5 will use either an **S-V-O word order strategy** or **event probability** to comprehend passives and datives, which not only violate S-V-O ordering, but rarely appear in parental speech models to children. Thus, if the child can use knowledge of real-world events to properly interpret *The mouse was chased by the cat* or *Mary baked John a cake* (because Mary cannot bake John), she will do so, perhaps even at a very young age (Bridges, 1980). However, when the meaning cannot be derived without properly analyzing the syntax (such as in *The boy was hit by the girl* or *The mother showed the girl the baby*), children are likely to interpret the sentences as S-V-O constructions (Bever, 1970; Osgood & Zehler, 1981). Thus, they will act out or point to a picture of a boy hitting a girl and of a woman showing a girl *to* a baby. Similar problems may arise when a sentence's S-V-O structure is disturbed by an embedded clause, as in *The man* who lives next to my sister *is a doctor.* Children may assume that the object of the main clause *(sister)* operates as the subject of the phrase *is a doctor.* They adopt what some have called a **minimal distance principle.** They assume that the subject for any verb is the noun that immediately precedes it (C. Chomsky, 1968).

Combining Sentences

Children's first efforts to create compound sentences are likely to utilize the conjunction *and* and link objects, as in, "I like cookies and cake" (which is presumably based on the underlying notions *I like cookies* and *I like cake*). Those that link subjects, as in, "Jamie and Sabrina want to come," emerge later; earlier attempts are likely to resemble, "Adam wants to come, and John wants to come, too." More languages of the world permit the first type of conjoined structure, which is thought to involve forward deletion of the redundant subject-verb sequence *I like,* than the second, which requires backward deletion of the first verb phrase and adjustment of the verb.

The use of other conjunctions, such as *because, but, if, before/after,* and so forth, will require children to understand their particular meanings. Children may use them in appropriate syntactic frames yet fail to appreciate their semantic roles, as in "I fell down because I hurt my knee" (Bloom, Lahey, Hood, Lifter, & Fiess, 1980; Menyuk, 1969). In many cases, an **order of mention strategy** appears to apply both to production and comprehension of such strings, in which the event in the first clause is simply presumed to occur before the second.

Young children rarely produce embedded clauses in their conversational speech (Wells, 1985). Most of the research on acquisition of such structures has addressed the degree to which children are able to comprehend them.

As Hamburger and Crain (1982) have noted, these sentences pose great difficulty for children, probably for several reasons. Studies disagree both on the relative difficulty of the constructions, as well as the ages at which they tend to be accurately interpreted by the majority of child subjects. It is safe to say that children younger than age 6 find it difficult to accurately interpret such structures.

This whirlwind tour through the basic accomplishments of young children acquiring a first language cannot begin to touch upon the complexity of their task and the great wealth of information that has become available on the topic during the past two decades. Readers interested in a more complete picture of children's progress toward language competence may wish to refer to Berko Gleason (1997), DeVilliers and DeVilliers (1985), or Owens (1996), among other sources.

Some Later Acquisitions

Certain syntactic skills evolve later in childhood. As mentioned above, ambiguity can pose problems for children. Ambiguity based on syntax rather than word meaning is particularly difficult, as in the joke, *Can you jump higher than your house?* (The answer is Yes—your house can't jump.)

An important skill that develops during the later elementary school years is the ability to **paraphrase,** which allows children to write reports without "copying" from the book. Children must have fairly developed lexicons and syntactic abilities to re-state sentences in different ways.

Understanding idioms and figurative language is a later acquisition for most children. An **idiom** is a phrase that is not understood as the sum of its parts: a person who "kicks the bucket" doesn't actually do what the phrase says she does. The sequence of words now carries the meaning of a single lexical item: *die.* In general, children interpret idioms literally until age 7 or so (Clark, 1995). The same tendency is true of **figurative language,** in which words are used metaphorically, as in, "She is a cold-hearted person." Learning not to put literal interpretations on idioms and figurative expressions continues through the school years.

Metalinguistic Awareness

As discussed in Chapter 1, metalinguistic awareness is the ability to reflect on the nature of language and its use. This talent develops throughout our lives. Early on, children cannot appreciate the arbitrary nature of language and the absence of relationship between the name of an object and its appearance or function. As Pan and Gleason (1996) note, young children consider that the name of an object is actually one of its attributes, as though, ". . . If you decided to call a horse a cow, it might begin to moo."

Early in development, children also have difficulty understanding that words are decomposable into sounds (Fox & Routh, 1975), an important ability in learning to read in alphabetic writing systems. Still yet another late metalinguistic development is the ability to define the meanings of words, as opposed to using them appropriately to communicate (Snow, 1990).

LEARNING TO COMMUNICATE: EARLY SOCIAL USES OF LANGUAGE

When children have acquired linguistic principles such as conversational turn-taking and many semantic relations, much of their early speech is directed toward maintaining contact with caregivers and getting others to do things for them. These early *social intentions* have been described by researchers studying the pragmatic aspects of language (Bates, 1976; Halliday, 1975) and include *drawing attention* to the self (a good example at the one-word stage is *hi*); *showing objects (see, ball); offering* (for example, the child says, "There!" when offering the adult a toy); and *requesting* objects or activities (for example, "More!"). The purely social expression, "Bye-bye," is, in fact usually the first conventionalized communicative act that an infant engages in, in our society.

Many researchers have suggested that some children are more social than others in their use of language, yet these reported stylistic differences are difficult to interpret. For instance, Nelson (1973) found that some children are **referential** whereas others are **expressive.** The expressive children were thought to be more social in orientation, and the referential children more interested in labeling the world. Perhaps the child who spends her time labeling her environment is actually motivated by primarily social (and not taxonomic) reasons—perhaps it is just this behavior that attracts and holds the attention of her achievement-oriented, middle-class family.

Research on the potential contributions of the early social characteristics of children suggests that the acquisition of grammatical forms may not be determined exclusively by the syntactic, semantic, or cognitive complexity of the form (Brown, 1973; Slobin, 1985). The social motivational propensities of children and the adults with whom they interact may also influence what and when particular linguistic forms are acquired. Cross-linguistic research provides many examples to support this position. In Samoan, special marking of transitive subjects distinguishes them from intransitive subjects. Ochs (1982) notes that this marking is acquired late by Samoan children for what appear to be social rather than linguistic reasons. For example, in Samoan, the form is more characteristic of men's than of women's speech. "Samoan children do not acquire this marking early largely because they are not exposed to it in their social environment—the household setting—where women and other family members are primary socializing agents" (p. 77). Ochs points out that this contrasts with the relatively early acquisition of the same grammatical form by Kaluli-speaking children in New Guinea. Clancy (1985) also describes the importance of sociolinguistic factors in the acquisition of Japanese and how pragmatic factors pervade the grammar of the language through "word order, ellipsis, and sentence-final particles, as well as an elaborate system of socially defined statuses and roles which are expressed in verb morphology, pronouns, and sentence-final particles" (p. 377). Grammatical forms that express deference, politeness, and other social proprieties may be acquired early not because they are syntactically or cognitively less complex, but because they are a social necessity.

Children's acquisition of varied polite forms occurs in conjunction with explicit teaching on the part of adults (Snow, Gleason, & Perlmann, 1990). It seems obvious that children acquire polite forms partly as a result of their increasing cognitive capacities and partly because they are motivated (at some level) to be polite, and hence socially acceptable people. Additionally, active and explicit adult teaching to ensure that pragmatic socialization takes place appears to be pervasive. In a study of eight families at dinner (Berko Gleason, Perlmann, & Greif, 1984), even when the dinner was only 13 or 14 minutes long, the adults in every family structured explicit teaching episodes regarding how children should comport themselves. Every family used at least some politeness routines such as, "Thank you," and, "May I please be excused?" and six of the eight families used prompting techniques with their children such as asking them, "What's the magic word?" or, "What do you say?" When questions and prompts failed to elicit the required form, parents often modeled it for their child. The following example, drawn from a family with a 4-year-old daughter, contains some of these elements:

Child: Mommy, I want more milk.

Mother: Is that the way to ask?

Child:	Please.
Mother:	Please what?
Child:	Please gimme milky.
Mother:	No.
Child:	Please gimme milk.
Mother:	No.
Child:	Please . . .
Mother:	Please, may I have more milk?
Child:	Please, may I have more milk?

(Gleason et al., 1984, pp. 500–501)

Learning to Take Perspective: The Demise of Egocentrism

Young children sometimes show evidence of an inability to take the perspective of their listeners, a notion sometimes called **egocentrism** (Piaget, 1926). Although even very young children seem to understand general ways of speaking to certain types of listeners (for example, other young children), the content of their interactions sometimes indicates that they do not fully appreciate the perspective of their addressees. For example, when talking to people who can't see what they can see—on the telephone, for example—they may mention visual cues ("Look what's in my hand") (Glucksberg, Krauss, & Higgins, 1975; Lloyd, 1991). Warren and McCloskey (1996) discuss other late pragmatic developments over the course of childhood.

THEORIES OF CHILD LANGUAGE ACQUISITION

What Must Theories of Language Development Account For?

In reviewing the theories of language acquisition we present below, remember that each must account for some facts about child language development. First, children learn language rapidly. In only a few years, children progress from virtually no language comprehension or production to almost adult capacity. Second, across languages, some systematic regularities exist in what children learn both early and late, as well as some differences that require explanation. Theories must also account for the nature of children's mistakes, as well as their successes in early language use. Theories additionally must explain why predictable sequences occur in children's language acquisition: why some learning occurs sooner, some later. Finally, theories must explain how children learn language, given the language input they receive from the adults in their environment.

General Features of Theories

Developmental psycholinguistics is filled with lively theoretical controversy about how best to account for language development. At one extreme, scholars claim that language is a *learned behavior* that parents teach to children. At the other end of the theoretical spectrum equally dedicated researchers claim that the principles that underlie language are *innate,* or present at birth as part of the child's biological heritage.

Most people today who have not studied psycholinguistics also have a folk theory of language development: They theorize that children acquire language by *imitating* the adults around them. Children do imitate many adult behaviors, both naturally and experimentally. In a famous study, Bandura, Ross, and Ross (1963) showed preschoolers an attractive person who punched and beat a doll. When left alone with the doll later, the children also punched the doll, occasionally using the adult model's words when they did so. Although imitation or, more broadly, social learning theory seems quite plausible and surely accounts for part of language development, some of the problems with assuming that imitation is a *sufficient* explanation emerge if we try to imitate an unknown language, for instance a Greek radio program on any Sunday morning or a simple conversation between two waiters in a Chinese restaurant. Under those circumstances, imitation appears a difficult and complicated way to learn a language. Therefore we turn to more powerful theories to account for children's remarkable linguistic accomplishments.

Major Dimensions of Language Development Theories

Theories of language development differ in the weight that they ascribe to various dimensions that characterize language. Each of the following questions asks which end of the continuum is more important.

NATURE OR NURTURE?   Perhaps this is the major question that divides psycholinguists. To what extent is language *hardwired* into the human brain (nature), and to what extent is it learned through interaction with the environment (nurture)? Do parents teach children language, or does language simply unfold according to a genetic program?

CONTINUITY OR DISCONTINUITY?   Does language develop in a seamless flow, smoothly and with barely perceptible transitions, or does it proceed in stages that are clearly distinct from one another? For instance, does the infant's babbling slowly turn into words, or does babbling cease at one stage, followed by a stage at which talking begins?

UNIVERSAL COMPETENCE OR INDIVIDUAL VARIATION?   Is linguistic competence basically *invariant?* That is, can we assume that all unimpaired speakers of the language share the same linguistic knowledge? Or does individual knowledge vary greatly? Do all children acquire language in the same way? For instance, if we collect the first words and then the first sentences of 50 or 100 children learning English, will they all be basically the same?

STRUCTURE OR FUNCTION?   In studying language development, should we concentrate on *structure,* the grammar of the language that children acquire, or should we pay more attention to function, the ways that children use language in various situations? For instance, if a 4-year-old says, "It's hot in here, isn't it?" is it of greater interest that she is able to make the complex syntactic *tag question,* or should researchers study the interpersonal situations in which children learn to mitigate or hedge their statements with tag questions? Chapter 1 includes a description of the grammatical rules that underlie formation of tag questions in English. Note that English makes it particularly difficult for children to learn tags, whereas in languages such as French or German tags require no grammatical modulation at all: one simply appends *"N'est-ce pas?"* or *"Nicht Wahr?"* to any appropriate sentence.

AUTONOMY OR DEPENDENCY?   Is language a separate faculty of the human mind? Or is language development dependent on—or a part of—other kinds of development? For instance, are there cognitive prerequisites for language learning, or can language be learned by an individual who will never pass the usual cognitive milestones of childhood?

RULES OR ASSOCIATIONS?   Is the child who acquires language internalizing a set of abstract cognitive principles or is the child learning language without recourse to *rules,* but merely as a set of *connections* or associations built on past experience? For instance, when a child learns that the past tense of *melt* is *melted,* has he learned a *rule* for adding the ending or has he simply processed the statistical observation that words ending in /t/ tend to be followed by /əd/ if they are conveying past-tense information?

These are just some of the kinds of questions that have led to research, theory, and heated controversy in the field of developmental psycholinguistics.

Linguistic/Innatist Theory

An early psycholinguistic study was conducted in Egypt in the 5th century B.C. (According to the Greek historian Herodotus, a contemporary of the playwright Sophocles), a king named Psammetichus performed an experiment in order to find out which human language was the first. Psammetichus gave two infants to a shepherd, who was instructed to treat them well but to keep them in isolation and never to speak to them. The king wanted to know what the children's first words would be if they were left to their own devices in this way. (This is an unethical experiment! The ancient Egyptians did many things that the National Institutes of Health would never allow.) This king's linguistic theory was perhaps the first and most extreme example of **innatism.** He believed that at a given moment the children would simply begin to speak the language that was innate to them (**innate** really means *present at birth*), and he hoped that the language would be Egyptian, because that would back up his proud claim that the Egyptians were the original race of humans. According to

Herodotus, the shepherd arrived to take care of the children one day, "after the indistinct babblings of infancy were past," and they held out their hands and said, "Bekos," which was a word he had never heard. The shepherd went to the king, who made inquiries all over the country, and eventually was told that *bekos* was the Phrygian word for bread. The king then claimed that the Egyptians were surely the *second oldest* race, because obviously the Phrygians must have come first.

No researcher today believes that a particular language is inscribed on our neurons, but linguistic/innatist theorists do believe that the principles of language are inborn and not learned. Why make such an assumption? Most simply put, it is because "one . . . still want(s) to know why young children arrive at successful grammars so much more readily than professional linguists" (Lightfoot, 1982). In other words, linguists can study a language for years to discover its rules, while children intuit the rules of language quickly and, for the most part, accurately.

Children universally acquire the major proportion of their mature language capacity between approximately 1 and 6 years of age. They can do so, according to some observers, without access to either the kind of models or responses to poorly formed attempts at language that should permit rapid achievement of such a complex system of behavior. In a modern-day parallel to Psammetichus's experiment, they point to research on deaf children who have not been exposed to any language. Goldin-Meadow and her colleagues studied a group of deaf children (Butcher, Mylander, & Goldin-Meadow, in press; Goldin-Meadow & Mylander, 1990). The children's parents did not want them to learn sign language, and the children had not yet entered a program that would teach them lip reading and oral skills. Goldin-Meadow found that the deaf children, even with no exposure to any kind of language, developed their own systems of manual sign communication that incorporated many of the formal features of language.

Other evidence of children actually creating language is offered by Bickerton (1984), who studied the properties of Hawaiian pidgin. A **pidgin** language is typically one that develops in a situation where speakers of many different languages need to find a common means of communication; as such, the pidgin may be quite simplified and lack features found in complete languages (Mühlhäusler, 1986; Romaine, 1988). Bickerton found that Hawaiian children who heard only pidgin gradually transformed that pidgin into a **creole,** which is a true language, and actually produced grammatical forms that were more complex than those in their parents' speech. The work of Goldin-Meadow and Bickerton is controversial, because, for instance, Goldin-Meadow studied only a small number of children and Bickerton inferred the course of creole evolution from historical data. Both, however, provide provocative support for the notion that some linguistic categories may be part of the way humans will inevitably want to organize their experience.

Of course, most children do not acquire language under the conditions studied by either Goldin-Meadow or Bickerton. Even so, many researchers are concerned that children could not extrapolate all of the rules of their language and only the rules of their particular language merely by reliance upon adult models or adult feedback to linguistic efforts. Lightfoot (1982) lists three major concerns that underlie the assumption that language learning is critically dependent upon specific biologically determined abilities and processes. All of them contribute to the deficiency or **poverty of the stimulus problem.**

First, some observers note that not all language addressed to or overheard by young children consists of complete, well-formed utterances. Given the fact that children cannot, at the beginning, distinguish between good and poor examples of language use, how do they proceed? Lightfoot provides the analogy of attempting to learn chess by watching many games into which a few illegal moves are introduced without being labeled or penalized. Second, children come to use and understand sentences that presumably never occur in their language learning environment, such as multiple clauses strung together endlessly, as in, *The horse the cow kicked was chased by the bull the farmer bought,* and so forth. Perhaps most importantly, because children do eventually master language structures they probably have not heard before, why do they not, at least in syntax, attempt to form certain ungrammatical constructions? Some people have called this last problem one of **negative evidence:** No one supposedly ever tells you, "And by the way, don't try doing the following things in English, they're not grammatical." Pinker (1991) discusses these limitations on the cues provided by the child's environment in detail.

Even when adults in the child's environment do attempt to actively teach language, linguists note that children fail to make use of such information unless they are at the particular stage of linguistic development to profit from the feedback. McNeill's example has become perhaps the most often cited example of the phenomenon:

Child:	Nobody doesn't like me.
Mother:	No, say, "Nobody likes me."
Child:	Nobody doesn't like me (eight repetitions of this dialogue).
Mother:	No, now listen carefully: say, "Nobody likes me."
Child:	Oh, nobody don't likes me.

(McNeill, 1966, p. 69)

Linguistic theorists rely heavily on theories of mind and on special abstract mental mechanisms such as a postulated **language acquisition device (LAD)** (Chomsky, 1965, 1972, 1982) to reconcile rapid, successful language acquisition with these deficiencies in data to which the child is exposed. The language acquisition device, according to Chomsky, makes it possible for children to *attend* to the language that the adults around them speak, *make hypotheses* about how it works, and *derive an appropriate grammar.* Chomsky himself eschews the term "innateness" when discussing the theory of language acquisition. As he points out, all theories of learning presume some innate capacities that probably are unique to the human experience. A horse cannot be trained either to use language or to calculate the odds on horse races. Thus, a linguist finds it noncontroversial to assume that the human mind possesses certain inherent properties, tendencies, and initial assumptions. The task is to specify them. Innatist theory claims that many aspects of language development are *preprogrammed* in the individual and a child does not require explicit teaching or experience in order to acquire language. The language that infants hear provides data for their grammatical hypotheses, but the LAD does not require *specialized input* to do its job—any reasonable sample of language will do, according to the theory. Thus, nativists view language as a hardwired **bioprogram** that develops when the infant is exposed to language.

The principles that underlie all possible human languages are considered innate and constitute the concept known as **Universal Grammar (UG).** Chomsky (1975) defines Universal Grammar, which we first discussed in Chapter 1, as "the system of principles, conditions and rules that are elements or properties of all human languages not merely by accident but by (biological) necessity . . . " (p. 29). Because UG specifies the basic linguistic possibilities from which individual languages derive, and because language reflects properties of the human mind, we can hypothesize certain initial states and paths toward language competence.

Linguists point out that children everywhere learn to talk—in fact it is just about impossible to suppress the development of language (Lenneberg, 1967). Because children are reared around a world in which thousands of different languages are spoken and different child care practices prevail, and because children come with obvious individual differences in intelligence, temperament, motivation, personality, and so forth, universal patterns of language development provide strong evidence that the *mechanisms* underlying language development are inborn or innate. Thus, acquiring language is rather like learning to walk—it happens in just about every intact individual, with or without explicit training.

Of course, every child learns a particular language, and we must explain *how* children proceed from the initial state (which specifies more structural possibilities than any individual language will permit) to competence in the language spoken in their community. According to the linguistic view, infants may be innately endowed with linguistic switches or *parameters* that they set once they hear the adult language around them For instance, children may note that English is a subject-verb-object or S-V-O language, or that it has articles before its nouns (Hyams, 1986), and set their parameters accordingly.

In the linguistic view, language is an *autonomous* faculty, separate from intelligence, that infants are innately driven to acquire. The various subsystems of language are internalized as sets of algorithms or rules that allow the child to produce new utterances that she has never heard before. For instance, a child of 3 or 4 years can produce the plural of a nonsense word *gutch,* which she has never heard before, if shown pictures such as the ones in Figure 8.6.

If a child knows that the plural of *witch* is *witches* he may simply have memorized the plural form. If, however, he tells us that the plural of *gutch* is *gutches,* we have evidence that he actually knows, albeit unconsciously, one of those rules that the descriptive linguist, too, would set forth in his grammar (Berko, 1958, p. 47).

Language acquisition involves internalizing the rules that underlie the various subsystems of the language. We can know one set of rules (the phonology, for instance) without knowing another set of rules (the inflectional system, for instance). In this sense linguistic knowledge is *modular*—the units are to a large degree independent of one another. Linguistic/innatist theory suggests the possibility of a *critical*

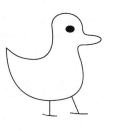

This is a *gutch.*

Now there is another one.
There are two of them.
There are two _____.

FIGURE 8.6

When a child pluralizes a nonsense word, she demonstrates knowledge of a rule of English. Source: Berko, 1958.

or *sensitive period* during which the language acquisition device and parameter setting can optimally function. When the critical period has passed (usually when the individual reaches puberty) acquiring a first language may become difficult or even impossible.

Learning Theory

Behaviorists, or *learning theorists* (for example, Skinner, 1957, 1969; Whitehurst, 1982), claim that language is acquired according to the general laws of learning and is similar to any other learned behavior. Behaviorists see spoken-language development as a result of adults' reinforcement and gradual shaping of infants' babbling, and they apply the general principles of learning to later developments—for example, learning how to make a past tense of a new verb is a result of generalization based on past experience with similar words.

Learning theory includes at least three kinds of learning: **classical conditioning, operant conditioning,** and **social learning.** Each of these kinds of learning can be called upon to explain some part of language development.

CLASSICAL CONDITIONING.   An infant may learn the meaning of a word through **classical conditioning.** In the famous conditioning experiments conducted by Pavlov

(1927) dogs learned (were *conditioned*) to react to a bell as if it were meat powder. Initially, the dogs were presented with meat powder—the **unconditioned stimulus (UCS)**—and their **unconditioned response (UCR)** was to salivate. The experimenter then rang a bell (the **conditioned stimulus**) just before giving the dogs meat powder. Eventually, ringing the bell alone caused the dogs to salivate (the **conditioned response**). In a sense, the dogs reacted to the bell as if it were the meat (even though their response was not complete—they did not attempt to eat the bell). In the beginning, the meat powder was the *stimulus,* and salivation was the *response.* Soon, through *association* with the meat powder, the bell alone became sufficient to evoke the salivation response.

Learning the meaning of a word is thought to be a similar process. An infant fed with a bottle, for instance, has many reactions to the bottle, such as anticipation of drinking (or perhaps even salivation). If every time she is fed, her mother holds up the bottle and says "bottle," the child begins to *associate* the word *bottle* with the object. Ultimately, when someone says "bottle," the child responds to the word in some sense as if it were the thing—by expecting to see a bottle, becoming physiologically prepared to drink (perhaps salivating), and so on. The word evokes the same response as the bottle, and in this sense she knows the meaning of the word.

OPERANT CONDITIONING. The basic principle of **operant conditioning** (also called **instrumental learning**) is that behavior that is rewarded—or *reinforced*—will be *strengthened.* This kind of learning is called "operant" because the subject "operates" on the environment in order to get a reward, or **reinforcement.** Behavior that is not reinforced will become **extinguished.** In the behavioral view, parents and others teach children language through operant conditioning by *rewarding* their early attempts at language. At first, parents are happy and react with reinforcing smiles and attention if their child makes any language-like noises at all, but in time the parents become more demanding and reward only closer approximations of the target language. This *selective reinforcement* gradually *shapes* the child's linguistic behavior. For instance, an infant who wants some water may say something like, "Wawweee!" and get results from happy parents. At age 3, if the child says, "Wawweee," the parent is liable to say, "What did you say? What do you want?" and not react favorably until the child says, "Water!"

By the time the child is 4 or 5, "Water!" won't do any more; now the parent says something like, "What's the magic word?" and holds out until the child says "Please, may I have some water?" The child's early utterances have gradually been *shaped* until they reach adult form.

SOCIAL LEARNING. **Social learning** takes place when the child *observes* and *imitates* others. The basic principle involved is that children need not be rewarded themselves in order to acquire a behavior—they also learn to behave like appropriate models. Older people who are seen as powerful, nurturing, and similar to the child (for example, the same gender) are most likely to be imitated. Little boys learn to talk like their fathers, and little girls imitate the speech (and other behaviors, of course) of their mothers. Thus, according to learning theory, through a combination of classical and operant conditioning, as well as imitation and social learning, the child moves from babbling infant to speaking adult. Because *observable* and *measurable behavior* provide the data for learning theorists, they are not concerned with abstractions such as whether children or adults at any stage have concepts underlying their language.

As we noted in Chapter 1, learning theory models cannot easily explain many aspects of children's language acquisition because children (1) say things they have never heard before, such as, "I holded the baby rabbits"; and (2) do not say some of the things they hear most commonly—for instance, infants' first utterances do not contain articles, even though *a* and *the* are the most common words in the English language. As a human activity, language development cannot be impervious to the laws of learning, however. Most likely some parts of language (for example, the politeness system or other social routines) may be explicitly taught, whereas others (for example, the phonology and syntax) may be acquired in a less obvious way.

Moerk (1990), in a reanalysis of Brown's original transcripts of Eve and her mother, has urged a reconsideration of stimulus-response-reinforcement mechanisms in language acquisition. In his alternative view, which contains elements of both operant conditioning and social learning paradigms, maternal utterances serve as model and stimulus; the child's utterances, which tend to be highly imitative in part or whole, are considered responses; and the following maternal response is considered reinforcement. If reinforcement is operationally defined as an acknowledgment (*yeah, right,* and so forth), evidence from Eve's interactions suggests a high proportion of self-repetition of rewarded utterances, an increase in the rewarded behavior. Similarly, maternal expansions of the child's utterances, which are extremely frequent, are hypothesized to provide reinforcement to the child's attempts, as well as corrective feedback.

Cognitive Theory

Cognitive theorists (Bates, 1979; Bates & Snyder, 1985; Macnamara, 1972; Piaget, 1926, 1954; Sinclair-deZwart, 1973) believe that language is a subordinate part of cognitive development, dependent on the attainment of various concepts. According to this view, children learn about the world first, and then map language onto that prior experience. For example, an infant first attains the concept of **object permanence** and then begins to note the disappearance of objects (such as milk) by saying, "All gone" (Gopnik & Meltzoff, 1987). Or an infant has experience with the family cat, knows that it meows, is warm and furry, eats in the kitchen; he develops a cat *concept* first, and then learns to map the word *kitty* onto that concept.

The fact that children develop in many ways at the same time creates special problems in developing theories of language acquisition. It is difficult to know to what extent language development is dependent on or part of other development, and to what extent it is separate, or **autonomous.** Adults learning a second language, for instance, already have their basic concepts in place: For an English speaker to learn that a horse is called *cheval, caballo, pferd,* or *ló* in French, Spanish, German, or Hungarian requires learning some new sounds, but we already have the concept *horse* on which to map these new words. Children who are acquiring their first language are acquiring their first concepts at the same time.

Controversy is inevitable among researchers about the extent to which developments that take place in cognition as well as in other spheres are necessary before language can blossom. The temptation to mistake *correlation* for *causation* is particularly strong when we study children—because different kinds of developmental milestones may occur at about the same time. For example, children's first words and first steps occur near their first birthdays, and children's first word combinations occur late in the second year, often around the time they gain sphincter control. Though these events *are* closely correlated in time, few would argue that toilet-training "causes" language development. It is certainly easy to assume, however, that before a child can converse about something, she needs to *know* what it is. Or the existence of general *cognitive prerequisites* for language: For instance, that the ability to use the future and past tenses depends upon a prior understanding of future and past. Cognitive theorists believe that language is just one aspect of human cognition (Piaget, 1926; Sinclair-deZwart, 1973). According to Piaget and his followers, infants must learn about the world around them, which they do through active experimentation and *construction*. For example, the infant crawls around the floor, observes objects from all angles, and slowly develops a *sensorimotor* (literally, "through the senses and motor activity") understanding of the space in which she lives. Primitive notions of *time* and *causality* develop, as well as an understanding that people and objects continue to exist even when they are out of sight *(person permanence* and *object permanence).* From Piaget's perspective, language is mapped onto an individual's set of prior cognitive structures, and the principles of language are no different from other cognitive principles.

Some studies have observed parallels between linguistic and cognitive development. For the most part, researchers have attempted to link Piagetian stage acquisition with the emergence of language skills in children. For example, Kelly and Dale (1989) suggest that late stage 4 or early stage 5 sensorimotor skills appear to signal the onset of single-word utterances by children. Stage 6 sensorimotor capacity closely precedes the emergence of combinatorial language. Bates, Bretherton, Snyder, Shore, and Volterra (1980) linked symbolic play behavior to greater progress in language development in children. Associations between cognition and language may be stronger in the domain of language understanding than language production. Bates, Dale, and Thal (1995) note that, "most cognitive variables correlate with what the child *knows* about language (indexed by comprehension), as opposed to what the child *does* (indexed by production)."

More recently, some have suggested that attempting to evaluate the role of cognition in language development by defining children's cognitive progress solely in Piagetian terms may obscure real relationships between the two domains (Cromer, 1991). Further, some researchers maintain that *skill,* rather than *stage* mastery, sets the stage for the acquisition of particular linguistic behaviors. For example, object permanence may be required before words such as *all gone* are used (Gopnik & Meltzoff, 1987).

Cognitive theory is challenged when cases arise that suggest a possible *dissociation* between cognitive and linguistic development—for example, some children who were born during the 1950s to mothers who had taken a supposedly mild tranquilizer, *thalidomide,* during pregnancy had limbs missing and were unable to have the sensorimotor experiences thought to be prerequisite to language development. Yet these children developed full, sophisticated language capacity. More recent reports document children with substantial intellectual impairments (such as an IQ of 50) who have complete and sophisticated language capacity (Curtiss, 1982; Yamada, 1990).

Social Interactionist Theory

THE LANGUAGE-LEARNING ENVIRONMENT: BABIES HEAR A SPECIAL KIND OF LANGUAGE.   The speech infants hear is different in many ways from the language shared between adult speakers. What are these differences, and what are their implications? The work of Fernald (1985) has shown that mothers use typical intonation patterns in speaking to infants; the prosodic envelope carries information about such things as approval or disapproval in the early weeks. Fernald's work in several language communities has shown that mothers use quite similar patterns to tell their children "no," or to encourage them. Additionally, research suggests that infants may use the prosody of speech to segment major syntactic units (Kemler-Nelson, Hirsh-Pasek, Jusczyk, & Cassidy, 1989; Bernstein Ratner, 1986).

Speech to infants in our society is marked by *slow rate, exaggerated intonation, high fundamental frequency,* many *repetitions, simple syntax,* and a *simple* and *concrete vocabulary* (Snow & Ferguson, 1977). Parents may say, "See the birdie? Look at the birdie! What a pretty birdie!" These features probably make it easier for the infant to decode the language than if he heard, "Has it come to your attention that one of our better looking feathered friends is perched upon the windowsill?"

Child-directed speech (CDS), or **babytalk (BT),** exists in one form or another in all societies studied. But it is not uniform from society to society; rather, it is culturally determined. CDS is one of numerous speech registers speakers can use. Although it has some features that are determined by the needs of the hearer infant, it varies from society to society. For instance, high fundamental frequency often appeals to infants (perhaps high voices are less threatening than low voices) and it is frequently a feature of CDS, but some languages reserve high fundamental frequency for other purposes (Bernstein Ratner & Pye, 1984). In Quiche Mayan the babytalk register is characterized by *low* fundamental frequency, and high fundamental frequency is used in speech to social superiors. However, Quiche Mayan utilizes its own particular BT register, designed to call the child's attention to ways of producing well-formed Quiche utterances. Thus, babytalk registers are pervasive, though their individual forms vary. According to Gleitman, Gleitman, Landau, and Wanner (1988), "There is a natural coadaptation at work here, in which the mothers are inclined to provide a particular data base, and the babies are inclined to attend particularly to this."

Whether BT is necessary, helpful, or irrelevant to the process of language development is still a matter of spirited debate. The relative contribution made by the BT register to the process of language acquisition continues to be one of the critical questions in developmental psycholinguistics. The fact that some form of BT is universal in all cultures strongly suggests that it can influence language learning, or may in fact, enable it. Experimental evidence does suggest that infants would rather listen to CDS than to adult-directed speech (Fernald & Kuhl, 1987). It is possible that some of the prosodic and syntactic characteristics of BT may allow children to "bootstrap" their progress in language acquisition. For example, prosody that makes word and phrase boundaries more evident to the child should facilitate the child's subsequent attempts to decode the lexicon and grammar.

RELATING INPUT TO LANGUAGE LEARNING.   *Social interactionists* (for example, Bruner, 1985; Berko Gleason, Hay, & Cain, 1989; Farrar, 1990; Snow, 1981) do not deny the existence of special neuropsychological endowments, but they also hold that biological factors, although *necessary,* are *insufficient* to ensure that language will develop. They place less reliance on postulated hardwired and time-limited neural structures (such as the language acquisition device) for which there is no anatomical evidence.

According to some social interactionists, no biological "critical period" for language acquisition exists (Snow, 1987). They point out that *some* parts of language, such as a correct accent, may be more difficult to learn as one gets older, but that little evidence indicates that adults are worse language learners than children. Nor is language development seen as simply one aspect of cognitive development. Instead, social interactionists view language as a facet of communicative behavior that develops through *interaction* with other human beings. Bruner (1985) offers the term **LASS (language acquisition socialization system)** as an alternative to Chomsky's LAD.

According to this interactionist view, children acquire language in part through the *mediation* and help of others, rather than purely through their own mental activity in processing adult language. Thus, *interaction,* rather than *exposure,* is seen as necessary. Children cannot acquire language simply by observing adults in conversation with one another or by watching television or listening to the radio. Social interactionists point to special ways of talking to young children all over the world and that the special language used by adults appears *tailored* or *fine tuned* to the cognitive and communicative needs of the children. This child-directed speech is believed to make the job of segmenting the speech stream and decoding the language easier for children acquiring language (Kemler-Nelson, Hirsh-Pasek, Jusczyk, & Wright-Cassidy, 1989; Bernstein Ratner, 1994).

According to this view, children are not little grammarians, motivated to decode the syntax of the language around them through the operation of their LAD, but social beings who acquire language in the service of their needs to communicate with others. In stressing the functional basis of language, interactionists study (1) the interpersonal reasons that children have for speaking in the first place, (2) the ways that older speakers tailor their linguistic interactions with infants in order to facilitate language acquisition, and (3) the effect of different kinds of input on children's developing language.

Social interactionists disagree with the view that children receive no *negative evidence* about their ungrammatical utterances, because research has shown that parents tend to respond in a variety of ways to unsuccessful language attempts. They are apt to react with puzzlement to ill-formed utterances, to **recast** them (or repeat them in corrected form), and to provide other cues to grammar (Bohannon, MacWhinney, & Snow, 1990; Farrar, 1992). Additionally, social interactionists focus additional attention on those aspects of language competence less often studied by proponents of linguistic theories of language development, who generally study the acquisition of syntactic ability. They focus on additional areas such as phonology (Bernstein Ratner, 1993), the lexicon (Masur & Gleason, 1980; Kavanaugh & Jirkovsky, 1982), and pragmatics (Berko Gleason, Hay, & Cain, 1989). Data suggest that parents make efforts to tailor articulation to young children to maximize phonemic contrasts (Bernstein Ratner, 1987) and respond to immature pronunciation (Bernstein Ratner, 1992). Further, the acquisition of a lexicon (vocabulary) seems inherently tied to interactional experience; one cannot extrapolate the name for an item using rules, unlike syntax or morphology. Finally, the very nature of pragmatic competence suggests the inherent role of social interaction within one's language community in its development.

Various interactional features appear positively associated with children's language acquisition. For example, joint attention focus (the amount of time that the mother talks about topics that the child is already focused on) correlates with early vocabulary size. Children's first word usages tend to mirror those contexts in which their mothers frequently use such words, although later vocabulary acquisition does not show this pattern (Barrett, 1995).

Connectionist Models

Connectionist or **parallel distributed processing (PDP) models** explore how information may be built into a system (in this case the child's brain) through *neural connections*. In particular, the human ability to make connections or associations between elements distinguishes the human mind from computer memory, which holds discrete bits of information at a specified address, available for retrieval and input to computations. To illustrate a nonconnectionist system, Potter (1990) uses the analogy of a television screen, in which a meaningful display can be generated by turning pixels off and on at discrete locations. The pixels' activity, however, is controlled by commands to each, and the pixels do not communicate with each other. People are different from computers and televisions; clearly activation of one concept in our minds has the capacity to bring up another.

Human memory for experiences appears to be distributed widely across what may be termed *processing units*. These units are "a little like idealized brain cells. They can perform only the same simple computation. The power of the system comes from how the units are connected" (Johnson-Laird, 1988, p. 174). A child develops such connections over time through exposure to the forms of the language associated with external events. For example, a child may hear the word *bottle* under varying circumstances and thereby establish neural associations to the word, to the initial sound /b/, to the word *milk,* and so forth. Ultimately those interconnected associations become the "meaning" of the word. Information in such a *neural network* is conveyed through many interconnected units or nodes. The nodes have activation levels or thresholds that can turn them on or off, and learning consists essentially of adjusting the strengths of the connections in a direction that produces the desired outputs. In the case of word recognition, for example, the word's stimulus properties activate various nodes and their corresponding connections to produce a pattern or state of activation. When this pattern reoccurs, the system can be said to "recognize" the stimulus. Eventually, even an incomplete or degraded stimulus may be sufficient to activate the full pattern.

In such a model, many operations can take place simultaneously or in parallel. No manipulation of symbols or higher "cognitive" activity is required. Connectionist theories thus model language acquisition at the neuronal level. In particular, they have been used to describe how particular grammatical structures such as the inflectional system may be acquired (McClelland, Rumelhart, & PDP Group, 1986).

Connectionist theory assumes that sufficient exposure will lead to the establishment of neural networks, and McClelland and his colleagues have somewhat successfully modeled in a computer how a child might acquire simple past tenses in English. In doing so, the "processor" (child or machine) simply tallies the input frequencies of the phonological characteristics of word stems and the corresponding phonological patterns in the suffix. If a particular sequence is statistically likely, the model will extend previously noted regularities to the new data. Thus, *showed, mowed, towed,* and *glowed* may imply the statistical likelihood that *growed* is the correct past tense of *grow.* In particular, forms such as *rowed, maked,* and *goed* seem to appear (in either computer simulations or actual children) after the initial lexicon (consisting of frequent but typically irregular verb forms) undergoes dramatic expansion, resulting in the input of a wider array of forms that follow more predictable patterns of root affixation. PDP models assert that connections, not "rules," underlie language development.

A rare introductory level discussion of parallel distributed processing models is provided by Johnson-Laird (1988). Pinker (1984, 1989, 1991) and his associates, however, argue that connectionists have not modeled everything that even a 4-year-old can do, and that the most parsimonious explanation for the acquisition of grammar is still that the child internalizes a set of *rules* or principles. In a recent formulation, Pinker (1991) has proposed that connectionist models can explain children's acquisition of irregular past tenses and why children and adults in "wug"-like experiments will create nonsense irregular forms rather than regulars when confronted with a hypothetical phrase such as, "This man is fringing; Yesterday, he _____." He suggests, however, that rule induction underlies the regular inflectional system, and that children do possess important underlying knowledge about verbs that goes beyond mere tallies of their phonological properties. For example, [rIŋ] is the present-tense pronunciation of *ring* (as in a bell, or to border something), as well as *wring.* These three verbs take three separate past tenses, implying the necessity for more sophisticated analysis of past-tense formation, which may, as Pinker suggests, require knowing whether a verb is irregular or has been historically derived from a noun root.

This controversy about the nature of mental representation may appear abstract, but it underlies much current thought in psycholinguistics. If children are acquiring rules and principles, then language can be seen, as Pinker has said, as the "jewel in the crown" of cognitive development; if they are simply establishing neural connections that are automatic and unrelated to their higher abstract abilities, then language loses some of its special status. Pinker is impressed with children's sensitivities to principles of language that are not easily captured in statistical terms.

It has become increasingly plausible to many researchers that multiple mechanisms may be involved in the full range of language skill acquisitions (MacWhinney, 1978, 1982; Moerk, 1989). Thus, rote learning, pattern abstraction, and rule learning may all contribute to children's eventual language development.

It should be clear at this point that we should add another feature of theories to the list presented in the first section of this chapter: theories are *selective*. Each of them concentrates on only some of the phenomena under consideration and has little to say about the others.

Theories, of course, ultimately require data. Because young children do not possess the *metalinguistic* ability that would allow them to describe for us their linguistic systems, we rely upon various forms of observation, experimentation, and assessment in the study of children's acquisition of language. Thus, the search for new sources of data and new ways to evaluate old sources of data continues.

PERSPECTIVES: WHAT DO THE DATA TELL US ABOUT THE THEORIES?

We come to this point in the chapter having discussed a variety of theories. We have also listed some of the major questions that divide otherwise friendly groups of psycholinguistic researchers. Some questions are still unanswered, but our rapidly growing understanding of psychology and linguistics points us toward ways to synthesize certain types of information.

NATURE OR NURTURE?   Clearly, the answer to this question is a resounding, "Both." Clearly, some properties of the human mind must guide the child through her rapid acquisition of this immensely complex system of behavior. However, certain types of knowledge, such as vocabulary and the social use of language, clearly are "taught" either explicitly or through directed exposure. Additionally, even in the area of syntax, particular parental language models do appear to affect some aspects of children's language development. For example, frequent parental use of Yes–No questions does appear to facilitate the child's acquisition of the verbal auxiliary system in English (Newport, Gleitman, & Gleitman, 1977).

BIOLOGICAL BASES.   Research during the past 30 years has provided us with a large data base as well as evidence of *universal processes* in language development.

Linguistic capacity relies upon, among other things, *neuroanatomical structures* that are unique to our species (see Chapter 2). Left hemisphere specialization for language appears innate; *cerebral asymmetries* have been noted as early as the 18th week of gestation (Witelson, 1977). In particular, the *planum temporale* (temporal plane) of the left hemisphere is larger than its homologue on the right; ultimately, the left temporal plane develops into **Wernicke's area** (in the medial and superior left temporal lobe; see Chapter 2). Wernicke's area is involved in processing incoming speech, and damage to Wernicke's area in an adult speaker results in a typical language deficit—Wernicke's aphasia. Other areas of the brain are also intimately involved with language: These include **Broca's area** in the posterior inferior left frontal lobe and the **arcuate fasciculus,** a band of subcortical fibers that connects Wernicke's area to Broca's area.

Thus, human infants are born with neuropsychological endowments in place that make ultimate perception, comprehension, and production of language in all its forms possible. We have no evidence that any other creatures have this kind of linguistic capacity, not even our close relatives, the chimpanzees.

BIOLOGICAL, COGNITIVE, AND SOCIAL INTERACTION.   Assuming an intact neurological system, infants' *cognitive* and *affective* propensities lead them to acquire language relatively rapidly during the first few years of life and with remarkable similarity across languages. As we have noted, during the first year of life children progress through some typical early communicative stages, and much of this development is maturational or determined by neuropsychological development. Someone who is unfamiliar with the immense research literature in developmental psychology might think that during a baby's first year she is best described as merely "prelinguistic," as if the main task of that period were to lie about engaged in phoneme discrimination, learning to babble, and so forth. But it is important to emphasize that during infancy children are also developing socially and emotionally. These social and affective characteristics may actually *cause* changes in the psychological mechanisms that undergird language and make language development possible.

Babies' innate social and affective dispositions lead them to be intensely interested in other human beings and to seek and maintain social contact with them. For example, much research indicates that babies are more interested in people than in objects. They are especially interested in the normal human face, which they prefer to look at when given a choice of various stimuli. They prefer an undistorted human face to a rather Picasso-like "face" with scrambled features, and they prefer the scrambled-feature face to a similarly complex but inanimate picture (Fantz, 1961; Lamb & Sherrod, 1981).

Infants' ability to hear fine auditory distinctions was noted earlier. Their preference for the human voice also appears early on; in fact, it seems quite likely that infants are innately predisposed to attend preferentially to human speech versus other sounds (Gibson & Spelke, 1983). Even more remarkable is the finding of DeCasper and Fifer (1980) that newborn infants prefer to hear their own mothers' voices! Infants were given the opportunity to suck a pacifier in order to evoke either the voice of the mother or that of a stranger; 8 out of 10 newborns adjusted the pauses in their sucking in such a way as to hear their own mother's voice. It is thus possible that children become attached to their own mother and their own mother's voice while still *in utero* and thus begin their language development prenatally.

Language development depends on much more than cognitive attainment—it is predicated on a complex base of social and emotional development as well, and it arises in an intensely interactive arena.

Interpretation of the same child language data varies with the theoretical stance of the researcher. How, for instance, do we interpret the actions of a child just learning to talk who points at her favorite toy, high on a shelf, and says, "Want dolly"? According to learning theory, the child has been rewarded in the past for speaking and has been reinforced for producing successive approximations of the phrase *want dolly* in the presence of the toy and a listener.

This behavior is explained by cognitive theorists and innatists as an example of the child's exercise of cognitive and linguistic proclivities: The child is seen as driven to categorize and name concepts and to understand the permissible organization of nouns and verbs in sentences in her language.

A social interactionist theorist sees this behavior as socially and emotionally motivated as well: The child uses language to get and hold the attention and affection of another person and to achieve a goal. This is not to deny cognitive activity, or the fact that the child is learning to categorize the world and acquire the lexical system of English. Still, the act of requesting the toy is an interactional phenomenon and an extraordinarily successful behavior for capturing the notice of parents and others. Like other attachment behaviors (smiling, following the parent, crying when the parent leaves), early language serves the social and affective needs of both infants and their parents. Like language itself, attachment is a universal phenomenon and is biologically based (Bowlby, 1969).

CONTINUITY OR DISCONTINUITY? This is one question that appears to have an answer, and the evidence is on the side of continuity in the domains that have been investigated, most particularly in children's progression from babbling to speech. Earlier theorists had postulated the existence of a stage of babbling, followed by a silent period, and that only then did true speech evolve (Jakobson, 1968). Current studies of babbling reveal a considerable overlap between babbling and speech (DeBoysson-Bardies & Vihman, 1991). Likewise, children's acquisition of syntax, although characterized by stages, does not appear to be markedly discontinuous, changing radically in underlying organization. Language is unlikely to be a "today you're a tadpole, tomorrow you're a frog" phenomenon.

UNIVERSAL COMPETENCE OR INDIVIDUAL VARIATION? We all learn to talk, just as we all learn to walk. But beyond the fundamentals we share, we show variation in our language, much as in our gait. Much of psycholinguistic theory and research is based upon a belief that all speakers are alike and share identical representations of language. Early child language studies also sought to find these universally shared aspects of language, and clearly there are universal, possibly innate, constraints on what an infant can acquire. However, even if language were entirely innately determined, we would expect it to vary from individual to individual. Just as no two individuals have the same brain (Lieberman, 1991), neither do they share exactly the same experiences. Studies of children's language continue to reveal differences in their style, rate, focus, and ultimate communicative competence (Goldfield & Snow, 1997).

STRUCTURE OR FUNCTION?   How shall we understand the bases of language development? Are children acquiring syntactic structures, or are they learning to communicate? Clearly, they are doing both. Grammatical mechanisms may activate when they hear language over which they have no control. At the same time, they are driven by social and affective forces that lead them to want to use language to establish and maintain contact with other humans. The adults in a child's environment also have certain beliefs about their own role in their child's language development, as well as what the child should be capable of to perform adequately within society at various stages of maturation. We cannot say what researchers *should* study: information about *syntax, phonology, the lexicon, morphology,* and *the social uses of language* are all necessary to complete our understanding of language acquisition.

AUTONOMY OR INTERACTION?   Is human language a separate faculty, or is it just one of the mightier weapons in our general cognitive armamentarium? Are complex vocabulary and syntax our crowning intellectual achievement, evidence of abstract abilities and advanced cognitive development'? This is one of the most intriguing puzzles that faces the developmental psycholinguist. Innatist/linguistic theorists believe that linguistic capacity is autonomous, whereas others see it as dependent on social or cognitive factors. To answer this question, we need much more information on atypical populations. Recent studies (Yamada, 1991) have described dissociations between linguistic and other development. For example, Yamada studied a young woman named Laura. When asked to name some fruits, Laura, age 16, named pears, apples, and pomegranates. In referring to a recent distressing event at around the same time, she said, "He was saying that I lost my battery-powered watch that I loved; I just loved that watch." These responses are unremarkable—except that Laura's general intellectual abilities are extremely depressed, with a full-scale IQ of just 41. Laura was given extensive batteries of tests of linguistic, cognitive, and neuropsychological functioning, and her language was analyzed. Her language has always been far in advance of her other abilities. Data of this nature support at least in part the conclusion that language is an independent, or *modular* ability. At the time of testing, even though Laura could talk about pomegranates and produce complex sentences with multiple embeddings such as the one cited above, she performed essentially at the preschool level on most standardized tests of intellectual functioning. She could not read or write or tell time. She did not know who the president of the United States was or in what country she lived. Her drawings of humans resembled potatoes with stick arms and legs, and, unlike many 2-year-olds, she did not know her own age.

Ultimately, our theories will have to account for the remarkable dissociations that can exist between an individual's understanding of the world and ability to produce complex language.

RULES OR ASSOCIATIONS?   How do human beings mentally represent language? As we noted earlier, this is one of the most contentious areas of modern linguistics.

Some of this text's authors' early work was predicated on the notion that children acquire rules (indeed, one of us once wrote that if a child can tell us that the plural of *gutch* is *gutches* we have evidence that he has a rule for the formation of the plural).

Now models of plural formation call upon neural nets rather than abstract principles, and they are also persuasive. Perhaps, for the time, our best answer is to say, as we did at the beginning of this chapter, that we can describe *what* children learn, but we don't really know *how* they do it. The answer to how they do it will involve understanding not just the complexity of linguistic systems, but children's unique biological endowments, as well as an understanding of the cognitive and social characteristics that they bring to the task. Bohannon and Bonvillian (1997) provide extensive discussion of the many theoretical approaches to language acquisition and evaluate the extent to which each approach can answer the questions posed earlier in this section.

SUMMARY

Young children acquire language rapidly and apparently effortlessly during their first three or four years. Researchers do not agree on how to account for language development, and a variety of theories have been called upon. These include linguistic/innatist theory; behavioral/learning theory; cognitive theory; information processing theory; and social interactionist theory. Each of them has something to offer, but none of them is complete. Psycholinguistic research can be conducted experimentally or observationally; early studies consisted mainly of diary reports, but contemporary researchers are able to study data on many children by using the Child Language Data Exchange System (CHILDES). Research on children reveals universal characteristics in early words and early sentences. When children begin to acquire the grammar of their own language, they all tend to follow roughly the same course. Language development relies upon both innate mechanisms that are specific to language, such as specialized parts of the brain, and more general propensities of children, such as the need to form bonds of attachment with their caregivers. In this sense, language is a biologically based attainment that relies upon social, cognitive, and affective processes.

KEY WORDS

Developmental psycholinguistics
Metalinguistic
Longitudinal studies
Cross-sectional studies
Observational studies

Naturalistic
Controlled observational studies
Experimental studies
Experimental group
Control group

Categorical perception
Habituation
High-amplitude sucking paradigm (HASP)
Voice-onset-time (VOT)
Cardiac deceleration
Conditioned head-turn procedure
Bootstrapping strategy
Perceptual loss
Protodeclaratives
Protoimperatives
Open syllables
Holophrastic stage
Content word
Function word
Negation
Recurrence
Nonexistence
Notice
Referential use of language
Basic level categories
Overextension
Underextension
Mismatch
Extendibility
Object scope
Categorical scope
Novel name–nameless category strategy
Conventionality
Semantic features
Prototypes
Concrete vocabulary
Relative concepts
Absolute meaning
Ambiguous words
Syntagmatic association
Paradigmatic association
Preferential looking paradigm
Telegraphic speech
Parameters
Mean length of utterance (MLU)
Overregularization

Passives
Datives
Compound sentences
Complex sentences
S-V-O word order strategy
Event probability
Minimal distance principle
Order of mention strategy
Paraphrase
Idiom
Figurative language
Referential children
Expressive children
Egocentrism
Innate/innatism
Pidgin
Creole
Poverty of the stimulus problem
Negative evidence
Language acquisition device (LAD)
Bioprogram
Universal Grammar (UG)
Classical conditioning
Conditioned/unconditioned stimulus
Conditioned/unconditioned response
Operant conditioning/instrumental learning
Reinforcement
Extinguish
Social learning
Object permanence
Autonomous
Child-directed speech (CDS)
Babytalk (BT)
Language acquisition socialization system (LASS)
Recast
Connectionist/parallel distributed processing (PDP) models
Wernicke's area
Broca's area
Arcuate fasciculus

SOMETHING TO THINK ABOUT

1. Compare and contrast the cognitive and social interactionist approaches with respect to the dimensions of nativism–empiricism, structuralism–functionalism, and active–passive children. What predictions would each make if children were exposed to language only through television? What predictions would you make?

2. How might you design a study to compare the abilities of adults, children, and adults who are learning English as a second language to use lexical prefixes (such as *re-, un-,* and *uni-*), and grammatical suffixes such as the plural and past and present-progressive tenses? Which do you think are easier to acquire? Why?

3. How might you determine what 2-, 4-, and 8-year-old children think the word *boat* means?

4. Consider the processes of *understanding* sentences, *producing* well-formed sentences, *judging* the well-formedness of other people's sentences, *correcting* ill-formed utterances, and *explaining* why sentences are ungrammatical. Think about which of these skills might emerge earlier and later in development, and why. Develop a method for verifying your predictions.

ACTIVITIES

1. Tape record language samples from a 1-year-old, a 3-year-old, and a 5-year-old as each child looks at a picture book such as *Frog, Where Are You?* by Mercer Mayer with a parent. How do the children's samples differ phonologically, lexically, syntactically, and pragmatically? How close is the 5-year-old to adult language performance?

2. Do parents' speech samples differ when speaking to these children of different ages? How? Do any aspects of the parents' interactions appear to have the potential to aid the children's language development? Might any of their behaviors hinder the children's linguistic progress? Explain.

3. Find a children's joke book. Engage a 5-year-old and a 10-year-old in joke and riddle telling. How do their responses reflect differences in their language abilities? Do both children find the jokes funny? How do they differ in their ability to explain *why* the jokes, riddles, or puns are funny?

4. Test the hypothesis that 3-year-old and 8-year-old children will differ in their abilities to understand sentences that do not follow S-V-O word order.

5. Surf the net! Access the CHILDES archive (see a copy of their web page in Figure 8.2b). Using data and analytical programs from the archive, compare some specific aspect of the spontaneous language of children at two different ages of development. (How do these children compare to age-matched children with language impairments, whose data are also included in the archive?)

REFERENCES

Aksu-Koc, A., & Slobin, D. I. (1985). The acquisition of Turkish. In D. I. Slobin (Ed.), *The crosslinguistic study of language acquisition: Vol. 1: The data.* Hillsdale, NJ: Erlbaum.

Anglin, J. (1977). *Word, object and conceptual development.* New York: Norton.

Bandura, A., Ross, D., & Ross, S. (1963). Transmission of aggression through imitation of aggressive models. *Journal of Abnormal and Social Psychology, 63,* 3–11.

Bar-Adon, A., & Leopold, W. F. (1971). *Child language: A book of readings.* Englewood Cliffs, NJ: Prentice-Hall.

Barrett, M. (1995). Early lexical development. In P. Fletcher & B. MacWhinney (Eds.), *The handbook of child language.* Cambridge: Basil Blackwell.

Bates, E. (1976). *Language and context: The acquisition of pragmatics.* New York: Academic Press.

Bates, E. (1979). *The emergence of symbols: Cognition and communication in infancy.* New York: Academic Press.

Bates, E., Bretherton, I., Snyder, L., Shore, C., & Volterra, V. (1980). Vocal and gestural symbols at 13 months. *Merrill-Palmer Quarterly, 26,* 407–423.

Bates, E., Dale, P., & Thal, D. (1995). Individual differences and their implications for theories of language development. In P. Fletcher & B. MacWhinney (Eds.), *The handbook of child language* (pp. 96–151). Cambridge: Basil Blackwell.

Bates, E., & Snyder, L. (1985). The cognitive hypothesis in language development. In I. Uzgiris & J. M. Hunt (Eds.), *Research with scales of psychological development in infancy.* Champaign-Urbana: University of Illinois Press.

Bellugi, U. (1967). *The acquisition of negation.* Unpublished doctoral dissertation, Harvard University.

Benedict, H. (1979). Early lexical development: Comprehension and production. *Journal of Child Language, 6,* 183–200.

Berko, J. (1958). The child's learning of English morphology. *Word, 14,* 47–56.

Berko Gleason, J. (Ed.). (1997). *The development of language* (4th ed.). Boston: Allyn & Bacon.

Berko Gleason, J., Hay, D., & Cain, L. (1989). The social and affective determinants of language development. In M. Rice & R. Schiefelbusch (Eds.), *The teachability of language* (pp. 171–186). Baltimore: Paul Brookes.

Berko Gleason, J., Perlmann, R. Y., & Greif, E. B. (1984). What's the magic word? *Discourse Processes, 7,* 493–502.

Berman, R. (1985). The acquisition of Hebrew. In D. I. Slobin (Ed.), *The crosslinguistic study of language acquisition: Vol. 1: The data.* Hillsdale, NJ: Erlbaum.

Bernstein, M. (1983). Formation of internal structure in a lexical category. *Journal of Child Language, 10,* 381–399.

Bernstein Ratner, N. (1986). Durational cues which mark clause boundaries in mother–child speech. *Journal of Phonetics, 14,* 303–309.

Bernstein Ratner, N. (1987). The phonology of parent-child speech. In K. Nelson & A. van Kleeck (Eds.), *Children's language, Vol. 6.* Hillsdale, NJ: Erlbaum.

Bernstein Ratner, N. (1988). Patterns of parental vocabulary selection in speech to young children. *Journal of Child Language, 15,* 481–492.

Bernstein Ratner, N. (1993). Maternal input and unusual phonological behavior: A case study and its implications. *Journal of Child Language, 20*(1), 191–198.

Bernstein Ratner, N. (1995). From "signal to syntax": But what is the nature of the signal? In J. Morgan & K. Demuth (Eds.), *Signal to syntax: Bootstrapping from speech to grammar in early acquisition.* Hillsdale, NJ: Erlbaum.

Bernstein Ratner, N., & Pye, C. (1984). Higher pitch in babytalk is *not* universal: Acoustic evidence from Quiche Mayan. *Journal of Child Language, 11,* 515–522.

Bever, T. (1970). The cognitive basis for linguistic structures. In J. Hayes (Ed.), *Cognition and the development of language.* New York: Wiley.

Bickerton, D. (1984). The language bioprogram hypothesis. *Behavioral and Brain Sciences, 7,* 173–221.

Bloom, L. (1970). *Language development: Form and function in emerging grammars.* Cambridge: MIT Press.

Bloom, L., Lahey, P., Hood, L., Lifter, K., & Fiess, K. (1980). Complex sentences: Acquisition of syntactic connectors and the semantic relations they encode. *Journal of Child Language, 7,* 235–262.

Bohannon, J. N. III, & Bonvillian, J. (1997). Theoretical approaches to language acquisition. In J. Berko Gleason (Ed.), *The development of language.* Boston: Allyn & Bacon.

Bohannon, J. N. III, MacWhinney, B., & Snow, C. E. (1990). No negative evidence revisited: Beyond learnability, or who has to prove what to whom. *Developmental Psychology, 26,* 221–226.

Bonvillian, J., Orlansky, M., & Novack, L. (1983). Developmental milestones: Sign language acquisition and motor development. *Child Development, 54,* 1435–1445.

Bowlby, J. (1969). *Attachment and loss: Vol. 1: Attachment.* New York: Basic Books.

Braine, M. (1963). The ontogeny of English phrase structure: The first phase. *Language, 39,* 1–13.

Bridges, A. (1980). SVO comprehension strategies reconsidered: The evidence of individual patterns of response. *Journal of Child Language, 7,* 89–104.

Brown, R. (1973). *A first language: The early stages.* Cambridge, MA: Harvard University Press.

Brown, R., & Bellugi, U. (1964). Three processes in the child's acquisition of syntax. *Harvard Educational Review, 34,* 133–151.

Brown, R., & Berko, J. (1960). Word association and the acquisition of grammar. *Child Development, 31,* 1–14.

Bruner, J. (1985). *Child's talk: Learning to use language.* New York: Norton.

Butcher, C., Mylander, C., & Goldin-Meadow, S. (In press). Displaced communication in a self-styled gesture system: Pointing at the non-present. *Cognitive Development.*

Carey, S. (1982). Semantic development: The state of the art. In E. Wanner & L. Gleitman (Eds.), *Language acquisition—The state of the art.* New York: Cambridge University Press.

Carey, S., & Bartlett, E. (1978). Acquiring a single new word. *Papers and Reports on Child Language Development, 15,* 17–29.

Chomsky, C. (1968). *The acquisition of syntax in children from 5 to 10.* Cambridge: MIT Press.

Chomsky, N. (1965). *Aspects of the theory of syntax.* Cambridge: MIT Press.

Chomsky, N. (1972). *Language and mind.* New York: Harcourt Brace Jovanovich.

Chomsky, N. (1982). *Lectures on government and binding: The Pisa lectures.* Dordrecht, Netherlands: Foris.

Clancy, P. (1985). The acquisition of Japanese. In D. I. Slobin (Ed.), *The crosslinguistic study of language acquisition: Vol. 1: The data.* Hillsdale, NJ: Erlbaum.

Clark, E. (1973). What's in a word? On the child's acquisition of semantics in his first language. In T. Moore (Ed.), *Cognitive development and the acquisition of language.* New York: Academic Press.

Clark, E. (1985). The acquisition of Romance, with special reference to French. In D. I. Slobin (Ed.), *The crosslinguistic study of language acquisition: Vol. 1: The data.* Hillsdale, NJ: Erlbaum.

Clark, E. (1993). *The lexicon in acquisition.* Cambridge: Cambridge University Press.

Clark, E. (1995). Later lexical development and word formation. In P. Fletcher & B. MacWhinney (Eds.), *The handbook of child language.* Oxford: Basil Blackwell.

Cromer, R. (1991). *Language and thought in normal and handicapped children.* Cambridge, MA: Blackwell.

Curtiss, S. (1982). Developmental dissociations of language and cognition. In L. Obler & L. Menn (Eds.), *Exceptional language and linguistics.* New York: Academic Press.

Dale, P. (1991). The validity of a parent report measure of vocabulary and syntax at 24 months. *Journal of Speech and Hearing Research, 34,* 565–571.

de Boysson-Bardies, B., & Vihman, M. (1991). Adaptation to language: Evidence from babbling and first words in four languages. *Language, 67*(2), 297–319.

DeCasper, A., & Fifer, W. (1980). Of human bonding: Newborns prefer their mothers' voices. *Science, 208,* 1174–1176.

Dennis, M., Sugar, J., & Whitaker, H. (1982). The acquisition of tag questions. *Child Development, 53,* 1254–1257.

DeVilliers, J. G., & DeVilliers, P. A. (1973). A cross-sectional study of the acquisition of grammatical morphemes in child speech. *Journal of Psycholinguistic Research, 2,* 267–278.

DeVilliers, J. G., & DeVilliers, P. A. (1985). The acquisition of English. In D. I. Slobin (Ed.), *The crosslinguistic study of language acquisition: Vol. 1: The data.* Hillsdale, NJ: Erlbaum.

Dromi, E. (1987). *Early lexical development.* Cambridge: Cambridge University Press.

Eimas, P. (1974). Auditory and linguistic processing of cues for place of articulation by infants. *Perception and Psychophysics, 16,* 513–521.

Eimas, P., Siqueland, E., Jusczyk, P., & Vigorito, J. (1971). Speech perception in infants. *Science, 171,* 303–306.

Fantz, R. L. (1961). The origin of form perception. *Scientific American, 204,* 66–72.

Farrar, M. J. (1990). Discourse and the acquisition of grammatical morphemes. *Journal of Child Language, 17,* 607–624.

Farrar, M. J. (1992). Negative evidence and grammatical morpheme acquisition. *Developmental Psychology, 28*(1), 90–98.

Fernald, A. (1985). Four-month-old infants prefer to listen to motherese. *Infant Behavior and Development, 8,* 181–195.

Fernald, A., & Kuhl, P. (1987). Acoustic determinants of infant preference for motherese speech. *Infant Behavior and Development, 10,* 279–293.

Fox, F., & Routh, D. (1975). Analyzing spoken language into words, syllables, and phonemes: A developmental study. *Journal of Psycholinguistic Research, 4,* 331–342.

Fremgen, A., & Fay, D. (1980). Overextensions in production and comprehension: A methodological clarification. *Journal of Child Language, 7,* 205–211.

Gentner, D. (1982). Why nouns are learned before verbs: Linguistic relativity vs. natural partitioning. In S. Kuczaj (Ed.), *Language development, Vol. 2.* Hillsdale, NJ: Erlbaum.

Gibson, E. J., & Spelke, E. S. (1983). The development of perception. In J. H. Flavell & E. M. Markman (Eds.), *Handbook of child psychology: Cognitive development.* Volume 3. New York: John Wiley & Sons.

Gleitman, L., & Gillette, J. (1995). The role of syntax in verb learning. In P. Fletcher & B. MacWhinney (Eds.), *The handbook of child language.* Oxford: Basil Blackwell.

Gleitman, L., Gleitman, H., Landau, B., & Wanner, E. (1988). Where learning begins: Initial representations for language learning. In F. Newmeyer (Ed.), *Linguistics: The Cambridge Survey. Vol. III. Language: Psychological and biological aspects.* Cambridge: Cambridge University Press.

Glucksberg, S., Krauss, R., & Higgins, T. (1975). The development of referential communication skills. In F. Horowitz (Ed.), *Review of child development research, Vol. 4.* Chicago: University of Chicago Press.

Goldfield, B., & Snow, C. E. (1997). Individual differences: Implications for the study of language acquisition. In J. Berko Gleason (Ed.), *The development of language* (4th ed.). Boston: Allyn & Bacon.

Goldin-Meadow, S., & Mylander, C. (1990). Beyond the input given: The child's role in the acquisition of language. *Language, 66,* 323–355.

Golinkoff, R., Diznoff, J., Yasik, A., & Hirsh-Pasek, K. (1992). How children identify nouns vs. verbs. International conference on infant studies.

Golinkoff, R., Hirsh-Pasek, K., Cauley, K., & Gordon, P. (1987). The eyes have it: Lexical and syntactic comprehension in a new paradigm. *Journal of Child Language, 14,* 23–46.

Golinkoff, R., Mervis, C., & Hirsh-Pasek, K. (1994). Early object labels: The case for a developmental lexical principles framework. *Journal of Child Language, 21,* 125–155.

Gopnik, A., & Meltzoff, A. N. (1987). Early semantic developments and their relationship to object permanence, means–end understanding, and categorization.

In K. E. Nelson & A. van Kleeck (Eds.), *Children's language, Vol. 6*. Hillsdale, NJ: Erlbaum.

Halliday, M. (1975). *Learning how to mean: Explorations in the development of language.* New York: Arnold.

Hamburger, H., & Crain, S. (1982). Relative acquisition. In S. Kuczaj II (Ed.), *Language development: Syntax and semantics.* Hillsdale, NJ: Erlbaum.

Haviland, S., & Clark, E. (1974). "This man's father is my father's son": A study of the acquisition of English kin terms. *Journal of Child Language, 1,* 23–47.

Hirsh-Pasek, K., & Golinkoff, R. (1996). *The origins of grammar.* Cambridge, MA: MIT Press.

Hirsh-Pasek, K., Kemler-Nelson, D., Jusczyk, P., Cassidy, K., Druss, B., & Kennedy, L. (1987). Clauses are perceptual units for young infants. *Cognition, 26,* 269–286.

Hyams, N. M. (1986). *Language acquisition and the theory of parameters.* Dordrecht: Reidel.

Jakobson, R. (1968). *Child language, aphasia and phonological universals.* The Hague: Mouton.

Johnson, C. (1991). *Emergence of "subject" in monolingual acquisition of Mexican Spanish.* Unpublished doctoral dissertation, University of Maryland at College Park.

Johnson-Laird, P. (1988). *The computer and the mind: An introduction to cognitive science.* Cambridge, MA: Harvard University Press.

Jusczyk, P., Luce, P., & Charles-Luce, J. (1994). Infants' sensitivity to phonotactic patterns in the native language. *Journal of Memory and Language, 33,* 630–645.

Kamhi, A. (1986). The elusive first word: The importance of the naming insight for the development of referential speech. *Journal of Child Language, 13,* 155–161.

Kavanaugh, R., & Jirkovsky, A. (1982). Parental speech to young children: A longitudinal analysis. *Merrill-Palmer Quarterly, 28,* 297–311.

Kelly, C., & Dale, P. (1989). Cognitive skills associated with the onset of multiword utterances. *Journal of Speech and Hearing Research, 32,* 645–656.

Kemler-Nelson, D., Hirsh-Pasek, K., Jusczyk, P., & Wright-Cassidy, K. (1989). How the prosodic cues in motherese might assist language learning. *Journal of Child Language, 16,* 55–68.

Kessel, F. (1988). *The development of language and language researchers.* Hillsdale, NJ: Erlbaum.

Kuhl, P. (1980). Perceptual constancy for speech-sound categories in early infancy. In G. Yeni-Komshian, J. Kavanagh, & C. Ferguson (Eds.), *Child phonology, Vol. 2: Perception.* New York: Academic.

Kuhl, P., Williams, K., Lacerda, F., Stevens, K., & Lindblom, B. (1992). Linguistic experience alters phonetic perception in infants by six months of age. *Science, 255,* 606–608.

Lamb, M., & Sherrod, L. (1981). *Infant social cognition.* Hillsdale, NJ: Erlbaum.

Lecanuet, J.-P., & Granier-Deferre, C. (1993). Speech stimuli in the fetal environment. In B. de Boysson-Bardies, S. de Schonen, P. Jusczyk, P. MacNeilage, & J. Morton (Eds.), *Developmental neurocognition: Speech and voice processing in the first year of life.* Dordrecht: Kluwer.

Lee, L. (1974). *Developmental sentence analysis.* Evanston, IL: Northwestern University Press.

Lenneberg, E. (1967). *The biological foundations of language.* New York: Wiley.

Leopold, W. (1948). Semantic learning in infant language. *Word, 4,* 173–180.

Lieberman, P. (1991). *Uniquely human: The evolution of speech, thought, and selfless behavior.* Cambridge, MA: Harvard University Press.

Lightfoot, D. (1982). *The language lottery: Toward a biology of grammars.* Cambridge: MIT Press.

Lloyd, P. (1991). Strategies used to communicate route directions by telephone: A comparison of the performance of 7-year-olds, 10-year-olds, and adults. *Journal of Child Language, 18,* 171–189.

Locke, J. (1993). *The child's path to spoken language.* Cambridge: Harvard University Press.

Macnamara, J. (1972). Cognitive basis of language learning in infants. *Psychological Review, 79,* 1–13.

MacWhinney, B. (1978). The acquisition of morphology. *Monographs of the Society for Research in Child Development, 43.*

MacWhinney, B. (1982). Basic syntactic processes. In S. Kuczaj II (Ed.), *Language development: Vol. 1: Syntax and semantics.* Hillsdale, NJ: Erlbaum.

MacWhinney, B. (1995). *The CHILDES Project.* Hillsdale, NJ: Erlbaum.

MacWhinney, B., & Snow, C. (1985). The Child Language Data Exchange System. *Journal of Child Language, 12,* 271–296.

Masur, E., & Gleason, J. B. (1980). Parent–child interaction and the acquisition of lexical information during play. *Developmental Psychology, 16,* 404–409.

McClelland, J., Rumelhart, D., & PDP Research Group. (1986). *Parallel distributed processing: Explorations in the microstructure of cognition: Vol. 2.* Cambridge, MA: Bradford.

McNeill, D. (1966). Developmental psycholinguistics. In F. Smith & G. Miller (Eds.), *The genesis of language.* Cambridge: MIT Press.

Mehler, J., Jusczyk, P., Lambertz, G., Halsted, N., Bertoncini, J., & Amiel-Tison, C. (1988). A precursor of language acquisition in young infants. *Cognition, 29,* 143–178.

Menyuk, P. (1969). *Sentences children use.* Cambridge: MIT Press.

Mervis, C. (1983). Acquisition of a lexicon. *Contemporary Educational Psychology, 8,* 210–236.

Miller, W., & Ervin, S. (1964). The development of grammar in child language. In U. Bellugi & R. Brown (Eds.), *The Acquisition of Language Monographs of the Society for Research in Child Development, 29,* 9–34.

Moerk, E. (1989). The LAD was a lady and the tasks were ill-defined. *Developmental Review, 9,* 21–57.

Moerk, E. (1990). Three-term contingency patterns in mother–child verbal interactions during first-language acquisition. *Journal of the Experimental Analysis of Behavior, 54,* 293–305.

Mühlhäusler, P. (1986). *Pidgin and creole linguistics.* Oxford: Basil Blackwell.

Murray, A., Johnson, J., & Peters, J. (1990). Fine-tuning of utterance length to preverbal infants: Effects on later language development. *Journal of Child Language, 17,* 511–526.

Nelson, K. (1973). Structure and strategy in learning to talk. *Monographs of the Society for Research in Child Development, 38.*

Newport, E., Gleitman, L., & Gleitman, H. (1977). Mother, I'd rather do it myself: Some effects and non-effects of maternal speech style. In C. Snow & C. Ferguson (Eds.), *Talking to children: Language input and acquisition.* Cambridge: Cambridge University Press.

Ochs, E. (1982). Talking to children in Western Samoa. *Language and Society, 11,* 77–104.

Osgood, C. E., & Zehler, A. (1981). Acquisition of bitransitive sentences: Prelinguistic determinants of language acquisition. *Journal of Child Language, 8,* 367–383.

Owens, R. (1996). *Language development: An introduction* (4th ed.). Boston: Allyn & Bacon.

Pan, B., & Gleason, J. B. (1996). Semantic development: Learning the meanings of words. In J. B. Gleason (Ed.), *The development of language* (4th ed.). Boston: Allyn & Bacon.

Papandropoulou, I., & Sinclair, H. (1974). What is a word? Experimental study of children's ideas on grammar. *Human Development, 17,* 240–258.

Pavlov, I. (1927). *Conditioned reflexes.* (G. Anrep, Trans.). New York: Dover.

Piaget, J. (1926). *The language and thought of the child.* New York: Harcourt Brace.

Piaget, J. (1954). *Origins of intelligence.* New York: Basic Books.

Pinker, S. (1984). *Language learnability and language development.* Cambridge, MA: MIT Press.

Pinker, S. (1989). *Learnability and cognition.* Cambridge, MA: MIT Press.

Pinker, S. (1991). Rules of language. *Science, 253,* 530–535.

Polka, L., Jusczyk, P., & Rvachew, S. (1995). Methods for studying speech perception in infants and children. In W. Strange (Ed.), *Speech perception and linguistic experience: Issues in cross-language research.* Timonium, MD: York Press.

Potter, M. (1990). Remembering. In D. Osherson & E. Smith (Eds.), *An invitation to cognitive science: Vol. 3: Thinking.* Cambridge, MA: MIT Press.

Rescorla, L. (1980). Overextension in early language development. *Journal of Child Language, 7,* 321–335.

Rescorla, L. (1989). The language development survey: A screening tool for delayed language in toddlers. *Journal of Speech and Hearing Disorders, 54,* 587–599.

Rice, M. (1987). Preschoolers' QUIL: Quick incidental learning of words. In C. Snow & G. Conti-Ramsden (Eds.), *Children's language, Vol. 7.* Hillsdale, NJ: Erlbaum.

Romaine, S. (1988). *Pidgin and creole languages.* New York: Longman.

Scarborough, H. (1989). Index of productive syntax. *Applied Psycholinguistics, 11,* 1–22.

Sinclair-deZwart, H. (1973). Language acquisition and cognitive development. In T. Moore (Ed.), *Cognitive development and the acquisition of language.* New York: Academic Press.

Skinner, B. F. (1957). *Verbal behavior.* Englewood Cliffs, NJ: Prentice-Hall.

Skinner, B. F. (1969). *Contingencies of reinforcement.* New York: Appleton, Century, Crofts.

Slobin, D. I. (1973). Cognitive prerequisites for the development of grammar. In C. Ferguson & D. I. Slobin (Eds.), *Studies of child language development.* New York: Holt, Rinehart and Winston.

Slobin, D. I. (Ed.). (1985). *The crosslinguistic study of language acquisition, Vols. 1, 2.* Hillsdale, NJ: Erlbaum.

Slobin, D. I. (Ed.). (1992). *The crosslinguistic study of language acquisition, Vol. 3.* Hillsdale, NJ: Erlbaum.

Slobin, D. I., & Welsh, C. (1971). Elicited imitation as a research tool in developmental psycholinguistics. In C. Lavatelli (Ed.), *Language training in early childhood education.* Urbana: University of Illinois Press.

Snow, C. E. (1977). The development of conversation between mothers and babies. *Journal of Child Language, 4,* 1–22.

Snow, C. E. (1981). Social interaction and language acquisition. In P. Dale & D. Ingram (Eds.), *Child language: An international perspective.* Baltimore: University Park Press.

Snow, C. E. (1987). Relevance of the notion of a critical period to language acquisition. In M. Bornstein (Ed.), *Sensitive periods in development.* Hillsdale, NJ: Erlbaum.

Snow, C. E. (1990). The development of definitional skill. *Journal of Child Language, 17,* 697–710.

Snow, C. E. (1995). Issues in the study of input. In P. Fletcher & B. MacWhinney (Eds.), *The handbook of child language.* Oxford: Blackwell.

Snow, C. E., & Ferguson, C. A. (1977). *Talking to children: Language input and acquisition.* Cambridge: Cambridge University Press.

Snow, C. E., Perlmann, R. Y., & Berko Gleason, J. (1990). Developmental perspectives on politeness: Sources of children's knowledge. *Journal of Pragmatics, 14,* 289–305.

Tager-Flusberg, H. (1996). Putting words together: Morphology and syntax in the preschool years. In J. Berko Gleason (Ed.), *The development of language* (4th ed.). Boston: Allyn & Bacon.

Tager-Flusberg, H., & Calkins, S. (1990). Does imitation facilitate the acquisition of grammar? Evidence from a study of autistic Down's syndrome and normal children. *Journal of Child Language, 17,* 591–606.

Warren, A., & McCloskey, L. (1996). Language in social contexts. In J. B. Gleason (Ed.), *The development of language* (4th ed.). Boston: Allyn & Bacon.

Wells, G. (1985). *Language development in the preschool years.* Cambridge: Cambridge University Press.

Werker, J., & Tees, R. C. (1984). Cross-language speech perception: Evidence for perceptual reorganization during the first year of life. *Infant Behavior and Development, 7,* 49–64.

Whitehurst, G. (1982). Language development. In B. Wolman (Ed.), *Handbook of developmental psychology.* Englewood Cliffs, NJ: Prentice-Hall.

Wiegel-Crump, C., & Dennis, M. (1986). Development of word finding. *Brain & Language, 27,* 1–23.

Witelson, S. F. (1977). Early hemispheric specialization and interhemispheric plasticity: An empirical and theoretical review. In S. J. Segalowitz & F. A. Gruber (Eds.), *Language development and neurological theory.* London: Academic Press.

Yamada, J. (1990). *Laura: A case for the modularity of language.* Cambridge, MA: MIT Press.

Chapter 9

A PSYCHOLINGUISTIC ACCOUNT OF READING

Maryanne Wolf
Tufts University

Frank Vellutino
State University of New York, Albany

Jean Berko Gleason
Boston University

INTRODUCTION

Just as the development of oral language made us a unique species, the acquisition of written language changed our species in numerous ways. It changed our cognitive capacity (Olson, 1980, 1986); it changed the kinds of knowledge we could have (Havelock, 1976); and it may even have changed our neuroanatomy (Geschwind, 1974). Perhaps no other human activity has so altered the course of individual and cultural development. The structure and development of written language and our remarkable ability to process it—to read—are the content of this chapter. We will begin with a brief *historical overview of writing systems.* This is followed by a *psycholinguistic account of the subprocesses that underlie reading.* In a third section, we describe the *natural course of reading acquisition.* The chapter concludes with a discussion of *current models of skilled reading.* In several places we provide examples of what occurs when written language is largely inaccessible, for instance in individuals with **dyslexia.** Our goals are to underscore by illustration the extraordinary complexity of the reading process and to bring to life its invaluable place in human activity.

Throughout the chapter, we will note connections between oral and written language development, because only when these systems are studied in tandem can the development of written language be understood in all its complexity.

A HISTORY OF WRITING SYSTEMS

The history of written language is relatively recent and varies somewhat in chronology; early writing appears to have evolved independently in different parts of the world. The earliest system we know of was devised about 3100 B.C. by the ancient Sumerians, who lived in Mesopotamia between the Tigris and Euphrates rivers. The Sumerians used **pictographs,** or small pictures, to represent objects or concepts. These oldest precursors to writing were cuneiform inscriptions on clay tablets; *cuneiform* means "wedge-shaped," from the Latin *cuneus,* "wedge," which describes the characteristic shape of writing strokes made by pressing a stylus into wet clay. The Sumerians used their writing system for practical purposes, for instance, to keep account of livestock shipped from the country to the city. A typical Sumerian document might consist of a list of animals, with marks before each to show how many there were, and the name of the owner. If the Sumerians had a particularly important clay tablet that they wanted to preserve, they baked it. About 100 years later, Egyptians living in the Nile River valley also developed a pictographic writing system. In the early Egyptian writing system, for example, the concept "ox" was represented by a small picture of the head of an ox.

Chinese **ideograms** (pictures that symbolize ideas or objects but not particular words for them) have been found on bones and turtle shells that trace to the second millennium B.C. These apparently were used to ask questions of the gods—questions perhaps best unuttered in oral language. An early Mayan picture writing system emerged as a means to chronicle major events. Each of these precursor writing systems became a way to preserve, accumulate, and transmit cultural knowledge across distance and time (Wang, 1991), a feat that oral history could not accomplish.

With time these early systems became less picture-like and began to represent actual words of the language rather than objects or ideas. This step to "one-word-one-symbol" marks the beginning of true writing systems (Ellis, 1984, p. 3). Various scholars have proposed a relatively orderly progression in the development of writing systems, beginning with concrete pictographs. The next historical step was the development of somewhat more abstract **logographs,** such as, Egyptian hieroglyphs, which correspond to words and sounds. Contemporary Chinese writing is also logographic (see Figure 9.1). The most recent developments are **syllabaries** (for example, the Japanese Kana writing system, where a written symbol stands for each syllable in the language); and **alphabets** like our own, in which a set of **graphemes,** or written letters, represent each phoneme in the language.

A major assumption by historians of writing was that with each of these transformations writing systems became more abstract, more efficient, and at the same time more cognitively demanding for the learner. The reality is more complex. As Schmandt-Besserat (1991) noted, even the early Sumerian systems were used for various transactions and may have been somewhat abstract, because they may not have represented particular words. Furthermore, logographic systems, as exemplified by present-day Chinese, are quite cognitively demanding. They make greater phonological demands than previously realized (Mann, 1986), and they make immense memory demands upon the learner. For example, at least 3,000 symbols must be learned in

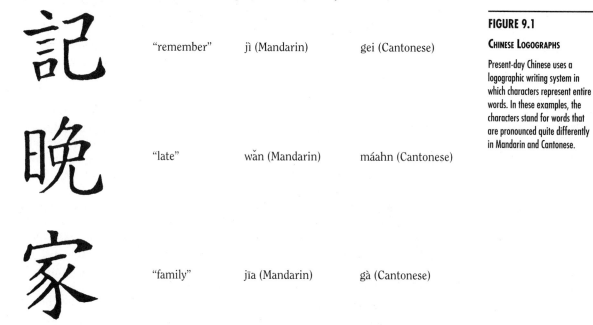

"remember"   jì (Mandarin)   gei (Cantonese)

"late"   wǎn (Mandarin)   máahn (Cantonese)

"family"   jīa (Mandarin)   gà (Cantonese)

FIGURE 9.1

CHINESE LOGOGRAPHS

Present-day Chinese uses a logographic writing system in which characters represent entire words. In these examples, the characters stand for words that are pronounced quite differently in Mandarin and Cantonese.

order to attain basic Chinese literacy (Stevenson, Stigler, Tucker, Lee, Hsu, & Ketanusa, 1982). Syllabaries, by comparison, make relatively few demands on memory, and the alphabet makes even fewer; thus, these systems increase cognitive efficiency in one way. On the other hand, the alphabet makes increased demands on the learner's *representation abilities,* particularly during the acquisition stages.

This brief discussion of writing includes two critical points: First, writing systems used around the world today represent oral language in quite different ways and make different requirements of the learner. Second, as Adams (1990, p. 43) noted, the discovery that "symbols can represent the sounds of language, rather than its referents," transformed the history of writing.

THE ALPHABET

Nowhere is this transformation more obvious than in the introduction of the Greek alphabet, upon which all modern alphabets are based. The emergence of the Greek alphabet represented "a psychological and epistemological revolution" (Havelock, 1976, p. 49) in Western culture and thought. The Greeks took a syllable-based Phoenician system, adapted it to provide a separate character for each phoneme, and invented the alphabetic principle (Ellis, 1984). Havelock proposed three conditions for a true alphabet:

1. Each phoneme in the language must be represented by the writing system.
2. Ideally, an unambiguous one-to-one correspondence should exist between phoneme and grapheme.
3. The total number of graphemes must be limited so as not to tax memory processes. An ideal number is between 20 and 30 if literacy is "democratic" (that is, accessible to most members of the society).

Havelock added that if the last condition is met, the act of reading can attain the status of "unconscious reflex" (1976, p. 24) or what cognitive and psycholinguistic theories refer to as **automaticity** or **fluency** (see discussions in LaBerge & Samuels, 1974; Logan, 1988; Stanovich, 1990; Wolf, 1991a). The Greek alphabet was able to meet all three conditions, and in the process "invented literacy and the literate basis of modern (Western) thought" (Havelock, 1976, p. 44).

With the dissemination of the alphabetic principle, writing began to make explicit some of the *tacit* aspects of knowledge carried by oral language (Olson, 1980). In the process, two critical consequences resulted across cultures: First was an ordering and thus a rethinking of previous knowledge. Second, written language made it easier to form a new distinction between factual information and the interpretation of that information (Olson, 1986). Olson explained that writing "split the comprehension process into two parts; that part preserved by text, the given, and . . . interpretation" (1986, p. 120). The consequences of such a split are the basis, he claimed, for

FIGURE 9.2

Literacy makes it easier to distinguish between what we know to be true and what we only believe to be true. This distinction underlies much of scientific thought.

modern science and an awareness of subjectivity, two of the most fundamental aspects of Western education and thought. Becoming literate makes it more likely that as individuals we can distinguish between *what we actually know to be a fact* and *what we only believe or suppose* (see Figure 9.2). Scientific thought is not possible in the absence of this distinction.

Alongside the overwhelming contributions of the alphabetic principle to intellectual growth, the cognitive costs must also be considered. The alphabetic principle may be difficult to acquire, depending on the language. For example, written Serbo-Croatian is easier to acquire than English because it contains a transparent relationship between a word's spelling and its pronunciation. That is, a less variant correspondence exists between graphemes and phonemes in written Serbo-Croatian. English orthography with its many irregular spellings barely satisfies Havelock's (1976) second condition for an alphabet, that of an unambiguous one-to-one correspondence between grapheme and phoneme. A major reason for this apparent lack of correspondence is historical: The English writing system attempts both to represent all phonemes in the sound system and to preserve lexical or etymological relationships among its morphemes (Chomsky & Halle, 1968; C. Chomsky, 1972). Thus, words such as *signature* and *sign, bomb* and *bombardier* are orthographically connected in a way that makes their etymological relationships clear, which would not be the case if they were spelled strictly phonetically—for example we might not recognize the relationship between *sign* and *signature* if the words were spelled *sayn* and *signuhcher.*

THE UNDERLYING ELEMENTS OF READING

The number of processes involved in reading, the complex nature of each, and the daunting demands posed by their rapid interaction help us understand the difficulty of acquiring the alphabetic principle. This discussion will be divided into a description of the *representational systems* that support *word recognition* within an alphabetic orthography, and of the *cognitive systems* involved in reading and learning.

Representational Systems in Word Identification

LEARNING SYSTEMS.   As a child learns to read, printed words—at first just marks on paper—gradually become invested with various linguistic properties, which may be more or less salient, depending on the child's stage of reading development. These properties are derived from corresponding linguistic *codes,* which are the *abstract mental representations* of the different subsystems of language that have been described in earlier chapters: *phonological codes, semantic codes,* and *syntactic/grammatical codes.*

PHONOLOGICAL CODING.   Phonological codes are mental representations of the individual sounds of spoken and written words (phonemes) and the implicit rules for ordering and combining them (Chomsky & Halle, 1968). As Chapter 8 on the development of language made clear, in order to acquire words in a language, children must be able to discriminate and represent the phonemes of the language. In other words, they must be able to code information phonologically.

Phonological coding ability is also important in learning to identify printed words. Knowledge of phonology makes it easier to associate as a whole unit the string of letters in a printed word and a known spoken word. Phonological coding also aids **segmentation** of spoken and printed words and thus facilitates detection and use of grapheme-phoneme and other spelling–sound correspondences that can be used for word decoding (for example, to distinguish between *cat* and *fat, train* and *pain*). In addition, it facilitates use of letter sounds to aid in discriminating and sequencing letters in words (for example, *pot* versus *top*). It promotes development of **morphophonemic production rules.** These rules help a child arrive at correct pronunciations of *derived words*—words that have common root morphemes but vary in form class (for example, *decide, decision*). A final function of this phonological knowledge is that it aids the process of attaching the appropriate sounds to common segments such as bound morphemes *(-ed, -ing)* and syllables *(-ove* in *love* and *dove).* Thus, facility in phonological coding is critically important in learning to identify words in an alphabet-based orthography.

SEMANTIC CODING.   Semantic codes are the interconnected mental representations of the meanings assigned to units of language. These codes refer either to the meanings of individual words or to the broader meanings conveyed by groups of words. In order to learn to associate a spoken word with its counterpart in print, children must have an adequate grasp of the meaning of that word, both in and out of sentence contexts. They must also be able to make clear-cut distinctions between the word's meaning and the meanings of other words, distinguishing among, for example, words that are similar either in referential meaning (for example, *cat* and *kitten*) or functional meaning (for example, *add* and *plus, him* and *he*). Adequate knowledge of the meanings of spoken words is important at the beginning stage of reading, because the child relies heavily on likely word meanings in learning to identify words initially encountered (Biemiller, 1970; Ehri, 1992; Vellutino, Scanlon, & Tanzman, 1990; Vellutino, Scanlon, DeSetto, & Pruzek, 1981; Weber, 1970). Semantic coding becomes increasingly important as the number of new words encountered in print expands, especially in learning to identify those that cannot be readily decoded using regular spelling–sound correspondence rules (for example, *was, saw, their,* and so forth).

SYNTACTIC/GRAMMATICAL CODING.   *Syntactic codes* are abstract representations of the rules for ordering words in the language—the rules for making sentences. *Grammatical codes* represent a word's form class (for example, noun, verb), and they define its function in sentences. Related to both of these codes are representations of bound morphemes (usually inflectional morphemes), which modify words for case, gender, tense, mood, and so forth. The child must learn to apply syntactic rules in order to segment sentences into their grammatical constituents and then determine how those constituents relate to one another. The grammatical constituents contain the substantive components of a sentence, and the syntactic rules order them in ways that facilitate comprehension.

Competence in the grammar and syntax of language facilitates word identification in at least three different ways. First, competence helps the child comprehend sentences and use the sentence context to anticipate which words might appear in given sentence frames. Second, competence aids the process of assigning to printed words what might be called *function codes*. Function codes are representations that mark a word's unique role in sentences. Function codes are especially important in distinguishing among non-content, function words such as *if, and, for, from,* and *of.* They, along with phonological codes, are also important in acquiring morphophonemic production rules that facilitate correct pronunciations of derived words such as *bomber* and *bombardier* and inflections such as *-ed* and *-ing.* The knowledge of morphophonemic production rules is a third way in which grammatical and syntactic competence aids printed word identification.

THE VISUAL SYSTEM.   In order to learn to read, children must come to discriminate among (literally) thousands of printed words, some differing in only a small feature of one letter (for example, *snow/show*) or in the way their letters are ordered (for example, *was/saw*). Children must also learn to recognize words written in different cases, fonts, and writing styles. How can children accomplish this feat relying on visual memory alone? The answer is that they do not because they cannot, at least not in an alphabetically derived orthography that contains so much visual similarity. The load on visual memory is much too formidable.

Successful developing readers acquire numerous synthesizing strategies that reduce the load on visual memory posed by alphabetic orthography. They do this with the aid of the language systems we have just discussed, especially the phonological system. If children are taught or discover and use the alphabetic principle (that a letter on the page stands for a sound in their spoken language), and if they have adequate ability in phonological coding, they soon learn to take advantage of frequently encountered spelling–sound correspondences and begin to develop the following strategies:

1. They begin to store rules for the order in which letters may occur in the orthography.
2. They store rules for ordering the letters in words.
3. They store representations of redundant combinations of letters with invariant spellings and pronunciations (for example, *at* in *cat* and *fat*).
4. They make increasingly fine-grained discriminations among visually similar words.
5. They store unitized representations of subword morphophonemic units that have invariant spellings and pronunciations (for example, *ing, tion*).
6. They store as units representations of redundant combinations of letters (for example, *th, sh, ch*).
7. They begin to identify new words generatively and through the recombination of elements they already know.

Each of these helps to reduce the load on visual memory in a slightly different way. Collectively, they constitute a powerful set of mechanisms that not only aid the child in negotiating the written system but also assist in the process of internalizing representations for identifying words that are familiar and those that are unfamiliar.

Research indicates that in word identification the visual system takes its lead from the language systems. The language systems confer meaning on the visual symbols representing printed words and determine how they will be analyzed and interpreted. The language systems also help the child synthesize the vast amounts of visual information that must be stored in order to acquire fluency in word identification. This suggests that reading may be acquired by children with a wide range of individual differences in visual ability if they have the linguistic coding ability to capitalize on the spelling-sound redundancies of the orthography, and to use code-oriented as well as meaning-based strategies for word identification.

MOTOR SYSTEMS. Children typically learn to read using an oral reading method, and they learn to relate visual symbols to internalized representations of the *speech-motor executions* used in vocalizing the names associated with those symbols. It is, however, likely that the role of the motor systems in learning to read is actually quite minimal. Although speech-motor and visual-motor representations normally become part of the information stored in memory about a printed word, little evidence indicates that success in word identification depends on the availability of high quality representations of speech-motor and visual-motor executions. It is more important for the child to grasp the concept that letters have sounds, as a prerequisite to success in alphabetic mapping, than to articulate those sounds physically.

Cognitive Processes Involved in Reading and All Learning

In addition to the representational systems and processes specifically involved in reading, general cognitive processes are involved in learning to read, as well as in all learning. Dysfunction in each of these processes has been suspected as a cause of reading disability.

ATTENTION.   Success in learning any new relationship, such as learning to read, depends on our ability to *attend selectively* to the distinguishing attributes of what we are attempting to learn. It is also important that we come to distinguish between *variant* and *invariant dimensions* so as to become increasingly efficient in how we search for their distinguishing attributes. Gibson (1969) calls this type of processing **perceptual learning.** However, as she points out, efficiency is not ensured simply by looking at or listening to the target. Efficient selective attention requires an extensive period of analysis that is influenced by three related contingencies:

1. An affective or emotional state that makes attention possible
2. Conscious motivation to learn
3. Sufficient knowledge to facilitate attention and make critical discriminations

The first contingency relates to the intactness of those components of the central nervous system responsible for degree of emotional arousal. The second contingency relates to the child's volition and deliberate intent. Without sufficient interest in acquiring knowledge in a given domain, the child will find it difficult to attend in a way that optimizes the likelihood of learning. No doubt many children have difficulty learning to read because of a lack of inherent motivation. The third contingency is more subtle. It involves the role of prior knowledge in new learning situations. For instance, young children who are familiar with the printed word *lion,* when first presented with the new word *loin,* are apt to misname this word because of their prior experience with its visually similar counterpart. After they add *loin* to their vocabulary, they begin to attend to the way its medial letters and those in *lion* are ordered. Subsequently, their means of processing these two words changes in a way that ensures selective attention to the order of their medial letters.

During the initial stages of discrimination, processing requires a good deal of cognitive effort, but in time it becomes *automated.* LaBerge and Samuels (1974) have shown that accurate discrimination of distinguishing attributes and selective and effortless attention to those attributes are related benchmarks of automatic processing of letters and words (see also Perfetti, 1985; Stanovich, 1991; Wolf, 1991b). Conversely, less accurate discrimination of distinguishing attributes and nonselective and effortful attention in searching for those attributes are benchmarks of nonautomatic processing. It follows that the child who fails to steadily and systematically acquire the types of knowledge that lead to more precise analysis of orthography (knowledge such as word meanings, spelling–sound rules, and such) will have difficulty attending selectively to critical differences in letters and words. The child who acquires this knowledge becomes increasingly more efficient in attending selectively to distinctions among letters and words.

ASSOCIATIVE LEARNING.   The ability to associate one entity with another is a basic cognitive mechanism that is critically important for learning in general and for word identification in particular. It underlies our ability to establish bonds between written words and their counterparts in spoken language. In a real sense **association** underlies one of our most fundamental cognitive abilities, the ability to *symbolize.*

When we symbolize, we have one element represent another; and each may prompt a reaction common to both. For example, we attach the same meaning to a word, regardless of whether it is spoken or printed. How we learn associative relationships—whether through *insightful discovery* of the distinguishing and mediating attributes or through gradual accretion of *connective bonds* through practice and reinforcement—is a controversial issue with a long history that we need not address here (Gibson, 1969). Contemporary theories of learning and memory suggest that each of these conceptualizations may have some validity.

Associative learning seems to involve a form of search for and "discovery" of **implicit mediators** (often called *retrieval cues*) that may link two associates in a component of memory called the **semantic network** (Tulving & Pearlstone, 1966). Associative learning often appears gradual, perhaps because of the need to eliminate competition from associates with similar attributes. This involves discovery and encoding of distinguishing attributes. Children appear to come by this associative capability quite naturally.

CROSS-MODAL TRANSFER.   When connective bonds are established between encoded information stored in different representational systems, and when accessing one type of information from memory becomes the occasion for accessing the other, we have what has been alternately called **cross-modal transfer** and **intersensory integration** (Bryant, 1974; Gibson, 1969). Reading involves connecting representations stored in one system (such as the mental representation of a spoken word) with representations stored in another (such as the mental representation of a written word). Connecting these auditory and visual representations is one type of cross-modal transfer.

This ability to associate symbols that are stored in different representational systems is a basic mechanism for learning that arrives early in life (Bryant, 1974; Gibson, 1969). Reading typically involves the use of rather arbitrary sets of visual symbols, but it could as readily involve the use of other types of symbols such as the *tactile* symbols of Braille. Cross-modal relations vary with the writing system. For example, the types of equivalencies established in a logographic writing system such as Chinese differ from those established in an alphabetic writing system such as English. Logographic systems rely primarily on word names and meanings to form connective bonds between visual and linguistic symbols, whereas alphabetic systems rely more heavily on connections between visual symbols and letter sounds.

PATTERN ANALYSIS AND RULE LEARNING.   One of the most important of all of our cognitive abilities is the ability to detect *patterned invariance*. Even a small infant, for instance, soon learns that her mother has certain invariant characteristics (such as her facial features), as well as features that vary from day to day (such as her clothing). Gibson (1969) suggests that humans are naturally inclined to search for invariant features in new learning situations to aid them in reducing the amount of information they must otherwise store and to help them detect distinguishing attributes in subjects that have overlapping features. She also suggests that we are naturally endowed with mechanisms that allow us to store representations of invariant relationships in the form of rules we can use generatively. In regard to reading, she argues that the ability to detect and use patterned invariance makes the development of word identification something more than simple paired associate learning. She suggests that, even without explicit instruction and because they are naturally *programmed* to search for invariance, developing readers will eventually detect and use spelling–sound correspondences and other forms of orthographic redundancy.

SERIAL MEMORY.   **Serial memory** poses a question of some importance to students of cognition—just how do we remember the order in which elements occur? A related question is whether memory for the individual elements in a given array or system is distinct from memory for the order in which those elements occur. Some suggest that serial memory is a generalized ability that determines the order in which we process all information. For example, largely on the basis of clinical studies of neurologically impaired adults, some investigators (see Luria, 1966) have assumed that serial memory in general is a neurologically based capability that depends upon the integrity of the left hemisphere (Das, Kirby, & Jarman, 1975). According to this point of view, the left hemisphere is responsible for representing and processing ordered information of all types (see Tzeng & Wang, 1984). This includes representation of diverse types of information, such as the order in which elements of a stimulus array are presented on memory tasks, the ordering rules for complex systems such as the language systems, mathematical systems, and so forth. By the same account, the right hemisphere is responsible for representing and processing simultaneously arrayed information, for example, spatial concepts. This division of labor has been called *successive* and *simultaneous processing,* respectively (Luria, 1973).

An alternative view of serial memory is that of different neurological structures that support *modality-specific* sequencing abilities (Johnson & Mykelbust, 1964). For instance, the ability to sequence visual information is believed to be distinct from the ability to sequence auditory information.

Thus, some clinical descriptions of ordered recall have indicated that serial memory is a general ability, whereas others have indicated that it may be a collection of modality specific abilities. Research conducted by cognitive psychologists, however, supports the conclusion that serial processing is, indeed, a generic cognitive function, but that it varies with the type of information serialized. It is also clear that how we represent the serial order in which items occur differs from how we represent the items themselves (see Bower & Minaire, 1974; Healy, 1974; Houston, 1976, for experimental documentation). This facet of cognition is illustrated by the distinction between the syntactic and semantic components of language: syntax embodies abstract rules for the order of words in grammatical utterances, and semantics embodies the meanings of words in terms of their conceptual attributes.

A more relevant illustration for our discussion is the distinction between the invariant order in which the letters of a printed word appear and the individual letters themselves. The rules that govern the order of letters in words are inherent in the writing system, not in the encoded representations of the letters themselves. The writing system contains orthographic conventions largely determined by the various ways that the alphabetic characters map onto their sound counterparts.

Another important generalization that has emerged from the study of item and order processing is that no invariant way exists to encode serial information. Patterned information is typically serialized by implicit rules inherent in a particular representational system. For example, the syntactic rules for the order of words in a language are quite different from the mathematical rules that order the quantities in a number system. We need to know the ordering rules for the particular system before we can encode the serial order of information in that system. However, when we must serialize information that has no inherent ordering rules, we must devise strategies, which will vary both with the unique properties of the ordered set and with our particular organizational and coding abilities. Such strategies will, therefore, be highly individualized.

The strategies we use in serializing randomly ordered items have been the object of extensive inquiry by memory researchers (see Bower & Hildgard, 1981, for a review). Two strategies frequently used to serialize random arrays are *chunking* and *recoding*. Chunking involves reducing the size of an array by grouping information into units that are easier to code. For instance, breaking a telephone number into several "packages" makes it easier to recall. Three packages of numbers such as (617) 555-1212 are easier to remember than the "unchunked" string 6175551212. Recoding involves assigning these units superordinate codes that facilitate recovery of position as well as item information.

These latter points bring into focus a final generalization that has emerged from the study of serial memory: Serial recall is almost always rule-based. If the material to be ordered does not exceed the limit of short-term memory (about 7 items, plus or minus 2) then serial recall is possible without the aid of organizational devices. But when the material to be ordered exceeds short-term memory limits, it is ordered by rules that are implicit, induced, or invented anew. The child learns the serial order of the letters in printed words largely by encoding representations of spelling-sound relations and orthographic redundancy and not by some inherent ability to serialize in the general sense.

Two questions inevitably emerge as a result of this discussion of constituent processes in word recognition. First, how does the child use these underlying systems in the various stages of reading acquisition? Second, how do these processes interact with the rapidity necessary to produce skilled reading? These two questions will frame the next two sections on reading development and models of the reading process.

THE DEVELOPMENT OF READING

The Protoliteracy Period

A child's attainment of reading ability is rooted in spoken language skills. Barron (1992) described this early period when the precursors of written language are laid down as the *protoliteracy period*. Several decades of cross-cultural research indicate that the two most powerful predictors of later reading achievement are a child's phonological skills and ability to recognize letters (Adams, 1990; Bradley & Bryant, 1983, 1985; Chall, 1967, 1983; Liberman, Shankweiler, Fischer, & Carter, 1974; Roswell & Natchez, 1971; Snow, 1973; Vellutino & Scanlon, 1987; Vellutino, Scanlon, & Spearing, 1995).

Perhaps the greatest influence on the development of these abilities is being read to. This seemingly simple experience helps the child understand that print on a page is related to words that can be spoken; this prepares the child to extract meaning from print (Marsh & Desberg, 1983). In the phonological domain, reading introduces rhyme, alliteration, and sound segmentation: the child begins to understand that words are made of phonological parts. Bradley and Bryant (1983) have shown this knowledge to be a powerful predictor of early reading (see also Bowey & Patel, 1988; Bryant, MacLean, & Bradley, 1990). And finally, children who are read to develop larger vocabularies.

Marsh and Desberg (1983) suggest that some of the earliest reading experiences occur when children turn from listening to others to making attempts of their own to read the pictured texts; this *linguistic guesswork* is the basis for children's first understanding of meaning-print connections. Another important kind of linguistic guessing that can prepare children to read is found in some children's *invented spelling* (Read, 1981). Read (1981) and Snowling (1987) demonstrated that children's earliest spelling often reflects what they hear or do *not* hear in the speech stream. For example, nasal consonants are difficult to detect in speech and are often omitted in children's invented words: *numbers* is written *nubrs.* Frequently children use the letter name as the basis of their efforts: *lady* is written *lade,* and *genius* becomes *gnus* (Bissex, 1980; Treiman, 1993).

PHONOLOGICAL SKILLS.   During the protoliteracy period phonological awareness emerges, not as a whole, but rather as a varied set of skills. For example, as Snowling (1987) and Treiman (1985) have shown, segmentation skills are not an all-or-none phenomenon. The ability to segment *syllables* is acquired first, followed by an intermediate level where the *onset* (for example, initial consonant of the syllable) and *rime* (for example, vowel and final consonants) are learned, followed by a final ability to segment individual phonemes.

·Barron suggested that each level of segmentation skills has a particular relationship to different aspects of reading development. He and others have emphasized the *bidirectional character* (Barron, 1992) of the segmentation/reading relationship, whereby some levels of segmentation proficiency influence the acquisition of reading and some are then themselves influenced by reading practice (Bertelson & De Gelder, 1989; Dickinson, Wolf, & Stotsky, 1993; Perfetti, Beck, Bell, & Hughes, 1987). A fascinating example of this bidirectional character is seen in cross-cultural comparisons of segmentation skills. Chinese-speaking adults who are literate in their logographic system (Read, Yun-Fei, Hong-Yin, & Bao-Qing, 1986) and Japanese children fluent in syllabaries (Mann, 1986) cannot initially segment words at the phonemic level, which English-speaking children can do by grade 2 after exposure to the alphabet. Another example is found in a study by Vellutino and Scanlon (1987), who showed that segmentation training can improve the reading acquisition process in young disabled readers. Thus, we see the developmentally interactive, level-specific nature of the relationships between phonological skills and later reading.

VOCABULARY KNOWLEDGE.   Similar developmental, bidirectional relationships with reading show up in the formation of both vocabulary and letter-recognition/ letter-naming skills. Beck, Perfetti, and McKeown (1982) suggested that development of vocabulary knowledge represents a continuum in which individual words move from unfamiliar, to acquainted, to established categories (see also Kameenui, Dixon, & Carmine, 1987). This vocabulary development both pushes and is pushed forward by reading acquisition.

Curtis (1987) also described the interconnectedness of reading and vocabulary development, where advances in each influence the other. Conversely, Stanovich (1986) described a *reciprocal causation* relationship that exists in older impaired readers, where these readers developed problems in vocabulary knowledge as the result of delays in reading, which then became further impeded because of increasing vocabulary deficits.

LETTER RECOGNITION AND NAMING SPEED ABILITIES.   Numerous letter-recognition studies have shown the predictive nature, apart from phonological skills, of the simple ability to recognize letters (Vellutino & Scanlon, 1987). Stanovich and West (1989) have shown that even in adulthood, skill at letter recognition accounted for the observed variance in word recognition—quite independent of phonological abilities. Barron (1992) discussed the particular predictive importance of one form of protoliteracy skill: knowing the difference between letters and their names *(B* pronounced *bee)* and letters and their sounds *(B* pronounced *buh)* (Barron, 1992, p. 16).

The predictive value of *letter-naming*—which requires rapid integration of letter-recognition, letter-sound associations, and phonological skills—has been the subject of considerable discussion (Walsh, Price, & Cunningham, 1988). In a seven-year longitudinal study, Wolf (1991a) demonstrated that in kindergarten children the *speed* of naming either letters or numbers was a powerful predictor of later reading ability, specifically of word-recognition. Wolf and her colleagues (Wolf, Bally, & Morris, 1986) have demonstrated that after average readers acquire reading, their letter-naming speed quickly reaches almost adult levels of fluency or automaticity, a finding suggestive of the bidirectional influence of reading on naming. A deficit in naming speed is a *specific* deficit (independent of phonological problems) found in dyslexic readers from kindergarten to adulthood, and this early separate deficit in naming speed may be linked to later failure in orthographic skills.

What emerges from the research in the protoliteracy period is that the child brings to the reading acquisition process a vast number of phonological, semantic, and orthographic skills that both influence development and, in turn, are influenced by it as these skills become practiced, integrated, and established over time.

Stages of Literacy

The actual stages of literacy acquisition are a matter of continuing discussion. Considerable variation in learning to read exists, based on factors such as early exposure to print, individual learning strategies, patterns of strength and deficit, and method of teaching. Within this context, we will consider three theoretical accounts of stages of reading development—those of Chall (1983), Ehri (1985), and Frith (1985). These accounts provide both areas of overlap, which reinforce one another, and differences that complement one another and provide a fuller picture.

The earliest stage of reading, according to both Ehri (1985) and Chall (1983), focuses on letter discrimination and knowledge; the child can recognize a few rudimentary words such as her own name. Ehri and her colleagues (Ehri, 1985; Ehri & Wilce, 1985) suggested that young children build up a repertoire of letter-sound associations that provides the basis for their move from prereader to reader. Chall (1967, 1983) emphasized the importance at this stage of letter-naming and the skills discussed earlier (Wolf, 1991a).

In the next stage, which Frith (1985) characterized as the **logographic phase,** the child visually recognizes highly familiar words but finds novel or unknown words inaccessible. Bradley and Bryant (1978) demonstrated that during this general period a dissociation between reading and spelling strategies can occur. Some readers use *visual* (whole-word) strategies for reading but phonological (individual-sound) strategies for spelling. These children progress in invented spelling, but they cannot read the very words they spell. Other children do little spelling during this stage. Ehri's *semi-phonetic strategies* emerge during this time as the child begins to apply some phonemic knowledge in both reading and spelling.

The first formal reading stage in Chall's (1983) model comes next: it begins when the child begins a more systematic learning and application of these grapheme-phoneme rules. Frith (1985) refers to this period as the *alphabetic phase.* Decoding is the central emphasis (across all three theories), as the lower-level skills in reading (for example, feature extraction, letter/pattern recognition, grapheme-phoneme correspondence, word recognition, lexical retrieval) are practiced and made automatic.

This alphabetic stage is characterized by changes in both reading and spelling. The child has begun to learn the specific connections between particular letters and sounds (for example, grapheme–phoneme correspondence rules).

We have an insufficient understanding of the mechanisms that drive the move from the logographic to the alphabetic phase, when children learn correspondence rules and "crack the code" (Snowling, 1987, p. 40). This move is more or less difficult depending on the invariant nature of correspondence in the various language systems. English contains, according to Gough and Hillinger (1980), approximately 577 letter–sound correspondence rules. (Recall George Bernard Shaw's famous lament that in the English language *ghoti* can spell *fish: gh* as in *laugh; o* as in *women;* and *ti* as in *tion.*) Although, as we noted earlier, English orthography embodies a living etymological history, the resulting lack of invariant correspondence rules is a major impediment in learning to read for English-speaking children. Gough and Hillinger (1980) suggested that we look at reading in these early acquisition stages as an "unnatural act," which inevitably needs intervention (teaching) by an outsider who pushes the child from an early paired-associate form of learning toward analytic processing. This characterization underscores an important historical dispute in reading theory: whether the achievement of word recognition skills proceeds from "bottom-up processes of spelling-to-sound decoding and direct visual recognition, or (from) top-down processes of expectancy generation and contextual prediction" (Stanovich, 1992, p. 2).

The question of how developing readers access their mental lexicon is important to consider within a developmental framework. Many models of fluent reading (Coltheart, 1982; Humphrey & Evetts, 1985) suggest the possibility of dual routes to the mental lexicon. Within the dual-route view are two possible access procedures in reading. In the indirect (nonlexical) route to meaning via phonology, a phonological representation of the word is assembled by application of letter-sound correspondence rules; and the direct (orthographic or lexical) route involves no phonological recoding and uses an orthographic input register to access the word's meaning (Bertelson, 1986, p. 14). More simply, in the phonological, indirect-access route the reader must access the word's phonological representation to get to meaning. In direct-access models, the reader goes directly from the printed word to its meaning, without having to access the word's phonological representation.

Barron (1986) reviewed evidence supporting various hypotheses concerning whether children employ a direct or indirect route or, in fact, use both in the reading acquisition process. He found that "rudimentary letter-sound/name knowledge and knowledge obtained from applying analogies" (for example, learning new words by using the sound and spelling similarity between the new word and a known word) are most central to the reading process (Barron, 1985, p. 110) (see work on analogies by Goswami, 1985; Marsh & Desberg, 1983). These types of knowledge, in turn, correspond to two basic types of orthographic units used by children: (1) letter-sound units (for example, consonants) and (2) letter-cluster sound units that represent the medial and final portions of a syllable. Barron (1985) contended that neither direct nor indirect routes were a "satisfactory characterization of these units in the orthographic lexicon of beginning readers" (p. 111). He went on to suggest a single-route model of lexical access that allowed for (1) the retrieval of different levels of orthographic units, (2) the application of grapheme–phoneme correspondence rules in various stages of development, and (3) the interaction between phonological and orthographic information.

Debate over whether children learn to read using an indirect, bottom-up route, or a direct, top-down route, or both at different times, has become polarized because of the implications for methods of reading instruction (Adams, 1990; Chall, 1967, 1983). Educators who assume an indirect, bottom-up route emphasize phonics instruction with its explicit teaching (see work by Liberman, Liberman, Mattingly, & Shankweiler, 1980). Those who favor top-down, direct-access use "look-say" (whole-word or whole-language) approaches (see work by Goodman & Goodman, 1980; Raines & Canady, 1990; Smith, 1980). The best evidence to date—the complexity of the reading process, and the developmental individual differences among readers—supports the thoughtful combination of *both* approaches (see Adams, 1990; Nicholson, 1991; Vellutino, 1991b).

Many investigators believe that developmentally influenced transitions—characterized by reliance on one or the other access procedure—depend on the child's individual learning strategy, background, and instructional experience (see also reviews in Bertelson, 1986; Jorm & Share, 1983). To bring to life some of the complexities involved, one need only imagine an average child with significant exposure to print beginning with a rudimentary direct-access, paired-associate strategy for word identification; then as phonics instruction progresses, moving to a more analytic, indirect strategy for most, but not all, words. Finally, as she acquires fluency in word identification, direct-access procedures may predominate, supplemented with indirect procedures when difficult or low-frequency words are encountered.

The final stage of literacy acquisition is characterized by increasingly greater fluency in word identification along with greater emphasis on comprehension processes. In Frith's schema this move into a final **orthographic phase** is characterized by the use of analogies, pronunciation rules dictated by context, morphophonemic knowledge, and what she calls *fluent, orthographic reading.* Ehri (1985) emphasized both the use of *morphemic strategies* and the consequent shift from sight vocabulary to *orthographic neighborhoods* of related words in this transition. Chall (1983) breaks this period into several stages: stage 2 (grades 2.5 to 4) where attention is increasingly directed to meaning and the use of inferential skills; stage 3 (grades 4 to 8) where lower-level processes are consolidated and comprehension of various kinds of material is the focus; stage 4 (secondary school) where inference and recognition of perspective dominate in comprehension processes; and stage 5 (college and beyond) where comprehension involves the active synthesis, integration, and critical analysis of different bodies of knowledge and the formation of novel thought.

Chall's final stage of reading in adulthood invokes Havelock's (1974) and Olson's (1986) powerful discussions of the ultimate contribution of literacy—that is, the production of the "novel or unexpected statement, previously unfamiliar and even 'untaught'" (Havelock, 1976, p. 50). In our final section on models of skilled reading, we examine the complexity of fluent adult reading, the true basis for the production of most new or novel thought.

MODELS OF SKILLED READING

Research with skilled readers has primarily concerned the question of how one recognizes and identifies printed words. This focus provides excellent motivation, because reading is critically dependent on facility in word recognition (Just & Carpenter, 1987; Perfetti, 1985; Rayner & Pollatsek, 1989). Accordingly, we describe briefly the major word-recognition models. Each of the models deals with one or more of the following related questions:

1. Are words recognized by accessing whole-word representations in the mental lexicon or subword representations such as features, letters, or syllables?
2. Are words identified through direct access to their meanings or through phonologically mediated access to word meanings?
3. Does word recognition involve serial or parallel (simultaneous) processing of letters?

4. Is word recognition primarily a context-driven, top-down process, or is it a stimulus-driven, bottom-up process? Or is it interactive?
5. Does recognition involve the use of a single mechanism for accessing the lexicon or multiple mechanisms for doing so?
6. Does word recognition take place through activation or through "search" processes?

Because of space limitations, our discussion of the various models must necessarily be brief. Moreover, we will not consider here models of reading comprehension but refer the reader to discussions of language comprehension in Chapter 5, on sentence processing (see also an excellent treatment in Just & Carpenter, 1987).

Context-Driven, "Top-Down" Models

Top-down models of word recognition assume that information about the context can directly affect the way lower-level stimulus information is perceived and interpreted. Contextual information includes domain-specific knowledge, knowledge of the semantic and syntactic constraints inherent in language, and implicit knowledge of orthographic redundancies and constraints (for example, *u* always follows *q; th* occurs frequently; *xz* never occurs).

Smith proposed a prototypical context-driven model (1971). In this model, the representations that uniquely define printed words in memory are the features (lines, curves, angles, and such) that define the letters in those words, and it presumes separate, "functionally equivalent feature lists" for letters that appear in different cases and fonts, such as those in Figure 9.3.

When a printed word is encountered, features are extracted in all letter positions simultaneously and word recognition occurs when a *criterial set* of features is successfully matched with its counterpart in memory. However, feature extraction is a selective process—it is influenced both by knowledge of orthographic structure and by the ability to use the linguistic context to predict words in the text being read ("The cat chased the _____"). Thus, in this model, word recognition is largely a matter of confirming one's predictions about what the word is, and neither letter recognition nor phonological recoding (accessing word names) is involved.

Empirical support for Smith's model is weak. The role of linguistic context gathers some support from studies that demonstrate that facility in word recognition can be affected by semantic congruence between the text and a target word (Morton,

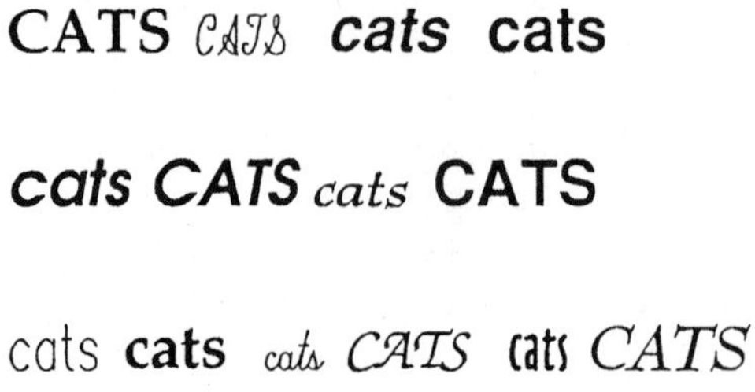

FIGURE 9.3

According to Smith's (1971) model, in recognizing words we call on functionally equivalent mental feature lists that allow us to read words printed in different cases and fonts.

CATS *CATS* *cats* cats

cats **CATS** *cats* **CATS**

cats **cats** *cats* *CATS* cats *CATS*

1964; Perfetti & Roth, 1981; Stanovich, 1980; Tulving & Gold, 1963; Tulving, Mandler, & Baumal, 1964). Yet, the role of context must be limited, because even highly skilled readers can, at best, predict only 1 out of every 4 words encountered in text (Gough, Alford, & Holley-Wilcox, 1981). Moreover, eye movement studies have shown conclusively that even highly skilled readers make little use of prediction, because they fixate on virtually all of the words in a passage, except for short, high frequency functors such as *the* (Rayner & Pollatsek, 1989; Just & Carpenter, 1987).

It has also been shown that word identification among skilled readers is a rapidly executed *modular* process. A modular process such as word recognition is relatively *autonomous,* that is, it is "not controlled by higher-level processes or supplemented by information from knowledge structures not contained in the module itself" (Stanovich, 1990, p. 82). Perfetti (1985, 1992) and Stanovich (1980, 1990) have, in fact, shown that most contextual effects are comprehension effects that take place after words have already been identified.

Smith's other claim, that familiarity with *orthographic redundancy* aids word recognition, has been validated many times over (for example, Adams, 1979; Massaro, 1975; Smith, 1969). Moreover, it has been repeatedly demonstrated that skilled readers have little difficulty recognizing printed words that appear in different or even mixed cases and fonts, which is consistent with Smith's assumption that word recognition involves the use of functionally equivalent feature lists (Coltheart, 1981; Rayner, McConkie, & Zola, 1980; Smith, Lott, & Cronnell, 1969). However, these results can also be taken as support for the possibility that a word's letters are the units of recognition, rather than the features that define those letters. Thus, Smith's model remains somewhat tenuous.

Stimulus-Driven, "Bottom-Up" Models

A basic assumption of stimulus-driven models is that word recognition depends primarily on information contained in the stimulus, the actual printed word, and not on the linguistic context. A second assumption is that recognition takes place in discrete, hierarchically ordered and noninteractive stages. Information at one stage is *encoded* (transformed) for use at the next stage. Virtually all bottom-up models postulate a *sensory stage* in which visual features are extracted, a *recognition stage* in which a representation of the word is accessed, and an *interpretive stage* in which the word's meaning is accessed. The models differ, however, in their conceptualizations of how we mentally represent and identify printed words.

Whole-Word Models

Whole-word models of word recognition commonly assume that printed words are represented mentally as psychologically indivisible wholes and that a word is recognized by virtue of the unique patterns formed by its component letters, just as a face is recognized by its pattern of features. Johnson's (1977) *pattern unit* model is prototypical (see also Cattell, 1886; Theois & Muise, 1977). This model postulates that stimulus features are extracted from all letter positions in parallel, but the letters themselves are not perceived because their collective features are assigned a *unitary encoding* during the sensory stage of processing. This mental representation is compared with the stimulus word and, if they match, the word is recognized and its meaning is accessed. In cases where no match for a string of letters is found, then that string would be parsed using orthographic rules that assign encodings to lower-level units. Thus, *xqz* would be encoded as individual letters and *snick* would be encoded as somewhat larger units, allowing for decoding of unfamiliar strings.

Support for the pattern-unit model came from classic research suggesting that a word may be perceived more readily than its component letters (Cattell, 1886). Especially notable is the **word superiority effect** (Reicher, 1969)—a highly reliable phenomenon whereby a letter embedded in a word seen only briefly (*work*) can be verified ("Did the word contain *k* or *d?*") more accurately than when it is embedded in a non-word (*Qrk*) or when seen alone. This, among other findings (Johnson, 1977), led to speculation that a word has cohesive perceptual properties that transcend its letters. However, later studies (for example, Mesrich, 1973; Johnston, 1981) showed that the word superiority effect occurred only under brief exposure and **backward masking** conditions (for example, when the stimulus word is obliterated by noise patterns shortly after viewing), which suggested that it may not be a true perceptual effect but, rather, a short-term memory effect facilitated by one's ability to remember the name of the stimulus word. This and other findings (see Vellutino, 1982) greatly weakened the pattern-unit model, and it has been all but discarded. The current view is that a word derives its cohesiveness not from the visual patterns made by its letters, but from the higher-level cognitive and linguistic information bonded to those letters.

Component-Letter Models

Component-letter models postulate that printed words are represented as uniquely ordered arrays of graphemes and that all of a word's letters must be recognized if that word is to be recognized. For example, Gough (1972) suggests that feature extraction and letter recognition take place through *serial processing* (letter by letter), and word identification takes place through phonemic recoding of each letter in turn, using *grapheme–phoneme correspondence (GPC) rules* to access word names and meanings (Venezky, 1970). In contrast, Massaro (1975) suggests that feature extraction and letter recognition take place through *parallel processing* (simultaneously) and that one uses implicit knowledge of orthographic redundancy to facilitate perception of letters not fully processed (for example, medial letters masked by adjacent letters). This *primary recognition* process becomes input to a *secondary recognition* process that accesses word meanings directly rather than through phonological mediation.

The evidence for these models is mixed. Their common assumption that letter recognition is a prerequisite for word recognition is supported by the studies cited earlier that demonstrate that words can be readily recognized in different or mixed cases and fonts, and it is now generally agreed that letter recognition is a necessary condition for word recognition. However, the serial processing component of Gough's (1972) model is questioned by studies that demonstrate that words are not readily recognized when their letters are presented in tandem (Kolers, 1970; Travers, 1973). These findings are more in keeping with Massaro's suggestion that a word's letters are processed in parallel, which is a widely accepted view.

The phonological recoding component of Gough's model is not so easily dispensed with (Gough, 1984). Although evidence indicates that phonological code activation is a component of working memory that facilitates reading comprehension (see Daneman, 1991; and Perfetti, 1985, for reviews), some debate continues, as we noted earlier, as to whether or not phonological code activation occurs before or after a word's meaning is accessed. The prevailing view is that skilled readers access word meanings directly, but empirical support exists for each point of view.

Support for the direct-access view comes from studies demonstrating that word meanings are accessed even when phonological coding is impaired (Barron & Baron, 1977; Kleiman, 1975). Also supportive of a direct-access model is the fact that one can readily distinguish the meanings of *homophones* such as *new* and *knew* from the differences in their spellings (Baron, 1973). However, other studies have shown that homophony slows both semantic and lexical judgments ("Are *pear* and *pair* both fruits?" see Van Orden, 1987; Van Orden, Johnston, & Hale, 1988) ("Is *brane* a word?" see Rubenstein, Lewis, & Rubenstein, 1971). Such findings, among others (Perfetti, Bell, & Delaney, 1988), have been taken as support for the contention that word identification necessarily involves phonological recoding. The common observation that skilled readers can decode *pseudowords* better than less-skilled readers has also been cited as evidence for Gough's (1972) suggestion that GPC (grapheme–phoneme correspondence) rules are used to identify real words (Gough & Tunmer, 1986). Yet, we tend to identify real words more rapidly than pseudowords (Forster & Chambers, 1973; Perfetti & Hogaboam, 1975), which is more in keeping with a direct-access view. Moreover, the fact that GPC rules fail with many words (for example, *have, put, bough, cough*) militates against any strong version of the phonological recoding theory, and some (for example, Coltheart, 1978) have taken such inconsistency as evidence for the coexistence of both direct and phonologically mediated access mechanisms, as we will see below. Thus, the issue is controversial and remains open.

Multilevel and Parallel Coding-Systems Models

These models differ from those already discussed in that each postulates more than one unit of recognition rather than a single unit and each incorporates alternative vehicles for word identification.

LaBerge and Samuels's Multilevel Coding Model.   The LaBerge and Samuels (1974) model includes hierarchically ordered "codes" (representations) for features, letters, spelling patterns, and words.

Through a process called *perceptual learning,* lower-order codes are integrated and *unitized* (perceived as a unit) to form a new set of codes at each successive level. Perceptual learning involves focal attention, which is conceived as a limited cognitive resource that cannot be allocated to two processes simultaneously. As our ability to recognize unitized codes at a given level becomes *automatized,* we redeploy our attention to the task of unitizing codes at the next level. The gradual emergence of both word and subword codes and the integration of their visual and sound counterparts facilitate the use of both direct and phonologically mediated vehicles for word identification in developing readers. Skilled readers, however, have fully integrated a vast inventory of both types of codes and can therefore allocate cognitive resources primarily to comprehending connected text. Thus, skilled readers typically identify words through direct visual access, but knowledge of letter-sound correspondences provides them with a mechanism for identifying unfamiliar letter strings.

In initial tests of their model (shown in Figure 9.4), LaBerge and Samuels (1974) demonstrated that shifts of attention from familiar stimuli (for example, *b-d*) to unfamiliar stimuli (↕ ↕) exacted a cost in speed of processing on initial learning trials, but not on later trials. Because attentional shifts between two sets of familiar stimuli did *not* disrupt speed of processing, it was inferred that automatic processing consumes no attentional resources and may be defined by this criterion. (For an alternative view—that automaticity is a continuum—see Logan, 1988; Stanovich, 1991.) LaBerge and Samuels's (1974) claim that lower-level codes are gradually integrated into higher-level codes is given some support in studies showing that disparities in speed of pro-

FIGURE 9.4

LaBerge and Samuels' model (1974).

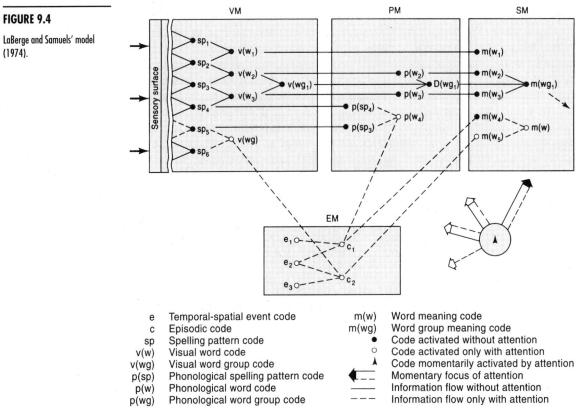

e	Temporal-spatial event code	m(w)	Word meaning code
c	Episodic code	m(wg)	Word group meaning code
sp	Spelling pattern code	●	Code activated without attention
v(w)	Visual word code	○	Code activated only with attention
v(wg)	Visual word group code	⌄	Code momentarily activated by attention
p(sp)	Phonological spelling pattern code	⬅ _ _	Momentary focus of attention
p(w)	Phonological word code	——	Information flow without attention
p(wg)	Phonological word group code	– – –	Information flow only with attention

cessing long words versus short words are substantial in children in the lower grades, but not in children in the upper grades (see Samuels & Kamil, 1984, for a review).

Support for the existence of intermediate-level codes comes from studies documenting that both letter clusters and syllables may function in word recognition (Adams, 1979; Greenberg & Vellutino, 1988; Petersen & LaBerge, 1977; Prinzmetal et al., 1988; Spoehr & Smith, 1973; Taft, 1979). Thus, the model enjoys considerable empirical support.

PARALLEL CODING-SYSTEMS MODELS.   The prototypical *parallel systems model* is Coltheart's (1978) *dual route* model. Discussed briefly in our section on development, the central assumption of this and related models (Carr & Pollatsek, 1985; Rayner & Pollatsek, 1989) is one of separate coding systems that independently carry out recognition operations. Coltheart (1978) postulates two such systems, one that uses word-specific associates to directly access lexical representations, and another that uses grapheme–phoneme correspondence (GPC) rules to access them indirectly. Both of these systems are activated by a letter string, and, depending on the nature of that string, one or the other system may bring about identification. Thus, highly familiar words would be identified through a direct visual route, whereas less familiar words and pseudowords would be identified through an indirect route using GPC rules. But, because the output codes of the GPC system must be *assembled* before identification can take place, it is the slower of the two processes.

Two different types of evidence have been cited in support of the dual route model. One type comes from studies of brain-damaged patients who have suffered an apparent selective loss of either the direct visual or phonologically mediated access routes. One group of patients—called *deep dyslexics*—appear able to read most words but have severely limited ability to read pseudowords, make many semantic confusion errors (for example, calling *cat*—"*kitten*" and *orchestra*—"*symphony*"), and have difficulty reading functors (for example, *if, and, but*). This symptom pattern suggests that the direct route is intact in these patients, whereas the phonologically mediated route is impaired (Coltheart, Patterson, & Marshall, 1980). *Surface dyslexics,* by contrast, often decode pseudowords and regularly spelled words (for example, *cat, fat*) more readily than they can decode irregularly spelled words (for example, *epoch, ache*) and often *regularize* words with exceptional pronunciations (for example, *have, put*), which suggests that they have lost word-specific connections that allow them to use the direct access route (Patterson, Marshall, & Coltheart, 1985). Because the strengths and weaknesses observed in these acquired dyslexia patients are relative rather than absolute (performance is never totally deficient nor totally adequate), critics have suggested that their performance patterns on decoding and naming tasks may simply reflect different types and levels of impairment of a single, lexically based access mechanism, rather than selective impairment of one of two separate mechanisms (for example, Humphrey & Evetts, 1985; Van Orden, Pennington, & Stone, 1990).

A second type of evidence for the dual route model comes from naming tasks with skilled readers. It has consistently been found that skilled readers are able to name printed words faster than they decode (sound out) pseudowords and that they name high-frequency words faster than low-frequency words (for example, Broadbent, 1967; Forster & Chambers, 1973; Perfetti & Hogaboam, 1975). This suggests that familiar words "use" the direct route, whereas less familiar words and pseudowords use the assembled route. It has also been consistently found that regular words are, in general, named faster than exception words (for example, Baron & Strawson, 1976). But, whereas high-frequency regular and exception words are both named with equal speed, low-frequency regular words are named faster than low-frequency exception words (Seidenberg, Waters, Barnes, & Tannenhaus, 1984; Waters & Seidenberg, 1985). Presumably the direct route always "wins the race" in the case of high-frequency words. With less familiar low-frequency words the indirect route is better able to compete with the direct route, and this conflict affects the exception words more than the regular words.

This account may be oversimplified. Glushko (1979) found that a pseudoword such as *tave,* which is spelled similarly to the exception word *have,* takes longer to name than a pseudoword such as *feal,* whose real word "neighbors" all have regular pronunciations (for example, *real, heal*). Glushko (1979) also found that regular words whose neighbors all have consistent pronunciations were named faster than regular words whose neighbors include words with inconsistent pronunciations. In addition, Seidenberg et al. (1984) found that low-frequency regular/consistent words were named faster than low-frequency regular/inconsistent words. Glushko (1979) and others (Humphreys & Evetts, 1985; Seidenberg et al., 1984; Van Orden et al., 1990) have interpreted these results as evidence for a single mechanism for lexical access (see also Barron, 1986) that identifies a word by "synthesizing patterns of activation" from other words with similar spellings (for example, identifies *fat* by analogy with *cat* and *fan*). The implication is that this mechanism mimics the apparent rule-based properties said to be characteristic of the GPC mechanism. Thus, the issue is controversial and remains unresolved.

Activation or Logogen Models

Most of the models discussed thus far imply that a printed word acts as a stimulus that energizes or activates a code or set of codes representing that word in memory. However, none of these models has been explicit in describing the activation processes. The class of models we now illustrate is more explicit in doing so.

MORTON'S LOGOGEN MODEL.   Activation models basically are fashioned after a model of word recognition initially proposed by Morton (1969). Morton coined the term **logogen** (from the Greek word *logos,* "word") to characterize an inferred *neural entity* that represents a printed word. Logogens function as threshold-type detection devices that incrementally register information derived from both sensory input and linguistic context. And, like neurons, they fire when a criterion threshold has been reached. When this occurs, the word is recognized and its meaning is accessed. In their *resting state,* logogens have threshold values for each represented word determined by their frequency of occurrence in print. Thus, logogens representing high-frequency words have lower thresholds of activation than do logogens representing low-frequency words. Linguistic context can also serve to lower or raise threshold values, depending on whether or not it contains information related to a word's meaning(s). Word recognition is believed to result from the interaction of stimulus and contextual information, and a word's meaning becomes available when a logogen is activated.

Support for Morton's (1969) model came largely from studies demonstrating that highly constraining contexts can facilitate word recognition, whereas incongruent contexts tend to impede recognition (Morton, 1964; Tulving & Gold, 1963; Tulving, Mandler, & Baumal, 1964). However, except for some later work (for example, Murrell & Morton, 1974), which suggests that logogens may be sensitive to morphemes rather than words (for example, *walk/ing*), Morton himself provided limited documentation of his model.

Interactive-Activation and Connectionist Models

Morton's model was pivotal in framing later models that provided greater specification of how logogens might work—the *interactive-activation model* of McClelland and Rumelhart (1981) (see also Rumelhart & McClelland, 1982a, b). In the latter model, word recognition is believed to result from the interaction of competing excitatory and inhibitory activations from interconnected logogen-type detectors *(nodes)* that correspond with features, letters, and words (see Figure 9.5). Each node is believed to have a "resting level" threshold that depends on frequency of activation over time. The activation level of a given node is said to be determined in part by excitation from the stimulus word and in part by excitatory and inhibitory activations from neighboring words. The greater the overlap in spelling, the greater the activations stimulated by given neighbors. Linguistic context may also influence activation level. The momentary activation of a given node is said to have a real numerical value that changes over time, depending on the relative weights carried by excitatory and inhibitory activations. Thus, in mathematical terms, word recognition is determined by the algebraic summation of excitatory and inhibitory inputs, which yields a net activation value that is a simple weighted average of these inputs. Because the excitatory activations prompted by a printed word stimulus are typically greater than the inhibitory activations prompted by neighboring words, the logogen for that word fires and the word is recognized.

The cardinal evidence for this *connectionist* model (the term reflecting its structural features) comes primarily from impressive computer simulations of some of the major word-recognition phenomena documented in empirical research (McClelland & Rumelhart, 1981; Rumelhart & McClelland, 1982a, b). The most notable is the word superiority effect discussed earlier, in which letters embedded in words are verified more accurately than those embedded in nonwords (Reicher, 1969). Moreover, the model rather handily accommodates Glushko's (1979) finding that pseudowords spelled like words with inconsistent pronunciations (for example, *tave/have*) take longer to pronounce than pseudowords spelled like words with consistent pronunciations *(feal/real)*. The underlying assumptions of the model are quite in keeping with Glushko's contention that words are identified by synthesizing patterns of activation from words with similar spellings.

FIGURE 9.5

McClelland and Rumelhart model
(1981).

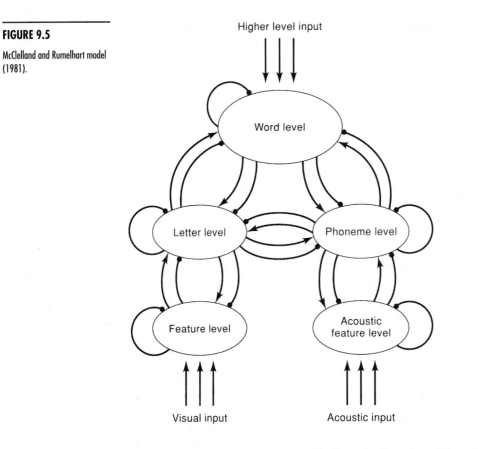

FIGURE 9.5

McClelland and Rumelhart model (1981).

But to complicate matters, a radically revised version of the interactive-activation model, proposed by Seidenberg and McClelland (1989), dispenses with word level nodes altogether and substitutes a **parallel distributed processing (PDP)** format, whereby nodes for three-letter spelling patterns are directly connected to nodes for the phoneme values of those spelling patterns (for example, the word *heat* is represented *-he, hea, eat, at-,* the dashes here representing word boundaries). Thus, there is no mental lexicon, and no assumptions are made about the role of linguistic context in word identification. And, using processing parameters similar to those outlined in McClelland and Rumelhart (1981), Seidenberg and McClelland (1989) were able to simulate an even broader range of word recognition phenomena—for example, the interaction between word frequency and regularity in word spellings, documented by Seidenberg et al. (1984); the pseudoword and regular/exception word pronunciation effects documented by Glushko (1979); and so forth. Seidenberg and McClelland (1989) conclude that words are identified using a single nonlexical coding mechanism that makes use of distributed representations that encode the spelling–sound redundancies inherent in the orthography.

However, it should be noted that the corpus of words used in the simulations reported by McClelland and Rumelhart (1981) and Seidenberg and McClelland (1989) included only four-letter words; thus, their results may not readily be generalized to more complex words. Moreover, in a critique of the PDP model, Besner, Twilley, Mc-Cann, and Seergobin (1990) compared the Seidenberg and McClelland (1989) simulations with performance of skilled readers on tasks not reported by these investigators and found that the two data sets did not correspond as closely as they should have. For example, the model did not name pseudowords as well as skilled readers. Based on such findings, among others, Besner et al. (1990) concluded that the standard dual route model still provides a better account of most word-recognition phenomena than does the PDP model. (See response to such criticisms in Seidenberg, 1992.)

Lexical-Search Models

Whereas activation models postulate that printed words are identified by passive and automatic activation of letter and word detectors, *search models* postulate that word identification is the culmination of an active and ordered search for lexical addresses where information about given words is stored. Such a model was initially proposed by Forster (1976) and later extended by Taft (1979). In the current model, a word's lexical address is assumed to be located in an **orthographic access file,** in one of several "bins" containing representations of words with similar orthographic descriptions. Entries in each bin are ordered by frequency, with those representing high-frequency words at the top of the bin and those representing low-frequency words at the bottom of the bin. The bin that contains a word's lexical address is located with the aid of an **access code,** which is defined as the first syllable in a stem morpheme. This unit—called the *basic orthographic syllable structure (BOSS)*—is isolated through left-to-right iterative parsing that maintains *orthographic* and morphological integrity. In prefixed words, parsing commences after the prefix has been stripped away. Thus, the BOSS of *prefix* is *fix,* and the BOSS of *vodka* is *vod* (*vo/dka* and *vodk/a* are both illegal). Similarly, the BOSS of *sunset* is *sun* because the parsing process gives morphemes preeminent status. When the bin containing the lexical address of the stimulus word is located, all codes in the bin are matched with that word in order of their frequency. When the appropriate code is found, the word's lexical address is accessed and a full orthographic description of the stem morpheme becomes available. A postaccess "check" is made to compare this representation with the stimulus word, and, if they match, the word is identified and its meaning is accessed.

Support for the search model came initially from Forster and Chambers's (1973) observations that real words can be identified more rapidly than pseudowords and that high-frequency words can be identified more rapidly than low-frequency words. However, such findings can also be explained by activation-type models (McClelland & Rumelhart, 1981; Seidenberg & McClelland, 1989). Moreover, most of the research conducted to evaluate the search model has been devoted to validation of the access code, and such research provides only indirect support for the model. Although considerable support exists for the idea that skilled readers are sensitive to both orthotactically and morphologically defined units in complex words (orthotactic parsing—*vod/ka;* morphological parsing—*sun/set; walk/ing;* see Feldman, in press; Lima & Pollatsek, 1983; Murrell & Morton, 1974; Prinzmetal et al., 1988; Taft, 1979; Taft & Forster, 1975, 1976), such findings do not constitute *prima facie* evidence for either access codes or search processes. In sum, the evidence for the BOSS unit is equivocal (Inhoff, 1989; Jordan, 1986; Lima & Pollatsek, 1983; Taft, 1979). Thus, whether words are identified through activation or search processes remains an open question (see Paap, Newsome, McDonald, & Schvaneveldt, 1982, for a model that incorporates activation as well as verification and search processes).

SUMMARY

In this chapter we have reviewed the history of writing, and we have discussed the kinds of complex abilities that humans have that allow them to read written language. We have traced some of the accounts that describe children's acquisition of reading, and we have summarized some of the most prominent models of the reading process itself. Although humans have been a language-speaking species for tens of thousands of years, writing is a relatively recent phenomenon. Our earliest evidence of writing dates from as recently as the 4th millennium B.C. Literacy has, however, changed the human species dramatically by providing us with an objective means of considering our own language and thought and of connecting ourselves to other worlds of knowledge, across time and space.

Spoken language is the fountainhead, as the great linguist Edward Sapir noted, from which all other forms of language flow. And writing is no exception. English writing is based upon an alphabetic principle: each written letter is meant to stand for a sound in the spoken word. This is the major principle that children must grasp. When children have grasped this principle, they bring into play various complex skills as they move through the stages of literacy acquisition.

Study of the reading process involves, in part, answering questions about how printed words are recognized. Many of the questions that have motivated the study of the word recognition process remain unanswered, but in addressing these questions we have, nevertheless, learned a great deal about how skilled readers recognize and identify printed words. We know, for example, that words are not recognized on the basis of shape cues or supraletter patterns, that word recognition depends initially on letter recognition, and that a word's letters are recognized in parallel rather than through left-to-right serial processing. We also know that, although the skilled reader may use both stimulus and contextual information in identifying printed words, the weight given these two types of information appears asymmetric insofar as skilled word identification has been shown to be an automatic, rapidly executed, and modular process, regardless of whether words are identified in isolation or in sentence contexts.

We have, in addition, good reason to believe that skilled readers have internalized unitized representations of redundant spelling patterns that they can use to decode unfamiliar letter strings; they also seem sensitive to both orthotactic and morphological boundaries in identifying familiar strings. Whether or not such boundaries define access codes that mediate word identification, and whether identification takes place through activation as opposed to search processes, through direct or phonologically mediated access mechanisms or through both types of mechanisms operating independently, are among the questions that remain open.

KEY WORDS

Dyslexia	*Implicit mediators*
Pictographs	*Semantic network*
Ideograms	*Cross-modal transfer*
Logographs	*Intersensory integration*
Syllabaries	*Serial memory*
Alphabets	*Logographic phase*
Graphemes	*Orthographic phase*
Automaticity	*Word superiority effect*
Fluency	*Backward masking*
Segmentation	*Logogen*
Morphophonemic production rules	*Parallel distributed processing (PDP)*
Perceptual learning	*Orthographic access file*
Association	*Access code*

SOMETHING TO THINK ABOUT

1. Do teaching methods that emphasize phonics concentrate on "top-down" or "bottom-up" processes? What are the advantages and disadvantages of such an approach?

2. Describe the kinds of experiences that adults can provide for children that enhance children's attainment of reading. What are some early predictors in children of later reading success?

3. Discuss the kinds of intellectual advantages that the establishment of writing brought to the human race, with particular reference to the kinds of thought available to literate societies that may not be found in purely oral cultures.

4. Models of reading processes have become increasingly complex and various. What are some of the basic components in most models, and why are theoretical models important for real children?

ACTIVITIES

1. **Interpreting a "Simple" Sign**

Consider this picture:

FIGURE 9.6

If the proverbial visitor from Mars landed in Boston, what kinds of information would she have to acquire to read and interpret the sign correctly? Make a model that includes a mental lexicon, bottom-up feature processing, and inferential processes.

2. **Parking Department Writing**

Consider the sign that follows:

FIGURE 9.7

What does this sign mean? How many and what kinds of writing does this sign exemplify? What are the advantages to such signs? The disadvantages?

REFERENCES

Adams, M. J. (1979). Models of word recognition. *Cognitive Psychology, 11,* 133–176.

Adams, M. J. (1990). *Beginning to read: Thinking and learning about print.* Cambridge, MA: MIT Press.

Baron, J. (1973). Phonemic stage is not necessary for reading. *Quarterly Journal of Experimental Psychology, 25,* 241–246.

Baron, J., & Strawson, C. (1976). Orthographic and word-specific mechanisms in reading words aloud. *Journal of Experimental Psychology: Human Perception and Performance, 2,* 386–393.

Barron, R. W. (1986). Word recognition in early reading: A review of the direct and indirect access hypothesis. *Cognition, 24,* 93–119.

Barron, R. W. (1992). Proto-literacy, literacy and the acquisition of phonological awareness. *Learning and Individual Differences, 3,* 243–255.

Barron, R. W., & Baron, J. (1977). How children get meaning from printed words. *Child Development, 48,* 586–594.

Beck, I. L., Perfetti, C. A., & McKeown, M. G. (1982). Effects of long-term vocabulary instruction of lexical access and reading comprehension. *Journal of Educational Psychology, 74,* 506–521.

Bertelson, P. (1986). The onset of literacy: Liminal remarks. *Cognition, 24,* 1–30.

Bertelson, P., & De Gelder, B. (1989). Learning about reading from illiterates. In A. M. Galaburda (Ed.), *From neurons to reading* (pp. 1–23). Cambridge, MA: MIT Press.

Besner, D., Twilley, L., McCann, R. S., & Seergobin, K. (1990). On the association between connectionism and data: Are a few words necessary? *Psychological Review, 97,* 432–446.

Biemiller, A. (1970). The development of the use of graphic and contextual information as children learn to read. *Reading Research Quarterly, 6,* 75–96.

Bissex, G. L. (1980). *GNYS at work: A child learns to write and read.* Cambridge, MA: Harvard University Press.

Bower, G. H., & Hildgard, E. R. (1981). *Theories of learning.* Englewood Cliffs, NJ: Prentice-Hall.

Bower, G. H., & Minaire, H. (1974). On interfering with item versus order information in serial recall. *American Journal of Psychology, 87,* 557–564.

Bowey, J. A., & Patel, R. K. (1988). Metalinguistic ability and early reading achievement. *Applied Psycholinguistics, 9,* 367–383.

Bradley, L., & Bryant, P. E. (1978). Difficulties in auditory organization as a possible cause of reading backwardness. *Nature, 271,* 746–747.

Bradley, L., & Bryant, P. E. (1983). Categorizing sounds and learning to read: A causal connection. *Nature, 301,* 419–421.

Bradley, L., & Bryant, P. E. (1985). *Rhyme and reason in reading and spelling* (IARLD Monographs, No. 1). Ann Arbor: University of Michigan Press.

Broadbent, D. E. (1967). The word-frequency effect and response bias. *Psychological Review, 74,* 1–15.

Bryant, P. E. (1974). *Perception and understanding in young children.* New York: Basic Books.

Bryant, P. E., MacLean, M., & Bradley, L. L. (1990). Rhyme, language, and children's reading. *Applied Psycholinguistics, 11,* 237–252.

Carr, T. H., & Pollatsek, A. (1985). Recognizing printed words: A look at current models. In D. Besner, T. G. Waller, & G. E. MacKinnon (Eds.), *Reading research: Advances in theory and practice, Vol. 5* (pp. 1–82). Orlando: Academic Press.

Cattell, J. McK. (1886). The time it takes to see and name objects. *Mind, 11,* 63–65.

Chall, J. S. (1967). *Learning to read: The great debate.* New York: McGraw-Hill.

Chall, J. S. (1983). *Stages of reading development.* New York: McGraw-Hill.

Chomsky, C. (1972). Stages in language development and reading exposure. *Harvard Educational Review, 42,* 1–33.

Chomsky, N., & Halle, M. (1968). *The sound pattern of English.* New York: Harper & Row.

Coltheart, M. (1978). Lexical access in simple reading tasks. In G. Underwood (Ed.), *Strategies of information processing.* New York: Academic Press.

Coltheart, M. (1981). Disorders of reading and their implication for models of reading. *Visible Language, 15,* 245–286.

Coltheart, M. (1982). The psycholinguistic analysis of acquired dyslexias: Some illustrations. *Philosophical Transactions of the Royal Society of London, 298,* 154–164.

Coltheart, M., Patterson, K., & Marshall, J. (Eds.). (1980). *Deep dyslexia.* London: Routledge & Kegan Paul.

Curtis, M. E. (1987). Vocabulary testing and vocabulary instruction. In M. G. McKeown & M. E. Curtis (Eds.), *The nature of vocabulary acquisition* (pp. 37–51). Hillsdale, NJ: Erlbaum.

Daneman, M. (1991). Individual differences in reading skills. In R. Barr, M. L. Kamil, P. B. Mosenthal, & P. D. Pearson (Eds.), *Handbook of reading research (Vol. II).* New York: Longman.

Das, J. P., Kirby, J., & Jarman, R. F. (1975). Simultaneous and successive syntheses: An alternative model for cognitive abilities. *Psychological Bulletin, 82,* 99–114.

Dickinson, D., Wolf, M., & Stotsky, S. (1993). Words move: The interwoven development of oral and written language. In J. B. Gleason (Ed.), *The development of language* (3rd ed.). New York: Macmillan.

Ehri, L. C. (1985a). Effects of printed language acquisition on speech. In D. R. Olson, N. Torrance, & A. Hildyard (Eds.), *Literacy, language and learning: The nature and consequences of reading and writing* (pp. 333–367). New York: Cambridge University Press.

Ehri, L. C. (1985b). Sources of difficulty in learning to spell and read. In M. L. Wolvaich & D. Routh (Eds.), *Advances in development and behavioural pediatrics.* Greenwich, CT: Jai Press.

Ehri, L. C. (1992). Reconceptualizing the development of sight word reading and its relationship to recording. In P. Gough, R. Treiman, & L. C. Ehri (Eds.), *Reading acquisition* (pp. 107–143). Hillsdale, NJ: Erlbaum.

Ehri, L. C., & Wilce, L. S. (1985). Movement into reading: Is the first stage of printed word learning visual or phonetic? *Reading Research Quarterly, 20,* 163–179.

Ellis, A. W. (1984). *Reading, writing and dyslexia.* London: Erlbaum.

Feldman, L. B. (1991). The contribution of morphology to word recognition. *Psychological Research, 5*(1), 33–41.

Forster, K. I. (1976). Accessing the mental lexicon. In R. J. Wales & E. Walker (Eds.), *New approaches to language mechanisms* (pp. 255–287). Amsterdam: North Holland.

Forster, K. I., & Chambers, S. J. (1973). Lexical access and naming time. *Journal of Verbal Learning and Verbal Behavior, 12,* 627–635.

Frith, U. (1985). Beneath the surface of dyslexia. In K. Patterson, J. Marshall, & M. Coltheart (Eds.), *Surface dyslexia* (pp. 301–330). London: Erlbaum.

Geschwind, N. (1974). *Selected papers on language and the brain.* Boston: Reidel.

Gibson, E. J. (1969). *Principles of perceptual learning and development.* New York: Appleton, Century, Crofts.

Glushko, R. J. (1979). The organization and activation of orthographic knowledge in reading aloud. *Journal of Experimental Psychology: Human Perception and Performance, 5,* 674–691.

Goodman, K. S., & Goodman, Y. M. (1980). Learning about psycholinguistic processes by analyzing oral reading. In M. Wolf, M. K. McQuillan, & E. Radwin (Eds.), *Thought & language/Language & reading* (pp. 253–269) (Harvard Educational Review Reprint series no. 14). Cambridge, MA: Harvard Educational Review.

Goswami, U. C. (1985). *The role of analogy in early reading development.* Paper presented at the Society for Research in Child Development, Toronto, Ontario, Canada.

Gough, P. B. (1972). One second of reading. In J. F. Kavanagh & I. G. Mattingly (Eds.), *Language by ear and by eye: The relationship between speech and reading* (pp. 331–358). Cambridge, MA: MIT Press.

Gough, P. B. (1984). Word recognition. In P. D. Pearson, R. Barr, M. L. Kamil, & P. D. Mosenthal (Eds.), *Handbook of reading research, Vol. 1* (pp. 225–253). New York: Longman.

Gough, P. B., Alford, J. A., & Holley-Wilcox, P. (1981). Words and contexts. In O. J. L. Tzeng & H. Singer (Eds.), *Perception of print: Reading research in experimental psychology* (pp. 85–102). Hillsdale, NJ: Erlbaum.

Gough, P. B., & Hillinger, M. L. (1980). Learning to read: An unnatural act. *Bulletin of the Orton Society, 30,* 179–196.

Gough, P. B., & Tunmer, W. E. (1986). Decoding, reading, and reading disability. *Remedial and Special Education, 7,* 6–10.

Greenberg, S. N., & Vellutino, F. R. (1988). Evidence for processing constituent single and multilevel codes: Support for multilevel coding in word perception. *Memory and Cognition, 16,* 54–63.

Havelock, E. A. (1976). *Origins of western literacy.* Toronto: The Ontario Institute for Studies in Education.

Healy, A. F. (1974). Separating item from order information in short-term memory. *Journal of Verbal Learning and Verbal Behavior, 13,* 644–655.

Houston, J. P. (1976). Item versus order information, proactive inhibition and serial recall. *American Journal of Psychology, 89,* 507–514.

Humphrey, G. W., & Evetts, L. J. (1985). Are there independent lexical and non-lexical routes in word processing? An evaluation of the dual-route theory in reading. *The Behavioral and Brain Sciences, 8,* 689–740.

Inhoff, A. W. (1989). Lexical access during eye fixations in reading: Are word access codes used to integrate lexical information across interword fixations? *Journal of Memory and Language, 28,* 444–461.

Johnson, D., & Mykelbust, H. (1984). *Learning disabilities* (2nd ed.). New York: Grune & Stratton.

Johnson, N. F. (1977). A pattern-unit model of word identification. In D. LaBerge & S. J. Samuels (Eds.), *Basic processes in reading: Perception and comprehension* (pp. 91–125). Hillsdale, NJ: Erlbaum.

Johnston, J. C. (1981). Understanding word perception: Clues from studying the word superiority effect. In O. J. L. Tzeng & H. Singer (Eds.), *Perception of print: Reading research in experimental psychology* (pp. 65–84). Hillsdale, NJ: Erlbaum.

Jordan, T. R. (1986). Testing the BOSS hypothesis: Evidence for position insensitive orthographic priming in the lexical decision task. *Memory and Cognition, 14,* 523–532.

Jorm, A. F., & Share, D. L. (1983). Phonological reading and acquisition. *Applied Psycholinguistics, 4,* 103–147.

Just, M. A., & Carpenter, P. A. (1987). *The psychology of reading and language comprehension.* Newton, MA: Allyn & Bacon.

Kameenui, E. J., Dixon, R. C., & Carmine, D. W. (1987). Issues in the design of vocabulary instruction. In M. G. McKeown & M. E. Curtis (Eds.), *The nature of vocabulary acquisition* (pp. 129–145). Hillsdale, NJ: Erlbaum.

Kleiman, G. M. (1975). Speech recoding in reading. *Journal of Verbal Learning and Verbal Behavior, 14,* 323–340.

Kolers, P. A. (1970). Three stages of reading, In H. Levin & J. P. Williams (Eds.), *Basic studies on reading* (pp. 90–118). New York: Basic Books.

Kolers, P. A. (1973). Some modes of representation. In P. Pliner, L. Krames, & T. Alloway (Eds.), *Communication and affect: Language and thought.* New York: Academic Press.

LaBerge, D., & Samuels, S. J. (1974). Toward a theory of automatic information processing in reading. *Cognitive Psychology, 6,* 293–323.

Liberman, I. Y., Liberman, A. M., Mattingly, I. G., & Shankweiler, D. (1980). Orthography and the beginning reader. In J. F. Kavanagh & R. L. Venezsky (Eds.), *Orthography, reading and dyslexia.* Baltimore, MD: University Park Press.

Liberman, I. Y., Shankweiler, D., Fischer, F. W., & Carter, B. (1974). Explicit syllable and phoneme segmentation in the young child. *Journal of Experimental Child Psychology, 18,* 201–212.

Lima, S. D., & Pollatsek, A. (1983). Lexical access via an orthographic code? The basic orthographic syllable structure (BOSS) reconsidered. *Journal of Verbal Learning and Verbal Behavior, 22,* 310–332.

Logan, G. D. (1988). Toward an instance theory of automatization. *Psychological Review, 95*(4), 492–527.

Luria, A. R. (1966). *Higher cortical functions in man.* New York: Basic Books.

Luria, A. R. (1973). *The Working Brain.* London: Penguin.

Mann, V. A. (1986). Phonological awareness: The role of reading experience. *Cognition, 24,* 65–92.

Marsh, G., & Desberg, P. (1983). The development of strategies in the acquisition of symbolic skills. In D. A. Rogers & J. A. Sloboda (Eds.), *The acquisition of symbolic skills.* New York: Plenum Press.

Marshall, J. C., & Newcombe, F. (1973). Patterns of paralexia: A psycholinguistic approach. *Journal of Psycholinguistic Research, 2*(3), 175–199.

Massaro, D. W. (1975). *Understanding language: An information processing analysis of speech, perception, reading, and psycholinguistics.* New York: Academic Press.

McClelland, J. L., & Rumelhart, D. E. (1981). An interactive activation model of context effects in letter perception: Part 1. An account of basic findings. *Psychological Review, 88,* 375–405.

Mesrich, J. J. (1973). The word-superiority effect in brief visual displays: Elimination by vocalization. *Perception and Psychophysics, 13,* 45–48.

Morton, J. (1964). The effects of context on the visual duration thresholds for words. *British Journal of Psychology, 55,* 165–180.

Morton, J. (1969). Interaction of information in word recognition. *Psychological Review, 76,* 165–178.

Murrell, C. A., & Morton, J. (1974). Word recognition and morphemic structure. *Journal of Experimental Psychology, 102,* 963–968.

Nicholson, T. (1991). Do children read words better in context or in lists? A classic study revisited. *Journal of Educational Psychology, 83*(4), 444–450.

Olson, D. R. (1980). From utterance to text: The bias of language in speech and writing. In M. Wolf, M. K. McQuillan, & E. Radwin (Eds.), *Thought & language/Language & reading* (pp. 84–108) (Harvard Educational Review Reprint series no. 14). Cambridge, MA: Harvard Educational Review.

Olson, D. R. (1986). The cognitive consequences of literacy. *Canadian Psychology, 27*(2), 109–121.

Papp, K. R., Newsome, S., McDonald, J. E., & Schvaneveldt, R. W. (1982). An activation–verification model for letter and word recognition: The word-superiority effect. *Psychological Review, 89,* 573–594.

Patterson, K. E., Marshall, J. C., & Coltheart, M. (Eds.). (1985). *Surface dyslexia.* London: Erlbaum.

Perfetti, C. A. (1985). *Reading ability.* New York: Oxford University Press.

Perfetti, C. A. (1992). The representation problem in reading acquisition. In P. Gough, L. Ehri, & R. Treiman (Eds.), *Reading acquisition* (pp. 145–174). Hillsdale, NJ: Erlbaum.

Perfetti, C. A., Beck, I., Bell, L. C., & Hughes, C. (1987). Phonemic knowledge and learning to read are reciprocal: A longitudinal study of first grade children. *Merrill Palmer Quarterly, 33,* 283–319.

Perfetti, C. A., Bell, L. C., & Delaney, S. M. (1988). Automatic (prelexical) phonetic activation in silent word reading: Evidence from backward masking. *Journal of Memory and Language, 27,* 59–70.

Perfetti, C. A., & Hogaboam, T. W. (1975). The relationship between single word decoding and reading comprehension skill. *Journal of Educational Psychology, 67,* 461–469.

Perfetti, C. A., & Roth, S. (1981). Some of the interactive processes in reading and their role in reading skill. In A. M. Lesgold & C. A. Perfetti (Eds.), *Interactive processes in reading* (pp. 269–297). Hillsdale, NJ: Erlbaum.

Petersen, R. J., & LaBerge, D. (1977). Contextual control of letter perception. *Memory and Cognition, 5,* 205–213.

Prinzmetal, W., Treiman, R., & Rho, S. H. (1988). How to see a reading unit. *Journal of Memory and Language, 25,* 461–475.

Raines, S. C., & Canady, R. J. (1990). *The whole language kindergarten.* New York: Teachers College Press.

Rayner, K., McConkie, G. W., & Zola, D. (1980). Integrating information across fixations. *Cognitive Psychology, 12,* 206–226.

Rayner, K., & Pollatsek, A. (1989). *The psychology of reading.* Englewood Cliffs, NJ: Prentice-Hall.

Read, C. (1981). Writing is not the inverse of reading for young children. In C. H. Frederiksen & J. F. Dominic (Eds.), *Writing: The nature, development and teaching of written communication.* Hillsdale, NJ: Erlbaum.

Read, C., Yun-Fei, Z., Hong-Yin, N., & Bao-Qing, D. (1986). The ability to manipulate speech sounds depends on knowing alphabetic writing. *Cognition, 24,* 31–44.

Reicher, G. (1969). Perceptual recognition as a function of meaningfulness of stimulus material. *Journal of Experimental Psychology, 81,* 275–280.

Roswell, F., & Natchez, G. (1971). *Reading disability: Diagnosis and treatment.* New York: Basic Books.

Rubenstein, H., Lewis, S. S., & Rubenstein, M. A. (1971). Evidence for phonemic recoding in visual word recognition. *Journal of Verbal Learning and Verbal Behavior, 10,* 645–657.

Rumelhart, D. E., & McClelland, J. L. (1982a). An interactive model of context effects in letter perception: Part 2. The contextual enhancement effect and some tests and extensions of the model. *Psychological Review, 89,* 60–94.

Rumelhart, D. E., & McClelland, J. L. (1982b). Interactive processing through spreading activation. In A. M. Lesgold & C. A. Perfetti (Eds.), *Interactive processes in reading* (pp. 37–60). Hillsdale, NJ: Erlbaum.

Samuels, S. J., & Kamil, M. J. (1984). Models of the reading process. In P. D. Pearson, R. Barr, M. L. Kamil, & P. Mosenthal (Eds.), *Handbook of reading research, Vol. 1* (pp. 185–224). New York and London: Longman.

Schmandt-Besserat, D. (1991). The earliest precursor of writing. In W. S.-Y. Wang (Ed.), *The emergence of language: Development and evolution* (pp. 31–45). New York: Freeman.

Seidenberg, M. (1992). Dyslexia in a computational model of word recognition in reading. In P. Gough, R. Treiman, & L. Ehri (Eds.), *Reading acquisition* (pp. 243–273). Hillsdale, NJ: Erlbaum.

Seidenberg, M. S., & McClelland, J. L. (1989). A distributed developmental model of word recognition and naming. *Psychological Review, 96,* 523–568.

Seidenberg, M. S., Waters, G. S., Barnes, M. A., & Tannenhaus, M. K. (1984). When does irregular spelling or pronunciation influence word recognition? *Journal of Verbal Learning and Verbal Behavior, 23,* 383–404.

Smith, F. (1969). The use of featural dependencies across letters in the visual identification of words. *Journal of Verbal Learning and Verbal Behavior, 8,* 215–218.

Smith, F. (1971). *Understanding reading: A psycholinguistic analysis of reading and learning to read.* New York: Holt, Rinehart and Winston.

Smith, F. (1980). Making sense of reading—And of reading instruction. In M. Wolf, M. K. McQuillan, & E. Radwin (Eds.), *Thought & language/Language & reading* (pp. 415–424) (Harvard Educational Review Reprint series no. 14). Cambridge, MA: Harvard Educational Review.

Smith, F., Lott, D., & Cronnell, B. (1969). The effect of type size and case alternation on word identification. *American Journal of Psychology, 82,* 248–253.

Snow, C. E. (1973). Literacy and language: Relationships during the preschool years. *Harvard Educational Review, 53,* 165–189.

Snowling, M. (1987). *Dyslexia.* Oxford: Basil Blackwell.

Snowling, M. (1990). *Dyslexia: A cognitive developmental perspective.* Oxford: Basil Blackwell.

Spoehr, K. T. (1978). Phonological encoding in visual word recognition. *Journal of Verbal Learning and Verbal Behavior, 17,* 127–141.

Spoehr, K. T., & Smith, E. E. (1973). The role of syllables in perceptual processing. *Cognitive Psychology, 5,* 71–89.

Stanovich, K. E. (1980). Toward an interactive-compensatory model of individual differences in the development of reading fluency. *Reading Research Quarterly, 16,* 32–71.

Stanovich, K. E. (1986). "Matthew effects" in reading: Some consequences of individual differences in the acquisition of literacy. *Reading Research Quarterly, 4,* 360–407.

Stanovich, K. E. (1990). Concepts in developmental theories of reading skill: Cognitive resources, automaticity, and modularity. *Developmental Review, 19,* 72–100.

Stanovich, K. E. (1991). Word recognition: Changing perspectives. In R. Barr, M. L. Kamil, P. Mosenthal, & P. D. Pearson (Eds.), *Handbook of reading research, Vol. II* (pp. 418–452). New York and London: Longman.

Stanovich, K. E. (1992). Speculations on the causes and consequences of individual differences in early reading acquisition. In P. Gough, L. Ehri, & R. Treiman (Eds.), *Reading acquisition* (pp. 307–342). Hillsdale, NJ: Erlbaum.

Stanovich, K. E., & West, R. F. (1989). Exposure to print and orthographic processing. *Reading Research Quarterly, 24,* 402–433.

Stevenson, H. W., Stigler, J. W., Tucker, G. W., Lee, S. Y., Hsu, C. C., & Ketanusa, S. (1982). Reading disabilities: The case of Chinese, Japanese, and English. *Child Development, 53,* 1164–1181.

Taft, M. (1979). Lexical access via an orthographic code: The basic orthographic syllable structure (BOSS). *Journal of Verbal Learning and Verbal Behavior, 18,* 21–39.

Taft, M., & Forster, K. I. (1975). Lexical storage and retrieval of prefixed words. *Journal of Verbal Learning and Verbal Behavior, 14,* 638–647.

Taft, M., & Forster, K. I. (1976). Lexical storage and retrieval of polymorphic and polysyllabic words. *Journal of Verbal Learning and Verbal Behavior, 15,* 607–620.

Theois, J., & Muisee, J. G. (1977). The word identification process in reading. In N. J. Castellan, D. B. Pisoni, & G. R. Potts (Eds.), *Cognitive theory, Vol. 2* (pp. 289–321). Hillsdale, NJ: Erlbaum.

Travers, J. R. (1973). The effects of forced serial processing on identification of words and random letter strings. *Cognitive Psychology, 5,* 109–137.

Treiman, R. (1985). Onsets and rhymes as units of spoken syllables: Evidence from children. *Journal of Experimental Child Psychology, 39,* 161–181.

Treiman, R. (1993). *Beginning to spell.* New York: Oxford University Press.

Tulving, E., & Gold, C. (1963). Stimulus information and contextual information as determinants of tachistoscopic recognition of words. *Journal of Experimental Psychology, 66,* 319–327.

Tulving, E., Mandler, G., & Baumal, R. (1964). Interaction of two sources of information in tachistoscopic word recognition. *Canadian Journal of Psychology, 18,* 62–71.

Tulving, E., & Pearlstone, Z. (1966). Availability versus accessibility of information in memory for words. *Journal of Verbal Learning and Verbal Behavior, 5,* 381–391.

Tzeng, O., & Wang, W. S.-Y. (1984). Search for a common neurocognitive mechanism for language and movements. *American Journal of Physiology, 246,* 904–911.

Van Orden, G. C. (1987). A ROWS is a ROSE: Spelling, sound and reading. *Memory and Cognition, 15,* 181–198.

Van Orden, G. C., Johnston, J. C., & Hale, B. L. (1988). Word identification in reading proceeds from spelling to sound meaning. *Journal of Experimental Psychology: Learning, Memory and Cognition, 14,* 371–385.

Van Orden, G. C., Pennington, B. F., & Stone, G. O. (1990). Word identification in reading and the promise of subsymbolic psycholinguistics. *Psychological Review, 97,* 1–35.

Vellutino, F. R. (1982). Theoretical issues in the study of word recognition: The unit of perception controversy reexamined. In S. Rosenberg (Ed.), *Handbook of applied psycholinguistics* (pp. 33–197). Hillsdale, NJ: Erlbaum.

Vellutino, F. R. (1991a). Dyslexia. In W. S.-Y. Wang (Ed.), *The emergence of language: Development and evolution* (pp. 159–170). New York: Freeman.

Vellutino, F. (1991b). Introduction to three studies on reading acquisition: Convergent findings on theoretical foundations of code oriented vs. whole language approaches to reading instruction. *Journal of Educational Psychology, 83*(4), 437–443.

Vellutino, F. R., & Scanlon, D. M. (1987). Phonological coding, phonological awareness, and reading ability: Evidence from a longitudinal and experimental study. *Merrill Palmer Quarterly, 33,* 321–363.

Vellutino, F. R., Scanlon, D. M., DeSetto, L., & Pruzek, R. M. (1981). Developmental trends in the salience of meaning versus structural attributes of written words. *Psychological Research, 43,* 131–153.

Vellutino, F. R., Scanlon, D. M., & Spearing, D. (1995). Semantic and phonological coding in poor and normal readers. *Journal of Experimental Child Psychology, 59*(1), 76–124.

Vellutino, F. R., Scanlon, D. M., & Tanzman, M. S. (1990). Differential sensitivity to the meaning and structural attributes of printed words in poor and normal readers. *Learning and Individual Differences, 2,* 19–43.

Venezky, R. L. (1970). *The structure of English orthography.* The Hague: Mouton.

Vygotsky, L. S. (1962). *Thought and language.* Cambridge, MA: MIT Press.

Walsh, D., Price, G., & Cunningham, M. (1988). The critical but transitory importance of letter naming. *Reading Research Quarterly, 23,* 108–122.

Wang, W. S.-Y. (Ed.). (1991). *The emergence of language: Development and evolution.* New York: Freeman.

Waters, G. S., & Seidenberg, M. S. (1985). Spelling-sound effects in reading: Time course and decision criteria. *Memory and Cognition, 13,* 557–572.

Weber, R. M. (1970). The linguistic analysis of first-grade reading errors. *Reading Research Quarterly, 5,* 427–445.

Wolf, M. (1991a). Naming speed and reading: The contribution of the cognitive neurosciences. *Reading Research Quarterly, 26*(2), 123–141.

Wolf, M. (1991b). The word-retrieval deficit hypothesis and developmental dyslexia. *Learning and Individual Differences, 3,* 205–223.

Wolf, M., Bally, H., & Morris, R. (1986). Automaticity, retrieval processes, and reading: A longitudinal study in average and impaired readers. *Child Development, 57,* 988–1000.

Wolf, M., & Obregon, M. (1992). Early naming deficits, developmental dyslexia, and a specific-deficit hypothesis. *Brain and Language, 42,* 219–247.

Chapter 10

BILINGUALISM AND SECOND LANGUAGE ACQUISITION

Catherine E. Snow
Harvard Graduate School of Education

INTRODUCTION

For most of us living in North America, the topic of bilingualism or second language (SL) acquisition seems rather remote from issues of language processing or language use. Of course, many Americans study a foreign language in high school or at university, but they often discover when traveling to the country where that language is spoken or seeing a movie in that language that their proficiency is extremely limited. Because few North Americans consider themselves bilingual, it is perhaps hard to realize that being monolingual is actually atypical; most people in the world are, in fact, bilingual to some extent. Some of these are bilingual because they have grown up in officially or pervasively bilingual societies, in which the citizens are expected to learn more than one language (for example, Quebec, Belgium, Switzerland). Some are bilingual because their own language is not the language used in their nation for schooling, for politics, or for economic exchange. For example, Zulu speakers in South Africa must learn English, and Malayalam; speakers in India must learn both Hindi and English if they wish to go to school, read signs, or get good jobs. Immigrants to a country that does not use their traditional language often become bilingual, such as Spanish or Khmer speakers in the United States. Colonization can impose another language, as it has imposed Spanish, for example, on the Quechua and Aymara speakers in Peru, Equador, and Bolivia. Some people are bilingual because they are members of an educated elite and have benefited from tutors and travel. Others are bilingual because they see economic or professional advantages to acquiring foreign languages, such as the Korean business executive studying English or the aspirant diplomat learning Arabic. And some people are bilingual because they grew up in households where two languages were used regularly; these we might think of as "native bilinguals."

Given the vast array of situations in which one might learn a second language, it is important to start out by defining what we mean by *second language learning* or *bilingualism*. Identifying someone as *bilingual* is often taken to mean "perfectly" bilingual. In fact, as we will see, the concept of being perfectly bilingual is of little use; few bilinguals use both their languages equally for the same sort of task. For example, the Mexican-American boy living in California probably finds it easier to talk about school in English, and about visits to his grandparents in Spanish. It is said that the great French mathematician Pascal always did arithmetic in French but algebra in English, because he had studied first in French and then in English schools. For the purposes of this chapter, then, we will use the term *bilingual* to mean anyone who actually functions to any degree in more than one language. This would exclude English speakers who use foreign words only to impress other English speakers (as in "Clinton, the *soi-disant* leader of the western world, makes up through *machismo* what he lacks in *savoir faire*") but would include English speakers who use high school French to talk to taxi drivers or waiters in Paris.

Another term we should define is *second language acquisition.* Does it differ from *foreign language learning?* What about third and fourth languages? What about two languages learned simultaneously? Broadly speaking, we refer to second language acquisition when describing cases in which a learner who already has some degree of control over one language system is introduced to a second (or third or fourth). We are interested in second language acquisition whether it occurs in a situation where the later-learned language is widely used or not, including contexts of exposure that may emphasize or be limited to either oral or to literate uses. We use the term to include second language acquisition in **submersion** settings (one learner surrounded by native speakers), **immersion** settings (a group of learners taught through the medium of the second language), or formal foreign language classrooms. One of the interesting questions that arises is the differences in the processes of studying a second language and of picking it up naturally. Thus, the phenomenon of second language acquisition is defined here as encompassing all the following sorts of cases: a Vietnamese-speaking 5-year-old in the United States who starts kindergarten in a bilingual program; the Sesotho-speaking South African 8-year-old who simultaneously learns conversational Xhosa from playing with neighbor children and literacy in English in school (See Figure 10.1); the upper-class Peruvian 10-year-old who learns

FIGURE 10.1

South African parents who speak African languages at home are increasingly seeking schooling in English for their children. They see English as a language of economic opportunity.

English and German from his governess and tutors; the American doctoral student who takes a course in "Reading Spanish" to pass his university's language requirement; and the Anglophone Canadian civil servant who enrolls in an evening French course in order to keep her job. The phenomenon is meant to include cases of second language acquisition that result in stable bilingualism, those that result in only transient or limited retention of the second language, and those that result in loss of the primary language and its replacement by the second language as the speaker's stronger language. However, if two languages are learned simultaneously from birth, we will call that **native bilingualism** rather than second language acquisition.

A good portion of the research on second language acquisition has been motivated by practical questions:

How can we improve foreign language teaching?

How can we predict who will be a successful foreign language learner?

How can we improve academic achievement for children who start school unable to speak English?

How can we decide if children should be in mainstream classrooms or taking classes in English as a second language?

Is it confusing or too difficult for children to grow up learning two languages simultaneously?

Other lines of research, though, have attempted to use the special characteristics of the bilingual speaker or the bilingual brain to test hypotheses about psycholinguistics:

Do bilinguals take longer to process sentences because they know more words?

Do they experience interference between their two language systems?

Is language localized in bilinguals' brains in the same way as in monolinguals' brains?

Is learning a third or a fourth language faster than learning a second?

Is it possible to learn a second language as an adult and become a native-like speaker?

In this chapter, we will address these and other questions. First, we will review research on native bilinguals—children growing up exposed to two languages from birth. Then, we turn to what we know about second language learners and the process of second language acquisition. Thinking and research on second language acquisition have been done by several rather separate groups of researchers whose work has not been integrated into a single view. We will distinguish four major lines of research on second language acquisition and review the contributions of each separately.

Growing Up Bilingual

Traute Taeschner grew up in a family that had emigrated from Germany to Brazil. As a child, she spoke German with her parents and many of her parents' friends and their children in the sizable German immigrant community of Brazil, but she spoke Portuguese at school and with other friends. When she grew up, she moved to Italy, where she married an Italian and started studying language development. Her own children, Lisa and Giulia, were perfect subjects for a study of native bilingualism, because they heard almost exclusively German from their mother and Italian from their father. Taeschner wrote a book about her children's language development called *The Sun Is Feminine;* the title refers to her 3-year-old daughter Giulia's insistence on saying, "la sole," when speaking Italian (instead of the correct *il sole),* presumably because she knew that *sun* was feminine in German *(die Sonne)* (Taeschner, 1983). Despite such transient errors resulting from being bilingual, Lisa and Giulia both became fluent, native-like speakers of both German and Italian, as is typical if a child's parents are consistent in using the two languages.

As one might expect, during the earliest stages of language development, Lisa and Giulia often made mistakes in which language they used with German- and Italian-speaking adults. In fact, of Giulia's first 90 words, only 7 Italian words had direct German equivalents: *scotta (heiss), grazie (danke), tutto-tutto (alle-alle), fatto (fertig), la (die), no (nein),* and *si (ja).* Only in the second stage of language development, after about 18 months of age, did Giulia or Lisa start to systematically acquire translation equivalents and thus become able to say everything in both languages. As is common with bilingual children, they became quite insistent on knowing such equivalents, sometimes refusing to believe that proper trademark nouns such as Tic Tac or

Kleenex could not be translated. Furthermore, even native bilinguals who are not as well balanced in their bilingualism as Lisa and Giulia demonstrate that they know which language to use with various adults. If they are much less proficient in one language than the other, they may use the better-known language most of the time with everyone. Such children will, however, more often use their less-proficient language with native speakers of that language than they do with other people, thus displaying their understanding of the difference between their two languages from an early age (Genesee, Boivin, & Nicoladis, 1996).

Lisa and Giulia also produced utterances that used elements of both German and Italian; these are called **code-switches** and often are considered evidence that bilinguals speak neither language really well. In fact, though code-switched utterances sometimes occur because the speaker has forgotten or does not know a word in the language being spoken, children often correct their code-switches, which indicates that they know both languages but have experienced a sort of bilingual slip of the tongue. Furthermore, code-switching is fairly common in families where two languages are spoken, as speakers select words from either language that best express the intent. Mario, a boy who grew up mostly in the United States with his Bolivian mother and his Italian father, both of whom spoke Spanish with him, was considered by his linguist father to be more proficient in Spanish than in English until at least age 7 or 8 (Fantini, 1985). Nonetheless, he produced many sentences like the following:

Sabes mi school bus no tiene un stop sign.

Hoy, yo era line leader en mi escuela.

Ponemos cranberries y marshmallows y despues se pone el glitter con glue.

Clearly, Mario used English words for experiences that were closely associated with English for him—activities at school and American foods. If an entire community is bilingual, similar to communities of Puerto Ricans who live on the mainland, then code-switching as Mario does becomes a community norm—a way of identifying oneself as a member of this bilingual community. It is not surprising, then, that in Puerto Rican Spanish, as spoken both on the mainland and on the island, certain words of English origin have become the norm, such as *brown* (instead of *marron),* *super* (for *superintendent),* *la carpeta* (to mean *carpet,* not folder), *la boila (boiler),* *lonchar (to lunch),* and so forth (Zentella, 1981).

Mario, Lisa, Giulia, and other children who grow up with two languages often display a rather precocious understanding of language and how it works. They develop metalinguistic skills earlier than monolingual children because they know that names for things and ways of expressing ideas are arbitrary and different in every language (Hakuta & Diaz, 1985; Reynolds, 1990). Do such children suffer any deficits from being bilingual? Many preschool and primary teachers, speech pathologists, and pediatricians worry that bilingual households produce language delay or contribute to language problems, but no evidence supports this. Children who are learning two languages may show vocabulary scores in each language that are slightly below normal during the preschool years, but that is simply because such tests are normed on monolingual children and do not take into account that bilinguals are learning almost twice as many words in the same time. Of course, children growing up bilingual may not have had the experience of talking about every topic in both their languages, and their vocabulary knowledge will reflect that, but their comprehension and production skills put them in an excellent position to continue learning both languages in other settings as when, for example, they visit relatives who use those languages.

Mario, Giulia, and Lisa maintained their bilingualism at least through their school years, in part because their parents were quite insistent on maintaining the home language and thus provided them considerable exposure to it. A study of children growing up in the Miami area suggests that children need at least 20 hours of exposure to a language per week to acquire productive skills in it (Pearson, Fernandez, Lewedeg, & Oller, in press). Miami children exposed to either Spanish or English less than that amount spoke exclusively the other language (though they may have understood both languages). Thus, producing bilingual children is not easy, and neither is maintaining their bilingual skills when they are living in an environment that uses only one of their languages. Children, like adults, tend to lose languages they don't often use, a phenomenon called **language attrition.** Even adults who go many years without speaking or hearing their native tongues can experience language attrition. For children, language attrition can occur even faster. When they attend school and have many friends with whom they use the societal language, they may start to forget the less useful language or even refuse to speak it. It usually requires visits from monolingual grandparents or spending time where that language is spoken to ensure maintenance, let alone continued growth.

One of the lessons we can learn from native bilinguals is that the notion of bilingualism is a relative one. Even for children who, like Mario, Giulia, and Lisa, can all use two languages extremely well, situations arise when one language is easier or more accessible than the other. They are unlikely to be equally good in all aspects of both languages (Grosjean, 1982). They might read better in one language, tell jokes or play games better in the other, and discuss dinosaurs better in one and geography in the other. When Mario went to school, his English became stronger than his Spanish; spending time in Bolivia and Mexico strengthened his Spanish while his English receded temporarily. If even native bilinguals have fluctuations of skill in their native languages, perhaps we should worry less about second language learners' mistakes and difficulties and focus instead on how effectively they can communicate in their second language.

THEORIES OF SECOND LANGUAGE ACQUISITION

Five major groups of researchers have contributed to our understanding of second language acquisition. The first group were foreign-language educators worried about their students' progress. The second were child-language researchers who noticed that second language acquisition might be similar in interesting ways to first language acquisition. A third group were linguists who wanted to use second language acquisition to test notions about language universals. A fourth group were psycholinguists who were interested in language processing issues. A fifth group were sociolinguists and anthropologists interested in how language is used in various social settings. Because of differences in their backgrounds and training, these five groups of researchers have focused on different questions about second language acquisition and have used different groups of second language learners in their research. It is important to keep these differences in mind when thinking about their various contributions.

In reviewing these five lines of research, we will keep returning to some major questions about second language learning and learners:

1. Is there an **optimal age** for starting second language acquisition?
2. How long does it take to learn a second language?
3. Do optimal conditions exist for acquiring a second language?
4. What are the characteristics of excellent or unsuccessful second language learners?
5. To what extent does second language acquisition resemble first language acquisition in terms of (a) stages or intermediate steps, (b) underlying acquisition processes, and (c) predictive or facilitative factors?
6. Can learners function as efficiently and as competently in communicating, learning, and reading in a second as in a first language?
7. To what extent is performance in a second language positively or negatively affected by the structure of the first language?
8. To what extent is performance in a first language facilitated or impeded by the acquisition of a second language?

Foreign-Language Educators' Contributions

The oldest tradition in second language research is one based strongly in foreign-language teaching; this approach derives from an age-old interest in issues of pedagogical efficiency and effectiveness in foreign-language training. The best methods for foreign-language teaching have been discussed at least since the time of the Roman Empire, when Greek slaves were kept in upper-class homes to ensure that Roman children would acquire knowledge of Greek. During the Middle Ages, monastery schools struggled to teach future monks and priests enough Latin to be able to say their prayers and read the Vulgate Bible. Today, foreign-language teachers still flock to conventions to learn about the latest methods for ensuring their students' success.

People who teach foreign languages tend to think about knowledge of a second language as what they teach rather than what students learn—the product of the curriculum, like knowledge of trigonometry or American history. Prototypical second language learners for this research tradition are students in language courses who are acquiring a second language through formal study and are typically adolescents or adults rather than younger learners. The major research activities are dictated by the problems those learners have. Foreign-language speakers typically have noticeable accents. They also make many errors in grammar, in morphology, and in word choice. Foreign-language learners may progress quite slowly, or they may learn at a reasonable pace but then slow down or even stop before they achieve either error-free or fluent use of the foreign language. Students often find foreign language classes boring (the drills, the vocabulary lists) or threatening (the dialogues, the conversation lessons).

In attempting to solve these problems, teachers keep trying new methods of teaching foreign languages. Popular teaching methods show regular patterns of alternation between what are called **grammar/translation methods** and **direct methods.** Grammar/translation methods involve teaching about the foreign language in the students' first language, with assignments that involve a lot of reading and translation of the foreign language but relatively little use of it in conversation. Direct methods (such as the audiolingual method) may ban the use of the first language in the classroom; they emphasize direct aural/oral encounters with the second language, submersion in it, and avoidance of stating formal rules (see Coleman, 1929; Handschin, 1940, for a historical perspective). Nowadays, most foreign-language teaching involves some mixture of these two extremes, but considerable question remains about the best methods and whether they are the same for all learners.

A dominant theme in research based on foreign-language teaching has been the value of **contrastive analysis** as a basis for teaching and as a predictor of aspects of learning. Contrastive analysis involves analyzing two languages to see where they differ and then using the differences as the basis for predicting errors and for developing curriculum. The assumption of contrastive analysis is that language is a set of habits; the habits established in one's first language might work well in a second language (**positive transfer**), but they might also produce errors called **interference errors,** caused by **negative transfer.** Thus, for example, contrastive analysis would predict that Spanish speakers would have little trouble learning English plurals or progressive verb forms, because Spanish has similar forms. The English possessive, on the other hand, is structured differently from the Spanish possessive *(John's mother* versus *la madre de Juan).* Contrastive analysis predicts that Spanish speakers will find it difficult to learn this English structure and suggests that it should be taught and drilled extensively.

Research based on foreign-language teaching has identified many of the specific phenomena that continue to intrigue researchers. This research tradition has alerted us to the difficulty of perfect second language learning and to the likelihood of **fossilization** of nonnative features in the speech even of advanced learners (Selinker, 1972). The nature of typical errors has been extensively probed by foreign-language researchers (for an overview see Nemser, 1971; Hatch, 1983). Typical errors and areas of difficulty for learners of English include the following:

1. Japanese and Chinese speakers have particular difficulty learning where they should use articles *(a* and *the)* in English (Thomas, 1989), presumably because their native languages contain no articles and because even native English speakers find it hard to explain the rules for article use.

   Using *do* and getting the order of auxiliary verbs right in questions and negatives seems particularly hard for many groups of English learners: Spanish (cited in Hatch, 1983), German (Wode, 1978), and Chinese (Huang & Hatch, 1978) (see additional cases documented in Gass & Selinker, 1983, and in the second section of Bailey, Long, & Peck, 1983). Errors such as, "Know you where the bus stop is?" can be seen as direct interference from German or French but also as related to the intrinsic difficulty of figuring out how and where to use *do* in English.

2. German and French speakers may have difficulty with the order of adverbials in English and produce sentences such as, "I go tomorrow to school," which mimic the order of these elements in their native languages ("Ich gehe Morgen nach Schule"; "Je vais demain à l'école").

3. Hebrew speakers have difficulty acquiring the correct use of the English perfect and progressive forms because Hebrew marks only tense (present, past) and makes no distinction between ongoing and punctual actions *(I ate,* versus *I was eating),* nor between past completed actions and past actions with continued relevance to the present *(I was married eight years,* versus *I have been married eight years).*

A major problem that confronts foreign-language teachers is that of enormous individual differences in speed and ultimate attainment of learners. Some students in foreign-language classrooms seem to make great progress, whereas others never get beyond the limits of vocabulary lists and predictable drills. In attempts to explain these differences, researchers have sought to develop measures of foreign-language aptitude (Carroll, 1981), perhaps under the assumption that students with low aptitude should be excluded from foreign-language classrooms. Carroll's aptitude test reflects four factors that predict success in foreign-language learning: associative memory, sound–symbol association, inductive ability, and grammatical sensitivity. One study of an exceptionally skilled foreign-language learner—a young man who spoke four foreign languages fluently after only relatively brief study and exposure—revealed that he had extremely good memory for new symbol systems, which was Carroll's first aptitude component (Novoa, Fein, & Obler, 1988). However, it should also be pointed out that Carroll's Modern Language Aptitude Test is far from a perfect predictor of foreign-language progress, and that it may work much better for students in foreign-language classes than for those learning a language outside the classroom.

Predictions from the Modern Language Aptitude Test are greatly improved if one adds a measure of how much the learner wants to know the language in question. Motivation plays a particularly important role in second language acquisition, as was first discussed by Gardner and Lambert (1972). They related progress in learning French to students' views of French speakers and French culture. In Quebec, where Anglophones looked down on local French speakers, high school students had a harder time learning French than in the United States, where French was associated with the high culture of France rather than with the lower-status Quebecois. Gardner and Lambert suggested that U.S. students were benefiting from **integrative motivation,** or the desire to identify with the culture of the language being learned. Although it is clear that integrative motivation can be a powerful help to the student struggling with a second language, other motives can also work. **Instrumental motivation,** the students' sense that they needed to learn English in order to get a good job, worked much better as a predictor of progress in the Philippines than did integrative motivation; in fact, Americans are quite unpopular in the Philippines, and if learning English depended entirely on integrative motivation students would have little chance of making much progress. Fortunately, instrumental motivation can be quite powerful.

The shortcomings of research based on foreign-language teaching derive from its focus on learning as something that happens in classrooms. In this rather limited view, a second language is defined by what the curriculum includes rather than as an abstract system of knowledge. Progress in learning is defined as eliminating errors from one's speech. This basic assumption of research in this tradition is undermined by current views about the nature of language and language learning (see Chapters 1 and 8). We now know that any language system is extremely complex, that many aspects of the grammar have never been described and thus cannot be directly taught, that the knowledge acquired by a competent speaker goes far beyond the information given in the input, and that the active, creative role of the learner is more important than the role of the teacher in any successful language learning process. At some level foreign-language-teaching researchers acknowledge the active role of the learner and concede that foreign-language classrooms at best provide knowledge that learners can draw upon in situations of real SL processing to generate proficiency in the SL. Still, the research activities they carry out do not fully reflect these understandings. Furthermore, this research focuses more on the product than the process of acquisition and casts little light on the nature of second language acquisition for nonformal learners. Nor does it attempt to approach issues such as the consequences for the learner of being bilingual.

Child Language Researchers' Contributions

The research on child language acquisition reviewed in Chapter 8 presents a picture of children as **active learners** who at every stage of language acquisition generate hypotheses and try to organize into a system what they know about language. Language acquisition researchers love the errors that children make because such errors reveal children's hypotheses and rules. This basic notion of language acquisition as an active process was recognized in the early 1970s as applicable to second language learners as well. Whereas foreign-language teachers cringe at students' errors, child language researchers believe that *errors are a sign of progress, learning involves reorganizing knowledge, not just storing it,* and *language acquisition is a developmental process.* This different view of language learning caused a minor revolution in foreign-language teaching and in the kind of research done on second language learning.

A defining question for child language-based researchers is whether second language acquisition is a simple recapitulation of first language acquisition, and if not, why and how it is different (Ervin-Tripp, 1974). Child language researchers are trying to determine if there is an **innate language acquisition capacity,** and if so, how it relates to the role of the learner's linguistic environment and specialized ways of using that environment. In the earliest research on language acquisition, three areas were identified as domains of study: the child's language acquisition device **(LAD),** the language acquisition social support system **(LASS)** available to the child, and the nature of the language system that emerges. The process could be summarized in a simple equation: LAD + LASS = Language. A persistent source of controversy among first-language-acquisition researchers has been the relative weights that should be assigned to the LAD and to the LASS, and whether the LAD is specialized for language or reflects general information processing and complex learning systems. First language researchers have extensively described the nature of language input to young children; understanding the role of language input in second language acquisition was seen to be just as important.

The prototypical second language learner for first-language-based researchers is a young child moved to a second language setting, or an older learner engaged in untutored acquisition. If such learners display the same pattern of acquisition as first language learners, it can be argued that the same processes of hypothesis testing and rule generation operate for both. The following kinds of evidence are offered in support of this position:

1. ***Developmental errors*** *by second language speakers, such as errors that are overgeneralizations based on features of the target language rather than interference from features of the native language.* As young children sometimes do, learners of English as a second language produce forms such as *hided* or *foots.* Even more strikingly, second language learners avoid transfer of idiomatic forms and highly marked structures from their first language, even sometimes in cases where these are acceptable in SL (see Jordens, 1977; Kellerman, 1977). For example, a French speaker learning Spanish might produce, "Estoy hambre," rather than, "Tengo hambre," despite the fact that the structure in French, *J'ai faim,* is the same as in Spanish.

2. *Recapitulation of the same order of acquisition shown by first language learners.* For example, Hakuta (1976) studied a Japanese girl who showed the same order as native English speakers in acquiring the 14 frequently used inflectional morphemes of English. English speakers learning Dutch acquired the rules governing allomorphic variation (Snow, Smith, & Höefnagel-Höhle, 1980) and those governing word order (Snow, 1981) in much the same order as native Dutch speakers. Cancino, Rosansky, and Schumann (1974, 1975) studied Spanish speakers learning English, and found stages like those of native English speakers for developing control over negation and question formation.

3. *Similar acquisition for speakers of different language backgrounds.* If speakers of languages as different as French and Thai show similar errors or similar orders of acquisition in English, this argues that the target language exerts a greater effect on acquisition than habits brought over from the native language. Dulay and Burt (1974) found that Chinese and Spanish speakers acquire English morphemes in much the same order, despite the fact that Spanish closely resembles English on morphological marking and Chinese is quite different. Fuller and Gundel (1987) showed that speakers of Chinese, Japanese, and Korean, all topic-prominent languages, were no more likely to use topic-fronting rules in English than speakers of Arabic, Farsi, and Spanish, which, like English, are subject-prominent languages. These researchers have

argued that the order of acquisition, though not necessarily the same as that of first language learners, reflects developmental processes governed by the way English works rather than interference effects from the learners' own first languages.

4. *Identifiable strategies of acquisition that mimic those of young first language learners.* Just as young first language learners often acquire some handy phrases in which to put new words, second language learners also use imitated chunks or **modular patterns** as a first strategy for communicating, then move on to analyzing syntactic structure in these chunks (Rescorla & Okuda, 1987; Wong Fillmore, 1976). Just as first language learners gradually increase the length of their utterances, so do young second language learners (Huang & Hatch, 1978).

Questions about the nature (Long, 1985; Snow & Hoefnagel-Höhle, 1982) and helpful qualities (Tomasello & Herron, 1988, 1989) of **input to second language learners** have become an important topic. It is clear that learners in a foreign-language classroom receive different input from first language learners and might be expected to show a different order of acquisition and maybe even different sorts of mistakes. But what about the child submerged in a second language classroom? What about the immigrant adult learning English from coworkers? What can we say about how their linguistic environment helps them learn?

First, quantity of input is important in determining speed of second language acquisition. Classroom-based language learners who seek opportunities to practice with native speakers outside of class learn much faster than those who don't (Seliger, 1977). The good second language learner also elicits particularly helpful input by trying to talk and receiving feedback from native speakers (Day, 1985). It is interesting to think about whether classroom contexts replicate optimal environments for language learning (Faerch & Kasper, 1985) and how they might be changed based on what we know about first language acquisition. Foreign-language teachers are interested in such issues of optimal input and natural order of acquisition. For example, Tomasello and Herron (1988) have shown that letting SL learners make overgeneralization errors and receive corrections produces better and longer-lasting learning than preteaching the rule that would preempt the error. In effect, they found gains from letting teachers make the kinds of responses that parents make to young children's errors (see also Krashen, 1985, for examples of foreign-language teaching devices borrowed from mothers' behaviors with their children). On the other hand, a large quantity of input is insufficient to ensure native-like outcomes; children can spend as many as 9 years in Canadian French immersion programs, for example, and achieve high levels of comprehension of French and native-like French accents, but still make many grammatical errors (Wesche, 1994).

Because child language researchers have a basic interest in development, they have emphasized the consequences of second language learning for the learner—that young bilinguals and second language learners have advantages in certain types of tasks (Hakuta & Diaz, 1985; Reynolds, 1990), particularly metalinguistic and language analysis tasks. They have also emphasized the interdependence between performance on first language and on second language tasks. It seems to make sense that a child who was a fast and untroubled first language learner will have an easier time with a second language. Cummins (1979) has even argued that certain levels of achievement in a child's first language constitute a threshold for the easy addition of a second language. Others (Johnson, 1989; Malakoff, 1988; Snow, 1990) have suggested that if conditions of acquisition for a first and a second language differ greatly (for example, one learned at home and the other at school), patterns of second language skill may not resemble or depend on primary language skills to any great extent.

Linguists' Approaches to Second Language Acquisition

Linguists tend to focus on the abilities displayed or errors produced by SL learners when they are relevant to testing hypotheses about the extrapolation of Universal Grammar to second language acquisition. A major starting point for linguists is that, at every stage of acquisition, the learner is operating with an organized system of knowledge. Second language learners are likely to encounter many such systems en route to full control of the target language grammar (if that is ever attained); each of these can be called an **interlanguage grammar** (Selinker, 1972). One question is whether these interlanguage grammars display the same constraints as first language learners' grammars or include "unnatural" or impossible sorts of rules or structures. If they include such rules or structures, then presumably second language learning is not subject to Universal Grammar—perhaps because the learner is past some critical period, as Long (1990) argues (but see Snow, 1983, 1987; Snow & Hoefnagel-Höhle, 1978, for counterarguments).

There is no clear orthodox position among Universal Grammar adherents about its relevance to second language learning. Researchers hold a variety of views about how powerfully Universal Grammar operates in second language acquisition (see White, 1990; papers in Flynn & O'Neil, 1988). Given the close identification of Universal Grammar with an acquisition device (the LAD) that many believe becomes inaccessible after the critical period, it would be perfectly possible to argue that adult second language learners operate differently from first language learners because of lack of access to Universal Grammar (Clahsen & Muysken, 1986). However, most linguists suggest that Universal Grammar may be at least partially available to the second language learner, though perhaps mediated by the first language in ways that may make it relatively inaccessible. Universal Grammar differentiates between two components of LAD—the principles, which are universal and should still be available to constrain language acquisition at any age, and the parameters, which constitute a set of options that may be more or less irreversibly set by exposure to a first language. If the first language causes learners to set a parameter in a "marked" or more inclusive way, they may find it especially difficult to reset the parameter to the less marked or more neutral setting. Examples of difficult-to-reset parameters for which second language acquisition research has proffered evidence include head direction—for example, whether heads precede (as in English) or follow (as in Japanese) the rest of the material in the structure. As a right-branching, or *head-first* language, English dictates that prepositions come first in prepositional phrases (*in* the bathtub), head nouns precede their relative clauses (*the boy* who is taking a bath), and matrix sentences normally precede their adverbial clauses (*I saw him* when he jumped in). In Japanese, these constituents are reversed. Flynn (1987) has shown that Japanese learners of English have persistent difficulty with imitating and correctly interpreting heavily right-branching structures when compared to learners who speak Arabic, which matches English on head direction. Hyams (1986) has similarly argued that English speakers should have less problem learning to reset the agreement parameter to allow pro-drop (the omission of redundant verb-agreement marked subject pronouns) in Spanish *(veo el arbol* instead of *yo veo el arbol)* than Spanish speakers attempting to reset their parameter to always supply the subject pronoun in English ("Is a very nice day today, no?").

The linguists' research on second language acquisition has contributed enormously to our understanding of the complexity of the grammatical knowledge that learners must acquire and of one route for first language influence on the process. Linguists are uninterested, though, in many aspects of second language skill that learners consider important: vocabulary, socially useful expressions, conversational rules, and so forth. Linguists are also not interested in the learner's communicative effectiveness nor in differences associated with motivation, aptitude, input, or instruction.

Psycholinguists' Approaches to Second Language Processing

One way to consider language acquisition is as a special sort of information processing (McLaughlin, Rossman, & McLeod, 1983) or psycholinguistic processing. Under this view, learning a language and understanding a language are not so very different from one another; both involve parsing an auditory stimulus and connecting that parsed string to a semantic representation. For skilled speakers of a language, as for learners, some strings are hard to parse whether because they contain novel lexical items, acoustically unclear elements, or obscure referents. The major difference between skilled speakers and learners, in the view of the psycholinguist, is that skilled speakers more readily question or reject a string if interpretation proves difficult, whereas learners are under greater pressure to try to incorporate all newly encountered structures into their system.

If learning a language is simply a matter of efficiently processing certain kinds of information, one might expect that learners who have already acquired several languages would be more skilled than monolingual learners. In fact, support for the notion of language learning as a processing skill at which one can get better with practice is supported by findings that "expert" (that is, multilingual) language learners do much better than "novice" (monolingual) learners in acquiring a novel, artificial language. Researchers use artificial languages in this sort of work to exclude any positive transfer from any of the languages known by the multilinguals (Nation & McLaughlin, 1986).

Psycholinguistic processing approaches to language acquisition acknowledge the likelihood of interference, but argue that interference from a first language to a second language operates at the level of processing tendencies, not habits (as the foreign-language teacher might think), rules (as the child language researcher thinks), or parameters (as the linguist thinks). One psycholinguistic processing model extensively applied to SL research has been the **competition model** (Bates & MacWhinney, 1981; MacWhinney, 1987). The competition model proposes that sentence interpretation is governed by accumulated knowledge of the likelihood that certain cues indicate certain semantic roles. In English, for example, the first noun in a sentence is likely to indicate the actor: *The dog ate the bone.* Thus, the hypothesis that first noun = actor has a high probability for any speaker of English, though it can be undermined by conflicting or competing cues, for example, that the first noun is not animate: *The bone ate the dog;* that it does not agree with the verb: *His parents above all loves the good boy;* or that it is pragmatically unlikely: *The patient cured the doctor.*

Competition theory suggests that the cue strengths from the first language are likely to be carried over into the early stages of second language processing, at least if the same cues are available in the second language. If the cue strengths of the first and second language match, this may operate in the learner's favor. However, quite often they do not match, even in closely related languages. English, Italian, and Dutch all have animacy, position, and agreement available as cues to the actor; but if these are in conflict with one another in the same sentence, then English speakers choose to rely on first position as the strongest cue. In Italian animacy is much more important, and in Dutch agreement plays a much more dominant role (Gass, 1987; McDonald, 1987; Kilborn & Cooreman, 1987). Acquisition of a second language can be impeded by the processing tendencies we import from our native language, and even quite far into second language acquisition we might display a processing "accent." Further developments can go in many directions; some SL speakers manage to develop systems that closely mimic native speakers' systems, whereas other speakers, particularly in social settings that permit a lot of code-switching, develop for use in both languages a merged system that represents a compromise between the systems of monolingual native speakers of both languages.

Psycholinguistic processing approaches to second language acquisition completely break down the distinction between comprehension and learning. Furthermore, under psycholinguistic processing approaches, learning a second language is just like learning a first language except that we start with more information. Psycholinguistic processing models focus on performance rather than competence, strategies rather than rules. Even native speakers of a language can show alternate patterns of preference for various cues (Harrington, 1987), which suggests that the notion of "the native speaker" has somewhat less central status in psycholinguistic models than in competence-based models, and that the distinction between first and second language speakers is also less sharp. No threshold of proficiency defines a native speaker or a perfect bilingual, because acquisition is considered a continuous and likely response to new information in any language.

Because processing speed and ease are functions of the amount of information available, it seems reasonable within a psycholinguistic processing perspective to expect processing costs in becoming bilingual. Bilinguals show slightly depressed reading speed—presumably because of their increased lexical retrieval times (Mägiste, 1979, 1987)—and may well end up completely unable to separate their phonetic (Caramazza, Yeni-Komshian, Zurif, & Carbone, 1973; Mack, 1984) and syntactic judgment systems (Mack, 1984). On the other hand, such deficits are minor and evidently are restricted to situations in which both languages are in relatively constant use. Psycholinguistic processing approaches have little difficulty in accounting for the widely reported ebb and flow of skill in language as a function of its use (see Grosjean, 1982, for examples) or even for significant amounts of attrition in one's first language (see Cohen & Weltens, 1989; Mägiste, 1987) because recent processing history clearly has a strong effect on the accessibility of lexical items or syntactic structures in a language.

Psycholinguistic processing approaches have little to say about learner factors that affect the speed or course of second language acquisition. They instead focus on the relation between the first and the second language in the learner's reliance on various cues. Learning a second language is simply a matter of experiencing it and making attempts to comprehend it. Such approaches hold no expectation of large individual differences in style or strategy of acquisition unless input experiences differ widely. Psycholinguistic processing approaches reduce second language acquisition to a problem of input and processing efficiency, with little attention to the larger cultural and social context within which it occurs.

Sociocultural Approaches to Second Language Learning

When psycholinguists, developmental psychologists, and linguists think about second language acquisition, they emphasize the cognitive side of the picture—the problems the learner faces in acquiring a complex system that has more or less overlap with complex systems already acquired. Sociologists, social psychologists, anthropologists, and sociolinguists, on the other hand, think about the societal context of bilingualism. They point out that multilingualism is common across the world and that a majority of children are expected to learn two languages. They point out that language use is tied closely to personal identity, to cultural identification, to national or ethnic pride, to specific communicative tasks or situations, and to a set of attitudes and beliefs that influence the course of second language acquisition. They point out that becoming too proficient in speaking a second language can threaten the personal identity of the learner—that speakers can have reasons for remaining less than perfectly bilingual if the second language has some negative associations for the learner. At the same time, perfect control over accent or grammar may not relate to effectiveness in achieving communicative aims in the second language. One study showed that, among immigrants from Europe to the United States during the period before World War II, psychiatrists retained their German accents longer than those in other professions; we can only speculate that their professional credibility was actually enhanced by the maintenance of a foreign accent!

For those who approach second language acquisition from a sociocultural perspective, speaking two languages is simply an extension of what monolinguals do when exploiting the potential for variability within a language. Adjustments of vocabulary choice, grammar, and morphology to different addressees and situations are within the competence of all language users. Socially appropriate speakers of English may use an expletive to express anger to a colleague but say, "Darn!" to a child or a minister; similarly a bilingual says, "chair," to an English listener and, "silla," to a Spanish listener. Failure to make these sorts of adjustments might reflect feelings of hostility to the addressee or a need to project a certain kind of personal and social identity for oneself. It need not be seen as a failure of "proficiency."

Many seemingly intractable issues within the more cognitive and psycholinguistic approaches to second language acquisition are easily dealt with from the sociocultural perspective. Whereas the other approaches identify a linguistic norm, typically defined by the competence of the **native speaker,** toward which the learner is presumably moving, sociocultural approaches recognize the social nature of language use and the impossibility of identifying better or worse varieties of any language. Around the world, for example, regional varieties of English, now known as **world Englishes,** are becoming established in countries such as India and Nigeria; these are spoken in those countries only as second languages, and they have many nonstandard features (which might be considered errors by British or American English standards). Nonetheless, these varieties are the appropriate acquisition targets for speakers in those countries, who actively reject British, American, or Commonwealth varieties of English (Lowenberg, 1986).

FIGURE 10.2

In countries where many different language groups coexist, a language of wider communication such as English is often chosen for use in public communication.

Within sociocultural approaches, notions such as **language proficiency** are replaced by notions such as **communicative effectiveness** and **social appropriateness.** Whereas first-language-based researchers struggle with the question of whether adult second language learners can become perfect bilinguals, sociocultural approaches emphasize the effective functioning in second languages of children and adults all over the world; because control over a first language includes much variability in performance, it is not of central theoretical interest that such is also the case for second language users.

Sociocultural approaches are particularly helpful in understanding the social and cultural pressures affecting second language learners in situations where the social value attached to their first and their second languages differs greatly. Why is it that children of immigrant families in the United States switch so rapidly to function better in English than in their parents' language? Simple psycholinguistic analyses cannot easily answer this question, but an answer can be found in calculating the stigmatization associated with traditional languages and the value attached to speaking English as a marker of being an American. Why is it that in two-way bilingual programs, Spanish speakers learn English faster than English speakers learn Spanish? Perhaps even kindergarten-aged children are well aware of society's negative evaluation of Spanish speakers. Furthermore, when Spanish speakers in those two-way programs learn English, they are likely to lose Spanish (**subtractive bilingualism**), whereas English speakers who learn Spanish will retain English (**additive bilingualism**)—a distinction that makes sense only when we understand the social context. How could a tiny Anglophone minority survive for generations in Quebec without learning any French? It seems impossible until we consider the sociolinguistics of the relations between French and English speakers and the relative power and status of the two groups. Why is it that Quechua-Spanish bilingual programs are on the decline in Peru, even though Quechua-speaking children perform better in such programs than in Spanish-only classrooms? A culturally based analysis suggests that Quechua-speaking parents do not see Quechua as an appropriate language for the school sphere (Hornberger, 1987, 1988). Understanding the patterns of language choice and language proficiency for an individual or a community requires understanding that language is a sociocultural phenomenon and not just a cognitive achievement.

Sociocultural approaches to second language acquisition deemphasize the importance of grammatical or phonological correctness, but they open up an additional domain of complexity for the second language learner—the rules governing communicative effectiveness and social appropriateness. These rule systems are complex and as language-specific as are rules for word order or morphology, though like grammar they have been described as having a universal "core" (Brown & Levinson, 1978). Cultural systems differ sufficiently that, though one can translate many words from one language to another with reasonable success, one can hardly ever translate "speech acts" directly without inviting miscommunication (Blum-Kulka, 1983). "We must have lunch sometime," is a friendly way of saying "good-bye" in American English, but its translation into French would be considered a sincere invitation (Wolfson, d'Amico-Reisner, & Huber, 1983); it is not surprising that French speakers think

Americans are unfriendly and insincere, if they hear many such invitations that never come through! In English it is appropriate to use indirect or polite forms with those serving you. A boss might say, "Would you mind typing this?" to a secretary, and a customer in a restaurant might say, "May I please see a menu?" In Spanish, "Bring me a menu," is perfectly appropriate; the Spanish speaker who translates that speech act (and its associated implications for social relationships) into English would be considered arrogant. It is not surprising, in light of such differences, that highly developed bilinguals think of themselves as having different personalities in their different languages.

Sociocultural approaches to second language acquisition make clear that, in some sense, more than just acquiring a new system of grammar or a better accent, learning a second language means joining a second culture. Speaking a new language means participating as a member of a certain group, engaging in a variety of novel social interactions, and establishing an enhanced or a changed personal identity.

SUMMARY

In order to summarize what we know about second language acquisition from each of the five groups of researchers who have tackled the problem, let us return to our list of eight major questions and see how each question is answered by each of the lines of research.

1. *Is there an optimal age for starting second language acquisition?* Foreign-language teachers typically encounter adolescent and adult learners, so their research does not directly address this question. However, evaluation of programs with preadolescent foreign-language students (for example, the Foreign Language in the Elementary School [FLES] programs) reveals that younger children are considerably slower than high school-aged children or adults at learning languages through formal teaching. Child language researchers have pointed out that, contrary to what is generally believed, older learners also acquire second languages faster than younger ones in untutored settings (Snow, 1983, 1987; Snow & Hoefnagel-Höhle, 1978). However, older learners also are more likely to encounter fossilization and persistent accents (Krashen, Long, & Scarcella, 1982), so their ultimate attainment may be lower. Linguists, because of their commitment to the notion of a biological substrate for language, are inclined to believe in the **critical period hypothesis,** which states that "normal" language acquisition must occur in (early) childhood. Neither the psycholinguists nor those taking sociocultural approaches to second language acquisition take much interest in the issue of an optimal age for learning; they see the process as gradual and incremental at all ages.

2. *How long does it take to learn a second language?* Foreign-language teachers point out that it takes more time to learn a distant language than one closely

related to the learner's first language; thus, English speakers should expect to spend more time acquiring Chinese than Spanish. Becoming a proficient second language speaker takes 2 to 4 years of college-level classroom exposure, plus a period of immersion to achieve full fluency. Child language researchers point out that a child requires 10 to 12 years to achieve full control over oral and literate uses of a first language; starting somewhat later means somewhat faster acquisition, but nonetheless it is quite normal for school-aged children to take as long as 6 or 7 years to function like first language speakers, though some manage in only 2 or 3 years. Linguists have paid little attention to this issue, and psycholinguists think of acquisition as something that continues throughout the learner's lifetime, though it slows down as fewer and fewer new structures are encountered. Sociolinguists lack clear criteria for deciding on native-like proficiency, so they consider this an uninteresting issue.

3. *Do optimal conditions exist for acquiring a second language?* Clearly, the foreign-language teacher thinks that a well-designed curriculum implemented by a native-speaking teacher and supplemented by many opportunities for practice is the optimal condition. Child language researchers would emphasize providing second language learners with conditions that resemble those for young first language learners: opportunities for conversations on topics of interest to the learner with native speakers who provide input adjusted to the learner's level, who provide conversational responses that build on learners' attempts, who are genuinely interested in communicating with the learner, and who have a positive affective relationship with the learner. Linguists are relatively uninterested in individual differences in speed of acquisition and have not addressed this question. Psycholinguists would identify optimal conditions for learning with the opportunity to hear lots of sentences paired with information about meaning, perhaps with some manipulation of cue conflicts to sharpen learners' hypotheses. Finally, the sociocultural theorists would argue that conditions of social equality between members of the learner group and the target language speakers are optimal, and either mutual respect or perhaps personal intimacy between the learner and some native speaker interlocutors is desirable.

4. *What are the characteristics of excellent or unsuccessful second language learners?* Foreign-language teachers think good learners are like good students in any subject—those who work hard, are motivated, and score high on the Modern Language Aptitude Test. Child language researchers emphasize the learners' capacity to elicit input from native speakers—outgoing, talkative, uninhibited learners are probably better at this—and their willingness to generate and test hypotheses about the target language based on partial data, that is, to make mistakes. Linguists emphasize the sensitivity of the learner to information about the target language, and perhaps a gift for metalinguistic analysis as well. Psycholinguists would not predict large individual differences except those associated with efficiency of information processing. Sociocultural theorists would emphasize openness of the learner to other cultures,

willingness to try on alternative social selves, and willingness to risk one's dignity in sincere communicative attempts.

5. *To what extent does second language acquisition resemble first language acquisition in terms of (a) stages or intermediate steps, (b) underlying acquisition processes, (c) predictive or facilitative factors?* The first language researchers and the psycholinguists come down most strongly on the affirmative in response to this question, assuming in both cases that the conditions of acquisition for the first and second languages are somewhat similar. Foreign-language teachers emphasize the differences introduced by prior knowledge of a first language, whereas linguists emphasize as well the possibility that post-critical-period learning might be quite different from first language learning. Sociocultural theorists don't much care about this question but would see both first and second language acquisition as strongly driven by communicative and social needs.

6. *Can learners function as efficiently and as competently in communicating, learning, reading, and talking in a second language as in a first language?* Foreign-language teachers, child language researchers, and linguists agree that some small percentage of second language learners become native-like, though these three groups would disagree on the reasons why most learners do not. Psycholinguists and sociocultural theorists downplay the notion of "perfect competence" for the native speaker, pointing out that even a native speaker may still be adjusting to the system as an adult; in this way, second language learners differ little from first language learners.

7. *To what extent is performance in a second language positively or negatively affected by the structure of the first language?* Foreign-language teachers and linguists would be most prone to argue for a transfer effect from first to second language, though psycholinguists and sociocultural theorists also acknowledge such effects, in processing tendencies and communicative rules, respectively. Child language theorists are the least likely to attribute a large role in second language acquisition to transfer, focusing instead on the influence on the learning process of specific areas of difficulty in the language being acquired.

8. *To what extent is performance in a first language facilitated or impeded by the acquisition of a second language?* Neither linguists nor foreign-language teachers confront the possibility that a first language might be affected by a second language—they attribute a different, special status to one's mother tongue. Child language researchers, on the other hand, often see cases of language attrition and conversely see the positive effects from learning a second language of heightened metalinguistic skills in a first language. Psycholinguists have documented cases in which bilinguals achieve a merged processing system for their first and second languages, possibly with some negative

consequences for speed of processing in the first language. Finally, sociocultural theorists acknowledge the possibility of first language attrition under conditions of low status, but also of the bilingual's enhanced understanding of communicative situations across both languages.

Clearly, many of the disagreements and differing conclusions by researchers from these varying groups reflect their interests in different aspects of the phenomenon of bilingualism and second language acquisition. Perhaps future research will be able to merge two or three of these perspectives to ensure that full attention is paid to the role of the learner, the environment, and the broader social context in understanding what second language learners acquire and how they acquire it.

KEY WORDS

Submersion
Immersion
Native bilingualism
Code-switches
Language attrition
Optimal age
Grammar/translation methods
Direct methods
Contrastive analysis
Positive transfer
Interference errors
Negative transfer
Fossilization
Integrative motivation
Instrumental motivation
Active learner

Innate language acquisition capacity
LAD
LASS
Developmental errors
Modular patterns
Input to second language learners
Interlanguage grammar
Competition model
Native speaker
World Englishes
Language proficiency
Communicative effectiveness
Social appropriateness
Subtractive bilingualism
Additive bilingualism
Critical period hypothesis

SOMETHING TO THINK ABOUT

1. Why does the average American view learning a second language well enough to speak it fluently as such an impossible task?

2. Discuss the arguments in favor of a critical period for second language acquisition. Discuss the arguments against this notion.

3. Describe the various mechanisms by which attitudes toward speakers of any particular language group affect the acquisition of that language by members of another group.

ACTIVITIES

1. **Bilingual Families' Beliefs and Practices**
   Locate a family with at least 1 child 2 to 12 years old in which at least 1 parent speaks a language other than English as a native language. This might be a family that is visiting the United States for several years from another country, an immigrant family, or a family in which one of the parents is a proficient speaker of a language other than English. Interview the parents to determine answers to the following sorts of questions: Did they plan for their child(ren) to grow up bilingual? Do they use the other language with their child(ren)? What difficulties, if any, do they encounter in maintaining the other language? How would they estimate the child(ren)'s proficiency in the other language? In English? If you establish rapport with the parents, ask if they will tape record a family dinner table conversation for you. Then listen to the recording and find answers to the following questions: Who speaks English at dinner? Who speaks the other language? When the other language is used, who switches back into English? Do particular topics seem to trigger switches into English?

2. **Second Language Learners' Errors and Reflections on Errors**
   Record a conversation between you and a friend who is not a native speaker of English (with the friend's permission, of course). Then transcribe utterances produced by your friend that have errors in them. Classify these errors as interference errors (based on the structure of the first language) or developmental errors (errors caused by areas of particular difficulty in English). Review the list of utterances with your friend. For each utterance, ask if your friend can (1) identify the error, (2) correct the error, and (3) comment on what might have caused the error.

REFERENCES

Bailey, K., Long, M., & Peck, S. (Eds.). (1983). *Second language acquisition studies.* Rowley, MA: Newbury House.

Bates, E., & MacWhinney, B. (1981). Second language acquisition from a functionalist perspective: Pragmatic, semantic, and perceptual strategies. In H. Winitz (Ed.), *Annals of the New York Academy of Science Conference on Native and Foreign Language Acquisition.* New York: New York Academy of Sciences.

Blum-Kulka, S. (1983). Interpreting and performing speech acts in a second language: A cross-cultural study of Hebrew and English. In N. Wolfson & E. Judd (Eds.), *Sociolinguistics and language acquisition.* Rowley, MA: Newbury House.

Brown, P., & Levinson, S. (1978). Universals in language usage: Politeness phenomena. In E. Goody (Ed.), *Questions and politeness: Strategies in social interaction.* Cambridge, MA: Cambridge University Press.

Cancino, H., Rosansky, E., & Schumann, J. (1974). Testing hypotheses about second language acquisition: The copula and the negative in three subjects. *Working Papers in Bilingualism, 3,* 80–96.

Cancino, H., Rosansky, E., & Schumann, J. (1975). The acquisition of the English auxiliary by native Spanish speakers. *TESOL Quarterly, 9,* 421–430.

Caramazza, A., Yeni-Komshian, G., Zurif, E., & Carbone, E. (1973). The acquisition of a new phonological contrast: The case of stop consonants in French-English bilinguals. *Journal of the Acoustical Society of America, 54,* 421–428.

Carroll, J. (1981). Twenty-five years of research on foreign language aptitude. In K. Diller (Ed.), *Individual differences and universals in language learning aptitude.* Rowley, MA: Newbury House.

Clahsen, H., & Muysken, P. (1986). The availability of Universal Grammar to adult and child learners: A study of the acquisition of German word order. *Second Language Research, 2,* 93–119.

Cohen, A., & Weltens, B. (Eds.). (1989). Language attrition. Special issue of *Studies in Second Language Acquisition, 11,* 127–216.

Coleman, A. (1929). *The teaching of modern foreign languages in the United States.* New York: Macmillan.

Cummins, J. (1979). Linguistic interdependence and the educational development of bilingual children. *Review of Educational Research, 49,* 222–251.

Day, R. (1985). The use of the target language in context and second language proficiency. In S. Gass & C. Madden (Eds.), *Input in second language acquisition.* Rowley, MA: Newbury House.

De Houwer, A. (1995) Bilingual language acquisition. In P. Fletcher & B. MacWhinney (Eds.), *The handbook of child language.* Oxford, UK: Blackwell.

Dulay, H., & Burt, M. (1974). Errors and strategies in child second language acquisition. *TESOL Quarterly, 8, 129*–138.

Ervin-Tripp, S. (1974). Is second language learning like the first? *TESOL Quarterly, 8,* 111–127.

Faerch, C., & Kasper, G. (Eds.). (1985). Foreign language learning under classroom conditions. Special issue of *Studies in Second Language Acquisition, 7,* 131–248.

Fantini, A. (1985). *Language acquisition of a bilingual child: A sociolinguistic perspective (to age 10).* San Diego: College-Hill Press.

Flynn, S. (1987). *A parameter-setting model of L2 acquisition: Experimental studies in anaphora.* Dordrecht: Reidel.

Flynn, S., & O'Neil, W. (Eds.). (1988). *Linguistic theory in second language acquisition.* Dordrecht: Kluwer.

Fuller, J. W., & Gundel, J. K. (1987). Topic-prominence in interlanguage. *Language Learning, 37,* 1–18.

Gardner, R. C., & Lambert, W. (1972). *Attitudes and motivation in second-language learning.* Rowley, MA: Newbury House.

Gass, S. (1987). The resolution of conflicts among competing systems: A bidirectional perspective. *Applied Psycholinguistics, 4,* 329–350.

Gass, S., & Selinker, L. (Eds.) (1983). *Language transfer in language learning.* Rowley, MA: Newbury House.

Genesee, F., Boivin, I., & Nicoladis, E. (1996). Talking with strangers: A study of bilingual children's communicative competence. *Applied Psycholinguistics, 17,* 427–442.

Grosjean, F. (1982). *Life with two languages: An introduction to bilingualism.* Cambridge, MA: Harvard University Press.

Hakuta, K. (1976). A case study of a Japanese child learning English as a second language. *Language Learning, 26,* 321–351.

Hakuta, K., & Diaz, R. (1985). The relationship between degree of bilingualism and cognitive ability: A critical discussion and some new longitudinal data. In K. E. Nelson (Ed.), *Children's language (Vol. 5).* Hillsdale, NJ: Erlbaum.

Handschin, C. (1940). *Modern-language teaching.* Yonkers-on-Hudson: World Book.

Harrington, M. (1987). Processing transfer: Language specific processing strategies as a source of interlanguage variation. *Applied Psycholinguistics, 8,* 351–378.

Hatch, E. (1983). *Psycholinguistics: A second language perspective.* Rowley, MA: Newbury House.

Hornberger, N. (1987). Bilingual education success but policy failure. *Language in Society, 16,* 205–226.

Hornberger, N. (1988). *Bilingual education and language maintenance: A southern Peruvian Quechua case.* Dordrecht: Foris.

Huang, J., & Hatch, E. (1978). A Chinese child's acquisition of English. In E. Hatch (Ed.), *Second language acquisition.* Rowley, MA: Newbury House.

Hyams, N. (1986). *Language acquisition and the theory of parameters.* Dordrecht: Reidel.

Johnson, J. (1989). Factors related to cross-language transfer and metaphor interpretation in bilingual children. *Applied Psycholinguistics, 10,* 157–178.

Jordens, P. (1977). Rules, grammatical intuitions, and strategies in foreign language reading. *Interlanguage Studies Bulletin, 2*(2), 5–76.

Kellerman, E. (1977). Towards a characterization of the strategy of transfer in second language learning. *Interlanguage Studies Bulletin, 2*(1), 58–145.

Kilborn, K., & Cooreman, A. (1987). Sentence interpretation strategies in adult Dutch-English bilinguals. *Applied Psycholinguistics, 8,* 415–431.

Krashen, S. (1985). *The input hypothesis: Issues and implications.* London: Longman.

Krashen, S., Long, M., & Scarcella, R. (1982). Age, rate, and eventual attainment in second language acquisition. In S. Krashen, R. Scarcella, & M. Long (Eds.), *Child-adult differences in second language acquisition.* Rowley, MA: Newbury House.

Long, M. (1985). Input and second language acquisition theory. In S. Gass & C. Madden (Eds.), *Input in second language acquisition.* Rowley, MA: Newbury House.

Long, M. (1990). Maturational constraints on language development. *Studies in Second Language Acquisition, 12,* 251–286.

Lowenberg, P. (1986). Nonnative varieties of English: Nativization, norms, and implications. *Studies in Second Language Acquisition, 8,* 1–18.

Mack, M. (1984). Early bilinguals: How monolingual-like are they? In M. Paradis & Y. LeBrun (Eds.), *Early bilingualism and child development.* Lisse: Swets & Zeitlinger.

MacWhinney, B. (1987). Applying the competition model to bilingualism. *Applied Psycholinguistics, 8,* 315–328.

Mägiste, E. (1979). The competing language systems of the multilingual: A developmental study of decoding and encoding processes. *Journal of Verbal Learning and Verbal Behavior, 18,* 79–89.

Mägiste, E. (1987). Further evidence for the optimal age hypothesis in second language learning. In J. Lantolf & A. LaBarca (Eds.), *Research in second language learning: Focus on the classroom.* Norwood, NJ: Ablex.

Malakoff, M. (1988). The effect of language instruction on reasoning in bilingual children. *Applied Psycholinguistics, 9,* 17–38.

McDonald, J. L. (1987). Sentence interpretation in bilingual speakers of English and Dutch. *Applied Psycholinguistics, 8,* 379–414.

McLaughlin, B., Rossman, T., & McLeod, B. (1983). Second language learning: An information processing perspective. *Language Learning, 33,* 135–158.

Nation, R., & McLaughlin, B. (1986). Novices and experts: An information processing approach to the "good language learner" problem. *Applied Psycholinguistics, 7,* 41–56.

Nemser, W. (1971). *An experimental study of phonological interference in the English of Hungarians.* Dissertation, Indiana University, Bloomington.

Novoa, L., Fein, D., & Obler, L. (1988). Talent in foreign languages: A case study. In L. Obler & D. Fein (Eds.), *The exceptional brain: Neuropsychology of talent and special abilities.* New York: Guilford.

Pearson, B., Fernandez, S., Lewedeg, V., & Oller, D. (1997). The relation of input factors to lexical learning by bilingual infants. *Applied Psycholinguistics, 18.*

Rescorla, L., & Okuda, S. (1987). Modular patterns in second language acquisition. *Applied Psycholinguistics, 8,* 281–308.

Reynolds, A. (1990). The cognitive consequences of bilingualism. In A. Reynolds (Ed.), *Bilingualism, multiculturalism, and second language learning: The McGill conference in honor of Wallace E. Lambert*. Hillsdale, NJ: Erlbaum.

Seliger, H. (1977). Does practice make perfect? A study of interaction patterns and L2 competence. *Language Learning, 27,* 263–278.

Selinker, L. (1972). Interlanguage. *International Review of Applied Linguistics, 10,* 219–231.

Snow, C. E. (1981). English speakers' acquisition of Dutch syntax. In H. Winitz (Ed.), *Native language and foreign language acquisition. Annals of the New York Academy of Sciences* (Vol. 379). New York: New York Academy of Sciences.

Snow, C. E. (1983). Age differences in second language acquisition: Research findings and folk psychology. In K. Bailey, M. Long, & S. Peck (Eds.), *Second language acquisition studies*. Rowley, MA: Newbury House.

Snow, C. E. (1987). Relevance of the notion of a critical period to language acquisition. In M. Bornstein (Ed.), *Sensitive periods in development: An interdisciplinary perspective*. Hillsdale, NJ: Erlbaum.

Snow, C. E. (1990). Diverse conversational contexts for the acquisition of various language skills. In J. Miller (Ed.), *Progress in research on child language disorders*. New York: Little, Brown.

Snow, C. E., & Hoefnagel-Höhle, M. (1978). Critical period for language acquisition: Evidence from second language learning. *Child Development, 49,* 1263–1279.

Snow, C. E., & Hoefnagel-Höhle, M. (1982). School-age second language learners' access to simplified linguistic input. *Language Learning, 32,* 411–430.

Snow, C. E., Smith, N. S., & Hoefnagel-Höhle, M. (1980). The acquisition of some Dutch morphological rules. *Journal of Child Language, 7,* 539–553.

Stubbs, J., & Tucker, G. (1974). The close test as a measure of English proficiency. *The Modern Language Journal, 58,* 239–241.

Taeschner, T. (1983). *The sun is feminine: A study on language acquisition in bilingual children*. Berlin: Springer-Verlag.

Thomas, M. (1989). The acquisition of English articles by first- and second-language learners. *Applied Psycholinguistics, 10,* 335–357.

Tomasello, M., & Herron, C. (1988). Down the garden path: Inducing and correcting overgeneralization errors in the foreign language classroom. *Applied Psycholinguistics, 8,* 237–246.

Tomasello, M., & Herron, C. (1989). Feedback for language transfer errors: The garden path technique. *Studies in Second Language Acquisition, 11,* 385–396.

Wesche, M. (1994). Input, interaction, and acquisition: The linguistic environment of the language learner. In B. Richards & C. Gallaway (Eds.), *Input and interaction in language acquisition* (pp. 219–249). Cambridge: Cambridge University Press.

White, L. (1990). Second language acquisition and Universal Grammar. *Studies in Second Language Acquisition, 12,* 121–134.

Wode, H. (1978). The L1 versus L2 acquisition of English interrogatives. *Working Papers in Bilingualism, 15,* 37–57.

Wolfson, N., d'Amico-Reisner, L., & Huber, L. (1983). How to arrange for social commitments in American English: The invitation. In N. Wolfson & E. Judd (Eds.), *Sociolinguistics and language acquisition.* Rowley, MA: Newbury House.

Wong Fillmore, L. (1976). *The second time around: Cognitive and social strategies in second language acquisition.* Unpublished doctoral dissertation, Stanford University, CA.

Zentella, A. C. (1981). Language variety among Puerto Ricans. In C. A. Ferguson & S. B. Heath (Eds.), *Language in the U.S.A.* New York: Cambridge University Press.

Glossary

Acceptable. A sentence or utterance considered possible or permissible by native speakers of a language. Acceptable utterances may or may not be grammatical, as in the partial phrase, "No, she isn't"; conversely, a sentence that may be grammatically correct may not seem acceptable to some speakers because of length or processing constraints, as in "The horse raced around the barn fell."

Access routes. In models of lexical access, pathways or processes used to retrieve targets.

Access code. In lexical search models of reading, the first syllable in a stem morpheme; used to locate the word's lexical address in the mental lexicon.

Acoustics. The study of the physical properties of sound, such as intensity, frequency, and duration.

Acoustic cue. Property of a sound signal that provides information about its identification.

Active learner. A view of the child or second-language learner that presumes that the learner generates hypotheses about the language and tries to organize what she or he knows into a system of rules.

Additive bilingualism. Learning a second language while maintaining active mastery of the first language.

Affix. A bound morpheme. Affixes can occur before a word stem, as in the prefix *run;* they may occur after the word stem, as in the suffixes that signal the past tense, plural, or possession. In some languages, they appear within words (infixes).

Affricate. Sounds produced by an initial stop closure followed immediately by a gradual release of the air pressure. The articulatory gestures needed in the production of affricates are those for stops followed by a fricative. The sounds that begin and end the words *church* and *judge* are voiceless and voiced affricates, respectively.

Agnosia. [*G. no perception*] Loss of ability to properly interpret sensory stimuli.

Agrammatism. The absence of function words and word endings in some types of Broca's aphasia (*See also* **Broca's aphasia**).

Alexia without agraphia. (*See* **pure alexia.**)

Allophone. One of a phoneme's variant realizations. The phoneme /t/ has many possible realizations (aspirated, flapped, checked, and so on), depending upon surrounding phonetic context and position within a word or utterance.

Allophonic variation. The individual allophones in a phoneme category represent the allophonic variations permissible in that phoneme category.

Alphabetic phase. Penultimate stage of reading development, when the child begins a systematic learning and application of grapheme–phoneme rules. Followed by the **orthographic** (final) phase.

Alveolar. Refers to any consonant made with the tongue near or touching the alveolar ridge, which is behind the upper front teeth. In English the alveolar consonants are: [t], [d], [n], [s], [z], and [l].

Ambiguous. A word or sentence that has more than one meaning, as in *bill* or *Visiting relatives can be a nuisance.*

American Sign Language (ASL or Ameslan). A manual language used by many deaf Americans; one of the world's manual languages, characterized by its own phonology, morphology, lexicon, and grammar.

Amplitude. The height of a sound wave, from peak to trough. Its perceptual correlate is loudness.

Analysis by synthesis. A model of speech perception. The listener guesses the possible identity of a speech signal, mentally synthesizes its acoustic characteristics, and compares the result to the input signal. If there is a match, the signal is accurately identified.

Anaphora. Reference to earlier elements in text or discourse.

Anarthria. Loss of speech without loss of intellectual functioning.

Angular gyrus. [*Brodmann area 39*] An area in the parietal lobe that may be involved in word retrieval as well as reading and writing.

Anomia. A disturbance in naming due to brain damage.

Anosognosia. [*G. no disease knowledge*] Denial of illness, a behavior that may follow brain damage.

Anterior. A descriptor used in the distinctive features system of classifying speech sounds. Sounds produced at the front of the mouth, from the lips to the alveolar ridge are +anterior. All other places of articulation are anterior.

Anticipation error. Speech error in which a segment to come later in the utterance inappropriately appears earlier than intended.

Aperiodic. An event that occurs at irregular intervals; not cyclical. In acoustics, the turbulent noise associated with voiceless fricatives ([f], [θ], [s], [ʃ]) is aperiodic.

Aphasia. [*G. no speech*] Language disturbance caused by brain damage.

Apraxia of speech. The loss of the ability to voluntarily position the articulators appropriately for speech, in spite of preserved muscle and sensory function.

Arcuate fasciculus. A nerve tract connecting Broca's area and Wernicke's area (part of the superior longitudinal fasciculus).

Argument. (a) Dispute; (b) assertion in the propositional structure of a dispute; (in syntax) one of the complements of a verb, for example the subject or object.

Aspirated. A sound produced with audible breath release, as in English initial voiceless stops *(pin, tin, kin)*.

Association. Cognitive process that underlies the ability to symbolize, or have one thing represent another. Each may prompt a reaction common to both.

Ataxia. A breakdown in muscular coordination caused by brain damage.

Attrition. In language, the loss of language skill through disuse. For instance, a person who moves to a new language environment may lose his or her native language through lack of practice.

Automatic speech. The retained ability in aphasia to produce overlearned materials.

Automaticity. The potential of a process to be completed without conscious attention and with great speed after long practice. When a cognitive process becomes automatic, it requires no extra time or processing capacity.

Autonomous. Not controlled by higher-level processes or supplemented by information from knowledge structures not contained in the module (*see* **modular**).

Axon. The nerve fiber carrying impulses away from the nerve cell body.

Babbling. Prespeech vocal behavior by infants, usually consisting of strings of syllables that the child uses either communicatively or in sound-play.

Backward masking. Experimental condition in which the stimulus is obliterated by noise patterns timed to occur shortly after presentation.

Basal ganglia. A mass of gray matter above and surrounding the diencephalon, mediating both motor and cognitive function.

Bilabial. Sounds produced by bringing both lips together. The articulation of [p]. [b] and [m] require these gestures; they are consequently described as bilabial.

Bilingual aphasia. Language disturbance that involves two languages following brain damage.

Bilingualism. The ability to use two languages.

Borrowing. Using a word or phrase from another language.

Bottom-up processing. 1. A listener's perceptual analysis of the physical sound pattern of speech "upward" from the level of the recognition of phonemes to eventual comprehension of sentence meaning. 2. A hypothesized mode of processing information. In speech perception, bottom-up processing follows this sequence: auditory analysis followed by phonetic analysis, then phonological, semantic, and syntactic levels of analysis.

Bound morpheme. A morpheme that cannot stand alone as a word, as in prefixes such as *un-* and *re-,* and suffixes such as the plural, past tense, and such.

Brain stem. A structure at the very base of the brain, which controls vital functions such as respiration and heart beat.

Broca's aphasia. Nonfluent, agrammatic language output caused by brain damage.

Broca's area. [*Brodmann areas 44 and 45*] An area of cortex originally defined by Broca as encompassing the third frontal gyrus.

Burst. A short, high-amplitude noise that accompanies the release of stop consonants.

Carotid artery. A major arterial system that supplies blood to the anterior two-thirds of the cerebrum.

Carrier phrase. A fixed phrase in which target words are inserted, for example, "*I see a _____ .*"

Categorical Scope Principle. In children's word learning, the premise that an object label may be extended to objects other than the original referent that occupy the same basic level category as the referent.

Categorical perception. A term that describes a special pattern of results in identifying and discriminating speech stimuli that differ systematically along a phonetic continuum. In categorical perception, listeners can discriminate only between stimuli that are identified as members of two phoneme categories. This pattern of response is suggestive of perceptual discontinuity across a continuously varying physical dimension.

Caudal. [*L. tail*] Toward the tail, posterior.

Caudate. [*L. tail*] One of the structures that make up the basal ganglia.

Central nervous system (CNS). Those parts of the nervous system enclosed by the bony coverings of the skull and vertebral column.

Cerebral spinal fluid (CSF). A normally clear **fluid** produced in the ventricles and central canal of the spinal cord.

Cerebrovascular disease. Disease that affects the blood vessels of the brain and that can cause death of neurons by depriving them of oxygen and glucose.

Characteristic features. Features of a stimulus that are typical but not necessary for the stimulus to be included in a category (for example, gray hair is typical of grandmothers, but grandmothers need not have gray hair).

Child-directed speech (CDS, babytalk, motherese). The speech register used when addressing language-learning children, characterized by higher pitch; exaggerated intonation; special vocabulary; and shorter, repetitive, and paraphrased syntactic patterns.

Choreas. [*G. dance*] A class of hyperkinetic neuromotor disorders characterized by continual rapid, jerky movements.

Cingulate gyrus. [*L. belt*] An arch-shaped band of gray matter lying above the corpus callosum.

Citation form. Speech that is produced with clear and deliberate enunciation. Acoustic studies of speech have used samples of natural speech produced in citation form. Compare with **underarticulation.**

Classical conditioning. A form of learning first described by Pavlov, in which previously neutral stimuli (such as words) that are repetitively paired with other stimuli eventually come to elicit responses to those stimuli.

Closed-class words. Function words such as articles and conjunctions *(the, a, and).* These are called closed-class words because their ranks are unlikely to expand.

Coarticulation. The influence of adjacent segments on the articulation of a given segment. Such influence consists of overlapping speech motor gestures that involve more than one point in the vocal tract.

Code-switching. Changing language or dialect within an utterance.

Codes. Abstract mental representations of the different attributes of the units of language; these include semantic, phonological, and syntactic grammatical codes.

Cognates. **1.** Words that have similar forms across languages (for example, *teatro/theatre/theater*) because of borrowing or historical derivation. **2.** Sounds that differ in only a single feature (for example, in voicing).

Cognitive economy. In theories of the mental lexicon, the assumption that some features that unite a lexical class are stored with the superordinate term rather than with each of the subordinate members' lexical entries. For instance, a feature such as *+breathes* is stored with the term *animal,* but not with every possible type of animal in the category.

Cognitive psychology/neuropsychology. The study of reasoning, memory, language, and other mental processes. Cognitive neuropsychology studies the neurological underpinnings of cognitive functions, often by examination of preserved and damaged abilities in neurologically impaired populations.

Coherence graph. A network of connections that expresses the relations among the propositions ("idea units") of an utterance.

Coherent. Composed of relevant turns that are thematically related.

Cohesive. Linguistically connected by devices such as pronouns or conjunctions.

Cohort model. A model of lexical recognition in which available information (contextual, acoustic, and such) creates a class of possible candidates (the cohort) for recognition that is progressively narrowed by subsequent information.

Commissure. A collection of nerve fibers that connects the two hemispheres of the brain.

Commissurotomy. The surgical cutting of a commissure; the cutting of the corpus callosum is sometimes referred to as "split-brain" operation.

Competence. The knowledge of their language that all native speaker–hearers possess (see **performance**).

Competition model. A model of language development based on **PDP networks** that assumes that various cues in the language environment compete with one another. The most available and reliable cues will be learned first.

Complex sentence. A sentence that consists of a main clause and one or more subordinate clauses.

Compound word. A word that is composed of two or more free lexical morphemes, such as *blackboard* or *merry-go-round.*

Compound sentence. A sentence that consists of more than one main clause or contains compound subjects, verbs, or objects.

Comprehension. Understanding of language.

Computerized transaxial tomography (CT scan). A form of x-ray imaging that can provide displays of sections of live as well as dead brains.

Conduction aphasia. A type of aphasia, first suggested by Wernicke, characterized by an inability to repeat (see **arcuate fasciculus**).

Connectives. Joiners of clauses; conjunctions, discourse markers.

Connectionism. A position in cognitive science that uses the analogy of the network of neurons in the brain to explain cognitive processes.

Constituent. A linguistic unit that is part of a larger grammatical construction, such as a noun phrase or a verb phrase.

Constraint satisfaction model. In sentence comprehension, the premise that more than one syntactic analysis of a word sequence may be generated during comprehension, though not all are activated at a level of conscious awareness.

Constriction. A narrowing of the vocal tract.

Content word. [synonym: *lexical*]Nouns, verbs, and modifiers within a language are considered content words; words such as articles and auxiliary verbs are considered **function words** or **functors.**

Context. 1. Situation, participants, activities, setting of speech. **2.** Surrounding verbal text.

Contextualization. Cues that suggest background for interpretation.

Continuant. One of the components of sound production used in the distinctive feature system of classifying speech sounds. Sounds produced with continuous air flow are described as *+continuant;* those produced with a stoppage of air flow are described as *-continuant.*

Contralateral. Referring to the opposite side of the human body.

Contrastive analysis. The prediction of second-language learning successes and difficulties by comparison of similarities and differences between the native and second language.

Conventionality principle. In language acquisition, the assumption that speakers expect a conventional form to be used to convey certain meanings.

Conventional request. The desired act or object is not directly specified but is clear because of conventions familiar to both speaker and hearer. Questions such as *can you?* are usually interpreted as requests rather than queries about ability.

Coordinate clause. Clauses in same tense linked by *and, but,* or *so.*

Copula. A linking verb with virtually no independent meaning. In English, the only copular verb is *to be,* as in *The apple* is *red.*

Coronal. A term used in the distinctive feature system of classifying speech sounds. Sounds produced by placing the tongue in contact with the palate are described as *+coronal.* Examples in English are [t], [d], and [n].

Corpus callosum. [*L. callused body*] The major commissure connecting the two hemispheres of the brain.

Corpus. [plural: *corpora*] Body of data used for linguistic analysis.

Cortex. [*L. bark*] The convoluted mass of gray matter covering the surface of the two cerebral hemispheres.

Cortical motor aphasia. See **Broca's aphasia.**

Cortical sensory aphasia. See **Wernicke's aphasia.**

Cranial nerves. Nerves of the peripheral nervous system that exit directly from the cranium.

Craniometry. Measurement of skulls and brains.

Cranium. Skull.

Creole. A **pidgin** language that becomes the native language of a community and is acquired by children growing up in that culture.

Critical period. A span of developmental time best suited for acquiring a particular behavior.

Cross modal priming. Refers to presentation of a priming word in one modality (for example, spoken) and then testing its effect on a related word presented in a different modality (for example, visual presentation) (see **lexical priming**).

Cross-modal transfer. The cognitive process by which information accessed through one sensory medium (for example, sight) becomes available to other systems. Also called **intersensory integration.**

Cross-over stimulus. A term used in categorical perception experiments. The stimulus on the continuum that marks the boundary between two phoneme categories.

Crossed aphasia. An extremely rare form of aphasia caused by damage to the right hemisphere in right-handed individuals.

Cytoarchitecture. The organization of nerve cells; their morphology (shape) and layering.

Dative. A sentence that contains an indirect object relationship. In English, basic dative order is subject-verb-direct object-indirect object (as in *He baked a cake for Mary*); sentences that are ordered subject-verb-indirect object-direct object are usually more difficult to process and more difficult for children to acquire.

Decussation. [*L. decem = Roman numeral X*] A crossing of nerve fibers from one side of the body to the other.

Deep dyslexia. Reading disorder characterized by the ability to name most words, but not pseudowords, and by the production of many semantic errors.

Deep structure. In transformational grammar, the underlying syntactic and semantic representation of a sentence.

Defining features. Features of a stimulus that are considered necessary for the stimulus to be included within a given category (for example, blood and having a heart are necessary features of animals).

Degeneracy (of input). In child language acquisition, the term used by some linguists to characterize the fragmented, unsystematic, and sometimes ungrammatical utterances a child is exposed to; although seen as a problem for models of language development by nativists, other groups of child language researchers argue the scope and influence of degeneracy.

Dementia. A gradual deterioration of intellectual abilities caused by brain disease.

Dendrite. [*L. tree*] Branch-like extensions from the nerve cell body upon which many synapses occur.

Derivational morphemes. Affixes used in word formation. Derivational morphemes change the grammatical class of root forms (for example, *happy + ness → happiness*).

Derivational theory of complexity (DTC). Early psychological attempt to link the derivation of sentences under Transformational Generative (TG) grammar to the time taken to process such sentences.

Developmental error. An speech or language error typical of those made by children learning their first language.

Developmental psycholinguistics. The study of language acquisition in children.

Dialect. A regional or socially conditioned variant of a language. Dialects may vary in their phonological, lexical, grammatical, and pragmatic conventions.

Diaschesis. [*G. to split through*] Loss of function in an apparently normal area of the brain caused by a lesion in another part of the brain.

Dichotic listening. Simultaneous presentation of different sounds to each ear.

Diencephalon. [*G. between brain*] The most centrally located part of the brain, a relay station for most sensations and motor functions.

Diminutive. Affix signaling "little"; in English, diminutives such as *-ie (doggie)* are conventional in the babytalk (BT) or **child-directed speech** (CDS) register.

Diphthong. A *vowel + glide* combination.

Direct methods of instruction. In foreign language instruction, emphasis on exposing the learner to the second language through immersion. In this method, the learner is not given formal rules for using the second language, and use of the first language in the classroom is discouraged.

Discontinuous. A grammatical construction interrupted by the insertion of another constituent or phrase.

Discourse. A spoken or written text of some length monologue or dialogue.

Discourse markers. Words whose main function is to indicate relations between propositions, actions, or global text features, for example *oh, well, but, because, so, okay.*

Discourse operators. See **discourse markers.**

Discrimination. A perceptual task in which the subject has to indicate whether two stimuli are the same or different.

Discrimination peak. The highest level of accuracy in the discrimination of pairs of stimuli sampled from a continuum. In categorical perception the discrimination peak coincides with the phoneme boundary.

Disfluency (also **dysfluency**). Break in the flow of spoken language. Disfluencies include pausal and hesitation phenomena, repetitions, retracings, and so forth.

Displacement. The ability of language to refer to events that are distant in space or time or concepts not triggered by the immediate environment. One characteristic that distinguishes human language from animal communication systems.

Dispute. Dialogue in which disagreement continues three or more turns.

Dissociation. The separation of functions in the brain based on the effects of lesions.

Distinctive feature. A term developed by linguists to describe the components of speech sounds. In phonology, each phonetic segment is associated with a specific pattern of distinctive features. Each distinctive feature refers to a minimal contrastive unit that has a positive (+) and a negative (-) state. For example [p] is +oral, -continuant, -voice, +anterior.

Dorsal thalamus. [*G. bed chamber*] A major part of the diencephalon.

Dysarthria. [*G. disjointed*] A class of disturbances of speech sometimes following brain damage, in which articulation is impaired by paralysis, loss of coordination, or spasticity of the muscles used in speaking.

Dyslexia. A class of disturbances of reading, some of which are acquired, and some of which are developmental.

Echolalia. Inappropriate repetition of part or all of an utterance.

Electrical stimulation of the brain (ESB). An experimental technique that usually involves direct electrical stimulation of the cortex or other brain structures.

Electroencephalogram (EEG). A measure of the electrical activity of the brain in action. An EEG represents a plot of voltage fluctuations over time produced by large numbers of neurons and recorded by electrodes placed on the scalp.

Ellipsis. Conversational deletion of a noun or verb phrase. (for example, *"Where is he? "____ Gone." "Who will go to the library?" "I will ____ ."*)

Encoded. In speech, the term is used to refer to coarticulated phonetic segments. Consonant-vowel (CV) syllables that begin with a stop consonant are described as being highly encoded because the acoustic information for the consonant and the following vowel are merged together.

Encoding. Process of transforming information at one stage for use at the next stage.

Event-related potentials (ERPs). Scalp-recorded electrical activity that can be referenced to or synchronized with an external event, such as the presentation of an experimental stimulus.

Exchange. Speech error in which two segments reverse positions.

Exchanges. Series of moves in a dialogue.

Explicit request. Request that mentions desired act or desired object.

Expressive aphasia. See **Broca's aphasia.**

Expressive style. A speech style seen in some toddlers that is characterized by the use of many personal–social terms, such as greetings and routines.

Extension. The class of known items or concepts to which a word applies.

External capsule. A band of outgoing (efferent) and incoming (afferent) nerve fibers surrounding the basal ganglia.

Extrastriate cortex. Portion of the cortex containing visual association areas.

Family resemblance theory. In theories of meaning, a premise of prototype theory. Instances of a category are linked through family resemblance, in which members overlap in some traits but not others.

Feature view. The most popular view of conceptual meaning, in which the concept is viewed as a composite of more primitive featural meanings.

Femoral artery. A major artery located in the thigh.

Feral child. A child raised in the wild, or isolated from human contact.

Filled pause. Nonsilent pause filled by a vocalization such as *um, uh,* or *well.*

Fine-tuning. Term used in describing changes made in the **child-directed speech** (CDS, babytalk, motherese) register to accommodate the child's changing linguistic abilities.

Fissure. A deep valley in the cerebral cortex's landscape (see **sulcus**).

Fluency. 1. Ability to speak a language with native-like proficiency. **2.** The characteristic of spoken language unimpeded by repetitions, interjections, revisions or silences and spoken at a natural rate.

Foramen magnum. [*L. big hole*] A large hole at the base of the skull through which the brain and spinal cord interconnect.

Foregrounded. In the main clause.

Formant. A band of resonant frequencies. Resonant frequencies are determined by the shape of the oral cavity through which air flows during speech production. The first three bands of resonant frequencies (formants) are considered more important than the remaining formants in defining the identity of phonetic segments.

Formant transition. Change in resonant frequencies as a function of a change in the shape of the oral cavity. Formants change in their spectral composition as individuals produce two adjacent phonetic segments in a syllable.

Fossilization. The maintenance of an early, incorrect language learning form despite subsequent language exposure and learning.

Fractionation. The concept that brain damage results in deficits to specific components of cognitive processing.

Framing move. Move that sets up preparatory situation for request.

Free morpheme. Morpheme that can stand alone as a word.

Frequency effects. In psycholinguistic research, response time variations on tasks that arise as a function of how often a word is used in written or oral language.

Freudian slip. Speech error in which the speaker chooses a word that means the opposite of what was intended, or the speaker's ongoing thought process results in an inappropriate lexical selection.

Fricative. Sound produced by creating a small constriction in the oral cavity and forcing air through it. This creates a turbulent (aperiodic) sound that is characteristic of fricatives. Some English fricatives are [v], [f], [s], and [z].

Frontal eye field. [*Brodmann area 8*] The area of frontal cortex related to conjugate eye movement.

Function word (functor). Word that plays a purely grammatical function in sentence constructions, such as articles, auxiliary verbs, and conjunctions.

Functional magnetic resonance imaging (fMRI). A procedure that measures functionally induced changes in brain tissue—such as level of blood oxygen concentration—that occur during brain activity.

Functional neuroanatomy. The relating of neuroanatomical structures to behavior.

Functionalist hypothesis. The view that a stimulus's function, rather than its physical nature, determines in which hemisphere it is processed.

Fundamental frequency (F0). The rate at which the vocal cords vibrate during phonation.

Garden-path sentence. A sentence whose structure is ambiguous to the point of being misleading or uninterpretable.

Gating. A technique for studying word recognition in which listeners are asked to identify words based only on hearing varying amounts of the word onsets.

Generalization. Production of a learned response in a new environment, as in a child's ability to form the plural of an unfamiliar word.

Generics. Generalizations about how things nominally are.

Genre. Cultural type of text that has name, regular structural features.

Glial cells (glia). [*G. glue*] One of the two basic types of cells that make up brain tissue (see also **neuron**).

Glide. Speech sounds produced with little or no obstruction in the air flow through the oral cavity. The sounds [j] and [w] are glides. In articulating these sounds the tongue moves rapidly ("glides") either away from or toward the adjacent vowel.

Global aphasia. Loss of virtually all language abilities as a result of destruction of the perisylvian language area.

Global structure. Major units of discourse, episodes, asides.

Globus pallidus. [*L. pale globe*] One of the structures making up the basal ganglia.

Glottalized. Made in the larynx, by closing or narrowing the glottis, the space between the vocal cords.

Glottis. The location in the larynx where the vocal cords meet.

Government and binding (GB) grammar. A model of grammar descended from earlier Transformational Generative models. It proposes only one type of transformation (movement of elements), the specification of possible grammatical frames for lexical items and their mapping onto the syntax of sentences, and universal constraints on possible syntactic rules, among many other notions.

Grammar/translation methods. In this type of foreign language instruction, students are taught in their first language, with an emphasis on reading and translation from the first to the foreign language. Less emphasis is placed on conversational use of the foreign language.

Grammatical. Construction that conforms to the rules of the language. Ungrammatical constructions are conventionally preceded by asterisks in linguistics texts.

Grammatical class. The classification of words into major linguistic categories, such as noun, verb, preposition, and such.

Grapheme. The minimal contrastive unit in writing systems. In English, an alphabetic system, graphemes are letters.

Gray matter. Gray-brown masses of nerve tissue, especially in the brain and spinal cord, as opposed to nerves, cordlike bundles of fibers found throughout the body.

Gyrus. One of the hills of the cerebral cortex's landscape.

Habituals. Verbs that refer to recurrent events or acts.

Hard palate. The anterior, bony portion of the palate, which separates the oral and nasal cavities.

Harmonics. Even multiples of the **fundamental frequency** (F0).

Hedge. Qualifier or phrase that reduces the strength of an assertion.

Hemidecorticate. A patient who has had half of the cerebral cortex surgically removed.

Hemiplegia. Paralysis confined to one side of the body.

Hemispherectomy. Surgical removal of one cerebral hemisphere.

Hemispheric specialization. See **lateralization of function.**

Heschl's gyrus. [*Brodmann area 41*] The highest (most rostral) cortical area devoted to hearing.

Hesitation. Category of spoken behaviors, including **filled pauses,** unfilled pauses, and other **disfluencies.**

Hidden units. In connectionist models of language processing, a link between input and output units whose weight can be modified by training.

Hierarchical network model. In models of semantic representation, the premise that concepts are organized in our minds as "pyramids," with broader, superordinate concepts (such as *animal*) at the top and more specific, sub-ordinate concepts (such as *poodle*) at the bottom. Basic-level categories (such as *dog*) are presumed to be stored at a more intermediate level of organization.

Holistic view. A view of conceptual meaning in which the concept is viewed as an unanalyzable whole rather than as a sum of parts.

Holophrase. Single-word utterance used by children at the earliest stages of language acquisition that appears to carry the meaning or intent of a longer utterance, given its context.

Homo sapiens sapiens. [*L. man most wise*] Present-day human beings.

Homophones. Pairs of words that have different meanings but sound alike.

Homunculus. [*L. little man*] On some illustrations of the primary motor cortex, a superimposed, disproportionately shaped figure of a person, to emphasize the uneven proportion of motor cortex devoted to particular functions such as speech and hand movement.

Huntington's chorea. An inherited hyperkinetic neuromuscular disease characterized by speech disorders as well as cognitive disorders.

Hydrocephalus. [*G. water + head*] A disease characterized by excessive accumulation of cerebrospinal fluid in the brain.

Hyperkinesia. Characterized by too much movement.

Hypertrophy. Excessive growth of an organ.

Hypokinesia. Characterized by too little movement.

Ideational content. Thematic information, content of propositions.

Identification. In speech perception tasks, labeling or determining the identity of a stimulus (for example, "write the word/sound you hear.")

Ideograms. Writing that consists of pictures that symbolize ideas or things, but not particular words for them.

Ideomotor apraxia. Brain-damage–induced inability to carry out individual limb or facial movements.

Idiom. An phrase or expression whose meaning can not be determined from the meanings of its individual words (for example, "to "kick the bucket" meaning to die, rather than to hit a pail with one's foot.)

Imageability. The degree to which a concept can be visualized. Highly imageable words are more easily accessed than low imageability words.

Immersion. Settings in which students learn a new language through the medium of the second language.

Implicit mediators. In associative learning, implicit mediators (or retrieval cues) link two associates in a component of memory called the **semantic network.**

Indirect request. 1. Request that does not refer to desired act. **2.** Conventional request.

Inference. A conclusion derived from facts and premises. For example, if an object is not where it was left, we infer that it has been moved.

Inflection (inflectional affix). Morpheme that signals grammatical concepts such as plurality, past tense, and possession.

Innate. Inborn, as in the nativist belief that language is a biologically conditioned ability in humans.

Input language. See **child-directed speech.**

Intension. The meaning of a term (for example, a *chair* is an item of furniture that can be sat upon).

Interactive Models of Language Processing. The suggestion that knowledge gained at different levels of processing interacts freely in sentence processing as the sentence is being heard.

Interdental. Sounds produced with the tip of the tongue between the teeth. The initial sounds in *thin* and *then* are interdental.

Interlanguage grammar. For second language learners, one of many grammars they employ en route to full control of the target language grammar.

Instrumental motivation. In second language learning, motivation to learn in order to obtain a tangible benefit, such as a better job or to earn more money.

Integrative motivation. In second language learning, motivation to learn based on desire to identify with the culture of the language being learned.

Interference error. An error in second language learning that derives from faulty application of a rule of the native language to the second language, as in a Spanish-speaking English learner producing, *"the mother of Juan"* for *"Juan's mother"* by employing Spanish possessive structure.

Internal capsule. A band of afferent and efferent nerve fibers in the area of the **diencephalon** and **basal ganglia.**

Intersensory integration. See **cross-modal transfer.**

Invariance. An attribute *not present* in speech sounds. If speech sounds were produced in exactly the same way in all contexts, they would be invariant. The complex effects of coarticulation result in the diversity characteristic of speech sounds.

Invariant dimensions. Distinguishing and unchanging attributes. For instance, the **phoneme** /p/ has some characteristics that remain constant (invariant) in all environments.

Invented spelling. Children's **linguistic guesswork** about how words are spelled, based in part on their phonological insights.

Ipsilateral. Referring to the same side of a structure such as the human body.

Irregular. Form that is an exception to a general rule of the language.

Isolation of the speech area. See **mixed transcortical aphasia.**

Jargon aphasia. A fluent form of aphasia that is largely unintelligible because of substitutions of inappropriate words.

Jargon agraphia. A fluent form of agraphia that renders the patient's writing largely unintelligible because of substitutions of inappropriate letters.

Key. Mood or style of discourse.

Labiodental. Sounds produced by touching the front teeth to the lower lips. Articulatory gestures for [f] and [v] require the touching of the lip *(labio-)* with the teeth *(-dental).*

Language acquisition device (LAD). The innate mental mechanism that, according to linguistic theorists, makes language acquisition possible.

Language Acquisition Socialization System (LASS). The social mechanism that, according to social interactionists, fosters language and communicative development through interaction with other human beings.

Language attrition. Loss of a language through disuse.

Language play. Use of language to convey humor, such as in jokes, children's rhymes, etc

Larynx. Commonly called the "voice box," it is an anatomical structure that contains the vocal cords.

Late closure principle. A principle of language comprehension that proposes the listener attempts to attach all incoming material to the phrase currently being processed, thus building the largest possible clausal structure.

Lateral geniculate nucleus. A portion of the metathalamus involved in visual processing.

Lateralization of function. The observation that each cerebral hemisphere may control different types of behavior.

Learnable. Able to be acquired through experience, rather than through genetic endowment.

Lemma. Used in Levelt's model of speech production to refer to the semantic and syntactic properties of lexical items, as opposed to their phonological properties.

Lesion. An area of damage or pathological change.

Lexeme. An individual item in the **lexicon.**

Lexical access. The process of recognizing or producing a word stored in the mental lexicon.

Lexical decision. 1. A task in which subjects are asked to respond whether a stimulus is a legal word or a nonword (that is, a string of letters). **2.** The speed (or accuracy) with which a person can decide whether or not a presented letter string forms a real word.

Lexical priming. A means of testing whether the meaning of a word has been activated by testing the speed with which a related word can be recognized or distinguished as a real word versus a meaningless letter string.

Lexicon. 1. [*G. dictionary*] Refers to all the words that a person knows. **2.** The vocabulary of a language.

Line. In a typed or printed text, a single line, usually numbered.

Linguistic aphasiology. The study of the breakdown of language structure caused by brain damage.

Linguistic guesswork. The basis for children's first understanding of meaning-print connections.

Liquid. Speech sounds produced with some obstruction of the airstream in the oral cavity, but not enough to create friction noise. The sounds [l] and [r] are liquids.

Listening for mispronunciation (LM) task. In speech perception, an experimental task in which listeners must push a button whenever they hear a deliberately inserted mispronunciation. The LM task is used to evaluate the joint contributions of top-down and bottom-up processing in speech perception.

Literal meaning. Word-for-word meaning of a phrase or utterance. Antonyms: *nonliteral, figurative, metaphorical, idiomatic.*

Local ambiguity. Situations in which the syntactic function of a word, or how to parse a sentence is temporarily unclear until more of the sentence is heard or read.

Lobe. A more or less distinct region of the brain.

Local system. Turn-by-turn unplanned accommodations.

Logogen. In Morton's model, a theoretical "scoreboard" for a word that keeps track of all incoming information to determine whether it will be accessed.

Logographic phase. Early stage of reading acquisition in which highly familiar words are recognized visually, but novel or unknown words are inaccessible.

Logographs. Somewhat abstract writing symbols that represent whole words and sounds, for instance, Egyptian hieroglyphs.

Logographic phase. In reading, the developmental stage in which the reader can visually identify highly familiar words, but cannot accurately identify novel or unknown words.

Logorrheia. [*G. word flow*] excessive talkativeness caused by brain damage.

Manner of articulation. Features of phonemes that specify the way the air stream is obstructed as it travels through the vocal tract in the production of speech sounds. Stop, fricative, affricate, liquid, nasal, and glide are manners of articulation.

Massa intermedia. In the brain, a bridge of gray matter connecting the two thalami.

Mean Length of Utterance (MLU). Computation that measures in morphemes the average length of utterances in a child's language sample.

Medulla. [*L. marrow*] A part of the **brain stem** containing motor nuclei for the control of speech (namely cranial nerves IX, X, XI, and XII).

Meninges. Layers of membrane wrapping and protecting the **central nervous system.**

Mental lexicon. The memory store of words and their meanings.

Mental grammar. Internalized knowledge of the rules of one's language.

Metalinguistic ability. Ability to reflect on one's language use and knowledge.

Metaphor. A form of nonliteral meaning; a figure of speech in which a word or phrase that literally denotes one idea is used in place of another to create an analogy, as in the phrase *"a heart of stone."*

Metathalamus. The portion of the diencephalon containing the lateral and medial geniculate bodies involved in visual and auditory processing respectively.

Midbrain. A portion of the brain stem containing nuclei involved in visual processing.

Minimal attachment principle. The hypothesis that listeners or readers attempt to interpret sentences in terms of the simplest syntactic analysis that is consistent with the input. Simpler structures will contain fewer phrase-structure nodes.

Minimal pair. A pair of words that are identical with the exception of a single phoneme in a set position, as in *pear/bear, bed/bet.*

Mitigation. Softening by vocal tone, hedges, address, politeness routines.

Mixed transcortical aphasia. An aphasia characterized by retention of only the ability to repeat.

Modality-specific abilities. Abilities that are limited to one sensory domain, for example, to sight or to hearing.

Modularity. 1. The view that cognition, and ultimately the brain, is made up of a number of independent processing units. 2. (Of mind or language) presumes that the mind or language consists of a number of discrete subsystems, each with its own properties. 3. Modularity theorists are those who believe that input processes, such as word-meaning activation or syntactic analysis, occur automatically and independently without further mental activity.

Morpheme. The smallest meaningful unit of language (for example, *dogs* is composed of two morphemes: *dog* and *-s*, which signifies plurality). A morpheme is the minimal grammatical unit. Morphemes consist of words and affixes.

Morphologically complex. Word that consist of more than one morpheme; also *multimorphemic.*

Morphophonemic production rules. Rules that help speakers arrive at correct pronunciations of **derived words;** words that have common root morphemes but vary in form class, for example, *decide, decision.*

Motherese (babytalk). Term used to describe the register adults use when speaking to young language-learning children (see also **child-directed speech; input language**).

Motor strip. [*Brodmann area 4*] The highest (most rostral) area devoted to motor functions.

Motor theory of speech perception. The assumption that speech is identified by reference to the motor speech movements that generate speech sounds.

Motor transcortical aphasia. An aphasia comparable to that of Broca's aphasia, but with retained ability to repeat.

Motor homunculus. The inverted motor figure fashioned by Penfield to represent the functions of the motor strip [*Brodmann area 4*] obtained by electrical stimulation.

Multiple sclerosis. A neuromotor and cognitive deficit produced by destruction of **myelin** in the brain.

Myasthenia gravis. A neuromuscular disease that involves depletion of receptor sites for the neurotransmitter acetylcholine.

Myelin. A fatty covering of nerves produced by **glial cells.**

Narrative rounds. Series of stories on related themes by different speakers.

Narrative clauses. Propositions referring to two or more serial events.

Nasal. Speech sounds produced with air flow through the nasal passage The sounds [m], [n], and [ŋ] are nasal consonants. In English no other sounds require air flow through the nasal passage; they are oral.

Native bilingualism. Bilingualism dating from simultaneous learning of two languages during the initial stages of language acquisition.

Native speaker. A person who speaks a language fluently. Typically, native fluency is achieved only when a person has used a language since early childhood.

Nativism. In language acquisition, a theoretical approach emphasizing the innate, possibly genetic contribution to language development.

Natural kind terms. Terms, such as *animal* and *iron,* that refer to inanimate and animate things found in nature, as opposed to artifacts that refer to person-made objects.

Negative evidence. Feedback from competent language users to children regarding ungrammatical or unacceptable constructions in the language. Nativists contend that children do not receive such information and that this presents problems for certain accounts of the language acquisition process.

Negative transfer. The result of using habits established in a first language to incorrectly predict second language forms. For example, an English speaker might predict that adjectives will precede nouns in French, when in fact they follow them.

Neologistic jargon. Speech characterized by use of nonexistent words in a language (see **jargon aphasia**).

Neurolinguistics. The study of the relationship between language structure and brain function.

Neurologist. A physician who specializes in nervous-system disorders.

Neuron. A nerve cell that consists of a cell body (soma), dendrites, and one axon.

Neuropathology. The study of diseases of the nervous system.

Neurotransmitter. A chemical agent that transmits information from one neuron to another.

Nominal terms (artifacts). Terms such as *chair* and *table* that refer to person-made objects.

Nonautonomous. Unable to function independently.

Nonliteral meaning. Meaning not derived from the denotative meaning of words. Antonym: *literal.*

Notice. In child language, the intent to call attention to something, as in greetings.

Noun ellipsis. Noun omitted; demonstrative, possessive, numeral, or adjective remains.

Novel name/nameless principle. In first language learning, the assumption that novel words that the child hears map to currently unnamed concepts or categories.

Nucleus ambiguous. [*L. the ambiguous nucleus*] The brain stem nucleus for the cranial nerves that control phonation (namely, IX, X, and XI).

Object permanence. The ability of a child, developed in the latter part of the first year of life, to understand that objects continue to exist even when they are not visible to the child. Cognitive ability described in detail by Piaget.

Olfaction. The sense of smell.

Oligodendroglia. A **glial cell** in the **central nervous system** involved in the process of myelination.

On-line processing. The comprehension of the words of a sentence as they are actually being heard. This is contrasted with off-line analyses of a sentence that occur later in memory.

Onset. Initial consonant of a syllable. The onset of *hat* is *h.*

Open-class words. Any word with "content," such as nouns, verbs, adjectives. The term open-class -presumably refers to our ability to think up new words to refer to things or properties (for example, *minivan* and *computer* are words that have arisen in the last century).

Open syllable. A syllable that consists of a consonant or consonant cluster followed only by a vowel.

Operant conditioning. Term used by Skinner to refer to the learning process in which behaviors that are followed by reinforcement occur more frequently, whereas those that are punished occur less frequently or are extinguished over time.

Optic chiasm. [*G. chi = Greek letter X*] The crossing of the optic tracts from the eye to the occipital lobe of the brain.

Optic tectum. [*L. roof*] A portion of the midbrain involved in visual processing.

Oral cavity. The portion of the vocal tract containing the lips, teeth, tongue, palate, velum, and uvula.

Ordered recall. See **serial memory**.

Orthographic access file. In lexical search models of reading, the location of a word's lexical address. Orthographic access files are presumed to be bins containing representations of words with similar orthographic (written) characteristics.

Orthographic phase. Final stage of reading, characterized by the use of analogies, pronunciation rules dictated by context, and morphophonemic knowledge. Also called **fluent, orthographic reading.**

Orthotactic. Based on spelling.

Overextension. In child language, the use of a word to refer to an overly broad number of referents, as in *daddy* for all men.

Overgeneralization. In child language, the application of a rule to exceptional cases, as in *goed* for *went*.

Palatal. Sound produced with a raised tongue against the hard palate. This location is posterior to the alveolar ridge. English has two palatal fricatives, [ʃ] and [ʒ], where the constriction for producing the friction noise is made at the hard palate.

Parallel distributed processing (PDP). A computer-based model applied to grammatical development in children that compares development by analogical reasoning to the kinds of associative links that computers make.

Parallel processing. Carrying out several computations or cognitive tasks simultaneously.

Parallel search model. A theoretical model of word access that claims that items in the lexicon are activated simultaneously, or in parallel, in an attempt to find the correct lexical item.

Parallel transmission. More than one source of information available at the same time. In a stop-initial CV syllable (encoded consonant), acoustic information about the consonant and the vowel is available at the same time and is transmitted in parallel to the listener.

Parameter. A principle of grammar that may be characterized by one of a finite number of values along which languages are free to vary. For example, the so-called pro-drop parameter distinguishes languages such as English and German, which do not permit omission of lexical subjects, from languages such as Spanish or Italian, which do.

Paraphasia. The substitution of incorrect sounds (literal paraphasia) or words (verbal paraphasia) for appropriate sounds and words in aphasia.

Paraphrase. A sentence with the same meaning as another, having different form (for example, *Mary gave the present to Bill/Mary gave Bill the gift*).

Paresis. Partial or incomplete paralysis.

Parkinson's disease. A hypokinetic neuromotor disturbance that involves both speech and cognitive functions and is caused by damage to the substantia nigra (a part of the **basal ganglia**).

Paroxysmal aphasia. A reversible form of aphasia caused by epilepsy.

Parsing. (Sentence parsing, linguistic parsing) The process by which a listener or reader assigns the words of a sentence to their appropriate linguistic categories so as to determine the syntactic structure of the sentence.

Participation structure. Turn-taking system; roles allowing speech.

Passive. In English, a sentence where the first noun phrase (normally the subject) is the logical object of the verb and the second noun phrase is the logical subject, as in *The meal was prepared by skilled chefs.*

Pausal phenomena. In spoken language, hesitations and other discontinuities in speech fluency.

Perceptual learning. A type of processing that makes it possible to become increasingly efficient in searching for distinguishing attributes and attending selectively.

Performance. What a speaker does when producing or understanding language. Language performance may be limited by factors such as attention, stress, and memory. Antonym: *competence.*

Periacqueductal gray. The gray neuronal cells surrounding the cerebral aqueduct in the midbrain.

Periodic. An event that is repeated regularly and cyclically. The vibration of the vocal folds during phonation is periodic.

Peripheral nervous system (PNS). Those parts of the nervous system that lie outside the skull and vertebral column.

Perisylvian area. The area of the cerebral cortex surrounding the Sylvian fissure (the principal language area in the dominant hemisphere).

Perseveration error. Speech error in which a segment early in an utterance reappears in an incorrect location later in the utterance. Also a naming error consisting of repetition of the previous response.

Pharynx. The throat cavity, made up of the nasopharynx, oropharynx, and laryngopharynx.

Phonation. The action of vocal cord vibration to generate sound.

Phone. Physical realization of a phoneme.

Phoneme. The smallest unit of sound. For example, /k/ and /p/ are single phonemes. A phoneme is a minimally contrastive unit within the sound system of a language.

Phonemic restoration. A perceptual phenomenon in which a missing or distorted phoneme is "filled in" by the listener.

Phonemicization. The stage of speech production at which the phonological structure of morphemes is specified.

Phonetic bias paradigm. In speech production, an experimental task in which subjects are led to produce speech errors by training an expectation of phonetic sequences which is then violated.

Phonological codes. See **codes.**

Phonology. The study of the sound systems of languages.

Phonotactics. Rules that govern sound sequences in a language.

Phrase structure tree. A tree diagram of a sentence that illustrates its linear and hierarchical structure. (See example, p. 18)

Phrenology. A view developed by Gall that bumps on the skull might reveal **hypertrophy** of underlying neural areas of the brain subserving diverse human abilities.

Physical anthropology. The study of the fossil evidence for human evolution and any other physical, as opposed to cultural, aspect of human development.

Pictographs. Pictures used to represent an object or concept; this precursor to writing was created in the latter part of the fourth millennium B.C. by the ancient Sumerians.

Pidgin. Language variant formed when two mutually unintelligible communities attempt to develop a communicative system. Pidgins are characterized by some aspects of each contributing language, but show reduced grammatical and lexical complexity when compared to them. Over time, if a pidgin becomes the native language of a community, it becomes a **creole.**

Place of articulation. In the production of speech sounds, the part of the vocal tract where the airflow is most constricted. Labial, interdental, dental, palatal, and velar are examples of places of articulation for English speech sounds.

Planum temporale. [*L. the temporal plane*] A region of the temporal lobe lying posterior to **Heschl's gyrus** that has been demonstrated to exhibit left/right asymmetries.

Plasticity. The presumed ability of undamaged parts of the brain to assume the functions of damaged areas.

Polarity question. Yes/no question.

Pons. [*L. bridge*] A portion of the brain stem containing motor nuclei for the control of speech (namely, V and VII).

Positron emission tomography (PET). A neuroimaging technique that utilizes radioactive isotopes of various elements to measure changes in brain metabolism correlated with behavioral tests or neuropathology.

Pragmatics. The study of the use of language in social context to accomplish the speaker's conversational intent.

Priming. A method for decreasing reaction time by preceding the presentation of target words by the presentation of related words.

Pro-drop language. Language in which the subject may be optionally deleted from sentences; usually some information about the subject is conveyed by verbal inflections.

Programmed. Genetically or biologically predisposed (or "wired") to behave in certain ways, for instance to search for invariance in one's surroundings.

Pronominal reference. The function of pronouns; to refer to previously established concepts.

Propositional representation. The meaningful relationships between the objects, actions, and events in a sentence.

Propositions. Assertions made in clauses in sentences.

Prosody. 1. The intonation contour, stress pattern, and tempo of an utterance. **2.** A general term that includes the melodic intonation pattern of a sentence, the pattern of stress received by each of the words, and the timing of the words in the utterance, such as where pauses are placed as a sentence is spoken.

Protoliteracy period. The period when the precursors of written language are being laid, usually during the preschool years.

Prototype. The central figure of a category that shares many features with other members of the category and few features with members of other categories (for example, a robin is a prototypical bird).

Pseudowords. Words that, according to word formation rules, are possible in the language, but that do not actually exist.

Psycholinguistics. The study of the cognitive and processing issues that underlie language comprehension and use.

Pure word deafness. A type of agnosia involving the inability to interpret the speech sounds of one's native language.

Pure alexia. Impairment of reading ability alone caused by brain damage.

Putamen. [*L. shell*] The most lateral structure in the **basal ganglia.**

Pyramidal tract. A major collection of motor nerve fibers controlling fine motor movements of the digits (fingers) and articulators.

Reaction time. A measure used in experiments to gauge how long a cognitive process takes, such as response time in choosing whether a stimulus *(cat)* is a member of a given category *(animals)* or not.

Recasting. Adult response to a child's utterance in which the grammar is rephrased or corrected, although the message content is maintained.

Reciprocal causation. Relationship that exists in older impaired readers who, early on, developed problems in vocabulary knowledge as the result of delays in reading and then became further impeded in reading because they lacked vocabulary.

Recurrence. In child language, an intention that signals notice of or request for more of something—usually signaled by the use of words such as *more, another,* and *again.*

Recursion. A property of human languages in which grammatical phrases of the same type can appear within themselves, leading to the infinite creativity of language. Example: NP → (det) (adj) N (PP), in which PP → prep NP).

Redundant. 1. A concept implied in rule or context by another concept. As examples, the phonetic feature *+voice* is redundant with the feature *+nasal;* the semantic concept of mammal implies the feature of animacy. **2.** Information that is multiply specified, as in cues to the recognition of speech sounds.

Reference. The philosophical view that words stand for the objects to which they apply; they point to or *denote* those objects.

Reference theory of meaning. The belief that the meaning of a term is the object to which that term refers in the real world (its referent).

Referential style. In child language, an early language style characterized by relatively high frequency of naming behaviors.

Regional cerebral blood flow (rCBF). Changes in blood flow in the brain correlated with different behavioral tasks.

Register. Variant of a language used in certain social contexts or with particular classes of addressee, as in *babytalk* or *foreigner talk.*

Reply markers. Words used to index a reply.

Representation abilities. Cognitive capacities that make it possible to store and access mental correlates of spoken or written language.

Resonance. The frequencies that are enhanced in a complex acoustic signal. The bands of resonant frequencies of speech sounds are called **formants.**

Retracing. Behavior seen when a speaker notes his or her speech error and "backtracks" to the beginning of the constituent to rephrase it.

Retrieval cues. See **implicit mediators.**

Rime. The latter part of a syllable as in the *at* in *bat.*

Rostral. [*L. beak*] toward the beak; anterior.

Schemata. Mental structures or organizing principles.

Schwann cell. A **glial cell** in the **peripheral nervous system** involved in myelination.

Segmentation. Correct division of either spoken or written language into its constituent elements. The learner who believes that in English there is a fruit called "a napple" has made a *segmentation error.*

Selective attention. The ability to focus on a target's distinguishing attributes while ignoring irrelevant cues.

Self-correction. When a speaker notices a speech error and corrects it.

Semantic codes. See **codes.**

Semantic network. Mental organization of the lexicon whereby words and concepts that share some meaning are related both hierarchically and laterally.

Semantic priming. The tendency for a word to activate other words associated in meaning (for example, table/ chair), making those other words easier to recognize.

Semantic processing. Determining the meaning of an utterance.

Semantically opaque. In multimorphemic forms, or words that can be interpreted as multimorphemic, inability to derive meaning by sequentially combining the meaning of the individual morphemes. For example, in English, words such as *butterfly* and *strawberry* are semantically opaque.

Semantically transparent. In multimorphemic forms, ability to ascertain meaning by combining the meanings of the individual morphemes. For example, in English, a word such as *buttonhole* or *teacup* is semantically transparent.

Semantic relations. Relations in terms of word meanings.

Semantics. The study of meaning.

Semiphonetic strategies. Early literacy skills used as children begin to apply some phonemic knowledge in both reading and spelling.

Sensory transcortical aphasia. An aphasia comparable to that of Wernicke's, with retained ability to repeat.

Sensory stage. In bottom-up models of reading, early stage in which visual features are extracted.

Sentence processing. The process by which listeners or readers determine the structure of a sentence and gain access to its meaning.

Sequential transition markers. Global markers of side sequences, episodes.

Serial memory. A generalized ability to determine the order in which information was received.

Serial search model. A theoretical model of word access that claims items in the lexicon are searched serially, or one at a time, until the correct item is found.

Shadowing. A psycholinguistic research technique in which subjects are asked to listen to spoken passages and to repeat aloud what they are hearing word for word as they hear it.

Side sequences. Going off main topic for asides, repairs.

Sign. Something that represents something else intrinsically—by its very nature—(for example, smoke is a sign of fire).

Slip of the tongue (slip, Spoonerism). Speech error in which sounds or words are mispronounced or rearranged; such errors are useful in constructing models of the speech production process.

Sociolinguistics. Study of spoken language in terms of social features of speakers and of context.

Speaker normalization. In speech perception, the ability to use pattern recognition to understand speech produced by different speakers.

Speaker independent. In speech perception, a speech recognition system that can process input from numerous speakers. Typically, speaker-independent systems can only recognize a limited lexicon.

Speaker dependent. In speech perception, a speech recognition system that can only process input from a single speaker on whose speech the system has been trained.

Spectrogram. The visual display produced on a spectrograph.

Spectrograph. An instrument used in acoustic phonetics for speech analysis. The instrument provides a visual representation of auditory stimuli, including speech, in which frequency is on the vertical axis, time is on the horizontal axis, and amplitude is indicated by the intensity of the markings on the display.

Spectrum. The full range of frequencies at different amplitudes in a signal.

Speech act. In pragmatics, the function accomplished by an utterance, such as requesting or promising.

Speech error. A mistake in speech production, such as switching the order of sounds in a phrase (for example, *"You have hissed all my mystery lectures."*). Synonyms: *Spoonerism, slip of the tongue.*

Speech perception. The process by which people decode spoken messages.

Speech synthesis. Generation of speech sounds with the use of specialized machines, usually computers. Synthetic speech is different from natural speech, which is generated from the human vocal tract.

Spinal cord. Part of the **central nervous system** that controls all motor and sensory functions from the body and back of the head.

Spinal nerves. Nerves of the **peripheral nervous system** that exit directly from the vertebral column.

Spoonerism. See **slip of the tongue.**

Standing ambiguity. Situations in which sentences remain syntactically ambiguous even when all of the lexical information is available.

Standing behavior patterns. Regular expected actions for a role in a setting.

Statistical approximations. Word sequences that in themselves convey no meaning, but that maintain the mathematical regularities of the language.

Steady state. A term used in connection with vowels that are produced in a deliberate and elongated fashion. When the **formants** do not change in frequency over time, the signal is in steady state.

Stop consonant. A consonant produced with a period of stoppage of the air flow and then a sudden release of the impounded air. In English the stop consonants are [b], [p], [d], [t], [g], and [k].

Subcategorization constraint. Specification of the grammatical frames appropriate to a lexical item, as in the requirement that a transitive verb be followed by a noun-phrase object.

Subcortical motor aphasia. A type of nonfluent aphasia postulated by Lichtheim involving a disconnection of Broca's area from the motor strip.

Subcortical sensory aphasia. See **pure word deafness.**

Subglottal system. The lungs and associated muscles involved in speech production.

Submersion. Settings in which a second language learner is surrounded by native speakers.

Subtractive bilingualism. Bilingualism characterized by the loss of one's original language while learning a second language.

Sulcus. One of the valleys in the cerebral cortex's landscape.

Supplementary motor area. [*a portion of Brodmann area 6*] A medial area of frontal cortex intimately involved in movement initiation.

Surface dyslexia. Reading disorder characterized by the ability to decode pseudowords and regularly spelled words more readily than irregularly spelled real words.

Surface structure. 1. As opposed to deep structure in Standard Transformational Theory, the final stage in the derivation of a sentence, which most closely resembles the actual sentences we hear and say. **2.** The specific words of a sentence that must be analyzed to determine the "deep structure," or meaning, of the sentence that underlies the surface structure.

Syllabary. Written system in which each symbol stands for a complete syllable in the language, rather than a single speech sound (for example, the Japanese Kana, or the Devanagari syllabary used to write Sanskrit).

Syntactic/semantic codes. See **codes.**

Symbol. In semantics, something that arbitrarily represents or stands for something else (for example, the word *cat* is a symbol for the concept "cat" in English; the word *chat* is a symbol for the same concept in French).

Synapse. [*G. connection*] The minute gap that separates output and input between neurons.

Syntactic autonomy. The proposal that syntactic analysis of a sentence can be carried out independently from the semantic analysis of the sentence where functional relationships are determined and the meaning of the utterance becomes available.

Syntagmatic. Reflecting a linearly ordered relationship between sentential constituents.

Syntax. The study of how words are combined to make grammatical sentences.

Synthesized speech. Speech generated by a machine or computer.

Tachistoscope (T-scope). A device used for rapid presentation of visual stimuli to the visual fields.

Tag question. Question appended to the end of a statement; used in English to request listener agreement with the speaker, as in, *That's a nice dress, isn't it?*

Taxonomy. A way of classifying concepts into a category such that two members are related through nesting relationships (for example, *bird* is nested within the category *animal*) as opposed to a category in which members are related through color, theme (for example *baseball* and *bat*), and such.

Telegraphic speech. In child language, speech characterized by a general lack of function words and inflections; rather like a telegram.

Telencephalon. [*G. far brain*] The part of the brain that includes the **cerebral cortex, basal ganglia,** and limbic system.

Text. The language record of a spoken or written encounter.

Top-down processing. 1. The use of prior knowledge or linguistic expectations to facilitate word recognition and rapid sentence comprehension. **2.** A hypothesized mode of processing information. In speech perception, top-down processing refers to the effect of higher levels (semantics and syntax) on perception of syllables and words. This mode of processing contrasts with **bottom-up processing.**

TRACE model. A neural network model of speech perception based on a system of processing units called *nodes*. Nodes exist for phonetic or distinctive features—phonemes and words—and are highly interconnected. When input to a node is sufficiently consistent with the unit that the node represents, it is activated and can excite or inhibit other nodes. For example, the excitation of nodes for phonemes [b] and [o] will excite lexical nodes that have [bo] as their initial representation (for example, *boat, bowl*) while inhibiting excitation of competing nodes, such as those that represent [p] or [i].

Trace theory. The presumption that, when linguistic elements are moved from one position to another as the words of a sentence are organized for production, a covert representation or trace of the word remains at its original position.

Transactional encounters. Task-oriented talk for a common impersonal goal.

Transcortical aphasia. Any type of aphasia characterized by the retained ability to repeat.

Transformational grammar. Grammar in which surface structure is derived from deep structure by the application of transformational rules.

Transparency. The ability to ascertain readily what linguistic functions have been lost through brain damage.

Trauma. [*L. wound*] Injury to the skull and brain produced by external force.

Tumor. [*L. to swell*] An abnormal growth of brain tissue that may be cancerous (malignant).

Turn. The speech of one person continued until another takes the floor.

Unbounded states. Verb category describing nonvolitional states.

Underarticulation. Speech that is produced without full pronunciation of all segments. For example, relaxed conversational speech is underarticulated in comparison to speech that is clear and deliberate.

Unfilled pause. In speech production, a hesitation not filled by words.

Universal grammar. Hypothetical set of restrictions governing the possible forms human languages may take.

Universal. Any property assumed to characterize all human languages.

Unreleased. In speech sound production, the failure to complete articulation of a stop consonant by releasing air, usually found at the ends of utterances. Synonym: *checked.*

Unvoiced. See **voiceless.**

Utterance. A speaker's output, which may be less than a full sentence, as in exclamations, responses to questions (*I didn't*), warnings (*Don't*), and such.

Uvula. Small fleshy mass that hangs from the back of the soft palate.

Velar. Speech sound made by making contact between the back of the tongue body and the soft palate or velum. In English, /k/, /g/, and /ŋ/ are velar speech sounds.

Velum. The soft palate, located behind the bony or hard palate.

Ventricle. [*L. belly*] A cavity in the brain that produces and contains cerebrospinal fluid.

Vocal folds. Also known as vocal cords. Two muscular, almond-shaped masses that run from a single point inside the front of the thyroid cartilage ("Adam's apple") to the front ends of the arytenoid cartilage. The space between them is called the **glottis.** The vocal folds and the glottis are part of the **larynx.** The action of their vibration produces sound **(phonation).**

Vocal tract. All cavities above the **larynx.** These include the pharyngeal, oral, and nasal cavities.

Vocative. Name used to identify the addressee (for example, "Hey, lady!").

Voice-onset-time (VOT). The interval of time between the release of air pressure in the production of word-initial stops and the onset of vocal cord vibration associated with the voicing of the following vowel. This duration is conventionally given positive values if release precedes voice onset and negative values if release follows voice onset.

Voiced. Speech sounds that require vocal cord vibration in their production. Examples of voiced speech sounds include all vowels and consonants such as [m], [b], and [z].

Voiceless. Speech sounds that require no vocal cord vibration in their production. Examples of voiceless speech sounds are [p], [t], and [s].

Wernicke's area. [*a portion of Brodmann area 22*] An area of the temporal lobe defined by Wernicke as encompassing the posterior third of the first temporal gyrus.

Wernicke's aphasia. Fluent but largely meaningless language output caused by brain damage.

White matter. Nerves that displaying a whitish appearance because of their **myelin** coating.

Word primitive. The smallest form in which a word is stored in the lexicon. Some theorists argue word primitives are words themselves, other that words are built up out of morphemes, which are word primitives.

Word superiority effect. Phenomenon whereby a reader who is only briefly shown a letter embedded in a word can verify the presence of the letter (for example, *work:* Did the word contain a *k* or *d?*) more accurately than when it is embedded in a nonword *(Qrk)*.

Word-initial cohort. The number of words in the language that share the same initial sounds.

Working memory. A combined temporary memory and mental work space in which recent stimuli are briefly held, either for rehearsal and recall or for meaningful integration with other knowledge.

World Englishes. Regional varieties of English, such as those in India and Nigeria, that contain some nonstandard features when compared to American or British English.

Wug. Nonsense word and creature invented by Berko (1958) to test children's productive knowledge of plural forms.

ACKNOWLEDGMENTS

PHOTOS

Chapter 1
Figure 1.7: © Leslie Starobin/The Picture Cube.

Chapter 2
Figure 2.1: Roger Voillet/Gamma Liaison. Figure 2.2: Signoret, J. L. P. Castaigne, F. Lhermitte, R. Abelunet and P. Lavorel. "Rediscovery of Leborgne's brain: Anatomical description with CT scan." *Brain Language. 22.* 303-319 (1984). Academic Press. Figure 2.3: Courtesy of Dr. Terence H. Williams. Figure 2.4: © Fred Hossler/ Visuals Unlimited. Figure 2.5: Fig. 14 from Poizner, Klima, & Bellugi, *What the Hands Reveal About the Brain.* Cambridge, MIT Press, 1987. Figure 2.6: Marcus E. Raichle, MD—Washington University School of Medicine. Figure 2.7: Marcus E. Raichle, MD—Washington University School of Medicine. Figure 2.8: Shaywitz, et al., 1995 NMR Research/Yale Medical School.

Chapter 3
Figure 3.6: Photo courtesy of Archives of Haskins Laboratories and reproduced by permission of Williams and Wilkins.

Chapter 7
Page 313: Rev. William Spooner. The Bettmann Archive. Page 314: "Wizard of Id" by permission of Johnny Hart and Creators Syndicate, Inc.

Chapter 8
Figure 8.3: © J. Wilson/Woodfin Camp & Associates.

Chapter 10
Figure 10.1: © Louise Gubb/The Image Works. Figure 10.2: © Michael Dwyer/Stock Boston

FIGURES AND TABLES

Ablex Publishing Corporation
Figure 4.5: From "Putting Knowledge in Its Place: A Scheme for Programming Parallel Processing Structures on the Fly," by J.L. McClelland, 1985, *Cognitive Science, 9,* p. 115. Reprinted by permission.

Academic Press
Figure 3.6: Two formant syllables produced on the Pattern Playback synthesizer identified as (di) and (du). From A. M. Liberman, 1970, "The grammars of speech language," *Cognitive Psychology,* 1, 301-323. Reprinted by permission. Figure 4.2: The logogen model by John Morton, from "A functional model of human memory" in D.A. Norman (ed.) *Models of*

INDEX

Staats, A., 36
Standard English, 290
Standard Theory, 20, 22
Standing ambiguity, 238
Stanovich, K. E., 412, 417, 422, 424, 427, 430
Stark, R., 138
Statistical approximations, in English, 230–231
Steady states, 121
    in vowel identification, 125–127
Steklis, H., 67
Stemberger, J. P., 315
Sterling, C. M., 162
Stevens, K. N., 112, 134, 144, 145, 358
Stevenson, H. W., 412
Stigler, J. W., 412
Stimulus, 382
Stimulus-driven, bottom-up models, of reading, 427
Stine, E. A. L., 236, 260, 262
Stone, G. O., 431
Stop, 9
    glottalized, 12
Stop consonants, 116, 127, 135
    identifying, 112
Stop-consonant spectrographic displays, 122
Storage, 166
    of master lexicon, 172
    of morphemes, 163–164
Stotsky, S., 421
Straf, M., 165
Strange, W., 125, 126, 135, 136
Strawson, C., 432
Stress, 317–318
Structural properties of sentences, 229–232
Structure
    deep, 21
    vs. function, 377, 392
    in language, 229
    of sentences, 232–233
    surface, 21
Studdert-Kennedy, M., 130, 134, 139, 143
Subcortical sensory aphasia, 70
Subcortical structures, 90–91
Subglottal system, 113
Submersion, 454
Substitution, 277
Subtractive bilingualism, 470
Successive processing, 419
Suffixes, inflectional, 166
Sugar, J., 355

Sumerians, 410
Summerfield, Q., 128
Sun is Feminine, The (Taeschner), 456
Supplementary motor area (SMA), 88
Surface dyslexics, 431
Surface forms, of sentences, 242
Surface structure, 21, 232–233
Sussman, H. M., 112, 145
S-V-O (Subject-Verb-Object) word order, 5, 16–17, 365, 370–371
Swinney, D., 180, 204, 206, 207, 235, 254–256
Syllabaries, 34, 411
Syllable, 316
    open, 358
    segmenting, 421
    speech perception research and, 113
Sylvian fissure, 68
Symbols, 181
    associating, 418
    foreign language study and, 461
    words as, 5
    writing and, 412
Synonyms, 160
Synonymy, 160
Syntactic ambiguity, 237–241
Syntactic autonomy principle, 244
Syntactic/grammatical codes, 414, 415
Syntactic knowledge, assessing, 364
Syntactic parsing, and retention of phrases, 258–259
Syntactic processing, 232–237
    clausal processing, 235–237
    competence vs. performance and, 233
    sentences structures, 233–235
    surface vs. deep structure and, 232–233
    syntactic resolution, comprehension, and, 232
Syntactic processor, 253
Syntactic Structures (Chomsky), 37
Syntactic theory
    in 1960s, 20–27
    in 1970s and 1980s, 24
    in 1990s, 28
Syntactic understanding, models for, 365
Syntagmatic responses, 364
Syntax, 3, 16–27, 79
    monostratal theories of, 28
    processing of, 244–245
    word perception and, 140–143
Synthesis, 109. See also Speech synthesis

Tabossi, P., 206, 256, 257
Tachistoscope (T-scope), 76, 163
Taeschner, T., 456–458
Taft, M., 162, 164, 431, 435, 436
Tager-Flusberg, H., 354, 364, 369
Tag question, 30, 288
Tallal, P., 138, 139
Talmy, L., 210
Tanenhaus, M. K., 3, 23, 27, 36, 37, 204, 206, 207, 240, 241, 252
Tannen, D., 28, 286, 288–289
Tannenhaus, M. K., 432
Tanzman, M. S., 415
Tartter, V. C., 110
Task, 192
Taxonomic categories, 198
Taylor, A., 230–231
Teeth, 113
Telegraphic speech, 366
Telencephalon, 78
Terrace, H., 6
Testing, of speech perception, 124–125
Text. See also Discourse
    discourse and, 277–282
TG model. See Transformational Generative (TG) grammar
Thai, 135
Thal, D., 360, 367, 384
Thalamus, 63, 90
    dorsal, 60–61
Thalidomide, 385
Tharp, D. A., 165
Thematic associations, 209
Theois, J., 427
Theory-based theories. See Knowledge-based theories
Thermometric crown, 86
Thibadeau, R., 248
Thomas, M., 460
Thought, language of, 311
Three-stage model, of processing nonliteral meaning, 257–258
Threshold, 173
Tibetan, 17
Time, 384
Time course of activation, 206–207
Time course of sentence contexts, and word pairs, 207
"Tip-of-the-tongue" (TOT) phenomenon, 170
Titone, D. A., 257, 258
    "Sentence Processing," 227–274
Tkacz, S., 170
Toddler. See Children